MR. BARUCH

American Family Tree
of
Bernard M. Baruch

Bernard M. Baruch, born Camden, S.C., 1870

son of
Dr. Simon Baruch, Posen, East Prussia
and Belle Wolfe Baruch, Winnsboro, S.C.

daughter of
Saling Wolfe of Prussia
and Sarah Cohen Wolfe of Charleston, S.C.

daughter of
Hartwig Cohen of Jamaica
and Deborah Marks Cohen of Charleston, S.C.

daughter of
Sarah Harris of London, England,
and Samuel Marks of New York City

son of
Isaac Marques of the Continental Army

son of
Jacob Marques of Barbados, B.W.I.

son of
Isaac Rodriguez Marques of Denmark
and New York City

Mr. Baruch

MARGARET L. COIT

BeardBooks
Washington, D.C.

Library of Congress Cataloging-in-Publication Data

Coit, Margaret L.
    Mr. Baruch / by Margaret L. Coit.
        p. cm.
    Reprint. Originally published: Boston : Houghton Mifflin, 1957.
    Includes bibliographical references and index.
    ISBN 1-58798-021-5 (paper)
        1. Baruch, Bernard M. (Bernard Mannes), 1870-1965. 2. Statesmen--United States--
Biography. 3. Capitalists and financiers--United States--Biography. 4. United States--
Politics and government--20th century. I. Title: Mister Baruch. II. Title.

E748.B32 C6 2000
973.91'3'092--dc21
[B]   00-040404

Printed in the United States of America

To the memory
of
William Watts Ball

PREFACE

LIKE MY EARLIER STUDY of John C. Calhoun, this biography of Bernard Mannes Baruch is also a portrait of America.

The story of Calhoun began with the birth of our republic and ended with the testing of that republic in the fires of civil war. The story of Bernard Baruch begins in the aftermath of that war and stretches into the shadow of the Atomic Age. Both eras are sides of the same coin. Calhoun's was the cause that was lost and Baruch's is the cause that has won. The transformation of the United States from an agrarian republic to an industrial democracy can be told through the lives of these two South Carolinians.

What Calhoun represented met with defeat; what Baruch has represented, with victory. Calhoun fought the spirit of his time and lost; Baruch rode the mainstream of his time and won. Calhoun saw the future and opposed it; Baruch saw the future and embraced it. Calhoun — a simple and intense man of thought — dealt with the America that was; Baruch — a complex and subtle man of action — dealt with the America that is today.

MARGARET L. COIT

ACKNOWLEDGMENTS

THE FINANCING of the tremendous research which this book involved was in large part made possible by the generosity of Brown University, which awarded me a President's Fellowship in 1952 and a George A. and Eliza Howard Gardiner Fellowship the succeeding year. For this help I want to express my utmost thanks and gratitude. My gratitude also goes out to my publishers, Houghton Mifflin Company, for financial and moral support, and especially to my editor, Craig Wylie, for the infinite patience and insight he put into the editing of this book, also to Paul Brooks, Mrs. Arthur A. Bright, Jr., Miss Helen Phillips, and all the others at Houghton Mifflin who have worked so hard on *Mr. Baruch*.

This book was undertaken at the suggestion of Mr. Baruch, and he made available to me over a period of some five years his large collection of papers. He also was willing to discuss with me many aspects of his career, to read various passages of this book, and to allow me to see and visit him both in New York and South Carolina, whereby I gained an insight into his daily life and met many of his friends and associates. Several members of Mr. Baruch's staff have also helped me at his direction, particularly Harold Epstein and Miss Mary A. Boyle.

Although various manuscript collections besides the Bernard M. Baruch Papers were consulted, much of the material for this book was the result of "leg work" among Mr. Baruch's acquaintances and friends. These comprise most of the public figures in the worlds of politics, high finance, sport, and society throughout the last half-century. Many who helped most during this six-year effort did not live to see the completion of the book. They are, however, owed great thanks. They included Dr. J. W. Corbett and Marion Heyman, both of Camden, S.C.; William Watts Ball of Charleston, S.C.; Marquis James of Rye, N.Y.; Robert E. Sherwood, Shaemas O'Sheel, John Hancock, and John Golden of New York City; Senator Robert A. Taft and Chief Justice Fred N. Vinson of Washington, D.C.; and Garet Garrett of Tuckahoe, N.J.

In Mr. Baruch's native South Carolina, help came from relatives in the Camden-Winnsboro area. These included Mr. and Mrs. Ulysse Ganvier Des Portes, Mr. and Mrs. Gabriel Baum, and Mrs. Eva Baum. Other South Carolinians assisting with advice and information were former Governor and Mrs. James F. Byrnes, Mrs. Christie Benet of Columbia, Mr. and Mrs. David McGill of Kingstree, Creola Bracey of Camden, Dr. G. H. Aull of Clemson, Rabbi Allan Tarvish, Thomas Jefferson Tobias, Miss Beatrice Ravenel, Herbert Ravenel Sass, Peter Manigault, and Mrs. Melton A. Goodstein, all of Charleston. Mr. Sass and Mr. Manigault have both read portions of the book in manuscript and have offered many valuable insights and corrections.

In Mr. Baruch's adopted home of New York City, I was generously assisted by Wayne Andrews, Curator of Manuscripts for The New-York Historical Society; Otis Cooper, Mrs. Fleur Cowles, Dr. Donald Covalt, Mr. and Mrs. Ferdinand Eberstadt, Miss Jinx Falkenburg, Arthur Godfrey, Dr. Oliver St. John Gogarty, Max Gordon, Governor Averell Harriman, former President Herbert Hoover, Eliot Janeway, Dr. Alvin Johnson, Mrs. Clare Boothe Luce, Sam Lubell, Mrs. Franklin D. Roosevelt, Judge Samuel Rosenman, C. R. Van Sappe, Mrs. Robert Samstag, His Eminence Francis Cardinal Spellman, Herbert Bayard Swope, and Mrs. Jerome Van Ess.

In Washington, D.C., I was assisted by President Dwight D. Eisenhower, Senator Harry F. Byrd, General Levin Campbell, Thomas Corcoran, George Carroll, former Senator and Mrs. Homer Ferguson, Associate Justice Felix Frankfurter, Philip Hamer, Senator John F. Kennedy, Arthur Krock, David Lawrence, Dr. Elizabeth McPherson, Miss Frances Perkins, Mrs. Anna Rosenberg, Walker Stone, David Stowe, Senator Stuart Symington, and former President Harry S. Truman.

More help came from Mrs. Clayton Hoaglund and Mrs. Eugene Ingalls, both of Rutherford, N.J.; Dr. Peter Sammartino, President, and my colleagues at Fairleigh Dickinson University who read portions of this book in manuscript — Dr. Loyd Haberly, Dr. Nasrollah S. Fatemi, and Dr. Herbert Gutman; Dr. Claude M. Fuess of Boston, Mass.; former Ambassador Joseph P. Kennedy of Hyannisport, Mass.; Curtis K. Thomas of Ring's Island, Mass.; Mrs. Robert Towne of West Newbury, Mass.; Dr. Jacob R. Marcus of Cincinnati, Ohio; E. Austin Benny, Haverhill, Mass.; Joel Kudly, Irvington, N.J.; Rabbi Malcolm H. Stern of Norfolk, Va.; and Mrs. Raymond Everitt of Philadelphia, Pa. A special word of thanks is also due my parents, Mr. and Mrs. Archa W. Coit of Charlottesville, Va., without whose aid the galley-reading task would have been impossible.

I want to express my gratitude to the library staffs who were of assistance, including Miss Virginia Rugheimer and others at the Charleston Library Society; the staffs of the public libraries of New York City and of Newburyport, Mass.; Mrs. Louise R. Crowell, Charles M. Fleischner and the staff of the Haverhill, Mass., Public Library; Miss Bella VanDyke and the staff and the public library of Paterson, N.J.; also Mrs. G. Harold Thurlow and the public library in West Newbury, Mass. Special help was also given by the town fathers of West Newbury, Selectmen Albert E. Elwell, Fred L. Knapp, M. Paine Hoseason, and Harold T. Daley.

Finally, I want to thank those friends and acquaintances of Mr. Baruch who have let me use quotations from their letters to him, as indicated in the notes, also to thank the McGraw-Hill Book Company, Inc. (Whittlesey House) for permission to quote from *Bernard Baruch: Park Bench Statesman* by Carter Field; Harcourt, Brace and Company for permission to quote from *Bernard Baruch: Portrait of a Citizen* by William L. White; and Houghton Mifflin Company for the quotations from Grosvenor B. Clarkson's *Industrial America in the World War: The Strategy Behind the Line*, 1917–1918. Acknowledgment is made in the Bibliography and Notes of the sources of my shorter quotations from a number of books and various periodicals and pamphlets.

PUBLISHER'S NOTE

This biography was undertaken at Mr. Baruch's
suggestion, but he is in no way responsible for
the interpretations in it or for the facts that
the author has derived from the Baruch Papers
or other sources. Mr. Baruch has always insisted that this should be Miss Coit's book in
every sense of the word.

CONTENTS

1

WHEN THE REDSHIRTS RODE

South Carolina — 1870!

In Columbia, a boy of fourteen, spindling, freckled, bespectacled, stood staring down at the ruins of a city, the rotting remainder of Sherman's March to the Sea. Behind him, from the shell-scarred white capitol, burst the sound of drunken laughter; in his ears echoed the shuffle of footsteps as troops in blue coats marched on parade.[1] Before him lay the city, block after smoke-charred block, and looking on the desolation, Thomas Woodrow Wilson, son of a Confederate chaplain, knew that he hated war.[2]

Thirty miles to the north, in the little town of Camden, a dark-haired young woman labored in the pains of childbirth. She was the wife of a former Confederate surgeon, now Camden's "country doctor," and the boy born on that August 19 was her second child. The son she held in her arms on that summer day in Camden was named Bernard Baruch, which means a brave little bear blessed in the sight of the Lord.[3]

The room in which Bernard Baruch was born was on the second story of a rambling old whitewashed house on Broad Street, with a hipped roof and big chimneys and a door opening in the Charleston style onto a shaded gallery. Long a landmark in Camden, the house was only recently destroyed. Bernard's first memories would be of this little world of home: the great shade tree in front, the breath of sun-warmed pine and ancient brick-walled flower gardens, blowing through windows open eight or nine months of the year; cows wandering down the sandy streets toward the courthouse basement in the evening — as the *Kershaw Gazette* observed: "It is said that cows have more business in the Courthouse than anybody else" [4] — and always there was the melody of Negro voices floating upward.

It was a world of peace within and terror without — a dark and bitter time for a child to be born. For in 1870 South Carolina was a military district, not even a state, and little Camden had been in "Sherman's track," that forty-mile belt of blackened and empty country side, in which five years before "not . . . one living thing, man, woman, or animal" remained, and only the gaunt chimneys stood "to show that any man ever trod this road before." [5]

Burned and rebuilt, Camden had survived. In the wake of Sherman, only a few hours before the courier brought the news of peace, had come "Potter's raiders," smashing windows, turning the cotton bales into mountains of flame, looting all that was left to loot; and after them the Yankee officers, "smiling, suave, well-dressed . . . who regretted it all so much." Then came the scattered and stunned refugees from the plantations, their hearts "filled with brotherly hate." The community was cut off, every rail line destroyed, only an occasional letter brought in by a man on horseback.[6] This was the town to which Belle Baruch had come as a bride.

But she held her baby unafraid. Gallant and gay, she was of a generation of Southern women who had seen their world fall about them and had built a new one, creating little sanctuaries around the battle-wearied men in gray. Yet when "Miss Belle" Wolfe came to Camden in 1867, she had never even dressed herself alone.[7]

She was a child of the Old South. Back in Charleston, her grandmother had danced with Lafayette on his triumphal American tour in 1824, and her grandfather, the Reverend Hartwig Cohen, a Jamaican of "priestly descent," was twice rabbi of the city's historic Sephardic congregation of Beth Elohim.[8] In November 1845, the seventieth year of American Independence, according to the old marriage contract, Belle's mother, Sarah, had become the bride of Saling Wolfe, a Fairfield County planter, like herself of Jewish extraction. With her she brought a marriage portion of an ornate wardrobe, furniture, and bedding valued at a thousand dollars.[9] Thus, in the lush years "before the war," the young couple had begun their life together.

Saling Wolfe was a native of Prussia.[10] He was a handsome man, dark-eyed and tall, and to his young grandson, Bernard, looking on him years after the "Confederate War," with his ruddy face and the proud carriage of a man born to the saddle, he seemed the very picture of a John Bull.[11] Although he has been described as an up-country man, Fairfield County, with its rich, rolling fields, valued even in the 1850's at thirty and forty dollars an acre, had been overrun by the fortune-seeking, malaria-fleeing planters of the coast. There, in the red clay hills, they had sown their seed and built their mansions, fusing their blood with the hardy Scots-Irish of the region.[12]

Proudly among them stood Saling Wolfe and his Charleston bride. He owned not one but several plantations, slaves, cattle, and a columned mansion. Thirteen children were born to the couple, and old reminiscences describe little Belle on her first day of school as "very sweet and pretty." [13]

"Miss Belle" was only eleven when the guns fired on Sumter, but the strain and excitement of the war years matured her quickly. She was not too young to have a soldier sweetheart, Dr. Simon Baruch, just out of the Medical College of Virginia; nor to write him letters that followed him from Gettysburg to the Wilderness; nor to paint his portrait during his furloughs home. Then came February 1865, with the refugee trains pounding into Winnsboro and the horizon blazing red from the fires of Columbia seventeen miles away. Down upon the Wolfe plantation swept the army of Sherman shouting and singing.[14]

Like locusts, the soldiers swarmed through the house, halting sharply by the well, where several of the more simple-minded Negroes were moaning that they were going to find the family silver, which they inevitably did.[15] One piece was salvaged; days later, neighbors found the great soup tureen, lying slashed and scarred in a cow pasture. Made of three hundred silver dollars melted down, it had been too heavy to carry away.[16] The army was not wanting in plunder, however. General Sherman already had "gold and silver enough to start a bank," [17] Union Lieutenant Thomas J. Myers wrote home, adding that he could already boast of "a quart of jewelry for you and the girls." [18]

Huddled on the lawn, Belle Wolfe and her young brothers and sisters heard the roar as their house went up in flames, smelled the charred timbers and the burning cotton. All that had meant home and happiness and security to them was burning in that fire; in the hiss of flame — the tainted air. That night the mother and the children came as refugees into Winnsboro — the father was away at war — and were taken in by the Rion family.[19] There, Belle could look down on streets "blue with Yankees . . . wagons filled with loot and Negro wenches." Nothing was left amidst the smoking ruins, no groceries, no vegetables, no cattle, no mules, no telegraph lines, no train — nothing. Winnsboro was a stricken community of women and children, with not six able-bodied men in town. But Belle was one among those girls who could stand defiant on a gallery singing: "Oh, yes, I am a Southern girl; I glory in the name." She could go out with the others to pick cowpeas or to gather the corn left by the horses for boiling down into lye-hominy. She could join in a grim May Day celebration in the ashes; and later at one of those "tournaments" surviving from the old romantic days of the "cause," where, decked out in rags and tags of attic finery, the young men fenced for their ladies' favor.[20]

And not all the Yankees were so terrible, after all. When the garrison moved out that spring, Belle Wolfe's letters followed it. Legendary in the Baruch family is the story of Miss Belle and the portrait of Dr. Simon Baruch, which was torn from her hand during the burning, trampled on and destroyed by a Yankee soldier. In hot fury, Belle told him what she thought of him, at which the soldier slapped her face. A moment later an enraged officer was flailing the private with his sword. He was Captain Cantine, and when young Dr. Baruch came back from the war, it looked as if he might have lost not only his health and his cause but his sweetheart too. Nevertheless Belle Wolfe was loyal — although she never forgot the Yankee captain. Years later, a young man handed a note to Bernard Baruch, then chairman of the War Industries Board. He was a nephew of Captain Cantine, and Miss Belle had written her son that she knew he would do what he could for him.[21]

The sensitive, scholarly Simon Baruch had hated war, and fled the militarism of his native East Prussia when only fifteen years old. Earlier two brothers, Herman and Mannes Baum, friends of Simon's from his birthplace in Schwersenz, near Posen, had emigrated to Camden, South Carolina, where they became owners of a small store. There young Simon Baruch came, and at night studied the new language by the light of a candle, an American history book open beside him. Mannes Baum's bride looked on admiringly. She was a Charleston girl, a daughter of Rabbi Hartwig Cohen, and to her husband and brother-in-law she insisted that this bright youth deserved to be "something better than a book-keeper." So the young Prussian was sent down to Charleston and enrolled at the

Medical College of the State of South Carolina in time for the last few lectures before the war, and from there he went on to the Medical College of Virginia.[22]

Whether it was the soft-spoken, self-effacing "Uncle Herman" or the more blustering "Uncle Mannes" who was Simon Baruch's benefactor has long been a point of dissension in the Baruch and Baum families. Bernard Baruch has always believed that it was Mannes, whose name he bears, but an undated letter from Dr. Baruch gives us a clue. As long as he lived, he wrote Herman's wife, he could never forget Herman's services to him. Without his help, the doctor could never have completed his medical education. However, the scrappy little Camden shopkeeper, Mannes Baum, who, scalp streaming with blood, once hung on with his teeth to a bully who had thrown him down, played a characteristic role. He gave the young Baruch his bright new Confederate uniform and sword.[23]

Simon Baruch knew nothing about "the cause" for which he would fight and almost die. But the Baums and their friends were his people now, and joining their side was the natural, human thing to do. His was the decision made by thousands of other confused and saddened young men in the sixties. "South Carolina," he told his colleague Dr. Benjamin Taylor, "gave me all I have. I'll go with my state." [24] So he was off for Second Manassas with the men of Kershaw's Brigade, stopping only to caution his seventeen-year-old brother, just over from Prussia, to keep out of the fighting. When they met again, nine months later, the youngster was wearing the uniform of a Confederate cavalryman.

Simon Baruch had marched northward with the Third South Carolina Battalion, arriving in time to join Lee for Sharpsburg. He was commissioned an assistant surgeon — this youth of twenty-two — and startled his superior by taking time before surgery to wash his hands and dip his scalpel in boiling water. Finicking niceties, these seemed, in the blood and sweat of the battlefield. Neither Baruch nor his associates knew the connection between death and dirt, yet the young doctor had sensed the cause and effect. It was not all luck that gave him the title of "lucky surgeon." He was commended for the skill with which he performed his first operation, although, as he always said, until that time he had never even lanced a boil!

The stories that he told would haunt his son Bernard's imagination seventy-five years afterward. He, too, could see that blood-spattered table in the churchyard at Boonsboro, hear the bullets shrilling overhead, and the guns of Sharpsburg rocking the earth below. Down the one road left had streamed the Confederates, and after them thundered the Union cavalry, while young Dr. Baruch worked on and on, a Union surgeon at his side.

He had been taken as a prisoner to Baltimore, given the freedom of the city, entertained at dances, and two days later exchanged and sent back to Longstreet's Corps. It was a gentleman's war, he always said in retrospect. He was remembering perhaps that hour when his weary comrades stood, heads bared and bowed, as by Lee's orders a Federal ambulance rolled in under a white flag and bore away the body of the Union Major General James S. Wadsworth. The doctor still thought it a gentleman's war when, once more a prisoner after Gettysburg, he was sent to Baltimore, worn out from two days and nights in a creekside tavern where he was ordered to remain with the wounded as the heartbreaking retreat back to Virginia began.

In Fort McHenry, overlooking that harbor where Francis Scott Key had watched the bombs bursting in air, Simon Baruch also took up his pen to write a paper entitled "Two Penetrating Wounds of the Chest," * which, his son Bernard was told during World War I, was still a standard work on its subject. Time passed quickly; the Baltimore belles came out by day, and in return for a simple *parole d'honneur* a young Confederate officer could dance the night away at the "best houses" of the city.

Two months later Dr. Baruch was back in Virginia, wading through the red mud, shivering in the cold and the rain that so often fell after battle, the rain that fell at Shiloh and Pittsburg Landing and on the long line of retreat from Gettysburg, the rain that fell too late on the burning swamplands of the Wilderness. Dr. Baruch, a captain and a full surgeon now, was detached from the Army of Northern Virginia and sent south to the Thirteenth Mississippi Regiment to prepare hospital facilities for the wounded in the wake of Sherman. He was on duty in March 1865 as the telegraph keys began clicking the news of 280 wounded men on their way back from a little-known but bloody skirmish at Averyboro.

Dr. Baruch issued his orders quickly. Every old man and boy in the neighborhood was pressed into service. Pews were stripped from

---

* This is the correct title of the paper commonly known as "Bayonet Wounds of the Chest." Baruch Number, *Library Bulletin of the Medical College of the State of South Carolina* (September 1944).

two churches, pine knots gathered, girls from a female academy set to stuffing straw into bags for mattresses. From house to house Dr. Baruch moved, pleading for home-baked bread, the last supplies of bacon and rye coffee.

The little train clattered through the night. By the light of the hissing pine knots you saw them — men, barefoot men, exhausted men, hungry men, piteously wounded men, ranged in rows on the jolting floor of the boxcars, thrown on piles of loose cotton, black and clotted with their blood.

Yet, somehow, all were made comfortable, were washed and fed and laid in beds. For two hours, Dr. Baruch slept. Then, under his direction the grim repair work began. Day and night the operating and the amputating went on, never ceasing until the wounds of every man were dressed.

Simon Baruch was ill. His head was pounding. He had just strength left to write a telegram, asking to be relieved from duty, and then, head reeling, he lapsed into darkness. Two weeks later, he struggled up out of the fever and delirium of typhoid. Lee had surrendered; Johnston had surrendered; he himself had been captured, nursed, paroled, and released, though he remembered none of it. Too weak to walk, he made his way homeward on crutches to Camden. All was gone in the ruins, even the case of surgical instruments which an admiring Northern physician had given to him during one of his prison terms in Baltimore. The war was over.[25]

Simon Baruch's marriage to Belle Wolfe was a happy one.[26] Four sons were born to the couple.* She ran the home; she gave singing and music lessons; her dark beauty graced every amateur theatrical production in town. She even ran a dairy to make butter and cheese for her neighbors. Seventy years and more after she had left Camden, her memory was still cherished in the little town; "the most charming woman I ever knew," reminisced the eighty-nine-year-old Dr. "Joe" Corbett; and ninety-one-year-old Creola Bracey, "de old Camden prophet" who had worked for the Baruchs when there were "only two little boys," still remembered the great willow baskets of food that Miss Belle sent home to Creola's "twenty-one-head" of brothers and sisters.[27]

Out of the plenty of cherished ante-bellum days, breakfast in bed

* Hartwig, b. 1868, d. 1953; Bernard M., b. 1870; Herman, b. 1872, d. 1953; Sailing, b. 1874.

was the one little luxury Mrs. Baruch could not give up. Early among her son Bernard's memories was a daily preschool inspection — the four boys lined up in their mother's room, hands extended, and the bombardment of questions. "Let me see your fingers. Did you wash behind your ears? Did you wash your feet? Did you clean your teeth?" [28] Often, for one or another, this meant a hurried trip back to the washbasin and a worried return to the mother's bedside, ears tingling no more from scrubbing than from shame.

In the long winter evenings, after an early supper of bread, milk, and preserves and a thorough scrubbing in the tin tub, the children would gather again in their parents' room. Never to be forgotten was the warmth and security of those early days, as in their long flannel nightgowns the little boys romped before the fire, the flames dancing pink lights across the ceiling, and their tired father stretched out on his bed as the children played around him. So, too, in later years would Bernard Baruch rest among his own children. At last, came the good-night kisses; then away the boys would romp, put out their kerosene lamps, and tumble into bed.[29]

There was also Mammy, a mammy to all the boys of course, but Bernard, or "Bunch," as the stubby, freckled youngster was called, was her "chile." Her name was Minerva; she was as black as swamp water, a low-country Negro of a type now almost never seen except on the remote sea islands. For her the woods and the waters and the fields were alive. She would tell of Br'er Rabbit and the Tar Baby, of "hants," like the fearsome "Plat-eye." Against the lights and shadows of Baruch's childhood memories, the dark bulk of Minerva moved; and it was perhaps with her that he attended his first camp meeting, thrilling to the rise and fall of the voices, the clapping hands and stamping feet, the black shadows swaying. The picture was forgotten until years later when services at the little church at his plantation, "Hobcaw," resurrected it all again. At night, with the rain soft-dropping on the roof, young Bernard would lie for hours, trembling and fearful over the fate of Bolem, the lion who had lost his tail. Over and over again, as if in echo, he would hear Minerva's never-ending chant.[30]

Minerva was never married, but she had plenty of children.[31] Her mistakes, as explained to Miss Belle, accounted for plenty of little black boys and girls for the Baruch children to play with; and their special favorite was Frank, who knew the calls of the birds and could beat them all at fishing and hunting and catching game. When Grandmother Wolfe came down from Winnsboro with some little presents for her grandsons, Frank even piped up, "Grandmother, what you brung me?" [32]

These carefree days did not last long. Even in boyhood Bernard began to realize "the bottomless chasm that separated the white and black races," and for him it was a shattering revelation. It was not something he learned at home. Never there did he hear the term "nigger"; never from his father and mother did he hear a word derogatory to Negroes. He could not understand why it was that Frank and the butler's daughter Henrietta were "different," why his playmates could be his playmates no more. Like thousands of Southern white children before him and since, Bernard was caught in that tangled web of racial relations which lets the white child drink its milk from the black woman's breast, but denies her the use of his drinking fountain. It was the dilemma of the whole South. [33]

Visits to Grandmother and Grandfather Wolfe in Winnsboro were a special delight. It was an adventure to tumble out of bed in the darkness and pile into the buggy just as the sky was paling at 4 A.M., before the great heat of the day. It was a six- or seven-hour ride to Winnsboro, across the bare, burned-over country of "Sherman's track," but mostly in the woods, with no sound but the soughing of the pines and the cry of the whippoorwill and the scratching of the underbrush against the buggy wheels.

Even today Winnsboro, with its faded ante-bellum houses straggling along the line of the Southern Railway and its brick courthouse of Robert Mills design, looks very much as Bernard Baruch saw it three-quarters of a century ago. It was a sleepy little Southern town. Red dust blew in clouds around the wheels of the wagons and buggies, dulling the leaves of the tall old trees overhanging the sidewalks, where old men shifted checkers in the shade, powdered the bellies of the "houn' dawgs," circled around the country stores as barefooted Negroes and poor whites stumped in and out to swap poultry and eggs for corn. Still standing on Main Street is the old "DuBose place," burned and rebuilt after Sherman, a white-painted, double-galleried house, where Saling Wolfe had moved his family after the war.

Inside, there were a few vestiges of vanished glory: a large silver candelabrum above the fireplace and another gleaming from an old

Colonial sideboard. A white-haired butler moved from chair to chair
with all the dignity of slavery days. Here the clan gathered for
Thanksgiving dinner, stately Grandfather Wolfe folding back slice
after slice of oyster-filled turkey; Grandmother Wolfe, with her sweet,
serene face, presiding over all, ribbons fluttering from the lace square
on her silver head.[34]

Outside, the old-fashioned garden was pungent with boxwood,
and under the apple and apricot trees that grew among the flowers,
Bernie could play with his brothers and his young tomboy aunt,
Sarah,* who had shocked the neighbors during a visit to Camden
by dangling head-down by her toes from the Baruch boys' trapeze.[35]

The rail line cut across the rear of the property. Snuggled deep in
his featherbed, Bernard could hear the cry of the whistle sounding
down the night; and by day, mounted on the fence, his bare feet
twined around the rails, he could wave to the engineers and chuck
stones at the old boxcars lumbering past, and dream of the far-off
names and places, and of the day when he would be a man and own
his own railroad.[36]

Grandfather Wolfe had never rebuilt the burned mansion-house
on the plantation outside of town. But he was planting cotton
again out there, as the neighbors observed, and Bernard could
hear that his grandfather had been a rich man, back before the war.
Bernard believed it the day he went rummaging in an old wardrobe
and found money, rolls and rolls of it, hundreds and thousands of
dollars crammed into a drawer.[37] He stared, awed. These were hard
times, when a silver dollar looked as big as a wagon wheel, as the
Winnsboro boys said. Money was important because it was something nobody had. Back home in Camden, the Baruchs had about
as much as everyone else, which was almost none at all. Pay for the
doctor was on a kind of barter basis: a cord of wood perhaps, maybe
some chickens, a day's work in one of his fields, or maybe a dog,
which was more of a joy to the children than to the father. This
way almost all the people of South Carolina lived, from hand to
mouth and day to day.

So here was the money in the wardrobe drawer, and what did it

---

* Sarah Wolfe Des Portes, b. 1865, was the only member of the Wolfe family
to remain in Fairfield County. She married Ulysse Ganvier Des Portes of Winnsboro, and had two sons, the late Fay Allen Des Portes, diplomat and legislator,
and Ulysse Ganvier (Jack) Des Portes of Winnsboro.

mean? Only years later, when he understood the story of the Lost Cause would Baruch realize what had happened to the money of a nation that printed paper dollars without gold backing — a lesson in fundamental economics that he would remember long after his schooldays.

The Negroes would not even take their pay in Yankee paper money now. Near the Wolfe house stood a shed, crammed with foodstuffs, and here on Friday mornings the field hands assembled for their rations of cornmeal, sugar, coffee, prunes, rice, and bacon. Only too eager to help in the distribution were the Baruch boys, for they knew what their reward would be at the end — a handful of brown sugar. White sugar they had never seen.[38]

Something of the old ways still lingered in this quaint plantation custom, and glimpses of that already legendary Old South were caught, in their passing, by an eager and perceptive little boy. There was his grandfather, riding out on his horse; there rolled the hills; there lay the fields, ridged and red in the spring when the seed was new in the ground, flaming red again in the sunset blaze of the summer when the cotton was in flower. Wounded and scarred though it was, this was a beautiful land. Even years later, gutted, eroded, and despoiled, it still held a beauty that could catch your throat. But for young Bernard Baruch these red hills were not so beautiful as the lower, more mellow country around Camden. Like a rabbit's, his young nose quivered and tingled to the breath of the longleaf pine. He knew the black swamp pools that turned a boy's body bronze when he bathed, and the feathery veils of Spanish moss, swaying and dancing from the intertwined branches, crossed like swords overhead. This was his land, the land he loved.

Out of his love of the land came his love of country, a heritage he came by naturally as a Southern farm boy. Always, he would remember his own father's cottonfields, the heat and the sun and the corn blades flashing. Years later, he could still feel the hot powdery sand sifting and scraping up between his toes, and the weight of the cotton bag on his wet back as he moved up and down the rows, picking the cotton.

Although never a planter or a large landholder, Dr. Baruch had gradually acquired a few acres near his home for experimental purposes. There was no help from the state; the state did nothing but oppress and steal. It was Dr. Baruch who experimented and devised, who had the best crops of cotton, corn, oats, and cane in the neighborhood, the prize-winners at the country fair.[39] It was Dr. Baruch who had the pile of yellowing farm journals, and who, tired though he might be from an all-night vigil at a bed of death or birth, was somehow never too tired to help and advise a farmer neighbor.

For him, as for his entire generation, "the war" had been the high-water mark of life. Its heroes came to the house: General Kershaw of the famed Kershaw's Brigade, even the great Wade Hampton himself. Voices flowed on unceasingly during the long summer evenings on the porch. History was lived again by the men who had made it, and history to the Baruch boys came to be part of their own experience. A whole generation of boys was growing up hearing of raids and sorties and cavalry charges — of Shiloh and Malvern Hill and Seven Days, the flames of Atlanta licking at the Southern night, and muskets too hot to load and fire — of Lee and of Stonewall, Stuart and Beauregard, they learned from men who had known all this at first hand.[40] Always the men talked of war, always of the war.

There were family heroes, too, like Marcus Baum, brother of Herman and Mannes, and already something of a legend in South Carolina. He had been a courier on Jackson's staff and had vanished into the mist one night at Chancellorsville. And Bernard would never forget the singsong voice and banjo of Uncle Fischel Cohen of Charleston, telegraph operator for Beauregard, thrumming the notes of "The Bonnie Blue Flag." [41] But for Bernard, two heroes stood above all others — his father and Robert E. Lee — and even when he was an old man he could not speak the name of Lee without emotions rising to choke him. When past eighty he was asked by three New York schoolboys to list his heroes. Stonewall, Pickens, and Marion were written down, to the children's mystification, but first of all was the name of Lee.

In his young manhood Bernard Baruch once stood at his father's side in the peach orchard at Gettysburg. There, through the old Confederate's eyes, he saw it all for himself: the wall and the ridge, Pickett, with his long hair streaming, those straggling gray lines sweeping up and breaking against the wall, the mist of battle that settled over the fields, punctuated by red bursts of flame. Bernard Baruch always remembered his father that day, a tall, erect man, gesturing with his black slouch hat, his gray beard cut like Lee's, and long white hair flowing in the wind, the steady blue eyes looking back and inward — and suddenly, for his twenty-year-old-son, the hero-images merged, and Lee and his father became one.

Dr. Baruch was always a hero to his sons, and never more so than on that summer day when, rummaging in an old horsehair trunk in the attic, Hartwig and Bernard found not only the faded and beloved uniform of Confederate gray, but white robes, long and flowing, emblazoned with the scarlet cross of the Knights of the Ku Klux Klan. Their searching hands halted. Silently, they gazed at each other. To think that their father was one of that legendary band, spoken of only in whispers. The brothers were rapt, their father exalted in their eyes. They did not hear their mother's step upon the stair. But when they looked up, they saw her face —

It was a terrible secret they had uncovered. The Klan was an outlaw band; rewards were posted; betrayal would bring good solid Yankee dollars in silver or gold. But there were no quislings among the Southern people. All over the South, thousands of women had sewn and fitted these white uniforms and sent their men out into danger, but not one had betrayed them. The two boys crept down the stairs from the attic feeling as if they had suddenly grown up.[42]

The Ku Klux Klan of Baruch's boyhood bore no resemblance to that mongrel outfit of the twentieth century, which burned a fiery cross near the property of Baruch, himself, son of a Confederate soldier and Klansman. The Klan of the seventies was created to free the South from the Reign of Terror of Reconstruction, where order was nonexistent.

In violation of the Bill of Rights, the North had quartered Federal troops in Southern homes. Union troops — sometimes bullying, black Union troops — elbowed their way into the shell-pitted houses and herded young girls off to jail.[43] All over the South women were sleeping with loaded pistols under their pillows.[44] "You wouldn't take the only pistol with which a woman could defend herself?" a terrified Laurens resident demanded of a Negro company, busy sweeping up firearms. But they did. All over the South, women huddled in their homes, terrified and alone; the poor-white farm women traveled in convoys to take their produce to market.[45] Even today it is lonely in the great stretches of swamp and pine-barren and sandhill country, and in that black and empty land of Sherman's track, it was lonelier still. The "natural protectors" were dead. Fifteen thousand young South Carolinians had died for the cause they never knew was lost.[46] "There is one recourse when all is lost — the sword," wrote Dr. Baruch. "What boots it to live under such a tyranny . . . when we can be much happier dying for such a cause?" [47]

The South had had to surrender, to relinquish its entity as a nation; but the horrors of Reconstruction united it as war had never done. It was Reconstruction that gave birth to "the legend of the Lost Cause." [48] The South would not readily accept outside protection, and it was out of this tradition Baruch later thought that it learned to stand on its own feet and fight its own battles.[49] Out of this tradition, too, came the South's propensity for violence, for taking the law into its own hands.

Undoubtedly this background of heroes and hero-worship raised in Baruch a thirst for military glory; one of his most vivid memories is the night he sat up until dawn reading a biography of Robert E. Lee. For the great American generals of the twentieth century — Pershing, Eisenhower and Marshall — he would feel something of the almost reverential admiration that was stirred in childhood by Lee and Jackson.

Despite his romantic background, Bernard Baruch grew up with no illusions about war. Wars, he knew, there had always been and he believed that nothing could ward them off in the future but preparedness and strength; nothing was worse than defeat and conquest.

Better even to lose the ideals you fought for than to lose the war. Better to adopt the methods and means of your conqueror than to bow to the horrors of defeat. Conquest was worse than a Lost Cause. These beliefs were deeply implanted in the young Baruch, growing up in the aftermath of a "dead civilization and a broken-down system," [50] in a country of roads leading nowhere, of shuttered and rotting plantation houses, dank with moss, overgrown flower gardens swallowed into forest, fields and parks lost in wilderness. Bernard Baruch was only eleven when he left South Carolina, yet he never forgot what he saw there. High in the buggy, wedged between the Negro driver and his tired father, whose head was nodding against his chest, young Bernard watched as scene after scene flashed across the sensitive film of his mind. Here, sun-dappled in a tiny clearing, was a cabin, windows tight-shuttered against the peering Plat-eye. Here stood the blackened shell of a mansion-house, chimney and columns looming out of the ashes, a row of straggling cabins in the rear.[51]

Out here, too, were the "sandlappers'" shanties, where looms creaked and women wove with corncobs for spindles; and pale, scrawny "shirttail boys," and girls, too, tumbled about the dooryards, naked except for a single garment of sacking. Baruch saw the faces of these children, the faces of hunger, half a century before the chroniclers and photographers recorded them. These were a people thrown back a hundred years. They were a people so dependent that one blight or the rise of a single stream could reduce them to bankruptcy. Black and white together were hungry, sick, ridden with fever. Nothing was left to live for but the sheer animal necessity to live, to beat off starvation. Bernard and his brothers could watch them hunched over the counter of a store, hear their tired, patient voices arguing dispiritedly for credit for medicine, clothes, seed, fertilizer, and food, which the merchant got from the jobber and the jobber from the wholesaler, who in turn got his money from Northern capitalists at high interest rates. Then, in the fall of the year, the boys stood watching as the wagons creaked up and the dingy bales were lifted out, the bills paid, and at last the farmer dragged himself away, as hungry, as empty-handed, and as debt-ridden as before.[52] Bernard Baruch saw; he did not understand, but he did not forget. In later years these scenes of hunger and misery colored his political thinking.

What he was living through — although he did not know it — was the end of one era and the beginning of another. The war had won freedom, not only the freedom of the slaves, but also the North's freedom from moral responsibility for the slaves. It had not freed the South from economic responsibility for the Negro.

This the Southern whites were slow to discover. "The Negroes are a good riddance," triumphed a bitter Camden woman. "A hired man is far cheaper than a man whose father and mother, wife, and twelve children have to be fed." [53] But Southern whites could not ignore the filthy shack towns, mushrooming and rotting around virtually every city, breeding disease, despair, and black progeny: pestilence in the shanties meant pestilence and death to their own children. The Negro was free, you could not make him work; and meanwhile the farms and fields were slipping back into underbrush. Ten years since the surrender — and yet the price of cotton was still but a third of what it had been before the war. And what of the great rice plantations? Rice required daily care, and how could it be grown when the hands, drunk with the joy of two or three days' pay, would throw down their tools and take off for a week? [54]

Leases, squad systems — these were some of the makeshifts devised by trial and error to fill the vacuum left by slavery. Ceaselessly men debated: Should the tenant supply his own needs or the planter advance them, and where was the planter to get his capital but from the conqueror? And even if you had the wherewithal, how could you do business with totally ignorant people who often preferred one-tenth to one-half of the crop, because, they said, ten was a bigger number than two? [55] A new word, share-cropping, was turning over on the planters' tongues. A new slavery was rising out of the war for freedom, the bondage of the tenant to the planter, and of the planter to the Northerner — a slavery for whites and Negroes alike.

The Negro, as young James Pike pointed out, rested like "an incubus" upon the whites. "The Africanization of the South," or the specter of open race-war raised by Calhoun thirty-odd years before, loomed as a very real possibility in Bernard Baruch's boyhood. The Thirteenth and Fourteenth Amendments had altered the status of the races but had done nothing to change their nature, nor to establish a new relation in the place of slavery. Men had laughed once at Calhoun's haunted prophecies. Now they did not laugh — not as they watched the mob massing and marching through the streets of Charleston shouting, "De bottom rail's on de top. And we's gwine to keep it dar." [56]

Race battled race, with raids, murders, with gin houses and dwellings flaming red against a midnight sky. Nearly a decade after the "peace" of '65, South Carolina was still aflame. Even a black "Radical" might sometimes warn a white man. "When you-all had de power you was good to me," one old freedman told his former owner, "and I'll protect you now." [57] But for the majority of whites there was all too much truth in the chanted warning:

> "Go way, white folks, you're too late.
> We'se de winnin' culler." [58]

Bernard Baruch knew nothing of ruined Columbia, nor of the legendary Black Parliament, where South Carolina's elected representatives waved peanuts in one hand and made oratorical gestures with the other, as an occasional planter in homespun would lean over the rail and mutter, "My God, look at this!" [59] But around the fire-side and at the store, you could hear the murmuring undercurrent of these desperate years: of the carpetbaggers, of Robert Kingston Scott, "by the grace of bayonets, Governor of South Carolina," and of his aide, rat-faced "Honest John" Patterson. John was not as honest as he claimed, according to Camden's Negro State Senator, Frank Adamson, for when Adamson sold him his vote, Patterson forgot to "pay off." [60] As the Camden *Journal* would comment in retrospect, "The Negroes never did rule South Carolina . . . she was ruled by a few cunning and unscrupulous white men." [61]

Then came the summer of 1876. It was one hundred years since the birth of the nation; it was the year of South Carolina's own Declaration of Independence from the Rule of the Robbers, who had picked the bones of the state clean.[62] It was the year of the Red-shirts' Ride.*

Bernard Mannes Baruch was only six that August, but he was old enough to stand, bare toes sunk in the dust of a country road, shout-ing "Hampton! Hampton!" as between sidewalks black with Negroes the red-shirted legions roared by.

What a day that was for an excitable boy! Three-quarters of a century later, it would all come back to him: the dust and the heat and the thunderous pounding of hoofs, row after row of Redshirts flaming past, six-shooters gleaming, foam-splashed horses rearing, and, over all, the cry that had sounded at Chancellorsville and Shiloh and shrilled across the peach orchard at Gettysburg — the ear-tingling, spine-chilling rebel yell! [63]

The young men were rising in their anger. All over South Carolina, men too young to have worn the gray now donned the red. A new generation was rising from the ashes of defeat, and by the side of fathers and uncles was riding to South Carolina's liberation, riding from the mountains to the sea, and singing as it rode:

> "We'll hang Dan Chamberlain ** to a sour apple tree,
> As we go marching on." [64]

---

* The Redshirts' Ride of 1876, headed by the noted Confederate general Wade Hampton, has been credited with liberating South Carolina from the last vestiges of carpetbag Union rule. Some Negroes actually rode with the Redshirts, and Georgians joined the ranks to swell the needed vote on election day. See Bibliog-raphy, Kirkland and Kennedy, II, 223.

** Daniel Chamberlain was the Radical governor of South Carolina from 1872 to 1876, when he was defeated by Hampton.

On Hampton Day in Camden, the cannon boomed, old cannon of the Revolution, silent now for ninety years. Resin barrels flamed on the street corners. Hampton bestrode the scene, Hampton, the giant, whose very name evoked memories of the old campfires and tattered battle flags, Hampton, with the golden beard of a Viking. You heard the song, the wonderful song with the swear words that even Bernard Baruch could sing with no fear of punishment:

> *"Hampton eat de egg,*
> *Chamberlain eat de shell,*
> *Hampton go to heaven,*
> *Chamberlain go to hell."* [65]

Out of that chaos of murder and bribery and fraud and intimidation that was a Southern election in the seventies, Bernard Baruch was to learn his first lessons in politics, not exactly those found in the textbooks. In after years, his father would tell and retell the story of that fantastic election day when the Redshirts rode from polling booth to polling booth, voting in masses as the carpetbaggers voted the Negroes, defeating the outlanders at their own game. Here, at one center, tickets were distributed to an out-of-town circus. At another, a shot exploded into the air. In the melee the polls were closed until order was restored and the election boxes switched about, so the Negroes who could not read put their ballots into the Hampton box.[66] Then came the months of aftermath, when Congressmen flashed arms on the floor of the House, and the "snarling rejoinders" of members and the sullen galleries were ominously reminiscent of the days of 1860–61. It has been almost forgotten today how dangerously near Americans came to a second civil war in 1876, with troops massing for a march on Washington to inaugurate Samuel J. Tilden by force of arms.[67] In South Carolina, every street corner and fireside was a public forum, the whole state "quivering on the edge of an explosion . . . so terrific that the outbreak of 1860–61 will be almost forgotten," a writer in the *Atlantic Monthly* believed. This was worse than 1861. The Southern people were not merely outvoted; they felt they were being defrauded of the nation's choice.[68]

Bernard Baruch, of course, was too young to have clear memories of '76 but that dark and bitter time took long to clear away in the Deep South. From a clamor and maze of impressions stands out

Baruch's recollection of one election night * and his mother's command to the boys to get their guns.

They were alone in the house, the mother and the four young children: Hartwig, ten or twelve years old; Bernard, two years younger; and the two little children. The doctor was away, for even after 1876 there still was work for a surgeon on election night in South Carolina. Outside, the din became louder, closer.

The boys moved for their guns.[69] They took them down: two old single-barreled shotguns and they loaded them and there on the gallery they stood, two staunch stubby little figures, guns lifted. Before them, like a nightmare, a mob was milling, Negroes and carpetbaggers and scalawags, all the riffraff of the town, dead-drunk on cheap whiskey. Nothing was real, nothing but the sound of their mother's voice — "Don't shoot unless I say so." [70]

As if in a dream, Bernard saw a Negro stagger out from behind a large tree and fall to the ground. Then, still like a dream, the whole mob dissolved and faded from view. The men and the women, the Negroes and the whites scattered in all directions. The pounding feet and shrieking voices died away. All was quiet. Nothing was left but the empty street with the resin barrels flaming, and the dark shape of the Negro, lying there beneath the tree, his head outlined in blood.

His head had been split open, as you might smash a coconut, Baruch has recalled. Someone had struck him a hideous blow from behind. Bewildered, the Baruch boys crouched beside him; then their mother came up with water. Tenderly she bathed and dressed the terrible wound, but little could be done.[71]

It is all history now, that dark and troubled time almost as dim and far distant as the battles of the *Iliad*. Yet living on, even into the Atomic Age, were Southerners who had known fathers who had fought at Sharpsburg as well as they had known grandsons returning from Salerno; who had grown up in the bloody days of Reconstruction and all their lives long were to battle with the problems arising out of that time.

For out of the "peace" of Reconstruction came the pattern of twentieth-century American race relations, of the conflicts between North and South, of party alignments; and, most important of all,

* Baruch is uncertain whether this was in 1878 or 1880.

perhaps, the basic motivations of a generation of American Southerners, of whom Bernard Baruch was one. There can be no understanding of this man without an understanding of the Reconstruction
South from which he sprang.

Only as the dust settles does the Tragic Era come clear. And as
we rebuild our latest enemies from later and more bitter wars, it may
be well to look back and remember the "peace" that Americans gave
their fellow countrymen.

In the seventies the North had yet a very real fear that the South
might salvage victory from defeat, combining with the New West to
challenge the East's industrial and financial empire. Furthermore,
some Southern leaders themselves, men to whom agriculture was a
business, not a way of life, stood ready to cast aside their old agrarian
spokesmen, if only they could share in the rich harvest of the Northern plutocracy. Others sincerely thought the only hope of their section lay in recognizing the facts of defeat and trying to make the most
of what could be made. These so-called Southern Redeemers, the
businessmen or "Cotton Snobs" of the prewar South, actually joined
with the North in programs which defrauded both Negroes and
poor whites of economic opportunity, fanned the flames of racial
hatred, and set them at each other's throats.

Even some Northern radicals, their political battle won, could
throw the mask aside, calling the Negroes "ignorant, narrow-minded,
vicious, worthless animals." From South Carolina the "New Southerner" Pitchfork Ben Tillman exulted: "The brotherhood of man
exists no longer . . . You shoot Negroes in Illinois when they come
into competition with your labor, and we shoot them in South
Carolina when they come into competition with us in elections." [72]

Traditional Southern leaders like Wade Hampton had not wished
to deprive the Negro of his new political status. "If there is a white
man," said Hampton, "believes that when I am elected Governor I
will . . . grant him any of the privileges and immunities that shall not
be granted to the colored man, he is mistaken." [73] And at a Democratic county convention in Barnwell, South Carolina, of the 203
members, 49 were Negroes.

In any event, the "Great Betrayal" came, which condemned the
South to colonial status in the Union for three-quarters of a century,
and in the shadow of which Bernard Baruch passed his formative
years.

When he was five years old he was sent to school. School in the postwar South was a hit-or-miss affair, ostensibly provided for in the new state constitutions; somewhat less provided for in tax revenues.[74] Segregation offered more problems. South Carolina experimented with integrated schools under Reconstruction, but by 1874, of the state's 200,000 children of school age, only 75,000 were attending schools at all.[75]

Among the numbers of small private schools formed was Mr. Wallace's establishment beside the DeKalb monument in Camden. It was a mile and a half from the Baruch house by road or only a mile as the boys went, across country and creeks, tin lunch boxes swinging at their sides. One of Bernard's early memories was of the Wallaces' kitchen, where meals were endlessly cooking, surroundings which might later come back to him as he read *Nicholas Nickleby* or *David Copperfield*. Stomach-down on the floor, he spelled out his letters, all the while seeing Mrs. Wallace, her baby on her knee noisily gulping its porridge to the drone of the ABC's and a sudden hiss from the stove.

The school itself was different. It was a small-town school, typical of the thousands of one-room schoolhouses all over the country that shaped the American man and leader of the first quarter of the twentieth century. It had long benches and high old-fashioned desks that opened on top, and in the corner a bundle of hickory sticks, peeled and waiting. Of books there were almost none; the few left were read ragged and passed from one child to another.

But young Bernard's eyes were riveted on the center of the room where Mr. Wallace stood, rigid and unyielding as the rule in his outstretched hand. From the boys' viewpoint, he was a hard teacher and a rigid disciplinarian, but Schoolmaster Wallace was goaded by a conscience no less Presbyterian than his name. He knew the effort, the actual privation many parents suffered to send a child to school. He knew the desperate need for education in this war-torn land. So, the slightest inattention brought the sharp sting of the ruler against the unruly knuckles or palm; and any real negligence, a beating. Mr. Wallace's enforced study habits were to stand Bernie in good stead as he went on to graduate from the College of the City of New York.

These were his schooldays, hot, dusty days in the Reconstruction South of the seventies. It would all seem incredible to him later on — that this freckle-faced, shabby little country boy, bare feet swinging

from a knife-scarred bench, should, scarcely twenty years later, have
a seat on the Stock Exchange in New York.[76]

Schoolmaster Wallace's precepts remained with him. Perhaps it
was even Mr. Wallace's Presbyterian conscience reinforcing his own
that spelled the outcome of his first and only theft, committed right
there in the classroom.

He had seen it when the other boy opened his desk — a big piece
of store candy, the kind you got only at Christmas or New Year's,
which grew continually bigger in his imagination. He could not forget it; he could not stop thinking about it. Late in the day, when the
schoolhouse was locked and empty and the dust had sifted back upon
the desks and floor, Bernie wriggled underneath the building, forced
up one of the wide floorboards, slipped through, seized the candy, and
fled to the woods, where he ate it in a gulp.

Never had sweetness tasted more bitter. The memory of candy
lying heavy in his stomach and even more heavily upon his conscience
lingered with him. Years later in Wall Street, when a young man
offered him $1500 to make a favorable report on a company, the
lesson was still in his mind as he rejected the bribe. In telling the
story later, he made no claim to moral courage. He had decided that
it took far more courage to do wrong and that it paid to do right. A
guilty conscience hurt. When past eighty he could still say that that
childhood theft was one of two sins that he had regretted all his life.
As for the other — "I've never told anyone," he would drawl, eyes
twinkling, "and I'm not going to tell you now." [77]

The weekly elocution programs at school were sheer torment.
Washed and starched and compressed into his "Sunday best," he
struggled hopelessly while "The boy stood on the burning deck" or
"The Conquered Banner" waved again. It was the age of recitation
in America — of "Curfew Must Not Ring To-night" and "You'd
scarce expect one of my age," and as the son of the most talented
amateur actress in Camden, Bernie's plight was all the more deplorable.

Hartwig was here in his element — so good, in fact, that not ten
years later he would be declaiming professionally behind the footlights. But Bernie was terrified. Only his mother could bring him
forward and had she told him to creep into a lion's den and pull out
the tongue of the beast by its roots, Bernie would have done it for
her.

One terrible night the boy faced a gathering in the Mannes Baum home. He knew his lines; he had been reciting them up and down the house for weeks. Slowly, he began: "On Linden when the sun was low — " As the singsong started, with Bernie momentarily pausing for breath, his father in a sudden effort to correct him pressed his finger to the side of his nose and let loose a sound resembling nothing so much as *ta-dah — ta-dah — ta-dah — ta-dah.*

Dr. Baruch never forgave himself for the result. With a howl Bernie burst from the stage and out into the night — of which he was terrified — ran all the way home, sobbing, and crawled into bed, where he cried himself to sleep. Not for years would he attempt public speaking again, and he would never be a "Southern orator" in the popular meaning of that term. Long afterwards, when he lamented to President Woodrow Wilson his incapacity for oratory, the President silenced him. There were too many, he said, who liked to speak, "and too few to do things. I wouldn't advise you even to try." [78]

On the whole, Bernard Baruch was a happy child. He had a wholesome family life, parents who adored him and each other, and a houseful of young brothers to play with. Above all, and what is rarest for a Jewish child, he had a sense of belonging, of identification with the community. Without knowledge of this, understanding of Bernard Baruch, either as a Jew or as a man, is not possible. "He was one of us," said the Charleston newspaper editor William Watts Ball, of Baruch's father. [79] It did not matter that Dr. Baruch came of an alien land and an alien faith. He had married a Southern girl; he had worn the Confederate uniform; he had fought and suffered for his adopted state. As "one of us" he had stood with the men of the South.

The Baruchs were leaders in their little community. The preacher, the teachers, and the doctor were the "big men" in a small town, and of them all it was the doctor who was most closely involved with his neighbors. In Camden Dr. Baruch presided at births, eased the dying, and was a discreet and confidential friend. [80] He doctored everyone, without stint and often without pay, carpetbagger and Confederate, white man and black. [81] "Oh, he was a fine, good old doctor," Creola Bracey has recalled. "All out in the country, he nursed the poor colored people, walking and stepping about." The poor Negroes "looked upon him as a god; they came trooping in to see him"; no

one else cared for them, or tended them. When he moved north in
1883, "de folks, dey died like flies," survivors told his son Bernard
years later.[82] Consistently he upheld the highest ideals of his profession. "Do not enter the medical profession to make money," Dr.
Baruch would tell his classes in later years. "Study medicine only
with the idea that . . . you will help your fellow man. Do not expect
gratitude and you will never be disappointed." [83] He was the living
embodiment of his words. But South Carolina was grateful, and
when he was only thirty years old elected the former immigrant boy
head of the State Board of Health and of the State Medical Association.

The Baruchs were beloved for what they were. They were intelligent, attractive young people, and inspired everywhere a feeling of
affection.[84] Everyone knew them. Everyone liked them and their
children.

It has been said that Bernard Baruch never knew that he was
Jewish until he was past eleven years of age, and in one sense this is
true: he never knew that it mattered. Realization was not forced
upon him. That the Baruchs were Jewish was of no more interest or
consequence in the community than that the Wallaces were Presbyterians, or others, Episcopalians. If the Baruch boys were irked at
having to wear their oversized copper-toed shoes on both Saturday
and Sunday, and were confined to their yard Saturdays, these were
again mere religious practices, of no more note or significance than
the foot-washing rituals of the more simple neighbors, or the total-
immersion ceremonies in the "Race." As few Jewish children can be,
the Baruch boys were accepted for themselves, and thus grew up
psychologically sound and healthy.

This is not to say that the boys were denied religious instruction.
Miss Belle was especially devout; all forms of worship had her respect,
and hence her boys wore their Sunday best out of respect for their
neighbors' Sabbath as well as their own. Old residents of Charleston
recall the Baruchs and the children in attendance on holy days at the
synagogue of Beth Elohim, but Bernard has no memory of these
early journeys.[85] That they occurred is probable, for there was no
synagogue in Camden. Dr. Baruch proposed the founding of a
Hebrew Sabbath School in the town, which his four sons attended.[86]

The historical and ethical precepts of his faith, more than the
strictly religious doctrines, stirred Dr. Baruch. He was a charter

WHEN THE REDSHIRTS RODE

member and president of the Hebrew Benevolent Association, the only organized Jewish group in town, and his beautiful letter of resignation in the winter of 1880 illumines the philosophy that would be reflected so vividly by his famous son.

"As parents and Jews," he admonished the group before his departure for the North, "it is your most solemn duty to educate your children not only mentally but morally also . . . Thus only will you enable them to become useful citizens . . . who by their upright lives and moral excellence will afford examples . . . to other sects and shed lustre on Judaism." The doctrines of the Bible, "as expressed in the book of Leviticus and especially in the Ten Commandments form the basis of the moral laws of all civilized nations." Thus it was a solemn responsibility to hand down the sacred book to the children, to teach them the history of the Jews and the Laws and precepts of their faith. Above all else must be instilled into their minds "the grand fundamental idea of Judaism," the belief in one omniscient and omnipresent God, who weighed in the balance of justice "our every action and thought and to whom we must at last render an account of our lives . . . Teach the children to observe the Sabbath day inviolate if you would have them honor you in your grey hairs . . . Let them keep that one day to the welfare of their souls, while the other days are devoted to their bodies."

His son might have made the final plea: "I beg of you to show the people of other sects you can, as Jews, be good, upright, moral men and useful citizens. This has been my great aim in the community and I can at this moment allude to my ample reward without egotism. Do not allow yourselves to entertain a prejudice against any sect, but remember the persecution of our people in former times and even at the present day; each man has a right to worship God according to his own belief and education." [87]

This was the intellectual climate of ethics and faith in which Bernard Baruch was nurtured.

He was playing outside the house one day when a traveler with a long gray beard and a pack on his back paused and pointed to the name on Dr. Baruch's sign. Bewildered, the ten-year-old backed up against the house as the stranger advanced toward him smiling. Just then the doctor rode up, mud spattered across his saddlebags. He took the stranger into the office, where for hours Bernard could hear the murmur of their voices — strange words in a strange tongue.

The visitor stayed all night. The next morning, after he had gone, Dr. Baruch took Bernard aside. Then, for the first time, the boy heard the story of the Wandering Jew, of the Jews who were scattered all over the world and the age-old prejudices against them. "You must always remember the sufferings of these people from whom you are descended," Dr. Baruch said. "We are even now suffering from intolerance. Sometime, son, you must take up this question and do something about it." Then he quoted the words of Robert E. Lee, "Do your duty in all things." It was your duty to "always remember your fellow man." This was the principle of medicine.

"Help these unfortunate people," Dr. Baruch continued, "but always remember your first allegiance is to the flag . . . Never forget that the American Constitution is the finest thing man has invented . . . that comes first and nothing else." He added, smiling, "Don't you ever let 'em touch a stick or a stone of it, or I'll come back to haunt you." [88]

The charter for Baruch's future relationship with the faith from which he sprang is in these words, which might have been paraphrased: "Render therefore unto Caesar the things which are Caesar's; and unto God the things that are God's." Here was a statement that would guide him but also, because it established divided loyalties, would often be misunderstood. Yet these principles alone might have carried little weight had it not been for the mixed quality of his heritage. If on his father's side he was one with the more recent immigration, on his mother's side he was part of the established American life.* As "one of us," he could lay claim to a heritage and an identification with the past that few Jewish Americans could ever share. Emotionally he was incapable of seeing the Jew as differentiated from any one of the other immigrant groups from which the American people sprang. America was the homeland of the Jew no less than of the onetime Dutchman, Frenchman, German, or Scot. There was neither room nor need for Zionist movements among Americans. Emotionally Baruch was never able to understand why he was not consistently accepted on his own terms by Zionists or old Americans. He lacked the background for prejudice. Seeing himself always as first a Southerner and an American, Baruch could never understand those who insisted on considering him primarily a Jew.

---

* "Belle Wolfe's family was one of the oldest and most distinguished in South Carolina." See Bibliography, Henning.

Nor would his fellow Jews ever quite understand that when he said "my people," he meant his fellow Americans and South Carolinians.

The most painful hurts of his early childhood had nothing to do with religious matters. He never forgot the cruelty of a woman visitor from New York, who peered through a lorgnette at the scrubbed but bare feet of the Baruch boys and then tossed them a dime to buy some shoes. They bolted for home, mad and humiliated.[89]

Such happenings were rare. The Baruchs were as well-to-do as anyone in the community, but everyone was poor. There was almost nothing to buy — cloth, shoes, coffee, tea, and salt were about all. Residents made their own brown sugar and candy; oranges or raisins were treats for great occasions like birthdays or Christmas.[90]

But the Baruch family lived high on "hawg and hominy" as Baruch would say afterwards. For them also were lettuce and greens, fresh from their own garden, berries, sweet in the wintertime with the taste of summer still upon them. They would shake the dew from the Damson plums as they picked them, or, under Minerva's direction, belabor the big mulberry tree in the garden to insure its bearing another year. And fall after sun-drenched fall, they would hear the papery crunch of dry leaves under their feet, know the smells of forest and swamp, watch the ripples across the fishing holes, and ransack the woods for hickory nuts. They trapped and hunted, Bernie carrying an old gun with a leather pouch for shot, and powder in a cow's horn.[91] These were his proudest possessions, paid for by moving up and down the cotton rows, or by gathering bits of scrap metal left in the wake of the armies, not only of Sherman, but Cornwallis and Greene, too.

For Camden had been a battleground in that earlier war, and the red clay streets were stained, so the Negroes said, with the blood of patriots butchered by Cornwallis' men. There was "Cornwallis house" up on Magazine Hill; Pickens and Sumter, and Marion and his swamp soldiers were real to the Baruch boys,[92] and still living were those who could recall the old stories their fathers had told — of the battles of Cowpens or King's Mountain, or of Camden, perhaps the most crushing defeat ever suffered by Americans on American soil.[93]

Up on Hobkirk Hill the old graves hunched beneath long grass and the shadow of a crumbling wall. A boy, looking hard, could even discern the faint outline of the stockade jail where the thirteen-year-old prisoner Andrew Jackson, soldier of the Revolution, burning with fever and a festering wound in his head, peered out to watch the onslaught of battle. There were other mounds, too, covered with whortleberries, and the year that Bernard Baruch was six, one caved in and tumbled onto the road its tragic bundle of skeletons, whose buttons were those of the Eighty-third British Regiment. As late as 1900 little boys could pry loose the bullets of Greene's or Marion's men from the old trees, or amidst the underbrush of Parker Old Field unearth some moldering relics — buckles, buttons, bullets, even old flintlocks and cannon balls lost a century and more before.[94]

Spring was a wonderful time in Camden. Floods roared down the Wateree, turning familiar fields and hills into "undiscovered islands." It was time for country boys to build rafts and bob downstream, or to watch the yellow waters climb along the banks of the riverside cemetery, up, up almost to the sunken tomb where "Agnes of Glasgow," a Scottish Evangeline, lay.[95]

This was the heritage of young Bernard Baruch. It was an American heritage, steeped in legend and tradition. It was a heritage of beauty: old residents would say that there "is more charm here than in a dozen South Carolina towns this size." [96] Walls festooned in roses and wisteria framed old gardens, like that at Lusanne, where inside the house hung a Peale portrait of Washington. Springs were pink with peach bloom and autumns vivid with the flaming blackjack. Elms lined the wide sandy streets, their leaves hanging in streamers, dripping slowly after a storm to dimple the fast-sinking pools of water below.

Through the green shone the soot-charred columns of mansions like Pine Flat and the Kennedy place. Closer to the roadside crowded the old double-galleried Charleston-style dwellings, of which a few still stand today. Of them all, stately and white, with its pediment across the columned doorway, none was more beautiful than the house where Bernard Baruch was born.

Historic and beautiful, too, was the old Robert Mills courthouse, dating back to 1824, its four huge Doric columns shading the iron stairway to the gallery. The site was historic, for there, in an earlier courthouse, a "Little Declaration of Independence" was prepared in November 1774.[97] Camden was a city of parks and statues, and of memorials like the Lafayette cedars, planted by the general during his American tour in 1824. Mary Young, who had been one of the girls in white from the Female Academy who had strewn flowers in his path, was still living in Camden during Baruch's boyhood. She remembered Lafayette very well and delighted in recounting her sight of him, red-haired and quite lame, "one of the homeliest men she had ever seen." [98]

A white marble horse trough marked the place where Hampton spoke during the Redshirts' Ride. In Kershaw Square, where a fountain plashed softly into a little pool and four old Revolutionary cannon stood at the corners, was a miniature Pantheon, vines outlining its pergola. Each of the six white columns bore the name of a Camden general of the Confederate War: these were the heroes that were dead but there were, too, the heroes that were living. Youngsters like Bernard could thrill to the daredevil exploits of youths like the six-foot-four-inch "Bully Billy" Cash. Hidden in the underbrush, near Factory Pond, a small boy could watch breathless as young Cash perfected his marksmanship for future shooting affrays, by firing again and again at the outline of an "Iron Man" fastened to a nearby tree.[99]

Of all in Bernard Baruch's youthful gallery of heroes, none could compare with his brother, Hartwig. "Harty" took to fighting with a relish and was something of a local champion. Harty could do anything. Harty was the leader of the gang wars between the "uptown" and "downtown" boys, which flared into battle after baseball games behind the jail when Bernard, like most of his crowd, usually got a good beating.

Yet it was Bernard, not Hartwig, who, as the boys stood in a barnyard waiting tensely for an announced attack, swung down from the gate and made for the barn. He was going to cut a hickory stick, he shouted back, and whale the daylights out of the downtown boys.

Whooping with joy, the others came pounding after him. Even the older boys thought Bernie's idea had merit. Quickly they pried the spokes from an old wagon wheel, hid, and waited. The rout was complete.[100]

This was the first time, Baruch has recalled, that he was ever of any particular use to his gang. It was a triumph that he needed. Like many "middle children," he was constantly overshadowed by his older brother. His rages were ungovernable; in fights with boys his own size, he invariably lost his head. Once, when Hartwig borrowed his prized fishing rod, he hurled a rock at the older boy, striking him in the mouth.[101] Bernard was all normal small boy. His was a kind of Tom Sawyer or Huckleberry Finn childhood. Growing up was a time of caves and rafts and of frenzied games of baseball or marbles, of peanuts and pink candy and of lemonade and of tagging happily after a little country circus parade. He was one of the pack of boys, shucking off shirts and pants on the run as they made for their swimming hole, Factory Pond, on the steamy summer days. Still on the run, they would dive from their clothes and into the water.

First Stump — Second Stump — Third Stump, and Flat Stump, strung out across the pool. These were the successive measure of a boy's athletic attainments. Harty gained them all. Bernie was too little and too young. But the thrill of the first time he swam to First Stump lingered for a lifetime.[102] Seventy-five years later he would still remember that cool water closing over his skin, the rush and purr of the dam, and the names of the boys who swam beside him, echoing in memory like a roll call: Workman, Zemp, Wittkowsky, Moore, DePass, Boykin, Cantey, Wallace.

For the children's elders, too, there was inward peace in that troubled time. An amateur play, a Shakespearean reading, a single copy of a magazine from New York — out of these rose discussions to fill an entire evening. Only a few books had been salvaged from destruction, but like the tattered magazines or stray copies of the Charleston *Courier*, they were treasured articles, passed from house to house.

Then Dr. Simon Baruch's hard-won calm was shattered.

It all rose out of a law case, a case of fraud, so it was charged, between the dueling E. B. C. Cash, father of Bully Billy, and Colonel William Shannon of Camden, a man so popular that Cash's side of the story could only get a hearing in Republican newspapers. Words and notes were exchanged, honor assailed. In the end, Shannon challenged Cash to one of the last duels to be fought in the South, one of the last two fatal duels in the United States.

The meeting was set for July 5, 1880, at Dubose's Bridge in Darlington. The news had spread and a "motley" crowd of about a hundred sensation-seekers had gathered. Dr. Baruch, Shannon's surgeon, stood watching as he saluted his opponent, took a last look at his wife's picture, then aimed low and fired. The sand sprayed up harmlessly around Cash's feet. Almost deliberately, Cash waited, as the crowd became tense. Did they remember his pledge? "If Colonel Shannon does not disable me, I will shoot my ball through his heart." [103]

Slowly, Cash lifted his hand and pistol. Slowly and deliberately, he fired. Shannon dropped. A moment later, Dr. Baruch was kneeling over him.[104]

The next day, hoofbeats pounded to a stop before the office of Simon Baruch. Out the doctor came to confront six of his neighbors, mounted and armed. Young Bernard, backed up against his father's arm, watched them. The spirit of lynch law was astir in Camden. Once more Dr. Baruch saw the ugly passions violence can rouse. And only his own urgings prevented the posse from swooping down on Colonel Cash and hanging him in his own front yard.

Involvement in duels was no shockingly new experience for Dr. Baruch, who had once himself accepted a challenge from a lawyer whose client had been convicted through the doctor's medical testimony. Stoically Dr. Baruch had continued his practice as the date approached, even delivering a baby to the daughter of his antagonist. Fortunately, a few days before the duel was to be fought the attorney learned that Dr. Baruch's testimony had been quite truthful and the challenge was withdrawn.[105]

But since the age of fourteen Simon Baruch had been seeking peace and had found very little. Now this new sign that bloodshed and hatred was still so much the pattern of local life in those bitter times may have been a decisive influence. He was weary of violence and feared its effect on his children. Of course there were other reasons for moving away — reasons which must have been weighed and debated over a long time. Hydrotherapy was more and more in his mind. The North would offer far better opportunities for research than South Carolina.

The boys were growing up. Where would they get their schooling and what would they learn? Not until twenty years after the war would an effective public school system be established in South Carolina. Meanwhile a whole generation of white children was being reared, picking up, as William G. McAdoo later remembered of his own childhood in Georgia, "a little education here and there, like a bird picking up crumbs." [106] Could not Dr. Baruch do better for his sons? He traveled north to see, and in 1881 the family followed him. For Bernard and his brothers, the first chapter of childhood was ended. Gone were the sleepy days, echoing only to the *clop-clop* of hoofs and the slow creak and strain of the wagon wheels, the long warm twilights, broken only by the far-off shouts and the crack of a bat against a ball.

It was heartbreak to say goodbye to Minerva. And the parting from Sharp would always remain one of the poignant memories of Baruch's life. It was from Sharp that Bernard had learned what it really meant to love a dog. Sharp was an English mastiff. He swam with the Baruch boys, he hunted with them, he followed them to school. He rooted out the rats from under the corncrib. He was the standard by which they judged every other dog in town. Yet this was a comradeship that Baruch would only find again in after years when he had returned to South Carolina, when he came back home.[107]

Now he was going from the place where his heart would always be. There was no room for Sharp in the old family buggy with its load of boys and baggage. The horse pulled forward . . . dust whirled around the wheels. They must have gone by Winnsboro, Bernard thought in later years, for his last memory of South Carolina was of Grandmother Wolfe's cookies in the food hamper. So long and crowded was that trip, over three-quarters of a century ago, that all memory of it has faded from Bernard Baruch's mind, except for what a typical boy would remember — a stopover in Richmond, where he ate the most wonderful food he had ever tasted.[108]

Then came an evening when a river glowed like opals in the sunset and the waters purred softly around the prow of the ferry. Not until he read a novel of the nineteen-twenties by Garet Garrett [109] did that forgotten memory flash again across Baruch's mind. Then he saw it all once more, as he had seen and felt it forty-odd years before. It was, he said, one of the three great thrills of his life. Out of the mist and shadows rose the enchanted city, windows blazing with sun. The din of scows and tugboats shrilled about him, and gulls wove shadow-patterns at his feet, as ahead of the big ferry loomed the slips where the boats were berthed in stalls. Bernard watched the narrowing of the strip of water ahead. Upward the ship heaved, and down into a whirling froth of whiteness, and there was a soft thud as gently it touched shore. The gates burst open, and the close-packed people streamed out. The long trip was over. Bernard Baruch's first impression of New York City was of the El with its chugging steam engines.[110]

2

GROWING UP WITH NEW YORK

ANCESTRALLY speaking, to arrive in New York was a kind of home-coming for "Miss Belle" and her children. Few American families have had older roots in the city than the Marques, or Marquise, strain from which Belle Wolfe Baruch had sprung.[1]

Isaac Rodriguez Marques was the first American ancestor. He was a skipper and shipowner of Spanish and Portuguese ancestry, sailing in to the port of New York from Denmark as early as 1695. That he was in the slave trade is possible; that he may even have been a pirate his great-great-great-great-great-grandson jocularly likes to believe.[2] In the reform wave that rolled over New York a year or so later, several of the city's foremost citizens, including special friends of Captain Marques, were ruined and haled to the gallows. Piracy had gone out of fashion, but the newcomer remained rigidly within the law and out of jail.[3]

But this was later. New York City was a freebooter's paradise back in 1695, rivaling even Charleston and Newport; and its mayor, William Merritt, a shrewd sailor-of-fortune, was blessed of all ship-owners for his liberal attitude toward "the trade." Hand-in-glove with the jovial mayor was the florid and flamboyant Governor Benjamin Fletcher, with his estate at Whitehall and his dinners at the Executive Mansion, where mariners were ever welcome, and over a drink Captain Marques might discover even Thomas Tew to be a most pleasant companion.[4]

It was only a generation since Peter Stuyvesant had stumped across the stage of New Amsterdam, ostrich plumes waving, the silver bands and nailheads of his wooden leg glittering in the sun.[5] New York was a bustling boomtown at the end of the seventeenth century, with some 3500 inhabitants tucked behind the great city gates and the nine-foot wooden wall. Only the burghers dreaming on Bowling Green remembered the canals and the windmills of the old days, the smell of pear blossoms on the "Bouwerie," and the tulips, lacquered and bright.[6] Of a different and more worldly world was the seafaring Captain Marques.[7] His three ships shuttled regularly between New York and England, or alternately to England, the Gold Coast, the West Indies, and home. Wheat and skins he carried to England; from England, he brought manufactured goods; sugar and rum from Barbados; and to the West Indies, ivory and Negroes from the Guinea coast. Yet, however much profit he may have reaped from human flesh, his descendants paid for it amply in the War Between the States.[8]

In his day, however, the trade was considered legitimate enough, and as for piracy, virtually every shipmaster sailing out of New York was under suspicion. On Broad Street, Mayor Merritt's store welcomed cargoes of every description without any carping inquiries.[9] Great was the indignation in society when an "honest seaman" like Captain Kidd was hanged in London on palpably trumped-up charges.

Captain Marques, however, early chose respectability. So on a bright September day in 1697 he repaired to Coenties Slip and the City Hall, and there from the steps, with the stocks, pillory, ducking stool, and like accessories standing as if in warning before him, the Captain by official examination and Act of the Mayor and Aldermen, was duly sworn in as a "freeman" of the city upon payment of five pounds.[10]

Only "gentlemen" were eligible for the privileges of a freeman — to vote and to bear arms. It was on a gentleman's estate that Captain Marques settled down in a large brick mansion house on old "Paeral" Street, where the paving of oyster shells made your eyes ache in the sunlight, and the fields swept down to the East River shore.[11] One account has it that Captain Marques was at that time New York's richest man.[12]

It was a pleasant neighborhood, this cradle of Bernard Baruch's family in America. In the "dark time of the moon," streets were lighted by lanterns hung from poles in front of every seventh house, the costs divided among the residents. Watchmen patroled, their bells sounding, calling the weather and the hours. A block away from Captain Marques' house rose the De Peyster mansion, and

across the street lived the widow and children of the late lamented
Captain Kidd. A sugar importer named Nicholas Roosevelt was
alderman of the ward, and other neighbors included the shipowner
and builder Rip Van Dam, later New York's first native-born mayor,
and William Peartree, who was to inaugurate the first free public
school in the city.

Most of Captain Marques' neighbors were of the old Dutch stock.
Yet there were many, too, of Sephardic origin like his own, such as
his rabbi, Abraham du Lucena, or New York's leading Jewish citizen,
the wheat exporter Luiz Gomez, who traced his ancestry back to the
old Spanish nobility.

The Rodriguez Marques family was large and prominent, descended
from ancient Hebrew lines or, as family legend had it, from the
House of David itself.[13] The wandering, high-spirited Sephardic
race of artists and scholars, poets, surgeons, and navigators, who have
put their imprint on the cultures of Portugal and Spain, and who,
caught in the toils of the Inquisition, were tortured, slaughtered, and
driven across the earth, are among the most cultured citizens of all
Europe. Of these early families few were better known in Rotterdam, Amsterdam, London, Paris, Madrid, and the Indies than the
clan of Rodriguez Marques.[14]

Yet, after a generation or so in America, Captain Marques' line
drops temporarily from sight. His two daughters died young; his son
Jacob migrated to Barbados. Jacob's son, another Isaac, forty-four
years old in the year of the Declaration of Independence, returned
to marry a Long Island girl, and to fight through the Revolution as
a private with Colonel Van Rensselaer's Fourth Albany County Regiment of militia.[15]

A last link with these old days was Bernard Baruch's great-grandmother Cohen. She had been born Deborah Marks (Marques) in
Charleston, South Carolina, eighteen years after the surrender at
Yorktown, and could remember the gunfire of 1812, and a ball at
which the Marquis de Lafayette had bowed over her hand. She
was eighty-two when the Baruchs moved to New York, a fastidious
old lady in her shawls and mitts (half-hands, little Bernie called
them) but between her and her eleven-year-old grandson was a link
that spanned time. She could remember more wars than one — the
ugly days of Nullification, the great Calhoun addressing the tense
crowds in Charleston's Harmony Hall Theater; the bugles and

banners as the men of South Carolina marched off to the Mexican
War; Fort Sumter and the shells bursting through the streets of
Charleston, the Stars and Bars bright against the Southern sky.
Often she told the story of her own mother, London-born Sarah
Harris, who had died nearly fifty years before Bernard Baruch was
born. She had grown up in New York during the aftermath of the
Revolution, in a gutted city where flames in 1776 had eaten away
at the little red-brick Dutch village below the "wall" that Captain
Isaac Marques had known. From her family, friends, and future
husband she would hear the story of New York under siege, and the
footfalls of the retreating Continentals, and the groan and creak of
their guns.

Now, a century and more later, the great-grandson of Sarah Harris
was seeing and hearing it all again — the cockfights and bullbaiting
and ring of hard British gold on the counters; "The Roast Beef of Old
England" roaring from the windows of Fraunces' Tavern; and under
it all, the dark river of misery flowing through a city of defeat —
the tents and shanties on the fire-ruins, men dying on the pews of
the churches and synagogues, rumors of the Delaware crossing and
Benedict Arnold, and what a ruddy-cheeked schoolmaster from Cov-
entry, Connecticut, named Nathan Hale, had said the morning he
was hanged, over in Rutger's Orchard on East Broadway.[16] And then
had come the twenty-fifth of November, 1783, with the British trooping in file onto their ships and the great sails swelling and the
Continentals marching in from Westchester "by way of the Bowery"
in all their dirt and rags and laughter. Even now, a hundred years
later, you could see the old tavern and the Long Room, where a week
after Evacuation Day the toasts were drunk and Washington had
kissed his generals goodbye before descending to the East River
shore for the voyage home.[17] And it was the son of Isaac Marques,
one of Washington's returned Continentals, that Sarah Harris married. He was young Captain Samuel Marks, born a decade before
Bunker Hill,[18] officially a privateersman on the run from Barbados
to Charleston, but rumored to be unofficially not so far from the
traditions of his pirate ancestor. He and Sarah met in New York and
moved to Charleston, where Marks settled into the more peaceful
pursuit of running a store.

But what a heritage they had left for an imaginative and impres-
sionable little boy! Seeing and listening to their daughter, his great-

grandmother, it was as if the whole terrible parade had passed in review before Bernard's own eyes. It was as if he had seen the Continentals and his own great-great-grandfather marching along the Bowery, or heard Lafayette tell again the words that Washington had said. It was as if the whole American Revolution was a part of his own memory. He, too, would live to be very old. His life would bridge the years between the Lost Cause and the Atomic Age. He would not only live through history, but he would make it, and he would feel and grasp the sweep of it around him. Looking always to the future, he had lived through the past; through the eyes of his great-grandmother he had seen America from its beginning. This was his heritage.

From the sun-dappled lanes and the big airy house in Camden to New York City and two furnished rooms in a brownstone front on West 57th Street was like a trip from freedom into prison for the Baruch boys, Bernard especially. The city frightened him.[19]

One comfort was Mrs. Jacobs, their landlady. She was a large kindly-looking woman, with a row of stiff curls marching in procession across her forehead. She had hands that knew how to dive into a boy's pockets and leave a gumdrop or a peppermint behind, and a heart that knew the emptiness of a boy's stomach when he came racing home from school and how to fill that emptiness with raisins and fruit, left waiting on the dining room table.

Miss Belle adapted herself quickly. Here in New York were organizations that she could enjoy, even a Wade Hampton Chapter of the United Daughters of the Confederacy. A born "joiner," in her mature years she was regent of the Knickerbocker Chapter of the Daughters of the American Revolution, president of the Washington Headquarters Club and of the Southland Club of New York.[20]

The boys had yet to make a place for themselves. Vaguely, they sensed that each must learn to stand alone and unafraid in this world of "great noises" into which they had been hurled — of wails and roars, of horsecars that lumbered and elevated railways that shrieked, and boys and girls — never had they imagined there were so many boys and girls in the world.

Even to the boys of the nineteen-fifties, New York Public School No. 59 on West 54th Street, between Sixth and Seventh Avenue, is a terrifying place. Rearing three stories high in its soot-stained

Gothic and brownstone, it has changed little in the three-quarters
of a century since Bernard Baruch was entered there. The gaslights
are gone. Bone-breaking cement now seals the playground, walled
in by brick like a prison courtyard. The old schoolrooms are still
there and the Doric columns and perhaps even some of the old
desks and the cracking plaster walls, grime-covered under layer after layer of highly varnished paint. It was a new building in 1881.
Even so, it was a formidable place for the country-bred Bernie and
his brothers. But there was the reassuring principal, Mr. Matthew
J. Elgas, waiting for him. And there was his teacher, Miss Katherine
Devereux Blake.

"She was so nice and beautiful and young," her most famous pupil
recalled some seventy years afterward. She was then twenty-two
years old. Her voice was so soft it could lull the fears of an admittedly
terrified little boy, and her dark eyes were soft too, but searching.
They looked deep into the eyes of the stately young woman who was
shepherding her son into the classroom. To her own mother, upon
her return home that evening, Miss Blake commented, "A real lady
visited the classroom today."

Now she looked gently upon her new charge. A solid, well-built
boy with a round face and wide-spaced eyes looked up at her. He
looked about him, at the staring faces, heard voices drilling in unison.
He clung tighter to his mother's skirt. Then Miss Blake spoke.
"Now, Bernard, I am so happy to have you here." A hand was on
his shoulder. The soft voice continued, "I am sure the other boys
are also pleased. Will you sit in this seat?" Bernard sat down and
relaxed, momentarily. But it turned out that Miss Blake also knew
the terrors of the long walk home, for at the end of the day she
asked, "Will some boy volunteer to take Bernard home and call for
him in the morning until he knows his way?" The volunteer was
Clarence Housman, who would be Baruch's partner in Wall Street
years afterwards. Forty years later, when one of the Baruch children
was ill, a specialist was called. Baruch stared at him in amazement.
It was Fred Sondern, another classmate, whom he had not seen
since Commencement Day in 1884.

Bernard Baruch never forgot Miss Blake. He looked back on her
not only with affection but almost with reverence. Students were
spurred on by the joy of pleasing her. Always she would say that
a boy who had done his best had equalled the efforts of any other —

no boy could do more. Only later did Baruch realize how painstakingly this beloved teacher had smoothed his way, encouraging him in his studies and holding up to him the precepts that he should follow. Later he was to feel that if he had helped his fellow man in any way her inspiration had made it possible.

In Miss Blake's classroom appears the first evidence of Baruch's mental superiority. So far there had been little to distinguish him from the average youngster whooping across to the store where you could get a lot of candy for a penny. He was a little more imaginative, with here and there a flash of ingenuity, as in the wheelspoke row at Camden, but on the whole, he was just a normal small boy. Yet here he was, eleven years old and in the tenth grade at school. Less than three years later he would be graduated as salutatorian of his class and have a gold medal duly pinned upon his chest — a recognition which seems to have made little impression upon him. Something far more significant had happened.

Of all the prizes and honors heaped upon Bernard Baruch in half a century of public life, never would he receive one so dear to him as the gift given him by Miss Blake at the end of that first school year. It was a copy of *Oliver Twist* and *Great Expectations*, inscribed to Bernard Baruch for "gentlemanly deportment and general excellence." It was the first prize he had ever received. He treasured it all his life and in later years upon rereading the inscription would reflect that if one could only live up to that inscription he would have lived a useful life.

Katherine Devereux Blake lived for ninety-two years, teaching and inspiring pupils almost to the end. Admittedly, Baruch did not see as much of this "beautiful character" as he felt that he should have, but he visited her occasionally and helped to get her a promotion, and on their partings, she would always say, "And now, Bernard, I know you have been a good boy." She died in New York in 1951, and at her memorial service, Bernard Baruch arose, eyes wet, choked with emotion, to hope that when he too died he would go where "Miss Blake will meet me and lead me to my seat." [21]

Even in the city there were peaceful vistas. From the car windows of the Third Avenue El or the horsecars of Second Avenue, you could see white-painted dwellings, green lawns, and trees. On lower Fifth Avenue at 19th Street, cows grazed undisturbed on a site soon to be valued at two and a half million dollars. Roaming westward, South Carolina country boys could still find fields scarred with the plow and corn tassels growing, and smell the breath of the fruit orchards at 47th Street and Seventh Avenue.[22] Eastward a few blocks, by the summer of 1883 workmen were leveling ground for the grand new Metropolitan Opera House, but at twilight Times Square was still a restful spot with grass growing green between the tracks of the horsecar.[23]

Only in summer, however, was there real escape from the brown-stone and the asphalt. Then Dr. Baruch took over the practice of Dr. William Frothingham, and the family spread out into the Frothinghams' comfortable house at 157th Street and St. Nicholas Avenue. Bernard's room was in the rear, overlooking the woods where the Yankee Stadium now stands, with white-starred flowers of black-berry vines flashing and bright leaves of poison ivy glittering, and air sweet with the perfume of honeysuckle.

Now the Baruch children were country boys again, free to roam the woods and the fields, and to explore the grassy heights where Washington once had camped. To the north lay the Bronx, with its few scattered farms and open countryside. This too was a lonely spot, almost out of touch with New York, except by the Third Avenue El and a single line of horsecars.[24] Out there Bernie might hoist himself up to the old-fashioned trestle of the New York Central, sprawl in the sun, and entertain the local boys with wild stories of the South.

There were marshes where you could crab, and at "Uncle Pete Hunt's" place, a steep slope ran down to a beach and the river below. Bernie could pack a basket of sandwiches and fried chicken, hire one of Uncle Pete's big round-bottomed boats and fish and explore for hours. But it happened to him as it happened to almost every roving country boy. Laughing and chortling one day, he toppled from the boat's gunwale. The waters closed over him and he seemed to have swallowed gallons before being pulled out, sick and gasping, and was rolled over a barrel to dry.[25]

Bernard was growing up. He was losing his baby fat; he was "Bernie" now, and "Bunch" no longer. In his teens he pulled up into the long, hard muscle and bone of his manhood. He was a startlingly handsome boy. It is unfortunate that so few of his child-hood pictures have survived, but an imaginative "as he was" portrait by the New York artist Vergas, gives some idea of Bernard Baruch in the summer of 1883. Sprawling in faded overalls with a straw hat over his dark curls, he still had the look of a Tom Sawyer. Freckles powdered his fair skin; his eyes, shadowed and almost violet in color, were dreamy and the sphinxlike smile of his maturity played over his lips.

The gangs of New York, he was finding out, were different from the uptown boys and the downtown boys of Camden. Neither better nor worse than their twentieth-century successors, they roamed in packs among the vacant lots and squatter shacks of the Fifties, between Sixth and Seventh Avenues. Fair game were the Baruch boys with their soft-slurred speech: scrappy Sailing, dreamy Herman, freckled Bernie, and stalwart Harty with his fighting.

"Nigger, nigger," was the cry they hurled at the Southern boys, pouncing always upon the weakest of them. The ringleader was an Irish boy named Johnson. Hartwig thrashed him and thrashed him again, whipping him at last on the school steps. Whimpering, Johnson tattled to his teacher, and Hartwig was suspended from school.

But what a hero he was in Bernard's eyes! Hartwig was at his side when, hounded and outnumbered, the Baruch boys fled up the steps of their boardinghouse, with shouts and rocks flying after them. Then came a new word — "sheeny." They did not know what it meant. They had never heard it before.

Seventy years later Bernard Baruch could still see the face of his tormentor — the blue eyes, dark lashes sweeping the fat pink cheeks. For a moment the two stood, body to body and eye to eye. Then Hartwig came to the rescue, hurtling himself forward.

Undefeated, Harty roared that he would take on any two together. Up stepped one big boy and said that he would fight alone. Harty fell to with gusto and administered such a beating that he became famous in the neighborhood.[26]

This was not enough for Bernie. He could not stand forever in the shadow of his older brother. A man must learn to stand up and fight to protect himself. Bernie could not do it. He was strong and tall but his was an undisciplined energy. It broke like surf as he was swept by rages that left him limp and vulnerable. Mentally his resources were superior to his fellows', but what good was a brain without an educated fist?[27]

Down on the Lower East Side, young Alfred E. Smith was building muscles and vitality swinging from the rigging of the clipper ships, but Bernie found a different way. As he grew older, he got to hanging around Wood's Gym down on 28th Street, between Fifth and Madison Avenues. It was a fascinating place, strong with odors from the livery stable below and the racy talk of its frequenters. You met every type of humanity there, from preachers to plugs — all were equal in the ring. You could pick up pointers from the "champs" of past days like Tommy Ryan or Sailor Sharkey, and even the great Bob Fitzsimmons himself might spar a round or two with an amateur.

One of the instructors was a broken-down old pugilist named Billy McClellan. Billy had the gold-toothed smile and cauliflower ears of his trade. He swayed uncertainly on his pins, but he was still certain when he landed a punch. From him Bernie learned much of the finer points of leads, blocks, and ducks. Sometimes even Fitzsimmons would toss in a line.[28]

So young Bernard Baruch pounded the bag and Wood's other clients, and gained in strength and self-confidence. Now that he knew how to take care of himself, it was easy to be conciliatory. Appeasement, he had early learned, did not work, and no cause was so righteous but what a show of force made it stronger still. It was comforting to know that if negotiations failed, he could be there with the sock.[29]

Baruch liked the ring. For sheer love of the sport he lingered around the ropes and the punching bag, through college and beyond it, long after the challenges to his manhood were past. He gloried in his strength, in the power and poise of his body. At sixty-seven he was still able to lay out a refractory taxi driver with a single blow. Only when he had passed eighty did he give up his cherished round of shadow-boxing before breakfast. All his life, there was no more avid spectator at the ring in Madison Square Garden than Bernard Baruch.

As a young fighter he had more than power: he had grace and form. Several of the old-timers were watching him expectantly the night he took on a red-haired policeman, a strapping six-footer outweighing him by fifty pounds.

It was a slaughter at first. The officer was a good boxer, and he knocked young Baruch all over the ring, but the boy held on. Blood was choking him, running in a stream from his nose and mouth.

Valiantly, he used every feint, every trick he had learned. It was no use; he was being battered. But he plunged forward, shot his left to the stomach and a right to the jaw. The policeman sank down quietly. Bernie waited, his shoulders heaving with exhaustion. His antagonist lay quietly on the floor. He never moved until a bucket of water was emptied on his face.

A hand cracked across Bernie's damp shoulder. He turned and looked up into the freckled face of Bob Fitzsimmons. The Champ told him he had the makings of a professional boxer. He knew how to keep going when things were tough, and that was what a champion had to know.[30]

Bernard wondered sometimes whether he might take up Fitzsimmons' hint. It was hard to decide. Ambition for the Baruch boys had been born back at Armstrong's livery stable in Camden, where talk drawled and tobacco juice drained, and horses and mules were swapped, sold, boarded, and auctioned. All the Baruch boys had decided to be horse drovers when they grew up, taking stables of mules and horses across the country. It seemed a splendid way to see the world.

Miss Belle had other plans. Hartwig was to be a rabbi. Herman would be a lawyer. Sailing — she wasn't so sure about Sailing, but Sailing was sure. Upon arriving in the North, he decided he was going to be the driver of a horsecar.[31]

As for Bernard, he would be a doctor. Somehow he had always known that he was going to be a doctor, accepting the fact with more resignation than zeal. Perhaps he feared to tread in the footsteps of his father whom he loved with such reverential awe. His father was still his hero, still a man worth looking at, standing six feet tall, his piercing blue eyes mild but unwavering. In later years Bernard could never recall seeing him disheveled, or even in his shirtsleeves. He would walk from his bedroom each morning spruce and immaculate, as his famous son would walk in years to come. Yet he was no unbending martinet. At the Metropolitan Opera House one night the orchestra played "Dixie," and the doctor, tugging free from his wife's restraining hands, reverted across the years to the Wilderness, Gettysburg, and Sharpsburg, and let loose the bloodcurdling rebel yell.

To Bernard Baruch his father seemed the best and wisest man he ever knew.[32] How could he ever be like him? So he floundered uncertainly as the time of decision neared, and his mother looked on and understood, instilling in him the precepts by which she lived, not so much those of orthodox dogma as of spiritual awareness. Wise but skeptical, Dr. Baruch adhered to no creed. For Miss Belle, on the contrary, one of the joys of moving north had been the chance to attend services in a synagogue, and sometimes she would go to Christian churches as well.[33]

Out of this mixed heritage came young Bernard Baruch's reverence for the traditions of his ancestors and a tolerance for the beliefs of others. His mother had probably sensed that there was too much of his father in him for complete surrender, and in the conventional sense he would never become what is known as a religious man. Not mystical illumination but spiritual and ethical law would be of importance to him. The holy days he would keep holy not so much for their sake as for his mother's.

Meanwhile, his adolescent spiritual ferment did nothing to resolve the basic question troubling him and his parents — What was he to be? For want of a vocational guidance service, his mother took him down to "Dr." Fowler's office, opposite the later site of Wanamaker's store. The good doctor adhered to the dubious science known as phrenology, but with his "stately beard," and gold-rimmed glasses pressed over his eyebrows, he was none the less impressive. Slowly his questing fingers moved over the bumps of Bernard's skull; his eyes questioned Mrs. Baruch's.

"And what do you propose to do with this young man?"

"I am thinking of making him a doctor," Miss Belle said.

"He will make a good doctor," the phrenologist agreed thoughtfully, "but," and his fingers pressed harder, "my advice to you is to take him where they are doing things — finance and politics. He might make good there, too." [34]

Childhood was now over. Bernard was nearly six feet and still growing. Soon he would be strait-jacketed into the dignity of a "college man." He knew where he wanted to go. He had studied the catalogues through the summer of 1884. Yale had been Mecca for young Southerners ever since the days of Calhoun, and to go there, Bernie swore, he would gladly wait on table or do any other necessary work.

His mother said no. She had come north to be with her children, and had no intention of being separated from them now. In spite of his large frame and precocious intellect, Bernard was too young, she said, to go away from home.[35]

Of that little College of the City of New York off Gramercy Park where Baruch enrolled as a "Sub-Freshman" in the fall of 1884, nothing remains today but the memory and the tradition. The tradition is unchanged. Then, as now, City College was for the underprivileged but talented youngsters of New York, with all aid given to those who would work, and all haste given the departure of slackers. Then, as now, City College was a place where a youth who wanted an education could get a good one, but in the uninterested, City College had no interest at all. Books, notebooks, even pencils, were supplied free of charge, but the price was hard study. Examinations were held twice a term, and dismissal was the cost of one failure. Thus the burden on the taxpayers was not too heavy. Of that entering class of three hundred in 1884, only sixty reached graduation day.

City College in the eighties was at 23rd Street and Lexington Avenue, where today the towers of the Bernard M. Baruch School of Business and Public Administration poke their way into the sky. Here the whole little world of the college revolved, with a campus of busy paved streets, but with an occasional glimpse of old Gramercy Park with its rose-brick houses frilled in iron lace.

Bernard Baruch was no typical "college man." He was awkward in his height, vaguely adult and professional-looking in his father's cut-over suits, the trousers hiking up over slender ankles. When the trousers became too short to be worn, the coats were still made over for him. For entertainment, outings, and other dissipations of college life, he was supplied with the princely allowance of twenty-five cents a week. This was doubled during his senior year, and rainy days were a joy, for then he received a dime for carfare, which by walking and braving the storms he could add to his little hoard. He even got up at dawn and was able to walk the forty-three blocks through drifts on the morning of the blizzard of 1888, and was much surprised on his arrival to find so few of his fellow students there.[36]

Many of the students were earning their own way. Even the star engineering student, Gano (Ginkie) Dunn, was a night telegrapher at the Park Avenue Hotel. It was a brilliant class, the class of '89, and neither at the beginning nor the end was Bernard Baruch the top man. That honor was reserved for Frederick M. Pederson, later professor of mathematics at the college. It was from this class, in fact, that City College garnered a good portion of its future faculty members. Even Bernard Baruch at eighty-three delivered there a series of lectures in economics. The star pitcher on the baseball team, Ventura (Doc) Fuentes, was still serving fifty years later as a professor in the Spanish department. Scholarly Charles Horn would become a professor of English literature, and "Livvy" Schuyler was in the history department until his death. One classmate, Montague Lessler, went to Congress; another, Richard Lydon, who combined political flair with a sharp-edged legal mind, became in time a justice of the Supreme Court of New York City.

Lydon, a Roman Catholic, was Bernie's best friend. He also liked Louis Rothschild, nephew of the famous Straus brothers Oscar, Isidor, and Nathan, who were already cutting a wide swath through New York's financial district. Louis, Bernie would always happily remember, "borrowed" claret of the best brand from his father's cellar for the class graduation dinner.[37]

Personification of the traditions, the learning, and, above all, the dignity of City College was President Alexander Stewart Webb, "Grand General Webb," as the students affectionately called him. To Baruch, the Confederate captain's son, the bewhiskered "General" was a man to inspire awe, as well as respect. For he had won his spurs and his title at the "Bloody Angle" and he governed City College with military efficiency. And he looked beyond childishness and hot temper to detect the germs of leadership in young Bernard Baruch.[38]

The scene itself was hardly an auspicious one. It began on a staircase where Bernard was taunted and cursed by a fellow student. Rage filled him. His father's warning came back to him: "Son, never stand an insult." The "educated fist" shot out, and a moment later his tormentor crashed down the stairs.

Dazed and raging, the two boys were haled before President Webb. The General was disgusted. But young Baruch stormed out at him. His antagonist had insulted his mother.

The General looked at him and there was understanding in the gaze. Silently, he motioned Bernard into the inner office and went in after him. They talked things over, and although the upshot was that Baruch must be suspended, the General told him he would make good material for West Point.[39]

Suspension weighed lightly upon Bernie. West Point was the answer to his old dreams of military glory. He tackled the West Point examinations and snapped them off, one by one. Then came the impasse. His father examined him first, then sent him off to another doctor. The verdict was unmistakable. He was almost stone-deaf in his left ear.[40]

So this was the price of that glorious day up on Morningside Heights, with the boys of Manhattan College in the field and the bleachers cheering "Home run, Shorty! Home run!" Baruch sliding home smack into the catcher, the instant the ball hit, and then the riot, and the "tremendous wallop" of a baseball bat crashing down across his ear. He could never go to West Point — he would never be a general now. In after years as war fanned across the earth and he mobilized the economy of his nation, Baruch may have paused to muse how it might have been otherwise — how he might have been leading an army in the field. Generals would seek his advice, and chiefs of staff his counsel; but always the lost hope teased him. Yet, neither the blow nor the years could make him regret that great day.[41]

Military ambitions dismissed, Baruch buckled down to the college routine. Years later "happy memories" of those college days would break over him. The old City College building with its four Gothic towers embowered in ivy. The ordered security of morning chapel and Bible-reading. The voice of General Webb pontifically expounding Scripture. The faculty in all the dignity of side whiskers and morning coats grouped in a half-circle looking on. Then up a trembling sophomore would come for a "declamation," followed by juniors and seniors with "orations" of their own composition. With each one who spoke, the sympathetic Bernie agonized through it all.

The day of his own first junior oration came. He mounted the platform. He bowed to the president, then to the faculty. He bowed to the assembled students, sitting, waiting to laugh. It was a dreadful trial, but no one suspected how frightened he was, nor how his knees shook and his heart pounded, as in all his public appearances thirty and forty and sixty years later.[42] What he said was a foreshadowing of his future career. He expounded the fundamentals of good government and society, and an early wisdom and sadness sounded in his words "There is no joy without alloy." [43]

Although he first enrolled for the scientific course, his work was something short of outstanding. Chemistry was merely a glorious opportunity to mix up messes to drop into someone's pocket. The "ologies" he never particularly cared for, because he could not get on with the teacher. Professor Compton he immediately recognized as the great scientist that he was, but despite all his teacher's efforts he could not seem to master astronomy.

But he reveled in languages, even rising to the challenge of Professor Heberman, a great Latin scholar who failed many students, who liked him anyway.* As for Professor Tisdale of the Greek department with his waving side whiskers, Bernie liked working for him and did well.[44]

Dr. and Mrs. Baruch set their son to studying Hebrew with a Portuguese rabbi and German with old Herr Hofstadt, who took snuff and blew his nose noisily on a big, red handkerchief. Languages, living or dead, were all the same to Bernie, and for him out of a dead language rose a living joy known to few men, because he had an ear for the rhythms and cadences of style.[45]

There was real romance in the classroom of the French professor, Jean Roemer, a continental in the grand manner with a limp from an old dueling wound and, it was said, with the royal blood of France in his veins. You could hear a pin drop in his room. It is prophetic, however, of Baruch's future career that of all the teachers and classes his favorites were Professor George B. Newcomb and his course in political economy.[46]

Physically Professor Newcomb was unimpressive. He was a lovable eccentric who looked like an old-fashioned Englishman, peering through gold-rimmed spectacles and futilely endeavoring to sweeten his squeaky voice by sucking sugar. Intent on his message, the professor had no time to waste on "children" with no real wish to study. If they liked, they could sit in the back and play chess. Bernard sat up front.

It was from Professor Newcomb that young Baruch first heard of the law of supply and demand, which influenced his whole future thinking, and perhaps it is not too much to say that from him he derived much of his basic political and economic philosophy.[47]

---

* He did not flunk Baruch, whose standing in Latin and Greek was fourth and fifth in his class, respectively.

Professor Newcomb's objective was not to teach a subject but to teach men; not to turn out quiz experts stuffed with facts, but men who knew the use of facts, who understood what Baruch would later define as the end of education: "The application of what we know to what we do."

Today, as Baruch has pointed out, Political Economy would be "fragmented among several professors." Information would become confused with education; under specialization a man would become a far more efficient machine for the Machine Age, but would he be necessarily a whole man? Without an integrated education, could he have any understanding of the infinitely complex cross-currents of an increasingly complex and disintegrated world.

Baruch made a discovery of the interrelationship of government, education, and moral law — a discovery rare in modern secular education. The test of education, he saw, was its effect upon the whole man, the rounding and fulfillment of mind, spirit, and body.

"There is no substitute for duty," Baruch would later say, true to the precepts of the Calvinistic South from which he sprang. "There is no bounty-man for one's self." In the twentieth century, government would be based upon "man's weakness and unwillingness to correct conditions by correcting himself." Government control would replace self-control. The failure of moral law from within would bring on the external law of totalitarianism.[48]

It was lucky, perhaps, for Baruch, that he started college so young. He was in time to taste the last of a grand tradition. Already the great debate was on as to whether how to live or how to make a living was the goal of education. Already it was taken for granted that change was synonymous with improvement. Even at City College the splitting process was under way, for it was the heyday of Darwinism, and what meeting ground could be found between materialistic science and the Biblical precepts proclaimed at morning chapel services? Already thought was beginning to be compartmentalized, and the effects would show in the generation then rising — in the discrepancy between their ethics in business and politics on the one hand, and in church and home on the other.[49]

Scholastically Baruch was a good but not exceptional student. At graduation he stood fifteenth in a class of fifty; his average grade for the entire college course was 83. Of demerits he accumulated only fifty-one of the hundred necessary to bring him again before the bar

of President Webb. But these matters would have been of little
interest to his fellow students.[50]

What did count was that "Shorty" Baruch had the makings of an
"all-round man." The "educated fist" and healthy frame had won an
equally healthy respect from his classmates. He was a member of the
lacrosse team and of the baseball squad. Young though he was, he
already had something of the caressing, subtle charm that was to exert
so potent an effect on friends and enemies alike. A far better public
speaker than he knew, he was urged to try for class orator at graduation. That he "ran" the class politics from behind the scenes was not
generally known, but he spent much of his senior year busying himself with the election of Dick Lydon as class president, and with his
activities as chairman of the exercises for Class Day. His attachment
for his alma mater was not weakened by the years. Much later, when
offered the place of honor at a reunion, he merely said that he felt
his classmates would prefer that he sit with them, and this was what
he would do. He would go up to the dais and accept his award.

One wall, however, he could not scale. He was natural fraternity
material; yet year after year his name was turned down. When he
munched his sandwiches at noon, he sat apart from the fraternity
men.

It hurt bitterly. Your religion was nothing you were responsible for.
Baruch knew that many were embittered and made miserable from
the blackballing, although the strong ones may have become all the
stronger. But the wound was always there to bleed again at the
wounding of his own children. Nor, in later years, would he make any
bones about the fact that it was President Woodrow Wilson's fight
against the clubs and social snobbery of Princeton that first enlisted
him as a follower of the great statesman.

Here was a man after his own heart, to fight out against snobbery
and exclusion of those unable to fight back for themselves. Bernard
Baruch was still young enough when the club row broke out at Princeton to be stirred by the battle for those excluded through no fault
of their own. Perhaps it was then that the Democrat by inheritance
became a democrat by conviction.

Though Baruch himself did not see it, there may have been other
reasons for his exclusion from the ranks of the socially elect of the
college. "Girls" terrified him. A wedding to which he was invited
was almost his undoing; he became so panicky that he fled to the

basement and hid there.[51] Even worse was betrayal by his best friend.
When Dick Lydon went over his head to urge Miss Belle to persuade
Bernie to come to his sister Marie's coming-out party, Bernie was,
or pretended to be, furious.

Then came a comforting thought. He could not go; he had no
dress suit. Triumphantly he imparted this news to his mother, who
seemed not in the least disturbed. His father's suit, she assured him,
would do very well. Bernie was not reassured: his father was only six
feet tall. Already Bernie had outstripped him by some three inches.
His mother was still unperturbed.

Painfully he worked his way into his father's shirt, the dress collar,
the white tie. Then came the trousers — they were "highwaters."
His mother took safety pins and pieced out the suspenders. Now
the vest. It was too short; Mrs. Baruch anchored it down to the shirt.
But there was nothing that could be done about the coat, which
hiked up in back, or about the long bony wrists dangling from the
sleeves. Bernard stole a glance at himself in the mirror. He was
deathly white, soaking with perspiration. He looked at his mother
and she looked at him. She whispered to him to remember his good
looks, that the blood of princes ran in his veins. "Nobody is better
than you, but you are no better than anyone else until you prove
it." [52] He began to feel better. But his terrors gripped him again
when he arrived at the Lydon party. He had to walk around the
block three times before he could muster courage to go inside. At
the door he stopped. There stood a butler, and all he could see was
the butler's dress suit and how much better it fitted him than did his
own.

Bernie retreated. He escaped the butler, escaped the music and
the lights and the girls and the smart young college men in smartly
fitted clothes. He went upstairs to the cloakroom and sat there,
alone.

Then a voice sounded. A smile reached out for him; a hand settled
in his. Bessie Lydon, Marie's sister, was laughing with him, pulling
him gently out of the cloakroom and toward the stairs. There was a
silvery tinkle of pins falling, but she paid no heed. They were down
the stairs and out on the dance floor. Suddenly a vision in blue, a
certain Miss Guidet, was in his arms dancing with him, and in all the
world, he thought, there was no worse dancer than he. Around
them the pins tinkled musically. Suddenly he did not care. He was

young; he was happy. It was a coming-out party for Marie Lydon, he knew, but it was also something of a coming-out party for him. He was a boy no longer.[53]

The final fillip to his self-esteem was to be given by a more sophisticated young lady than Bessie Lydon. It happened near Long Branch, New Jersey, where from the tiller of a catboat, as he stood with brown chest bared to the wind, Bernard heard his masculine charms audibly and admiringly commented upon by a young lady on the shore, the most beautiful woman he had ever seen. He recognized her escort — the noted sportsman and hunter Freddie Gebhard, who had been racing his horse at nearby Monmouth Park. Then he knew who *she* was. Dizzy with excitement, he almost rammed the dock alongside, and went home that night his mind awhirl with thoughts of the compliment. The lady was Lily Langtry.[54]

The old sleepy days on the Heights were only memory now. It had been a long struggle, but Dr. Baruch was prospering at last, even gaining a measure of fame. So ably had the doctor preached hydrotherapy ideas that he was named to the College of Physicians and Surgeons of Columbia University. To the discredit of the medical faculty, they later repudiated their own daring, and dropped the innovator. Cold-water "cures" for typhoid fever seemed as ridiculous then as they do now, and in retrospect, hydrotherapy may have been overestimated as a branch of medical science. Yet Dr. Baruch clung to it with single-minded tenacity, and lived to see its widespread adoption. Many of the principles he voiced are still valid, and the place that hydrotherapy holds today in our hospitals and mental sanitariums is in large part due to the pioneer work of Simon Baruch.

Equally revolutionary were the doctor's ideas on treatment for the common and usually fatal complaint then known familiarly as "inflammation of the bowels." Ever since the Civil War, surgeons had begun to open and cleanse the abdominal cavity, but it was Dr. Baruch who insisted on the revolutionary theory that the cause of the trouble, the appendix, should be removed whether already ruptured or not. This was a revolutionary idea to a pair of fellow surgeons called in to consult with Dr. Baruch over a sinking patient.

"He will die if we do," said one of the doctors flatly, shaking his head. "He will die if we don't," Dr. Baruch answered. He was later credited with being the "first doctor in the world to diagnose, preoperatively, a case of ruptured appendix, in which successful operation was performed and the patient lived." Speaking before the New

York Academy of Medicine in 1894, the noted surgeon Dr. John A. Wyeth, himself a Confederate veteran, declared: "The profession and humanity owe more to Dr. Baruch than to any other one man for the development of surgery of appendicitis." [55] Ironically enough, Dr. Baruch's mother-in-law, Mrs. Saling Wolfe, died about this time in South Carolina of what had already come to be called appendicitis.

With increasing recognition, the doctor permitted himself one extravagance. In the summer of 1890 he went home to Schwersenz, East Prussia, and the mother and father he had left over forty years before. Bernard's making the trip was unplanned. He had gone down to the boat to see his father off, when someone asked the doctor why he did not take Bernie along. In those casual days of no visas or passports this happy impulse was possible. Bernard had only to dash from the gangplank to the nearest horsecar, hurry home with his mother to West 70th Street, hustle a few clothes into a bag, and race back again.

The trip itself held few memories for him. Those happy days when he could demand and receive an outside cabin were far in the unmapped future. He shared an inside room with three other boys, and at every heave of the ship, Bernard's insides heaved with it. Sick all the way, he was too exhausted and confused to perceive his surroundings, to separate England from France or France from Belgium. Only upon his arrival in Germany did full awareness return to him.

Young hussars dashed by on horses, or goose-stepped, strutting, and at sight of their smart uniforms and scarred faces, something tightened within him. For his was the heritage of '48; and this was the hateful Prussian militarism from which his father had fled.

He met his grandparents with eagerness. Here were the roots of his being. His grandfather was tall with ruddy skin and brown hair, dark eyes magnified by thick glasses. He was, as Baruch recalled afterward, an intellectual and dreamer, a student of Sanscrit and of the law, who liked nothing so much as to sit in a beer garden with his grandson and smoke and talk the afternoon away. They immediately became great friends.

Quite different was his grandmother, a hard-working, practical, earthy little woman. She was short and fair, her hair parted in the middle and drawn down on either side, eyes bright and blue as Bernard's own. She had been Teresa Gruen before her marriage. Of her antecedents Baruch knew nothing but believed her to be of Polish or Russian Jewish stock.

His grandfather's origins were no mystery. Gleaming from a shelf
in a closet was a human skull, uncounted centuries old. On it
wavered microscopic script in half a dozen languages: Hebrew and
Portuguese, Spanish and German, even tongues long forgotten and
spoken no more.

This was his grandfather's treasure. For here was the genealogy of
the Baruch family, crossing nations and centuries, back far beyond
Europe. Even in pagan Ireland, Baruch was one of the ancient
names.[56] Family legend told, too, of descent from that Baruch of the
Old Testament who was Jeremiah's scribe and wrote a book in
Babylon, and the Jews there "wept at the reading of it . . . For if
thou hadst walked in the way of God, thou shouldst have dwelled in
peace for ever." * [57] But Bernard's father did not respond. As an
American, he looked to the future, not the past. He had severed the
ties behind him.

"It is not so important where you come from," he told his son, "as
where you are going." [58]

Back at home, too, horizons were widening.

In the late eighties and nineties, the theatrical district was still the
old Rialto from Madison Square to 42nd Street, a tunnel of hotels,
bars, and theaters glaring under the new "Edison" lights. Even there,
gas lamps still marked every street corner, and you could watch an
era passing in the pause of the lamplighter to open the lamps, turn
the jet, and touch it into flame.

The Baruch parents were especially fond of Shakespeare, and under
their tutelage the boys saw some of the best plays of the day. But,
somehow, not even Ada Rehan in *As You Like It* could impress them
as much as Sam Bernard, or the well filled-out girls in tights in *The
Black Crook*, a musical extravaganza all gold and silver and unveiled
feminine beauty. It was the first of the big "girl shows," a display at
which the clergy thundered and elderly gentlemen showed a tendency
to imperil their souls repeatedly. Its first performance had been in
1866, but time could not wither its infinite variety. Still revived, too,
as late as 1890 was that valiant old melodrama, *The Octoroon*,[59] whose
lurid story of a near-white slave sold in shame on the block might
have re-echoed in Baruch's mind sixty years later as he read a historical novel on the same theme.**

* The Book of Baruch is in the Apocrypha.
** See Bibliography, Coker.

Then there was the minstrel-man, Neal O'Brien, who was "so funny Bernie couldn't stand him," one of Baruch's oldest and earliest friends, fabulous John Golden, has recalled. Baruch thought O'Brien the funniest man he had ever seen, and at first glimpse was racked and torn with laughter. Several times, as he got more prosperous, he would take six seats at the theater for himself, his mother, and friends and sit down. The instant O'Brien appeared, Baruch closed his eyes, rammed his fingers into his ears, jerked up his long legs and stuffed his head between his knees, all the while shaking in paroxysms of uncontrollable laughter and screaming, "Tell me when he's gone." [60]

Always to Baruch and his whole family, from the days of O'Brien to those of Danny Kaye, the theater was fascinating. Even in his twenty-five-cents-a-week days, Bernard and Hartwig would squander funds for a "two-bit" seat in "Nigger Heaven," or stand, shoving, in the lines around Niblo's Garden, or the old West 23rd Street playhouse. In funds or without, there was always "plenty of fun" for young Bernard. New York was his city, a multicolored jewel by night, a fantastic adventure by day.

There rose the soaring towers, higher and ever higher, and his own spirits soared with them. New York was a city eternal only in change, in the permanence of impermanence. The rapidly building towers were crowding out even the spire of St. Paul's, a landmark to sailors and ships at sea for one hundred and fifty years.

A man had to think, walking forty-three blocks twice a day as Bernard did to go to college. He had time to think and to feel, to look at what he saw and beyond, to soak up the sights and sounds of a great city almost through his pores. He knew his city, from the seventeen-million-dollar Frick mansion with its great art collection to the hellholes of the Lower East Side. From Fifth Avenue, smothered in a pall of brownstone, to the last of the clipper ships, thrusting their prows across the South Street landings.[61]

He knew his city, the sights and sounds and smells of it. The white skins of boys, flashing like flying fish in the sun, as they dived for the overripe bananas falling from the West Indian freighters. The scrape of the tea chests being dragged up the landing at the foot of Market Street. The spare, strong framework of the Brooklyn Bridge. Light on the wet sides of the fishing smacks at Fulton Market at dawn. St. Patrick's Day, and the feet echoing in parade from the Bowery to

23rd Street. "Danny by My Side" and "The Brooklyn Bridge on Sunday." The clatter of the goat wagons in Central Park. The clangor of
the El and the *clop-clop* of horses' hoofs pounding into Madison
Square Garden for the annual show. The swish of the bicycles along
the new asphalt at William and Wall Streets and in front of the Sub-
Treasury Building, where it looked on Sundays as if all New York
were out learning to ride. The hiss of gas jets. The fading signs of
the oyster houses, alternating white and red stripes around a two-
foot globe hoisted upward on a pole. The Croton residence at Fifth
Avenue and 42nd Street, like an Egyptian temple, with walls from
which you could see the city and the harbor and the skyline northward.* The smells of salt and the sea, chocolate, coffee, the open
roll of the country where cows lay in the fields around Yorkville and
Harlem. He could walk the old streets which Captain Isaac Marques
had walked nearly two hundred years before. He could watch the
stars come out and the lights come on; this was New York at the
close of the nineteenth century. This was his New York. This was
home.[62]

Looming upward in the dignity of Gothic and brownstone were
buildings to which the young Baruch might have given a glance or
two of interest. Quiet by day, at night their long-arched windows,
hung as if from coat hangers, glared with light, and on election days
and nights the whole buildings were beehives of activity. These were
the Democratic clubs, the headquarters of city government and
Tammany Hall.

Election day was a universal holiday in New York, but for the
Baruchs it held none of the sharp-edged desperation of the old voting days in Camden. New York would be saved or, more likely, "go
to hell in a hack," as the old-timers said, without any help from the
Baruch family.[63]

Unlike little Alfred Emanuel Smith, young Bernard Baruch did not
get his Democratic Party schooling in the classrooms of Tammany
Hall. Yet in later years, memories of those New York election battles
might come back to him, the great crowds milling around the polling
places, the sudden furies and fist fights, and at noon the little street
boys shouting as they touched off fires in the election huts.

At night the boys would shinny up gas lamps to look down on the
close-packed rows, oilskin capes wet with rain and glimmering in

* Now the site of the New York Public Library.

the light from the kerosene torches, hear the beat of marching feet and the chant:

> "*Blaine! Blaine! James G. Blaine,*
> *A continental liar from the state of Maine.*"

A few nights more and the Republicans would be answering back:

> "*Ma, Ma, where's my pa?*
> *Gone to the White House, ha-ha-ha!*"

— bitter climax to a campaign scarcely less corrupt and vicious than the bloody battle of 1876.[64]

Late at night more crowds would begin to gather to read the bulletin boards down in old Park Row on East Broadway. This was near the new-built Brooklyn Bridge, where the *Tribune* building towered eleven stories, and by 1889 the *World* would be building an office fifteen stories high with a gold dome that glittered down the bay. Yet, whatever the election returns, whichever the winner, in New York City election outcomes mattered not at all.

The New York of Baruch's boyhood was a wicked city, a stench in the nostrils of decent men, so the Reverend Dr. Charles H. Parkhurst proclaimed in 1892, steeped in vice that made it "the nation's principal pleasure resort." [65] Few young men could miss the invitation in the saucy glances of the "cruisers," swinging skirts and muffs under the gaslights all the way from Canal Street to Washington Square. Open invitations studded the personals column of the New York *Herald*, where young ladies of pleasure invited friends to inspect their new places of residence; and what distinguished visitor to the city had failed to receive his chastely engraved card from the "Seven Sisters" at their stately brownstone residence on 25th Street off the Avenue, known neither by lamp nor sign but by nationwide fame.

The New York of the eighties was but a generation removed from the draft riots of the sixties when the human sewers had overflowed the city, draft dodgers flailing the recruiting officers, the wounded Union troops of the Invalid Corps, with their own muskets, ferreting out and beating to death every Negro they saw. The year of Baruch's birth, 1870, was the year of the Tweed Ring scandals and of Tammany's easy re-election, despite the thumping of the *Times* and of

Harper's Tom Nast. "What are you going to do about it?" demanded Tweed, eyes cold as the diamond on his shirtfront.[66] Why should new men be put in to rob and steal? What of the moral tone of a time when the adulterous private life of New York's foremost preacher was laid bare, and he from his pulpit continued to issue moral judgments for youth and his parishioners; or when a young theological student opened a wide-open sporting house, where girls in red-topped boots, jingling with bells, were diverted from their activities to hear his latest sermons?

The only "absolutely honest" policeman of the city force was revealed to have distributed the entire proceeds of the graft racket to various officials without one penny sticking to his fingers.[67] Purgings of New York's interior mechanisms would occur three times in Baruch's life: the Lexow, the Seabury, and the Kefauver investigations. But it would be understandable if he regarded them as little more than a passing show. Reform, as a Tammany Hall senator observed, was like morning-glories, "look lovely in the morning and wither up." Even more dour was Theodore Roosevelt of the Board of Police Commissioners, forecasting that if an administration really carried out reform it would make an end of itself. "To Hell with Reform" was the slogan as Tammany Hall swept gaily back to power.[68]

In an earlier and nobler age, a young man of Bernard Baruch's talents might have aspired to public service, but now he could never have bucked the tide. No man from the impoverished South could have done so; money alone was the entree to real power, and furthermore, what incentive was there? [69] As "Boss" Croker of the iron-gray hair and the iron-gray eyes pointed out, you had to bribe a man well to get him to go into politics, for there was no honor in public service.[70] With few exceptions, the "governing class" had no place for a gentleman. In the small towns, politics were reserved for the broken-down tobacco chewers of the courthouse steps, to whom geniality came easier than money-making.[71] "Grooms, liquor dealers and low politicians," young Theodore Roosevelt was warned, for instance, would be his political associates. Science, literature, art, "none of these could count in business," and young men were warned away from any art or profession in which it was difficult to make money.[72] Half a century before, one of the giants of the past had seen the storm signals flying, but who heeded his warnings now? "If a community demands high mental attainments and allots honors and re-

wards that require their development, creating a demand for justice
. . . knowledge, patriotism, they will be produced," had said Calhoun.
But year by year America was allotting both her praise and her rewards to business leaders. The rising generation felt this "deadening
influence . . . the youths . . . who behold the road to distinction
terminating in a banking house, will feel the spirit . . . decay within
them." [73] So, too, had Alexis de Tocqueville seen in America's swing
to finance capitalism and industrial democracy the rise of a class
which, without the economic security of landownership, "would view
money as the key, both to power and society." [74]

Such insignificant figures as governors or senators had long since
been overwhelmed by the power and majesty of "the interests" —
the New York Central or Southern Pacific, cotton or coal — whose
collars they proudly wore.[75] Even President Cleveland, after four
years in Washington, had evolved a philosophy as capitalistic as that
of any Republican.[76] Were not the interests of business and the interests of the people identical? As for the business leaders, eyebrows
might have lifted a generation or so before at Drew or Jubilee Jim,
but today J. P. Morgan was the foremost layman in the Episcopal
Church, and Rockefeller had all the respectability of a country
parson.

Even in Puritan New England, where sunlight lay cut in lean bars
between the pickets of the fences and the white-pinnacled meeting-
houses soared upward as if to meet God, young men shifted uneasily
in old pews as men of faith offered them the worn-out texts of the
seventeenth century. They knew better. "Good" Americans did not
become rich; only "smart" Americans did. As Charles Francis Adams
said, Americans wanted a system that would work; decency no longer
counted. Had not Darwin revealed the laws of nature — and thereby
of God — in the "survival of the fittest?" Ethics were necessarily
different in the harsh realities of the business world. Slums, graft,
epidemics — all were "natural" outgrowths of the rampaging expansion after the Civil War; and "wholesale bribery of Negroes" or
60,000 new citizens in twenty-one days were guarantees of satisfactory
election returns.[77]

"Progress." "Social Darwinism." These were the catchwords, both
in New York and out in the little towns, in the comfortable, ugly
houses of carved gingerbread, garnished with ironwork and lightning
rods. There, amidst the polished walnut and golden oak, the steel

engravings and gilt mirrors, business dominated all. Against the hard-drawn lines of new realities, the old faiths fitted jaggedly. Men acknowledged that it was their own fault if they "lost their money" or a panic reduced their savings; and if the little, local industries seemed but cogs in a far-off wheel, was that not the price to be expected for more bathtubs and faster trains and clearer burning oil for the lamps, for the America where everyone was busier and richer and happier than ever before? [78]

Fear goaded this brave new world, the hideous, half-subconscious fear of poverty and oblivion. For poverty was not only a stigma in America at the end of the nineteenth century, it was almost a crime. Opportunity was the American ideal, but for those who failed to grasp opportunity there was neither pity nor protection. The government owed poor men nothing; it was not *their* money that supported the government. Men might escape the thralldom of poverty by working ten or twelve hours a day to provide for themselves in sickness or age. Yet heavy over the minds of men hung memories of the panic of 1873, when the starving were battered down by police clubs; the Haymarket riots of 1886; the ten months' strike at Fall River, where workers were literally starved into submission; soon the Pullman strike in 1894, and Cleveland's troops shooting down the rioters. [79]

As Jay Gould had seen years before, "the one sure way of escaping . . . was to get wealth and hold wealth" — this was the urge that drove men on. [80] Was not Baruch himself subconsciously driving toward the same goal? For painted on the backdrop of his mind were the faces he could never forget, eroded and empty as the worn-out, beaten land from which they had sprung — faces of children and men and women of the old cotton country of his boyhood. As a young man he took a trip back into the sandhills and clay. He saw again those pallid, hungry children, growing into worn-out, beaten men and women in a South still prostrate from the terrible wounds of a generation before. [81] Hideous indeed were the gulfs between poverty and plutocracy in America.

How was the change in values wrought? As far back as the eighteen-thirties "the art of making dollars" had given a man the highest status in his community. [82] But the Civil War had given a new release to money-making energies. Unrestrained by the check of Southern conservatism, the wartime tariff had made "protection" virtually a permanent policy of the government; and the National Banking Acts of 1863–64 had swept away the last vestiges of the old

Sub-Treasury system for a plan more "favorable to private bankers." [83] As for the Fourteenth Amendment, Roscoe Conkling told the Supreme Court that it was designated not so much to free persons of color as the "persons" of corporations, and so, under test, the Supreme Court voted.[84]

Massed corporate power meant massed profits, and in the Northeast, at least, men talked of millions as easily as they once had talked of thousands. Whatever the impetus, the value of industry was up 100 per cent from 1860 to 1870. In the five years after the Civil War, more rails were laid, more trees felled, more cloth woven, and more oil refined than in all our previous history.[85]

Not all these facts would have been known to young Baruch, but they were the factors that made up his world. His was the Gilded Age of James J. Hill, George F. Baker, and J. P. Morgan, of Carnegie, Rockefeller, Duke, and Harriman. New York itself symbolized the change by the contrast between the beautiful City Hall and the ornate City Court Building looming behind. There they stood — City Hall classic and unsullied as in the day of its building in 1812, with its hanging stairway of marble, up which Lincoln was carried to lie in state, and the desk at which Washington penned his first message to Congress; and there rose the ornate, rococo City Court Building, monument to the Tweed Ring, ten years and twelve million dollars in the building, from which contractors had emerged to pad their bills 100 per cent for the payoff; and tall, handsome, foulmouthed Judge George C. Barnard had dispensed the justice of Boss Tweed.

"Never talk about money and think about it as little as possible" had been the watchword of an earlier and more modest age. But now — what else was there to talk about? Money was the open-sesame, the magic key to the treasure houses of the world. Money was power and power was glory — and with the prospect of heavenly glories seeming ever more illusory under the impact of the materialism of the nineteenth century, all the more precious seemed the glories at hand.

This was the school in which young Bernard Baruch grew up in the latter years of the nineteenth century, and that he was not immune to its inducements is evidenced by the story of his mother, who on a walk paused before the William C. Whitney mansion at the 57th Street corner. "You will be living there some day," she said. The idea was not displeasing to him.[86]

3

HIGH STAKES AND BIG PLUNGERS

HIS SALARY was three dollars a week. It was 1889 and Bernard Baruch was nineteen years old. He had made his start. He was a man of business. He was office boy for Whitall, Tatum and Company, wholesale dealers in glass, at 86 Barclay Street. He ran errands for the clerks, indexed the letterbook, took invoices to the consular agents, and, in a hand more legible and painstaking than in later years, made copies of the outgoing mail. His days were full and the pay regular. Sometimes he was in the office before eight in the morning and often he was getting out bills of lading after dark.

This was not the spectacular career he had dreamed of in the classrooms of City College. This was just his first job, seized upon in desperation when, as it seemed to Bernard, his chance at glory had been blasted for all time.

It had been a discouraging summer that first year after graduation. Listlessly he had still toyed with the idea of going to medical school. He skimmed the books, attended some lectures, and hung around the dissecting rooms with his cousin, a medical student. But Dr. Baruch regretfully but finally warned him not to take up medicine unless it was because of a great urge to help people.[1]

This, at least, shook young Baruch out of his halfhearted dream.

Times were hard. He began to pound the pavements and the closed doors of the office buildings. But the writers of the "help wanted" notices wanted no help from young Bernard Baruch.

Then inspiration had struck him. Systematically he had listed the names of his father's patients, among them one Mr. Daniel Guggenheim. Baruch knew who he was. At Long Branch he had watched admiringly the exploits of old Meyer Guggenheim at the roulette table — Meyer Guggenheim, the little Swiss-born lacemaker who wore a frock coat and flowing burnsides which he stroked lovingly, who had sired seven sons and an industrial empire in America.

Seated before Meyer's son Daniel, a man as small as his father and with a smile as large, Bernard had suddenly become overwhelmed with consciousness of his legs and arms and his whole lanky longitude; but Daniel Guggenheim looked beyond these. He eyed the young man keenly, then submitted an offer that seemed the realization of Baruch's dreams — the chance to work as an ore buyer for the Guggenheims in Mexico.

Bernard went out, his head in the clouds, until his mother jerked him down to reality again. He was, she said, too young to go away from home.[2]

So to Baruch, the plate-glass windows of Whitall, Tatum and Company must have been like prison walls. This was the New York of the nineties, and southward lay "the Street," the vital artery through which flowed the lifeblood of a continent. Already the first generation of the great "robber barons" was passing off the scene — the new tycoons were closing in on a new prey. Vanderbilt was dead — the "Commodore" — dead with the word of God on his lips and $105,000,000 salted away in his coffers. Dead, too, was evil-talking, tobacco-chewing old Dan Drew, who looked on cards and theaters as things of the devil but for whom "lying, duplicity, thievery and greed were the passions of . . . life." Frail, pasty-faced Jay Gould, too, had gone to other than a financial reward — spidery Gould, with an "acute and sinister genius," [3] who had bought up Tweed and displayed President Grant in his box at the opera, and battled Vanderbilt in the bloody old railroad wars of the seventies. And down at the Grand Central, "America's most palatial hotel" with its glittery Crystal Ballroom and fat bronze cupids disporting themselves over the gilt mirrors,[4] people still paused to stare at the great rust-colored stain on the rug where the "peacock Fisk" had sunk into velvet and stillness, drilled through by Ed Stokes's bullets — Fisk, graduate of a Vermont peddler's cart and Tammany Hall, who had reaped a fortune selling shoddy blankets for the Union soldiers. Less flamboyant, but no less imposing was the British-born speculator and plunger James R. Keene. A mule skinner out of the West, he had struck into Wall Street in the seventies, battled his way with the Goulds and Fisks, and held his own twenty years later against the real giants of the street — Morgan, the Rockefellers, Thomas Fortune Ryan, and James Duke. Panic after panic broke against him and receded; he took his losses, asking neither sympathy nor quarter. To the young Baruch he was a figure of romance.[5]

To the generation that grew up with the New Deal these days seem incredibly remote — this age of the plunderers who fleeced and looted and skimmed the cream off a continent. This was the climax of the Frontier period of our history, in which three thousand miles of forest and plain were despoiled and subjected. The result was what Henry Adams called "the whole mechanical consolidation of force, which ruthlessly stamped out the life of the class into which Adams was born, but created monopolies capable of controlling the new energies that America adored." [6] The king of this new America was J. P. Morgan the elder. It was while working at Whitall, Tatum and Company that Baruch was sent on an errand to the banking house of Drexel, Morgan and Company on Wall Street and there saw Morgan himself.

There he was, "Morgan the Magnificent," with the head of a Titan. This was the man who strode down Wall Street as if he were the only man alive, or the owner of the world's highways; the man at whom the peasants of Europe gaped and whom New York mobs followed, running in packs alongside his carriage; the man for whom the trains of a nation were shunted aside as his "special" roared westward. There, from the shadow of his office he loomed, with a kind of medieval splendor, one mighty fist clenched before him, the other clasping the arm of his chair. Baruch saw his face. He saw his great blazing eyes, the huge beak of a nose, and he felt all the intensity and power of the man as he looked, and thought of Charlemagne on horseback. There they were, a boy and a man, each with his greatest strength and greatest days ahead of him — each to wield power unique in American history. It was a meeting any boy starting out in business would remember.[7] To Baruch it seemed that to work for Morgan would be a wonderful opportunity; yet already, he knew that he was barred from the Big Chief's citadel, if not his notice, because he was a Jew. This meeting, however, perhaps provided Baruch's final impetus toward a financial career.[8]

To him Morgan seemed a heroic figure, a poor hero after Lee and Stonewall, but the best, perhaps, that the time could offer. He was "the great financial Gorgon," the king of American banking.

Scarcely fifty people knew him personally, but the whole country knew of his moods and rages, of his blue-ribbon collies and his yacht *Corsair*, and of the flowers that he laid upon a tomb every St. Patrick's Day in memory of the love of his youth, the nineteen-year-old Mimi, whom he had carried in his arms downstairs to their wedding, and who had died in his arms four months later. The power that he wielded was no less fabulous than the man. Steel, rails, utilities — he commanded them all. At the peak of its power the House of Morgan with its associated banks held directorships or controlling interests in fully 112 banks, insurance companies, transportation systems, public utility and other corporations which had combined assets and capitalization of over twenty-two billion dollars, and was the nerve center of American business.[9]

Morgan had set the "pattern of American money-getting." Every company in his orbit marketed its stocks through his bank. Every company deposited its funds with the House of Morgan, and with these funds the firm made further purchases and further expansions. Morgan was in command "on both sides of the counter": as the banker, he represented both himself and the sources of supply to other companies. One company owned the others; one man bestrode them all. By fastening on industries already developed, he had "learned the trick of sharing their wealth with other men." [10]

Morgan had learned his lessons, and they were in turn learned by the generation after him. Costs of competition and advertising, costs of operation, the "high costs of price-wars" [11] could all be eliminated by combination, by pools and trusts and unified management. Thus power could be closely concentrated in the hands of a few men in the East who understood each other and acted together with accord.

Morgan fascinated Baruch, but it was industrialists like Rockefeller and the Guggenheims who were, he realized, the creators of real productive wealth, and in whose trails he hoped to follow. It was thus ironic that Baruch should have come to be popularly regarded as a speculator and a plunger. Since he was never a banker, providing funds for the development of industry, the financial district was never to regard him as a creator of wealth.[12]

Even Baruch's summers now were high-geared, edged with excitement. His father had a new summer practice at Long Branch, where before the dazzled eyes of his sons passed the fashionable world. Belmonts, Dwyers, Lorillards, Lillian Russell, and others, less fair and more frail, like the blue-eyed, golden-haired young lady who all of a sudden started appearing in her own carriage, lolling behind a coachman and footman. Just how this miracle occurred was a mystery to Baruch and his brothers until their young innocence was suddenly enlightened.[13]

Along the fairways they dashed, the tandems, the four-in-hands, the cabriolets; "Great Tenny, the swayback," in for the races at Monmouth, the sandy turf churned to powder beneath his racing feet. And there was another army, whose interest was as much in finance as in horseflesh. Touts, sports, sportsmen, bankers and brokers, merchants and bookmakers, and young Bernard M. Baruch bringing up the rear.

What was it that fascinated him? Was it the horses? Was it the thrill of the chase and the contest that set his heart pounding? Or the aftermath, when the coin won at the track clinked onto the tables of the gambling casinos? Was it gambling fever that set the blood racing in his veins — or the thrill of pitting his skill against chance and the knowledge of older and "wiser" ones? Whatever it was, something drew him to the track, where he flung his small savings to the winds; or to the gambling houses, where New York's top bankers tossed fortunes to chance in private rooms discreetly screened from the public gaze.

Was it skill or chance? This was a question that drummed in Bernard's mind — a question, in fact, upon which his own life, his own future fortune would turn. Certainly knowledge and skill played their part. Already he had found that he could never forget a card — an attribute that stood him in good stead in an early forbidden bout of penny ante, at which he had been "spectacularly successful." That his father had forbidden the game made no impression. He had been a "model" all his boyhood, and now suddenly there was a change.

Others besides his father were worried about him. You could not help noticing the tall young man with fine features and an almost Irish vividness of coloring. Pat Sheedy, gambler and sport, whose haunts ranged from the Bowery to Fifth Avenue, had seen the young man and begged him for his parents' sake to stop hanging around gambling dens.[14] But Baruch was deaf to the plea; the only reason he did not play was that he had no money.

At Phil Daley's at Long Branch, chips were a dollar apiece. But at his brother John's you could get them for fifty cents, and it was from this modest start one evening that young Baruch raised his stake to two dollars.

A hush fell over the room. Looking up, Bernie saw his father framed in the doorway. "Son," he said, "when you are ready we will go home."

At the hotel as he undressed Bernard thought again and again of the words of sorrow and shame that his father had used as they made their way home.[15] For hours he lay sleepless, remorse battling something within him. He was sorry to have hurt his father and bitterly ashamed. But he was caught in the surf of an irresistible impulse that he could neither understand nor withstand.

At last his mother came to him, as she would always come in times of trouble. He roused himself from a half-doze to find her arms around him. Gently she held him, whispering words of comfort and consolation, which made him more miserable than ever.[16]

He could sleep no more. At five he got up, dressed, tiptoed out of the house, and fled back to New York. The sun rose and his spirits with it. By afternoon he had so far reverted to his natural tendencies as to round up his cousins * for an all-day poker game. They were aroused from this pleasurable occupation by the sudden appearance of his mother. There she was, indeed, so excited that she paid no heed at all to the cousins, scuttling away with the evidences of crime. It was Bernie that she had followed to New York to comfort, for, as she explained, she had feared what he might do in his remorse. Bernie, head hanging, felt a new wave of shame engulf him and loved her all the more.

Mrs. Baruch, it turned out, had great news. Coming up on the train, she had talked with Julius A. Kohn, a retired wholesale clothing merchant who had gone into Wall Street. He had complained bitterly to Mrs. Baruch. Oh, the younger generation — it was so hard today to find diligent young men who would work their way up. After all, in Europe, an apprentice worked for nothing because he knew nothing, and nothing was all he was worth. If he could only find a young man willing to learn, a young man he could train and teach and make into a real businessman. Mrs. Baruch had told him that she knew her son Bernard was exactly the man.[17]

Bernard eagerly grasped this new opportunity. With Kohn he

* These cousins were members of the Heyman family of Chesterfield, S.C.

could continue his education. True to his word, the old German
paid him nothing, but in his office young Baruch mastered what was
to become one of the most profitable lessons of his life. For the Kohn
firm specialized in arbitrage — the trade in currency or securities in
different markets for the purpose of making a profit on buying where
the price was low and selling where it was high. The system worked
simply enough. Stocks might be quoted at one figure in New York,
another in Baltimore, still another in London or Amsterdam. Still
another aspect of Kohn's work involved the buying of old and defaulted securities and selling the new ones issued against them.

Bernard Baruch's eyes were opened. Here was adventurous work of
far more interest to him than the glass business. Feverishly he set out
to master the secrets of this new world. He began to study the stock
quotations on foreign markets. He learned to figure in different
currencies, until he could turn guilders into sterling, sterling into
francs, or dollars into marks as quickly and automatically as he could
recite the alphabet or the multiplication tables. It turned out that he
had a natural aptitude for this. The time would come, in fact, when
he would be "one of the leaders of arbitrage operations" in America.
Yet Wall Street, the citadel of his dreams, was as far away as ever.
His eyes scanned western horizons. He would leave the city
where paper represented wealth and seek the real wealth of the gold
fields.[18]

Cripple Creek, Colorado, in the summer of 1890 was still a wide-
open town. It was the Old West on a last fling, a roaring gully lined
with swingdoor saloons, false fronts, dance halls, gambling hells.
This was the scene that confronted young Bernard Baruch as he unfolded long legs from the westbound stage one afternoon.

He made his way to the hotel. Upon requesting accommodations,
he was assigned to a dormitory with twenty or thirty cots. The next
morning Mr. Bernard M. Baruch was at work in a shaft of one of the
gold mines. His job was to follow the blasting crew as they piled up
rock, gather it into a bucket, and take it away.

Although this was perhaps the only pick-and-shovel job of his life,
there was nothing soft about Baruch. Soon after he arrived he was in
a fight. He let go with a tough fist and the left that Fitzsimmons had
admired, and his opponent went quietly down. He was soon promoted to a tougher job, the blasting crew, where he held the drill,

going at it with all the high spirits and gusto of a college boy on a holiday.

Evenings, with no father looking over his shoulder, Baruch headed straight for the palaces of chance, and soon he hit upon an ingenious way to beat the law of averages. Watching the great wheels spin, he noticed how frequently the management won, and decided to place his small bets upon the side of the house. The system seemed to work, and he was congratulating himself upon the discovery of a new and steady source of revenue when his activities were noted. The manager drew him aside and told him, as Baruch retold it afterward, that he could dispense with his patronage. "He seemed very much in earnest," Baruch recalls, "so we left." [19]

What now? What ways to fortune? A onetime carpenter named Tom Walsh had made a quick profit in mining shares. So Baruch sank his little savings in a near-by mine, which did not "strike it rich," and ruefully the tenderfoot concluded that returns might be more dependable by way of the weekly payroll.

Baruch's western adventure did not last long. Back in New York a good opening was found through a friend of his mother's, and Baruch was ready. It was a job with A. A. Housman and Company, Wall Street brokers, and the salary was five dollars a week. Bernard Baruch's real career had begun.[20]

He was in "the Street" at last. That enchanted tunnel, scented by coffee and sugar and now and then by a vagrant gust of salt from the sea, marked for him the boundary lines of achievement. This little valley of finance, was the site of present riches and past glory, bounded to the north by jewelry, on the east by coffee and sugar, on the south by cotton and shipping, and on the west by Greek lace, ship chandlers, and Trinity churchyard. Here had walked Captain Isaac Rodriguez Marques. Here, classic and proud as the Greek temple that inspired it, soared the white columns of the Sub-Treasury, remnant of the days of Madison and the War of 1812, but Baruch noticed little of this. His whole being was concentrated on his work.

At the Wall Street station, morning after morning, he bounced down from the Sixth Avenue El and raced up Rector Street, a hand-wide thoroughfare under the south wall of Trinity. Halfway up, over the top of the soot-stained wall, you could see the tombs of Robert Fulton and Alexander Hamilton.

In the evening, on a late homeward rush, he might have had to stand aside for two men lugging a strongbox between them, followed by a third, fist ominously bulged in his pocket. There passed the wealth of the Street; there were massed the symbols, stocks, bonds, the vast outpouring of the Exchange, all packed off to great vaults for the night.[21]

Baruch began as a "runner." In the twenties he might have joined other young college graduates in selling and "instructing" the public on the values of inflated stock. In the benighted nineties he had work to do. His tasks were, in fact, little different from what they had been at the plate-glass company. He was the office boy, the comparison clerk, the utility man. He opened the office in the morning, changed the blotters and the pens. He filled the inkstands. He copied letters and indexed the copybook. Sometimes he helped get out the monthly statements. He studied; he soaked up knowledge. Slowly he was "correlating the facts of finance into a system." [22]

Promotion dangled alluringly in front of him. A bookkeeper's job was his goal, and to speed advancement he enrolled for courses in bookkeeping and law at night school. Also, he studied on his own. *Poor's Handbook* became his bible, this and the *Financial Chronicle*. They were the guideposts to researches of a more intensive kind. It was not enough to know where a corporation was and what was its function. Who formed it? Who owned it? Who ran it? Was there need for its products? Would it be superseded by competitors or new inventions? How was it affected by floods or drought, or freight movements? Were there railroads to transport the product to the most likely market? How could you know anything about the value of a company's stock unless you knew everything about it?

Baruch had to know. He was saturating himself with the industrial geography of the country and of its railroads. His own mind was a map of the United States; he was teeming with information, bubbling over with it — so excited that he even poured it all out to a girl who shared a bench with him in Central Park.[23] He was in fact, becoming a walking — or running — encyclopedia of industrial knowledge. It was a lot easier to ask young Bernard Baruch the data about a company, or a stock's earnings, dividends, and book value than to look it up.

Along Wall Street he was seen daily, long legs flashing by a window, a lanky youngster who bustled in and out of offices, always in a hurry. A story was told, retold, laughed over, and survived to become legend. "Young fellow, come down off that stool," growled an irritated clerk of the Jewett Brothers firm, as Bernard's head and shoulders shot up high over an enveloping crowd.

"I'm not on any stool."

"If you get fresh, I'll come out and box your ears," the clerk retorted.

"Come right on out," Bernie dared.

The clerk flung open the door. He stopped and stared. "Good God," was all he said.[24]

Baruch looked even taller because he was thin; the intensity of his drive was burning up more energy than he could restore. You saw him sometimes in Fred Ebling's cellar at noon, looking wistfully over a sandwich, his hunger whetted by the smells of good food and the sight of the well-fatted partners eating mightily around him. Five dollars a week did not go far. Only when he was invited out was his appetite appeased, and then he dived happily into slices of rich roast beef and piles of mashed potatoes.[25]

His struggles were not unnoticed. Inspiration came from two men, wise in the ways of the street and of mankind — men from whom, he said afterward, he learned more than from any others. In a sense, he was their protégé. One was Middleton Schoolbred Burrill, a brilliant young lawyer and the only amateur Baruch ever knew who always made profits in stocks. Through him Baruch met the other, already hailed as the greatest speculator Wall Street had ever seen. In years ahead, only one name would be bracketed with his — that of Baruch himself. He was James R. Keene.

But it was from Burrill that Baruch received his basic training in speculation, and this he learned by watching Burrill. You must always get the facts. This was the first and greatest commandment and, once learned, it encompassed all the rest.

Even facts were not enough, although Burrill sometimes cross-examined Baruch on these from *Poor's*. There was the human element too, the emotions and passions and psychology. There was money to be made on sudden bulges and fluctuations, which were not the result of reasoning.

Baruch carried this thinking a step further. If economic law was really man's law, the outgrowth of his greeds and fears, were there any economic ills that man himself could not overcome? Were there not opportunities that arose from disaster itself? It was a thought that struck his fancy — and came to fruition some forty years later.[26]

Meanwhile, at the moment prices were low and the public was

wary, as it always is of things that are cheap. But was not a panic the very time to buy? What matter if the bottom had not yet been hit? If you knew your stock and knew your values, your investment would return threefold. Had it not always done so before?

Hopefully Baruch scanned the future — a future that superficially looked dark in the depression year of 1895. Panic gripped the country; smokeless stacks stood against the sky. Coxey's army was marching on Washington, a ragtag, hobo army demanding a new right in the charter of freedom, the right to work. Strikes. Riots. Troops and Henry Clay Pinkerton's detectives massed, bullets cutting the strikers down. A new word on the American tongue — anarchy. A word as bloody and weighted in its implications as bolshevism or communism would be a generation later. A new word, and a new heresy, that gold itself was the source of all evil, that the metal was too precious, too limited for the needs of an ever-multiplying population and that money and prosperity for all would come from the free coinage of silver. Coxey was marching and Bryan was marching, a country lawyer out of the West, with a swinging mane and a silver tongue, "a puppet," warned the New York *Tribune*, "in the blood-imbrued hands of Altgeld, the anarchist, and Debs, the revolutionist." Fiercely he flung down his challenge to the cities and corporate wealth: "You come to us and tell us that the great cities are in favor of the gold standard; we reply that the great cities rest upon our broad and fertile prairies . . . destroy our farms and grass will grow in the streets of every city . . ." [27] So amidst the debris of scattered fortunes panic crept, and great men trembled, for had not even Theodore Roosevelt proclaimed that Bryan and his pack were like "the leaders of the Terror of France?"

Characteristically, Baruch was ready to gamble on the future: on the ambition and need of the American people. They were not seeking a minimum wage, but maximum opportunity. With returning prosperity, they would abandon their self-styled savior Bryan. It was no division of the crumbs they wanted but a chance at the loaf. Later, they might band together for their mutual protection, but not now. Prosperity would return. Baruch felt sure.

Now he turned his attention to railroad securities, a subject on which he had learned much back in the office of old Julius Kohn. Railroads were greatly overbuilt, yet there were some that would survive. Pamphlets on reorganization became his favorite reading.

Upon a railroad's reorganization new securities were issued and bought in anticipation of better management, or future developments of the property and territory. These new issues might pay. Even the old stock of bankrupted concerns might pay — under competent management. Money might be made out of old railroads, both by the seller and those wise enough to buy.

Baruch had no money himself, and how to sell the public upon these semi-defunct rail lines was a question. He copied names and wrote letters. No answers. He visited office after office on lower Broadway. Again — no answers. No one would see him. No one would talk to him.

He called on gray-bearded James Talcott, a merchant whose secretary saw her duty and ejected the young man from the office. So he waited on the street, literally cornering his prey on the way home, and pouring out a flood of sales talk over Talcott's obvious irritation and repeated protests that he was interested in nothing Baruch had to say.

Finally, to get rid of him, Talcott placed an order for a single Oregon and Transcontinental bond. Up it soared, and Baruch's prestige and self-confidence with it. His commission was one dollar and twenty-five cents. But he had gotten a customer.[28] Gradually he began to build up a little circle of customers who told their friends about the young man down at Housman's, who not only bought for them but advised them when to change. Slowly, orders began to increase and with them Bernard's salary — $5 a week — $10 — $20 — now, $25.[29]

He could parade on Sunday morning on Fifth Avenue, resplendent in Prince Albert coat, silk hat, striped trousers, but there were moments when he smarted as he viewed the tandems and traps of other young men of his age, scions of rich families, or those who had been more successful than he. He still could not resist spending his little savings on flyaway ventures — still had not learned that you cannot win millions on a shoestring. But he was learning, gradually finding out that you must always hold some money in reserve — a backlog for bitter times.

His new-found self-esteem took a sudden plunge one night as he was wildly cheering on his favorite fighting cock when the raid cry sounded. A. A. Housman's serious, conservative young employee went headfirst out the nearest window. He had a double jolt when he hit

the ground. A vision of himself haled before the police court somehow dulled his relish for the sport. The cockpit, after all, was no place
for a young man thinking of settling down in the world.[30]

He had first seen Annie Griffen as a terrified little girl with black
curls, fleeing down the street with a dog nipping at her heels. Afterward, the picture had faded from his mind, only to flash back the day
that he really saw her for the first time. This was in 1889, and they
were both nineteen years old.

She was not alone. Another girl was with her, as well as an acquaintance of Baruch's named Dave Schenck, but Baruch had eyes
only for Miss Griffen. So bedazzled was he that all thought left his
head, and she was gone before he remembered what he had forgotten
— to ask for an introduction.

To Baruch she seemed a goddess, statuesque and divinely tall; she
was fully six feet in height. Perhaps this played a part in her shyness
through life. She would seem proud to the world outside. Yet those
who knew her best loved her, and young as he was, Bernard Baruch
came to look beyond the shyness and the reserve and know that
here was a girl he might love.

But how to meet her — how to win her? He wrestled with the
problem methodically, as if he were gathering data on some speculative enterprise. She had been educated at a private school. Her home
was a twenty-two-foot brownstone house at 41 East 58th Street —
Bernard passed it almost every day. Her father was in the glass-
importing business; he had been a Phi Beta Kappa man at City College, where his son was studying now. Her grandfather was W. J.
Wilcox, a well-known lard merchant of Irish background. To his
surprise Baruch recalled that he had at least a speaking acquaintance
with one of her brothers, and presuming on this link, hat in hand, he
approached the young lady as she mounted her stoop, and asked if
she was not Miss Annie Griffen.

"No, indeed," she said, and with a toss of her head indignantly
entered the house. The rebuff hurt, but did nothing to daunt his
pursuit. Eventually Schenck arranged the introduction, and from
then on Bernard Baruch required neither devices nor assistance in
his courtship — a courtship that lasted some eight years.

Their meeting place was Central Park. Hours passed unnoticed.
But heavy problems confronted them. What prospects had Baruch
— a shoestring trader, flush one day and broke the next? How could

he support a wife? Slowly the years passed, eight long years of waiting and wanting, dreams of wealth and poverty making Baruch's life wretched. As for the girl Annie Griffen, she was interested in no other man, and her only fear was that Baruch might not wait for her. However, Baruch's determination was equally unshaken. On fifty dollars a week, he believed, he could support a bride very comfortably, but when the time came that he felt able to ask for such pay, Mr. Housman suggested a compromise of more prestige than money — partnership in the firm. Based on the previous year's figures, his earnings would be only thirty-five dollars a week, but times were once more good and he might even attain his fifty-dollar goal. Baruch worked; he waited; and at the year's end he counted out a $6000 share.

Further opportunity sounded in Congress. The stock of the American Sugar Refining Company was selling at $110, and Baruch scraped enough money together to take a margin flier. Meanwhile, Congress was considering the tariff. Would it be high or low? Would American Sugar be protected? Baruch waited, figured, finally decided that the new Republican Congress would not reduce the tariff. He guessed correctly. Up went the stock and up went the hopes and prospects of young Bernard M. Baruch, who emerged some $60,000 to the good.[31]

Now at last he could begin to think seriously of a wife and marriage. Now he could buy that $19,000 seat on the Stock Exchange of which he had dreamed. Now he could even boast a little to his mother, who, as she turned over card after card at solitaire, exasperatingly took it all as a matter of course.[32]

It was Hartwig she wanted to talk about. Hartwig had not precisely fulfilled the family's hopes of earlier years. He had chosen to magnetize his audiences from behind the footlights rather than in the synagogue — not, it is true, without some success and fame. As Nathaniel Hartwig he had played on Broadway in that old thriller, *The Corsican Brothers*. He had been Marie Wainwright's leading man in *Camille*, and was even on the receiving end of the famed Nethersole kiss.[33]

The theater was in the Baruch boys' blood. All had a natural forensic quality: "I'd have given any of the Baruch boys a job anytime," one of Broadway's foremost producers has said. Yet the really "consummate actor" of the group was not Hartwig but Bernard.

We have the opinion of John Golden on this, and Golden knew

the Baruchs when he was a $30-a-week fledgling and Hartwig a $90-a-week leading man. A sturdy live-wire youngster with shining eyes and a crop of thick black hair, Golden was beloved in the Baruch household, and Miss Belle affectionately called him her fifth son. No one would have seen in this eager youth the famous figure of theatrical glamour who would flourish in the great age of Frohman, Belasco, and Ziegfeld and outlive them all. It was Golden who first saw in young Bernard Baruch that theatrical quality which has kept him in the limelight for half a century. To Golden, Baruch never seemed a behind-the-scenes mystery man. "Before the footlights he has stood." Golden has added, "I'd have given him a job . . . if he could have gotten rid of his Southernisms." [84]

Perhaps it was an early experience that cured Baruch of any later desire to be even a theatrical "angel." The venture was an abortive production of *East Lynne*, performed before a three-row house at Centerville, New Jersey. The star was a lady, years Hartwig's senior, who had impressed him as a great actress, only temporarily out of an engagement. Even a real live baby in the cast could not make up for the fact that although the players may have been artists — as Hartwig said — they had not troubled to learn their parts.

The curtain jounced up. During the first act the audience was alternately amused and angry. By the second act it was just angry. By then Bernard had told the box office to refund the money — and with the costumed and grease-smeared cast trailing behind him, he had run all the way to the Centerville railroad station. They were on a train and off for the big city before the audience realized that the third-act curtain would never rise!

This was not the kind of life Miss Belle wanted for her sons. She missed Hartwig, she wanted him at home. She looked at Bernard, paused and waited. Bernard knew what she wanted him to say. He said it: he would give Hartwig that new, hard-earned seat on the Stock Exchange. Perhaps thus he could repay the faith his father had shown in him that time he lost $8000 of the doctor's savings in an abortive streetcar venture; and not even with a look had his father reproached him. On the contrary, he had trusted him again and, with Bernard's confidence at the breaking point, had handed him a check for an investment in Tennessee Coal and Iron. His father had understood and Bernard understood now.[35]

Then came the reaction. Nothing had ever hurt so much — not

even that seeming last chance for fame and fortune with the Guggenheims. All that night he lay sleepless, realizing what he had done to himself. Nothing counted so much in the life of a young man of finance. Nothing meant so much in prestige in the street as a seat on the Exchange, and now he had all the long, hard job to do once more. But he still had Annie Griffen. This would not stop his scheduled marriage.[36]

Money had not been the only obstacle to this union. In the old-fashioned, formal way, Baruch had visited Miss Annie's father and asked for her hand. We can see them now, across the span of fifty-odd years, facing each other in that Victorian drawing room of the Griffens' old brownstone dwelling. Baruch took little notice of his surroundings. His single-track mind always moved straight to its objective, whether in love-making or speculation. As he said, later, "I was always so busy I didn't have a chance to notice anything." Only of people was he sensitively aware. Now he sat waiting in his chair, opposite him the scholarly Mr. Griffen, courteous but obdurate, struggling for words.

He tried to be gentle; he tried to cushion the blow. Mr. Baruch was as agreeable a young man as had ever come to the house. But he had his religion and his daughter had hers, and if they married, the differences would prove a barrier.

So that was it! And there she was, waiting for him — and for the answer. Baruch told her, but nothing could end the understanding between them. Both were young and in love. They were children of the modern age. If religious differences did not concern them, why should they trouble Mr. Griffen? They could not understand, but in later years they did understand. In later years Baruch could daily come home and see his father-in-law enter the University Club promptly at 6 P.M., a club to which he could never belong. Annie Griffen Baruch would learn bitter lessons, too, and in the end Baruch would admit that although their love had been complete, in most cases Mr. Griffen would have been right.

Their wedding day was October 20, 1897. To the last, Mr. Griffen had withheld his consent. Unmoved, the young couple had held their ground. Bernard Baruch and Annie Griffen were married in the Griffens' dark-paneled living room, the golden light of autumn filtering through the windows. The bride's cousin, Henry Griffen, gave her away. Baruch's father and mother were there and his brothers,

Hartwig clutching the ring, but Baruch had eyes only for his bride.

Before them stood the Reverend Dr. Richard Van Horn, grand-father of the bride and descendant of an old Dutch family. Slowly he read the full Episcopal marriage service, up through "the Father, the Son, and the Holy Ghost." Bernard had wanted it that way. At the proper moment he groped for the ring, fitted it on a long, slender finger. Then confusion overtook him. Afterwards he would remember the next few days only in fragments — the train ride to Washington, the old Shoreham Hotel and the strange brassy smell from the newly painted radiators, then the boat trip to Old Point Comfort, where consciousness returned completely. Too much excitement, too many radiators perhaps — at any rate, he was "very sick" on that boat.

Marriage did nothing to weaken his speculative vigor. Luck was with him during those closing years of the nineties; for him, even history swung upward on fortune's wheel.[37]

He was at Long Branch, New Jersey, nursing a sore ear on the Sunday of July 3, 1898, when a call came through from one of Housman's senior partners — a reporter's "tip" from the firing lines. Admiral Sampson's fleet had done some "fancy battling" down in Santiago Bay. The Spanish fleet was finished. The war was over.

A memory flashed across Bernard's mind, a legend recalled from childhood — of the old Baron Rothschild who had gambled on the fall of Napoleon and, so legend said, from a hillock near Waterloo had watched the French tide surge and then retreat before the on-rushing British forces. Somehow he had gotten word to London and garnered his winnings hours before the official news came. Why could not Bernard Baruch do the same?

Tomorrow would be the Fourth of July. The New York Stock Exchange would be closed. But the London exchange would be open; you could get "the jump" on your colleagues before the market boomed. But how could he send the word? He had only thirty-six hours —

On that holiday weekend even the trains were stilled. So Baruch hired a locomotive and tender and coach and rattled through the night. Towns roared past; sleepy little villages huddled under gas lamps as if in fear of the bottomless darkness beyond.

Lower New York was empty and as silent as the Palisades. Only the racing footsteps of Baruch and his companions struck echoes in those quiet streets. Then came a horrible moment as they halted before the door of A. A. Housman and Company; they had forgotten the key. This was solved by hoisting Baruch's slenderly built young brother, Sailing, to his shoulders and through the transom. There was a thud — and the lock turned. Inside, they dashed to their stations, Housman cranking the telephone until his arm ached, Baruch writing the cables. Through the morning of July 4 they placed their orders, huge purchases, not only for themselves, but for their vacationing partners. When the Exchange reopened Tuesday, prices soared, and with them the fortunes of A. A. Housman and Company.[38]

So, too, did the fortunes of young Bernard Baruch — and not only in a financial sense. "Ryan's midnight broker," [39] the insiders of Wall Street were beginning to call him, after observing his equipage drawn up at a significantly late hour before a well-known building. His coup had brought him to the attention of one of the most fabulous and powerful figures in the history of the Street, Thomas Fortune Ryan.

A barefoot orphan boy from Virginia, Ryan had come up by way of a Baltimore dry-goods store. At twenty-two he had married the boss's daughter, whose small fortune had bought him a seat on the Stock Exchange; his own genius and good fortune did the rest. At his death his estate would be valued at some two hundred millions. Typical was his comment to the financier Clarence Barron that he had put money into Portuguese Africa looking for diamonds, "and just as somebody had warned me, my experts found oil." [40]

His political power was scarcely less impressive. He had a finger in everything from Wall Street to the Belgian Congo; his influence reached out to senators, governors, congressmen "by the score." Woodrow Wilson despised him. Yet his influence was at its peak during the First World War, and such men as House and McCombs were willing purveyors of the information he wanted the President to have.[41]

He spent no less lavishly than he earned. There was his town house on Fifth Avenue with a million-dollar flower garden, spectacular even in a New York accustomed to magnificent display. His wife loved flowers, and for her he wrested a garden from marble and concrete. Charles Yerkes, the transit king, had lived next door in a house valued at $1,239,000. Ryan bought it, razed the house to make room for the garden, but he left the thirty-two marble columns of the staircase, white as the flowers around them.

When Ryan met Baruch in the closing years of the nineteenth century he was not yet fifty years old. His wizard mind was planning one of the most daring coups yet to be attempted by an American financier — a raid on the giant "tobacco trust," the American Tobacco empire of James (Buck) Duke, the onetime snuff peddler from North Carolina, who like Ryan had struggled up out of poverty and Reconstruction to found an empire.

Duke was "the Trust." Eight years earlier, his W. Duke and Sons had swallowed up four competitors to form the American Tobacco Company, with a capitalization of $25,000,000. That took care of the cigarette firms. Next, Duke had turned his attention to the plugs. A year later, "the more important independents" had succumbed — except the Liggett and Myers Company of St. Louis.

In 1898 Duke formed the Continental Tobacco Company to take care of the American's plug business. He himself remained as president of both concerns. Yet Liggett and Myers was still holding out, resisting every attempt at merger, friendly or otherwise: price-wars, million-dollar campaigns, drive after drive for extermination.[42] But who could best Duke? Who could stand against him? James R. Keene had tried to carry out his announced determination to send Duke "back to mule-driving." [43] Secretly he bought a controlling interest in Duke's company but came up at last against Duke's own ultimatum that although Keene might own American he didn't own him, and all Duke had to do was to start another firm. Keene retreated.

Now a newcomer had entered the field. Inconspicuously organized by inconspicuous persons, who inconspicuously dropped from sight at the judicious moment, it was no secret in the Street that the real backers were of different caliber: Whitney, Widener, and, leading them all, that soft-spoken, gimlet-brained Southerner, Thomas Fortune Ryan. This would be a battle of giants — far transcending the limits of Wall Street.[44]

The moving spirit behind the Ryan forces was James George Butler of St. Louis. Duke had snapped up Butler's little independent firm several years before. Now Butler, still bitter at the tough-minded master, wanted to get back at Duke; and Duke suddenly girded for battle. So off to St. Louis his emissaries hustled, to dangle allurements before the Liggett and Myers stockholders. And hot in their wake trailed Ryan's representatives, Attorney William H. Page and a Wall Street broker named Bernard M. Baruch.[45]

How had it happened? How had a man of Ryan's stature entrusted negotiations so delicate to a man scarcely twenty-eight years old, almost unknown even in the Street? No one knew. But Baruch's plungings had not gone unnoticed by Ryan — he had watched his tracks on the ticker tape. "You young man over in the grass, you're pretty dangerous," he drawled.[46] Thus the spark was struck. Opportunity comes to those who seek, and Baruch saw opportunity. He knew that he was the man Ryan required. He knew Ryan would tolerate no high-pressure methods. So, of his own accord, he had sought him out, and as one Southerner to another, convinced him that he could be useful.[47]

St. Louis thirty years after the Civil War was still a half-Southern town. A few old houses still survived, the old memories and the old ways, and in the lobby of the Southern Hotel, where Baruch and Page established themselves, voices drawled, liquid and soft. So too at the Planters' Inn, where, accompanied by the aggrieved James G. Butler, they met short, stocky, jovial Colonel Mose Wetmore of Liggett and Myers and, as Page later reminisced, overwhelmed him with hospitality.[48]

The tactics consisted, first of all, in being agreeable socially. Juleps tinkling with ice and green with mint cooled the hot Southern air. Cards eased off the pack during the long sleepy afternoons at the Planters'.[49]

The city was excited. From the first the people sensed the truth — that the battle was between two empires locked for control. St. Louis cobblestones resounded to the marching feet of the local grocers' association, parading before the Liggett and Myers Company, placards waving. Newspapers hailed the victory of the "Trust" one day, of Ryan's forces the next, dredging into the past of Mr. Thomas Fortune Ryan and warming up all the unpleasant stories that one heard.[50]

Baruch disclaims credit for the results that ensued — although in retrospect it is of course Baruch that the old-timers in St. Louis remember. Page and Butler did most of the talking; Baruch was just their adviser. But the trio used tactics entirely different from those of Mr. Duke's advocates: they shrugged the ugly charges negligently away. As Baruch said, they had no hatred for Mr. Duke. In fact, they had only praise for Mr. Duke as a great man and a great manager, but they did feel that the interests of the Liggett and Myers stockholders would be better served by joining with Ryan. This approach, they believed afterwards, impressed Colonel Wetmore.[51] In any event, the objective was gained and Thomas Fortune Ryan's emissaries returned to New York with the Colonel's option on a controlling interest in Liggett and Myers.

Now the firing line shifted to Wall Street. A "raid" was on against Duke's subsidiary, Continental, with Bernard Baruch as general-in-charge, taking orders only from the field marshal himself. The scene of operations was the Curb Market on Broad Street in front of the Exchange, still in 1898 a huckster's warehouse, business transacted as openly as from the sidewalk pushcarts of the Lower East Side.

Baruch's job was to "raid" Continental by selling short and dragging the market price down. Every morning he repaired to Ryan's house on West 72nd Street to give his reports and get his instructions.

What manner of man was he, Baruch may have wondered, as the razor was stropped and Ryan's voice drawled on, so gentle, so soft, so great a contrast to the man himself.[52] All America was wondering what manner of man he was, for the tobacco war was nearly over, and strange rumors were afloat in the Street. The killing had been a mighty one. Ryan had reeled in Liggett and Myers; he had raided Continental; his choice now was to compete with American, or to demand a gigantic price for a sellout.

Had the whole scheme been a cooked-up plot on the part of Duke himself to gain control of Liggett and Myers? Was there a secret understanding between Ryan and Duke — and was Ryan actually working for Duke all along? Baruch never thought so, but rumor said so, and in the spring of 1899 the bomb exploded. At a directors' meeting, Duke's trust gobbled up the last competitor, the short-lived Union Tobacco Company. Union was merged with American, and Liggett and Myers was taken over by Duke's Continental company. Subsequently, American bought from Continental the cigarette business of Liggett and Myers.

Ryan was elected to the American company's board of directors. At a swoop, the shrewd Virginian and his friends had broken into Duke's inner circle. Poor Butler, who had wanted to humble the tobacco trust — no more is heard of him.[53]

Personally, Baruch emerged from the fray enriched, both in worldly

wisdom and by the sum of $50,000. That was his payment for serv-
ices rendered, but he would not sell himself to Ryan. In later years,
he was even to become friendly with Duke, whom he saw as one of
the great men of his age. They never had financial dealings, but
personally Duke often talked with the younger man about how he
felt his own mighty fortune should be spent.[54]

As for Ryan, Baruch's final evaluation of him was that he was a
man who never broke his word although he played the Wall Street
game.[55] It was not the way Baruch played. It was a strange and
tenuous friendship they had, almost as if Baruch were a young son,
battling his way in a harsh world. Baruch might do the things Ryan
had wanted to do, go farther than he had gone. Ryan understood even
when Baruch refused to join him in a drive to put James R. Keene
behind the bars — he saw that the younger man had his loyalties. For
Keene had been Baruch's friend back in his junior clerk days, his
mentor and teacher before Ryan had entered his life. He would not
turn on him now, although he did warn Ryan when Keene began
spreading false gossip about him. He refused to appear before the
Grand Jury on behalf of either antagonist. Despite his refusal, Ryan
trusted him more than ever.[56]

He had trained in a tough school — young Bernard Baruch —
with Ryan, Whitney, Aldrich, and Keene. He trained with them, yet
was not of them.[57] And he held their friendship. He last saw Ryan
in a New York office building at the height of the boom days of the
twenties. Ryan was then past seventy but glowing with vigor and as
well groomed and spruce as if he had his hair cut every day. Gaily
he strolled up to Baruch, linked his arm in his, and suggested that
they should get together on a scheme to set Wall Street talking.

And Baruch almost bowed to his impulse to go along.* [58]

With his profits from the Liggett and Myers deal, Baruch bought
his second seat on the Exchange, at a cost of $39,000 — no small ac-
complishment for a man not yet thirty years old. Now recognition
admitted him to that informal circle known to Wall Street as the
"Waldorf crowd." It was the fraternity of success, the brotherhood
of high stakes and big plungers. Now, before 1899 shifted into 1900,
Baruch was included. He was no longer a "coming man." He had
arrived at last.[59]

* Baruch has no memory of the particulars of this plan.

4

THE GOLDEN TOUCH

THE SOO LINE — the Minneapolis, St. Paul, and Sault Ste. Marie — at the end of the last century was a wheat route. Straight across the prairies it stretched, a glitter of rails shining through a green and waving sea. In 1904 word came to Wall Street that it was reaching farther, throwing out a line from Thief River Falls, Minnesota, to Kenmare, North Dakota, where plows were ripping at the unbroken prairie. Would this prove permanently profitable to the railroad? In his office Baruch pondered the question and was satisfied with none of the answers; he must go west to see for himself. He returned to find Soo selling at sixty and on the rise. He began to buy the stock.

It is significant of his standing in the Street that there were enough insiders confident of his judgment to come in with him. Meanwhile, the stock continued to rise. A bumper wheat crop was harvested that fall. Up went the traffic of the railroad some 50 per cent, and up zoomed Soo from $60 to $110. Then a negative voice sounded through the excitement — that of Bernard M. Baruch.

He distrusted panic-buying. And he distrusted enthusiasm. The stock was still rising. Baruch did not care. He began to sell. It hit $135 before the peak was reached; Baruch had got out some thirty points below the high. Disagreeing with the insiders, he had concluded that the Thief River extension would be of small permanent benefit.

This was how Baruch played it safe, just by patient research, he insisted. The game was not too difficult if you were willing to work and followed the rules.[1]

Some of this wisdom was derived from a new friend, a man who "knew what was going on west of Hoboken." Henry C. Davis, a new member of A. A. Housman and Company, knew little about stocks and bonds and ticker tape. But he knew America, the whole great country, and found his answers there.

He had been a rod boy with the engineering corps that laid the line of the Northern Pacific, laboring under the armed guard of Federal troops, alert to hold off the Indians of the Plains. Baruch's soaring flights sometimes led him into dark descents; the friendship of Davis was like a bright, clean wind from the plains, sweeping out the shadows. They took an instant liking to each other. Each year Davis took a trip around the Union, and Baruch began to join him. Broadly the panorama of America spread before them. From the observation car they saw the opening West, the great fields of oats, barley, wheat, and corn. They saw whole states parched by drought and knew what that would mean in the Exchange centers of the world. Through Davis, Baruch met the big, redheaded "Tim" Shaughnessy, later Baron Shaughnessy of Montreal and Ashford and president of the Canadian Pacific Railroad. Once Davis and Baruch even hired a private car and took Baruch's aging father and mother as far west as the Yellowstone, and Dr. Baruch mused on how far his son had come from the older simple Carolina days.[2]

More than ever now Baruch played his canny hand. He had learned his lessons. It had been a sober and most chastened young man who had stepped into the dawn of the new century with little left to him in the world but his seat on the Exchange. That seat had been such a fillip to his spirits that he was aglow with pride. Then he had fallen for a market "tip." He had bought just as the market sagged, sent good money after bad, and had been "cleaned out."

He had had to go home to tell his young wife that they would have to let their servants go and the horses and the cabriolet with the two on the box.[3]

Tips, he had had to conclude, were a very costly affair.

The Waldorf-Astoria Hotel at the end of the nineteenth century was the American dream come true. To the "gold-plated aristocrats" it offered the opulence of the Vanderbilts and the Astors. It offered the clean shave and the rose-shaded candles, the chafing dish and the Waldorf salad; for the Tammany elite a dinner table centered with a pool banked in lilies and orchids, jeweled perfume bottles for the ladies, jeweled matchboxes for the gentlemen, blue raspberries, chestnut purée, terrapin.

It was a cavalcade, a panorama from 3 P.M. to midnight — Peacock Alley, where along the great marble and amber corridor moved a parade of fashion and form — the Palm Garden, its velvet rope sealing off the "swells" from *hoi polloi* — the more lowly Empire Room, the Rose Room, and the tall thick-set figure of Oscar, bowing in recognition. To be noticed by Oscar, to be granted his personal attention to your food and drink was an accolade — but alas, it was noted that these delicate attentions were conferred alike on bluebloods and men of the Golden Touch.[4] Oscar was the prophet of the New Era; not only did he know the social distinctions; he knew when to ignore them. It was this encroaching democracy that spelled the end of the "Old Waldorf." An "indiscriminate throng," society found distasteful.

By 1910, the Waldorf's brief feverish hour was already fretting toward its close. Only memories remain of the gilded splendor, the multiprismed chandeliers and ceilings encrusted with gilt, the sinking carpets, the men's café, like a gentleman's club, with its darkly paneled walls, ample armchairs, cards, tobacco, and big four-sided bar.

But in the first decade of the century, the Waldorf was at the pinnacle of its glory.[5] The Men's Bar was an uptown extension of Wall Street. Here came the sports and the speculators, Hawley, Housman, Keene, little German-born Jake Field, who, when asked if he liked Balzac, thought it was the name of an unlisted stock.[6] These were one-track men — men of undivided attention and single aim. And here moved Bernard M. Baruch. For years he was a regular habitué, realizing that here you could pick up, better than anywhere else, news of the speculative trends.[7]

Not all was business. At the bar a weary young broker could quench his thirst on any one or several of hundreds of varieties of liquor; if hungry, appease his appetite on smoked turkey and hot casseroles, steaming on the buffet, or fresh-cut slices of Virginia ham, curling back pinkly from the blade.

Morgan, the great high priest of finance, was there only occasionally, his dark eyes brooding. But in a single afternoon, almost, a young "comer" like Baruch could have had the thrill of "bottoms up" with the flame-haired, mustached, onetime river boatman Samuel Clemens, hear talk of the sweaty swamps of Cuba from Richard

Harding Davis, see the gold braid of Admiral Dewey wink in the gaslight. He could have brushed shoulders with "Diamond Jim" Brady and "Gentleman Jim" Corbett; handsome, laughing Charlie Schwab, Carnegie's boyish protégé, a joy because he never talked business out of business hours; and dour Judge Elbert Gary.[8]

Over with the "Western crowd," his bald dome and black eyes shining, sat Dan Reid, later of the United States Steel Corporation. A strapping six-footer, Reid raided stocks to the point where he had everyone, including the bankers, afraid of him.[9] But the "king of the Waldorf crowd" was none of these. He was John W. (Bet-a-Million) Gates, a bumptious, loud-mouthed Chicagoan who drank standing up, one foot hooked over the rail. With his flashy vests and glittering watch chains, his brown derby aslant, he still looked the former Western drummer, the barbed-wire salesman who had started a rival firm and forced his boss to buy him out. For the public, it was hard to distinguish between big business and big gambling; for Gates, there were no such distinctions. He would gamble on anything, from the fall of a raindrop to the sprint of a horse — and in later years Baruch saw him in London, stuffed heavily into striped trousers and Prince Albert, waistcoat unbuttoned and silk hat tilted back on his head, making a little bet of seven thousand pounds at Ascot. Nothing but the grandiose appealed to him — he was the greatest plunger of his time. He would play forty-eight hours straight without food or sleep.[10] If he lost, there was a scene in the $20,000-a-year suite which he shared with his wife, and tears that only a $50,000 brooch could dry. If he won, however, Mrs. Gates would flip flapjacks happily for all comers. Baruch liked him, but their friendship was determinedly social. As Baruch said afterward, when Gates threw his arm over your shoulders and said "Bernie, listen to me," that "was a good time to put your watch in your shoe." [11]

Yet he was no mere plunger. He was selling ideas to Morgan now, instead of barbed wire to the hardware dealers.[12] His mind had conceived a gigantic thought while he was jostling pool balls in the billiard room of the Waldorf. Later, in a private dining room, he and silent Henry Clay Frick, Charlie Schwab, and the cold, precise Gary mapped details of the scheme, but it was Gates who conceived the United States Steel Corporation. His idea was for an eighty-million-dollar American Steel and Wire Corporation, and Gary passed on the suggestion to Morgan. But Morgan disliked Gates and his type — and mistrusted them.[13] Gates and Gary had to go on with their wire trust alone. Only later did Morgan decide to combine the combinations, buy out Carnegie, and come to terms with Gates, buying him off by taking over his American Steel and Wire Corporation.[14] Gates demanded a tremendous sum in this transaction, yet, plunger that he was, in the end he confessed that he would have to go back into business to square his accounts.[15]

The bull market roared along in that triumphant, cocksure spring of 1901. "Never lower the flag" was the watchword from the White House. The Spanish War had opened the door to empire. The Atlantic began to look to American eyes like an American lake. A new era of wealth and glory had begun. People were in the market now who had never played stocks before.[16] Baruch could feel the feverish throbbing, the tension in the air. Women were in the market now for the first time, and over the teacups you heard the babble of their voices, of rumors and tips and what steel or copper or Union Pacific was going to do.

On Friday, May 3, the market dipped some seven to ten points. Baruch thought it would drop farther, but waited before taking a short position.

Saturday, lightning struck. Northern Pacific, which three years earlier had been selling at 19, rocketed upward, closing at 110. On Monday it opened four points higher.

In all his years on the Exchange, Bernard Baruch was never to see such an opening again. Frenzy swept the Exchange. It was a wild, runaway market; like an unbroken colt, the stock bounded upward in leaps and rushes. The rush to cover was like a football scrimmage. By two o'clock the "shorts" were "shaken out": Northern Pacific was at 133.[17]

What had happened? Neither the directors nor the bankers knew the answer.

Baruch knew. He had spent Monday at the arbitrage desk. During the afternoon, Talbot J. Taylor, son-in-law of James R. Keene, stopped by, and Baruch told him that Northern Pacific could be bought in London several points lower than in New York.

Taylor looked at him thoughtfully. Was Baruch buying Northern Pacific? he asked. When Baruch admitted that he was, Taylor, giving no reason, advised against it. Baruch did not ask why. Taylor hesitated, then gripped Baruch by the shoulder and drew him aside. He had something to tell him.

The information was invaluable.[18] A furious battle was shaping up. This was no small-scale raid, no mere tussle of the bulls and bears. This might be one of those terrific contests for control that take place once or twice in a decade. This might lead to anything. Baruch thought of the panic of 1873 and Black Friday and the Chicago and Northwestern corner of Jay Gould twenty-nine years before. This was to be a struggle of giants — the greatest of them all — Morgan and Harriman and James J. Hill.

Since the early nineties, Hill's Great Northern Railway Company and Morgan's Northern Pacific, which Hill had helped reorganize, had worked in close collaboration. But there was no collaboration between them and Edward H. Harriman and Jacob Schiff of Kuhn, Loeb and Company. For Harriman, too, was king of a railroad empire. It was he who had taken the Union Pacific when it was but "two streaks of rust" and built it into the greatest railroad of them all. To it he had added the Illinois Central. He had set his sights on the Chicago, Burlington and Quincy — for a complete tie-up to Chicago and St. Louis. Morgan and Hill had had the same idea, and they got there first. Nevertheless, Harriman's exploits, climaxed by the final purchase of Southern Pacific, had made him loom up at last as one of the most important forces in the railroad world.[19]

Harriman, like Morgan, was one of Baruch's heroes.[20] That "two-dollar broker," Morgan dismissed him contemptuously, this frail, secretive clergyman's son from Long Island, who at twenty-one borrowed money from an uncle to buy a seat on the Stock Exchange. But to Baruch he had the talents of Morgan and Ryan combined. He was the most versatile man he had ever seen in the Street, and the only one to whom he would apply the overworked word "genius." Harriman's self-confidence was never shaken and his consecrated energy, his razor-sharp mind and lightning plunges were the embodiment of what young Baruch wanted to have and to be.[21]

Now Harriman, with Kuhn, Loeb backing and with the Standard Oil empire's blessing, could meet Morgan as an equal at last.[22] He had knocked for admission at the door of the House of Morgan: a third interest in Northern Pacific was what he suggested, but Morgan had neither taste nor tolerance for a rival. He had slammed the door in Harriman's face.[23]

Harriman was not to be thwarted. For weeks he had been moving to purchase under cover in the open market a majority of the Northern Pacific stock, parent line of the Chicago, Burlington and Quincy.

So secret were his maneuvers, that even Morgan, now placidly vacationing in Europe, was fooled into thinking public interest alone was
responsible for the demand.[24]

But not James J. Hill. He was soon suspicious of the sudden rise
of Northern Pacific. Well aware that he and Morgan did not control
a full 50 per cent of the stock, he chartered a special train and rushed
to New York. He arrived on Friday, May 3, 1901. There he found
that Harriman already owned a majority of the preferred, but only
about 370,000 of the 800,000 outstanding shares of common. Yet
Morgan and Hill owned but 260,000 of those shares.

A cable was rushed to Morgan, who, at Aix-les-Bains, lifted his
voice loudly, and not in hymns. The order he transmitted to New
York was for 150,000 shares of Northern Pacific, but this was Saturday and the purchases could not begin until Monday morning, the
Exchange being already closed. Late that Saturday also came a rush
order by Harriman to grab up more common. His order for 40,000
shares was placed with Jacob Schiff, who accidentally or purposefully
attended divine worship at the synagogue on Saturday until the Exchange was closed. Schiff, so it is presumed, had decided enough was
enough.[25] On Monday the onslaught began and continued until
Morgan and Hill had between them "cornered" the stock — no more
was available — in fact more had been sold than actually existed.

As for Baruch, he got in the market too late and out too early,
but neither too early nor too late to sell short a number of other
issues than Northern Pacific. Fortunately, he kept out of Northern
Pacific, as James R. Keene had advised him to do. But he knew the
rules of a corner and of a panic, and how money could be made on
the short side, generally, when the whole list declined as deluded
short purchasers of Northern Pacific liquidated their other assets to
be able to pay up.[26]

Tuesday, May 7, the Exchange opened in a frenzy with brokers
grappling to pay $700 for a day's "loan" of one share of Northern
Pacific.

"I'll give a thirty-second for five hundred shares of Northern
Pacific," someone shouted.

"A quarter for five hundred."

"Three-eighths for two hundred." Looking down, Bernard Baruch
saw something that he had never seen before and might never see
again. Desperate men, surging like flood waters, hands waving, voices

roaring in a crescendo of sound, driven by all the primal emotions: greed, lust, fear. Here was what gold did to men. Here was a mad mob.

"Let me go, will you," shrieked a broker, tackled by a flying leap that nearly cracked his ribs. "I haven't a share of the damned stock." Then Al Stern, a robust young broker, looked in and naïvely inquired, "Who wants to borrow Northern Pacific? I have a block to lend."

The shout that went up left Baruch's ears tingling. Panic became a stampede. Across the floor they raced, hats bashed in, coats and collars dangling, stamping, trampling, screaming, and through the melee the cry of one little man: "Lift me up, will you? Lift me up ... I'm little and I can't yell loud enough."

"Three per cent for five hundred."

"I want a thousand, give you two per cent."

Around a chair the crowd parted, and for an instant you could see Stern's face. It had the look of one who dies at his post. There he was, huddled in his chair, his back to the mob, struggling to note down his transactions, and to fight off his tormentors. "Don't stick your finger in my eye," he protested; "Put back my hat," as someone began to beat a tattoo on his skull. "Don't make such a confounded excitement." It was no use; it was like trying to hold back the sea. A few minutes later, his last share loaned, he broke away, white-faced, his clothes disheveled, while bids of 9 and 10 per cent shrilled impotently about him.[27]

Baruch now knew what gold and the greed for gold did to men.[28] Here was the outcome of "tips," of "dope," of "inside information." Anyone could lead this mob. Anyone could destroy them who played on the primal emotions. Anyone could better them who kept his head when they were losing theirs. "Your people, sir," had said that great American who lay undisturbed around the corner in Trinity churchyard, "your people, sir, is a great beast." [29]

Wednesday was another terrible day. Northern Pacific opened at 155, twelve points over the closing. In the middle of the morning came a public announcement that Harriman had won control. Up shot the stock to 180, but neither happening served to restore public confidence. For this was war to the kill; here was no room for pity, for generosity, or quarter. If Morgan fell, under the combine of Harriman and Standard Oil, the world of finance would fall with him.[30]

Baruch was still making money on the short side of stocks that fell as Northern Pacific soared. Yet even his resilient young nerves were jangled. Rumor pounded upon him; fear, alone, now had taken over, and when the professionals were frightened, the public would no longer buy. One emotion swayed men now — not greed, not power, but fear, and there was a cold contagion about it that chilled your nerves.

Uptown at the Waldorf the corridors were jammed. In the bar you saw John W. Gates keeping up his jovial front, although his millions were in jeopardy.[31] All elegance — the silk hats, the white ties, the swish — was gone. The women were gone; this was no women's world. Gray cigar ash lay splashed across the carpets like bird droppings. In locked rooms, up and down the corridors, voices rose and fell — the Kuhn, Loeb and Morgan people were conferring through the night.[32]

It was worse Thursday morning. Baruch's self-confidence melted as he looked on the tired and white-faced men standing in silence, in rows. They were quiet, so quiet, so quiet.

Onward the stock reeled — to 190; an hour later, 400; before noon, 700; and shortly afterward, word came of a sale of 300 shares at $1000 a share. All sanity, all values were gone. Crazily, the whole list plunged downward, as Northern Pacific zoomed skyward, and recklessly men hurled good money after bad, selling everything at any price and fighting for a foothold like survivors on an overcrowded raft. There were pitiful scenes in the brokerage offices — a man, head sunk in his hands, shoulders heaving; another, arms thrown back, face contracted with desperation and pain. Now and then you heard a muffled cry. Baruch caught a fleeting glimpse of his friend Fred Edey hurtling back and forth from the floor to the offices of the House of Morgan. Loans must be made, collateral be found, or there would be twenty failures by nightfall. Through the crowd threaded a rumor that Arthur Housman had dropped dead. Tense with excitement, Baruch watched his partner fighting his way, inch by inch, through that swirling mob to show himself, faces turning upward in relief and amazement as he passed.

It was too much. Baruch was engulfed with pity at this wild, ruthless drive for power, where the innocent suffered the most of all.

At 2.15 Al Stern mounted a chair. Like a whip, his voice cracked across the uproar. His firm, at least, would not enforce delivery of the purchased shares. Eddie Norton followed him. Down the stock came to 300, a figure at which you could do business. Slowly, it steadied there. Something had happened, but what? The answer came at five that evening as crowds milled around a bulletin board at the Waldorf. On it was a brief word from Morgan and from Kuhn, Loeb. They would give stock to those "short" at $150. This, Baruch thought, was better treatment than most could have hoped for. Friday morning the Exchange opened in an atmosphere of almost funereal calm. The panic was over.

Back in the shambles, the survivors rested and licked their wounds. John W. Gates had had a bad day, but he held court that night in the Waldorf bar, still chipper with an effort.[33]

Who had won? No one knew. Slowly, the missing pieces began to fall into place. The brokers, having sold stock that was nonexistent, could find no one from whom they could either borrow or buy — hence the wild, runaway demand. To get money to buy and deliver the promised shares of Northern Pacific, they had had to sell every other stock they could lay their hands on, hence the collapse of the whole list.

Harriman had not won control. Morgan would not surrender to him. Harriman would have fought on indefinitely, but his bankers had had enough, and Morgan and Hill had had enough. Harriman had won something, however: he did get representation on the boards of both the Burlington and the Northern Pacific. Furthermore, the new Northern Securities Company which evolved represented both the Northern Pacific and the Great Northern.[34]

They called Baruch "the Lone Eagle." Men turned to whisper as he passed, runs a highly colored account of Baruch at the end of the century, "tall, aquiline, smiling, but uncommunicative among the excited stock dealers."[35] He was alone. He was always alone. He was deaf to tips, indifferent to advice or information. Ruefully, Otto Kahn, no mean money-maker himself, told the story of the young Baruch bursting out to him the instant they shook hands not to tell him any market rumors — they might confuse his own judgment.[36]

His self-confidence might have been laughable had it not been so justified. To hardened old-timers Baruch seemed a part of the eternal mystery of Wall Street. They did not know the hours and years of study he had spent on subjects unfamiliar to him, the patient sifting of the trivial for the bedrock of fact, the soul-searching, the self-discipline that had produced the phenomenon that was Bernard Baruch. They called it genius; he knew it to be, in large part, hard work.[37]

Silence was not easy for a naturally gregarious young man.[38] His role during the Northern Pacific "corner" had raised his prestige with the Waldorf crowd, but out of the debacle, also, he had gleaned a philosophy that would make him millions. Eternal suspicion was his motto — not only of panics, crowds, tips, or unsolicited information, but also of "insiders," whether amateur or professional. The men with ample credit, big bank accounts, and "sure tips" went broke nine times out of ten.[39]

Now position and influence in the Street hung tantalizingly before him. But he spurned all offers. Realizing that if you played with others you had to do it their way, he preferred to go it alone. He was beholden to no one, and no one owed him anything. Some called him smug; others thought him selfish, but he continued on his own way. He did not want to know what "the other fellow" was going to do, for he was confidently sure that his own clear brain could figure out the answers better than those on the inside, too much swayed by emotion.[40]

Yet his aloofness aroused little animosity. The boyishness of his smile, the twinkle in the keen scrutiny of his eyes tempered antagonisms toward him. Furthermore, to those he respected he was as receptive and humble as a child, self-confident, but without arrogance. To such as Thomas Fortune Ryan and James R. Keene, his ears were always open. Had he been known as a donor and receiver of tips, he would never have received the one or two that really counted. Never did he break a confidence, even to his own associates or family. For him, it was a good rule. Never would he have been told to stay out of Northern Pacific if it had not been known that he would not tell.[41]

Furthermore, if he "knew" too much, he might have to abandon a well-mapped plan simply because it could look as though he were using information against the very people who had given it to him. He had no right, he was convinced, to lose anyone's money but his own. If you went your own way you were free of responsibility to others. For you would inevitably be wrong some of the time. To save yourself, you had to be ready to duck out and run to shelter without consulting associates.[42]

Hardest of all to shake off were the free riders — the bankers, lawyers, merchants, sometimes even your own friends and relatives. Cynicism must have edged Baruch's smile in those first flush days before his reputation for imperturbability was established. People, he found, would entertain him socially in order to get tips for their own benefit or for someone else's. It would have been cheaper sometimes, Baruch must have thought grimly, to have given them the money.[43]

The market was no place for amateurs. Denouncing Wall Street, the mysterious "thems" and "theys" who supposedly manipulated secret forces, Baruch thought, was like fighting shadows. The Street was not to blame. No one was to blame but the greedy lambs themselves, who ventured into the pen and remained to get shorn. Playing the market was as technical a business as manufacturing — which no amateur would attempt.[44] Yet the same person would throw his bankroll into a market dominated by professional financiers.

Baruch was a success at his profession, so amazing a success that his legend has persisted for fifty years. It is true, as we have seen, that he did go broke once or twice before his fortunes stabilized, and this would be due to the violation of his own rules. The rules worked; there was no magic secret to the game.[45] There were other wonder boys in Wall Street, like Morton Schwartz, who came out of Louisville, Kentucky, to make a million before he was twenty. But Baruch was one of the few successful speculators of his generation, not so much because of what he made as because of what he was able to keep.[46] Not his services as presidential adviser, nor his relations with the New Deal, nor his behind-the-scenes exploits as "elder statesman," but "how he made his potatoes" is of primary interest to the public mind. He was the American dream come true. He was the American success story, the aspiration fulfilled of every young man off the farms, or out of the little towns and villages, who dreamed of conquering the city and of amassing wealth and fame and power. If he did it — maybe they could too. And so they dreamed, forgetful that the rules change in fifty years and that even the game itself would be recognizable no longer.

Many versions of Baruch's rules of success have been given. It would take a book to list them all. Yet it is possible to reduce them to general principles. It was no question of blind jumps in the dark. To be a successful trader you would have to (1) know mankind,

(2) know yourself, (3) know your world and your time, (4) know the stock, the market, and the rules of the game.

It was possible, Baruch admitted, to make money and be wrong — some of the time. If you were right five times out of eight, you could make money. If you were right only six times out of ten, you could make a good deal of money, and if you knew how to retrench and cut your losses, you could make money, even if you were right only two or three times out of ten. Baruch was right far more.[47]

When was a stock good? The answer was the key to fortune, but there was no one answer. Sometimes it took six months to find the answers, but Baruch waited until he was sure.

He would study a company's board of directors, especially their range of activities. It was not big names he was looking for, but names that did not appear too often. When a man spread himself too thin, he was of less use to all the industries he served. Director-ship was a big job; no man could serve as front man or smoke screen to a number of companies and do justice to any one of them. Two or three directorships was the most any prudent man could handle. Baruch preferred a working director, even of slight fame and modest attainments, to a potent name anytime, if he were really capable and absorbed in the interests of the company.[48]

There were other questions to answer. The product — Was it useful? Was it necessary? What about the men with the ideas, were they the masters of the firm?

There were rules, too, by which you could tell a good stock. As old James Keene would point out, you couldn't hold a good stock down. Like water, it inevitably sought its own level; a good stock was its own best advertisement. The stock that was the first to rise and the last to fall was usually a good stock, although artificial manipula-tions could send poor stocks up and sound ones down — but the natural trend could not be withstood for long. Great was Baruch's disillusionment when Thomas Fortune Ryan, with the look of a disappointed father at a wayward child, warned him not to depress a certain stock.[49] Baruch desisted, but the stock continued its down-ward way. Not even Ryan could reverse the rules of the game. The good stock would snap back, once the pressure was off, but not the tenderest fostering care could hold a poor stock up above its value. Natural laws were indifferent to man's contrivings, and no scrupulous man would push a stock above its true value. In fact, Baruch was always to have a kindly word for the "bears," whose periodic raids brought the market down, and the hopes and fortunes of men with it; such raids he thought, had a most salutary effect. Good stocks would bounce back easily enough, but the laggards would have tumbled in time anyway, and perhaps from far more disastrous heights. No speculative raids had any permanent effect on a good stock.

If you had to study the market to learn your stocks, the rules of the market could conversely be learned by study of the stocks. Stocks were, in fact, a barometer for the market's changes. The fall of good stocks on a rising market was a storm signal. On the other hand, the end of a long decline might be signaled by the inching upward of a few good stocks.[50]

Cheap stocks were no bargain. Baruch early learned that a stock quoted at its full worth was also no buy. The old rules still held — and hold today — to buy low and sell high, but the question was in knowing just when a stock had reached the high- or low-water mark. This was the area where rules could no longer operate, nor knowledge suffice, and you were alone in the twilight world of your own instincts. When in doubt, sell was the only safe rule; and it was the small and carefully garnered profits, not the big coups that totaled up to wealth in the end.[51]

Baruch has said that never in his life did he buy at the bottom and get out at the top. All his life, in fact, he got out too soon. This was his canny judgment. Satisfied with the smaller and surer profit, he did not share the risks nor the heartbreak of those who waited too long and too late. Although in general he would advise the average trader to buy on a rising market and to sell on a falling one, for himself, like Ryan, he reversed the rule.[52] It was not that he lacked the courage to take risks. Time and again he struck out into uncertainty, bolstered by his understanding of the inevitable economic law. He had the courage and the backlog to buy low and watch the stock sink lower, to hold on, confident in himself and in the stock and in the inevitable comeback under economic law. But this was his own game, played for himself alone, by one who could afford the lesser profit. He was deeply regretful when his conservatism made him sell out too early for certain friends. This was why he hated to take care of other people's transactions.[53]

If the policies of the government were bad, that narrowed your range for choice. The canny Wall Street speculator could not survive with his nose in Wall Street. He had to have an eye out to Washington.[54]

But one gamble you had to make — on the future. You not only had to know the other fellow; you had to know the trends of your time. This was where Baruch's talent came into play. For talent alone was not the answer. This was what no "rules of success" could ever teach. This was what he could not transmit, could not even explain. Study was not enough. As he would say: "I tell you, making money is purely and simply a faculty." [55]

Baruch was, in fact, essentially an artist in finance. Neither in talent nor in temperament did he conform to the pattern of the average businessman. He made money quite simply and naturally as other men might have composed music or painted pictures. One writer has described Baruch's brilliant intuitions as some kind of fourth mental dimension, "some two or three extra senses that have been schooled out of most men." "I can't imagine anything that Baruch can't accomplish if he puts his mind on it hard enough," Mark Sullivan once observed.[56]

But even these insights were enriched by study. You must know people, not only politically and economically, but psychologically, in the mass and individually.[57] You must know yourself also. The trader's life was a hard life. A man had to go into training for speculation; he had to keep well and fit, his brain clear and keen. Always he must have complete control of his emotions; he could give way neither to elation nor despair. Baruch was no mere calculating machine; he had the sensitive nerves that made his acute perceptions possible. He sometimes gave way to overconfidence after a big killing. This was the danger. He had to get away to rest and to cool off. The dulled and tired brain could fumble the controls, and in a moment undo all the work of hours of thought and consecration.[58]

It was not the lure of money-making alone that held him enthralled with the Street for so many years. It was the thrill of the game. Wall Street was legalized gambling and would endure so long as the love of something for nothing was inherent in humankind. You could control the excesses of Wall Street; you could not redirect the course of human nature. The law could protect a man from being exploited, but not from the penalty of his own stupidity, his belief that he could outsmart the other fellow — the irresistible urge to try to beat the game.

Baruch was always to feel that the ethics of Wall Street were no less high than those of any of the traditional professions. Never did he know a trader to repudiate a contract. Often a deal involving millions was concluded without a word in writing. Wall Street generally kept its own house in order, and as a member of the law and governing committee, Baruch sat on trials and judgment of delinquent Exchange members. The Exchange, he believed, usually operated for the public's good. Often it forced information from fly-by-night corporations so that investors might be informed. Baruch believed it did more toward its own self-regulation than that which was accomplished by its critics, but it did not go far enough.[59]

Baruch would admit as much. In the thirties, surveying the debacle of the preceding six years with the perspective of forty, he conceded that the Exchange had had its opportunities, and some of the regulations that were forced upon it were justified. Regulations sufficient for the bulls and the bears had not protected the lambs, who had tumbled, bleating, into the pen, the gold dust in their eyes. Even the old traders were sometimes bedazzled by the glitter of the New Era. The excesses of the Exchange made the Securities and Exchange Commission necessary.[60]

Finally, in 1929 when the market crashed, the faith of the people crashed with it. Human greed was not blamed, only the instrumentalities by which greed was fulfilled. It became a stigma to be a Wall Street man. None knew this better than Baruch, or suffered more from it; yet he always kept pride in his profession. It was the greed and excesses of men, not the Street that was to blame.

As for himself, he amassed a fortune by the rules, in conformity with the laws of his time. It was a rough time and a rough game, but as the rules changed, Baruch's practices changed with them. Baruch's guide was the law. He was too sophisticated not to realize that right and wrong were relative, according to time and place, and he liked to apply to himself the story of the man who when young was known as a gambler, later a speculator, and finally a banker, although he had been doing the same thing all along.[61]

In old age he would look back, repeating: "You can't do it today. You don't know what to do; the government can upset all your calculations." Yet the general principles were still the same. And men were still fools to play the market, unless as a lifetime career.[62]

Not all his killings could be reduced to formulas. There was, for instance, his coup in Amalgamated Copper.

It all began according to prearranged plan. During the summer of 1901 Baruch had had a long talk with a hardheaded, piercing-eyed German coffee merchant named Herman Sielcken, who knew a lot about copper. He told Baruch that because of the small demand for copper in peacetime, overproduction had glutted the market. Copper was due for a fall. With Amalgamated Copper, particularly, all was not well. Nothing but the genius of Thomas Lawson, plus a lot of oversubscribed stock (in which, as it turned out, the organizers had not risked a penny of their own money), had sustained it this far.[63]

So in the big talk of boom, Baruch began to sell short, and he was already enough of a figure in Wall Street so that his move attracted attention. Thomas Fortune Ryan issued a warning: "Bernie, I hear you are short of Amalgamated Copper. I just want to let you know that the big fellows in it are going to twist your tail." [64] Keene, he warned, was "long" of the stock.

Baruch was unmoved. His instincts were now at work. Nothing mattered or could matter but simple economic forces. He was indifferent to inside opinion. He paid no heed to the taunts about the moral wickedness of those who were ruining the market and tearing down a great enterprise. He said nothing and the Wall Street insiders understood his silence.

True to his expectations, Amalgamated Copper began to drop. On September 20, 1901, the directors of the company cut the dividend from 8 to 6 per cent. The stock then broke seven points, with Baruch comfortably on the short side.

The crisis was expected Monday. On the Saturday of that weekend, Miss Belle called the office. "Son, do you know that Monday is Yom Kippur?"

Baruch knew, but he had forgotten. Yom Kippur, the Day of Atonement — that belonged entirely to his family. And on Yom Kippur no business could be transacted.

Baruch went home to observe his holiday. On Monday the telephone began to ring and it rang all day. Baruch never lifted the receiver from the hook. After a while the calls ceased.

What happened? The stock had opened at 100, dropped to 97, then rallied. Had Baruch been there, he would have given orders to sell out. But he was not there. In the afternoon the stock sagged again. Eventually it dropped to 60. And when Baruch did close out the next September, his profits were some $700,000.[65]

Not all that Baruch touched turned to gold. Sometimes he met disillusionment. This time he misjudged the knowledge and capabilities of another man, instead of following his own rule and trusting himself. He had made a fortune on Amalgamated Copper by listening to the rugged old coffee merchant, Herman Sielcken. Surely Mr. Sielcken should know about the coffee. Since the panic of 1903 coffee prices had been rising steadily, and with the prospects of crop control by the Brazilian government, plus a severe drought, Baruch bought heavily on margin and sat back, trusting nature for high prices. Nature did not cooperate. Nature, in fact, came through with a tremendous crop, and somehow in the middle of Brazilian politics, crop control did not come through at all. Down went the price of coffee and with every fraction of a point it dropped, Baruch's capital dropped — by thousands of dollars.

Sielcken told him to hold on. He held on, watching the profits of years dwindle away. He became a one-man panic. Every rule that he had taught himself or learned from hard experience was forgotten as he frantically sought to strengthen his position, hurling good stocks after bad, even selling his Canadian Pacific to increase his holdings. Coffee dropped even faster than before.

Bernard Baruch became emotionally and even physically sick. Rallying his shattered forces he took stock. He could afford his losses. What had really suffered was his self-confidence. Never had he suffered such indecision. What had he done wrong? In the first place, he had neglected to study the field. He had taken the opinion of an insider too involved in the commodity for perspective, instead of doing the groundwork himself.

His self-confidence was shaken, but he would recover. He would come back. Many never did. Long since, he had learned, "You have to take it or you can't give it." No man could succeed without bitterness and hard work, ridicule, and taunts, the sneers and threats and sleepless opposition of other men (for who could succeed as he did without inciting envy and rivalry?). All this he could take.[66]

In spite of this setback, he had made his mark in the world — and he celebrated. Now drivers of buggies began to clench bridles and clear the way as Baruch's monster of a Panhard speeded by — a glittering long-distance winner of the race from Paris to Bordeaux, its gas exploding like a gun. Later, after the Panhard, came the Mercedes, a $22,000, forty-horsepower, mile-a-minute model, like William K. Vanderbilt's. It raised young Baruch to such eminence as a personage that the *Herald* printed his picture at the wheel.[67]

The cars were only superficial marks of his achievements. He had his town house in the West End, and in summer the Baruchs moved out of town. At Elberon, New Jersey, near Long Branch, thirty-year-old "Getty" Reilly would rush to watch as Annie Griffen Baruch made her stately promenade, "she was so beautiful." A step or two behind came her husband, his eyes fixed upon her in admiration, "never moving from her form or face." Even at the opera, in the hubbub surrounding Mrs. Vanderbilt's "entrance," kicking a jewel swung from her waist by a rope of pearls, heads turned to look at Annie Baruch, the pearls her husband had brought her from Paris glinting around her throat. The Baruchs had their box at the horse show, but Miss Reilly noted that the people that visited them were, of course, "his own kind." And although her schoolmate Irma Kuhne attended the little reception and housewarming the Baruchs gave to open their new house, Miss Kuhne never called again. There were too many of "his kind" there.[68]

This was what Mr. Griffen had tried to tell Baruch and his daughter. The walls of Mrs. Astor's ballroom, enclosing the select Four Hundred, were unyielding. It was not that the young Baruchs were garish with their wealth; it was a garish Gilded Age. An earlier, more rigid society might have ignored William Henry Vanderbilt's ninety millions, or the dry-goods merchant A. T. Stewart's white marble palace, with its drawing room where no one was ever received, or its art gallery which no one ever saw. Now, the younger generation could ignore Society. Dullness was the unforgivable sin, so one hostess might present Paderewski as an after-dinner attraction, and another command the orchestra to play "Home Sweet Home" when bored with her guests, or send a baby elephant to pass out peanuts.[69] The social walls were not unscalable. "We cannot fight Wall Street," was the sad cry of the Old Guard. But what of the young Baruchs? They had charm, education; the look of breeding and distinction. As for their antecedents, who could claim the heritage of old New York more than they — Annie with her Dutch strain, Baruch of the line of Isaac Rodriguez Marques? Yet prejudice made the citadel unattainable to them.

It hurt. It hurt then and rankled in Baruch fifty years later. It was not for himself that he suffered. He has said, and intimates have confirmed the fact, that in his youth he scarcely knew there was any such thing as the *Social Register*. But his wife knew it, and this may in part have accounted for her shyness and for her seeming more interested in her own home than in anything else. They had the nicest circle of friends in New York, Baruch has said of these years. Yet, he admits that when he got into social life there was a difference; "in business there was a great prejudice. There were more difficulties when I married." There were moments when bitterness must have burned within him, when he recalled that "down South, my mother and father were the top"; or might have reflected, as did Disraeli, that his ancestors were priests in the temple of their God, when those of the Anglo-Saxons were running loose in the forests. "It hurt my wife"; he knew that, and this particular kind of discrimination was "the worst thing anyone could do. It makes a difference with children," and the children were coming along now.[70] First was Belle, a wistful-eyed girl, named for her grandmother; then "Junior," the much-desired heir; and finally the pretty Renée. The girls were baptized in the Episcopal Church, but that made no difference. The world condemned you for what you were, and condemned you all the more for trying to be something else.

What could Baruch do for his wife? He tried to make it up to her. He showered her with jewels, bought her all the pretty, graceful things her fancy could desire. Her whim was his law.

There were sides to him, of course, that she could not share. He was primarily a man's man, battling upward in a world of fierce competition; too little sleep and too long hours, too much work and too much play. He was not what he calls a "goody-goody man." He was full of bounce and beans, placing $1000 bets on horse races and prize fights, glorying in being young, strong, and successful. As athletic as in boyhood, he punched the bag and dogtrotted around Central Park, and often a pugilist came to spar with him.

His days were now falling into a kind of routine, that of the financier-sportsman and young man-about-town. Behind him now was the Duke tobacco deal, the Northern Pacific corner, and his "killing" in Amalgamated Copper. Soon he would be setting up in business for himself. He was less closely associated with Ryan now, but during those first years, he often dropped by the Ryan house for consultation and instructions. When Baruch's first child was on the way, Mrs. Ryan would be sitting by, knitting baby things.

Afternoons were reserved for the Waldorf bar. Every holiday and usually every Saturday and Sunday afternoon, Baruch and his friend John Black would make it a foursome at golf against Richard Lydon and James P. Traverse. Evenings, Baruch would sometimes go down to the boys' club on West 69th Street, as he had done ever since college. Here he would play games or pinch-hit as gym teacher.

Probably his family saw less of him than they could have wished during those years, something that he would regret later on, both for their sake and his own. To his younger daughter Renée, brought up under the strict care of a Fräulein, Baruch seemed a fabulous and faraway figure, at once the most lovable and the most awe-inspiring of parents. He was always sympathetic toward her small problems; as father and daughter they had "a lot of fun together," and yet somehow, he was a remote and godlike figure who could do no wrong. "I always wanted to please him," Renée has recalled. He seemed to her the handsomest man she had ever seen in her life. As a little girl, she would have fleeting memories of her father and mother, fairylike figures sweeping in to say good night, tall and beautiful and glittering with jewels. She could remember the smell of perfume and the sense of excitement, scored by the echo of hasty footsteps, off for a concert or a first night.[71] At the Metropolitan the Baruchs held the same three seats for over forty years. Although Baruch himself has never made any pretensions toward great interest in music, his wife played the piano well, and as the children grew older "musical evenings" became a family institution, with Mrs. Baruch at the piano, the girls at the violin and bass viol, and the boy with a cornet.[72]

In these early years Baruch's was the world of Wall Street and Broadway, but Broadway was also a woman's world. Beauty won its salute from the gipsy fiddler at Martin's, as Lillian Russell, her silks whispering, moved into the spotlight to the tune of "Come Down, May Evening Star." Or Maxine Elliott, the toast of the younger generation, made her entrance in all the dark beauty of hair, black and glossy as Josie Mansfield's had been, so the old-timers said, and tragic, shadowed eyes. She walked, head high, in a cloud of legend — whispers — of her town house in London and her gold dinner set and her loves — two kings on two continents, it was rumored, Edward VII and J. P. Morgan.

Beauty won its tributes, whether known or unknown. Gazes might turn toward the tall young Baruchs as they moved in the wake of a headwaiter. An early picture shows us how she looked at that time, with her proudly held dark head and high-massed hair, eyes glowing brightly, her figure, now in the richness of her early thirties, set off by the bouffant gowns of the period. As for Baruch, his height gave him a dignity beyond his years, and splashes of gray at his temples and cobwebbed across his dark hair added to the distinction of his appearance — even at Rector's, the rendezvous of the distinguished. For Rector's, the long, yellow building along the block from 43rd Street to 44th, was the headquarters of Broadway's elite. There was no name above the door, any more than at Mrs. Astor's. "If a table at Rector's could talk," sang the chorines from the Roof-top Theater in the Ziegfeld Follies of 1907 — what a story it could tell! [73]

A table at Rector's at midnight was proof that you had "arrived." There, in the corridor of mirrors, running from floor to ceiling and back into space, you saw the infinite reflection of chandeliers and celebrities magnified upon themselves in shattered prisms of light. Laughter frothed like champagne; a snatch of song might ripple across the conversation, "Tell Me, Pretty Maiden," or that theme song of Broadway and the gilded era, "I Want What I Want When I Want It."

Rector's was the after-theater show of the show world. Bald, tubby Charles Frohman might pause a moment at the entrance with regal Ethel and Byronic Jack. Victor Herbert was there, his laughter billowing upward, and Richard Harding Davis.[74]

It was the show people that fascinated Baruch — they and their world. From the boyhood thrills of *The Black Crook* to *Gentlemen Prefer Blondes*, the theater was always a joy to him. He liked show people, their warmth, their camaraderie. His potentialities as an "angel" would, of course, have won him respectful attention in theatrical circles, but these potentialities were seldom fulfilled. It was Baruch's gusto and easy charm that made show people accept him as one of themselves. None more enjoyed the gambols of the "Lambs." None enjoyed more the talk of Broadway: of Frankie Bailey's legs, copyrighted at the Library of Congress; of Lillian Russell with top hat and cigarettes singing "coon songs" at Weber and Fields' music hall; of the millionaire husband of the Floradora Queen, who dropped dead with excitement before a performance. Baruch enjoyed the sights of Broadway — dark, lean "Mephistophelian" Florenz Ziegfeld, making his entrance at Rector's with his French Anna Held on his arm — Anna of the milk baths and incandescent eyes, whose "Won't You Come and Play Wiz Me?" had titillated New York with the allurements of sin in France.

Or Baruch might watch, goggle-eyed, as Diamond Jim Brady leaned over the bar to down three or four dozen oysters as a before-dinner appetizer, and then, huge napkin around his neck, settled back to a dinner of twelve crabs, half a dozen lobsters, a giant-sized steak, coffee, and a whole tray of French pastry! Rector's called him the best twenty-five customers they had. Page and Shaw might have said as much, for their standing order was for a special assortment of ten or twelve varieties of chocolates of a pound each, done up in a single package and delivered at Brady's apartment every day.

Diamond Jim was King of the Great White Way. He had the showmanship of Billy Rose, the geniality and flamboyance of Jimmy Walker. He was "the Harlequin of Broadway." He was gourmet, greeter, and guardian angel of the theater, a walking sideshow, a one-man carnival, a figure of fun and tomfoolery. He had the first electric automobile in New York, which snarled traffic for two hours on Fifth Avenue, and at its eleven-mile-an-hour speed frightened so many horses that he was forbidden to use it, except at night. He had a gold-plated bicycle, too, with silver spokes and mother-of-pearl handles, and his initial in diamonds and emeralds on the side. He had a matching one made up for Lillian Russell and they cycled together on Sundays in Central Park while the talk buzzed around them. "Being a sucker is fun — if you can afford it," Diamond Jim said. He could afford it. There was a kernel of wisdom in those layers of fat, and to Bernard Baruch his displays did not hold so much interest as the brains that made them possible. Baruch had real respect for the hard-working efforts by which this illiterate son of a West Side saloonkeeper had struggled up out of poverty, and through shrewd coups in the sale of equipment to rising railroads, and later in speculation, had assembled a fortune on which he could live very comfortably with an income of a million dollars a year.[75]

Yet there was tragedy behind that boyish and tentative smile. All knew the Broadway quip of "Beauty and the Beast" that followed Brady and Lillian Russell, knew that Miss Russell accepted Brady's admiration and attentions but gave no return. Not even the blond and flamboyantly beautiful Edna McCauley, for whom he settled as second best, would give him love or loyalty, and once, in bitterness, Brady burst out, "There ain't a woman on earth who'd marry an ugly-looking guy like me." [76]

There was no malice in him. Baruch found him to be a truly kind person. Brady yearned for Lillian Russell, yet never spoke disparagingly of a rival. The heart that she spurned he opened to all. As a host he was delightful, as Baruch came to know. Sad himself, he enjoyed making others happy.

Baruch and Brady knew each other well. Once he asked Baruch if he thought his wife would like to see his jewelry, and gave a dinner party for the occasion. Twelve attended, and never did Baruch eat a better meal. Out of courtesy Brady ate no more than his guests, but the dinner was not without its extravagances. At each course a gift was served for each lady, a trinket or a jewel. After dinner, the guests had the freedom of the apartment, the wardrobes lined with Paisley shawls, the racks of suits in gray, navy, blue, black, and plum. In the guest bathroom the tub was of solid silver, and the toilet set in the dressing room was of gold.

Then the valet brought out the jewel sets, and before the fascinated eyes of the company they were laid out. Here were the glories that blazed on Diamond Jim like the show window of a Broadway jewelry store: the collar buttons, studs, cuff buttons, and waistcoat buttons, scarf pins, watch chains and fobs, suspender clasps, belt buckles, rings, lead pencils, glasses cases and card cases, and removable heads for his canes — all in matched sets of diamonds, sapphires, opals, emeralds, rubies, pearls, every imaginable stone or combination of stones, not excluding one set in gun-metal gray for funerals.

"Them as has 'em wears 'em," Brady said cheerfully.[77]

5

EASY MONEY

IT WAS ONLY a small party that evening at the Waldorf. From his height Bernard Baruch watched the faces white under the gaslight, like the chips scattered before them on the table.

Ohio Columbus (Hi) Barber, president of the Diamond Match Company, was the guest of honor and, like Baruch, had come for a good time, not a trimming. The game was baccarat; the white chips were the cheapest — at $1000 apiece. But at the table were two hard-playing, high-betting bankers, Loyal Smith and John W. Drake, and that incorrigible big-time plunger, John W. Gates.

Baruch's own limit was $5000. Up went the betting — sixty, seventy-five, eighty thousand — until Baruch, fascinated, for the first time in his life saw $100,000 risked by one man on the turn of a card.

Gates picked up his chips. He chinked them together and then, with a single movement of his stubby fingers, piled two equal stacks before him, each standing ten yellow chips high, one million dollars in all. He spread his hands. This was his bet.

No one breathed. It was so quiet you could hear the hissing of the gas in the jets and the fall of the ash from Gates's cigar. For a moment the spell held — then John Drake broke it. He wanted to take Gates up.

Drake dealt, deathly pale, but his hands steady. Smith stood behind him, white as a ghost, and Baruch saw the gleam of the sweat on his forehead. On one side Gates lifted his cards. On the other Baruch looked at his and laid them down, exposing a natural nine. Gates had won his first bet — a half-million dollars — but his cards did not suit him and he drew from the pack. A moment later, he lost his second bet to the bank.

The big betters had broken even. Drake was satisfied, but not yet Gates. They played on. For the small players, the evening was a costly one. One lost $72,000. Baruch himself was down some $10,000. But that night in that room he had seen Bet-a-Million Gates get his name.[1]

As he was to recall it years afterwards, Baruch as he emerged felt sick with a sudden "revulsion of feeling." It was not a feeling that lasted very long, for Baruch is not an introspective man. The lure of money-making had too tight a grip upon him to be abandoned for the mood of the moment. But there is no doubt about his immediate reaction.[2] His head was dulled with tobacco smoke; he was empty and tired and suddenly disgusted with the thought of those $500,000 bets and the easy money tossed around, and his knowledge of what money meant in toil and worry to most Americans.[3]

It is too much to say, of course, that a single evening of cardplay turned the direction of Baruch's life, but it marked the beginning of a turning point. In his memoirs, as originally written some thirty years afterwards and colored by the social consciousness engendered by the Great Depression, he exaggerated the impact of this night — but nevertheless a seed had been sown. Something was lacking in his life. Something was beginning to trouble him; something was out of joint in the world around him.

How the other half lives — it was all there to see in his city: the dirt and the vermin and the foul rookeries of Cherry Hill, once George Washington's home; the thirteen-cent stew dinners on Orchard Street; aristocratic Chelsea sinking into the squalor of Hell's Kitchen; the two tiny rooms in the six-story tenements, littered with filthy bedding, scraps of food, and tobacco, where father, mother, twelve children, and six "lodgers" ate, slept, bred, and worked out their lives for a few cents a day.[4]

Easy money!

No city on earth, so the muckrakers cried, had such poverty, such misery, so many dark and stinking hallways where crime was plotted but a wall removed from rooms where babies slept and children were growing up and reaching out toward the world around them.[5] No city on earth had more "old-law tenements," forgotten and unseen at the end of alleys, rammed up against the sun-baked brick of the building on the street, with scarcely an air space between; gullied with corridors of rooms like medieval cells, without windows, without lights, without air, without space even to breathe. This was the New York of the "Lung Block," once a fashionable quarter, then sinking finally into sailors' lodginghouses and bordellos, and at last divided and subdivided and rented out to the poorest of the poor in which to rot and die.[6]

Easy money!

It did not come easy to all men. Not below Houston Street on the Lower East Side, where the scent of tobacco filled the streets and, by working from dawn to midnight, a man could make 1500 cigars and one dollar a day. You could ride on the Second Avenue El up from the pier straight into the workshop of New York, into clouds of hot steam from which men and women, too, emerged winter and summer, half-naked, shabby, hunched with weariness after ironing and sewing into the night. This was the garment industry of New York — the reality of the dream dreamed on the steppes of Russia, in the ghettos of Poland, the wastes of Lithuania, the sunny villages of Italy.

Was this all? There was hope. Outsiders wondered at the apathy, the benumbed, animal-like acceptance of fate there on the Lower East Side. Yet there Darwin's law was seen working. A pair of fur-cutters, Marcus Loew and Adolph Zukor, were cashing in with the nickelodeon and a chain of the new money-making novelties called movie theaters. Power and passion and intellectual riches were crannied up there on the Lower East Side. Even uptowners were stirred by the art of the Yiddish Theater, or the majesty of Adler's performances as Shylock or the "Jewish King Lear." Weber and Fields were up from the Lower East Side, and so was silk-hatted Oscar Hammerstein. What they had done, others could do. They could hope and dream.

Was hope enough?

Bernard Baruch could not answer. Somewhere, something was wrong; somehow he felt a sense of questioning and constriction. This mood of disillusion was not new. It occurred and recurred like a kind of delayed growing pain.

He thought of his father. Never had he forgotten the day that he had gone to his father in the triumphant confidence of his thirty years to announce that he had made a million dollars.

Dr. Baruch's kindly face went quizzical. He was not very much impressed — in fact all he wanted to know was what good Bernard planned to do with his money.

What good was he going to do, indeed? Of what use were a million dollars unless you did something with them? The doctor's quiet words had sown the seeds of doubt in his son's mind. He was later to say that he had spent a lifetime trying to answer his father's question.

Was money the measuring rod of worth? What of his father? Baruch thought back to his childhood, the long, hard years of poverty and the dedicated toil his father had undergone. He thought of his father's love of humanity, the books that he had translated into French and German, the studies that he had made, all the service to which he had put his mind — the best mind, his son would later say, "with which I had ever come into contact, and his life the most useful that could be imagined." Suddenly, Baruch, amidst the empty triumph of his million dollars, wished with all his heart that he had not given up his dream of studying surgery, and in that moment he would have traded all his earthly goods for a medical degree.

He looked at his father, at the lines and shadows of fatigue on his face. Dr. Baruch was only fifty-nine, but already the years were showing.[7] He had never really done what he had wanted to do. For years he had hungered to devote himself to research; yet of necessity he still lived the hard-driven life of the general practitioner. Hardly ever did he know the luxury of a night's unbroken sleep; never could he attend a play or concert without leaving his name at the box-office door.

At last Bernard Baruch knew something that money could buy. On a July day in 1900, his father's sixtieth birthday, Baruch confronted the doctor in his office and asked him point-blank what he made in a year. He was shocked by the smallness of the sum.

"So that is all. Think how hard you work, day and night, while my money comes easy. I will give you twice what you make to retire."[8]

The plan was arranged. Baruch set his father up with a yearly income to free him for rest and research. The doctor did not want to cut himself off from all his old ties and retained a few of his patients, remaining at their call, day or night. But the burden of practice was lifted from him. He could now study and experiment and crusade for his lifelong dream of public baths for the occupants of cold-water flats, not tubs, not swimming pools, but sanitary showers.[9] Baruch could look on proudly through the years, as his father continued his research and his rise, graduates of his classes opening schools of their own, his judgment as to water cures vindicated, and he, himself, at last acclaimed as "one of the most famous surgeons in the United States." [10]

Baruch's money had helped foster his father's greatness. This did him much good, he admitted afterward. But you could not solve your personal problems by getting someone else to do something. He was still subject to spells of disappointment, dissatisfied with his work, his lot, and his attainments. Of one thing he was certain. He was through with easy money, playing and fattening on the losses of other men. Easy money was false money; it created nothing; it only violated economic law. Baruch turned down an offer from Gates to join a pool with him, Drake, Keene, Reid, and Hawley to "bull up" the market.[11]

According to Carter Field, when Baruch was thirty-two years old, he had $100,000 for every year of his life; but slowly he was beginning to realize how much there was that money could not buy. His had never been a money-making family. His was a heritage of scholars. What did he want? What should he do with the years that stretched ahead? His father suggested banking. He was not interested.[12]

At last he decided to go to Europe and sort out his thoughts. An idea had finally come to him during those months of soul-searching. Maybe he would devote his life to public service, study law, perhaps become an advocate of causes and a defender of the poor and unfortunate. Was he too old to begin?

He could not resist one more triumph of wealth. He decided to open an account at the National City Bank of New York and, visiting the bank unknown, asked to see the president, Mr. James Stillman. Instead, he was passed over to a vice-president, who told him that Mr. Stillman was busy.

Baruch explained his business. Unimpressed, the vice-president asked for identification. This was a blow to Baruch's youthful ego; he had thought that his activities in Amalgamated Copper were not entirely unknown. So he offered as reference the name of the coffee merchant Herman Sielcken. This, he could see, made an impression.

When the vice-president asked the amount for deposit, Baruch produced a certified check for one million dollars. The effect was satisfactory.[13]

This little business attended to, Baruch and his wife boarded ship for Europe. He found little peace in his travels, although sometimes there were a few hours of transitory diversion as he ran into an old friend. Charlie Schwab, for instance, took him to the Capucine Club in Paris, a private institution for members "duly proposed, posted, and elected." As he walked back alone to his hotel, he suddenly heard Schwab puffing after him. He had obtained Baruch's membership card. He had kept pointing at him and saying, "Diplomat. Diplomat!" [14]

Even Baruch's dream of service through the law vanished under the impact of reality. It was too late to redirect the course of his life. The years of study would be too long. Reluctantly, he was back now where he had started. What could he do? The answer came from home.

He struggled out of sleep to a thunderous pounding on the door of his room at the Ritz. Hastily he slit open the envelope of the cablegram. It was an SOS from A. A. Housman and Company. Ed Hawley, the president of the Minneapolis–St. Louis Railroad, had seriously overextended himself, endangering the fortunes not only of the firm but of Housman himself.

Baruch at once cabled that his private funds were to be put at Mr. Housman's disposal, then boarded the next steamer for home. The next few weeks he devoted to salvaging the affairs of the firm, which he did without the loss of a cent to anyone. He rejoiced that he could help the man who had given him his chance in Wall Street. Once all was in order, he had his chance for an easy exit from the firm.[15]

In May 1903, Baruch moved into his own office at 111 Broadway, at the foot of Wall Street. The thrill was like hitting that homer with the bases loaded, or Fitzsimmons telling him he had "the stuff." [16] He was still young enough to remember the landing of his first job, the selling of his first bond, the cutting of his first coupon. Here was the climax to these triumphs.

His prized possessions were three on the day of the "opening." His father gave him a photograph of himself, inscribed with words that for Baruch became a kind of moral code: "Let unswerving integrity always be your watchword." [17] His mother sent him a telegram of congratulations which he framed and hung on the wall. Also from his mother came a large green china cat, spotted with circles of red. The cat was still in its place of honor on the desk fifty-odd years later.

The change gave him new life. One close to him through the years recalls that he seemed in his element, "happier than at any other time in his life." [18] His plunges and coups became more spectacular; to his intimates, it seemed that he loved living on his crag, "like an eagle and swooping down on Wall Street." [19] Yet though he had the flair, he seemed to lack the incentive to become a very rich man by the Street's standards. It was not now so much the money that lured him as the trials of strength, the heat and the race.[20]

Underneath, his restlessness still surged. Often he still wondered as he looked out of his window at the serene spire of Trinity Church and the quiet graveyard where birds' wings flashed in the sunlight, and along the line of the fence, bootblacks with firm, outflung strokes soothed the nerves of tired brokers.[21]

Sometimes he would just sit, staring out of the window at the church and the graveyard and the long shining line of the Hudson. Sometimes he would wheel about and fix his eyes on his father's picture and his mother's framed telegram. Or he would rise to pace up and down, up and down, behind his chair, passing and repassing the window; or go down, across the street, and walk quietly in the churchyard.[22]

Wall Street, he knew, was not sinister, really. You could find great unselfishness there and loyalty, the best as well as the worst in men. But Wall Street, as a street, was no longer wide enough for him. He was weary of money-making for the sake of money-making, speculation for the sake of speculation. His thoughts were turning to the broad horizons his friend Henry Davis had shown him — to creative enterprise and constructive finance.[23]

A new friend now came into his life. This was Garet Garrett, short, stocky, bluntly individualistic and outspoken, at that time still in his twenties, and a columnist for the New York *Evening Post*. They became intimate friends quickly, and sensing Garrett's understanding, Baruch opened his thoughts to the younger man as he could not do to many people.[24]

Often Garrett dropped by in the late afternoon. Once he said suddenly, "You know, B. M., you are not really a Wall Street man at heart. You should go into public life, and some day you will."

Baruch stared at him. "Oh, nonsense, this is my life," he said.

Garrett nodded his head sagely. "You'll see. [25]

Meanwhile the old question still tantalized Baruch. What could he do with his wealth? There were two kinds of money, he knew. One possessed man. The other was possessed by him.[26] Baruch knew how money corroded, how the very fascination of it trapped men. On crossings to Europe he had seen rich men carrying little notebooks, gloating and pouring over their holdings. One man who had spent almost nothing on himself left a fortune of nearly $200,000,000, and not a cent to charity. Then there was the reverse side of the ledger. The great endowments by American millionaires were already beginning with the Carnegie libraries and the Rockefeller Institute. Was this conscience-balm? Or was it the spirit of man struggling to be free from the bondage of self, and to liberate and serve others? Could he also gather wealth to disseminate it among men?

What was wealth? It was not stocks, bonds, or paper dollars; it was the raw material in the ground. In later years, Baruch would come to see labor, too, as a source of wealth. Meanwhile he studied. He studied currencies of every sort and with every conceivable backing. Wealth, he decided, was raw materials, arable land, silver, and perhaps gold most of all.[27]

No investment, no source of wealth was sure. Even land could become depleted and eroded, or made worthless by superior agricultural competition. Scrubby lots on Manhattan Island became the highest-priced real estate in the world. With the opening up of the Orient and the ravages of erosion, Southern rice fields became liabilities for two generations. Bonds offered a fixed income, yet they were no better than the real wealth behind them. Baruch knew all about Confederate bonds. Plenty of money, he knew, was lost in bonds, though people talked more of stock losses.[28] No "security" was secure. What of stage lines and riverboats, canals, and streetcars — even the railroads — what was their future? Not the finished product but the raw material had true worth. And every kind of "wealth" could be destroyed by modern war.

Yet all was a gamble and a question mark. One raw material could be supplanted by another, like oil for coal.

Nothing endured but gold. Gold was good when Napoleon was

at his zenith, when Caesar's legions conquered Britain, when Alexander invaded India. Gold had outlasted history and time. India's
nabobs never went bankrupt, and they had no holdings of bonds,
stocks, mortgages — so-called securities. Theirs was merely the rich
earth and the storehouses of jewels and of gold, coins glinting silently,
lying there over the centuries drawing no interest, reaping no return.
But where would it have gone if invested? It could have been lost
twice or thrice in Baruch's own lifetime. Thus Baruch concluded
that when something holds good over the centuries it was apt to
remain so.[29] Here, gleaned from the classical lessons, we see the
origin of Baruch's belief in the sacred properties of gold.

Gold was sure, but there was no sure way of gaining it. A gold
mine was only a speculation.[30] Developed, it might become the
most secure of investments. So too might copper mines or tungsten.
They were not sure; nothing was sure. Life was change. There was
always the human variable, always the imponderables of time and
chance. But Baruch now could afford to take chances.

At the turn of the century, it was a moot point whether railroads
were a speculation or an investment. Yet since the old Winnsboro
days, when swinging from the back fence he had waved to the brake-
man and chucked stones at the freight cars, Bernard Baruch had
dreamed of owning his own railroad. Railroads had been his hobby
since he was an unknown office boy, listing in a little black notebook
the lines that he thought might survive rebuilding, and learning to
trace the routes and the resources of their territory.[31] All this was
still in his head as now in the early years of the new century he
studied the Louisville and Nashville, with its potential hookups to
Chicago, to the Atlantic Coast Line and the Seaboard. It had, he
was convinced, the makings of a great railroad. Few Americans
had holdings; most of the stock belonged to the Rothschilds abroad.
Baruch was driving for control and he asked his friends to come
in with him. A few did, but dropped away with their profits as
the stock rose from 95 to 100. Only Baruch kept buying — soon
to find himself the largest single shareholder other than the Rothschilds of Britain. Meanwhile, rumor had threaded through the business world. Who was behind this buying? Gates was away, Morgan
in Europe, Keene in Florida. "There were a number of guesses, none
correct." None suspected young Baruch.

But he could not swing the deal alone. Finally, Ed Hawley and a group of associates joined him. His other associates were Baruch's former partner, Housman, the Huntingtons, L. C. Weir, president of the Adams Express Company, and General Hubbard. Trailing after them, uninvited but eager, playing his own hand, was Bet-a-Million Gates.

Baruch planned his strategy carefully. He cabled London for the necessary option on huge blocks of stock. He talked much and said very little. He bought and bought, and buying along with him was Gates. Gates could not be shaken, so he had to be played along with. Since J. P. Morgan was getting interested, Gates was assigned to make a deal with him, which he succeeded in doing, and finally Morgan got control. The exploit was hailed as a typical Gates coup, the bold Chicagoan and his associates clearing some seven and a half million on the deal. But it had been Baruch's coup as much as that of the Johnny-Come-Lately, Gates.[32]

Baruch was now ready for a new challenge.

He could look back to the year when he was nineteen and his mother had thwarted his chance to go to Mexico to learn the ore-buying business for the Guggenheims. How different his life might have been if he had done that! Now he was too old to become a real mining man, but he might still do what the Guggenheims had done. The adventures of creative industrialism and constructive engineering were still open to him.

For the Guggenheims, speculation had been an art. They had had to guess as to how the prospective venture might be developed and operated, visualize its potentialities, the production, the use, the sale. There was the quality of folklore to their story.[33]

Although no one individual in the family had attained the eminence of a Morgan or a Rockefeller, as a unit they were fabulous — as creative industrialists. They were the copper kings.[34] Even the Rockefellers had bowed to their terms. They had transformed mining from a speculation to an investment. They had torn out the treasures of the earth and put them to the service of mankind.[35]

Little Meyer Guggenheim, so affectionately remembered by Baruch, was gone now, but his empire survived, and his sons. It had been Meyer who in middle life had determined to master personally the practical problems of mining, smelting, and refining, and to see that this knowledge was handed on to his sons. In the traditional European fashion, each of the seven sons was apprenticed to a branch of the industry — pick-and-shovel work, smelting, refining. One son, Simon, was a timekeeper in a refinery at Pueblo. The eldest, Daniel, succeeded his father as head of the empire.

Although Baruch had heavy holdings in the Guggenheims' American Smelting and Refining Company, the majority of the stock was held by the brothers. Could Baruch break into the circle? He wondered, and then opportunity sought him. It was an enterprise not unlike his mission for Ryan back in 1898. The Guggenheims had come into conflict with the Rockefellers, who were branching out into mine ventures, dickering for control of the Selby Smelting and Lead Company of California, and Tacoma Smelting of Washington. To Baruch, as a large stockholder in American Smelting and Refining, the Rockefellers were serious competitors.

The Rockefeller raid was as yet indecisive. Could Baruch, his interest in smelteries as yet unknown, help swing control of Tacoma to the Guggenheims? He determined to try.

Key man in the Tacoma holdings and a big stockholder in Selby as well, was Darius Ogden Mills. In his sedate office in the Mills Building on Broad Street, this gentleman, with his old-fashioned side whiskers and bare lips and chin, reminded Baruch of his grandfather, Saling Wolfe, the South Carolina planter. So they talked of the old days, the old man and the young, and for a while thoughts of options and mergers, big trusts and corporation wars seemed very far away. At the end, although Mills did not give an option on the Selby or Tacoma stock, he promised that he would not sell out to the Rockefellers.

From then on, negotiations moved rapidly. Early in 1905, Baruch and Henry Davis headed westward. At Everett, Washington, they met William Rust, president and operating head of Tacoma, who assured the pair that he had no prejudice against the Guggenheims; he might even help in the pursuit of their objective. He listened agreeably as Baruch, with all the amiable persuasiveness which had been used on Colonel Mose Wetmore back in St. Louis, presented an offer of $800 a share for Rust's holdings of the common stock. A few days later a forty-five-day option was in Baruch's hands.

Next, the group moved on to San Francisco. There the stockholders were scattered and the press wary; it was no secret now that Baruch was not acting for himself alone. A story broke on his interests in the American Smelting and Refining Company, but the Guggenheim connection was not yet known. With the combined aid of Rust in the West and Mills in New York, the options began to be transferred. It was a tense three weeks, and Baruch held his sights and his ground with delicate diplomacy. Not until the options of both Tacoma and Selby were transferred did the public learn that it was the Guggenheims who had checkmated the Rockefellers.

That Baruch would be "rewarded handsomely" for his effort had been stipulated from the first. The understanding was that he was to be paid in stock. However, since his journey to the coast, there had been a merger in the Guggenheim firm, and cash was now offered.

The attorney was shrewd Samuel Untermeyer, and as representative of the Guggenheims he was eager to get the best deal he could for his clients. Stubbornly he strove to force Baruch down; Baruch was unyielding. One million dollars was the amount of stock he had been promised. His work was done, and a million dollars he should have. One million dollars. The words hung suspended between them. When Untermeyer implied that his attitude was a holdup, Baruch picked up his hat and left the room.

A day or so later, Daniel gave his decision: "If Bernie says he ought to get a million dollars, that is what he will get."

It was not what he kept. Once the check was in his hands, Baruch divided it, sending $300,000 each to Rust and Davis. Both protested. But Baruch insisted that they had to take it, for never could he have closed the deal without them.[36]

Grateful though he was to the Guggenheims, Baruch was perturbed at the subsequent rise of Smelting and Refining stock.[37] It was with real regret that Baruch went quietly to the brothers as the stock hit 100 and warned them that he must tell his friends to sell.

His warning was not taken seriously. The stock rocketed on to 150 while Baruch's attention was momentarily diverted, as the Guggenheims engaged him for another deal, this time to purchase the National Lead Company, strongest of the independents in the open market. This accomplished, Baruch took a look around him. Smelting and Refining had hit 179. Then it broke — as drastically and completely as he had foreseen that it would, and the ensuing storm broke over his head.

The prophet of disaster is, of course, not necessarily its author, but he is often blamed. All over Wall Street the story buzzed — that the break was due to Baruch, the Big Bear who had raided the stock of the corporation that had given him his chance. What was worse, the Guggenheims themselves avoided him. Deeply hurt, Baruch heard at last that a Guggenheim had accused him of selling the stock short. Boldly, Baruch went to him and denied the charge, leaving him angry but mostly angry, perhaps, that he had not taken Baruch's advice.

But friendly voices reached the Guggenheims, and a brother came over to Baruch and apologized in the name of the family. Then a "cruel rumor" arose, challenging the stability of the whole Guggenheim organization. Now came Baruch's chance to prove the friendship he had claimed. He went straight to the offices of the brothers at 71 Broadway, and his offer of a $500,000 deposit as evidence of his confidence brought tears to Daniel Guggenheim's eyes. Baruch said he stood ready to help in any other possible way, and demonstrated his faith by large purchases of American Smelting stock. Daniel Guggenheim jokingly told Baruch that they were going to take him in "just like one of the brothers." [38]

Baruch was now free to seek another creative enterprise. His inspiration came from the wheels of his automobile. Despite the jeering crowds that howled "Get a horse, get a horse" as an automobile heaved into view, Baruch was convinced that motorcars had come to stay. They could be more than high-priced toys if it were not for the upkeep — if tires, for instance, were good for more than a few hundred miles.

Rubber was the key to the problem. But rubber had yet to be developed on a mass scale. It required a capitalist of vision and bold spirit to take over, as Rockefeller had done with Standard Oil. Here again the Guggenheims and Baruch came together. The idea was to develop new sources of more easily available rubber. Almost coincidentally a man named William A. Lawrence had devised a method of extracting crude rubber from guayule, a silvery-leafed shrub or weed growing wild in Mexico. This had even attracted the notice of the Rhode Island senator Nelson W. Aldrich and Thomas Fortune Ryan. Here was the union of talent and influence with the resources of the Guggenheims behind it all.

Baruch made an exploratory trip to Mexico. He saw more than the guayule shrubs, bending in the hot winds that seared the desertlike plains. He was struck by the color and contrasts of Mexico —

between the teeming, hopeless peons and the sophisticated land-
holders living in luxurious elegance. He was looking, although he did
not know it, upon the end of an era. He met the famed Carranza
and Terrazos families, whose acres and cattle could only be approxi-
mately numbered, even by themselves. Never, even in Europe, would
Baruch see such men as these with all the grace of the salon and the
untamed primitive vitality of the open range; or meet such a figure as
Señor Pablo Martínez del Rio, who spoke English, French, German,
and Italian like a native, who had the bearing of a prince and the figure
of a Spanish grandee, and a seething hatred and fear of the United
States. This was the Mexico of Porfirio Díaz, who in thirty years'
time had raised his country from the anarchy and despair in the wake
of Juárez to the status of a second-rate power. This he had done by
trading off his country's future, leasing or selling her untapped rich
potential to concessionaries from the outside.

The ensuing unrest Baruch could feel to some degree. He was
frank to admit that he did not realize then that imperialism would not
last. Social questions, admittedly, were then of little interest to him.

He was aware of the contrasts of Mexico — the hideous gulfs between poverty and plenty, the despair and resentment of a proud
people. Grimly Del Rio warned him that contracts such as he was
seeking would put Mexico at the mercy of Americans, might even
mean that an imperialistic president would seek to shift the frontier
southward. These were words that Baruch would remember afterward.

His immediate mission, however, was accomplished. He obtained
options on three million acres of land for the newly formed Intercontinental Rubber Company.[39]

Baruch, meanwhile, was again out looking for new ventures. The
search for new sources of rubber went on. Baruch's view now extended over the world. Under his direction expeditions were moving
through the upper reaches of the Amazon, across the Andes, into
Borneo and the Congo. One man was swept off a ship in the Carib-
bean; two dropped from sight in Africa; one disappeared in the
jungles of Venezuela. Yet, onward the caravans moved. The activity
of the American rubber kings stirred the grandiose ambitions of the
most ruthless robber baron of all time. This was Leopold of Belgium,
whose exploits had made the name of the Belgian Congo a synonym
for horror, and whose "red rubber," it was said, was soaked with hu-

man blood. Leopold could no longer ignore the outraged voice of public opinion. He wanted the shield of respectability, and sacrificing not a whit of his greed enlisted the aid of America's foremost Catholic capitalist, Thomas Fortune Ryan.

Thus was formed the American Congo Society. Whitney was in it and the Guggenheims, who prided themselves on their fair treatment of workers. Baruch held back — reform and Leopold, he was convinced, did not mix — but Ryan was ardent, enthusiastic, convinced that the atrocity stories were merely the maligning of rival imperialists. As it turned out, labor conditions in the Congo had improved. There was no rubber on the American concession, but there were diamonds, and these Ryan carried around in his pocket, showing them off with all the delight of a boy with a prize collection of marbles.[40]

Meanwhile, a series of blows struck the Intercontinental Rubber Company of Mexico. Just as its factory went into operation, the American Rubber Goods Company, which was to absorb the new rubber, repudiated its contract. Then the Madero revolution swept across Mexico, and the tender young guayule plants were smashed under the tramp of the armies. Yet the point had been proved — the soundness of guayule, if not of Mexican politics. New sources of supply had been opened up; the dream of guayule would be forgotten by many, but not by Bernard Baruch.

As "one of the brothers," copper was also on Baruch's agenda. Perhaps even if he had never known the Guggenheims, copper would have stirred his imagination after he had met Dan Jackling. For in his small experimental mill, Jackling, a strapping red-faced mining engineer, had found the way to refine low-grade porphyry copper at a profit and thus, potentially at least, to put the metal on a mass-production basis.

Hitherto the world demand had been small. But a greater supply would mean an expanded demand. The building program of the United States Navy would have to expand fast to keep up with the German fleet — a mighty force assembled against what enemy and to what end? Small wonder that the Guggenheims now became interested in expanding the new Utah Copper Company, formed at Jackling's recommendation in 1903, or that its bond issue was immediately oversubscribed.

Yet, it was a time to move cautiously. Storm signals were flying again at the Waldorf bar. Again there was all the old talk of tips

and millions. It was a new era, so everyone said, but Baruch looked
on with a cynicism rare at his age. He had seen the coming of new
eras before.

But this, in 1907, was worse than panic. It was ruin — for the West-
inghouse Electric Company and its hapless employees; for the Knickerbocker Trust Company and its president, who killed himself. It
looked like ruin for the "whole credit structure of the country," ruin
— so some feared — even for Morgan himself.

But Morgan was at the helm. Crisis was an old story to Morgan,
he who had got his start in the panic of 1857. Down Nassau Street
he barged, "the Old Man," the "Big Chief," with his black derby and
his hard-bitten cigar, crowds massed, as if for a fire, parting as he
passed. And in the evenings in his great library, there among the
Florentine paintings, he organized the banking community for the
fight — and finally the victory. What it amounted to was that under
the leadership of the House of Morgan the bankers took care of all
banks that were basically sound so that business could continue —
doing privately what was done publicly by the Federal government
during the panic of 1933. And "slowly, the great credit structure of
the country righted itself." [41]

Baruch was out of it. He could boast, and truly, that he had never
been caught in a panic. Copper was piling up by the railroad tracks,
and Baruch was buying. He knew that there would always be a need
for copper in the world.

His telephone jingled. The Guggenheims were on the line. They
knew their Baruch. To him they had come — an unattached operator
— for the cash no bank could give them. One-half-million dollars
was needed to meet their immediate payroll. Baruch was ready. Since
the panic had started, he had been increasing his cash balances and
had warned his banker that he might want his deposits at any
moment.

So there it was, the solid currency, ready to be boxed and shipped
by express to Salt Lake City and stuffed in pay envelopes. The Guggenheims came through to become the biggest copper-working concern in the world, and to develop the greatest man-made excavation
on the face of the earth. Baruch's part in their salvation was not to
go unnoticed, even by Morgan himself.

Baruch had also played a secret role in ending the crisis. Lying
sleepless, as the waves of panic crashed, Baruch had decided to offer

$1,500,000 to Morgan's pool to support the endangered banks. Unwilling to seem to be seeking publicity, he made the contribution in his bank's name. Had he done otherwise, he wondered later, would his relations with Morgan have been different — in the Texas Gulf Sulphur deal, for instance? [42]

Baruch's sensitivity in regard to Morgan was understandable. His former partner, Arthur Housman, was Morgan's friend; Baruch would have been happy to have been on a firm footing with the great banking house. Morgan's eminence was such that if anything big was going on, he was behind it.

But Baruch could not have been an insider had he wanted to be, and this exclusion, like his later exclusion from elective office, may have illumined and fortified his peculiar role. In addition to Morgan's prejudice against Jews and Jewish banking houses, there was his aversion to the flashy "Waldorf crowd" of which Baruch was a part.[43]

It was now impossible, however, for Morgan to ignore the young financier whom even Keene hailed as the greatest speculator of his time. Nevertheless, Baruch was surprised when in 1909 the Morgan firm called upon him to investigate the potentialities of a sulphur dome in Texas, they to furnish the money and Baruch the labor, profits to be shared on a 60:40 basis.

Accompanied by Seeley Mudd, a brilliant mining engineer, Baruch departed for Brazoria County. There, in the dusty Texas heat, he sat slapping mosquitoes, studying charts, and watching the drillers. They were not sure. Mudd said it was a 50:50 proposition. Baruch then confronted Morgan with his report and the necessary options for the purchase.

Baruch said that he would personally gamble half the purchase price. "I never gamble," the great J. P. Morgan said loftily, and lifted his hand in a gesture of dismissal.[44]

Morgan never gambled. Of course, when the price of steel was low, he might call in the brokers and issue a few weighted words on "conditions," after which orders were promptly placed for Morgan stocks. Morgan never gambled. Baruch observed that he had his own ways of influencing the market.[45] But Morgan's distaste for the word "gamble" deprived his firm of millions and cost it association in an enterprise which gave the United States control of the world sulphur market, enabling it to become the biggest and lowest cost producer in the world.[46]

Baruch's pride had been hurt. He knew that sulphur was essential to industry, probably the most important chemical for modern manufacturing. Baruch held on to the undeveloped property, and in 1916 decided to open up the mound. Before doing this, however, he felt that he should give the House of Morgan one more chance. So he offered, and sold, the firm a 60 per cent interest in his company. What was his horror to have them soon sell out at a profit to a competitor, giving Baruch no chance whatever to buy back the controlling interest.

Baruch considered this unfair and told them so. They would never have forgiven anyone for treating them in that way. But in the end they had hurt themselves far more than they had hurt Baruch. For the stock Baruch had sold them at $10 a share grew to an investment of 45 million.[47]

Although Texas Gulf Sulphur was a slow starter, not really beginning to produce until after the First World War, its history for the next ten years was spectacular. It outlasted its nearby competitors. It survived the fierce underground competition of the neighboring but unneighborly Union Company. It represented the attainment of Baruch's ideal — of creating wealth by taking it out of the ground. It was he, not Morgan, who had formed, pioneered, and financed it. Baruch retained his 40 per cent interest, and it turned out to be the most profitable enterprise of his entire money-making career.

Baruch was now, even by his own standards, a rich man and was attracting the attention of various leaders on the Street. He was flattered by a chance to join the executive committee of the Central Trust Company, an unusual offer to an independent operator, but he turned it down. He also declined a directorship in the Phoenix Life Insurance Company. He still stuck by his rules. As a speculator by choice and profession, he was convinced that he had no place as a director in charge of other people's money.[48]

Mining deals still held his first interest. His fame as a "buyer" was soaring, and on the recommendation of the San Francisco bankei William Crocker, scion of a pioneering family, he aided Senatoi George Nixon of Nevada, not only in dickering for the purchase of the Combination Mines adjoining Nixon's own Goldfield Consolidated, but in swinging the million-dollar loan necessary for the deal.

Crocker wanted Baruch to lend Nixon a million dollars, and personally guaranteed to stand behind it. Then Nixon could pay the price of $2,578,216 for the mines in three installments.

Meanwhile, Goldfield stock was tumbling in the wake of rumors that Nixon needed cash. As an antidote, Baruch suggested a table at the Waldorf. There Nixon was to sit, with a personal certified check of Baruch's for $1,000,000. This was to be shown with proper discretion and without comment to such persons as manifested interest in the Senator's financial concerns. If anyone inquired further the Senator should refer them to Baruch.

It is a tribute to Baruch's understanding of his times and his associates that this gesture worked. Goldfield began to rise again. Nixon left for the West. In New York Baruch snapped up the stock as fast as it came on the market. When the Combination Mines owners saw the demand for Goldfield, they were willing to take part of their payment in Goldfield stock.[49]

As for Baruch, his compensation for his part in the transactions was 100,000 shares of Goldfield, a prize well worth having.

"Who in hell's Baruch?" This was the query that came crackling over the telegraph wires from Nevada in 1910 as headlines blazed the story of the "only authentic gold-rush of this century," the richest treasure trove since "the days of the Comstock Bonanza in Virginia City." Who was behind it? The wires clicked out the names. William H. Crocker, the "Morgan of the West." United States Senator George Nixon of Nevada. Nixon's partner, George Wingfield, a poker-player, buckaroo, and onetime telegraph operator. And one more name, as yet little known beyond Wall Street — Bernard M. Baruch.[50]

Goldfield, Nevada, is a ghost town today, wind whining around the gutted and empty mine shafts, and flopping the loose boards of the false fronts. But in Goldfield in 1910, the Old West was riding off the scene in a clatter of hoofbeats and a shrill of bullets; and to the young French count, Roger de Perigny, peering over Baruch's shoulder on a warm summer evening, Goldfield was all the Western thrillers he had read packed into one. Even Baruch must have felt memories of his Cripple Creek days tingle down his spine.

There were three in the party: Baruch, Senator Nixon, and Perigny, who was thrilled at every mile of the route. The Count's blood was blue, but at each train stop it grew bluer, and by the time they reached Goldfield, as Baruch later recalled it, he had royal blood.

They did not arrive unwelcomed. Nixon's partner, the vice-president of the firm, George Wingfield, former gambler, jockey, prospector, a coming power in Nevada state politics, was awaiting them. He was a stalwart man, six feet tall, with a mask of a face. As the evening was warm, he wore no coat. This made it easier for him to reach the five revolvers he carried, two in front, two behind, and "one on his left breast." Four grim-faced men flanked him, front and rear — Pinkerton detectives, it was explained; there had been labor trouble at the mine. This armed bodyguard somehow failed to fill Baruch with any sense of security.

A Pinkerton detective accompanied the guests to their rooms. All would be well, he said, if they kept their lights turned off. Later the trio were shepherded through murky streets, ominously lined with silent, tough-looking men. Light splashed to their eyes in the big saloon and gambling house, where drinks were set up, friends introduced, and an explanation made of the "labor difficulties," which arose from the practice of stripping the men after work and jumping them over a bar so that any concealed gold might fall to the ground.

Order was maintained only by aid of the detectives. Once, Wingfield told his guests, when the IWW had kidnapped and beaten up several superintendents, he had gone to the desert after them and brought them back to have their wounds dressed. Strikers had hemmed in the automobile, jostling and shoving until Wingfield and all others looked toward the bank, where guns bristled from every window and a path suddenly opened for the victims and their rescuer. What if the mob had turned upon Wingfield? There would have been a massacre, Wingfield thought.

This talk of massacres also failed to contribute to Baruch's sense of security or pleasure, as he later confessed. Nor did the spectacle of Wingfield himself, eyes roving, hands continually moving over his guns.

The next day Baruch looked on as Wingfield whirled a bottle into the air and shot and shattered it on the way down. The Count, meanwhile, had discovered their landlord's wife, a lady who he felt would be an ornament to Paris itself. Baruch looked and agreed, but agreed also that the Count's education in this phase of American life had gone far enough. [51]

On that Wild West adventure, Baruch little dreamed that his own real adventure had scarcely begun. That George Wingfield not only would become his partner but one of his oldest and most trusted friends, that he himself would find gold in Goldfield, exceeding even his highest hopes, all this was beyond his imaginings or his expectations. Yet, so it was, and Wingfield's brute courage in the shotgun violence of the Old West was matched only by the fortitude with which he battled his way out of bankruptcy and the Great Depression of the thirties.

Railroads were still one of Baruch's greatest loves. And in 1911 came the offer he could not refuse. He was nearly forty-one then, past his first youthful hopes and illusions, and yet his heart still thrilled to his old dream of railroad empire.

To none but a dreamer or an optimist would the Wabash Railroad have looked like opportunity. For the Wabash, torn between warring factions, neglected and run down, was a sick railroad. None but a genius could save it — a mastermind like Harriman. And here was Jacob H. Schiff, one of America's most powerful bankers, telling Baruch that he might be that genius.

Baruch was elated; he felt as if the mantle of Harriman had dropped upon his shoulders. But was Schiff sincere? Baruch wondered, studying the urbane and persuasive man. Somehow, despite the animosity between them he preferred the forthright Morgan. He delivered his own ultimatum bluntly, demanding a free hand. Schiff's answer came suavely; as far as he was concerned, he said, Baruch should have one. With that Baruch had to be satisfied. He took a large holding of Wabash bonds and bent his energies towards a complete reorganization of the railroad.

He was not alone. Already at work were two committees of reorganization, at complete cross-purposes with each other. There were two rival chairmen. One was Winslow Pierce, director of the Equitable Trust Company and several of the Jay Gould enterprises, unofficial representative of Schiff's Kuhn, Loeb and Company and the very managerial policies that had made the railroad sick in the first place. The other was the hard-working and talented James Wallace, whose committee was organized by the Central Trust Company, not so much to salvage the railroad as to protect the stockholders.

Baruch's choice was difficult. To bring the committees together was impossible. To act without inside information was equally impossible. He must bore from within, and reluctantly he chose the

Pierce group. For he knew what the public did not know — that the railroad was in virtual receivership and that the Wallace committee, looking toward self-enrichment, was dickering for control.

Baruch's goal was simple: to reorganize the railroad and "put it on its feet." He made his point clear. Hostilities arose between himself and his fellow committee members in a series of lively exchanges, as he divested them of the idea that his was just another vote for those who had already ruined the road.

He then turned his attention to the ailing railroad. The Wabash looped in a series of short lines between Detroit and Chicago, Chicago and Toledo, Chicago and St. Louis, and St. Louis and Kansas City. Its equipment was a joke. Its management was a mystery, even to its own officials. Stockholders clamored for dividends, bondholders for interest, and bankers were scrambling to save their investment at the expense of everyone else. The Goulds, it was rumored, were heavily involved. The Wabash was not a railroad, it was a speculative enterprise. No one wanted to bear the expense of rehabilitation. New equipment was essential, new terminal facilities, new operating talent. Worst of all, the road had no credit.

First the committee members tried to "jolly," then to force Baruch down. In desperation he turned to Schiff, but the banker had deaf ears for his pleas. Determinedly he began to fight, and after hard words and bitter struggle obtained a few small concessions.

He reached an impasse. Fagged and discouraged, he would have resigned, except that he discovered this to be just what the bankers' committee wanted. The "interest" of the Pennsylvania Railroad only compounded the difficulty.

For Baruch these were bad days. They were days of defeat and even of despair, which dulled the fine edge of pleasure in life, and even corroded his pride in his past triumphs. He had dreamed of a railroad; the dream was becoming a nightmare. To cap it all, a vicious whispering campaign arose that he was in financial difficulties. He could neither fight it nor stop it. But now he was to know the reward of friendship. As he sat at his lonely lunch one day, he perceived the tall form of Thomas Fortune Ryan. A moment later the financier was at his side, assuring Baruch and anyone within earshot that he stood with him on the Wabash deal. This was enough to hearten a dying man. Ryan stood ready to take over half of Baruch's Wabash securities at what they had cost him, and although he did not avail himself of the offer, the news was not long in traveling.

At last Baruch got the two committees together. It was not as Harriman would have done — Harriman who had boasted that he could bring any ten men in America together. Baruch had got the committees together, but there must have been times when he wished he could have knocked their heads together instead. After three years' work the road was technically reorganized, but not as Baruch had hoped. The interest on the bonds had been reduced, some had been devalued, others exchanged for stock. Continually Baruch had been harassed by men whose only purpose was to hide their own mistakes.

He spurned a fee for his three years' work, for he had failed. Harriman, he kept telling himself, would not have failed. Harriman could have made the bankers jump through the hoops. Baruch had not been able to. Yet, if he had not gained the sweeping reorganization of which he had dreamed, he had done enough so that the Pennsylvania interests took over the railroad.[52]

6

SCHOOL FOR STATECRAFT

THEY WERE SITTING together in the lobby of the Plaza Hotel in New York, Bernard Baruch, his wife, and his brother-in-law, when Griffen turned sharply. "There's Prexy," he said.[1]

Baruch saw a man in a badly cut suit, not tall but looking tall because he was slender, with a springy step and eyes beautifully set and clear, "the color of black ink on gray blotting paper," color rising along the lean jaw of a face "cut out of wood and looking into light." [2]

So this was "the man from Princeton" whose battle against the "eating clubs" had roused the wrath of fraternal circles — Thomas Woodrow Wilson, who as early as 1906 had been hailed by such diverse voices as those of George Harvey of *Harper's Weekly* and the Charleston *News and Courier* as "the most promising of Southern candidates for the Presidency." [3]

Years later, Bernard Baruch was frank to admit the origin of his own interest in the man. He who had been barred from the fraternities of his own college was stirred by the blunt-spoken courage of this fighter against privilege and exclusiveness, this zealot who dared term the clubs the sideshows "swallowing up the circus." [4] But he shrank from an introduction. "No," he said, "I don't want to meet him." [5]

What restrained him? It was 1912. Forces more potent than the *News and Courier* were now backing Woodrow Wilson for the Presidency — Wilson, who had told Morgan to his face that there was a "higher law" than profit, and that bankers did not understand the country.[6]

Wall Street was the stumbling block. Wall Street, Baruch had heard, was anathema to Wilson. For Wilson had broken with one of his earliest and most enthusiastic supporters, Colonel George Harvey, because of his refusal to accept the support of Harvey's — and Baruch's — good friend, the Democratic Party "angel," Thomas Fortune Ryan.[7]

Much has been made of the story that only Baruch's acceptance of a trusteeship at the College of the City of New York (on the insistence of his father) enabled him to meet his fellow trustee William McCombs and eventually, through him, Wilson. But Baruch believes that the train leading to the friendship started when his mother joined the Southern Society of New York and there met a tall raw-boned man named William G. McAdoo.[8]

William Gibbs McAdoo is worth a pause for consideration, for he was a big man in his day. If far from the caliber of Wilson, he had a drive and fight and fire that extracted a million dollars from J. P. Morgan in ten minutes' time — a dynamism that inspired Bernard Baruch.

He was America incarnate. He was born at "Melora," a sagging, white-columned house in the red hills near Kennesaw Mountain, Georgia, and his mother had been a Floyd of the old slave-holding aristocracy. His father was of east Tennessee stock, out of the blue mountains, and the boy, with a heritage of Indians and campfires and Bible-reading Presbyterians, was brought up on stories of a bearded grandfather, who had fought with Jackson in the old Creek war, and of a father, the old Confederate, who in youth had gone down the Mississippi on a flatboat and shouldered a musket at Buena Vista in the war with Mexico.

Like Baruch and Wilson, McAdoo had grown up in the desolation of war's aftermath. In the dusty streets of Milledgeville, the men "pitched horseshoes and talked of the past." For him childhood was concerned primarily with the sheer "difficulty in keeping alive." [9]

Nothing, however, could daunt this fighting Scotch-Irishman. Like so many Southerners of his generation, he fought his way up, as if goaded by a compulsion to beat the Yankees at their own game. He sold stocks and bonds and, like Baruch, studied the industries and railroads of the country with the creative urge, the driving inner compulsion of an artist. If a tunnel could be driven ten feet under the Hudson, he argued, it could be driven a thousand feet. He raised three million dollars for the job and tunneled through, while the people of New York looked on in wonder.[10]

When Baruch met McAdoo, he was a forty-nine-year-old widower and father of six children, soon to be squiring young Eleanor Wilson at tennis games and tea dances. He was a lean and gangling six-footer, with crow's-feet radiating from hollow eyes and the grin of a Will Rogers. He was explosive with energy and untamed speech, redolent with the expletives of Andrew Jackson's time; he was one of the few men in the world, Carter Glass once said, who could "swear interestingly." [11] He was verbose and windy, made up in stubbornness what he lacked in profundity, was intrigued by men rather than ideas; but, as he himself said, he was one to "make the fur fly." Wilson once said that McAdoo was not fit to be President. Yet measured against the nominees of the nineteen-twenties he does not come off badly. In any event, his courage, his tenacity, his warmth and exuberance endeared him to Baruch.[12]

Baltimore, in that steaming convention week of 1912, was like "a country town on circus day." A hot wind blew, flicking dust across the endless rows of white steps. It twisted ties into strings, pasted shirts to round bellies or sweat-soaked backs. The clamor at convention headquarters at the Hotel Empire was like the murmuring onrush of a sandstorm. From the walls blazed great maps posted by the followers of the "houn' dawg statesman," Champ Clark, each Clark state colored red. Upon entering, Baruch would have noted familiar faces, that of McAdoo, and of William McCombs, hands shaking, and "on the ragged edge of a nervous breakdown." [13]

It was Baruch's first convention. Never before had he encountered that particular combination of mirth and tomfoolery, of side-show carnival and General Edwin Booth's entry into Heaven, by which the people in their wisdom make their choice for the republic's highest office. Yet, despite the brass and clamor of the professionals, it was an amateur show. Baruch had not come as a delegate. Seated on the platform, he was there as a "rooter" for a man now almost forgotten, whose colorful and cantankerous personality has faded into the razzle-dazzle of the city he loved — the New York mayor of O. Henry's time, William Gaynor.[14] It was Gaynor who had appointed Baruch a City College trustee. Although he was never associated with Tammany Hall, Baruch was a friend of the Wigwam leader, Charles F. Murphy, who, incidentally, was not a Wilson man. For Richard Croker, too, Baruch had respect, for Croker had helped his father in his program of public baths for New York City.[15]

Not until the onslaught of Wendell Willkie upon the Republicans twenty-eight years later did the nation again see drama like this. Even Wilson's campaign manager, McCombs, was an amateur, as was McAdoo, going "at it" with a fervor and a skill at horse-trading that dazzled the professionals. A one-man buffer between the hard-driven McCombs and the hard-driving "Mac" was Colonel Edward Mandell House, a man "of almost Chinese self-effacement," who the previous November had described Woodrow Wilson as "both the man and the opportunity" he was looking for.[16] It was he who smoothed the rough edges at headquarters with a grace which made McAdoo feel him to be one of the most agreeable and unobtrusive men in the world.

For Baruch the convention was the big parade, the passing show: "Alfalfa Bill" Murray, with his snapping galluses and bandana handkerchief; the quiet and quietly clever Oscar Underwood of Alabama, his votes nailed down for the bargaining table; Champ Clark, waving his broad-brimmed slouch hat, as feet began to pound the floor and galleries to resound with the refrain:

> *I don't care if he is a houn'.*
> *You gotta quit kicking my dog aroun'.*[17]

Baruch saw Cardinal Gibbons in his skullcap, light glinting off his silvery hair, and down in the Virginia delegation, the unspeaking and unmoving form of Thomas Fortune Ryan. But it was toward the delegation from Nebraska that all eyes turned, and the man with the Websterian brow and elflocks dank with sweat, a mouth like a dagger slash and brows twisted over a hawklike nose. This was the man, weighted with three defeats and the prestige of a following held by no Democrat since Jackson's time — Bryan, sitting there, fanning himself with a palm-leaf fan.

Baruch had never followed the Western Star. "Too emotional," was his summary of him,[18] but his opposition was rooted even deeper in his distaste for the great commoner's elementary concepts of economics. However "new" Wilson's ideas may have been, they still breathed hope into conservatives who wanted to "save" the country from Bryan. But Baruch knew, as all did, that Bryan held the key to the convention. It was a knock-down grapple between Wall Street — the Ryans, the Whitneys, and the Belmonts — versus the Bryans and the Watsons. And where did Wilson stand?

Or Champ Clark? Was Clark really the tool of those who would sell the Democratic Party out to yet another group of bosses and Wall Street? The Wilson forces claimed so, and had so informed Bryan earlier that summer. Bryan had been very much impressed by "Governor Wilson." But under the unit rule, his state delegation was pledged to Champ Clark. After fulfilling his instructions in good faith, he would, of course, be free to take any course that his conscience should dictate.[19]

On Thursday, the twenty-seventh, "all hell" broke loose in convention hall. Ponderously, Bryan mounted to his feet. Now it came, "the vast volume of sound," the eloquence out of an earlier age that could evoke memories of Webster and Clay; the oratory that had fired the delegates back in '96 and still sent chills down their spines sixteen years later. Bryan had loosed his bolt. John W. Owen, later editor of the Baltimore *Sun*, recalled it afterward as the tensest moment of his life. Openly Bryan denounced the nomination of any representative of J. Pierpont Morgan, August Belmont, Thomas Fortune Ryan, or any other member "of the privilege-hunting and favor-seeking class." [20]

The chaos exploded. The newspapermen ducked. "Hard-bitten, veteran reporters" slid low in their chairs, ready to dive under the nearest table. There was "murder in the air." Amidst the frenzy and uproar, the shouts, howls, groans, and cries of "Lynch him" and "Throw him out," the voice of Bryan sounded on, like waves beating at a rocky shore.[21] "We demand," he shouted, "the withdrawal . . . of any delegate or delegates constituting or representing the above named interests." [22]

For an hour longer it continued, voices roaring, men running wild up and down the aisles, even a fist thrust into Bryan's face. After concluding, he made his way to the platform, where he took a seat at the side of Baruch and picked up his palm-leaf fan. "That will fix 'em," he said.[23]

Bryan knew his politics. He was playing for more than he could get, and in return would get about what he wanted, which was, most of all, the defeat of the Tammany forces. The nomination of Wilson was assured by Bryan's speech, although none but the amateurs knew it.[24] Even McCombs had some bad moments, and told Wilson it was all over when New York switched its vote to Clark and launched its long-prepared demonstration. None but amateurs would have held on. None but amateurs would have disregarded the fact that not in sixty-eight years had a candidate failed of nomination after once securing a majority.[25] All the amateurs knew was that Clark was far short of the required two-thirds vote.

Saturday was a day of tense expectancy. Bryan arose again, amidst a chorus of jeers and boos. He would not follow the "ninety wax figures." He would withhold his vote from Mr. Clark "as long as New York's is recorded for him." Clark had his chance now — to repudiate bossism or risk defeat — he took the risk. Ballot by ballot, his vote began to fall. Meanwhile, into the Wilson headquarters burst a haughty young scion of the house of Roosevelt. This was Franklin Delano from Dutchess County, "the most attractive man I ever met," one observer described him. The regular Democrats just "gritted their teeth and endured him." [26] But he was "heart and soul for Wilson," and could he do some work? He could.[27]

On Monday, Indiana "went over the top" as the galleries roared with enthusiasm. By the thirty-seventh ballot, the count was Wilson, 494½, and Clark, 433½, with only the band wagon to wait for.

By Tuesday it was all over, with the switch of Illinois on the forty-third ballot and of Oscar Underwood's ninety-seven votes on the forty-sixth. The delegations sat fagged and limp, a yawning sea of white faces. Under the bald glare of the lights they sat at nine that night, still yawning, still whispering, glancing at timetables, with only a few moments to spare to select the vice-presidential candidate, who by the grace of God might have become President. It was said that Wilson had no preference, but McAdoo knew where the award should be made — to the bandwagon state of Indiana and Tom Marshall. The delegates yawned; they had no spirit, not even for Marshall's cracker-barrel humor. The convention was over. Bernard Baruch had had a firsthand lesson in the working of American democracy.[28]

Baruch's meeting with Wilson came in October 1912, and was arranged by McCombs. It took place on the sixth floor of the Plaza Hotel. Colonel House was present, and James Gerard was in the waiting room outside. But Baruch had eyes primarily for Wilson. They clasped hands, the upcountry zealot and the low-country courtier, both out of the war-ravaged South. Something flashed between them. Baruch's reaction was instantaneous. He was completely taken with the man.[29]

Baruch later recalled that they discussed the question of monopoly and centralization, Baruch asking flatly, "Do you believe that if a man makes a success he should be punished for it?"

"No," Wilson replied, adding that he believed that telephones, for instance, were "a natural monopoly." It was a good thing to have one system under private control, but he believed that it should be regulated.[30] These words struck home to Baruch.

It was a meeting that changed the course of Baruch's life and perhaps of history. He stepped from the elevator of the Plaza and to the street outside deeply moved by the experience. The next day he said, "I have met one of the great men of the world." [31] Nearly thirty years later he described his meeting with "the incomparable Wilson" as "one of the great events of my life . . . If I have been able to serve my country, it was he who planted the seeds . . . within me." [32]

He spoke the truth. It was Wilson of the New Freedom who released Baruch's talents, who gave the world the future statesman. With the one exception of his father, Woodrow Wilson was the greatest influence on Baruch's life, and for Wilson Baruch felt something of the veneration his father felt for Lee.

Usually a man of forty-two is not easily susceptible to personal influence; but Baruch had not yet really found himself. Even his posed portrait of the war years, with the scarf pin and the stiff collar, the eyes searching, is that of an idealist playing the role of businessman. Younger and more softly drawn, it is a face with a strange resemblance to Wilson's own. Baruch's idealism had already been put to the test: along with Charles Evans Hughes and others, he was fighting for the rights of duly elected Socialist legislators in New York to take the seats to which they had been chosen.[33]

Wilson and Baruch must have met almost with a sense of recognition — these two who had spent childhood years not forty miles apart. Baruch had seen that face before, with its jutting nose and sharp jaw; it was the face of the Presbyterian divine, who prayed daily as Wilson did, and saw man not as a creature of the drawing room or of the Stock Exchange, but as "a lonely, awful soul." He was of Covenanter stock, born in the blue hills of the upper Shenandoah, "the Valley," where Stonewall slept and Lee walked at the end. For Wilson, childhood in South Carolina had been "an ordeal of misery." He remembered fear and the dried cowpeas left in the wake of Sherman's "bummers"; he had seen Negroes drunk with freedom, and Columbia in the ashes of her desolation. As with Simon Baruch, the image of Lee was the inspiration of his life, and he cherished an early "delightful memory" of standing at the side of the great general and looking up into his face.[34]

He was an instinctive zealot, a "good hater," yet counterbalanced with a Scottish gift of "pure logic." [35] To the world he seemed a kind of thinking machine, and yet, as his wife Edith knew, he was a creature of high emotions.[36] He had visions, flights, a soaring creative power; an inflexibility which made him bar the door to a man who was five minutes late, and a rigidity which impelled him to play golf in the snow, with fingers too stiff to unbutton his coat.[37] But his Puritanism was overlaid with a gay grace; and, as he told the Sons of St. Patrick: "There is something delightful in me that every now and then takes the strain off my Scotch conscience . . . when I do not care whether school keeps or not." [38] There was, in fact, nothing of the schoolmaster about him. As McAdoo said, "He simply was not that kind of man at all." He was the mimic who could look more like McAdoo than McAdoo looked like himself; [39] the wag who would cakewalk with his students or clean the boots of a visiting snob; the lover who would break into a buck-and-wing and whistle "Oh, You Beautiful Doll" while waiting for Mrs. Galt. He had fallen in love at first sight with his first wife, a dark-eyed, honey-haired little girl, who might have stepped from the pages of a Jane Austen novel.[40] More sophisticated were the charms of Edith Bolling Galt, but with her, too, Wilson fell in love at first sight, offering her marriage one month from the time he saw her in a White House corridor in a Worth suit, a tricorn hat and shoes muddy from a country walk.[41]

Gossips have dealt harshly with Woodrow Wilson's supposed susceptibility to women — a matter which is of no importance to history. Admittedly the company of beautiful and vital women refreshed him. Often Colonel Starling, the White House Secret Service chief, would take him backstage at a theatrical performance so that he might have the pleasure of meeting the actresses, "observing their charm and inhaling their perfumes." This was as good as eight hours' sleep to him. In women Wilson found qualities of friendship lacking in men. One woman relative only wished that his innocent and beautiful correspondence with Mrs. Hulbert Peck had been published, simply as a contribution to literature.[42]

He charmed, too, no less than he was charmed. Like Franklin Roosevelt, he bewitched with his rich, vibrant voice, energetic and warm. Yet he inspired as a statesman far more than he intrigued as a politician; never would he be called the master politician of his time. "You stood in awe of Wilson; you didn't cheer him." [43] To those who knew both Wilson and Roosevelt — men like Baruch and his close associate, John Hancock, and David Lawrence, Wilson seemed incomparably the greater of the two.[44] It must be taken into account, however, that all these men were beyond the age of hero-worship when Roosevelt was in his full power.

Through McAdoo, Baruch was soon to meet others of the Wilson inner coterie. One was the conscientious Dr. Cary Grayson, whose task it was to keep the President functioning at peak efficiency, and who could not agree that the President's job was just "a vacation" for Wilson. Despite the executive efficiency by which he could turn out enough paperwork in a few hours to keep his office staff busy all day, the President had come into the White House virtually a sick man, and the doggedly loyal Grayson watched over him as if he were a baby. It was a distinct worry to him that Wilson did so much of his work before he came to the office. "He thinks," reported Grayson, "while he's exercising, while he's dressing or bathing." Relaxation was completely out of his power.[45]

No less solicitous of the President's political well-being than Grayson was of his health, was the other White House intimate, a "quiet man of velvet," with an aptitude for arranging situations — Colonel Edward Mandell House.[46]

The perspective of history and the publication of *The Intimate Papers of Colonel House* have thrown much light on the activities — or presumed activities — of the Colonel. That his influence on Wilson was great is undeniable, but the nature of that influence is less clear. Psychologists have seen the mouselike House as gratifying his own ego by his influence over the President; and such figures in Wilson's cabinet as Postmaster General Albert Burleson and Secretary of the Navy Josephus Daniels have endeavored to explode the House "myth" once and for all. Burleson, for instance, thought House merely a capable emissary, who would get his daily preview of what was foremost in the President's mind by a briefing from a favored Cabinet officer, and then a few moments later at the White House would deliver himself of exactly what the President had in mind.[47]

And House distrusted Baruch, with his Wall Street background. In fact the Colonel later went so far as to place a spy on Baruch's trail who could report only that the South Carolinian was doing an excellent job. In fact this man became so admiring, both of Baruch's accomplishments and of the man himself, that he broke down and confessed that he had been asked to give information. "I'm just a little ashamed," he said.[48] Baruch's final evaluation of the Colonel was that he had really "a great deal of influence on Wilson," perhaps because he agreed with him so much of the time. When he ceased to agree, when he became the critic instead of the aide his influence correspondingly diminished.[49]

House, McAdoo, and McCombs managed Wilson's 1912 campaign. The Governor sat on his porch at Sea Girt, New Jersey, receiving the stares of the passing motorists with the look of a man "sentenced to sit in a show window." [50]

As for Baruch, his party regularity long antedated his party service. As he said, "Of course, I was born a Democrat, a Southerner, and a Confederate." He could remember his joy when Cleveland was elected; to see the old Jeffersonian party back in power was his dream. Here, now, was a leader and a cause that could focus his energies.[51]

What could he do? He could and did contribute money. Although he did not later recall his exact donation, he was a very large contributor.[52]

"Billy," Baruch said to William McCombs, "I'll give you any amount of money you want; just tell me how much you'll need." [53] This meant much at a time when Bryanism had left the party coffers depleted. Then, as always, there were few wealthy givers among the Democrats, so the name of Baruch was blessed indeed.[54] Nor were his contributions solely on behalf of Woodrow Wilson. He had the money to build up the Democratic Party, this was what he wanted to do.

For Baruch more than his money was at stake. All his awakened idealism was in this struggle. "If Wilson is defeated, I don't know what I shall do," he told Garet Garrett, who had watched him in his long search for a consuming purpose. He supposed that he would have "to go back to Wall Street and play the game." [55]

He asked no return on his investment but victory, but with the victory won he was not for two years to come forward again. Then he strode to the Administration's side in a situation that threatened not only the prestige of the President, but of the whole party program. Cotton was at six cents a pound.[56] The cotton panic of 1914 was no fault of Wilson's. As war exploded over Europe, ships from across the world scuttled for their home ports, and produce lay rotting at the wharves. Panic struck the growers as the great staple of the South dipped three cents below the cost of production. In Mississippi, not only cotton overalls but suddenly whole suits of cotton were manufactured and worn. Markets must be found or the whole South would be plunged into want.

Wilson and Secretary William Gibbs McAdoo swung into action. Already, the German and neutral markets were lost; the Allies, too, were under blockade and ships would not sail unless bribed or subsidized. Wilson issued his orders: cotton was not contraband. If private ships would not sail, then the government would carry the cotton.

Furthermore, the price of cotton must be supported. Wilson's idea was a loan fund of 135 million dollars, to be raised by the bankers of New York, for which purpose Secretary of the Treasury McAdoo opened a special office. Toward the end of the drive, a tall man came before him.

"Mr. Secretary, I understand that you need subscriptions to complete your cotton loan fund?"

McAdoo assented. He was "still three million dollars short," he said.

"I will take the balance of it," replied Bernard Baruch. "I am a Southerner and am deeply interested in helping the cotton growers in their desperate emergency."

McAdoo jumped up. "That's wonderful," he shouted.[57]

As it turned out, Baruch was again waging psychological warfare. For he well knew, and told Paul Warburg, "Everyone will want to get in now. Jacob Schiff will want some." But as the rush got under way, Baruch insisted that he wanted to take "at least a million of this." His gesture, of course, did not go unnoticed in party circles.[58]

The relationship of Baruch to the New Freedom, so-called, is less of a paradox than might be supposed. When past eighty, he stated his credo: "I would rise and fall on what I call individualism." [59] Individual liberty was the cornerstone of the New Freedom, which was basically a program of common sense come to terms with human nature.

The New Freedom stemmed from deep roots: from Jefferson's sense of social obligation and Wilson's convictions of original sin. Not modern economic processes but the men who managed them were to blame for the state of the world. Through proper government, the forces of "special privilege" could and would be foiled. Power without personal responsibility was criminal; responsibility must be placed upon individuals, and men must be guaranteed against unprincipled competition.

This process worked two ways. Wilson had small sympathy for strikes and was a fierce partisan of the "open shop." Capital and labor, at their worst, he believed, were a double-headed menace, both the enemies of individualism and free enterprise. Labor unions, he thought, put a premium upon laziness when they looked merely to the laborer's interests rather than to the interests of the whole. Calvinism demanded of each individual that he do his best. Nor was Wilson unaware of the abuses of so-called "free enterprise." He was not against bigness for its own sake but only because of the abuses that had followed in the wake of unregulated corporate power. Men and systems should be free, so long as they permitted freedom to others. Where abuses occurred, the government should intervene. Wilson saw government as above all class interests, its function that of mediator or policeman to guard competition in a society where the employed could rise to become the employers.

Although Wilson has been called an idealist and theorist, it was the basic practicality of his plans that attracted Baruch. Wilson's was no blueprint philosophy, but a natural outgrowth of the times in which he lived. His theories were voiced in action, and only from the perspective of forty-odd years is the full scope of the New Freedom's achievements visible. As one historian has said, more sensational things were accomplished in the first hundred days of the New Deal, but many so fumblingly that they had to be done all over again.[60] The miracle of the New Freedom was its permanence. Not a single important act of its legislation was ever repealed. Hurtled through in two years, the New Freedom took shape in legislation still unrivaled in the annals of lawmaking.

It was more than a program of law; it was a social revolution. It threw the tariff lobbyists out of the temple and achieved the first real tariff reduction in fifty years. The Clayton Act substituted effective control for the inadequacy of the old Sherman antitrust law. Back in New Jersey, Wilson's old-age pension plan had been hailed as "Labor's Magna Charta," and now he struck a mighty blow for human rights in the provision of the Clayton Act exempting labor unions, to a great degree, from prosecution under the antitrust laws. For Wilson agreed with Samuel Gompers that labor was "not a commodity or article of commerce." [61]

The New Freedom brought a Federal income tax law under the newly approved Sixteenth Amendment, the first Federal child labor law,* and the Adamson Act of 1916, establishing the eight-hour day for workers on interstate railroads. The Federal Reserve Act — soon to survive the test of the First World War — kicked up the biggest financial row since the battle of the bank between Nicholas Biddle and Andrew Jackson.[62] Furthermore, the New Freedom had international as well as national implications. Wilson recognized the interdependence of world economies. America's destiny lay in world trade; there was no prosperity in economic isolation. The function of government, he believed, was not to divide men but to bring them together.

Philosophically the New Freedom laid the foundation for both the New Deal and the Fair Deal of the future. Their basic concept was the same: that government should take a positive hand in the direction of the national economy. This was a landmark in American political thinking — the substitution of public for private morality in the concerns of human interest.[63]

For it was the genius of Wilson to recognize that social change was inevitable and this was understood by Baruch. From the first, Baruch saw the goal of the New Freedom was to cut down privilege and to put men on a more equal basis before the law and opportunity, and the aim of Wilson was to serve his country through his party, not his party through his country.

Baruch's influence on the early Wilson program has sometimes been overestimated. In those first days he "kept away," [64] and by so doing insured his later entree. Numerous friends of the Guggenheims, for instance, were eager for Baruch's intercession with the President against the bill providing for government construction of an Alaska railroad which would compete with Guggenheim developments. This Baruch declined to do.

Money may have gained him an entree into Administrative circles, but it was the abilities that had made the money which now sought an outlet. Baruch was determined to earn his way to preferment not

* Declared unconstitutional by the Supreme Court in 1918.

by donations but by actions. He always "backed the President up in progressive ideas." [65] Sometimes he went farther than Wilson. Wilson, for instance, originally thought that readily available credit alone would answer the farmers' problems. It was Baruch who helped convince the Administration that the nation's consolidated banking system must reach into the agricultural areas.

As for the Federal Reserve bill, Baruch had his own quiet advice to offer, when McAdoo, Carter Glass of Virginia, and Senator Aldrich labored to transfer ultimate control of the monetary system from private banks to the government.[66] In the final test before Congress, Baruch persuaded the President to accept some amendments without which the bill would have been lost.[67]

Baruch has commented on this phase of his career: "I had a flexibility in action desirable to have." [68] Furthermore, he sensed the future. His old idol, Theodore Roosevelt, stirred his interest in preparedness, and Baruch's stalwart figure headed the Bankers' and Brokers' Division in "T.R.'s" Preparedness Parade down Fifth Avenue.

At a luncheon given by Henry Clay Frick during the winter of 1915–16, Baruch was seated next to General Leonard Wood, who talked of the rebuilding of Camp Plattsburg, then shut down for want of funds. The General was concerned, for the camp was badly needed for the training of volunteer officers.

How much was needed to reopen it? Baruch asked. "Ten thousand dollars," the General replied.

"You've got it providing you don't tell anybody," Baruch said.[69]

He was similarly generous in his contributions to the campaign chest of 1916. During a subsequent congressional investigation, someone wanted to know how much Mr. Baruch had contributed to Wilson's campaign. The figure made public had been $35,000.

"Fifty thousand dollars," Baruch said.

"I wish we had a lot more like him," one Democratic Representative observed.[70]

This time, Baruch knew that he was not betting on a sure thing. Such was his party loyalty that despite the failure of the party in New York to organize properly, Baruch had endeavored to help matters by offering $50,000 to the state campaign fund through the Tammany leader, Charles Murphy. The Boss refused it. "I wouldn't take your money," he said, "because Wilson can't carry the state." This prediction proved to be entirely correct.

Baruch's close friend Herbert Bayard Swope, one of few who never gave up hope, has recalled Baruch's despondency in the pale dawn following that uncertain election day. "I went up to the Belmont," the redheaded Missourian later recounted, "and there found Baruch, McCombs,* McAdoo, and little Vance McCormick, all in their shirt-sleeves," fagged, their faces hidden behind palls of smoke and gloom. Swope raged at them. "You fellows are a lot of damn quitters," he said. "California looks very, very like Wilson."

Wearily, they looked up at him. Odds were twenty to one on Hughes, and even Wilson had prepared his formal message of congratulations. They were too dazed, too tired to believe. Baruch went home to bed and slept until awakened by a telephone call from Henry Morgenthau, Sr. "Bernie, we're in," he said.[71]

Baruch was "in." Old friends — or kinsmen — began to see less of him. They would come to New York and find that he was "down in Washington, seeing the President." [72]

By the spring of 1917, Baruch became a frequent visitor at the White House. This is shown by Wilson's diary entries, recording that on March 4 he "saw Baruch"; and again on March 9 at 4 P.M., his only appointment of the day. Other entries were May 13, June 17, July 31, August 9, and September 3, 11, and 16.[73] As early as the summer of 1916 Baruch was admitting his growing feeling for Wilson. The President, in his turn, was acknowledging that he had learned to trust and admire Baruch. At Long Branch the President met Baruch's elderly parents, his handsome mother, and his father, the old Confederate, eager now to aid the American army with his knowledge of medical sanitation and rehabilitation of the wounded. "I was proud to fight for the Gray," he told Admiral Grayson; "I would be happy to fight for the Blue." Wilson shook hands and chatted with the couple and, as Baruch recalled it, "became enamored with them." [74]

Yet never would Baruch allow his support to be a source of embarrassment to the man — or the cause — he so much admired. On the personal side this was a pity. Mrs. Woodrow Wilson regretted that she and her husband had not known Baruch earlier.[75] For

* Baruch recalls that Thomas L. Chadbourne was also there, but has no memory of McCombs. The latter's personal role in the campaign was minor, because of some delicate intervention from Baruch. At the suggestion of Colonel House, Baruch had been able to persuade the temperamental McCombs that his health would prevent his serving as Democratic chairman in 1916. See Bibliography, Charles Seymour, ed., Vol. II.

Baruch gave to Wilson what was rare in the life of that great man —
not loyalty or service or devotion alone, but warm, understanding
friendship which Colonel House could never give. In Baruch's eyes
Wilson could do no wrong. House's undoing, as it finally turned out,
came from his criticisms of Wilson on the outside instead of to his
face. Baruch was not uncritical, but he was direct. Sometimes he or
Vance McCormick would say: "I don't agree with you, Mr. President.
Sorry, sir."

Then Wilson would answer, "I'll listen to your reason." [76] Wilson
never demanded unqualified agreement with his views. On the contrary, according to Baruch, he "constantly sought advice and the
opinion of others before making decisions." He willingly gave way
on matters of detail. "It was only on basic principles that he refused
to yield." [77] In all his long and intimate association with Wilson,
Baruch never found him "harsh and dictatorial," although Baruch
never hesitated to express an opposing view. Unlike Colonel House,
however, once policy was made, Baruch unfalteringly carried it forward.[78] Loyalty was what Wilson demanded.

Wilson slowly came to know and admire the Wall Street man
whose principles and politics came from elsewhere, who was a digger
for facts with an intensity no less than Wilson's own.[79] Slowly, the
President came to see in Baruch something he had not expected:
"a great intellectual and political resource besides his money." [80]

The Baruch-Wilson relationship gives the lie to the myth that
Wilson was incapable of holding friends. Baruch once said that
when Wilson broke with a friend he always suffered.[81] Yet he retained devoted friends to the end: Louis Brandeis; Vance Mc-
Cormick, who, after House, "undertook more confidential missions
than any other man"; the newspaperman Frank Cobb; Cleveland
Dodge; Cyrus McCormick. To the end, he was a hero to the loyal
Grayson, and to the fiercely devoted Josephus Daniels, who never
thought of him afterward but with the feeling that he was looking
back to glory, and to whom Wilson wrote "of our genuine affection
for one another." [82] It was understandable that the Southern group
should have been closest to his affections. Baruch he would always
love, and Glass and Claude Swanson; but there were also McAdoo,
Baker, and General Bliss. Less known than his celebrated "break"
with his secretary Joseph Tumulty was his effort to win Tumulty a
seat in the United States Senate as late as 1923.[83]

Baruch would never have gained such unofficial authority as he did, had he not been qualified to exercise it. In his search for sure investments, Baruch's mind had become, as we have seen, an encyclopedia of American industry. He knew the rail lines and the industries and the sources of raw material for those industries. He knew the markets, at home and abroad. He knew the tides and the cross-currents, the climatic fluctuations from year to year, the relationship between a canal route in Canada and a projected railway in the Northwest. He knew tariffs and credit, supply and demand; and most of all, he knew people. He knew America as an economic entity that in time of war might be grasped and used as a whole. Like Wilson, his love of country had grown out of his love of his state and of the South, and out of "an overwhelming sense of identification" with them.[84]

"His love of country," one intimate has said of him, "exceeded his love for any woman." Once he had used his brains and talents for his own advantage. Now he would turn them to the benefit of mankind.

From Wilson Baruch had caught a sense of the spiritual significance of America. With the shadow of war creeping nearer, Wilson looked more to Baruch, realizing that few men had his knowledge of the country's economy.[85] The President now knew that he wanted this man permanently at his side.

Baruch had been his own best advocate. The genesis of industrial mobilization for the United States * was long and the final form taken by the War Industries Board was the result of experience and the thought of many men. One of the basic ideas, however, came to Baruch one day as he lay back in a train chair, his eyes on moving space, and the wheels drumming toward San Francisco.

Baruch knew "all the copper, lead and zinc fellows." He knew their sources of supply, their price scales, their means of production. But did any central agency in Washington know about them? He carried his thinking a step farther. "Committees of industry," big business and small business, both represented in Washington, and both with Washington representation back home — this could be "the backbone of the whole structure." It would work on the principle of a faucet. Turned one way, data on the capacity, the potential,

* For a close scrutiny of the origins and development of the WIB, see Bibliography, Clarkson, Chap. II.

and the needs of industry would flow into Washington. Turned the other, the needs of government could be transmitted to industry. As it was later worked out, above all in the Commodities Section, all power was concentrated in the hands of specialists, operating through existing business mechanisms. Three hundred and fifty industries were represented by some sixty "sections." The approach to an industry was through the proper "section," acting for the government, and the answer came from a "committee," often staffed with the strongest men in the industry, operating jointly for their companies' and their country's welfare.[86]

The "sections" and "committees" were the key to the whole scheme. Baruch had no fears, as Wilson had, of the submergence of the government by big business. He knew that no important businessman could afford to work against his government in his own interests; his industry would know that he was false. "There could be no better watchman than one of their own kind." It was impossible "for any first-class kind of man to be false and make a deal and survive it." [87] But Baruch had taken no chances; the system of checks and balances that he had evolved was watertight.

As overseas the echo of Prussian goosesteps sounded louder, Bernard Baruch concentrated on plans for industrial mobilization for modern war. Just how big the concept was, Baruch himself may not have realized. But on his return from the West, at McAdoo's request, his plan was laid before President Wilson — one of the most clear-cut of the proposed plans.

In the autumn of 1916 Baruch heard of the possibility of his appointment to the projected new Advisory Commission to the Council of National Defense, and immediately hurried to Colonel House, begging him to get him off. "Well, it was your idea," was the Colonel's answer. Next, Baruch protested to McAdoo, pointing out that he was a Wall Street man. Both House and McAdoo remained unimpressed. President Wilson was away on a trip to Indianapolis. Before his return, the appointment of Baruch was announced from the presidential train.

The Senate was something less than amenable. "Who is Baruch?" was their attitude, and when told that he was a Wall Street man, they were hardly reassured. Senator Claude Swanson put a question to McAdoo: "How strong is this fellow?"

"Any goddam fellow tries to interfere with him, he'll knock his block off," McAdoo answered cheerfully.[88] More support came from Senator Charles E. Thomas. Baruch was everlastingly grateful when Thomas rose to explain that as an attorney for certain Baruch partners named George Nixon and George Wingfield, he had discovered that Baruch had stood by them in a time of grave financial disaster. Had he cared to do so, he could have taken over their mining enterprises for his own enrichment; instead, he had helped put them back on their feet. Thomas quoted their words: "No man ever acted with such generosity." [89] The Senate listened and voted for Baruch's confirmation.

Actually, the appointment of the "Wall Street man" stirred far less comment than was expected. To the country at large Baruch was almost unknown. This was quickly changed. Like a skyrocket, his name flashed before the people in a burst of pyrotechnics worthy of the man who was to remain silhouetted in the public mind for the next forty years. His was a worthy entrance, and it happened during the so-called "leak investigation" of 1917.

Officially it had begun on December 18, 1916, when Wilson dispatched his "Peace Note" to the Allied and Central Powers. Actually, it had started some three weeks before. As early as December 5 the rumors of peace negotiations started. On December 15, a bear raid on the Stock Exchange had driven the market down some four to ten points. Nearly two and a half million shares changed hands. There was more short selling on the eighteenth and on the twentieth, but on the twenty-second came the most violent slump in fifteen years. The list sagged from fifteen to thirty points.[90] Then in headlines across the country appeared the name of Baruch,[91] the man the President had just named to his Advisory Commission! "Baruch Made Fortune in Big Market Crash" — "Baruch Used 'Tip' Rumor House Hears." [92] From New York to San Francisco, the press trumpeted of a "big leak" on the President's peace message, of a private pipeline between the White House and Wall Street, and of a secret breakfast or luncheon meeting between the President's secretary, Joseph P. Tumulty, and Bernard Baruch, rumored to be the largest of the Democratic campaign contributors.[93]

Tumulty exploded. "Tumulty Demands Apology," rang the headlines. Why, he scarcely knew Bernard Baruch; certainly, he had never had lunch with him. From "Hobcaw Barony," Baruch's plantation in Georgetown, South Carolina, came the first of many communiqués

to the nation. In the form of a letter to the New York *American*,
Baruch explained that the only information he had received was in
the form of an ordinary stock market circular. Peace rumors were
in the air. He had never received a tip, nor had he ever eaten a meal
with Joseph Tumulty.[94] His self-assurance, however, was a veneer;
here perhaps was the end of the whole new life he had been building
for himself. Close to this time, his friend Garet Garrett found him
in tears.[95]

Garrett set himself the task of doing what he could to clear
Baruch's name, while Congress probed into the charges. In January
the "big leak" inquiry was launched, and from a New York pulpit
the Reverend Edward Young thundered a denunciation of "the
World, the Flesh, and the Devil" and of Wall Street as a "doubly
distilled extract of deviltry." [96]

In Washington, the "Red Devil" himself held the floor. Hard-
visaged, walrus-mustached Thomas R. Lawson, an ex-speculator
turned muckraker but still sporting a red devil on his letter paper,
bandied about the name of Baruch and others in his "leak" charges.
Garrett meanwhile warned him to retract and tell the congressional
committee the truth, that Baruch was clean, and that "none of this
ever touched him." [97] At last, Lawson agreed to do so.*

Baruch appeared at the hearings on the fifteenth of January, a
beautifully tailored black overcoat accentuating his height and slen-
derness. He had presence, an air of command. For the first time
he faced the crowding, the clamor, the close-knit tension of a congressional committee room. Flash bulbs popped into his face; voices
roared and echoed in his injured ear. With his inherent grasp of
histrionics, Baruch rose to the occasion. Almost casually, he stepped
before the table and gave his name. Then came the moment. The
chairman leaned forward and asked his profession. A half-stifled
gasp went up at the answer. Baruch lifted his head and spoke the
words his friend Eugene Meyer had advised him to use. "I am a
speculator," he said.

He elaborated to the newspapermen. "A speculator," he said,
thoughtfully, "is one who thinks and plans for a future event — and
acts before it occurs. And a speculator must always be right." [98]

---

* Years later, Lawson went broke and asked Baruch for a loan of a quarter of a
million dollars. Garrett advised against it on the grounds that the only favor
Lawson ever did for Baruch was to tell the truth. Baruch, who knew nothing of
Garrett's part in Lawson's reversal of testimony, also said, "My answer is no."
Otherwise, it would look as though he had been guilty.

His case was already half won, and he knew it. The congressional inquisitors had long been building up their "revelation" that this unknown member of the Advisory Commission was no banker or financier of respectability but a Wall Street speculator, and now the cork had been pulled from the bottle. Baruch stretched his long legs in front of him. His nerves had been tempered in fiercer fires than these, and in the first of his many congressional "appearances" he betrayed no sign of strain. It was as if he had inscribed a little circle of intimacy around himself and his accusers. It was as if he were there not for a grilling but as an honored guest, as if the Committee were not one of inquisition but of mere inquiry. He was obviously in high good humor. Congress, he was sure, could handle Wall Street, and this was "the finest body of men he had ever spoken to." [99]

Assuredly, this was not the usual manner of approach toward congressional committees. The reporters leaned forward with interest. This man, observed the Philadelphia *Public Ledger*, was "the best witness that has so far been on the stand," and the only one who made a good impression. [100]

Leisurely, in the favorite pose of his office, he leaned back in his chair. He clasped his hands behind his head. In the tone of a weather reporter, softened now and again by the drawl of the South, he began to talk. He was as "plain as an old shoe," one reporter observed. Laughter bubbled in the wake of his easy humor. Somewhat scornfully he brushed aside queries of tips and rumors. If such existed, they did not interest him. "I never pay any attention to Wall Street rumors," he said.

Pulling a long finger down a column of figures, he began to illustrate. Hundreds could have read what he did; he had known nothing about President Wilson's "Peace Note." Then he brought out the records of his brokerage house. He had begun to sell on December 10 during the up-flurry of peace talk, inspired by the German Chancellor, Bethmann Hollweg. Over the telegraph wires had come Lloyd George's official rejection, modified, however, by the word "but." That left the door open. "I went to it as light and fast as I could when I saw the word 'but' on the ticker."

The peace talk died down. Then he had made a mistake, and he offered his books to prove it. He had "covered" on December 20. Had he had advance knowledge of Wilson's note, he would have continued to "sell short"; he would not have switched to the long side. He had been in error. This he admitted, with all the regret of hurt professional pride.[101]

Someone interrupted at that point to inquire how much he had made on the entire transaction.

"My net profit amounted to four hundred seventy-six thousand, one hundred sixty-eight dollars and forty-seven cents," Baruch answered.[102]

A sigh rose across the silence of the committee room. Baruch sighed in his turn and leaned back wearily, and Congressmen and spectators gaped as he told of what he might have made had foreknowledge of the "note" been available to him. As for what he had done, he brushed off praise. "They were fair operations," he said, "but I've done better." To the *New York Times*, it seemed that he had done quite well indeed without help, but he was obviously mournful that he had missed an opportunity.[103] Shortly thereafter he was excused from further testimony, and almost at once, talk of the "note" and "the leak" was dropped from the papers. " 'Barney' Baruch about ended the 'leak' investigation," the Philadelphia *Public Ledger* commented.

Investigation of Baruch himself, however, was only beginning. For weeks he was the subject of editorial speculation and controversy. Not only the audacity of his testimony, but his unparalleled self-confidence had tickled the interest of a nation. As the *Public Ledger* observed, "He has a wonderful belief in 'Barney' Baruch." [104] Was it not justified? Alone among men, the Salt Lake *Tribune* observed, he had foreseen a peace drive; he alone had moved into the "upper atmosphere of prophecy and statesmanship." There was no need now to wonder why some men did not "need to work for a living." He had taken the money from his fellow speculators "as if he were taking candy from babes." [105] Later, the New York *Financial American* commented on the foolish wave of short selling which followed in the wake of the leak investigation. The attitude had been that if a man like Baruch did not think he could make money on the long side of the market, what chance was there for a little fellow? [106]

To each generation, its own war seems the most terrible and the last that a suffering humanity can endure. Yet there is truth in Ernest Hemingway's reflection that so far as the individual fighting man is concerned, there are "no worse things to be gone through than men have gone through before." [107]

The First World War was not alone the first of the new wars; it was also the last of the old. In that "Unknown War" on the Eastern Front, cavalry horses screamed and sank in the marshes, and men, untold miles from lights and roads and railways, fought and froze and starved and died on the same blood-soaked plains where the legions of Napoleon had perished little over a hundred years before.

No man of sensitivity could watch unmoved, even those who only in their imaginations saw the pock-marked fields and the red rockets spitting up against a black sky; or heard drumming the "ceaseless cannonade" in which "heroic human beings were torn to pieces," or the moans, groans, and "last screams of death." Later Winston Churchill, in stately cadences, would record what he had seen among the sand dunes of Belgium, the "snarling lines" of barbed wire, twisting down from Switzerland to the sea, entangled with corpses, swaying and lapped by seaweed and tide. They had lain there for months, groups of ten or twelve, still in their attitudes of slaughter and attack, until the sand had softened their outlines, and "it was as if Nature were gathering them to herself." [108]

To Churchill, doing penance in the lines for the disaster at Gallipoli, it seemed in retrospect as if all Europe were not only a battleground but a burying ground for the youth of a generation. What nations could endure such blows and survive? [109]

Over the width of an ocean, a certain perspective — and even objectivity — could be obtained. Machine warfare meant less mass warfare; wars, in the end, would be won by "the scientific application of industrial forces." [110] Bernard Baruch, even before America's entry into the conflict, had been building his famed fact-finding organization, keeping men busy "digging up facts, correlating them, relating them, particularly to the mobilization of national and industrial resources for the waging of war." [111] Baruch by heritage knew the German mind, knew that for Germany peace was merely an interval between wars; and that in America, in contrast, there had been no effective mingling of the industrial and military power. [112]

Despite the later ascendancy of isolationism and the understandable reluctance of the Wilson Administration, there seems to have been more of a national will toward defense than in the advance days of the Second World War. The idea of a Council of National Defense, for instance, had been broached by General Leonard Wood even before 1910, written into the Democratic platform of 1912, and partially provided for by the National Defense Act of 1916, which enabled the President to "place orders for war material directly with any source of supply," and under which the Council of National Defense was established. As evolved, this finally seemed to the Secretary of War "the most amazing baby that was ever put on the War Department steps." Even Wilson acknowledged, "This is admirable; this is extraordinary," — a real concession from him, for he was torn with conflict over peace and preparation.[113] Yet as late as 1916 an American army of 200,000 was deemed adequate; and to the impetuous urging of the Under-Secretary of the Navy that the fleet be fitted out and made ready, the President's answer was, "I am very sorry, Mr. Roosevelt, I cannot allow it."

Roosevelt pleaded; he could not budge Wilson. But as he started for the door, he stopped at the President's abrupt summons. "Come back. I am going to tell you something. I don't want to do anything. I don't want the United States to do anything in a military way, by way of war preparedness that would allow the definitive historian in later days to say that the United States had committed an unfriendly act against the Central Powers." [114]

Nevertheless, the Council of National Defense was pushed through at the quiet insistence of President Wilson and his Secretaries of War, Navy, and Labor, "avowed pacifists all." [115] The decision was reached in a tense Cabinet session, where Newton D. Baker, calling himself a pacifist, demanded, "How would we more effectively dissuade these would-be enemies than through preparation?" Josephus Daniels, his emotions breaking to the surface, repeated that he was morally, spiritually, and nationally opposed to war; yet, if destroyers of the peace attacked, there was but one answer — "repel them to the utmost limit." [116]

The Council of National Defense was composed exclusively of Cabinet officers, but an "Advisory Commission" to the Council was appointed by the President and became its operative part.[117] The first official meeting of the Advisory Commission was held in a Washington hotel room on the evening of December 7, 1916, in an atmosphere of uncertainty and confusion, no one quite knowing why he was there or what was expected of him. The membership was made up of the lean, classic-featured Dr. Franklin Martin, director-general of the American College of Surgeons; Julius Rosenwald of Sears, Roebuck, a "prince of good fellows" who made you like him more with each passing day; the president of the Baltimore and Ohio Railroad, Daniel Willard, with alert blue eyes and outthrust lower lip;

Howard Coffin, vice-president of the Hudson Motor Company, all ideas and ideals; Dr. Hollis Godfrey, president of the Drexel Institute of Philadelphia, who had been one of the earliest proponents of industrial mobilization; Bernard Baruch; and the man who above all interested the others, the aging, leonine Samuel Gompers.

Probably none of that group could in their wildest dreams have imagined the warmth of affection which Gompers was to inspire in them. Baruch was enchanted with the man; to him, he was soon the "dear Old Chief," just as he was to his "boys" in the union. Daniel Willard expressed the feelings of the group: "If anyone had told me that my personal antagonism towards Samuel Gompers would change within a week to ardent admiration and real affection, I would have pronounced that individual a fit candidate for an insane asylum." He won them from the first, this stocky little figure with the giant head and a personality equally large. British-born, Gompers when not yet in his teens had been laboring in the filth of a cigar-maker's shop and there heard the workmen debating slavery, freedom, Abraham Lincoln, and the Civil War, and now, telling that story, he won each of the Commission members.

The next morning the group met again, this time in the rococo corridors of the old State, War, and Navy building. A moment later they were ushered into the War Office, with its long windows, the walls dimmed with portraits out of the past. As Baruch came in, his gaze fell first upon the big mahogany table with the Council of National Defense grouped around it and the waiting row of chairs opposite. In the center, one foot curled beneath him and his little briar-root "pacifier" pipe tight clamped between his lips, Newton D. Baker, the "Little Giant," sat waiting. Neither then nor later was any love lost between Baruch and Baker, but for each other they had a certain professional respect. There was an impersonality about Baker that invited opposition.[118]

Baker had a look of bottled-up intensity. His dark eyes were sharp behind the pince-nez. His brief welcome to the "specialists" was gracious, but there was no reason, he said, to waste time on preliminaries. The question of universal military training was introduced bluntly by Rosenwald, who then questioned the members of the Council. The sentiment was evident, a show of hands rather than a vote, out of deference to Gompers, whose bitter sentiments on war and compulsory service were well known.

After a later meeting, lunch was at the Army and Navy Club.

There Secretary Daniels and Secretary of Commerce William C. Redfield regaled the members with fish stories and Southern hospitality. By afternoon they arrived at the White House, where Wilson greeted them cordially, one by one.

Next, Wilson asked the group to be seated, and sat down with them as a discussion ensued, led by Godfrey, but with the President "taking a lively part." Finally, he said that he "expected much help from us, bade us farewell, and retired." [119] Obediently the group left, scarcely more enlightened now as to "the business at hand" than they had been at their first meeting the night before.

Later afternoon sessions in the President's "study," the old Cabinet Room where Lincoln and his officers had debated freedom and slavery, peace or war, would become imprinted on Baruch's memory. The group would assemble in the Red Room, then mount the stairs to find Wilson waiting just inside the door, shaking hands with each as they passed, and adding a pleasant "How are you, Martin?" or "Hello, Baruch." The study was on the south side of the White House, overlooking the Potomac, and it was as simple and austere as Wilson himself. There was no table, only the well-ordered flat-top desk presented to the United States government by Queen Victoria, which on cold days reflected gleams from the flames of the fireplace. A simple green student lamp stood at one side and an office chair behind the desk.[120] There were a few comfortable chairs, but for the dubious benefit of the War Cabinet and Advisory Commission, the usual straight, back-breaking chairs were lugged in, while Wilson removed a bouquet of flowers from his desk and passed out cigars to those who wanted them. For the thirsty, there were drinks of water — not even Secretary Daniels' persimmon beer violated the Puritan austerity at the White House,[121] but the atmosphere was not wholly lacking in humanity. On noticing the lanky Baruch twisting his legs around the chair, Wilson might pause to ask if he were comfortable; or, like another great and hard-pressed President who had gazed on that same river from the window of that same room, might lean back and tell a story before launching into the factual details of the problems of peace and war.

Slowly, the Commission was becoming aware of the truth that no one quite dared put into words: "the business at hand" was that of preparing their country for war. Then, like other well-intentioned groups before and since, they became bogged down with the question of "seven different standpoints" on procedure alone. Darkness was filling the room with shadows. All were weary. Finally at five o'clock, Gompers said that he could dictate a plan that would crystallize the consensus if he only had a stenographer.[122]

Wearily, the tired men relaxed. Gompers threw his shaggy head against the back of his big chair, pressed his cigar more tightly between his lips and turned his eyes ceilingward. For fifteen minutes, scarcely stopping to breathe, he dictated, then broke off with a sudden "Please read that, Mr. Stenographer." The result, virtually "a miracle of perfection," evoked a spontaneous burst of applause. But the Old Chief brushed off praise. "To be a successful organizer," he said, "requires the lowest type of mentality." [123]

A course had been set through the uncharted seas, but the Commission was still vague as to its responsibilities. The members knew they were part of a virtual "War Cabinet" to help "plan, execute and direct" the activities of government in preparation for war. But what could they do? Not until February, at Secretary Lane's suggestion, did they divide into committees. Willard took transportation; Coffin, munitions, manufacturing, and industrial relations; Rosenwald, dry goods, clothing, and supplies. Gompers was in charge of labor, including the maintenance of the health of workers. Godfrey would undertake a survey of resources and engineers. Martin, of course, would supervise medicine, surgery, and general sanitation.

Raw materials were logically left to Baruch. "Raw materials looked the dullest; no one else wanted it," he said afterwards. Baruch wanted it; he felt it was "the key to everything." In choosing raw materials, he had taken another step toward becoming chairman of the War Industries Board. He told David Lawrence, "If you understand raw materials, you understand the politics of the world." [124] Baruch knew from his own dark memories of Reconstruction that wars were won not by armies alone but by the economic resources of the people. Sheridan had perceived this truth fifty years before, and so had Sherman, but the lessons of economic warfare in all-out war were not yet understood.

Another member of the Advisory Commission was also aware of the facts of survival. This was Howard E. Coffin, who from 1915 until 1916 not only headed the volunteer Committee on Industrial Preparedness, but also canvassed 20,000 manufacturers to discover their war potential and "to fill the gap that Congress had long ignored." [125]

The achievements of the later War Industries Board have overshadowed the very real accomplishments of the Advisory Commission. Without precedent, without power, the Commission drove ahead and gave the impetus, not only for the War Industries Board, but for the entire war effort. A committee of the House of Representatives reported that this committee of seven men planned the system of purchasing war supplies, a press censorship, a system of food control, with Herbert Hoover as its director; decided on a daylight-saving scheme, and, in short, had "discussed and settled upon" almost every war measure which Congress subsequently enacted, all before the United States had entered the war.[126]

Finally, one day in February, Gompers asked permission to make a personal statement. His voice was low, but its intensity held his listeners.

"I have always been uncompromisingly against war," he began. Even as a child, he had felt the suffering in the heart of Lincoln and had seen a vision of America, where slavery and war would be abolished for all time to come.

"Ten million men are now looking to me for guidance," he said. "Aggression is in the air . . . Another great President is struggling to find another way out. We have planned for war . . . and in this . . . I, too, reluctantly have been associated."

His weary head fell into his hands. His voice broke. Then suddenly he raised his head.

"By God's help I can no longer stand it. War to suppress crime is justifiable; and with all my energy and influence I will induce my boys . . . to follow me." [127]

The Advisory Commission to the Council of National Defense was more than a testing ground for methods and concepts of war. It was a proving ground for men. To know and accept Samuel Gompers had broadened the understanding of each man there. Old prejudices were breaking away. There was, for instance, Daniel Willard, whose strong distrust of Wall Street had centered on Baruch. Characteristically, Baruch "overlooked the whole thing." They became friends, Baruch meeting intolerance with tolerance.

Gompers, meanwhile, held to his word. At the session of March 23, he reported on a March 12 meeting where the heads of the trades unions had acclaimed Willard for his aid in a satisfactory settlement of the railroad strike. Gompers also said that credit was due to Commissioner Baruch. Up sprang Willard to point out that Gompers did not sufficiently stress his own part, adding, however, that Baruch had given valuable aid.[128]

It is noticeable in these meetings of the Advisory Commission how little talking Baruch did. He sat silent among his companions, yet struck bedrock from the start. In January, while Willard had been investigating how the railroads could be used in event of war, Baruch had sounded the keynote of the future War Industries Board. He had been privately studying the steel and metal industries, and wanted to consult further with authorities to find out from the trades what they could do and "how to get their resources together." Secretary Lane's suggestion of February 12 for conferences with leading men in essential industries was perhaps inspired by Baruch.[129]

At the meeting of March 12, Baruch had revealed that committees had already been formed in leather, rubber, steel, copper, wool, zinc, oil, and coal; that others were in the process of formation, and that stockpiles would be built of certain raw materials not found in the United States, such as nitrate of soda and rubber. The United States, he knew, was already lacking in metals of unmeasured value.[130]

Advice poured in on the Commission, and often that which was the least desirable was the most persistent. Now and then extraordinary matters invaded the sessions, as when Dr. Martin read aloud the recommendation of a military medical committee that sexual continence be advised as the best preventative of venereal disease. Furthermore, the prohibitionists had hit upon the war as an instrument in their long fought fight, and had no hesitation in speaking out on the matter. Baruch, like his fellow members of the Advisory Commission, arrived for the meeting of April 17 loaded with letters and telegrams of protest.

Samuel Gompers opened the business. Furiously he reared to his feet and thrust a finger in the direction of Dr. Martin.

"What have you been doing? Sold out to the so-called 'social hygienists' and prohibition fanatics . . . When have our fighting men been preached to on the value of continence . . . Real men will be men."

Fighting back a smile, Martin addressed the chair, declared Mr. Gompers to be out of order, and submitted the resolutions which he had prepared.

"Well, read them all," Gompers grumbled. Martin explained that he had done so and Gompers subsided, muttering that he did not see anything the matter with them. They were promptly adopted, plus one amendment by Gompers that alcohol and prostitutes be controlled, rather than prohibited. Later, noting the failure of law-enforced morality in the prohibition experiment, Baruch and Martin concluded that Gompers had been right.[131]

The Commission members tackled problem after problem. They considered the possible exploitation or Americanization of foreign-born workers; the tensions and overcrowding of war-boom cities; the maintenance of traditional standards of labor, all toward increasing the efficiency of workers. They read a telegram from Democratic committeeman Gavin McNab of California, urging that "idle lands, like idle hands, should be put to work"; and on Baruch's motion, urged the increasing of government oil reserves. This suggestion was later contravened by Josephus Daniels, who was convinced that "the drive was not purely in the interest of the government." [132]

A committee met with Baruch to increase the efficiency of the mines.[133] The "cost-plus" formula for government contracts was considered. Engineering resources were being coordinated, and by the first of April the Commission would even have suggestions on how to eliminate naval tie-ups in the harbors.[134]

Suggestions they had, but not authority. They were legally powerless and too often were actually ignored. Too often their tacit jurisdiction overlapped that of the General Munitions Board. Meetings were held in an atmosphere of increasing tension, doubt, and uncertainty. Again and again the members voiced the need for central authority. It was a need that grew ever greater as the darkness of war spread closer and closer —

War was coming.

They knew it on that second Inaugural Day, as streets flamed gay with bunting and were shadowed by somber faces. They heard it in the words of Wilson, weighted with foreboding, as he spoke of men "shaken . . . everywhere with a passion and an apprehension they never knew before." [135]

It was Wilson upon whom the burden lay; Wilson, facing perhaps the darkest hours yet to confront an American President.[136] Pressures were bearing in upon him: young Franklin Roosevelt, urging that the government arm merchant ships; McAdoo, beating the drums for dictatorial powers for the Presidency; March 1, and the State Department counselor, Frank Cobb, repeating that he did not see how

America could avoid a declaration of war now; March 5, and Baruch at lunch, brows knit with concern.

Almost two years earlier Bryan had foreseen the inevitable. One day Commander John Hancock had seen him outside the old State Department. His head was sunk on his chest. Hancock had little use for the leader of lost causes, whom he described as "a volume of sound with the mouth of a frog," but something in the dejection of the man caught his sympathy. A few moments later Daniels emerged and laid his arm around Hancock's shoulder. "Bryan is resigning today. I think that means war." [137] Hancock later learned that on that day the Cabinet had voted to send the *Lusitania* note.

On March 20 Wilson called the Cabinet into session for advice on the question that he alone could answer. All were tense, yet the President was smiling as genially as if it were an ordinary occasion.

McAdoo spoke first, softly, but with measured earnestness. War was certain; why delay? No doubts troubled Robert Lansing, Bryan's successor, who had spent the previous day preparing a letter on the advantages of entering the war right away. He spoke so loudly and with such vehemence that Wilson cautioned him to lower his voice — those in the hall outside might hear. Daniels was in tears.[138]

At last Wilson was alone with the decision. His was the responsibility, his the mind that whirled like a squirrel on a wheel as he lay sleepless, night after night. Where was the right and where the wrong in the duty before him? [139] He had said that war would be the supreme irony of his administration, the direct moral violation of all in which he believed. War would increase the domination of finance and big business over public affairs, "the insolence of aggrandized wealth."

Were American ideals or American dollars at stake? American capital had been sunk into huge speculative loans to the Allies, who, it now appeared, were too drained either to win or to pay. Were American lives to be hurled as dice for American dollars? Was German imperialism more foreboding to the world's future than the so-called ally of freedom, czarist Russia, which was "a lesser menace than Prussia, not because her morals were better, but only because her railroad system was worse. Europe, in its desperation, had to use the lesser barbarian in order to destroy the greater." [140] For Wilson there were no compromises.

So in the night silences the President wrestled, and just after mid-

night on the morning of April 1 he greeted his old friend Frank Cobb.
They talked, in a little circle of light pushing back the encroaching
darkness. Wilson was "sad beyond thought." [141] The cup was before
him, but could he drink? American belligerency, he said, would
mean the end of neutral opinion and the beginning of new wars; for
none would be left to invoke the terms that meant peace for the
future. "If there is any alternative," he cried out to Cobb, "for God's
sake let's take it." Cobb saw none. America's hand, he said, was
forced by Germany.[142]

Rain was falling softly on April 2, 1917. Like ants out of a hill,
crowds swirled around the White House, waving little ten-cent-store
flags. Senator Lodge had a fist fight with a pacifist; in the drizzle,
Wilson grimly played golf. In his bedroom, aided by his valet, Lacey,
Bernard Baruch dressed for the joint session of Congress, emerging
into the late twilight where the Capitol dome glimmered against a
waterlogged sky.

It was a night and a gathering "the like of which the capital . . .
had never seen," as Josephus Daniels recorded afterward. All were
there, the ambassadors in full dress, glittering like the jewels in the
crown of an Indian potentate; the Cabinet; the Supreme Court,
ranged in a dusky half-circle before the speaker's stand, the figure of
Chief Justice White "towering like Saul among prophets" — White,
the ex-Confederate, who wished now that he were thirty years younger
and could "join up" as a volunteer.

Baruch's sharp eyes could pick faces out of the melee: sober Champ
Clark; the ever serene Tom Marshall; North Carolina's Claude
Kitchin, who had taunted the House with the shout, "It takes neither
physical nor mental courage to vote for a war which someone else will
have to fight"; Lodge, sardonically smiling. It was an awed gathering
with a tense kind of stillness, as if there rested upon it "the life and
death of nations and peoples the world over." [143]

Then you heard the clatter of cavalry hoofs on the paving and the
rush and stir as the House rose for the ovation at the cry, "The President of the United States." Wilson moved forward. Years afterward
Starling, the Secret Service chief, remembered the sound of his heavy
step and the feel of his dead weight against his arm.[144] Baruch saw
him, erect and looking even taller than usual in his austere black, the
lines cut across his pale face as if by a saber. To Daniels he seemed
as one who "had come to that moment through great travail." [145]

The moment had come. For a flash the onlookers saw the President's white face lift toward the gallery where his wife and daughters looked down. A murmur of whispering followed in his wake; as he had walked in, word had come that the American ship *Aztec* had sunk under enemy attack.

Now he was ready for the "fearful thing to lead this great and powerful people into war." Calmly he turned to his manuscript, resting his arm on the high desk before him. Occasionally he looked up; he had no other gesture. His voice was husky, but the words and the meaning were clear. The look of the prophet was on him, the evangelist calling for a last crusade. "We will not choose the path of submission," he shouted, and up sprang the Chief Justice, tears shining on his face, and from his lips, echoing across the hall, came a cry that sent a chill down Baruch's back and Daniels' and Wilson's and all of Southern blood — the rebel yell, the war cry of Shiloh and Fredericksburg.[146]

Wilson continued and concluded: "America is privileged to spend her blood and her might for the principles that gave her birth and happiness and the peace that she has treasured. God helping her, she can do no other." There was the grim-faced Kitchin, and La Follette, rigid in unmoving silence as the applause thundered out, and up stepped Lodge to be the first to congratulate the Chief Executive. "Mr. President," he said, "you have expressed in the loftiest manner the sentiments of the American people."

That night, led by old Chief Justice White, the American people marched. Crazed by hate and lust for victory, they marched. Bernard Baruch could have heard them storming and shouting through the streets, the uproar drowned by the tinny notes of "Dixie" or "The Star-spangled Banner." Wilson heard them, too, as they crowded around the gates of the Executive Mansion. Sick with revulsion, he turned to Tumulty. "Think what it means, the applause. My message tonight was a message of death to our young men. How strange to applaud that!" And suddenly the President of the United States dropped his head on the table before him and "sobbed as if he had been a child." [147]

7

"GENERAL EYE"

SECRETARY OF WAR Newton D. Baker stumbled. Groping his way through the dark and dust of the basement of the old State, War, and Navy building, he had come up against a pile of crates, towering from the floor to the ceiling. As he peered through the dimness, he saw that each was marked for the Adjutant General's office. They were tightly sealed. What did they contain? A few moments later he had the Adjutant General on the telephone, and also the Adjutant General's explanation.

The crates, it seemed, contained typewriters. Typewriters were necessary for the war effort, so the Adjutant General had bought up typewriters! Because if he hadn't, the Surgeon General would have, and if not the Surgeon General, the Navy or the Treasury Department. He was sure that the Secretary of War would understand.

Secretary Baker did understand. The confusion in the basement was but one example of the general confusion across the country. In the stampede of rush orders by government bureaus, prices were rising to incredible heights; goods were piling up on the docks before the ships were built to transport them, or lying loose in freight yards and meadows waiting for the manufacture of new trains. Thus was competition working in a war economy, the competition of each single group to excel the other and win the war.

It was July in Washington, the hot, sodden July of 1917. On the eighth, Daniel Willard requested a meeting of the Advisory Commission. He faced the members with the light of accusation in his eyes. He had just visited his son in an army camp, and the weight of his responsibility for that young life and all the others to be offered up for freedom overcame him. The Commission was responsible to those young men — for food, equipment, life itself. Fiercely he challenged his fellow members. Was each doing his utmost? His hopes, his thoughts, his fears all flowed forth; looking on him, Baruch may have seen him as the perceptive medical officer Martin saw him: "an overworked man, with the horrors of sleepless hours of midnight and dawn in his mind." [1]

So Baruch and the others pondered. All that month the tension did not ease. Secretary Baker's reassurances only troubled them. What they had done was miraculous, he told them; yet how little had been done to solve the real problems! Every man should work sixteen hours a day. Again and again, Willard stressed the necessity for "central authority and decisive information." [2]

A reorganization began to get under way, and the name, if not the fact, of the War Industries Board was born. Baruch's part began as early as October 1915, when he drew up a plan for a defense, munition, or mobilization committee, the genesis of what later came to be the War Industries Board, and gave an outline of his plan to the President.[3] Now this new organization began to take shape, to be responsible to the Advisory Commission; also to take over the Commission's actual functions and to swallow up the overlapping General Munitions Board, whose "funeral" was held on July 31. The chairman of the new War Industries Board, Frank Augustus Scott, presided at the obsequies, and was hailed by the enthusiastic Rosenwald as "the Lloyd George of America." [4]

Besides Scott and Baruch, who was again in charge of raw materials, the personnel * included Robert Lovett, who first supervised priorities and in whom Baruch ran up against anti-Jewish prejudice, but this was soon overcome. In charge of finished products was the honest, courageous St. Louis philanthropist Robert S. Brookings, who shared Baruch's respect for centralized authority and his gift for striking through to fundamentals.

Guardian of the "human factor in production" was Samuel Gompers' representative, Hugh Frayne, a first-rate appointment,

---

* At the Armistice, the Board was composed as follows: Bernard M. Baruch, chairman; Alex Legge, vice-chairman; E. B. Parker and R. S. Brookings, price-fixing; George N. Peek, commissioner of finished products; Major General George W. Goethals, Army; Rear Admiral F. F. Fletcher, Navy; J. Leonard Replogle, steel; Hugh Frayne, labor; Leland Summers, technical adviser; H. P. Ingels, secretary; and Herbert Bayard Swope, Clarence Dillon, Harrison Williams, and Harold T. Clark, assistants to the chairman.

Baruch thought. With him on the Board, labor was on the "inside"; and there were no dealings with business in which labor was not represented. But although Frayne stood guard for labor, his patriotism came first.

Rear Admiral F. F. Fletcher represented the Navy. He was "a regular fellow," who won Baruch's heart by writing the shortest letters in Washington — and by demanding and getting action. Sitting in for the nominal Army representative, Colonel Palmer E. Price, was usually the hard-bitten, youthful future brigadier general, Hugh S. Johnson. For all his unruly emotionalism, Johnson caught Baruch's attention by the order and keenness of his mind. Johnson even had regulations for the draft printed and ready before the Selective Service Act was passed. The intelligent and highly geared young attorney for the group was Albert Ritchie of Maryland.[5]

Chairman Scott did not last long. Hard-driven and hard-driving as he was, not even the comparative youth of this Cleveland manufacturer could endure the pace he set. His nerves broke under the strain in November — he resigned and Daniel Willard replaced him.

But not even such a strong executive as Willard could make up for the lack of authority in the Board. Certain objectives were attained: in conservation, for instance; in the beginning of price-fixing; and in an appraisal of the labor and material resources of the country. Even the Inter-Allied Purchasing Commission now got under way. But all this was not enough for Willard or for Bernard Baruch. In the privacy of his room at night Baruch released his feelings in a few diary entries through the fall and winter of 1917–18. "The more committees, the more lack of coördination," he wrote. "No one wants to give the power to one man."

"All these men get everybody's advice, and then take the wrong advice," and, "I would rather do the wrong thing than wait till the right thing becomes . . . wrong . . ." "What is everybody's job is nobody's job."

"The confusion is greater and not less here." (This was on January 19.) "No one has a plan and all seem too tired to do anything except to criticize." [6]

His entries foreshadowed the exit of Willard, who really bore the burden of this first War Industries Board, and as Baruch knew, did everything that could be done without a real organization.[7]

For the "reorganization" that had set up the War Industries Board had been largely theoretical. Reckless commandeering flourished. "Perhaps in despair at the Board's lack of vigor," and facing Army ambitions, Secretary Baker for a while thought the Board should be replaced by an Army group.[8] The row finally burst into the papers, where Willard and Baruch's declaration was given as "Munitions Is One Man's Job," which was promptly countered by the headline that Baker claimed "Munitions Job Too Big For One." But the clamor continued, with the War Industries Board fighting for genuine powers to establish itself as a single, unified agency for all Army, Navy, and Federal purchasing, under a single "Industrial Dictator," as Baker disapprovingly commented.[9] The resignation of Willard brought matters into focus. He was infuriated with the new limitations that hamstrung him. He told Wilson that the President expected the impossible. No organization could have more authority than the board that created it. Any reorganized War Industries Board must be more than the creature of the Advisory Commission. It must derive its power from the President himself.

Wilson wondered. To him it seemed that only a superman could fill such a job. And where was such a superman to be found? [10]

Dr. Alvin Johnson, then a scholar-journalist endeavoring to survey the real needs of the warring governmental departments, first saw Baruch as he stepped out from a White House conference. "That man," said Johnson's companion, "is the biggest menace in America. Big capitalist, ruthless speculator, he leads the flock of big business cormorants that has settled down on Washington."

Johnson never forgot this first look at Baruch. "He seemed enormously tall against the White House door, straight . . . and slender as modernist sculpture, with a sunshine of content illuminating his strikingly handsome face." Around the offices of the War Industries Board, Johnson heard more stories. Baruch was a menace, indeed, he heard again, but this time "a menace to big business." He had stripped himself of all personal financial interests, had nothing to gain and no "special interests" to please. He had never played with the "inside." He had come to Washington with no axe to grind, seeking only to put his talents at the service of his country.[11] To Johnson he seemed relaxed, but the professor later realized that horizon-wide calculations were going on behind his quiet face.

At that period Baruch loomed among his fellows, wrote his associate Martin, "like a giant sequoia," and it was obvious that he was

assuming more and more of the burden of decision.[12] Few had a
more diversified knowledge of the American industrial economy than
he.[13] His associates knew their own fields, but Baruch knew the picture as a whole. Johnson, who was at sea in a storm of "monstrous
confusion . . . one power cancelling out another," saw "forty departments, more or less, each jealous of the other, each in a mad scramble
to gather up all the wool, all the copper — or all the surplus typewriters in the country." Before this time, there had never been such
an adequate survey of American economic power, and Baruch had a
concept of how that power might be made to work.[14] As Commander
Hancock of the Navy purchasing committee said, "Here was a man
who knew so damn many things I didn't even know were problems."
He knew the "key men" in every industry — not the "front" men,
but those lesser-known figures who knew the future of their companies. "If you wanted to get experts in any field, he knew where to find
them." He could deal with diverse groups, calmly and with understanding.

"Just a Wall Street speculator," [15] the politicians said, dismissing
him, or silently or verbally damned him for being a Jew. Yet the
same Wall Street that made him anathema politically had taught
him what it was now indispensable to know.

Baruch has been condemned for remaining silent in his own behalf. The official historian of the War Industries Board, Grosvenor
Clarkson, has written: ". . . the man who could certainly have done
in the fall of 1917 what he did in the spring of 1918 was passed over
for many months after he had demonstrated to all close, unprejudiced
observers that he was marked for leadership." [16] Already he had organized his raw-materials group the way he later did the War Industries Board. He was the one man you could go to and get action.
Once Josephus Daniels was short of zinc. Baruch called up the New
Jersey Zinc Company. Within a few hours, the zinc was rolling up
in a truck, still in hot ingots. At McAdoo's request Baruch once saw
the French Ambassador, who wanted gasoline. Within a few days,
the tankers had started.[17] Back in New York, Baruch had leased a
large office in a skyscraper to provide a central place where all plans
for ships, motors, and material could be scanned. He was slashing
the red tape of war production. His efforts cost him a fortune; and
yet he refused $85,000 in reimbursements.

His struggle with the copper kings during his days on the Advisory

Commission set the pattern for the industrial economic relationship of the entire war period. The demand for copper was outrunning the supply, even before the United States entered the war, and already at prices that made war financing look impossible. Copper had sheathed ships before Nelson's time. Now it was a necessity for airplanes, field wire, and Signal Corps telephones. In Germany, copper had been stripped from rooftops, house gutters, even from church bells; but as late as the fall of 1917, the United States had found no answer to the copper problem.[18]

Baruch visited his old friend Daniel Guggenheim to dicker over the question of forty-five million pounds. It passed into the folklore of the war how Baruch talked the Guggenheims into surrender and saved $3,700,000 for the government by mass deliveries of metal at approximately half the market price. It was a triumph, "a repudiation of profiteering," but Baruch knew how far short it fell of the ideal. The initial seventeen-cent-a-pound figure could not be maintained, and the industry fought for twenty-five cents, settling at last on a twenty-three-and-a-half-cent compromise. Small, high-cost mines could not have afforded the earlier figure. And the miners themselves, living hard and spending high, would have struck at any resultant lowering of wages by a dollar a day.

As for the copper kings, Baruch frankly admitted that they profited. At a congressional inquiry in 1916 he conceded that the War Industries Board had been vexed almost to the point of commandeering as Senator Bennett Champ Clark charged that the copper companies had "held a gun to Uncle Sam."

Baruch did not wish to seem to be defending the copper companies. By the end of 1918 it was acknowledged that the copper firms paid over $200,000,000 in dividends.[19]

To McAdoo, Baruch later explained that he had made the best deal he could on behalf of the country. You could be forgiven if you paid too much and got the stuff, but you could never be forgiven if you did not get it and lost the war.[20]

Despite exploits such as these, however, Baruch refused to push himself for leadership. As Clarkson has said, "The chances are that Baruch could have tipped the scales to action by a single picturesque sentence in his own behalf." This is to be "put down to his debit." He knew how few really dispassionate men there were. Of his own associates, both Willard and Lovett were then opposed to him. A proud and sensitive man, Baruch had, despite his surface self-confidence, an inferiority complex for which in later years he would overcompensate. He had even felt doubts as to the adequacy of his advice while on the board of trustees of City College.[21] So now he waited and let those with friends at court have their day.

Wilson knew what was going on and had his plans. "Sorry," he wrote McAdoo, who wanted Baruch to run the railroads, "but I can't let you have Baruch. He has trained now in the War Industries Board until he is thoroughly conversant with it . . . and as soon as I can do so without risking new issues on the Hill, I am going to appoint him chairman." Typical of the President's struggle were the protestations of an unidentified visitor: "He's a gambler and a speculator."

"Yes," came the surprising retort. "I understand he's a very good one."

He had even gambled on Mr. Wilson's re-election, the visitor pointed out.

"Yes, I understand so," the President said. "He showed great intelligence."[22]

Meanwhile, the ostensible search for a "superman" went on. Secretary of War Baker, although belatedly agreeing to an over-all director,[23] told Baruch that he had done the best work on the Board, but that he did not consider him qualified as an executive. His plan was to call in some great industrialist not even on the Board.

Subconscious resentment against Baruch may have smoldered in Baker. Once the "Little Giant" burst out, "If I was a big fellow like Baruch, they'd say I was a better Secretary of War."[24] In any event, one Saturday morning in February he called Baruch to his office: "Mr. Baruch, I wish you'd get in touch with John F. Ryan * and tell him we want him to be chairman."

"Very good, Mr. Baker," Baruch answered. "But you could just as well tell him yourself." He added, "I've always been loyal, but I don't think this is a very nice thing to do." Humiliated and rebuffed, he carried out his assignment, however, despite Alex Legge's angry "We'll get the hell out of here."

"We've got to stay and do our duty anyhow," Baruch said. But he could never quite forgive the Secretary and would not even accept the Distinguished Service Medal at his hands, receiving it later at the sickbed of Woodrow Wilson.[25]

The afternoon of his visit to Baker's office, Baruch called on Wil-

* Ryan was then president of the Anaconda Copper Company.

liam G. McAdoo, who had been ailing and whom Baruch found stretched out on his bed, his feet extending from his long nightshirt. At Baruch's story he reared up. "Goddam! I'm going over to see the President." It was not just that Baruch had been passed over which aroused McAdoo. That his friend should be made the errand boy for Baker, doing the work and exerting tacit control until he was replaced, was more than "Mac" could take.

At the White House, with the indignant McAdoo looking on, Wilson and Baker talked on the telephone. Baker repeated, "Baruch's got to stay there to show the new man how to run it."

McAdoo countered, "If he's good enough for that, why isn't he good enough for the job?" [26] The question was unanswerable.

Baruch thought he had no friend at court, but he was wrong. Josephus Daniels favored him personally but warned the President that Congress would not approve him. Justice Brandeis had nothing to do with his appointment, but he did tell the President that what was needed was an out-and-out speculator, independent of all the organized interests, who knew how to raid the vulnerable ones and trade with the powerful ones.[27] By coincidence, this description fitted Baruch perfectly, although neither then nor later was love lost between Baruch and the Kentucky-born Zionist.

There were powerful voices lifted for Baruch — not only McAdoo's, but Gompers' and Tumulty's. At a meeting of the Council of National Defense that February, Daniels led the fight for Baruch as chairman, and, strangely enough, Baker this time was inclined to agree. Houston and Redfield were opposed. Argument broke out over the statement of a former president of the United States Chamber of Commerce that Baruch's appointment would not be approved by businessmen. "I think," countered President Wilson, "that you will find that members of the two Houses are learning very fast to have very great respect for Baruch, and, after all, they are our only authoritative citizens." [28] Yet, before Wilson named his new chairman of the War Industries Board on March 4, 1918, he took the precaution of writing each Cabinet member to request his cooperation.

Baruch's appointment was received with approval by a smattering of newspapers and Wall Street publications. Baruch himself, confronted with the actual grant of power, was hesitant. "I never got a job anyone else really wanted," he said afterward, "but in wartime you've got to do whatever you're told." [29]

At the White House Wilson showed Baruch his letter of authorization. "Baruch, you read this letter. Will that do?"

"Yes, sir," came Baruch's answer, slowly. "But may I say this? When I make a mistake, call me in and close the door and give me the devil. Don't publicly repudiate me until I've had a chance to be heard." He added, "I'll be all right, if you don't overrule me."

"I won't overrule you," [30] the President assured him.*

So there it was — his — the "Grim Job," what came to be perhaps the greatest grant of power yet made to an American not in the presidential office. "Yes," he would say afterward, he had greater power than anyone else. Authority to establish the priorities for the needs of the Army, Navy, and for all war and peacetime agencies; authority over men, money, materials, and manufactures — even the final authority over Allied purchasing was in his hands. If the head of the draft board wanted men, he would have to go to the chairman of the War Industries Board to find from what industry men might be available. The location of new factories, the commandeering of fuel, the allocation of materials and resources — all came under his sway. Steel moved at his order; mines yielded up their treasure.[31]

In his letter of March 4, 1918, Wilson outlined the goals to Baruch. The Board would be responsible for the creation of facilities and for sources of supply, conversion, conservation, and advice on price levels, Allied purchases and priorities of delivery with the help of representatives of Food, Fuel, the Railway Administration, the Shipping Board, and the War Trade Board. All decisions, except the determination of prices ** should rest with the chairman. President Wilson was the only court of appeal from his decisions.

As for Baruch, his tasks were to act for the government departments, to let alone what was being well done, and to take action where there was any conflict. Also, the chairman should determine needs as far ahead of demand as possible.[32]

Yet the creation of this office was never specifically authorized by an Act of Congress.† When anyone wanted to know what Baruch's authority was, he answered, "That's my business."

* For President Wilson's letter, see Appendix.
** Baruch did not have actual power to establish the prices which the government would pay, but he could determine them indirectly by commandeering.
† The Overman Act of May 1918 gave the President power to reorganize the governmental agencies, but the new War Industries Board had already been established for two months.

Technically, his authority was to be found in Section 120 of the National Defense Act, which empowered the President to appoint a board to mobilize essential industry for war purposes. Other sources were such special legislation of Congress as the Transportation Priority Act, the Lever Act on price-fixing, and authority for commandeering.[33] The chairman was responsible to no one but the President, from whom his power was derived.

Leon Henderson explained it afterward: "You know, all that old speculator Baruch had was an old piece of paper. It got all soiled and worn being carried around. If he had to, he showed it to people. That was the way he settled disputes. That was practically the only power he had except a personality and the sense other people had of his leadership." It was enough.[34]

As Wilson had said, the War Industries Board was an administrative agency set up to act for him, and the chairman was the "general eye" of the entire war program.[35]

"More important than Baruch is his job, vastly more important than the country supposes," said a writer in *World's Work*. He was more "than an eye . . . a great deal more." Much, of course, would depend on his inherent capacity.[36]

"I don't know if you can get away with it, Bernie," observed his friend Vance McCormick, "a man from Wall Street and all that." He added that "they all talk about you being a speculator, but once you're appointed, they back you." [37] Yet, at this stage, Baruch had little confidence in himself. He felt that what he knew must be known by others.[38] Far from pretending to be any formulator of presidential policy, he told Wilson that he would always seek his direction on questions of large policy. However, he hesitated to bring any additional burdens upon the President who was so generous of his time.[39]

Privately then, as later, Baruch talked about himself, of "his philosophy of life . . . how liberal and advanced were his social views . . . how democratic he was with his employees"; and, most of all, the wonder of what had happened to him. "It all seemed amazing to him," one interviewer commented.

It was amazing. Because his mental processes were intuitive, he could wonder how all this marvel could have happened. "For Baruch," commented the same journalist, "the great romance is Baruch, the astonishing plaything of fate," who became, next to Wilson, "the most powerful man in Washington." Such a meteoric rise made it hard for him to feel that anything was impossible. Was Baruch now any farther away from becoming an American Disraeli "than was the Baruch of today from the Baruch of yesterday"? Because this was true, observers could declare that Baruch's unaffected delight in himself came from "real humility," [40] or, at the same time, that he was "the most conceited man" they had ever known.[41] A man who was not an industrialist and yet organized the greatest industrial combine the world had known; a man who was suspect by business and yet got on well with businessmen; an amateur in politics who played politics superbly — small wonder that he should marvel at how he had done it all. He had an answer: "I do things one at a time." [42]

He lacked the egotism which imagines the existence of massed enemies; people, he felt, were not thinking about him but about his job. He pledged himself to give all that was in him, but knew that he would need assistance and perhaps even prayers.[43] He resigned himself to becoming unpopular.[44] He only hoped that he could deliver some of the goods expected of him, and to this end he moved slowly. He wanted to take in the general picture before focusing on specific subjects.[45]

He was eager to learn. Herbert Hoover, who came to know him well in these years, has said that "of technology he knew nothing, nor of distribution . . . There were technical subjects on which he had no knowledge." [46] What Hoover — and all official Washington — wondered at was Baruch's "capacity for absorption," not knowing of his years of study in the past.[47] He hated detail, yet developed a talent for it. Papers wandered away from his desk, only to turn up weeks later in his pockets.[48] It did not matter; his mind was his filing cabinet, and it was said around Washington that he could recite verbatim every word of the vanished documents.

It was heartening to know that even Colonel House was publicly praising his vision and imagination, and later to hear from the lips of Clemenceau that almost coincidentally with his appointment France felt the "change in the situation." How much this was due to Baruch is problematical, but the fact remains that steel now flowed across the ocean for 165 million "75" shells, and food for twelve million Frenchmen for a year and a half. If this help had not come, the French armies might not have held. With pardonable pride, Baruch himself said of the "Grim Job," "I was made chairman and things commenced to hum." [49]

It is true that in its powers and structure, the War Industries Board was elementary compared to its World War II successor, the War Production Board. As the *Journal of Commerce* has observed, where Baruch was merely the "general eye" of the supply departments, Donald Nelson was "the 'eye' and the 'mind' and the 'hands' as well, with dictatorial power over production." The War Production Board was far larger and more complex, but the War Industries Board's importance as a trail-blazer must not be underestimated, or the precedents it laid down. Its power, in short, was what Baruch made it. [50]

The Board was housed in a rickety, tar-paper and clapboard makeshift building (still standing in the mid-fifties), with "paper walls so thin you could hear the man in the next room change his mind." [51] A permanent structure for the Board was rising, not far away, but it would not be completed until four months after the Armistice. [52]

Baruch plunged into his tasks with an almost boyish gusto. In the weary, war-fagged Washington of 1917, "his good humor was unfailing . . . His smile was perennial." That strange sphinxlike smile, which for Baruch bridged the years between youth and age, was a riddle to his associates. It seemed as if he was never too tired or too engrossed to smile, half perplexed though that smile might be, sometimes even making "a profound depression." [53]

"The strain was great, but it was a great game." Life for him was "a succession of big thrills," and having an outlet for his pent-up energies, Baruch was calm and cool. He knew that he had reached the climax of his life, and he gloried in it. He gloried in Wall Street's charge that he was "a Socialist in his devotion to the interests of the people as represented by the government."

Above all, he could "always relax, always talk, always make friends." Every associate commented upon his courtesy, under even the most extreme tension. "If Bernie had to cut off a head," an aide commented, "he would be polite." [54]

His dignity was in part a physical thing, for despite his good looks, he gave the impression of a man much older than he was. [55] Already, he had the aura of the "elder statesman." His hair had gone white and he compelled the respect automatically given to age. [56] The eyes, humorous, blue, searching, told nothing of himself, and went cold "and gleamed like a polished gun barrel when he spoke of money, production, or any of the various aspects of finance." It was the contrasts of the man that challenged. He was "a complex and fascinating person," aristocratic in appearance but democratic in manners.[57]

What inspired him under pressures that broke other men? To Hoover it seemed a "sixth sense." To Mark Sullivan, it was sheer artistic genius in the realms of money-making and politics.[58] To Commander John M. Hancock, the Navy representative on the Price Fixing Committee, he was the inspiration, the one who welded the men around him into a fighting team.[59]

Obviously, Baruch could never have done his job without first-rate backing, men like Leland Summers, George Peek, Hugh S. Johnson, Alex Legge, J. Leonard Replogle, and Herbert Bayard Swope. Not until fifteen years later, when another generation of young men descended upon Washington and rolled up their sleeves to rebuild a nation, did such a galaxy illumine the capital.

Some were chosen; some chose themselves. A brain trust, a later generation might have called them. Their backgrounds were widely diverse. Replogle, for instance, had been a water boy in the steel mills, and Legge a cowboy on the plains. Now they were the bright young men of big business, although their names were little known as yet in Washington. They were the leaders of the future. They had special knowledge in key fields, "but also the kind of broad-gauge vision that encompassed the problems of their neighbors." They had tact and patience, the "enthusiasm which could inspire, and inspiration which could accomplish." Baruch picked masterful minds and men — this was his secret that could not always be emulated in other wars.[60]

Baruch's second-in-command was the tall, raw-boned "Abraham Lincoln of industry," Alex Legge, who in the opinion of many was the real driving force of the Board, so far as the day-to-day decisions were concerned. Baruch's office window faced a park and the rear lawn of the White House, but it is characteristic that Baruch did not remember looking out. Below the glass top of his desk were the names of all the committees of the War Industries Board, and there was a bell to summon one of his "flying executives," Clarence Dillon, Herbert Bayard Swope, or Harrison Williams. These men, Baruch would sometimes say, multiplied himself by three. If he thought some particular job was not going well, he would assign one of them to straighten it out. If he had some new problem to tackle, one of these was delighted to study it and report. He also leaned very heavily on

Eugene Meyer, an expert on nonferrous metals whom he considered to be not only of extraordinary character and ability but "a fine public servant." On Meyer he depended especially for help with the copper, lead, and zinc problems.

Of these, none was more of an unsung hero than Leland Summers. The War Industries Board historian, Grosvenor Clarkson, has written that Baruch never had greater luck than when he found Summers.[61]

He was an "alchemist of the wizardry of war." Back in 1911, watching Germany amassing her materials of death, he saw that modern war would not be a matter of chemicals and weapons alone, but that it was rooted in industry as a whole. Raw materials were the key. Baruch, "stunned by his knowledge," called Summers in for help in 1916. He backed him up when he arranged to have the du Ponts assemble toluol for TNT. Later, at "Hobcaw Barony," Baruch offered Summers the same salary to join the Advisory Commission as he himself was getting.

"How much do you get?" Summers asked.

"Nothing and pay my own expenses."

"I'll go with you," Summers answered.[62]

Quite different talents were those of dogmatic, boyish-faced George Peek, who saw the world in violent contrasts of black and white. He fairly radiated energy. Always putting the public interest first, even at the risk of his own career, was young, vigorous J. Leonard Replogle. He knew steel and steel men, the costs of mining ore and making pig iron, the prices that big steel thought it had to have and the prices the War Industries Board knew that it could pay.[63] By no means the least conspicuous of the War Industries Board personnel was their future entertainer and host to Broadway night life, a young stenographer called Billy Rose. His job was to carry chocolate sodas to Baruch at three in the afternoon; his brashness carried him to the study in the White House, where he challenged the somber Wilson to a shorthand contest.[64]

Baruch was unyielding in his determination to get whom he wanted. From the first, he had set his sights on Alex Legge of the International Harvester Company. When he showed Summers a list of twelve suggested names for the Inter-Allied Purchasing Commission, the answer was: "There's the man for you . . . knows Europe, knows human nature . . . a very shrewd trader, and straight as a die . . . but you cannot get him."

"Why?" Baruch asked.

"Because he is the greatest brain in the International Harvester Company," Summers responded.

"He's the man we want," Baruch said.

When Cyrus McCormick notified him that Legge could not be spared, Baruch invited them both down to Washington. One look at Legge's calm, strong face, and Baruch knew that he had to have him. He knew also that McCormick would be very reluctant to let him go. To give up Legge would be a true patriotic sacrifice, Baruch finally convinced McCormick. Less convinced was Legge himself, who muttered: "Well, Baruch, if I could find the son-of-a-gun who got me into this, I would get my six-shooter after him."

Just then Summers came in by a side door. Baruch whirled and said, "There's the man."

Legge exploded, "My God, it's Summers," and said that he was a poor friend.[65]

So Baruch chose men, measuring them as he did Alex Legge, choosing them for their judgment and objectivity, their capacity to separate essentials from nonessentials. He never tired of praising them, and inspired in them an extraordinary loyalty.[66] One War Industries Board associate heard a young man on a club car to St. Louis making flippant charges that Baruch had "cleaned up" during the war. He said he had the inside dope. The War Industries Board man listened, simmered, then boiled over. Enraged, he identified himself, and tore the story to pieces, bit by bit. Then he pulled his watch from his pocket. "Young man, I shall give you two minutes to apologize to everyone in this car for slandering Mr. Baruch. If . . . not . . . then I will knock you down." [67]

Having chosen wisely, Baruch could lean back and delegate his authority. His men had the power of decision, with no fear of reversal. He let them alone. "You do what you think is right," was his stock answer to the seekers of advice.[68] An early morning joint committee meeting thrashed out problems common to all. Then each was on his own. At that period, Baruch would never publicly reverse or repudiate those around him. If something went wrong, he took the blame. To admit to outsiders that a subordinate had violated orders would destroy the morale of his organization.[69] The real mistake would have been his choosing the wrong man.

"Here is a job," he would scrawl in a memo to one of the "boys" outlining requirements but with no hint as to what ought to be done.

"I'm on the job," would come back the answer, "and nine times out of ten" that ended Baruch's concern with the matter.[70] His men fulfilled their trust, for he required of them the same loyalty and unstinted effort that he gave himself.

"You can't be a trimmer around him; you can't lie. He's too smart," Billy Rose observed afterward.[71] Having granted power, he kept out of sight, even out of committee meetings, intervening only when there was a failure to agree. Thus, Baruch was not hampered by petty details to blur his master plans. He was free to see and to steer the whole and to rove the scene. His task was to organize the great industrial combine, and perhaps because of what America did in time of war, the New Dealers would see better what could be done in time of peace. But Baruch was not thinking of the future now. He said: "There is only one business for America and Americans — war . . . War is the business of America." [72]

Baruch was now a part of the Washington scene. You saw him in the mornings, striding toward his office, spare and quick-moving in his formal black, towering over his fellows. On misty mornings in the spring, with the low-hung trees just filmed in green, and even the monument itself veiled from sight, you could see the army recruits taking setting-up exercises on the mall "Ellipse" behind the White House, "the whole scene . . . so fresh and beautiful one felt like crying out with delight."[73]

Of Wall Street he said, "I decided to close that page in my life. I closed it." [74] For the duration of the war he held to his resolution. He had given up his seat on the Stock Exchange. All of his salable stocks or bonds that might benefit in any way from government purchasing were sold. The dividends of those that were unsalable were distributed to charitable institutions. He had tungsten holdings, for instance, that could not be sold because they were not producing. However, he felt that if any tungsten was produced, it should be sold to the government at cost, and that competitors would have to meet that figure, even if it caused them a loss. Texas Gulf Sulphur was tapped as a potential source by the Federal Bureau of Mines. Here, too, Baruch ordered that the sulphur be sold at cost, or lower, if the cost price exceeded that of the lowest bidding competitor.

Baruch had drafted both himself and his dollars. During the first Liberty Loan drive he walked into McAdoo's office and wrote out a check for five million dollars worth of bonds. "I had more money on hand than usual," he explained to Clarence Barron, "and my affairs were very liquid." [75] No number of millions that he could have made in Wall Street could have given him the satisfaction he had in serving his country.[76] The *Independent* believed that "His past was forgotten by those who knew what he was up to."[77]

He was what is known as a dollar-a-year man. But many of his chief associates, like Hugh Frayne, could not afford to work on this basis. Much of the dollar-a-year breed Baruch considered of nuisance value. He knew what he wanted — and that it had to be paid for.[78]

Baruch's home in Washington was the Hitt house near Du Pont Circle — "a nice house, with a lot of room in it," one visitor has recalled.[79] Except for his servants, he was often alone. Mrs. Baruch went back and forth between New York and Washington, managing both establishments. Bernard, Jr., was at Milton Academy in Massachusetts, longing to run away and become a "powder monkey" with the Royal Canadian Air Force. Renée also was at school, and Belle was serving in the Women's Radio Corps. Meanwhile, their father was shadowed by the faithful Lacey, who came to be well and favorably known to Baruch's friends over a period of forty-two years. British-born, Lacey was not only well-mannered but highly intelligent and, as Baruch described him, "a fine gentleman." For Baruch, he provided a link of continuity with home. More than either a valet or a social secretary, Lacey's relation to Baruch was so close that his obituary notices "promoted" him to the War Industries Board itself.

As the heat of the Washington summer closed down, Baruch found other quarters. He moved out to a "new country place" owned by Charles C. Glover. There were tennis courts in the rear, and sometimes Admiral Grayson would join Baruch for a few sets. Baruch still loved dancing, but his springy, graceful figure would have cut too conspicuous a figure indeed on a Washington dance floor without his wife, so this was one more pleasure that he gave up when she was not in town. Occasionally he appeared at the usual Washington receptions, or at dinner at the home of Secretary Daniels, who would raise his hand and bow his head for the blessing, "and whose row of wine glasses maintained their virginity." [80]

Baruch would have disagreed with the patronizing estimate of Daniels privately given by his high-geared young Assistant Secretary, Franklin D. Roosevelt, as "bewildered . . . very sweet but . . . full of idealistic nonsense." [81] Next to McAdoo, Daniels was Baruch's favorite in the Cabinet and he knew him to be a far better Secretary of the Navy than many people supposed. Baruch, who had not turned a deaf ear to the sponsors of a "death ray," could have sympathized with Daniels' summoning of the Army and Navy engineers to watch a secretive little scientist, John Andrews, add "six or seven drops of a greenish-colored liquid" to the tap water which had been drawn into the tanks of some airplane engines. There was no explosion. No steam issued from the exhausts. Yet the engines ground into operation, developing about three-quarters of their usual horsepower. For two million dollars, the scientist volunteered to divulge the secret, but Daniels would not hand over the cash without the formula, and' the mysterious John Andrews dropped from sight.[82]

At meetings in the old State, War, and Navy building, Baruch might sometimes catch a glimpse of the "boy Secretary," Franklin Roosevelt, who was to boast in 1920 that he had broken enough laws during the war to go to jail for nine hundred years. He was tall, slender, and highstrung, but his haughty gaze and outthrust chin did not detract from the charm which had won Daniels at the Baltimore convention of 1912 and resulted in Roosevelt's appointment as Assistant Secretary of the Navy. A story about him was told and repeated. As early as 1913, Representative Edward W. Pou told Daniels, "Joe, you and I will live to see that young man elected President."[83]

Baruch, now established in his job, was beginning to sort and sift, to separate and divide, to bring order out of chaos. "Wars," he warned, "are fought and won — or lost — on the land, on the water, in the air and on those battle-lines behind the front where the civilian forces stand." [84] Delay, procrastination, and inefficiency were the bugbears. Industry, for all its protestations of patriotism, was stubborn, and as in a later war the toughest job was to get contracts signed and work under way.[85]

His energy perhaps made him overzealous. Like others in high places, he had to be warned against wooing clerks and specialists from other departments with offers of more pay. "We are a single family," Wilson cautioned.[86] The President and Baruch balanced one another, one symbolizing the political and the other the economic aspects of mobilization.[87] Always Baruch strove to do more than what was asked of him, and always Wilson answered: "You are doing all that it is possible for you to do to relieve me." [88] Together, Baruch and the President considered the question of supplies for the Allies or the shifting of new industrial enterprises southward.[89] They hit on a kind of pre-Prohibition, merely by denying the use of foodstuffs to the manufacturers of malt liquors.

The cornerstone of the industrial mobilization was Baruch's system of interlocking committees, representative of industry and government. It took a year to realize fully his idea of a single controllable outlet for each separate commodity. But now the plan worked, Washington putting forth the demand and industry giving out the supply. Not yet, however, had disastrous competitive buying been halted. In June the Requirements and Supply division was created to represent the purchasing agencies of all the government bureaus. Yet this was not enough. Although the War Industries Board was content to have all departments represented in its organization, it was soon found advisable that the Board, in turn, should have representatives in the departments.

So unrelenting was the pressure, so immediate were the needs, that it seemed impossible to look to the future. The Navy's quota of 100,000 men had suddenly been raised to a million; the Army was confused because it did not know its requirements, "even at the end of the war." Competitiveness left small place for impartiality. The harassed chairman of the War Industries Board would commiserate with the officer who had ordered cement from a plant 500 miles distant only to discover plenty available not ten miles away. He would search the round and deceptively innocent face of the naval representative, John Hancock, called "on the carpet" to account for the Navy's "kidnapping" of a cargo of beans.

"John, here you are again! You've grabbed something."

Patriotism triumphed over zeal. "Well, if the Army has a greater need, we'll give them to the Army."

Then it was Baruch's turn to assemble the facts for the consideration of the Priorities Board. Hancock commented in retrospect, "We damn seldom lost." [90]

The opposite view was supplied by the Army representative, General Hugh S. Johnson, who dismissed the War Industries Board as "obnoxious" at first, only to become its most zealous convert. Speaking of the Army-Navy controversies, he wrote, "We beat the pants off of them." [91]

Mobilization for total warfare was learned only by trial and error. No lesson was more bitter than that learned from the slow strangling of much of the industrial program by the breakdowns in the over-crowded factories of the Northeast. Three-quarters of the machine-tool industry was there, but the region was short in fuel, power, and transportation. For want of anchor chains, ships could not sail. Cranes that would have saved five days' work in unloading a ship were jammed onto docks too flimsy to bear their weight. Nothing was more trying than five heatless and lightless days in the bitter cold of a New England winter. No department knew its require-ments, only that it outran the supply. Occasionally there were no transports available to send troops to France, and sometimes there was inadequate material to maintain them after they arrived. "To an unknown demand there was nothing to do but to oppose an un-known effort." Should trains be assigned to Pershing to haul muni-tions — or to Chile to haul nitrates for making munitions? Should the nitrates, in their turn, be used for munitions or for fertilizer, steel for trucks or steel for munitions, cranes be sent to the American docks for loading or to the French docks for unloading? [92]

It was the War Industries Board that had to decide — to remember that the development of new facilities meant also the manufacture of new machine tools; to remember that older plants, using older processes at higher costs, still made up a large part of the nation's existing facilities. Baruch and his organization had to rob Peter and pay Paul, to conjecture as to the elements that went into the making of a single shell: ore from Minnesota, coal from Pennsylvania, coke from West Virginia, brass from Connecticut, copper from Arizona, chemicals from New York, explosives from Delaware, the milling machinery, the iron, the steel, plus the cargoes of freight, piled up and snarled to a point threatening collapse of the entire rail system. [93]

"Priorities" — an idea which Baruch always credited to Sir Wal-ter Layton of the Balfour Mission — and "clearance" were the foundations upon which rested all else. To be stricken from the priori-ties list "was to be damned; to be on it was industrial salvation." An unwritten law governed the land. [94] Like other divisions of the War Industries Board the Priorities Board functioned without disturb-ances and was subject to review only by Baruch himself.

Hugh S. Johnson once said that the best example of priorities was a basket of an unknown number of eggs. No one ever quite knew just how many there were to go around. Sometimes, not even the most desperate needs of Numbers 1 and 2 could be met, even by curtailing

3 and 4. But the rule was, Number 1 came first, taking what it had to have. Afterwards, Numbers 2, 3, and 4 could take or share what was left over, according to their relative importance. Replogle would say to the representatives of the Army, Navy, Shipping Board, and Allies: "Here's the steel . . . Let me know how much each of you is to have. There's exactly thirty-three million tons to go around." No one could be completely satisfied.[95]

Representatives of the Army, Navy, supply bureaus, the Inter-Allied Purchasing Commission, the Shipping Board, and the Fuel and Food Administrations studied the shortages, and how they could be met. In "clearing" a commodity or giving a plant the signal to go ahead, the questions were: (1) the commodity's importance to the war effort; (2) the urgency of the need; (3) the relation of supply to demand; and (4) the potential plant capacity.[96] Every section of the War Industries Board was informed of the clearances acted upon by other sections, and each government purchasing department informed of the purchases of other departments. Daily two lists were prepared, one showing items on which clearance was requested; the other, items cleared within the last twenty-four hours. There was also posted a list showing the articles or commodities that must be cleared before negotiations for further purchases might be started.[97]

Clearance did not always work kindly. For some, there was the pride and consolation of giving their industries as freely as they had sent their sons to war; but few were really big enough to sit by and see their factory chimneys go cold for lack of raw materials while their neighbors' were smoking hot. To them the appeal was made: "Will you take this material or will you let the boys in France have it?"[98] Jewelry could not win the war, and the little jewelry manufacturing town of Attleboro, Massachusetts, wondered if it was to be wiped off the map. Jewelry workers wanted tobacco, ice cream, silk shirts, and high wages. These demands, as well as patriotism, were potent incentives. Output, not motive, was what counted. It was frequently urged that all small businesses be stifled, and all nonessential enterprises, but Baruch, the "general eye," not only of industrial mobilization, but of civilian morale, withstood the demand. Temporarily, the war nearly dealt a deathblow to the building trade and the auto industry and the workers who depended upon them, but this was not Baruch's goal.

Priority must come first. The farmer's new barn could wait, and the old industrial plant make do, and even the little red schoolhouse could fade a year or so more in the sun and rain. A curt no to Mayor Hylan's promised school-building program for New York brought the local Democratic Party chiefs howling around Baruch's head. Once again, his figure towered high in a congressional committee room as patiently he explained the needs, the shortages, the demands — twenty-one million tons of steel for war purposes alone, measured against a total output of seventeen million tons. "It is," he said, " . . . the clear and simple duty of the War Industries Board to see that the war programme of this country is met . . . even if its fulfillment entails industrial loss as it does human loss." [99] Industry would come back; it was only the "spare parts" that were to be eliminated. At least the manufacturers now knew where they stood.[100]

Always, as Baruch said later, "the method sought was . . . one which would cause the least disturbance to the essential features of . . . industry." [101] He agreed that is was desirable to have "something left of what was worth fighting for." [102] It was the Chicago publisher A. W. Shaw who persuaded Baruch that nonessential industry should be "skeletonized," not destroyed. In return, manufacturers would voluntarily promise to observe restrictions.[103]

Shaw had not liked Baruch at first, and as they sat down for their first meeting, they frankly discussed the matter. Baruch liked Shaw; he liked a strong and forceful man with an idea, and Shaw was that. He wanted Shaw as chief of his Conservation division and got him. Later Shaw quipped: "We have two great sports down here — one is passing the buck, the other is chasing the nonessential. Since Mr. Baruch has been chairman, we have stopped passing the buck and we have found the nonessential." [104]

C. A. Otis, president of the Cleveland Chamber of Commerce, came up with an idea for the integration of industrial processes. Why could not a regional system be set up, he wondered, by which the making of all parts for one weapon or machine could be concentrated in a single section of the country?

"I'm sold," Baruch said. "You get your winter clothes and come to Washington." [105]

Together they mapped out twenty-one industrial regions, with a local Chamber of Commerce "adviser" representing the War Industries Board in each. Now the Board had another pipeline, not just to individual industries, but to the industrial clearinghouses for whole regional communities. Now Baruch could issue a ruling that before being cleared by the Board, any building project must first be approved at home. No longer could smooth talkers with blueprints win contracts; nor home-town incompetents start building new plants. You could ask somebody now in Oshkosh or San Francisco, "What kind of a fellow is Sam Perkins?" [106]

The War Industries Board was the shovel that cleared the tracks. And the tracks were beginning to clear. Week by week the interdependence of various industries became recognized more clearly. Withdraw toluol from explosives, for instance, and the whole program collapsed.[107] It had been a deadly malady, this lack of coordination: tanks without engines, plane bodies without wings, freight without cars, carloads without ships, cargoes without docks — it was perhaps "the worst tangle of disordered effort the world has known." [108] But it was not fatal. Priorities and clearances pulled in double harness and at least 300 applications were approved or declined in a single day.[109]

The War Industries Board even turned the tables on the dress designers. Women could stand curtailment of the manufacture of pianos, wringers, bicycles, coffins, and even engagement rings, but it was something else again when Mars denied war babies their buggies, pulled the steel from their mothers' corsets, and even began to specify the length and style of their drawers.[110] The drag-down battles with the steel and lumber interests were powderpuff affairs compared to the uproar that ensued. Nor were the ladies mollified by Baruch's happy observation that "the most patriotic woman will be the one who finds happiness in what she does without." [111] Yet it was because of Baruch, not Worth, that silhouettes were slimmed and doughboys overseas were tantalized by skirts lifted above shapely ankles. The rustle of silk was heard no more, for gone were the length and sweep of material and the traditional "weighting." However, the "Pershing" and "Victory" shoes of the trenches were not for milady. Baruch's dictate of one standard black shoe for all was fought to the death by the trade and a compromise on three shades finally accepted.[112]

The newly fashionable platinum wedding rings were in short supply for war brides, for platinum made the only kind of wire that could stand intense heat and was a necessity in the manufacture of surgical instruments. Its price had soared from $39 an ounce in 1915 to $108 an ounce by 1917; [113] and the United States was dependent on foreign sources. Ninety per cent of the world's crude platinum was produced in Russia, and from there the last two thousand ounces had seeped out in December 1916, with Russia on the brink of revolution.[114]

Nor was the platinum the only vital metal or mineral in short supply. In the West, old ghost towns experienced resurrections as long abandoned silver mines sprang into life once more. America was digging deep into the earth, often for inferior grades of metal; and although South American supplies were available, North American ships were not. Llamas could not transport cargoes between continents.[115]

The hitch was in the tremendous expansion of facilities to meet the war's needs and the huge surpluses left unused at the war's end. Looking at the question with hindsight, Baruch later wrote, "There are ample grounds for the belief that the price fixed by the government worked hardship." [116]

Lumber was a tough problem. The lumbermen, whose Southern Pine Association was far more of a lobby than a helpful committee of industry, were cast "in a rough mold." To them, the war was a "golden opportunity for filling their coffers." The entire black walnut supply of the country, for instance, was used for gunstocks and propeller blades. An order rolled off a typewriter in Washington one day and within a few hours, with whoops and screeching of saws, lumber was felled for the building of cantonments; and within twenty-four hours hundreds of freight cars might be rolling — twenty-five million feet of lumber cut, loaded, and shipped within three days.[117] The lumbermen's very zeal for business increased the almost unbelievable congestion of the lines, and only General Order Number 38 from McAdoo halted unsolicited shipments, sent vaguely to the United States Government.[118]

What aggrieved lumbermen was that no one was to sell or deliver lumber except for essential uses. Baruch soon found that diplomacy did not work with these men. It was time, he decided, that they found out that the war was not their private war. "Quite true," he snapped, to one diehard lumberman, who dared him to commandeer his mills and run them with any efficiency, "but you will be such an object of contempt and scorn in your home town that you will not dare to show your face there . . . your fellow citizens would call you a slacker, the boys would hoot . . . and the draft men . . . run you out of town." [119]

The problem of explosives, the very essential of the war-making mechanism, fell squarely on the shoulders of the War Industries Board. America had the burden of supplying more than half the Allied need. Vast plant facilities, nominally owned by Americans, had been built at the expense of the Allied governments, and America was to pay off the debt in explosives. American-made powder, for instance, "drove half the projectiles that rained on the Germans from Goritz to Ostend." Yet America worked under tremendous handicaps, despite the fact that this country produced most of the necessary basic raw materials except nitrate of soda. For the industries of dyeing and death were interrelated. Germany was the world's primary dyemaker and her "chemicals of color swarmed with devils of death." [120]

An American dye industry, started in 1900, had been choked off instantly as Germany flooded the market with low-cost derivatives. By 1915, this country was hard pressed; in the end, fifty-three plants, built at a cost of some $350,000,000, underscored the parsimony and wastefulness of prewar days. Victory was won in the American chemical laboratory, however, as the United States discovered an explosive that outdid TNT.[121]

To old soldiers, lolling dreamily in front of the Grand Army posts, memories of Civil War scandals which had put a stain on the whole textile industry were bitter. Now came a chance for redemption; and "shoddy" became a respectable word. For, with seven million men to be uniformed and outfitted — and with the fact that the British government in 1916 had snapped up the entire Australian and New Zealand wool output for a year — mixed fabrics were the only answer. It was found that they could be nearly as good and enduring as pure-wool textiles. Fifty million yards of cotton for uniforms alone were supplied in the summer of 1917. Despite all efforts prices soared, and the whole industry was called to account for its wasteful methods.[122]

Waste was not to be tolerated; conservation and substitutions were cornerstones of the war program. The substitution of paper wrappers for cartons, the saving of the shipping space of 600 boxcars by merely increasing the length of thread wound upon a spool, the salvaging of 395 tons of steel by the elimination of metal boxes for typewriter ribbons — these were some of the battles won behind the front lines.[123] Power was precious. Amidst a blaze of denunciation, Baruch turned New York into a "hick" town and dimmed the lights on the Great White Way. The only thing worse, Josephus Daniels thought, would have been not to have done it at all.[124] The War Industries Board's orders meant fewer deliveries from stores, robbed coffins of their brass and children's carts of their tin. There were fewer tires for horse-drawn vehicles, less manufacture of beard softeners and bust forms.[125] Discards like cotton "linters" and by-product molasses all had their work to do. Even some low-grade corn whiskey went to war.

Baruch was a "go-getter," as his friend Garet Garrett described him.[126] If he told Wilson he could get ships, he got them. His copper deal with the Guggenheims had been no isolated case. In his early days on the Advisory Commission he had obtained lead at eight cents a pound when the market price was eleven. With only two hundred tons of antimony on hand and the ordnance people demanding three thousand, Baruch and Eugene Meyer halted the runaway price jump from fourteen to twenty cents a pound. They did this by slow, piecemeal buying, at which the price subsided comfortably.[127]

Baruch had the courage to gamble: "In a crisis or emergency he was not a cautious man." [128] When the Mexican province of Yucatan attempted to "hold up" the United States in its need for vital sisal fiber, Baruch went into action. He got both the lower price and the product by using substitutes in the United States and by a deliberate withholding of purchases until financial collapse threatened Yucatan.[129]

Equally spectacular was Leland Summers' game with the price of Indian jute — an outrageous price, in Baruch's opinion. Could not the British do something about it? It seemed not. What control did Britain have over the subcontinent? Belatedly, Britain discovered its control, upon learning that the United States was about to ban the silver exports that bolstered India's currency. On the basis of depreciated rupees, the United States could buy jute on its own terms; and the Empire discovered that India could be brought to terms.

The War Industries Board had been in operation many months before its idea was applied to inter-Allied purchasing. When Baruch assumed power, the opportunity to integrate our industry with that of the Allies had already been lost. It might well be, as we claimed,

that the French guns were best, but the United States should have
used British guns that were in ready supply. Nothing was more
exasperating than the perpetual American yen for "making it better,"
with the resultant discard of models for planes, rifles, and machine
parts that were giving adequate service. As Leland Summers
roared, "It is ridiculous for our nation with its facilities to be in a
position of not having shipped a day's supply of ammunition" after
having been at war for some seventeen months. If we could not develop good detonators, we should have adopted the French or English ones.[130] In six months the United States produced but six million
shells, scarcely enough for ten days of firing, while Britain manufactured thirty million shells right in the United States in two months'
more time.[131] This was the cost of the Yankee zest for experimentation. Baruch himself has admitted that the American mobilization
program was not really completed until the midsummer of 1918,[132]
and years later, during the Second World War, President Roosevelt
twitted him about the War Industries Board's "failure" to send guns
to the front. The real failure was in the Ordnance Department, which
was concerned with improving the French models rather than giving
the go-ahead for guns of American design.[133] It has been said by
critics of the War Industries Board that everything got perfectly
organized for war but that this was not wholly accomplished until the
war was finished.

The conflicting demands, meanwhile, were impossible to fill. For
in the American zeal for achievement, we had graciously told the
Allies, "Help yourselves." Then once we entered the war, we grabbed
up everything in sight. As one young officer put it: "My instructions
are to go and get . . . regardless of . . . whom it hurts." [134] Only belatedly was it coming to be realized that supplies of war did not come
out of an international grab bag. Only hindsight would disclose that
if the Allies collapsed as America armed, the United States might well
have to fight for beachheads in Europe and fight alone.[135] Economically, if not militarily, however, the war did finally become "the war
in common," with material in every stage of production transferred
back and forth "as easily as two friends might share a luncheon
basket." [136] Britain ransacked its cupboards for the Americans in
France; Americans drew from "common factories"; America supplied
the guns and England the howitzers, and America, at last, came up
with the most deadly mustard gas.[137]

Meanwhile, the Allies had built up productive capacity beyond demand. The French Army was dwindling because of its great casualties. One million men of the Front of 1915 were not there in 1917. In retrospect, it is conceivable that France could have supplied many more of the necessary arms had we only shipped over the raw materials, and we could thereby have avoided much of the tumult of conversion. Instead, as we have seen, we had created an "absolutely independent supply scheme." [138]

Now, across the walls of Baruch's office, moved the shadows of the world's death struggle; across his desk passed cables, signed by a name to become ever more familiar to him. Churchill, that dogged veteran of British wars and politics, the onetime First Lord of the Admiralty, now, in the darkest hours of that icy winter of 1918 — "the coldest the world had known" — was on a civilian mission again, burning into his brain the hideousness of scenes that through his prose would forever haunt the conscience of mankind.

Into the grim, bitter, broken country of northern France, Churchill wandered in the rain, amidst the ruins and the mud, where in that last offensive more than one hundred thousand men had been killed or captured. "Scores of thousands of wounded were streaming through the hospitals," there to be patched up again for the shambles. The Germans were moving on Paris; two weeks later ninety of their finest divisions would be hurled against the British lines, "companies, battalions, even whole brigades . . . obliterated," in a prodigality of human sacrifice never before seen.

Ludendorff was making his last push; like lava from a volcano, the gray-uniformed soldiers were flowing forward across the old battle-fields they had laid waste. Nothing was left to win, nothing to gain, no cities to capture, no greening fields of spring. Nothing was left but the pock-marked meadows, the rotting bodies and skeletons looming white in the water-filled trenches, the blackened husks of villages, even the trees, shell-blown into grotesque "Dead Sea Fruits." [139] This was the supreme drive. As of January, Ludendorff had said that Germany had never been so strong, numerically, in proportion to its enemies. Yet Winston Churchill, military strategist no less than political genius, knew that for the first time the German casualties were greater than the Allies', greater than the monthly supply of fresh German reservists, fighting now in paper-and-wood-pulp uniforms. Had not the prisoners returning from Russia refused to fight at all?

Had not the winter of 1917–18 been the last real chance of German victory, during that "lengthy deadly interval" with Russia dropped out of the war, releasing a million troops for the Western Front, and America not yet present in effective force? Desperately the Allies had cried out for help. "We'll do our damnedest," Wilson promised, and half-equipped American troops had been hurled into the slaughter. Yet at Château-Thierry American troops had helped to halt the drive on Paris. They had held; the Allied lines had held. As Wilson said, "Back, back, back, always back for the enemies, always back." [140]

Churchill, on his inspection, turned into a dugout to get a match for his cigar. At the very instant the pathway ahead exploded from a shell.

At his headquarters, Marshal Foch, holding a big pencil as if it were a weapon, gestured at the map.

On the twenty-second of March, the Germans had broken through. "Oh! Ah! Oh! How big!"

On the twenty-third they had advanced again, but on the twenty-fourth they had gained less territory than the day before, and still less on the twenty-fifth and twenty-sixth. Each zone of advance was progressively smaller. Foch's voice dropped to a whisper. He waved, shrugged, leaped, gestured — "This poor, weak, miserable, little zone of invasion." Clemenceau clasped him in his arms and kissed him as Churchill looked on. The worst was over. The great effort had been made and failed. "The mighty onset was coming to a standstill." [141]

Was there a divine purpose behind this madness? Baruch found himself stirred by Wilson's words, delivered at Mount Vernon, shrine of a free country. "The Past and the Present are in deadly grapple and the peoples of the earth are being done to death between them. There can be no compromise." He had been "too proud to fight" for a selfish cause, but he could be "proud to fight for mankind." [142]

From the Republican side of the United States Senate echoed another voice of conviction, that of William E. Borah. To his rolling phrases, hardened Senate veterans listened with the almost reverent attention given two or three generations earlier to Webster or Calhoun. He compelled silence, this shaggy Westerner out of Boise, Idaho — like Wilson a "moral crusader," something of a poet, something of a scholar, Celtic and emotional, yet who, as one amazed correspondent put it, "neither drinks, smokes, nor plays." [143]

"We can no more quit than Washington could have quit," was his cry. This is "war unto death between two opposing theories of government . . . between . . . systems . . . peoples and nations, and . . . one or the other will have to go down." [144]

In the United States the manpower problem was becoming crucial. Baruch suggested the use of women in the factories. The question rose to a head at a dinner Baruch gave to the leaders of labor at his home. What would become of the men after the war, returning to find women in their good jobs? Suddenly Daniel Tobin of the Teamsters Union said: "Well, here is the way I look at it. If I am going home with my week's pay in my pocket and some fellow tries to hold me up, do I keep one hand on my wad and with the other try to defend myself? Or do I take both hands and lick the hell out of him. Let us go after those Germans with both hands . . . and if it's necessary to have women in our places, that is all right with me. We will look after our jobs when we get back."

Smoking away on his cigar, Samuel Gompers said quietly, "Well, that's the answer."

Churchill never underestimated the American industrial effort. "All that could be sent was given as fast and as freely as possible," he has recorded. To France alone, within eighteen months the United States sent ten million tons of food and raw materials. By the time American troops reached the Marne, the war had become a kind of long-drawn endurance struggle; the goal was to hold, while Germany was bled dry. A small war the conflict may have been from the American point of view compared to the Second World War; yet the American plans to swamp Germany may well have been "the chief reason why the German leaders asked for an armistice." [145]

Although personally, Baruch and Churchill were as yet unknown to each other, Baruch appreciated the power and wizardry of the forty-four-year-old man in the War Office in London, just as Churchill later remembered the clear cool mind in Washington making swift decisions and holding to them.[146] Churchill knew that Baruch was the main cog of the inter-Allied munitions program, although he may not have known that the American was spending his own money in its operations.

To Baruch, with American and Allied demands continually overlapping, the necessity of a central inter-Allied buying agency had seemed imperative. No War Industries Board funds being available,

Baruch furnished the money to send Leland Summers and a commission to London to investigate and build the framework for action. They had no congressional funds. When the cost of the mission was later disclosed as $63,752.25, an investigating Congressman demanded indignantly of the WIB counsel Albert Ritchie, "Are you aware that there was no authority for such an expenditure?"

"Yes, sir," Ritchie answered, "there was nothing for Mr. Baruch to do but pay the bill himself. The Mission had to go." [147] Baruch refused repayment. As he said afterward, "Our government benefited many thousandfold, but I had the great pleasure of being able to do something that had to be done." [148]

As a result of this mission, a scale was established by which the demands of both the Allies and the United States could be met. In addition, Baruch cracked down upon Britain's joint price scale, one for the government and one for civilians, with her American ally on the losing end of the line. American steel had been flowing into Britain's civilian market where prices on certain scarce items were not yet even under restriction. Baruch warned that unless prices were changed (and they were changed) "American financial support would be withdrawn." [149] Thereafter, Britain showed "a spirit of wholehearted co-operation," and there was vastly improved coordination in Allied purchasing. The War Program moved on.[150]

8

"DR. FACTS"

For Baruch in that Washington of 1918, there was nothing but work, work, and more work, with no end in sight.[1] His golf and golfing friends back in New York seemed very far away. Time was the most precious thing he had, and nothing irritated him more than correspondents mysteriously hinting of secrets that could only be disclosed in a confidential interview. Why would they not tell enough to let him judge whether the matter was of sufficient importance to take up his time? [2]

He worked around the clock.[3] Yet he thrived upon his labors, and perhaps for want of the golf games gained over twenty pounds. His good humor still was unfailing. When confronting the toughest industrial tycoons, he might show "the gleam of fight in his eyes," but he was always patient, and his personality had "the flavor of invitation rather than of challenge." [4] There was something most appealing about his gusto, his enthusiasm, his striding step through the streets of Washington very early in the morning or late at night, "at a gait to make you run." This was the man with "the padlock on his tongue," who filled out blank checks and told pretty women: "Thou shalt have no more high topped and fancy colored shoes." [5] There was no limit, the Baltimore *Sun* thought, to his recklessness.[6] His name appeared often in the headlines: "Baruch Joins To Take Over Power Plants"; "Baruch Solves Great Problems"; or details of "The Baruch Plan," which in those happy days had nothing to do with atomic energy.[7]

"He doesn't talk, he just works," the Buffalo *Times* reported.[8] Yet, during the busiest weeks of his entire two years in Washington, he claimed to be having the best time of anyone, anywhere.[9]

His personality was emerging before the country like "a lighthouse in a fog." One observer thought that there was less "thought of self" in him than in any other man in the inner circle. He just had in mind "the whole people." [10] One writer noted that, after all, since this was the trader who had played for high stakes with Duke and Ryan, "The Government's magician in raw materials" was still at the old game, only now with "the lines drawn a little tighter." [11]

He was up at dawn, bathed, ate, and often disposed of several callers before nine o'clock. His mornings were spent at the War Industries Board office; he spared himself ulcers by lunching alone at the Shoreham. Appointments for the typical day of May 21, 1918, ran like this: (1) Mr. Ingalls, (2) General Johnson, (3) WIB meeting, (4) Colonel Roberts, (5) Mr. Shaw, (6) Mrs. Haskins, (7) Governor Manning, (8) Price Fixing Committee, (9) Priorities meeting, (10) Mr. Yeatman, (11) Mr. Morgenthau, (12) Mr. Whitmarsh, (13) Mr. Legge.[12] He might be anywhere in the afternoon, but between six and seven he took a drive, talking business as he rode. Conferences often lasted until midnight.[13] The Buffalo *Times* gratified popular morality by reporting that when he was through at the office, Baruch went straight home "to a wife and three children." Actually, he often went home to wish that he were really home, and to think of how much he missed his wife and children.[14]

A newspaper at this time reported that Miss Belle Baruch was to be presented to Washington society at a reception, having made her debut in New York earlier that season. Although not the traditional fluttery little debutante, Belle the tomboy had grown into a magnificent woman, well over six feet tall, for whom the word Junoesque might have been invented.

Mrs. Woodrow Wilson described her and a friend, Evangeline Johnson, at the theater a few years later "as stunning-looking young creatures as I ever saw and so full of native vivacity and charm . . . like birds of brilliant plumage" in their velvet evening dresses.[15] Belle was willowy and slender, with the finely coordinated grace of an athlete. A young Princeton student, Dale Warren, later an editor at Houghton Mifflin Company, recalled that he had never met a girl at dances "as light on her feet as Belle Baruch." [16] Despite her casual manner, which was to grow more bluff and offhand over the years, she was shy and sensitive as very tall people so often are, and there was a look of sadness in her dark eyes. She and her father always shared much, a love of the land, of sport and good food, a hearty humor and stubborn independence, and between them, then and years afterward, there was always sympathetic understanding.

It was obvious that Baruch was his daughter's hero. It must have been obvious, too, at that Washington reception how proud he was of her. Already she was gaining recognition as a sportswoman. She was tirelessly busy with war charity and relief work. Later on her young enthusiasm for Wilson's dream of a League of Nations was no less than her father's.

Belle's reception was for Baruch a rare interlude of social life. He had not attended a dinner in honor of Secretary of War Newton D. Baker at the Army and Navy Club, only a few days after his appointment; but at the end of the war he accepted the invitation of Josephus Daniels to board the President's yacht *Mayflower* in the North River of New York to welcome and review the returning fleet.[17] He realized the almost impossible tasks under which he labored, and that he had little time for entertainments.[18] Swiftly he passed up chances to become a member of the Advisory Council of the American Agricultural Association, to join the board of directors of the American-Russian Chamber of Commerce, or, understandably enough, to serve on the Memorial Committee for the Grand Army of the Republic of New York. There was real regret in his note to the Shepherd of the noted theatrical club, The Lambs, that he could not attend their annual "Gambol" in 1918; and in a note to William A. Barbour, president of the Southern Society of New York, to whom he confessed that he always longed to be with people whose point of view he shared.[19]

He could not submit to the strain of attending a dinner for shell-shocked soldiers, although he gave money to them, to the Salvation Army, for the memorial prize essay at City College, for a country training school for Negro teachers in Georgetown, South Carolina, for the Knights of Columbus, and $20,000 for Jewish War Relief. Sometimes he was pressed beyond endurance.[20]

He did not want to see people with letters of introduction, he was finally forced to conclude.[21] He had to have some recreation, however, and despite his crowded time he accepted the golf privileges of Washington's Town and Country Club, although he seldom took advantage of them;[22] and he was among the laughers at the Gridiron Club dinner of December 8, 1917. What he liked best were quiet family dinners with old friends, such as his schoolmate Dick Lydon;

or with a new friend from the Southern group close to Wilson, who was to become very dear to him. This was an imperious former news-paperman named Carter Glass, who would soon invite Baruch to polish up his manners by dining with him.[23]

Deeper implications marked some of his social engagements. Al-though, as we shall see, he had no great fondness for Judge Gary, he did accept his invitation to the annual meeting of the American Iron and Steel Institute at the Waldorf on May 31, 1918 — if, as he wrote the Judge, he could be sure that he would not be called upon to make a speech.[24] Sundry speaking invitations were turned down. To a close friend he explained that he cared too much for him to make him listen to one of his speeches.[25]

Bonds of friendship were strained during Baruch's service on the War Industries Board, but his natural courtesy prevented them from being broken, as when he gave a gentle answer to an old friend angry because he was compelled to state the nature of his business in order to see him.[26]

Relations were eased with Newton D. Baker after a mutual ex-change of gifts: ducks from Baruch, a book, Frontiers of Freedom, from Baker. Later when Mrs. Baker went to a hospital, flowers ar-rived from the chairman of the War Industries Board.[27] As best he might, Baruch tried to cushion the blow to his friend Governor Christie Benet of South Carolina, whose son was reported killed in action days after the fighting was over. A week earlier, Baruch had been in touch with the Adjutant General's office, seeking news of an army private, missing for weeks. To the wife of a man who had died while working for the War Industries Board, Baruch wrote tenderly of her husband's sacrifice for his country, as great as that of a soldier falling on the battle front.[28]

No matter was too trivial for his attention if it involved winning the war. He might be planning to "Take Steel Materials On Requisi-tion," [29] but he was equally concerned with the confidential "tip" of a young kinsman from South Carolina that his own war plant was more interested in having winning baseball teams than in winning the war.[30] He took time to note on the appeal of a semiliterate applicant for a job as camp steward that he was a good man.[31] He would help an officer unjustly accused, or a young lieutenant drunk while off duty; try to find an Irish viscount missing in action, or save the life of a young French deserter who was willing now to return to his country's armed service.[32] Baruch's wife played her kind part, too, going before the judge advocate and Secretary Daniels to plead that the word "Ensign" be placed on the gravestone of young John van Wicheren Reynders, who died in his country's service before his commission was delivered.[33]

Baruch even paid heed to an old army comrade of his father's, who believed that the Confederate veterans' camp of New York had devised an article useful in aviation.[34] Continually, he pored over files of "desirable men" for an expanding War Industries Board. Anyone suggested was carefully noted down, even Dick Lydon's recommendation of a Long Island playboy who wanted to inspect horses for the cavalry.[35]

Members of the War Industries Board long remembered the day when a stately old man, who might have stepped straight out of a steel engraving of Robert E. Lee's staff, put his head in the office door. Baruch arose, left his chair, "kissed his father with all the affection of a child," and led him in. "Gentlemen," he said, "I want you to meet a great old man — my father." [36]

He was deaf, however, to any appeals for "pull" or "influence." And these were unending. Every cousin, kinsman, and connection, every friend and acquaintance of his life seemed to turn up with an appeal. Had Baruch filled all these requests, he would not have had time to steer the mobilization program. If men were privates, they wanted to be officers; if they were officers, they wanted promotions; if they were at boot camp, they wanted to be at Plattsburg; if they were on the sidelines, they wanted to be in the front lines.[37] If they were in the Reserves, they wanted to be in West Point, and if they did not seek special privileges, their mothers did for them.[38] A commission for every draftee seemed the goal, and Baruch, it was assumed, was a kind of Auxiliary War Department. Almost all shared the opinion of one New Yorker about his son, that his full capacities would not be utilized unless he was an officer.[39]

Not equal justice for all but "influence," it sometimes seemed, was what counted during the "patriotic" fervor of 1917–18. In the rush, even Mrs. Baruch and "Miss Belle" were pushed to intercede. Baruch refused to be swayed, even by his mother's recommendations; or to take too seriously the assertion of one correspondent that Mrs. Baruch had encouraged him to make his request. Poor Mrs. Baruch was even harassed upon a question of plumbing for United States ships.[40]

More typical was the plea from a South Carolina woman who almost tearfully urged Baruch to procure the President's signature on her son's application for Annapolis. One would-be officer and gentleman personally pointed out that he was prone to colds and throat infections, to say nothing of hemorrhoids, and would be of far more use anywhere than in regular trench life. Baruch undoubtedly agreed, but did not see how he could give the petitioner any guarantee of freedom from service.[41]

He had no hesitation in coming down hard upon his own relations, if necessary; and he sent a stern reproof to his "Uncle Henry" Lytton, a Chicago merchant who in a public advertisement, urged that everyone buy extra suits and overcoats while they were still available. But to one appeal he could not turn a deaf ear. Embers of memory smoldered again on a June day in 1917 as he glanced at a letter in his mother's handwriting to her beloved son. The bearer was the nephew of Captain Cantine, the Union officer who had befriended Miss Belle and her family back in that terrible February of 1865, and who had recently died.

The request, as it turned out, was worthy of a nephew of Captain Cantine, and Baruch helped the young man get to the front with the American Field Service.[42]

Smoothly oiled now, the War Industries Board machine moved into high gear. A headline summed up its spirit: "Baruch Warns the United States To Prepare for Hardships." [43] No doubts as to legal powers troubled Baruch. He spoke with a boldness impossible to a man in elected office.

He would not hesitate to take anything he needed, if it contributed to the war. Truck deliveries were limited to one a day. Civilians were put into uniform, and women were recruited for war work. For America, it was a great experiment; for the War Industries Board members it was "a glorious adventure," the high-water mark, as a new war would be to their sons and grandsons. Years later they looked back almost wistfully on "those glorious days when we were all so busy that some of us hardly knew what we were doing." [44]

Drastic as the methods may have been, the results justified them. As of the spring of 1918, the U-boat was checkmated. Fifty thousand tons of plate a week were available for the shipyards.

Labor was the War Industries Board's human problem — labor

struck for higher wages and although Baruch knew, no less well than
Gompers, that labor had a measure of justice on its side, the public
railed at men striking while their brothers fought. Gompers, true to
his word, had put the case to his followers in a dramatic scene in a
room at the Munsey Building in Washington. With great emotion
he spoke of his childhood, of the years in the sweatshops, for which,
he said, he had "never quite forgiven society," and yet, unfalteringly,
he called upon labor to come to its country's side.[45]

Production alone was what counted. The law of supply and demand in wartime might lead to outright profiteering, and the "cost-
plus" policy was accused of putting a premium upon inefficiency, because the price that gave a little profit to the small high-cost producer
might mean mass profits to great corporations. It also meant results.
Patriotism, unfortunately, did not always provide such incentive as
profits. Profits were the bait for the so-called "voluntary agreements"
by which the big corporations were eventually brought into line.
"Goodwill and cordial acquiescence" was the happy description General Douglas MacArthur gave to those agreements.[46] Baruch, studying the merchant chiefs from behind his desk, was getting rich lessons in the ways of human nature, or the gamut of human expressions,
when the captains of industry and the big chiefs were forced to
knuckle under.

Not all did so gracefully. "Mr. Stettinius, I am going to rely on you
for many things," was Baruch's prediction early in the war as he confronted the Morgan partner.

"Mr. Baruch, you can't rely on me for a thing," was the prompt
answer.[47] It is true that there were many who yielded with grace,
subordinating their own interests to those of their country.[48] But
there were others who wrangled over whether they or the government
should pay the costs of new plants for essential war materials. These
selfish men, despite their huge contracts, threatened to undo the real
accomplishments of the War Industries Board. So grave, for instance,
was the shortage of smokeless powder that Baruch summoned Dan
Jackling to Washington, and by September 1918 construction had
started on a federally owned nitro plant, where 4,533,000 pounds of
powder were manufactured by the time of the Armistice.[49]

President Wilson had sounded the watchword. "Those who do not
respond in the spirit of those who have given their lives for us . . .
may safely be left to be dealt with by law."

The trouble was in the law. A robust inflation was in full swing even before the United States entered the conflict. So a kind of improvised, piecemeal price-fixing had got under way, and as Baruch explained afterwards, he knew of no benefit that came from this lack of precision.[50]

The way of the price-fixer, Baruch admitted, was hard. Actually, of course, he had no authority to set prices at all. The Price Fixing Committee of the War Industries Board, headed by Robert Brookings, was the only independent committee of the War Industries Board — its relation to the Board has been described as comparable to that of the Supreme Court to the whole Federal government. The chairman reported not to Baruch but directly to President Wilson himself. Baruch merely sat in, as one of the nine members. Nor did the Board have any general price-fixing power; it could only decide what prices the government would pay. Its aim was not nearly so much to fix prices as to inspire production. It was, perhaps, more in retrospect, that Baruch saw how disastrous to war- or peace-time economy a soaring price structure can be. Regardless of the actual division of authority, in the public mind at least his was the responsibility for the rising cost of living. Furthermore, he well knew that even such prices as were obtained were by no means free-will offerings. As we have seen with steel, they were fixed only with the aid of potential Federal compulsion.

Perhaps in no segment of his entire experience did Bernard Baruch learn more than in his service on the Price Fixing Committee of the War Industries Board. Germany had nearly won the war by a neatly mapped plan of organization. What had America to lose by planning ahead for future eventualities? None knew better than Baruch how far short of the ideal the First World War program had been. Only the use of priorities or the threats of commandeering could restrain a company that had determined to flout Uncle Sam. In the drive for increased production, the consumer's needs and pocketbook had been forgotten. Out of what had not been done, Baruch began to see what could have been done. Thus arose his conviction that stand-by legislation should always be on the books, providing that at the imminence of conflict prices could be pegged where they stood. Critics might retort that this was like fastening a lid on a boiling pot. Baruch retorted that was an unnatural situation, and price controls could at least reduce the spread between the abnormal and normal price relationships. Each individual price was simply the resultant of the price of everything. The whole price structure was interrelated, and an over-all freeze was at least fair. Fragmentary price-fixing resulted only in a continual adjusting upward. Instead of abortive attempts to roll prices back to their natural level, why not hold them there in the first place? As Baruch has often said: "One method stops a runaway and keeps the whole team in line. The other submits to the runaway and then tries to keep some of the horses from running faster than the rest." [51]

As the "general eye" of economic mobilization, Baruch looked beyond production to the producers. High prices might inspire production, but wild inflation broke morale, especially among soldiers' families, persons on fixed incomes, and laborers, whose real hardships in fighting the jacked-up prices for slum squalor, cheap food, and shoddy clothes endangered the whole war program.[52] Small wonder that labor had struck.

Even in a war boom, Baruch noted, few low-wage earners could maintain their meager standard of living. He agreed with the report of the President's Mediation Commission that "with the exception of the sacrifices of the men in the armed service the greatest sacrifices have come from those at the lower rung of the industrial ladder. Wage increases respond last to the needs of this class." Through his affection for Samuel Gompers, his respect for Hugh Frayne, and his own open-mindedness, Baruch gained considerable understanding of labor's problems.

From Frayne especially Baruch learned much. With Frayne's help, labor was guided across the bridge from nonessential employment to essential, without wasteful turnover.[53] Speakers from the Labor Department were sent to war plants. Baruch joined Frayne in his plea to Wilson for a War Industries Board badge for workers who had wanted to be at the Front and whom the draft boards had had to convince that it was just as patriotic to work as to fight.[54]

Together he and Frayne could talk about their hopes for after the war — a board for the rehabilitation of labor, soldiers perhaps to be kept in uniform and on pay until jobs were ready for them, and the new emergency laws for the protection of women and children which must be kept on the books. Labor must not lose the summits it had gained.

If from the public's standpoint production delays were usually due to labor agitation, those on the inside knew how diverse the causes might be.[55] On delays, even God played a part; a sudden summer tornado on August 6, 1918, meant suspended production of 65 per cent of the nation's sulphuric acid for nearly three months. All was wrecked — old wells were plugged with molten sulphur, and new ones had to be drilled under conditions of limited material and limited manpower.[56]

However slow production might be, the War Industries Board had early realized that if the supply of labor and raw materials was not great enough for plants already operating, it was obviously useless to build new ones. Railway bottlenecks continued to tie up freight, almost to the end of the war. In April 1918 Baruch suggested to McAdoo that shipments produced south of the Potomac and west of Pittsburgh be routed out from Southern ports.[57]

Second only to the dynamics of labor in the war was steel — steel for the rails that pursued the Germans back to Berlin; steel for the barbed wire of no man's land; steel for ships to replace those flooring the sea. This was "a war of blood and iron," fresh bodies and fresh steel, Pittsburgh against Krupp, the fires of battle burning beneath the coke ovens.[58]

As for the steel leaders themselves, some were not cooperative.[59] There was, for example, Judge Gary, for steel was Gary and Judge Gary was Big Steel. A small, compact, primly neat man, devoid of humor,[60] Gary was admittedly a tough nut to crack. But he had his virtues. Baruch was willing to concede that he was perhaps the best executive he had yet encountered. Gary knew the difference between good and bad trusts. He paid good wages; he felt that the workers were entitled to a share in the company's profits, and had worked out a scheme to make them sharers and stockholders, "capitalists in a small way," but management came first. As for his postwar protestations, to Baruch, he seemed merely an over-talkative old man intent on showing that his company had won the war.[61]

It was another representative of Big Steel who, jumping to his feet, roared that Baruch was the archenemy of the steel people and that they would never forgive him as long as they lived [62] — although in fact Baruch was not the one to be forgiven, for the quarrels with the steel industry came in the late summer of 1917, months before he was named chairman of the War Industries Board.[63] Nevertheless, the steel men recognized the head of the Raw Materials Committee as a weighty obstacle in their path, who ultimately used the threat of commandeering — which won the needed concessions — with great effect.

According to Baruch's old associate John Hancock, the denouement of this particular test of strength came at the conclusion of a meeting from which Gary emerged, after ten minutes of silent introspection, and in a low monotone, his words spaced about ten feet apart, told the assembled newspapermen that although not a steel man there approved the government's views, they had, nevertheless, bowed to them.[64]

What had happened? Baruch later commented that the government had had to use a club until the steel industry understood, but when it did understand, it did wonderful work.[65] Gary himself, years afterward, disclosed that the government had merely hinted that if the necessary prices were not approved, it would have to go to the difficulty and pain of nationalizing the steel industry. So Big Steel decided to spare it this pain.[66]

"That's what you call voluntary agreements," Baruch later commented.[67]

Afterward Garrett asked Baruch, "How the hell could you make those decisions?"

"They had to be made," was Baruch's prompt answer. "As you say, God knows what the consequences will be. But once a decision is made, the whole damn world has to adjust to it." [68]

But few tears need be shed for Big Steel.[69] The steel men had more reason than they would admit to applaud the name of Baruch at their Institute dinner at the Waldorf on June 1, 1918. For, despite such a shortage of the vital metal that the United States could meet neither its civilian nor its military obligations, there was no shortage of profits.[70] United States Steel's net income, for instance, for 1917 alone had been $224,000,000, with dividends of $7.62 a common share, figures not to be approached again for thirty-seven years.[71] So large were the Federal contracts, that even with the fixed prices and an excess profits tax, some of the "high-minded and public-spirited steel men" came to Baruch expressing concern over the immensity of the profits.[72] These were the exceptions. As for the others — "let's make no mistake about it," Baruch wrote, afterward: prices were fixed with the aid of potential Federal compulsion.[73] Sternly Baruch told Clarence Barron, "The financial and commercial interests of the

country have not stood by me as they ought to." [74] Actually, steel
lost out by dragging its feet. The government would at one point
have settled for $3.50 or $3.75 a pound for ship plates, and the industry would not then take it. Finally it had to take $3.25.[75]

Later, Price McKinney of McKinney Steel admitted, "We are all
making more money out of this war than the average human being
ought to." [76] Yet, upon the small producers the "voluntary agreement" bore down hard; what was the bare cost price for them meant
huge profits for Big Steel. But the profit incentive could not be
withdrawn. In desperation Baruch told the steel men on August 22:
"The whole question on the western front is a question of metals. It
is not to get steel there in January or February — not even day after
tomorrow, but to-day. We must have the weight of metal." If the
goals could not be met, he would have to tell the military chiefs, "We
cannot support you." Steel could not be produced for anything but
the war.[77]

In some cases, cooperation was cruelly hard upon certain industries
— the automobile companies, for instance, who faced an edict of
100 per cent repression or conversion. They met with Baruch on
May 7, 1918, and the atmosphere in that closely packed room of grim
men, their backs to the wall, was highly emotional. Baruch tried to
ease the tension, pointing out that all were in the same boat, but
the blow could not really be softened. As Judge E. P. Parker put it,
"Would we give the boys in khaki their supplies or give the automobile industry theirs?" [78]

Stoutly Baruch, Legge, and Replogle faced them down. They stood
before them as men of business, answering men of business. Patiently,
they tried to describe the vicious circle closing around their country
and the whole Allied world. The blast furnaces were closing down
because they consumed too much coke; more steel would be produced, if there were more steel from which to build railway cars to
carry coke; there would be more steel, if there were more steel to
make up the components that went into the making of steel. In the
final analysis, only steel begot steel.

Faces remained skeptical. Finally, Alex Legge said, "If any of
you gentlemen have a notion this is a hobby, please get that out of
your minds and get the idea of just how serious it is." He broke
off suddenly. Baruch tried to be explicit. "The recent advance of
the Germans has put them in control of the coal fields in France.

I don't think you gentlemen realize — " He paused, then went on, "We don't propose to let any industry in this country suffer when it is not necessary to suffer."

"We are telling you things which cannot be made public," he continued. "This is the problem as we see it; you haven't seen it yet." One manufacturer now nodded, gravely. "We understand the seriousness of the game," he said.

Up spoke D. D. Dart of the Dart Motor Company of Flint, Michigan. Flint was absolutely dependent upon the automobile industry. "You paralyze absolutely that life. I am speaking for Flint, alone. It is so serious that we must consider it better . . . even dragging a bit on . . . the Government program."

Baruch spoke firmly and slowly. "These orders cannot be put aside," he said.[79] They were not put aside, although the final outcome was as it should have been — a compromise. The agreement was that the auto industry be permitted to make in the last six months of 1918 one fourth as many cars as were delivered in 1917, with the added right to buy enough materials and parts to complete stocks on hand. By 1919, the industry would have to shift to war construction entirely.[80]

So ended the first round in the battle with the automobile manufacturers. It was not the last. Steel remained scarce; the battle of the home front went on, and with tiresome repetitiveness, Judge Gary insisted that there was enough steel for war and the home market too.

There were no ships for manganese. Idle plant capacity did not necessarily mean potential production. First there had to be the components to go into production; and furthermore there had to be excess facilities for emergency demand.[81] So desperate was the situation that the War Industries Board even considered a strange plan for resumption of pig iron production, through the reopening of coal mines in the old Bell seam off the Ohio River in the Ozark Mountains. Not since Civil War days, when gunboats and paddle-wheelers had steamed down the Ohio and pack mules had footed their way down half-broken mountain trails carrying fuel for the steamers had the old mines been in operation. No roads led to the camp, no rail lines, yet the property was developed and ready to supply coal for the pig iron in St. Louis. As it turned out, the plan was impractical, but it was one of many possibilities considered by the Board.[82]

By that little worn-out "paper" of authorization Baruch had the

authority to act for the President. Clarkson tells of the auto manufacturer with ample supplies of coal and raw material on hand who
refused to convert. Baruch called in a naval officer and asked him to
commandeer the manufacturer's coal. "The amazed automobile man"
asked, "You wouldn't do that, would you?"

"So far as I am concerned," Baruch replied, "it is already done.
So far as you are concerned, it will be accomplished tomorrow morning." [83]

So Clarkson tells the story. Baruch's version is less dramatic. When
members of the auto industry would not play ball, he merely invoked
his power to commandeer steel, rubber, all the "makings that went
into a car." [84] Whatever else he may have lacked, it was not the
power of decision. "I was a speculator, by God," he said, "and I'd do
what I damn well thought was right." Paralysis he always deemed
more deadly than error. A word of backhanded praise came from the
temples of finance. His old friend Thomas Fortune Ryan wrote,
"You're doing a good job. All our friends here are kicking." [85]

There is high drama in the story of nitrates during the war. Worn-
out land cried for nitrates, and, as Baruch said, "every pound of
powder and every pound of shot must have nitro as its principal in-
gredient." [86] Thus the sinking "of a rusty old freighter wallowing
up from Valparaiso was of more moment than the destruction of an
Army Corps," or of a warship.[87]

What water is to steam, nitrates are to explosives. In the desolate,
sterile plains of Tacna and Arica in Chile, seven thousand miles from
the Western Front, lay the most important deposits of nitrates in
the world. Yet even these sources were insufficient for both America
and the European Allies, to say nothing of the Central Powers. So
Chile held the whip hand. As prices soared up, 33 per cent upon
the declaration of war, and another hundred per cent three weeks
later, Baruch considered what to do. He had begun on the day that
Senator "Cotton Ed" Smith of South Carolina stopped by his office
to remind him of the exhausted cottonfields of their native state,
and of their crying need for fertilizer. Smith had appealed to the
President, who in turn had sent him on to Baruch.[88]

Baruch's first move came with the aid of Naval Intelligence. Chile,
the Navy reported, had gold reserves in Germany, which that nation
refused to release. And there were German-owned nitrates in Chile,

free from the vast governmental monopoly. Why could not the Chileans be induced to seize those nitrates as compensation for their gold and sell them to the United States? Baruch found out quickly enough why not: it was against a British law. Technically, any purchase of German holdings violated the Trading with the Enemy Act.

Up at the White House Baruch exasperatedly poured out the facts to President Wilson, who agreed with him that the whole thing sounded like a lot of nonsense. To Baruch it seemed even worse, and with British cooperation the Trading with the Enemy Act was waived and the purchase concluded. As Baruch explained to Vance McCormick, the need for nitrates was so imperative, that even the black-list policy seemed of small importance.[89]

Meanwhile, four American nitrate plants were being built to experiment with the ammonia process of extracting nitrates from the air. The plan was not as novel as it seemed; Germany had already had some success with this method, and at Syracuse a small plant had experiments already in progress. Talk of nitrate "fixations" filled the air. It was considered a possibility that the Chilean source would become obsolete. With this threat to the speculators, and with the Allies now sharing in the erstwhile German nitrates, the overseas powers were willing to join with the Raw Materials division in forcing lower prices, the speculators having bid the price up to seven and a half cents a pound. Very simply, all Allied buyers withdrew from the market for the last three months of 1917. Their need, they announced, had been supplied. Chile was left with a record production and no market, and prices broke so rapidly that the South American republic was almost "overwhelmed with financial panic." The desired end was achieved. The Allies returned to the market and bought their nitrates at four and an eighth cents a pound.[90]

All this economic warfare was almost neutralized, however, by the Du Pont Company, which in some forehanded purchasing of nitrates for explosives, had "misunderstood" Baruch's orders to keep out of the general market. The du Ponts' belated promise to withdraw instructions to their agents to purchase some 15,000 tons a month, their agreement that the government could take over their supplies, even the assurances that Mr. Baruch could count on their full cooperation, were not assurances enough for Mr. Baruch. He called them on their protestation that the company should not be compelled to turn over purchases already made. He would insist that they do so. He further stated that he would not permit the du Ponts to profit from a situation caused by all other purchasers remaining out of the market. The United States Government should receive the benefits.[91]

There was still another move to be made. From the first, Baruch had recognized the international implications of the nitrates question and its concern to the Inter-Allied Purchasing Commission. His whole plan would be liquidated should the European powers continue to dicker in the Chilean market. So the International Nitrate Executive was formed, with representatives of France, Italy, Great Britain, and the United States on the board.[92]

The real hunch, according to Leland Summers, was the appointment of Winston Churchill as Nitrate chief. The idea was at once to appease England and to make an Englishman responsible for straightening out the problems which his government's opposition to our waiver of the Trading with the Enemy Act had brought about. The move was strategic. Not only did Churchill's appointment mollify Great Britain, but it impressed both the War Industries Board and the Inter-Allied Purchasing Commission upon the British imagination. The War Industries Board, Summers wrote Baruch, had been practically unknown in London and was often confused with the War Trade Board.[93]

Churchill gloried in his new responsibilities. "I now became the Nitrate King," he exulted, "the greatest there will ever be." Summers assured Baruch that he had won Churchill's admiration and that the Englishman wanted to win Baruch's, in turn.[94] With "masterly" efforts, Churchill fought down the British Foreign Office, and Baruch held off the State Department while the Trading with the Enemy Act was scuttled, and the Chileans went to work seizing the German nitrates. By the summer of 1918 the Chileans, in exasperation, were even offering nitrates not for money but merely for some necessary railroad equipment. "Through the intimate cooperation of Winston Churchill and Baruch the offer was accepted."[95] Churchill even induced the Chileans to seize interned German ships for the transportation of the nitrates. Apparently Churchill did succeed in winning Baruch's confidence, for the Englishman was entrusted with the United States nitrate purchases. Baruch did not forget "Cotton Ed" Smith, however, and a *sine qua non* of the agreement was that the United States must first get one hundred thousand tons for the Agricultural Department. Here again Churchill did a "masterly" job of joint buying, with an eye to American interests no less than to Britain's.

At home, perhaps because of his triumph in the "leak" inquiry, there was a certain congressional animosity toward Baruch. Yet, by the force of his achievements, his warmth, and his guilelessness, Baruch was chipping this feeling away. Sometimes, under congressional grilling, he would wonder if he had any congressional friend; sometimes, before it was all over, the Senators might rise spontaneously to take his hand.[96]

He still had a long way to go, however, before he would be accepted even by the entrenched Southern committee members. Baruch's apparent disdain for "the privileges Southern planters are entitled to under a Democratic control of government" was as bold, if not as spectacular, as one of his financial coups. "Mr. Baruch," declared a writer in the Philadelphia *North American*, "was apparently thinking only of the needs of the government and the general public." [97] Hence Baruch's proposal to "stabilize" the price of cotton brought a spate of headlines: "Baruch Causes Big Cotton Stir" — "Southern Senators Up In Arms" — "Fixing Cotton Stirs All Dixie." [98] The one Southerner who refused to be stirred was Bernard Baruch.

Another headline completes the story: "Baruch Not To Yield." [99] After twenty-two Southern Senators, as heated as their own cotton-fields on an August day, had grilled Baruch for two hours, the spokesman for the group, Hoke Smith of Georgia, told reporters, "We asked Mr. Baruch to kindly keep his hands off." But the "suave and frequently smiling gentleman whose principal business [was] to say 'No,' when people want him to say 'Yes,'" as a reporter described him, had again said "No." [100]

Not only did he make the Southern planters swallow their dose; they even came to like it. For when the New York *Tribune* announced: "Cotton Price Is 'Fixed' By Baruch Magic," the subhead ran: "Even the South Likes His Scheme. Stabilization Plan Even Aids Farmers." The dose was not so bitter after all, although one paper proclaimed it "the boldest thing domestically that this administration has attempted." [101] With the cotton price stabilized, manufacturers were next compelled to use the lower grades and to pay more for them. The price of upper-grade cotton had been too high;

that of lower grades, too low; and the stabilization in the long run boomed Southern prosperity.

Not all Baruch's exploits were so sensational. Petty details and obligations beset him. Every penny spent by the War Industries Board office was itemized, whether disbursed by Baruch or Uncle Sam. An Underwood typewriter disappeared from the office of the Inter-Allied Purchasing Commission in London, and Scotland Yard was sent in search of it. This care was understandable, for the Board operated on a comparative shoestring. In March 1918, for instance, Baruch had had to ask for $200,000 in emergency funds to cover expenses until June of that year.[102]

There were the courtesy luncheons or dinners for the Board's regional representatives. There were always the problems of affronted groups, like the horseshoers, who wanted to form their own trust to negotiate with the government; or affronted individuals, like one who sought special licensing privileges for castor oil! In contrast, there were examples of real patriotism, like that shown by Alfred C. Bedford of Standard Oil of New Jersey, whose efforts helped bring the cooperation of the entire oil industry.[103]

"You always hold your helm true," wrote Wilson to Baruch in the late fall of 1918.[104] Words such as these were encouragement for the tense days of waiting. Battles must be fought; plans must go on; men must die; yet the end of the war was in the air.[105] On Wednesday, November 6, a final meeting of the "War Cabinet" was held at the White House.[106] Wilson said: "The Germans have asked for terms. Gentlemen, I'd like to have your views."

The man who spoke first was Herbert Hoover. Baruch was last in line. He spaced his words slowly. "I've been thinking so much about war, I really haven't been thinking about peace."

But Wilson had. He lifted a sheet of paper. "This is what I am going to say." [107]

For November 11, Baruch had planned a full day. In addition to his usual duties, at three he had scheduled an important session with the representatives of the State Councils of National Defense, to be capped with a banquet in the evening. The "false armistice" rumors still ran like a current beneath the plans for a shipment here and a new plant there; but so geared were Baruch and his men to a war economy that it had become the pattern of reality. Did not the "experts" here and abroad say that the greatest battles of all might come in 1919?

But November 11 was real. Baruch awoke to the shrill of whistles and sirens, the squawk of tin horns, the ringing of bells, the screaming of newsboys and explosions of backfiring cars. At the White House, Wilson's hand moved across a piece of paper. "Everything for which America fought has been accomplished." Nothing remained now but to establish "just democracy through the world." [108]

In New York, the Barnard students were snake-dancing on Morningside Heights. Down in Wall Street a dummy of the Kaiser was washed with a fire hose, and on Broadway a boy was drawing pictures of the Kaiser on the sidewalk to be trampled upon by the jeering mobs. In Times Square, under the light of the November dawn, a girl was singing the doxology.[109]

At the old State, War, and Navy building in Washington, the casualty figures were still coming in; and on this day, as on days for weeks ahead, telegraph wires were clicking out the messages: "The War Department regrets — " Regrets for men dead when it was all over, dying now in the field hospitals, dead and not yet reported, dying in the hours of celebration before noon, when it was not yet "All Quiet on the Western Front." In the offices of the War Industries Board, the girls were at work, Baruch himself bending over his desk.

At one o'clock that day, Wilson stood before Congress. Watching from the floor, Baruch saw the lines that sorrow had cut into his face, heard the somber, weighted words of responsibility to the unknown future. There was no lightheartedness, no exultation here. "It is up to you and to me," the President said, "and to every patriotic citizen of the United States to stay on the job." [110]

The State Councils assembled as scheduled at three, Judge E. P. Parker presiding. Outside, a crowd swayed by, shouting. Up sprang Secretary Lane and, with all the jubilation that Wilson could not muster, proclaimed, "It is a great thing to be an American at this time . . . all the world looks towards Washington . . . Now we are going to lead [the world] into peace." [111]

But it was Baruch the company was waiting to hear. He stood before them at last, a little diffidently. He was no man for speeches; had he not told them so?

Now, half apologetically, he confessed that the group had been summoned to hear "our further plans for the restriction of the industries of the country." Had any secret information as to the peace been forthcoming, we would have "asked you not to come here,

because we know that you are all busy men . . . We will not ask you
to do any further restricting." The smile, boyish and ingenuous now,
flashed across his face. "Thank you for what you have done for us.
It has been perfectly wonderful." [112]

He spoke again that evening at the banquet with the section chiefs
and Cabinet officers. Also on the program was Herbert Hoover, his
features frozen into perpetual youth, and his expression into perpetual
maturity. His name, too, had loomed large in the war. Was he a
"coming man"? Meanwhile, Baruch's tall figure wandered to and
fro among the guests and his "boys." What would the future hold
for him? Was this an end or a beginning? Professor F. W. Taussig of
the Tariff Commission, on his own way back to the classroom, hoped
that this would not be the end of Baruch's public career, and drew
him aside to warn him about the futility of going back to a life of mere
money-making. In a few short months he had won the admiration
of those whose opinions he valued. Typical was the comment of
Albert Brunker of the War Chemical division, who took time out on
Christmas Eve to write Baruch that he was leaving "proud in the
feeling" that he had served under a great man.[113]

Seldom in the history of a Washington government agency has
there been anything quite like the affection between Baruch and the
members — down to the lowliest eighteen-year-old typist — of the
War Industries Board. During the weeks after the Armistice there
were banquets and dinners, presentations of a loving cup, a knife,
and sentimental tributes to the "great days." Four years later, one
member wrote Baruch that he cherished his association with the War
Industries Board more than anything in his life.[114]

Typical of the unabashed sentimentality of the goodbyes was the
final meeting of the Building Materials division, with the chairman,
Richard I. Humphrey, wondering aloud if all appreciated "what a
wonderful experience this has been" or shared that feeling of having
climbed "a big mountain peak."

From their cheers, it was evident that they did, and then Baruch
rose to his feet. "I am particularly embarrassed," he said, "when I
am complimented for doing something which I know myself I had
so little share in doing because you men are the men that did it . . .

"When there are a dozen kicks about the work of some Division
I know that they are doing a fairly good job, and when I receive a
hundred kicks I know that they are doing a mighty fine piece of

work . . . If a man down here was not called a scoundrel a thousand times, I immediately came to the conclusion that he was not doing a fine piece of work . . ." [115]

The breaking up of the Board reminded him of the last days of college; the friendships that he had found were like "associations in school." If only they could all get together again. This last hope came true, and in future years the renewal of these memories would ease his heart and mind, and make him wish to live through all eternity.[116]

Humphrey now resumed the floor and poured forth tribute to the inspiration of the Chief which had actuated every man to do more than he thought humanly possible. For each, what counted was "the personality of the man at the head."

Again Baruch rose and stammered, "If you are going to throw bouquets of that kind, I had better withdraw." [117]

It was his personality they would remember. One wrote that in the years to come he could see his children's children telling how "Grandpa was a friend of the great Baruch." [118] Tributes poured in to his "unfailing good nature," to the strength and force you could feel at meetings, even when he was not there, to his patriotism.[119] The explosive, warmhearted Herbert Bayard Swope felt that never in his life had he been so helped by the personal influence of one man.[120]

Glory had come to Baruch, but he shared it with those around him. His achievements in Washington, as in Wall Street, had arisen from his comprehension of human nature. Personal loyalty and team play had made the big achievements possible.[121]

To the Regional Advisers, to the firms that had loaned or donated men, he sent notes alike only in their graciousness. In a cable to Churchill, referring to the wartime relations between the United States and England, he pledged that he would do his utmost to perpetuate this friendship.[122]

Tributes poured in to Baruch throughout the winter. One of the great "human interest" stories of the war did not even then make the newspapers. Not until eighteen years later did James F. Byrnes tell the tale of Baruch's Christmas gift to the stenographers of the War Industries Board.

So quickly did the Board wind up its affairs that hundreds of girls — from Oshkosh or Wahoo, Cotton Plant or Morganfield, many of them in their teens and never before away from home — were left stranded in the capital. Their pay checks had stopped. Christmas was coming, and some had not even the carfare home. Beckoning them were all the temptations of the big city in a frenzied postwar jubilee. Then word was passed through the little furnished rooms of the Washington boardinghouses. The Chief would pay their fare; the Chief would provide a matron to see them off and send them home.

One girl wrote that she had returned home on Christmas Eve and was regarded as a Christmas present from Baruch.[123] He had requested that they let him know of their arrival; and they did, on picture postcards, or on violently hued pink or blue notepaper, and all of their communications he filed away. Few of the girls were of course known to him personally. Some saw him for the first time as he stood submitting to the clicking of cameras at the presentation of a loving cup, and yet they felt why he was so much beloved.[124] Years later, if his name or fame were assailed in a public gathering, there was always in the audience some girl from the old War Industries Board to rise in protest. So treasured were his farewell letters that one who lost hers wrote it out from memory and sent it to be signed again.[125]

It had cost Baruch $45,000 to send the girls home, and it had made friends for him across the country. It made him realize the joy to be had in spending money.[126]

Baruch did not forget Frank Scott, his weary predecessor on the War Industries Board to whom he wrote gratefully of the "almost" impossible job which he had faced with courageous patience without the reward of final victory.[127] To Winston Churchill in almost Churchillian rhetoric, Baruch expressed his great respect for England's fortitude in fighting through weary days for the right. He hoped that some day they would meet and become friends.[128]

Baruch's reward came from the man who was soon to characterize him as "one of the best friends I ever had." [129] Publicly, Wilson told him that the success of the War Industries Board was due to the chairman's "ability, tact, and devotion to duty." [130] Privately, he elaborated on how Baruch had won not only his confidence but his affection, and how he had learned to "value [his] counsel and assistance. It has been a delightful experience to know you and to work with you . . .

"But your letter sounds too much like goodbye," Wilson wrote Baruch the twenty-second day of November. "I do not mean to let you go yet if I can help it, because there is much remaining to be done, and I do not like to feel that I am going away and leaving it to be done by inexperienced hands. We will have a talk about this . . ."[131]

The talk was held, as rumors buzzed through Washington. In December, William G. McAdoo had retired from the Treasury. He resigned a poor man, his purse and his energy drained by the demands of his office. He had made a good record, and was acclaimed as the only man in the Cabinet with a "grasp of complex business problems." Outside the Cabinet, Baruch was the only official of like caliber.[132]

Baruch stood high; in the opinion of his more fervid admirers, even the Presidency was not beyond his grasp. No one had been more devoted to Wilson than he. Nor was anyone more vigilant in guarding Wilson's name.[133] At a Washington dinner party a friend heard people conjecturing as to McAdoo's successor, and burst out that the only man in the country who had the confidence of the American people was Bernard Baruch.[134]

Yet, documentary evidence to the contrary, despite the assertions of several historians of the era and innumerable letters of congratulation and newspaper stories, according to Mr. Baruch's own memory he was not offered the Treasury job in 1918. He was "spoken of" continually, but he headed off any outright offer of the position from Wilson by pointing out that he was unavailable because of his great wealth.* [135] Furthermore, he may have had his mind on more distant horizons. There was rather undue modesty in his assertions that he believed that he would not be burdened with after-war responsibilities.[136] For, even to the novice observer, it was obvious that Bernard Baruch was by temperament a born diplomat, with a passion for getting people together and getting things done — qualities Wilson had noted well.

Meanwhile, the glorious adventure was over — the War Industries Board died officially and quietly on November 18, 1918, and within a week all was still in the rooms where once had hummed the enterprise of a continent. A few clerks worked carefully, sorting out the papers so that they would be useful, unlike so many archives.[137] The

* See the next chapter.

War Industries Board was ended, but it had left behind a concept, a plan for fusing the diverse elements in an economy for a single purpose. In war, this idea had reshaped the life of a continent. Might it not also in peace reshape the pattern of its economic thought?

Only from the perspective of nearly forty years is it possible to evaluate the long-range effects of the War Industries Board. It left the blueprints and the record as a guide toward mobilization for modern war. Less attention has been paid to its reshaping of huge industrial units toward the economic collectivism of a later day. Least of all has its influence been appreciated toward making regional economic isolation, rather than political internationalism, the pattern for a world divided by curtains of bamboo and iron.

This last was not Baruch's goal. He dreamed of "an ordered economic world," a world community with common access to the storehouses of mankind. But after the Paris Conference and the ensuing peace that was no peace, doubts increased. Baruch warned Wilson on the eve of Christmas in 1919 that, since another war emergency might "arise in the future," essential to our military security was a "peacetime skeleton" War Industries Board, with stand-by powers to coordinate the resources of the country and the representatives of the Army, the Navy, the Shipping Board, and the purchasing agencies. Men should be in charge of raw materials, labor, planning, statistics, and priorities, with specialists in the various commodities empowered to name committees of industry for quick mobilization.[138] These should meet annually, serving without pay. Some kind of central agency for mobilization would thus force a liaison between the armed forces and industry.[139] Baruch realized, of course, that it was "impossible to foresee the precise circumstances and requirements of any future war." But the general principle of industrial mobilization was unalterable: the services must state what they needed, and civil control must umpire and allot it.[140]

To Baruch it all seemed perfectly reasonable and clear, but it would not seem so to Wilson, nor to Roosevelt, nor to Truman, nor to Eisenhower — all of whom in turn considered and rejected any idea of complete stand-by industrial mobilization. Nor did it seem reasonable to the people, with their "vested interest in error," their propensity for building anew, without utilizing the foundations of the past.

Nor did it appeal to Congress, even though it would involve funds for only one organization instead of half a dozen. The plans for the future did not seem reasonable to a Congress already embroiled in warfare over the peace. The time had come to put away the things of war. And among the first to be put away was the War Industries Board.[141]

Congress even turned a jaundiced eye on the preservation of the Board's records for public use, and the formation of a permanent agency to watch all industries of potential war value.[142]

But not even Congress could legislate the impact of the Board out of existence. Wartime conservation had reduced styles, varieties, and colors of clothing. It had standardized sizes. It had reduced waste in shipments.[143] It had outlawed 250 different types of plow models in the United States, to say nothing of 755 types of drills. Two hundred and thirty-two different types of buggy wheels had come under the eye of the War Industries Board, and as they rolled away into the soft dust of country roads, as yet untouched by macadam, an era faded into the cloudy horizon with them. Not "Yankee ingenuity," but the assembly line was becoming the ideal; not to be different, but to conform. Nearly 6000 different shapes and sizes of pocket knives vanished from the country stores and from the pockets and imaginations of country boys across a continent; mass production and mass distribution had become the law of the land. Mass production could save time and labor and lower prices at the cost of individual self-expression and variety. This, then, would be the goal for the next quarter of the twentieth century: "To Standardize American Industry," to make of wartime necessity a matter of peacetime advantage.[144] With the undoubted value of lower prices, the retiring Board urged formation of a permanent agency for conservation and standardization. The agency was not formed. But conservation and standardization became permanent.[145]

They would have become so, anyway; they cannot be laid to the door of the War Industries Board. America was on the assembly line. The horse-and-buggy age was over. On the way to oblivion was the era of rugged individualism and small business, the one-man shop and the one-man farm; even the New Freedom itself was shelved. Actually, the processes of modern technology had been evolving for a long time, as trends so often are, before reaching the attention of the public. What the War Industries Board did was to step up the trend, as trends are stepped up under the impact of war, perhaps to even speed it up ten years. What the War Industries Board did was to dramatize the trend for American people.

As for Baruch, himself, whatever his own sentimental yearnings toward the past might be, he knew that it was too late to go back. A new function of government, "certain new principles of supervision" [146] would have to be evolved to protect the public interest. The same massed power that could benefit private greed must be diverted to the public benefit. Waste and duplication could be eliminated. Mass tastes could be cultivated for "rational" types of commodities; mass production would mean more goods at lower prices.

The War Industries Board had taught lessons, perhaps even too many at one time; and the lessons that big business had learned were not easily unlearned. In eight short months there had been the near reversal of a generation's trend against trusts, monopolies, and massed corporate power. Had not "cooperation" indeed been the aim of the whole war program, beneficial not only to industry, but to the whole public? Proper legislation, George Peek thought, should be enacted to permit cooperation in industry.[147]

Business had combined for the public good; would it ever now be able to resist combination for its private welfare? [148] How far could the domination of an industry by any single great concern be permitted? Baruch knew well that such domination was possible without outright ownership; as, for instance, in Gary's control of the country's steel. Big Steel alone could probably put its minor-league competitors out of business, then peg prices where it wanted them. And this was a situation the War Industries Board had furthered.

In his subsequent book, *American Industry in the War*, Baruch analyzed the situation. The Sherman and Clayton Antitrust Acts had sufficed only for the simpler conditions of the past. As he wrote, to leave business with no more supervision than those old laws, would subject the leaders to "temptations to conduct their business for private gain with little reference to the public welfare." Vast monopolies might subtly influence production, keeping supply short and prices high. They could break the backs of infant unions, or, by "a meeting of minds," determine wage scales. Conceivably, big business untrammeled could enslave America to make itself prosperous and "free." Conversely, through control of huge sums of capital, the businessman could convert the natural wealth of mankind into a means of human happiness.[149]

What was the answer? In Baruch's findings we see the outlines of the future NRA. He suggested not the "busting," but the regulation of trusts and big business, perhaps by the Federal Trade Commission, or by a kind of "high court of commerce," as Wilson planned. The point was not to discourage big business, but to control it, and turn its profits to public advantage.[150]

America was drifting away from the old laissez-faire concept that government was merely a policeman. The power of modern industry made it necessary "for the Government to reach out its arms to protect competent individuals against the discriminating practices of mass industrial power." [151] Some central agency was necessary, "clothed with the power" to prevent abuse, and with power, also, to supervise and encourage production and conservation. "Such a plan should provide a way . . . of inviting industry to approach the Government." [152] Thus far had Baruch come from Wall Street.

One evolution, however, out of the combined impact of war and mobilization, he did not see. Nor was it even seen by the isolationists whose cause it would have upheld. A generation and more later, it would still not be recognized, although the scattered pieces of the puzzle were to be found, neglected and half forgotten in the files of the War Industries Board. There is no more ironic paradox in history than the fact that as the Parliament of Man first began to seem a possibility, as over and over into the minds of men was dinned the doctrine that the conditions of modern war made isolation impossible, the bases of economic nationalism were evolving out of those same conditions of war.

Up in Lawrence, Massachusetts, the Pacific Mills might gloat over the prospects for increased foreign trade; but the forecast was to seem slightly more than optimistic a decade or so later. Slowly, realization came that a market and a supply do not automatically go together. A war-wracked continent has needs, yes, but it has nothing to trade or with which to pay. Nor was American industry eager for the entry of rival products from abroad. As early as November 26, 1918, American dye manufacturers were demanding protection for their "infant industry." [153]

The fact that in 1914 the United States produced 591 tons of chromite, compared to 60,000 tons in 1918, is highly significant. Of what use to purchase the metal, of what use trade? Chrome and manganese, too, supposedly nonexistent in this country, were found in such large quantities that there was actually too much on hand. Brazil had been the source of our manganese, yet during the war our shipping was so involved in the transport of munitions that we could not even send to Brazil the coal to run her railroads. With over 150 nitrogen plants under construction at the war's end, the United States was, of course, freed from its dependence upon Chilean nitrates; and Chile, in its turn, was minus the dollars needed to buy the output of American factories. As the official report of the chemical industry observed, given a few months' time, you could get about anything you needed out of the American continent.[154]

What did this mean? It meant that as the gospel of internationalism was preached, the cornerstones of economic nationalism, or, at best, regionalism, were being laid. The instances cited are not the reasons for this "trend in self-sufficiency," observable in almost all of the disillusioned countries after the war, and nowhere more than in the United States.[155] They were the symptoms of the diseases, or, perhaps, the valid excuses for doing what it was already determined to do. The irreconcilable elements in the gospel of Wilson were his dual insistence upon internationalism, as exemplified by the League; and upon the self-determination of the nations and people who composed it. Self-determination is but a step away from nationalism, and in the dark days of the war's aftermath, with their credit exhausted and being forced by war's necessity to rely upon their own scanty resources, left only in the rags of their own national pride, a kind of international "austerity" gripped the nations of the world. France would not surrender her precious gold for American cars. Germany had no gold and few raw materials left. Britain was already belting in.

As for the United States, we had proved our self-sufficiency, and, as happens after every war, our war-born industries would not be sacrificed, not for the abstractions of an unnecessary world trade or for better world relations. We could stand alone. Thus, the circumstances of modern war which rendered political nationalism untenable were making economic nationalism more and more of a world reality.

9

WORLD TO WIN

To THE YOUNG, Paris is always young. The lament of those who mourn the gay Paris, the beautiful Paris of their youth, falls on deaf ears. For Paris is always young, Paris is always gay, Paris is always beautiful to those who have never seen it before.

Wounded, bleeding, "pierced almost to her heart," Paris in that sullen winter of 1918–19 was wonderful,[1] according to Baruch's colleague of the Advisory Commission, Dr. Franklin Martin. It was wonderful to those battle-stained young Americans from the Marne who had laid down their guns and picked up their books almost on the same day. They filled the shell-shocked capital with gusto and exuberance; they brought lights of hope into the eyes of the girls, although they could never tell the girls they could speak to from the girls they could not. Young Americans exploding out of classrooms of the staid Sorbonne. Young Americans who would drink nothing but water and young Americans who would drink nothing but wine. Young Americans who had taken up the fight at the eleventh hour. Young Americans, like York, the blacksmith and mountain preacher, the conscientious objector with a hunting rifle; these were men, these young Americans, "lifted out of their ordinary selves." [2]

In their wake came a second onslaught of Americans, young [3] also, although not as young, uplifted by the intensity of their purpose, by feelings they could scarcely put into words. Baruch had earlier spoken of them to Wilson — of the crusading zeal his cause had engendered.[4] A few weeks past, all Europe would have followed Wilson like crusaders — the enthusiastic young Americans and the war-worn young Englishmen, who together knew the dream at which Clemenceau smiled, of a world where all wrongs were "to be righted, all old injustices to be redressed." [5] The measure of their failure is the height to which they climbed.

Wilson had arrived on December 13, 1918. Never had there been such crowds, such cheers, as had followed his cavalcade — streets black with crowds — London — Rome — cascades of violets and yellow mimosa falling upon him, people who would be tearing down his picture as that of a devil only a few weeks later, struggling to clutch his hand. Paris, the Paris that had cheered Foch and Clemenceau and the haggard, wounded soldiers, now finding voice again. If you heard these voices, you never forgot them. Who could doubt Wilson's invincibility? He was a god, a Messiah. And following him were the young "crusaders," their dream not vengeance, but eternal peace. It was a New World of which they dreamed, but the new world was already locked in a death struggle with the old — with those who dreamed that everything would soon be as it was in 1914, "save the aching vacancies at every hearthside." [6] Many looked back happily to 1914; for many it had been a good world, which offered opportunity, if not equality; where a man in London had at his command the products of the whole earth, "cheap and comfortable means of transit to any country . . . without passport"; could draw his gold from the bank and spend it anywhere without interference.[7] Now all was "transformed utterly," as Yeats was writing,[8] and many cried out against this strange New World being born in forced labor. The brotherhood of man was the cause of the epoch, and the United States, through its President, was its chief warrior.[9]

And Baruch was there to help in the fight. On November 23, Governor W. W. Hobby of Texas, who had found a rare sympathy of thought and purpose on meeting Baruch in October, had telephoned Wilson urging that the chairman of the War Industries Board be named to the Peace Commission. No selection would more please the South or benefit the country.[10]

On December 11, Baruch had received word to hold himself in readiness for a call to Paris. His assignment was the sector of international economics and industrial affairs. Immediately, he had dispatched Alex Legge into Austria and Germany with Hoover to survey conditions. Legge, he thought, would be unequalled in assisting with the problems. On January 2, 1919, Baruch sailed on the *George Washington*. Mr. and Mrs. Franklin D. Roosevelt were also aboard. Upon leaving, Baruch was offered so many letters of introduction to this or that French official that he arbitrarily ruled against all of them.[11] More useful seemed a seasickness remedy suggested by a friend: plain butter sandwiches, sprinkled with cayenne pepper.[12] But these, alas, were of no avail. Vance McCormick, who was Baruch's cabin mate, recorded in his diary that his friend was "sick most of the way." [13]

At Brest, Baruch and McCormick were met with a private car provided by the French government and hurtled through the mud and rain to Paris. The city was damp, foggy, and alive with rumors. "Bolshevism," it was said, had infiltrated the disbanded German Army. Secretary of State Robert Lansing, who as early as November had predicted that Wilson would only weaken his influence both at home and abroad by going to Paris, was now exulting that the President had found himself confronted with a man-sized job. As for his idea of a covenant for a League of Nations, it would "never go, never." Colonel House, meanwhile, was imparting the news that the President did not look well.[14]

At the Crillon, where his business suite comprised some six rooms, Baruch soon saw that he was no longer the rich American on tour. The hotel, gaunt and gray as its atmosphere, requested guests to reduce tipping to a minimum: for breakfast, a half franc; for lunch and dinner, a franc each — although Memo Number 59, distributed to the Peace Commissioners from the office of Captain R. C. Patterson, Jr., informed them that arrangements had been made to pay the servants a flat wage, including tips. As fuel was short in Paris, another memo requested that all lights be turned off when not in use.[15]

The Majestic, with its garish foyer where teacups were ever clattering, was headquarters for the British delegation. There, by day and night, dance music rattled tinnily from below stairs, but to the overstrained young men who had stepped straight out of khaki into council chambers, this shell-shocked capital seemed a nightmare and everyone was morbid. While they were soldiers, in the febrile gaiety of wartime, Paris had been the oasis in a desert of death. Now, ghosts peopled the city.

Baruch and McCormick, officially classified as "presidential advisers," had arrived in time for the formal opening of the Conference at the Quai d'Orsay. There, in funereal black, with all the solemnity of a court, the eleven delegates of the major powers seated themselves at a U-shaped table. Clemenceau was at the head, Wilson at his right side. There was no applause. Behind the encrusted gilt and faded silks of the high, hot salon, with its rows of gilt chairs and maps and interpreters and secretaries, the crystal chandeliers and great red curtains, the red upholstery and the carpets, red as blood — behind all this throbbed the "fearful convulsions of a dying civilization" and the chaos of a world. Here indeed were the ghosts — the ghosts of ten million dead young men and all their unsown progeny.

Against this backdrop the peacemakers seemed insignificant. Clemenceau with his gloved hands and strange, animal eyes; Wilson with his high collar and Southern drawl and black buttoned shoes; Lloyd George and Orlando and the others, big men and little men, dwarfed by the immensity of the task before them.[16] Their charge was the future of mankind. From the moment Bernard Baruch had stepped from the gangplank of the *George Washington,* he was swept into the current of history and it seemed to him as if the very foundations of society were shaken. The people of Europe were not fearful of the future; they could see no future. The problems seemed almost insoluble, Baruch wrote his son, but solved they would have to be, if civilization were to continue.[17]

Meanwhile, time was frittered away. Wilson nominated Clemenceau as president of the Conference, and an agenda was prepared for the discussion of regulations, the order of the day, the responsibility of the authors of the war, and responsibility for the crimes committed in the war. A ruling was made that technical delegates, such as Baruch, could only speak to supply necessary information. But they could listen, and Baruch heard the multifold explanations of the two months' delay between the Armistice and the opening of the Conference. "We thought," explained Harold Nicolson of the British delegation, "that if we waited a little things might settle down." But "things" had no intention of settling down.[18]

Baruch heard the debate as to whether French or English should be the official language of the Conference, and whether the French-speaking peoples or the English-speaking peoples had done more to win the war. At last, Clemenceau observed that if so much importance was attached to such matters, it boded ill for the proposed League.

One day later came the censorship row. Clemenceau demanded either "total secrecy or complete publicity," and Wilson insisted on "complete publicity." The United States wanted open sessions. But here the realistic Clemenceau interjected a warning — agreements must be unanimous, or malicious forces would breed discord.

Would it not suffice, Wilson wondered, if newspapers were frankly told that the objective was agreement? Lloyd George demurred. With day-to-day news reports, he warned, a false impression would be made.

The decision was dictated by practical necessity. Strictly edited reports of "progress" were disseminated to the dissatisfied newspapermen. Of Wilson's stubborn fight for their interests, they knew nothing. David Lawrence, for instance, thought that Wilson believed there should be no town meeting when negotiating a treaty.[19] Wilson had not the surplus physical strength for press interviews. Every ounce of his energy had to be husbanded for the immense tasks before him; but this was known only to those on the "inside," and the false impression dealt a damaging blow to Wilson's public relations overseas.

The immediate question, however, was procedure. At the request of Clemenceau, a French plan was considered and divided into two parts, one dealing with guiding principles as to war guilt and reparations, the other, with immediate financial problems. From the first, there was divergence between the English and Americans on the one hand and the French on the other — the latter preferring to deal with broad general principles and the logic of their application; the Anglo-Americans with the immediate and practical facts. Agreement was difficult. As late as April, Alex Legge advised Baruch that the rules of procedure should be in writing. Progress was seriously delayed, in many cases almost entirely stopped, because of a lack of uniform understanding.[20]

There is no evidence that Baruch upon his summons was even informed what his role in the Conference would be. In his personal suite at the Ritz, where negotiations went on continuously as to whether or not his status was such as to permit him a telephone,[21] he pored over his commission, signed on January 18 by Secretary of State Robert Lansing. His titles, if not his duties, were impressive. He enumerated them in a letter to his son: Technical Adviser of the American Commission to Negotiate Peace; American Delegate and Economic Adviser to the Peace Conference; Chairman of the Raw Materials Section, Supreme Economic Council; Technical Adviser to the Economic Drafting Committee; member of the Economic

Commission; member of the Reparation Commission, and of the Inter-Allied Supreme Economic Council. On the last, he and Mc-Cormick had privately agreed not to push for an American as chairman, since they knew that whatever was finally accomplished would disappoint the hopes of the world.[22]

By Executive order on February 14, $150,000 was put at Baruch's disposal to carry out such activities as he found necessary.[23] He could now belatedly assemble a staff of eight or ten (Wilson's first instructions had been to bring no one with him), and within a few weeks they began arriving — his "boys" from the War Industries Board: Legge, Summers, F. W. Taussig, and Charles H. MacDowell, to name a few. They overflowed two floors at the Crillon; they exuded drive and bounce in the war-wracked city.

Despite his high-sounding titles already listed, Bernard Baruch's part in the Peace Conference was that of a technical expert in economic matters, including the problem of German reparations. Although he served, together with Norman H. Davis, as American representative on the Reparation Commission, and as sole official American member of the Economic Drafting Committee, it must be remembered that the American delegation together with all its technical advisers was very large, and the work of any individual below the top echelons, no matter how important, was inconspicuous.[24] It was the opinion of Senator Robert Taft, however, that "Baruch and Hoover pretty well ran the economic side" of the American delegation.[25]

What Baruch learned about the processes of international statecraft was probably far more important than anything he really did at Paris. In that madhouse of conflicts and crosscurrents, no one could see anything but his own sector of the background. Not for several weeks could Baruch write Joseph Grew of how pleased he was that the secret notes of the informal meetings of the Big Four were sent on to him.[26] And, at first, his advice was not asked, even on economic questions. He has confirmed the unimportance of his early role at the Conference. "There I sat," he said afterward. "I just sat around; nobody paid any attention to me." If his name appeared on a committee assignment, it was at least once written in, as an afterthought, in Wilson's own hand. It was perhaps in feigned amazement that Colonel House once confronted Wilson with the statement, "Bernard Baruch says you offered him the Treasury."

"Well, it is true," Wilson replied.* [27]

In any event, Baruch had ample time to listen, to read, to learn. What he heard was the conversation of the world's most brilliant men.[28] He was learning the facts of international economic life in the twentieth century. He was asking himself constantly what America's role could most usefully be.[29] The previous fall he had requested France, Belgium, and Serbia to supply lists of what was needed for their rehabilitation. The second day after his arrival he made the same request of Tardieu. By mid-April, not having yet received a reply, he pointed out to the governments concerned that the responsibility for the delay was theirs. But he was beginning to know the reasons for delay; he answered his own unspoken question. Perhaps the task was so great it was impossible. Meanwhile, he stood ready to do anything he could.[30]

Through the hallways and corridors he moved, a tall American with a crown of prematurely white hair, bringing a breath of new life into the halls of the Quai d'Orsay, "that . . . kindly individual whose smile encompassed everyone . . . and stimulated one's pulse rate and temperature," as his colleague Dr. Franklin Martin described him. In that atmosphere of resentment and intrigue, Baruch's frank blue eyes were not only friendly but "without guile, and that immediately struck a responsive chord of sympathy." [31] Mark Sullivan later observed that Baruch was "to an extraordinary degree for a man of so high a position in the world, thoughtful about others, and considerate of the personality of the humblest man." In the supersensitive Paris of 1919 this was rare praise indeed.[32]

But Baruch was not entirely unnoticed. This was the man who even Hindenburg was said to have claimed "won the war for the Allies." [33] Especially between Clemenceau and Baruch an instant attraction developed into friendship. Clemenceau liked Americans. As he once explained, "You are so very, very young and amusing . . . And because when we [came] within two fingers of disaster you came and saved my grey hairs from knowing defeat." [34] But in this particular American, Clemenceau found a kind of innate sophistication, an inbred wisdom, something of the quality that Paderewski had.

---

* According to Mr. Baruch's present memory of when he was offered the Treasury (that is, in 1920), it was after the last time that House and Wilson met, on June 28, 1919.[27] If the above exchange occurred, it would indicate that the offer was actually made when the documents indicate — in 1918.

Clemenceau questioned Baruch once on his Polish heritage, then leaned back, as if satisfied. To Baruch, Clemenceau seemed a noble and inspiring figure, "one of the truly great men I have met." In later years, when Baruch could write familiarly to the Frenchman of how together they could solve the world's problems, he added an ingenuous expression of gratitude for the Frenchman's friendship.[35]

The press closed in. Young Arthur Krock requested an interview, which was forthwith arranged by Herbert Bayard Swope. On the threshold of Baruch's suite Krock halted and stared. There lay Baruch, a magnificent figure, all six feet four inches of him, on a chaise longue, with a pretty manicurist at each hand, a barber at his head, and a bootblack at his feet. Around him milled men and talk on how to make the peace. Baruch's voice, Southern, slurred, a little harsh, cut through palaver. "We must work and save," he said.[36]

It was understandable that in the early days Baruch's concept of the problems of the peace was elementary. He thought as an American long before he began to think as a world statesman; and he thought first of the safety and interests of his own country. Nor was all of his work at Paris concerned with the making of peace. There were tag ends of business from the War Industries Board to be cleared up — for instance, the nitrate situation. By cable Churchill and Baruch had discussed the best way to handle the remaining nitrate stocks.[37] The hitch was the United States itself, frantically scrambling to sell its own surplus in competition with the world pool. At subsequent luncheons with Churchill, Baruch thrashed over the problem. England would not act for the United States in disposal of the overseas surplus if the United States competed with the pool.[38] Baruch got the War Department to agree to a more cooperative plan but had yet to hear from the Navy, and as late as May he had to cable a reminder to Franklin Roosevelt that only the Nitrate executive could sell the surplus stocks.[39]

Eventually the scheme got into operation. Germany and the Central Powers were the "natural market" for nitrates,[40] and so desperate was the German need for fertilizer that a drain on the world's food supply might well be eased if a way could be found for her to pay. Open sale to the enemy was, of course, *unthinkable*, but even before arriving overseas, Baruch had the idea that the neutrals could buy the surplus and, in turn, sell it to Germany.[41] The scheme worked.

Baruch was for "America first" — perhaps at first in a parochial way.⁴² To paraphrase Churchill in a later day, Baruch might well have said that he had not been appointed to preside over the liquidation of American trade rights across the world. With every famished state and even unborn states diving into the international grab bag, the United States must have its share — a view in which worldly-wise Colonel House concurred. Neither House nor Baruch may yet have realized, as Wilson did, that an age had ended and the world had changed. But both House and Baruch realized what President Wilson never did, that human nature itself was unchanging — a conviction heartily shared by Georges Clemenceau, whose only illusion was France and whose greatest disillusion was mankind.

In any event, Baruch thought that the United States should go after the trade that the French and the Germans, and perhaps even the English, used to supply. Germany, he knew, would be "out" for some time. The American manufacturer would be much better off aiming for Europe's former markets than in trying to supply Europe itself, whose countries required loans from the United States before they could or would buy. The French were suppressing imports. China and South America offered a growing market. In further elaboration, Baruch wrote George Peek that conditions abroad were somewhat different from what he had first imagined. Whole industrial plants had been destroyed; whole countries were without transport or supply. There were not enough people working to carry those who were idle. Worst of all, these depleted European countries could not establish credits with which to buy. The United States insisted on payments in solid currency. Slowly Baruch was realizing, as American businessmen in general had yet to learn, that "business as usual" could not be resumed in the postwar chaos. Deferred payments must now be the rule. Baruch wondered if individual notes, to be guaranteed by banks and governments, might be acceptable. Payment on national loans, he thought, should be adjusted by the Treasury Department, and the President empowered to relieve countries that could not even meet their interest payments without destroying their economic potential.⁴³

But all this was hypothetical. Baruch's interest at the moment was in undeveloped markets, and no warnings of shipping experts against the wasteful shipbuilding and no fear of alienating our recent allies by ruthless competition for world markets could dim his enthusiasm. Nevertheless, although the best markets were in the undeveloped countries, they no more than Europe possessed any "natural credit" or gold, being themselves subsidized from the treasuries of Europe. Would we, instead of trying to "sell America" to the world, adapt and design our goods for the markets where they were to be sold? Would we view undeveloped sectors as markets or dumping grounds? Europe was already there. Would we go there — to the flea-bitten, heat-sogged, moldering outposts of the world — stay there, live there, learn the languages, and risk the jealousy of other nations? [44]

The answers seemed obvious — at least to American industrial producers. European ground was, at least, familiar, and Baruch and the rest of the American delegation's technical advisers were bombarded with questions from home as to the European market. Automobiles, for instance. France was without transport; the American auto industry stood ready to supply it. Why were not the embargoes lifted, export licenses granted? The answer came in seven typed pages. Briefly, the auto manufacturers of France feared American rivals.[45]

Distillers. Why, demanded Fred Housman of Baruch, were 200,000 workers still unemployed in the United States and supplies of fuel, of barley, cereals, and corn still withheld by the government? Was not the world in crying need of spirits? [46]

Cotton. This was Baruch's own immediate concern. Peek reminded him of the sad plight of the American industry. Germany had been America's greatest prewar cotton market. Perhaps now a Finnish or Polish trade could be developed.[47] Here, again, the problem was credits, and every day's delay was critical to the hard-pressed cotton growers.[48] But if America was not yet willing to underwrite the war victims, she was even less enthusiastic about subsidizing her own "independent" cotton farmers.

Chemicals. Potash and German dye stocks were to be traded for food,[49] yet already a clamor was rising against letting nations get the dyes at a minimum price and then use them competitively in foreign trade.[50] America had its own dye industry now to think of. As for potash, it took all of Baruch's efforts to put through a plan to ballast American ships with potash on their outward voyages to France and Belgium and thus save the new industry at home.[51]

Alex Legge had come back to report from his tour with Hoover, and Baruch turned his attention to plans for American aid in the rebuilding of war-devastated areas. American builders stood ready by the legion — but were they scavengers? The United States had the methods, the material, and the experience to render valuable service, but it was important that our government apprise foreign governments of what was good and what bad in American methods. Already, the United States had an agency of the kind with "know-how" left over from the war. It could advise foreign states on the "merits of the varied and various propositions" that were sure to be made by American firms, some of questionable character. Such aid would secure the rebuilding of the devastated areas in the shortest time and at the lowest cost. These were the general outlines of the policy filled in by Baruch who, in an urgent message to Eugene Meyer of the War Finance Corporation, cabled demands for greater coordination by various American agencies involved.[52] To Wilson's financial adviser, Norman Davis, Baruch had suggested that there be established a central United States agency to which all foreign governments should apply and without whose approval no permit for exports would be granted. Rigidly he defended his primary aim: America was not to be given away. We should advance no money to a nation until its own resources were exhausted; and no rights or privileges should be given any country, which would not reciprocate. In a memo Baruch suggested that our national interests would be best served if all American advances were passed on at Paris, where information on the European situation was more easily come by.[53]

From the beginning Baruch had recognized what it took time for Wilson to concede — that the first objective of America, as of all countries, was her own national prosperity. Finally, however, the London *Morning Post* complained that "Wilson declared against tariffs in every country but his own. We admire Wilson; he's so sublimely unconscious of his inconsistencies. He proposes free trade while he supports the highest tariff." Wilson, it was charged, assumed that what was best for America was of necessity best for the rest of the world.[54]

Perhaps it was. In any case, there were sound reasons for the doctrine that the raw materials of the world must be available to all — that is, to all the winners of the war. Otherwise, geographical lines or spheres of influence might predetermine the distribution of goods. The guarantees against economic warfare must be sure. After all, as Wilson realistically told House, the United States could "force" the other nations to its way because "they will be financially in our hands." [55]

Furthermore, as the American realists perceived, if the dream of a

League of Nations dissolved and there was another war, access to the oil resources of the world "should . . . be safeguarded for the United States." France, England, Holland, all were closing in on the undeveloped areas — Mesopotamia, Turkey, the Balkans, even hapless Russia. What an irony it would be if in the future the American navy were dependent on unavailable foreign oil.[56]

On this matter Baruch moved swiftly. He cabled Peek on April 7 to head off an Anglo-French group that was seizing Rumanian oil properties, and on the eleventh he assured Josephus Daniels that we must, for the welfare of all countries, have our fair share of the world's oil. American oil production was already less than its consumption; a third of the then estimated stocks were exhausted; * we had no holdings except in Mexico and Rumania, and the Mexican properties were already confiscated. There would be no American aid for any country anywhere unless "equal opportunity" were given Americans.[57]

"Equal opportunity," but not special privileges. Baruch wrote one petitioner, for instance, that despite his sympathy for the protection of our new industries it was up to Congress to look after them.[58] The practical necessity of tariff walls for the victors should not supersede equal access to raw materials.[59] Ideally, he thought, trade barriers should be removed and the goal be the equality of trading conditions for all nations in all markets except our domestic one. He questioned Attorney General A. Mitchell Palmer as to the regulations the Allies were planning to clamp upon the business activities of former enemy aliens. Vigorously he fought the "preferential conventions" that were being entered into between England and France, and France's desire singly to exploit the Rumanian oil fields. The battle broke out during a meeting of the Economic Commission on March 15, where the French emissaries were reluctant even to discuss the question of equality of trade. Was not this a matter to be settled later by the League of Nations? Baruch and Alex Legge did not think so.[60]

For how could the Reparation Commission determine Germany's ability to pay, when all proposed amounts of reparations were based upon her prewar territories, many of which were about to be taken away, and upon prewar access to markets now to be barred to the defeated nation? [61] All through March, the Economic Commission worked on the idea of removing trade barriers from Germany once the

* Vast new reserves have, of course, since been discovered.

Peace was signed, but by early April it was plain that the restrictions and preferential agreements would reverse this work. Undeterred, Baruch continued with his original scheme, outlining to Wilson a full-scale plan for resumption of unhampered trade. America, he knew, was in the position of England half a century before. She, alone among the nations, could provide "foreign aid." But a condition of American aid to any nation should be equal trade, American credits in exchange for the cancellation of preferential treaties, and, in our own interest, loans to be made only for purchases from American nationals.[62]

To Baruch, the German question presented a simple choice: to offer Germany free trade and collect reparations; or to restrict her to a point where nothing could be collected. You could not have it both ways. But common sense could not overrule the claims of emotion.[63]

In Paris in that spring of 1919, all roads led to the President's house. All hopes, all hearts, all plans were centered in that hot, dry room in the Palais Murat. The fate of mankind was being deliberated in the dark and richly furnished study where between rows of books Rembrandts and Goyas looked down indifferently on the actors.[64]

Baruch's eye was always on the "human equation": South Africa's Jan Christiaan Smuts, with his wearied illusions and forced smile; the cultured, gracious Balfour, whom Baruch had already met in Washington; Lord Robert Cecil, with his closed mind. There was eagle-faced Baron Sidney Sonnino, who was in favor of the Old Order and all the new territories that Italy could grab. From the newborn state of Czechoslovakia came Masaryk and Beneš, shedding intellectual light;[65] and their counterpart, in whom the past and the future met in a whirlwind, the patriot of reborn Poland, Jan Paderewski. With tears in his eyes and the same passion he could loose from a keyboard, the flame-haired Pole told again the story of his ravaged homeland as if it were a tragedy that had happened only yesterday, until in his voice you heard the thunder of Napoleon's legions and the jabber of those earlier "peacemakers" whose partitioning blotted Poland from the map of Europe.[66]

Familiar faces, however, could give Baruch a feeling of reality and even of solidity in this shifting world of gigantic unrealities: jovial

Josephus Daniels; Robert Lansing, handsome, white-haired, and
"fussily precise"; Hoover, with all the stiffness of the man whose
nerves are at the end of their tether; the stolid, intelligent John Foster
Dulles.[67] There was Ray Stannard Baker of the American press
corps, "ever-present, ever-vigilant, like a faithful watchdog." Sometimes, you caught a fleeting glimpse of Mrs. Wilson, nearby in her
little sitting room, anxious eyes straying to the lined face of her
husband. Baruch knew, as few did, of the "incalculable help and
comfort that she was to him." [68] And hovering always, ever self-
effacing but ever present, was Colonel House, "that super-civilized
person . . . from the wilds of Texas . . . a good American, very nearly
as good as a Frenchman," as Clemenceau described him.[69]

There, ranged in a half-circle around the fire, the Big Four sat as
if on a stage — America, Italy, France, and England. These were the
Powers that counted — not the great, sprawling, mammoth Russia,
nor the Chinese, for whom only Wellington Koo spoke, reminding the unlistening, the unheeding. There was Orlando of Italy,
the weak link of the Four, with his pompadour of white hair,
eyes spilling over with tears as he eloquently urged his country's
claims. No one was ever quite sure what he wanted, except that like
Oliver Twist he "wanted more." [70] Across, on the right, sat Lloyd
George, "fresh and pink of countenance," springing up to greet new-
comers "with a bright, two-fisted smile." He was all "Celtic wit and
quicksilver enthusiasms" (and, as it was observed, scarcely more re-
liable than quicksilver).[71] He charmed you; he baffled you; he
amused you; he could, as Winston Churchill said, "almost talk a bird
out of a tree," or turn a cabinet around in ten minutes. Even the
supercritical Keynes acknowledged that Lloyd George had "six or
seven senses not available to ordinary men." [72] He knew not only
what you were thinking but what you were going to say. Yet it was
"his sixth sense for the changes in the pulse of public opinion" that
betrayed him at last. He had come to the Conference convinced on
the one hand that there must never be a new war, and on the other
hand that Germany must not be economically prostrated, for then
she could not pay reparations.[73] Facts were to deal harshly with his
theories.

But it was Wilson upon whom the observers' eyes most often
rested: Wilson "never . . . in better form; never so firm, yet never so
courteous. He drove things with a charm that won everybody." He

looked desperately tired sometimes, and yet younger than his pictures, fired with unquenched hope and dedication of purpose. Often on "pins and needles," he would pace up and down, up and down the carpet, kicking his neat black boots, or dash to the window for revivifying gulps of fresh air. "The difficulties here," he confessed, "would have been incredible to me before I got here." [74]

Or you might come upon him squatting, cutting up the map of Europe with an apparent abandon that horrified onlookers until, in answer to the mocking query of whether this was a game, he replied: "Alas, it is the most serious game ever undertaken." [75] Critics might gibe at Wilson as ignorant of Europe, but even Lloyd George blithely admitted never having heard of Teschen, "the bone of contention between Poland and Czechoslovakia." [76] Certainly what Wilson lacked in knowledge he made up in purity of purpose. Furthermore, he refused to make decisions until he had the facts; he knew much and he absorbed more. As Baruch observed, if there were those who did not respect him, even they feared and were jealous of him.[77] Yet Wilson was not the dominant figure of the Big Four.

The man was Georges Clemenceau. So wracked and bombarded and weary was France that it was hard to remember when there had not been war, or when the leader had not been Clemenceau. He was France incarnate, this powerful, wise, and weary old man who had seen everything, done everything, and felt everything; and all was reflected in the black eyes gazing pitilessly between ivory lids. He seldom moved. He almost never spoke, and then only a short, trenchant sentence, cutting through the diplomatic arguments like a whiplash. He was seventy-eight years old; his voice sometimes shook; but his faintest whisper penetrated a room.

He commanded admiration — the square, solid body in the square-tailed black coat, the gloved hands folded below his "great drum of a chest." He was old; he was very tired; yet one emotion — France — sustained him still.

What an era of history and space he spanned: born under a king of France, eleven years old when the second Napoleon mounted the throne, he could remember Paris with the barricades and the bloody street fights of 1848; and at the age of seven he had felt the earth tremble to the hoofbeats of the Polish legions galloping away to the abortive liberation of a homeland which was not to reappear for half a century and more. He had grown up among the old soldiers of

Moscow and Waterloo and the old statesmen who had resewn a torn Europe into unholy alliances but a generation before he was born. As a young Paris correspondent in Washington, he had learned something of "peacemaking" from the Reconstruction Congress of the sixties. At thirty he had seen Paris under the heel of the Prussian and in bitterness had resolved that this tragedy must never happen again.

He waited for revenge, for nearly fifty years watching the rise of German armed power. He lived to be very old, to feel the dark chill as the shadow of Hitler fell across Europe, and to pen a last warning against "the designs of German violence" to a general staff still musing over the tactics and strategy of Verdun — a warning to people somehow lacking the fierce moral strength of 1914. Germany was arming and France was disarming, so he wrote, but if Germany, "still obsessed . . . persists in her *Deutschland über alles,* well — let the die be cast. We shall take up the atrocious war again." [78]

Clemenceau was no cynical plotter mapping future wars. No one hated war more than he who had twice seen his country devastated. Yet who could deny his contention that an armed Germany was, by nature, an aggressive Germany? At the signing of the Armistice, he had wept; he had come to the peace table "hot from the fray," he who had hoisted the tricolor in 1917, in the darkest hour of Europe's history from Napoleon to Hitler, when Russia had reeled from the fight and the thunder of German guns had sounded in Paris. As would Churchill a generation later, Clemenceau had held on.

The dream was to make a new Europe, founded on right.[79] But could there be a reborn world without a rebirth in the hearts of men? Woodrow Wilson understood the facts of history that made a League of Nations necessary; Clemenceau understood the facts of human nature that made it difficult if not impossible. The showdown came at the third meeting of the Big Four, as Wilson repetitively voiced his dream of a "permanent peace." Clemenceau faced him. Did he mean what he said? Both Wilson and Lloyd George agreed.

"All right," snapped Clemenceau. "We can make this permanent peace. We can remove all the causes of war."

Bluntly, he continued. "We must first give up our empires and all hopes of empire." England must get out of India, France out of Africa, America out of Puerto Rico and the Philippines. All must throw away their keys to the trade routes, surrender their spheres of

influence. "Are you willing to pay these prices? No?" Clemenceau
sprang up, brought his fist down on the table. "You don't mean
permanent peace. You mean war." [80]

There was, Clemenceau knew, another possibility. If the causes of
war could not be eliminated, it might yet be averted by massed force,
by the fear of war more terrible than any man had yet undergone. It
may be true, as the jokers gibed, that Clemenceau's daily pill upon
arising was to mutter, "Now, Georges Clemenceau, you *do* believe in
the League of Nations." [81] He did believe in a league, but he knew
that no league was stronger than its guarantees, and what guarantees
were there in this proposed League, this thing of milk and water?
What did Wilson know about guarantees? He was "a nice man [who]
means well," but as Clemenceau told House, talking to him was
something like "talking to Jesus Christ — how could you reach understanding with a man who thinks himself the first man in two thousand years to know anything about peace?" [82]

What guarantees did the League offer, except that America at her
pleasure might come to Europe's aid again — after three long years? [83]
What guarantee could America give but words, and flimsy words at
that — what guarantee that her own people even would accept the
League, much less agree to military support for it? The French press
echoed these questions. What if another administration were to
break the pledges of the peace table? [84] Would not the United States
soon yield to her desire to return home, and tell Europe to get out of
her difficulties as best she might? [85] Why, then, should not France
demand the Saar as a safeguard and the Rhineland and perhaps the
Ruhr? Wrong might beget wrong, war breed war, but Baruch
through the years would more and more understand France's driving
need for security. She would not give up the Ruhr until she had an
equally good hostage.[86] Meanwhile, bitterness rose against Wilson.
What right had this American President, an interloper at the eleventh
hour, to dictate terms to a world still "reeling with shot and echoing
to gunfire" only a few miles from where the millions of young French
and English men had died? Let him see! Let him see the babies in
the hospitals at Budapest, living and dying testimonials to the effects
of malnutrition. Let him see the people, tens of millions of people,
who ate and yet starved, because they had not had the right kind of
food.[87]

Let him see. Let him think of the men in the American Hospital

at Neuilly, where he and his wife walked, trying to comfort American
soldiers with their faces gone, their noses gone, their eyes put out,
their jaws and lips and chins blown off, for whom the future held
neither love, nor joy, nor hope. Or let him hear the cry of the American nurse. "Let President Wilson come here . . . Let me show him
these horrors . . . Let him see the starving people . . . are we going to
allow . . . the villains to escape?" Let him see. Let him see the battle-
fields. Let him see the fiery furnaces where peace was to be tempered.[88]

It did not suffice that Wilson was working eighteen hours a day,
that he had not the strength, physical or emotional, to see those shattered regions. It did not matter that he thought "there should be one
man at this peace table who hasn't lost his temper." [89]

Baruch determined to see. He could not believe what he saw; he
doubted even his powers to describe it. Piles of unfired shells lay
around old carts or shattered baby carriages, and sickish-sweet odors
still hung in the murky air. The pock-marked cathedral of Rheims
was like a wreck in a storm of desolation. At Verdun, the great for-
tress of the dead towered above a sea of churned-up mud — a sea in
a storm, not a tree, not a house, nothing but a great, gray, rolling sea
of mud, white-capped by the flash of skeletal bone.

Baruch could not describe it; he could scarcely believe that the
ghastly wreckage was the work of human beings.[90] The French had
shrunk from bombarding their own villages, even to root out the
Germans; but not so the Americans. Amidst the desolation around
Château-Thierry a few trunks of trees loomed raggedly, snapped off a
few feet above the earth. Beyond stretched the waste of no man's
land, a vast shambles as big as a great city. Nothing could live above
the pallid ground; nothing was left but debris in the wake of the retreating lines — nothing but a few bedposts sticking up, or a sign
showing where a village had once stood.[91]

Baruch saw the incredible battlefield of Ypres, a ghastly and desolate spot — mile after mile of nothing, not even a field fit for the
plow. It was, Baruch wrote, so frightful that it could not be described.
Here the British had stood and never surrendered; and to Churchill
Baruch wrote that their courage before such odds could justly make
all men proud.[92]

At last Wilson saw it all. Twice he toured the battlefields, and in
May, at Suresneo, he stood before the crosses, beneath the Stars and

Stripes, his "tall, slight form tense with emotion"; he bared his head and one saw with shock how white his hair had grown. A sound of muffled sobbing rose from behind, and suddenly the President, too, almost broke down.[93] Both Wilson and Baruch understood now. What effect it all had on Baruch is illustrated by a letter he wrote his German-born father. France and Europe would have to be made safe from the Germans. The distinction between the German people and their government, so easy to preach at home, was now a hard one for Baruch to remember, having seen the horror of the devastation. The Germans must be allowed to work but forced to pay.[94] Of one thing, at least, Baruch was sure: the demands of the Allies might be unfair, but it was hard to expect reason when the sound of the guns had hardly died.[95]

Baruch was caught up in "cross-currents . . . against which principles and men, no matter how strong," could make no headway.[96] This was not the world he had known — the Paris he had known — "a city by night of myriad golden stars," of theatergoers streaming out from the hot, carpeted stalls and knotting for chatter, the white flash of the police officer's baton, the pull and pop of corks. The laughter. The tango. The bunny hug. High collars and low-cut dresses. Dawns fragrant with coffee and brioches.[97]

All was changed now, the sights and the sounds and the smells. Now there was the whine of planes above and the rattle of typewriters below, footsteps nervously clattering across parquet, and the crackle of Rolls-Royces across the courtyards; ragged gaps, empty as a tooth socket, torn by the shells of Big Bertha, dead flowers heaped around the Strasbourg monument. Now and then a watery sun glanced off the piles of German trophies — guns, tanks, planes — or lay caressingly across the shoulders of "pitiful shattered fragments of living death," who sat and stared, or clicked their crutches across an alleyway. Paris was a mourning city: a woman in a black shawl singing "Madelon" in front of a café; bony-kneed children in black playing listlessly in the gardens of the Tuileries or the Luxembourg; women in black moving with dignity amidst the teeming homeless, the refugees, the streetwalkers, the strange-looking men in strange-smelling clothes who had come each to remake his own little world — Kurds, Tatars, Letts, Poles, Arabs, Finns. Turbans and mantles and scimitar-shaped noses.

The Treaty of Versailles was not born "in the stilled and moderate

deliberation of a Council Chamber." No one, Baruch wrote a few
months afterward, could understand the Treaty who did not com-
prehend the human conditions under which it was brought forth. As
Baruch observed, "many preferred war with all its horrors to any
peace short of that which they demanded." In this sick and sorrow-
ing Paris of 1919, there was no place for cool reasoning, no belief in
peace, or in future happiness. As one writer put it: "We want . . . to
get a German into a corner and tell him all we think about him and
then kill him." [98]

The London *Observer* might well warn that "the botchers of this
generation would be the butchers of the next," that there must be no
surrender to blind appetites.[99] An even more ominous warning
sounded from the London *Graphic*. "The world is on the eve of a
new war," it proclaimed. "There will be no peace until Bolshevism is
overthrown," declared the *Daily Mail*. Even more prophetic were
the words of *The Times*: "If we don't have a Russian policy, Germany will, and when Russia awakes she will be an ally of Germany.
The prevention of such an alliance should be one of the first aims of
the Paris Conference." [100]

Thus was fair warning given.

To the fear of Germany was added the trebled fear of Russia, and of
a Germany allied with Russia. Fear of Russia was like a shadow-world
fear of the unknown. Of the Powers of Europe, excluding Germany,
only three really functioned at the Conference; and one was not even
there. The giant bulk of Russia, occupying one-sixth of the world's
land space, with 150 million inhabitants, was not there. "Is this
justice?" demanded Grand Duke Alexander.[101] Yet the silent shadow
of the Russian bear fell on the peace table; communism was
spreading across Europe — already, as it would be twenty-five years
later, the race was on for Germany as an ally, even before she was
punished for the crime of 1914. There could be no peace, it was said,
with Russia. Yet, as Lloyd George realized, until that issue was faced,
the world was not at peace.[102] For many, realization dawned more
slowly. Three years later, Baruch wrote Arthur Krock asking how we
could judge such powers as Russia and China without giving them a
fair hearing.[103]

Meanwhile, what thoughts about Russia stirred behind the parch-
ment skull of old Georges Clemenceau? Did his mind go back to
childhood and the old, old men who remembered the Revolutionary

mobs screaming and the heads of a king and a queen rolling on a Paris scaffold?

Distraught by their own peril, the Allies had not the least concept of their responsibility for the tragedy in Russia. Winston Churchill, although aware of "the foul buffoonery of Communism," a "sub-human structure" erected in Russia "upon the ruins of Christian civilization," [104] reflected even more bitterly upon Russia's "separate peace," which had left the Western Allies to face the full fury of Germany.

There was much sympathy at first for "The Birth of Russian Democracy." Baruch in the summer of 1919 had said he was available to assist the new Russian government at any time.[105] Churchill spoke of the "complete rottenness" that had preceded the upheaval, and Wilson knew that the Bolshevists had found "the soil already prepared for them." The delegates would be working against the principle of a free world if they did not give the Russian people a chance to find themselves and to settle their affairs in their own way.[106]

Wilson, perhaps agreeing with the opinion of the *New Statesman* that Lenin, who had already offered "real concessions," was the actual head of government in Russia, dispatched young William Bullitt to Moscow, whence he returned with proposals that might have meant peace. Offers were made by the Soviets that had not even been requested, such as the payment of the Russian debt, economic concessions, and agreements for the Soviet armies to abandon Siberia, the Urals, the Baltic states, Archangel, White Russia, and the Ukraine.[107] But to have accepted these would have meant recognizing the new regime.

What had to be done seemed clear to the gentlemen at the Peace Conference, as it did to the man in the street. How to do it was another question. Obviously, the half-dozen self-styled "leaders" of the various Russian governments in and out of exile must be brought together; and Wilson announced his willingness to meet with the Bolshevists. On January 22, 1919, he called for a conference of "every organized group that is now exercising or attempting to exercise political authority or military control in Russia" to meet on the little island of Prinkipo, where ancient kings were exiled in the days of Byzantium, and where from the two hills you looked down on the domes and minarets of Constantinople.[108] Despite acceptance by the

Bolshevists and all the "authority and prestige of Wilson," the other Russian elements refused an invitation to meet with those whom they considered traitors.

As Bernard Baruch observed, no money was appropriated to deal with Russian needs and problems.[109] The delegates could only collect data. They had to take the Bolshevists at their own word — that they could not survive unless the rest of the world was bolshevized. Despite Wilson's assertion that the Allies stood as ready to help Russia as an ally,[110] despite the delegates' protestations that their first principle was to avoid interference in the internal affairs of Russia, "their real end was to help Russia free itself from Red rule." [111]

How was this to be done? Marshal Foch had an idea, which was to march straight into Russia, with Polish, Lithuanian, and Czechoslovakian allies and put the Red menace down. The quality of troops was of no consequence, he told a secret meeting on February 25, if only the quantity was sufficient. "If this were done, 1919 would see the end of Bolshevism, just as 1918 had seen the end of Prussianism." [112]

But as it worked out just enough of this sort of thing was done to guarantee the perpetuation of communism — not enough to end it. "The war" was over; yet British soldiers were in Russia, being killed in action. Americans were in Russia, knowing neither what they fought for, nor why. The Toledo *Blade* summed up the story: "The present administration . . . has filled the soldiers . . . with bitterness and resentment. It has to its everlasting discredit the blame for the only mutiny which has occurred in the American Army in more than 100 years." [113] Russian communism might be no less dangerous than Prussianism, Lloyd George conceded, but he rejected any idea of putting it down by the sword. Two-thirds of Russia was starving; the Czechoslovaks had no desire to fight for a restoration of the old regime, and as for the British, if sent into Russia, "the armies would mutiny," as the Americans had already done. Wilson agreed: from the first there had been doubts in his mind as to whether communism could be checked by arms. The Allies could neither stop communism themselves, he told Churchill in debate, nor would the anticommunists use the arms we supplied.[114]

Nevertheless, Foch's dream at last became a nightmare, and an army of "the scurviest rascals in Europe" subjected Russia to "three years of horror the like of which the average American had never imagined." They could not conquer the Soviet Union but they maddened it. The separation from the West became irrevocable.

In one sense at least the war went on. The peacemakers sat and there was no peace. It was a virtual impossibility to keep people from fighting even after four years.[115] With Russia abandoned, the Germans were still struggling to hold their spoils from the Treaty of Brest-Litovsk, and Russia to regain them. Germany, the Peace Conference well knew, "had one face towards the West, where she had made peace, and another face towards the East, where she was organizing for war." Germany had not learned her lesson of defeat; she had not abandoned her dream of "Empire in the East." Helplessly, the Allies faced the dilemma — of subduing Germany or stemming communism, and no answers came. War still smoldered on the Eastern Front, where from 1914 until 1917 that "unknown war" of which Churchill would later write had raged — "incomparably the greatest war in history . . . in its scale, in its slaughter." Russia, with antiquated equipment and fantastically bad transport, had, as always, fought the war of a generation or a century before. Men died "in the mud, they perished in the snowdrifts"; the wounded lay "frozen in their own blood . . . uncounted, unburied," beside their dying horses. Back and forth across a continent the tides of slaughter had moved; and now in the winter of 1918–19, the returning soldiers wandered in a nightmare of iron cold and biting snow; warriors coming back to homes laid waste wandered forth again.[116]

There were no answers. There were no answers for the plight of the Baltic states, flooded by wave after wave of Germans and Russians and Germans again — Germans, here, as allies against communism; there, as allies of the Bolshevists. From Estonia, the Russians had been driven back, but not before they had taken everything that could be carried away. They had stripped houses to the bare walls, seizing a man's last cow, his last piece of clothing. The protestants received specialized treatment; their skulls were smashed to pulp, their heads scalped, their eyes put out and some were buried alive.[117]

In Latvia, German troops remained to fight the Bolshevists. If Germany withdrew, the whole country would be overrun. The German troops were living off the civilian population. And Latvia was starving.

What could be done? Mr. Hoover might want humane conditions

to prevail. Yet if you fed Latvia, you would feed the Germans, and if you fed Latvia, the Russians would return.[118]

The question was still under debate in May, and a month later Riga was in anarchy. The Germans had appealed to the British to cooperate in taking the city, they to operate on the land and the British from the sea. Lord Balfour commented that "it was rather a strong order to expect to march shoulder to shoulder with the Germans." Tartly, Lansing retorted that the Germans were there because the Allies did not wish them to leave; and conversation quickly shifted to the matter of starvation in Estonia. Balfour fired a parting shot — the Germans were "behaving disgracefully . . . for their own political ends." But "even if the Germans were devils in Hell the people should still be fed." [119]

For, with the advance of spring, the Four Horsemen were galloping across the devastated continent "from the Baltic to the Black Sea . . . to the Adriatic . . . disaster of the greatest magnitude," from Rotterdam to Constantinople. First cold and then hunger, then revolution and now pestilence — typhus, smallpox, syphilis. Rumania, besieged, fighting the Hungarians on her borders, was fighting want and smallpox within; in Poland, even American epidemiologists were falling victims. All Eastern Europe must be quarantined — death was spreading to the West. It was, as an International Red Cross report declared, "the darkest picture of widespread human misery in three hundred years." [120]

It was impossible to visualize, impossible to believe. You became saturated with it, waterlogged, numb — moving on automatically like a machine wound into motion and unable to stop, like those very hag-ridden armies that went on fighting and dying, because they had forgotten what it was like not to fight and to die.

From every country the story was the same — disease, hunger, butchery. There was Poland — buffer and battleground between Germany and Russia for a thousand years, now "scorched earth" across a hundred-mile swath, not a town, not a cottage but what was fired by the retreating Russians, old persons dying by the roadsides, trampled by the Cossacks' horses. Poland, read a report in late January, "resembles an island . . . trying to defend itself from being submerged." [121]

The resurrection of this vanished empire had posed problems grave enough even under peaceful conditions. Should the boundaries follow the line of "old historical Poland" of the seventeen hundreds? Should it include those "four or five million Poles in German Prussia?" What of Silesia, lost to the empire since the thirteen hundreds, yet 70 to 90 per cent of whose population had "kept its language and was strongly Polish." What of East Prussia that was completely German — and Poland's promised outlet to the sea?

Finally, there was the question of the Jews — always the scapegoats for a people's disaster. Stories were seeping out of Cracow and the Warsaw ghetto — the Dombie concentration camp, starvation, disease, "Polish soldiers given to all sorts of excesses, pogroms," the ghetto where soldiers who had escaped death on the battlefield came home to find their families "less fortunate." The Warsaw ghetto was a mass of "filth and rags and disease and starvation," and out in the villages, Jewish families were living "on grass and poison ivy soup." The whole race was being rooted out, came the cry from Warsaw — what was left would be good for nothing for fifty years.[122] A letter from a childhood friend of the Baruch family in New York, who had returned to Europe to live was ironic. He pointed out that when Baruch's father had been born in what was now Poland, it had belonged to the Germans — who had given the world its culture. The Poles were only good for persecuting the Jews.[123]

There is no record of Baruch's reply.

Self-determination, as applicable to a religion as to a nationality, was what the Jews of Poland demanded and what the Poles denied. In the fevered nationalism of the new Polish state, there was no place for those who might confuse their religion with their nationality. According to an American survey many orthodox Polish Jews although loyal were "indifferent" to the new Poland, and to the customs of their neighboring Catholics. Jews demanded respect for their Sabbath, yet persisted in working on Sunday. Jews had a monopoly of the food trade. With people starving, food was hoarded. Feeling the Polish cause lost, some Jews had sided with the enemy, charged the Polish delegation at the Peace Conference, and this "called forth a change of public opinion against them." The Poles had tried to embrace the Jews as far back as the eighteenth century — to release them from the ghettos and to give them civil rights. The Jews had refused. Now Poland again would offer full rights of citizenship to everyone.[124] But all must be loyal. As for special privileges for minorities, did Polish minorities have special privileges in Germany? [125]

Of the Jews who comprised 50 per cent of one little town and defended it against the Ukrainians, street by street and house by house,
the delegation did not speak.[126]

Where economic questions were concerned, Baruch was in on the
discussions. It was Baruch, in fact, who persuaded the Polish delegation to withdraw its opposition to a special customs agreement
between Austria, Czechoslovakia, and Hungary.[127] But the customs
question was nothing beside the over-all Polish question, which involved the over-all settlement of the peace of Europe.

If the Russians had pillaged Poland, now the Poles were pillaging
Russia, killing, burning, stealing, in the effort forcibly to widen their
boundaries. Paderewski had formed a government in the melee; few
thought it would last more than four to six weeks. He visited Posen;
the population turned out to greet him, and troops turned out with
machine guns. The Germans charged that his visit had been the
signal for insurrection. "The situation is most critical," came a report
on January 25.[128]

Meanwhile, the Germans refused the Allies use of their trains for
the relief and feeding of Poland. "The Teutonic Order" called for
"the extermination of the Slav population"; conversely, the Germans
would not recognize as Poles any who were born in Germany. At a
secret session on February 15, Clemenceau read a message from Warsaw, ambiguous, exaggerated, and yet true enough to illustrate the
confusion and the terror of that uncertain time. It read simply: "German troops have commenced offensive." It was signed, "Paderewski." [129]

Food for Poland was a necessity. But no trains could get through
to the cities; they would be halted on the way by a starving countryside. Could the Allies occupy the rail lines? If Poland was not assisted, it was forecast that she would be "crushed and submerged by
Bolshevism." Communist propaganda was even being disseminated
through the prison camps, with the tacit agreement of the German
authorities, representatives of that same unrecreant power that was
"saving" the Baltic states from Bolshevism. Now came the report:
"There is no hostility between the Germans and Bolsheviks." The
Germans were, in short, playing Russia and the West off against each
other for future advantage, as they were to do so ably and with so
much more fanfare a generation later. They knew enough to be silent, also, when the Allies started to wrangle over the Polish Corridor,

of "undoubted German nationality," and certainly the seed of future wars. Lloyd George posed a moot point: If the Germans went to the liberation of their countrymen in the Polish Corridor, were England and the United States prepared to go to war? [130]

The two powers who were not at Paris — Russia and Germany — were in reality dictating the terms of the Peace. Unless Russia became a vital partner in the League, all knew, there would be neither peace nor victory. There had been many who had wanted to fight on to complete the conquest of Germany but had dared not do so, otherwise "Bolshevism might have engulfed Europe." [131] General Tasker H. Bliss of the American delegation ventured a prediction: that an alliance of armed giants might crush a single giant, but if the conditions that made war were not changed, who was to guarantee that one of the allied giants might not replace the one destroyed? [132]

10

REHEARSAL FOR DISASTER

On the March day in 1919 when Woodrow Wilson returned to Paris after a few weeks in the United States, the wind blew. Carelessly, it tugged at a banner of cotton, rain-stained and bedraggled, bearing the words *Honneur à Wilson, le Juste*. This was the last reminder of a day that was gone, that incredible thirteenth of December when the sun had shone and the dancing chains of Parisians had woven in and out along the Champs-Elysées and the Place de la Concorde, laughing, cheering, chanting: "Vive Weelson, vive Weelson." That day all Paris had blossomed into welcome.[1]

Now the wind blew. A band blared sullenly. Ranged on a strip of red carpet, rigid as the potted evergreens behind them, were twelve frock coats topped by cynical faces — Lansing, House, McCormick, Baruch among them — wondering, waiting.[2]

No rejoicing greeted this "Second Coming." Hope was quenched beneath the starched shirt fronts. The waiting dignitaries knew that the man once hailed as a Messiah brought with him neither miracle nor mandate — even across the seas they had heard the echoes of dissension. When Wilson had first come to Paris, his prestige and moral influence were perhaps unequaled in history. Now the disillusion was so great that few even dared speak of it.[3]

That night President Wilson closeted himself in his cabin on the *George Washington* with Colonel House. Many versions have been given of the subsequent "break" with the suave Texan. Actually, this was only the beginning. But the air that night was charged with thunder. Rumors were stirring that House had made secret agreements with Lloyd George and Clemenceau, who had been using the attacks of the American Senate on the President as an excuse for their own. House had not been able to keep "under cover." He had held press conferences. He had preened himself over his title of "the genius of the American delegation." He had "given in" where Wilson would never have given in; Josephus Daniels contends that he even agreed to take the League out of the Treaty. Behind closed doors, House and Wilson had it out in a sharp exchange. Nothing was worthwhile in life, the President told House, that you did not have to fight for.

House countered: "Anglo-Saxon law is built on compromise."

Secret Service Chief Starling saw Wilson emerge from the interview "looking disturbed and walking rapidly." [4] He was pale and drawn. He said to his wife that night: "House has given away everything I had won before we left Paris. He has compromised on every side." Yet later he said to her: "Don't be hard on House. It takes a pretty stiff spinal column to stand against the elements centered here." [5] The hour was late; he was very weary. But he could not rest until he had read his nightly chapter of the Bible. He, at least, had kept the faith.

To Wilson it seemed that House had betrayed his trust; to Mrs. Wilson that he had betrayed the President. Later Mrs. Wilson called in the Colonel and showed newspaper articles sharply critical of Wilson. The Colonel seized the papers, blushing furiously, and quickly made his exit, and, according to Daniels, after Paris the President never saw him again. [6]

To outsiders, only the cracks of the "break" were showing. To Baruch, the whole affair could have hardly come as a surprise. Before he had sailed for Europe, Frank Cobb had warned him that Wilson had no chance, because the British had taken House into their camp. All this, even before the Peace Conference had begun. [7]

The supposed "sellout" was not complete. Wilson's singleness of purpose sustained him, but all House's sins were of course blamed upon Wilson. The French felt that the President favored the Germans and became almost virulent in their name-calling. [8] Writing to a French girl on February 27, Baruch observed that France had done more for the world than mankind could ever repay. He knew the effect of even the irresponsible French charges on wavering public opinion at home. And Wilson, he was still convinced, was a far weightier force than Edward Mandell House. [9]

He wrote to Senator Charles Thomas that things had gone better after a blunt talk with the French, who had been trying to put off the settlement. He differed from many political critics and future historians in his belief that nothing could have been more fortunate than the President's going to Paris in person.[10] On March 3 he told Clarence Barron, then in Paris, the French attacks upon Wilson and the League were so violent that unless they were halted the Peace Conference might have to be moved to some neutral ground.[11]

Secretary of State Lansing's confidential diary adds a strange chapter to the story. On the evening of October 6, 1921, an unnamed former Democratic senator told Lansing "an extraordinary tale" of the break between House and Wilson.

"You surely know," the Senator is quoted as saying, "that the getting rid of House was all planned and carried through by Baruch, Morgenthau and some others very close to the President."

Lansing replied that he had never heard this hinted.

"Certainly. I know that it was so," his informant continued. "I was in Paris at the time, and Baruch talked to me about it, said that House was a bad adviser and they were going to get rid of him."

Who was to be the new adviser?

Baruch allegedly had answered, "Lansing." [12]

Here the story moved into the ridiculous. Baruch thought little of Lansing, who had been badly treated by House but would have asserted himself against the Colonel, just as he himself had done, had he been a strong Secretary of State.[13] It is true, of course, that House did try to maintain control, keeping Wilson isolated. Baruch knew that House wanted to keep everything in his own hands and would exclude anyone who wasn't his own handpicked man.[14] His overweening jealousy of anyone who might threaten his pre-eminence as privy councilor to the President was almost neurotic.

With Baruch, House's surface relations, were seemingly good — because Baruch saw to it that they should be. He had no quarrel with House at this period, excusing his highhandedness because of his apparent loyalty to Wilson. He could even forgive House's "spying" on him during his service as chairman of the War Industries Board. Not until nearly a decade later was Baruch to learn from the published papers of House just where his loyalty to Wilson ended; and not until nearly forty years later were Baruch's staff assistants to uncover what House really thought of Baruch, deep in the files of the House papers. In 1919 Baruch knew nothing of this, and en-

joyed superficially pleasant relations with the Colonel, forgiving him
as he had forgiven Tumulty for any personal injustices. Even after
the Conference, Baruch tried unsuccessfully to bring the President
and the Colonel together again. But Wilson was adamant. "It's a
terrible thing," he murmured, "when a man you trusted could not
be faithful." [15]

There was more than stubbornness in Wilson's stand. Cary Grayson later told Baruch that once when Orlando murmured to House
that the President was only bluffing, House had calmly nodded his
head.[16]

To Baruch behavior such as this would have been the acme of
disloyalty.[17] But he did not know of the Colonel's private comment
to Lansing that "the President is hated by more people than any
other living American or any American who ever lived"; that Wilson
had no creative genius and was a thief of other men's ideas, and that
the man from whom his ideas were stolen was Colonel House.[18] How
the President had stood House's egotism as long as he had was a
marvel to acute observers when *The Intimate Papers of Colonel House*
was later published. Not only had the Colonel taken credit for
Wilson's policies, dealing with the affairs of three continents, but for
most of his major speeches as well.[19]

Josephus Daniels, who was in Paris during part of the Conference,
noticed that then and during the dark days thereafter, Wilson was
coming to lean more on "two friends whose judgment and affection
were an abiding rock — Bernard M. Baruch and Vance McCormick
. . . Admiration of Wilson was a passion with them . . . True and
tried and generous and steadfast to the end . . . they were affectionate
and loyal friends." [20] Baruch knew that it was not so much advice
that Wilson was seeking as a strong arm to lift the burdens from
his tired shoulders.[21] Purposefully, Baruch tried to keep everything
that he could from the President, strove to make Wilson believe that
all Baruch's problems were simple and that he could solve them all.
He thought it outrageous to run to him the way many men did,
wearying him with matters that would improve in time, or that they
could work out themselves.[22]

The last week of March and the first three in April were the "Dark
Period" of the Conference. Soon, the virtually ignored Lansing was
filling his time buying Dutch silver, reading novels, and enjoying

tête-à-têtes with "sprightly" Nancy Astor.[23] Two entries on April 4 agreed: McCormick wrote that all were tired and irritable, and Lansing that there was "gloom and depression everywhere." Before bed that night Baruch called on Lansing. He was angry at the Allied leaders on account of their unfair tactics, and also angry at the "Colonel's crowd," which, as its influence diminished, did not cease attacking the President to outsiders. "Imperialism is rife everywhere . . . militarism is stronger than ever," [24] McCormick wrote gloomily, and was seconded by Lansing a few days later.

Then on April 3 Wilson fell ill, and there came the "darkest moment" of all. He lay in his bed, fever-stricken, and out in the book-lined study the Big Three sat, considering the President's "ever-lasting no" conveyed in written messages.[25] Bullets had whistled through the streets of Paris, one piercing Clemenceau's lung, and the sound of his anguished coughing vibrated against the walls of the study. Hopelessly, Colonel Starling wondered if the peacemakers would indeed get out of Paris before the start of the next war.[26]

Mystery hung over Wilson's sick chamber, as it was to hang over the White House a few months later. "Influenza," the official report said, and Baruch agrees.[27] The President had fever and a heavy cold. Was that all? Herbert Hoover has recalled that when he emerged from his sick chamber Wilson "seemed to have changed greatly." There was a dulling of his fine intellect, a slackening of the wary alertness with which he viewed all efforts to divert or dissuade him.[28] Whether or not he had had an actual stroke — and Baruch is convinced he had not — is unimportant.[29] What matters is that according to Herbert Hoover he "relaxed in his battle except on the League." [30] It was as if he knew that his strength, physical and political, was running out. With increasing fatigue came increasing irritation, a worsening of his relations with the press corps and of his public relations at home.[31]

His waning energies flowed in one channel now. Sensing his weakness, the forces of reaction closed in in an effort to wear him down. Cynical smiles greeted his repeated threat to appeal to the people over the heads of their rulers. For whom did he actually speak? Not for "the people" of Europe with their cries for vengeance, and not for the people of the United States — he had lost his right to speak for them in the election of 1918. Lansing was horrified, writing of the attacks at home: "Apparently, they are seeking in every way to discredit him before the world even though by doing so they destroy American influences at the Peace Conference . . . To mortify the President, to humiliate him, to prove to everyone that he is distrusted at home and unworthy of admiration abroad are the supreme objects which animate these small-minded politicians who mouth their insults like a lot of hyenas whose jaws drip with . . . foulness." [32]

A kind of "helpless embarrassment" descended over the Conference, a vitiating suspicion that "the American people would not honour the signatures of their own delegates," Harold Nicolson recorded. The topic was never mentioned, but it was the "ghost at all our feasts." [33] Wilson was offering to mankind what his own country stood waiting to refuse — was asking of Europe sacrifices for an ideal "which his own country would be the first to betray." [34] All were coming to suspect this except Wilson himself, and without the support of America they knew the League would never work. We can understand Lloyd George's comment to Baruch that if Germany failed to accept the Treaty, neither the British Army nor fleet would move. Each must look to his own.[35]

The Conference dragged on. The sniping grew sharper, the clamor louder. The "Rehearsal for Disaster" had already started. It was true, of course, that the so-called Wilson goals were not purely Wilsonian. They had once represented the peace aims of all the Allied leaders, even of the Russians. The Fourteen Points expressed an ideal. Lloyd George himself had called for open covenants, free seas, and even self-determination for the Africans before the Fourteen Points were written. In reality it was the people who clamored for revenge.

The Fourteen Points had been an effective weapon in the disarming of Germany, but their interpretation in the "commentary" of Colonel House, written in the face of the realities as they unfolded, was to arm Germany with a new weapon, the accusation of betrayal. The Germans claimed that they had been tricked into peace, a peace which was dictated without a single German being heard. They had a solid and permanent grievance — that the conditions under which the Armistice had been signed were ignored. Yet Wilson had approved of House's commentary, as cabled to him from Paris in October 1918. He had realized that principles must accommodate themselves to realities. Open covenants did not exclude confidential diplomatic negotiations. If Belgium was to be indemnified, the German colonies could not have self-determination. Poland must have its Corridor.[36] Wilson had to recognize the "prearrangements" without which the Allies might have lost the war. If he had been a radical, he might have tried to impose his ideals by force. This he would not do.

The final settlement was bad enough with Wilson there, but Baruch sometimes shuddered to think what it might have been if he had not been there. In Wilson's own view, his Fourteen Points were, at least, ninety per cent accepted. Few of the new arrangements placed peoples under governments not of their own choosing. Poland, dead since the time of George Washington, was once more alive. The League may not have freed the seas, but that was only because the world failed the League.[37]

Perspectives of time illuminate Wilson's errors. When an international army (the only force that would have saved the peace) was urged by European Powers, Wilson shied away — partly because of his guileless faith in the illusion of "moral force"; perhaps more because he knew the Treaty would never pass the American Congress if it provided for an international police force. He argued for the equality of man — until the American race question was raised.[38] The world's first experiment in international government since the time of Charlemagne was built upon the rotting foundations of nationalism. Self-determination may have been pleasing to the peoples concerned, but to those with a knowledge of history and cultures it was somewhat less so. Natural boundaries, in terms neither of race nor nationality but of economic interdependence, had lasted for centuries; there was more than imperialism in such groupings as the old Austro-Hungarian or Ottoman empires — there was a recognition of realities.[39]

Were the Germans to be trusted as a people? Was the nature of a nation to be changed by calling it a republic and forcing upon it the very democracy that it had fought to destroy? Wilson said the evil of war sprang from the warmakers, a small military clique who had duped the people into aggression. Clemenceau always contended that Prussia was a people alien from the general culture of Europe and incapable of loyalty to Europe.

The people did not always understand Wilson. Groups turned on him almost overnight. In Italy he changed from a god into a devil when he ignored the Italian demand for self-determination for Fiume but not for the Brenner Pass. However, as Ray Stannard Baker observed, the President was never used by anybody or any interest.[40] To him came delegations from Siam and voiceless Russia, from Uruguay and Chile, with their petty claims, from Albania, Silesia, and South Carolina; Polish peasants from a forgotten corner in North Austria, wearing their Cossack caps and homespun woolen coats embroidered in red, leaving along the hallway and carpeted staircase the odor of their thick garments and of fresh-turned soil.[41] To Wilson appealed the Africans, who wanted the same rights as French citizens; Arabs, civilized when Europeans were still grubbing in caves; the Lebanese, half of whose population had been wiped out by the Turks and whose starving fragments wandered through desolated areas, tearing the flesh from a dead horse with their bare hands. For all of these, as for the Jews in Palestine, had come "the solemn hour awaited during the centuries." [42] The dream was perhaps to become a reality. For all the pressures crushing down upon him, Woodrow Wilson never lost sight of this ultimate goal.

The League was all. Upon the League there would be no compromise. His insistence upon putting the League into the Peace Treaty meant hasty drafting, and smeared the Covenant with the errors of Versailles. But the League was Wilson's bargaining power. Without the League he might not have sat at the peace table, and how infinitely much more harsh the peace might have been. With the League, the wrongs of the peace might be righted. The concessions he made to get the League in the end wrought its death. But this he did not foresee.

For Baruch, all was not toil and trouble. They had danced at Vienna a hundred years before; here in Paris they labored ten, twelve, fifteen, eighteen hours a day. But Baruch had his hours off, and once a dinner partner so beautiful that he "forgot to eat and actually missed two courses." [43] His talk was a mixture of French, Latin, Greek, oratorical English, Gullah, double negatives, street-corner slang, well-rubbed tags, and homely similes peppered with "ain'ts" for emphasis. An accent thick as South Carolina cornpone shifted suddenly into a kind of hand-hewn prose, nearly architecturally perfect. "We ain't out of the woods yet," he would drawl, and then, "Destiny is crouching on the doorstep." [44]

You saw him everywhere, at small dinner dances at the Ritz or at Count René de Rougemont's. Sometimes he was host at a large dinner party, or entertained the forty members of the Economic Commission.[45] Muscle-cramped delegates frequently joined him for tennis in the Bois, and when heat closed down on Paris there was coolness and calm for nerve-fagged emissaries at Baruch's quiet place in the country.[46] But Baruch did not use this retreat solely as an escape from work. It was his custom on Saturday at the country house, sometimes alone and sometimes with Frank Taussig, to review the work of the previous week.[47]

The arrival in February of Mrs. Baruch and Belle delighted him. Happily he wrote his son at Milton Academy that Mrs. Baruch was having her breakfast with him once more, while from the mantel the boy's picture was looking down on them.[48] He was proud of his son's playing on Milton's undefeated football team, and pleased when people admired his son's picture. He told young Bernard that he knew the boy would never be dishonorable or untruthful. He was depressed a few days later when his wife left, but was cheered by the hope that both his son and Renée would come back with their mother in the summer. Tentatively he broached the question — Would Bernard like to stay out of college a year? Perhaps in the back of Baruch's mind was the thought that this might help the boy find himself. Finally, there was the hope expressed by fathers before him — that his son would realize the necessity of hard work for a happy life.[49]

He wrote tenderly and affectionately to his own father, sending his love to his mother, his brothers, and all of the family.[50] He was delighted at his daughter Renée's eagerness to come over, since her sister's visit had been so successful.

Not all his thoughts of home were directed toward his family.[51] After two years in the public service, he fretted about his office continually in letters to his private secretary, Miss Mary Boyle, although she assured him that everything was going along well.[52]

While Wilson struggled with the over-all policy, Baruch labored at his own tasks on the Reparation Commission and on the economic sections of the Treaty. Through him, in part, there was some little liaison between the two mutually dependent organizations. For, without knowing what territories Germany would be made to cede, what trade restrictions would be imposed on her, what means of production would be left to her, how could you estimate what reparations she would be able to pay?

That Germany must pay, all agreed, although Baruch protested that if the peace was to be maintained, Germany must be restored as a sound business enterprise. To stop communism in Germany, she would have to obtain a food supply and the chance to work; if reparations were put too high, she would repudiate her debts, and, if too low, she might take over the trade of the world. Most important of all was a lasting peace, rather than temporary punishment of the enemy, and to this end, Baruch labored, often, it seemed, against tidal waves of opposition. His struggle was understood by one man.[53]

Years afterwards, Baruch often told the story of how once, when he reached a low ebb of discouragement, the word came that the President wanted to see him. Baruch found Wilson waiting with his hat and coat on. He would take Baruch home, he said. Puzzled, Baruch had followed him down the corridors, outside, and into the car.

Once seated, Wilson turned impulsively toward him. He knew that Baruch was not very popular at the moment and he knew the reason why. The President's jaw sharpened. "You go on and do your duty and I'll back you up." The car halted, and as Baruch got out the President followed him and took his hand. "After all, Baruch, our minds have met." Baruch walked away, as he remembered it afterwards, "on air." [54]

Thus girded, he returned to his job. On February 3 there was held the first meeting of the Reparation Commission in the office of the French Minister of Finance on the Rue de Rivoli. Five paramount questions lay before the Commission: (1) For what categories of damage was Germany liable? (2) What amount should she pay? (3) What proportions should the various Allies receive? (4) How should Germany pay? (5) How could she be compelled to pay?

For what should Germany pay? Obviously, this depended on what she was guilty of, and who was to bear the burden of the guilt. Had not Wilson said there was no quarrel with the German people, no feeling for them but sympathy and friendship? They had not created the hideous war; the Allies were fighting their cause against a warlike and tyrannical government.[55] Only a year had passed since Lloyd George had told the Trade Union Congress that there was no demand for an indemnity on Germany, but in that year had taken place the "khaki election" in England, with the rallying cries of "Hang the Kaiser," "The Fruits of Victory," and "The Loser Pays." In

Paris, stones hurtled through the windows, and the cobblestones echoed with angry shouts of "Down with Clemenceau!" whenever it was thought that he wavered for one instant in the determination to make the German people, who had twice in forty years invaded France, pay to the last sou.[56] Could even the hanging of the arch-criminal, the abdicated Kaiser, satisfy the blood lust of people who had suffered agonies for four long years? A proposal to hang the Kaiser was actually discussed but dropped, in fear that his guilt could not be established, and that to try, and perhaps to execute him, might establish grim precedents for future wars.[57]

But if the Kaiser was not guilty, then it must be the German people. A scapegoat must be found. Admission of this guilt would be extorted from the Germans, and the peoples' clamor would be heard. To no avail did John Foster Dulles protest that war, however hideous, had never been deemed an illegal act, and that to punish a state for acts which enlightened sentiment belatedly condemned would be punitive.[58] So Germany's guilt was officially proclaimed, and millions of young Germans growing up in the bitter years would have engraved on their souls the motto, "Versailles — never speak of it, but always think of it." What was bred was not repentance but defiance — "a sense of injustice and a reaction against the implied moral inferiority which was so intense as easily to lend itself to leaders who were adept at arousing and directing human emotions." [59]

Then, if guilty, for what should Germany be required to pay? As a practical measure, she obviously could not be made to pay the entire cost of the war. The massed suffering of four years of hell could never be reduced to sums of money, and it was recompense for this suffering which the Allied peoples demanded. Haiti sought recompense for six of her citizens lost from a torpedoed steamer; Armenia claimed over a billion francs for devastated areas; Poland, for workmen enslaved by the enemy; China, for ruined railroads; Greece, for forests and bridges; Portugal, for her lost foreign markets; Italy, for the suffering of prisoners and the keep of refugees, soldiers' pay while they were captives, workmen's pensions, inflationary living costs; Britain wanted Germany to repay the loans she had made to her allies; France, above all, sought indemnities for widows, orphans, maimed soldiers and civilians, bombed factories, and for the losses of the Franco-Prussian War. And so the roll went. Armenia, Czechoslovakia, Serbia, Australia. Payment for destroyed lands, "sterile forests," beasts of burden, silkworms, donkeys, furniture, hospitals, libraries, and a thousand other war casualties. From this welter of claims the Reparation Commission was to decide how much a guilty Germany should pay.[60]

And even here was bitter dissension, for America insisted that at least a figure must be fixed so that Germany should know the limits of what was demanded of her. Baruch and Thomas Lamont pleaded with Lloyd George, but with the "crazy echoes of the General Elections" still ringing in his head, the British Prime Minister dared not agree. He and Clemenceau could not face the explosions in their own countries if the sum fixed should fall below the expectations of an inflamed electorate. There was no answer to Baruch's argument that if a sum were set which was within Germany's ability to pay, there would be no possible excuse for her not to pay. Unlimited reparations would paralyze initiative.[61] In the end it was agreed that if Germany continued weak, her payments would be reduced; if she prospered, they would be increased. America had failed to get a fixed sum named. The gap to be bridged is indicated by the fact that whereas Baruch and McCormick had agreed that twenty-five billion dollars was a reasonable figure, the British talked of a hundred and twenty billion. Wilson listened to the discussion in silence, finally saying, "Well, Baruch?" The American rose and buttoned his coat. "Mr. President, let's take a trip to the moon." [62]

How were the payments to be apportioned among the victors? This was more easily settled after Dulles had shown that France would get a higher percentage if she were willing to forego the theoretical demand for the entire costs of the war.

How was Germany to pay? There were her coal mines, of course, her dyestuffs, her industrial equipment and output, and her rapidly dwindling reserves of gold. Some demanded payment in raw materials; yet Germany's colonial sources of raw materials were being stripped from her. Some demanded the output of German industry — and at the same time guarantees against the revival of German industry. Germany, in her turn, was willing to pay damages in gold marks, but demanded credits in return — a proposition that all recognized as self-defeating.

On March 11, Baruch sat in a meeting where the various possibilities were enumerated: a forced bond issue, forced labor (which Dulles saw as slave labor, and at which the French balked, having no desire to see Germans on their soil again, whether in or out of uniform),[63] seizures of property, of exports, raw materials, and, most of all, of the German reserves of gold.

In 1914 Germany's gold had amounted to 54 per cent of her paper currency, and now, the Reparation Commission noted, sensing the oncoming inflation and disaster, it was down to 9½ per cent.[64] The very threat of seizure would send available supplies into hiding, Baruch and the other experts believed. A cash indemnity through quickly convertible assets might be of value; but if gold *en masse* were seized, Germany would repudiate both her internal and external debt, and notes all over Europe would be defaulted.[65] To drain off German gold for reparations would destroy both her credit structure and her ability either to buy or to meet future liabilities. If she was to pay at all, she "must have working capital to start industries," and it was for the Allies to consider this and the ensuing results.[66] Furthermore, Germany could never pay in gold until she had a balance of trade in her favor. "We ought to see that Germany could put herself in a position where she could be punished," Wilson said. This was a formidable argument.[67]

Baruch heard Wilson's words and agreed. The United States was basing its case upon Germany's being allowed at least some "freedom of action." But the voice of France countered: France wanted no "freedom" which for her meant only freedom to perish.[68]

William Hughes, the Australian premier, agreed. For Germany to be allowed to reorganize her industries, he thought, would be "a monstrous perversion of justice," putting Germany "in a better position than those that saved the world." Wiser heads saw graver dangers. No just peace could be sired by injustice; no payment could be torn from a Germany stripped naked and unable to pay. This was the dilemma of the whole reparations question, and reparations were the key to peace. The economy of Germany was, of course, interdependent with the economy of all Europe. Before the war she had been Austria's best customer and France's third best; as for England, it had sent more exports to Germany than to any other country except India.[69] Crippling Germany would destroy the trade of France and England. And if refused any facilities for industry or trade, Norman Davis warned, German citizens would either repudiate their obligations or leave the country like "rats from a sinking ship."[70] Payment in manufactured goods was demanded in one breath, and in the next came terror lest Germany become the workshop of the world. Knowing the Germans, Baruch feared that they might find credit facilities to rebuild before the Allies.[71] Britain would not take their goods; but France wanted an option on all the industrial output of the enemy. Was the game worth the candle? Did the world want Germany in the export business? Conversely, would it not be of more profit to the world to trade with Germany than to boycott her? [72]

Wilson warned against the proposed German bond issue. It would build a shaky foundation for the new German economy; and if it was too large, it might delude people into thinking that it represented the total of the reparations.

"Special" property such as industrial equipment, still intact in Germany, could be taken and divided among the victors. This was Baruch's idea.[73] But the Americans balked against wholesale confiscation or property seizures. America, no less than the other nations, wanted German property to cover prewar claims. But Leland Summers thought that any wholesale property seizure might lay precedents for wealth seizures in the future.[74] Upon entering the war the United States had, indeed, seized and sold German property of private ownership, but the funds were being held against the possibility that the German government might eventually settle the accounts. Europe, on the other hand, wanted debts to her own nationals paid immediately by sale of German property located in the different countries. The United States opposed this. Ideally, the Americans thought, private citizens in Germany and outside should make their own adjustments. The final compromise incorporated some of the American suggestions but, like most compromises, pleased no one, the Germans least of all. All Allied property in Germany was to be restored immediately and, to compensate for what had been sold or damaged, the Allies might seize enemy property within their own countries. Of all the clauses of the Treaty of Versailles, one of the bitterest for the Germans was this assumed right of the Allies to liquidate private property to satisfy private claims, leaving the German owners to get their only compensation from their bankrupt government.[75]

The problem of German shipping went hand-in-hand with the private property question. Answers here typified the divergence between the Allies, with whom compromise was often the mere glossing over of an agreement to disagree. France suggested a pool of all ships flying the German flag, to be allocated to the Allies in proportion to their war losses. For France, shipbuilding had virtually ended during the war. But Lloyd George reminded listeners that shipping was the very lifeblood of the Empire. Prize ships seized during the war, he thought, should remain in the hands of the power that seized them. America put an oar in, demanding that only ships that had surrendered be placed in the pool. As the question was finally settled, all belligerents retained the ships they had captured. It was decided, however, that the value of these ships, if greater than that of the ships lost by each nation, must be counted as reparation payments.

Under this arrangement, the Americans got 600,000 tons. This was twice what they had lost, and it was commented acidly that it was hardly in accordance with Wilson's declaration that the United States expected nothing out of the war.[76] The United States had lost 350,000 tons of shipping and France 924,000 tons; yet France got only 450,000 and the United States 600,000. "Is not this scandalous?" commented *Démocratie Nouvelle*. "While our poilus fell by hundreds of thousands . . . Americans grew rich." [77]

This bitterness was typical. When Norman Davis reported, "Both Mr. Wilson and Mr. Lloyd George say that enslavement of Germany for one generation is enough," Monsieur Loucheur commented, as Bernard Baruch listened, "I do not think the matter could have been put up to them properly." [78] It was easy for America to err on the side of leniency; Americans had not had the Germans fighting within thirty miles of New York. It was easy for Americans to be lenient; it was not easy for Europeans.

Slowly the debate dragged on. Baruch prided himself on no hard and fast answers, writing a friend that he was fully aware that one of his recent memoranda was full of errors.[79]

It was upon raw materials that the war-ravaged countries set their hopes. Yet was Germany to be left sufficient lands and colonies to export raw materials, or would she herself have to be supplied? If her raw materials were seized to rebuild devastated areas in the world, would not the world in turn have to rebuild Germany? Germany needed everything, Baruch informed the United States Department of Commerce — tons of oil, fertilizer, hides, cotton waste, asphalt, all the supplies that she had destroyed in other countries and drained in her own.

Of all the raw materials under consideration, coal was perhaps the most important. During the war, the Germans had deliberately "wrecked and flooded the French mines of the departments of the Nord and Pas-de-Calais," so that French coal production at the war's end was only about half what it had been before hostilities commenced.[80] France felt, and there was no opposition to the demand, even on the part of Germany, that her recent enemy should be held responsible for making good the decrease in the output of her mines due to this vandalism. But in addition, France demanded further supplies of coal from Germany for many years to come, and here her claims became confused with attempts to cripple Germany industrially and to acquire territory. President Wilson had stipulated in the Fourteen Points that Alsace and Lorraine should be returned to France, and also that Poland should be reconstituted. Since the acquirement of Alsace and Lorraine gave France territory which before the war had produced for Germany 3,800,000 tons of coal annually, since German territory assigned to the newly re-established Poland had produced 43,800,000 tons a year, and since Germany's export of coal before the war had only been some 33,500,000 tons per annum, it is easy to see that she would under the new demands have very much less coal available for her domestic consumption than previously. Of course, the diminution of her territory carried with it a lessened need for coal, but not to any such degree. Now, in addition to the demands listed above, Germany was required by the Treaty to supply some 40,000,000 tons a year to France and other Allied countries.[81]

And this was not all. The Saar Valley had before the war produced 13,200,000 tons of Germany's coal. The French at first claimed this territory as a just restoration of land formerly French, although the fact is that she could only claim to have possessed the Saar from 1793 until 1815, when the Second Treaty of Paris had restored it to Germany. She also claimed the coal output of the Saar as a part of her reparations, and maintained that to guarantee the carrying out of this payment French sovereignty in the region was a necessity. The Germans claimed that the Saar was more than 99 per cent German as far as population went, and had been of German nationality for more than a thousand years, with the exception of the twenty-odd years during the French Revolution and Napoleonic periods.[82] The French had only very feeble answers to these claims and soon fell back on the argument of the necessity of possession of the territory to assure the required coal shipments.

On April 7, at a meeting at Lloyd George's apartment in the Rue Nitot, it was decided to form two expert committees, the first to consider "payment in kind — coal etc.," the second to take up the proposal of "utilizing German labor for the restoration of the devastated areas." It was as a member of the first of these committees that Baruch came into intimate contact with the Saar question.[83] Two days later he wrote to the President, foreshadowing the ultimate "solution" of the problem. The Treaty finally gave France possession of the mines in the valley, but put the government of the area under a League of Nations commission for a period of fifteen years, at the end of which there was to be a plebiscite to determine whether it would return to Germany or be incorporated into France. The justice of the German claim that the area was rightfully theirs as far as population was concerned was upheld when the plebiscite of 1935 gave a majority of 99 per cent for return to Germany.

Closely allied to the coal problem were many other questions of German production and reparations. Always the basic problem turned out to be a choice between allowing Germany the prerequisites for a flourishing economy or reducing her to a state where little could be extracted from her in the way of reparations. Baruch and the American experts tried to steer a middle line between the intransigence of France and the claims of Germany. To a certain degree they succeeded, but the problems which had to be settled under the prevailing conditions of hatred and fear were too great for wise and dispassionate solution. As the iron industry of Essen depended on coal which France demanded, so the factories of Alsace and Lorraine were impotent without German coke. If France received coal above her own needs, would she undersell England and other exporting countries in the world markets?

On this last problem Baruch's work was of the utmost importance and contributed largely to the solution that there should be two prices — the German pithead price for land deliveries of coal and the British for deliveries by sea.[84]

Next to the coal reserves, Germany's dyestuffs excited perhaps the greatest controversy. Besides being Germany's stock in trade, the dyes had enabled her to switch quickly from a peacetime footing into war. Now came the demand that she release the secrets of this industry.

Nor was she to sell her dyestuffs to compete with other nations, or even to use them to establish credits, except under the Allies' direction. Instead, the Allies in general and the Americans in particular took options on the German stocks.

But back in the United States, indignation rose high; it was charged that the plan favored Germany. Were German dyes to be dumped in the United States and the new American industry stifled? Baruch answered for the economic representatives, replying carefully but with firmness. The options had been taken for the very purpose of keeping Germany from dumping her dyestuffs by selling to neutrals at submarket prices, in exchange for food.[85]

This last phrase was the one that counted. Germany was desperate for food, as mounting riots and Communist demonstrations testified. At Rotterdam, tons of food lay spoiling. Germany was encircled by the iron cordon of blockade. Not even her herring fleets were allowed out of the harbors. There was street fighting on Unter den Linden — half-frozen, half-starved men in paper clothes were looting. A few coarse turnips, a few shreds of dried beef lay on the display counters.[86] There was no milk; the cows had been slaughtered long since, even those far gone with calves. Bullets scarred the stately houses along Unter den Linden and guns bristled from the windows of the Kaiser's former palace, and from government buildings the Red flag was flying.[87]

For four years the German people had been on a war ration of 1200 calories daily, less than half the normal amount; now they were down to 900 or 800. The sight of American soldiers gorging themselves on thick steaks almost maddened a starving population; and open mutiny was threatened by the British soldiers, who wrote home they would no longer be held responsible, "if children were allowed to wander about the streets, half starving." Meanwhile, the Conference continued to haggle. Regret was voiced for the suffering of German women and children. "But the blockade was maintained." [88]

There was growing up "a bloodless generation . . . with undeveloped muscles, undeveloped joints, and undeveloped brain." The young bruisers were growing up who marched for Hitler, who shouted and sang and made a cult of health. Their bodies repaired themselves. As a scientific experiment, comparable to the German scientific "discoveries" at Dachau and Buchenwald, it was learned how great are the restorative capacities of the human body. The American William Shirer would comment in the Second World War on the magnificence of the German physical specimens in contrast to the puny soldiers of Britain. Their bodies had forgotten — but what of their brains? What nightmares coiled darkly in their subconscious minds, as callous-eyed they lit the incinerator ovens at Dachau or slammed the doors of the death cars to Poland, or looked dispassionately on the rotting death of the Warsaw ghetto? Did they remember other unseeing faces, callous eyes — did they remember that they, too, had been victims, "punished" for a slaughter they never caused? Three and a half million "subnormal children" were counted by Hoover; in their distorted brains burned the vision of the Third Reich.[89]

Two fatal mistakes were made by the peacemakers of Versailles — the continued blockade and the "War Guilt" Clause of the Treaty. As Baruch pointed out, according to German interpretation the Armistice had tacitly agreed to feed the German people. Even the French conceded that the Allies had promised 270,000 tons of food.[90] Instead, there was blockade, punishment, betrayal. Versailles maddened Germany without destroying her.

Why was this tragic error committed? "It would be inadvisable," ran the report on food conditions in Germany, "to remove the menace of starvation by a too sudden supply. This menace is a powerful lever for negotiation." [91]

The Germans answered this turn of the screw with political blackmail of their own. Muttering sounded — "If we don't get food very soon, we'll smash everything up, plunder the rich, plunder the farmers, join the Russians and plunder Europe." The Allies would have only themselves to blame if communism were to sweep over the whole continent. "The danger," ran a report on conditions in Germany from February 1 to February 24, was "not as remote as might appear." [92]

But Clemenceau was implacable to the end. Bolshevism was a bogey, he said. He knew the Germans, and they must be treated firmly. It was not a matter of rewarding them if they stopped threatening the Poles, but of punishing them unless they desisted. Whatever was wanted "must be demanded in the form of an order and in a loud tone of voice." [93]

In the end it was Wilson who had his way, enforcing principle in the name of self-interest. As a realist, he argued that unless Germany were fed no reparations could be paid; and as a moral man, he had no intention of sitting by while Germany starved. Baruch, against the blockade from the first, felt that an army of occupation was the best means of enforcing submission and payment, although such an army should be withdrawn after twenty-five years.[94] Meanwhile, Germany was fed, early enough to save her children for the next war, too late to save their spirits. Germany was fed, but in an order in June, "every preparation" was made for reimposing the blockade and dispatching destroyers to the Baltic, to threaten the people into accepting "peace." [95]

Now the final document was being written. Word came from Germany that no real change of heart had taken place; Ludendorff was proclaiming that Germany would once more "try the hazard of arms," nor was she making the least haste to restore goods seized from the plundered areas. Meanwhile, on paper the peacemakers arranged for the restoration of Alsace-Lorraine and the internationalization of the Saar, for the severed colonies and shifted boundary lines, the razed forts and surrendered ships, the occupation, the unnamed, back-breaking indemnity, Germany's recognition of the League without a right to membership — and recognition, most of all, of Germany's "full responsibility for all damages caused to Allied and Associated Governments and nationals."

Did the Treaty mean justice? Yes, Wilson said, "justice for the dead . . . the German people . . . supported the war . . . obeyed every order, however savage . . . they shared the responsibility for the policy of their government."

Wilson called in the American delegation to hear the final draft. "Anybody got anything to say?" he asked.

Hoover belatedly offered the opinion that the Treaty was "too punitive." From Baruch's point of view, worse than the punitive clauses was the fact that, once imposed, they were never carried out; inspection was called for, but was never enforced. The Treaty of Versailles, he was always convinced, could have kept the peace if it had been enforced. As it was, it aroused the enemy's anger, but in the end lost even his respect.[96]

The time had come for the presentation of the Treaty to the Germans at the Trianon Palace Hotel in Versailles on the afternoon of May 7, 1919 — Lusitania Day. Less publicized than the more spectacular "signing" of June 28, this meeting was perhaps more tense, more charged with personal emotion. You could feel the electricity in the air. The room was small; outside the window each white blossom of a cherry tree was outlined in blazing light.

The Big Three sat like judges, Wilson at the right, Lloyd George to the left. Clemenceau was in the center with the two hundred pages of terms before him. Thus they waited for the German emissaries.[97] As they entered and moved forward, like shadow monotones in their correct half-mourning, the assembly arose. The Tiger, Clemenceau, bent forward, growling out his words. "The time has come when we must settle our accounts. You have asked for peace. We are ready to give you peace."

He "hurled" the document toward them.

A half-stifled murmur of protest arose, for Count Brockdorff-Rantzau sat down. He was, in fact, ill, almost too weak to stand, but the assembly did not understand this and read in his action what he may have indeed intended to imply — that he was not a criminal at the bar. Minute by minute he read, in mounting tension, the silence broken only by the dry scrape as he turned the pages. Finally, he arose, and the guttural German sounded out like a drumbeat. The pose, the tone, the authority, were undeniable. Germany was not guilty. The German people had fought in defense, and any confession that they were the only ones guilty of the war was a lie. "Imperialism," the Count warned, not without truth, had "chronically possessed the international situation . . . expansion and the disregard of . . . peoples." Russian mobilization had placed Germany's fate in the hands of the military. What of the thousands of innocents who had perished from hunger since the close of hostilities — on whose head was their blood? Germany was not the only guilty one. "Think of that when you speak of guilt and punishment."

Clemenceau's face was blood-red. "Has anybody any more observations to offer?" A more tactful speech might have left the door open, but now the challenge had been thrown down. The victors must defend their victory.

Lloyd George snapped a paperknife through his fingers. "It is hard to have won the war and have to listen to that," he said. Clemenceau was silent. When addressed by Brockdorff-Rantzau "in the language of the bearer of a challenge," a hideous abyss had opened in his mind.

The German, he knew, was "not a whit cured of his insane folly."
Europe would continue, without respite, "to be subjected . . . to the
same attack from the same enemy." [98] Back in Germany, the conduct
of the parliamentarians was so "haughty and insolent" that they even
sang "Deutschland über alles" at the end of an assembly; and so infuriated were the peacemakers that Baruch heard them actually considering the possibility of not renewing the Armistice.[99]

The Allies were thus confronted with the paradox of a people
wearied to death of war and a leadership still ready for one. No party
in Germany seemed willing to admit her fault. Germany's submission
was being obtained by "extortions." The Allies were warned by the
German press: any peace signed would last only so long as the Allies
kept the might with which to enforce it — only so long as the power
on which it was based was undivided. Headlines in the German
papers announced the news of young William Bullitt's resignation
from the American delegation in protest over the Allies' indifference
to Russia, and his forecast that Versailles would breed a new world
war. Few indeed were the German newspapers that conceded that the
war was lost, that Germany's "political religion of the past" had been
condemned by the majority of civilized mankind.[100] The Allies had
sown the seeds of hatred; they would be cultivated and reaped.

This was the note sounded by the formal German "replies" of
May 29, over which the peacemakers brooded in indignation and fear.
What if Germany refused to sign? Shrewdly, the German notes
struck to the core of the misgivings that lingered in the Allies' minds
— all initiative, they pointed out, would cease if the reward of labor
was only increasing burdens. If the output of their factories benefited
not themselves but strangers, "the German people would feel themselves condemned to slavery." Nothing would be left for the crippled
soldiers, schools, orphaned children. German democracy would be
strangled at birth "by the very ones who during the whole war never
grew weary of insisting they wanted to bring democracy to us." If the
war was fought for freedom, why was not Germany given the same
freedom as other nations? Violence had replaced right. Germany
must recognize her allies' claims against her, but must not enforce her
claims against her allies. The Treaty implied that Germany alone
could pay the costs of the war, but the experts knew that that was impossible. Where was right, where was justice? A nation could not be
compelled to sign its own death warrant.[101]

Almost simultaneously with the German reply to the terms, Winston Churchill arrived in Paris. For months Baruch had longed to meet that fabulous soldier of fortune, leader of disaster and of victory, his onetime "partner" in the nitrate negotiations. Early one morning, accompanied by Lloyd George, he called on Churchill at his hotel.

The Englishman was dressing and at the moment of his guests' arrival was carefully putting on a black satin tie. Baruch wasted no time on amenities. "We're going to discuss the Treaty," he said. "I want us to be a unit and not bust up in front of 'em."

Churchill turned from the bureau and dropped his hand. "If we could have gotten a peace on the terms the Germans offer us now," he said, "it would have been a brilliant peace."

Now was too late. The defeated enemy could not call the tune. The next day Churchill met Baruch in the Bois, stolid in his square-topped derby and clutching a walking stick in his hand. The air was raw and cold. As the two fell into step, Baruch heard his companion muttering, "Russia. Russia. That's where the weather is coming from." [102]

A day or two later, Baruch had breakfast with Lloyd George. Again the "one subject" was discussed; Lloyd George agreed with Churchill that the Germans had submitted a "masterly reply." Then, before Baruch had taken one sip of coffee or put a spoonful of egg in his mouth, the little Welshman leaned forward tensely.

"I cannot agree to turn down the German counterproposals," he said. The British Fleet and Army were too weary to fight; if the Germans refused to sign, they would not move. He paused dramatically for an instant. "What will Mr. Wilson say?"

Baruch got up. "I can find out," he said.

Colonel House was standing guard at Wilson's door. Mr. Baruch could not see the President, he said, and at that instant Wilson looked out. "I want to speak to you, Mr. President," Baruch shot in, and gave his message. Wilson got his hat and coat.

On their way to Lloyd George's residence, Baruch briefly outlined the picture. Lloyd George, he said, was trying to seize the moral leadership of the world, "and I'd let him have it." Wilson said nothing. In silence, he and Baruch walked up the flight of stairs, and after they were greeted at the threshold, Baruch offered to leave.

"I'm only going to tell him what I told you," Lloyd George said, and when the President added, "I have no secrets from Baruch," the financier "sat down with those two great fellows."

Now Lloyd George explained more fully. He was willing at last to agree to the American wish for a "fixed sum" of reparations for Germany; even to offer the Germans the chance to suggest the sum.

Wilson was not pleased. On the surface, Lloyd George's offer looked like capitulation. Here was what America had been fighting for, alone, month after month, but Wilson realized that since France would never give in, Lloyd George's move was a grandstand play, designed to give England credit for "generosity" toward Germany, and to weaken the Allied position — for it was a generosity induced only by her own war-weariness. Here was England, proposing to undo the work of months — with the Treaty finished. As Baruch noted in retrospect: "It was Lloyd George who made the most trouble at Paris, not Clemenceau and the French. If Lloyd George had played with Wilson and Clemenceau . . . we should have been much better off."

Usually Wilson was the ameliorating influence. Not now. He turned on Lloyd George. "You make me sick," the President said, "to want to make those changes which for four and a half months you have so consistently fought. Now you want to make changes America once wanted to make, after we've already agreed. It's up to you to get France."

"You talk to Mr. Clemenceau," Lloyd George said, wheedlingly. "If you can get the French to agree, I'll get Britain — "

"No, you do that. You're the one who's insisting on changes."

Later Baruch asked the British Prime Minister what the reaction of Clemenceau had been. "He nearly went through the roof of the automobile," Lloyd George said.[103]

But the Germans had to be answered. Joseph C. Grew, the Secretary General of the American delegation, had notified Baruch: "You have been named the American member on the Committee on Economic Clauses, established to deal with questions of detail, requests for explanation and the like . . . by the German delegation." This was on the twenty-sixth of May.[104]

Although only a routine working paper was called for, it required careful preparation, and Leland Summers worked with Baruch on the draft. They could not speak for themselves. This was not the Baruch who in private condemned the unfair burdens being levied upon the German people, and who even now privately wished that the Allies could set a fixed sum so that the German people would know what they had to bear. Now no concessions could be made, and any "answer" to the Germans must speak with the united voice of Allied power. Germany could not expect to be better off than her victims, but eventual restoration of her industrial life would be in the Allies' own interest.[105]

Draft after draft was considered. At length the document was completed. The revised copy of the projected reply, a British delegate wrote Baruch on May 18, followed Baruch's final draft very closely.[106]

This time, however, the Germans did not respond in diplomatic form. The real answer came not from the diplomats but from the hungry German workers, who would not submit to any policy that did not bring immediate peace. As predicted, the political value of the blockade now came into play in Austria, where order was maintained "by threat of cessation of the thin stream of food which kept the population alive." On May 5, at a meeting of the Supreme Economic Council, Baruch read a resolution, to be submitted in case the Germans refused to sign the peace: "That the blockade section . . . prepare immediately a plan for the instant application, in case of need, of the fullest possible pressure of Blockade upon Germany" — this almost at the exact moment that Herbert Hoover watched the rickety children of Germany tottering across the schoolrooms.[107]

Ten days later Baruch met with Wilson to discuss "our plan." Wilson demurred; he preferred military occupation to starvation. Germany knew nothing of his misgivings, and the fear of a resumption of the blockade was like a gun at her heart. Under this threat the ultimatum was accepted. But while Germany hesitated, only Wilson seemed as "calm and clear-headed as though he were not passing through the most anxious days of the Conference."

What had happened to the "peace without victory" for which Wilson had called? What had happened to Lloyd George's belief that "to shift the costs of conflict from one belligerent to the other would be a great breach of the public law of Europe?" It was not the peacemakers who failed at Paris. Individually they were "able and high-minded men." They were aware of their responsibility to history and to mankind. All who saw could feel the purpose that dominated the Conference, the burning intent to see that wrongs were righted, and the steps taken that would prevent another world holocaust. The spirit of the Conference, Baruch felt, was basically fair. The aim was for the common good and the great decisive questions were often left up to the Americans. No, the peacemakers did not fail. It was the human spirit that failed.

As Clemenceau said, the war still went on in the minds of the people to whom the statesmen were answerable. These were the "same minds that had made the war of 1914." Greed had bred one war; vengeance was breeding the next. If German children were starving, what of ravaged France, "devastated and subjected to the worst kind of savagery?"

Fear — that grim sire of war — was the uninvited guest at the peace table. Fear overrode all, for what protection did France have but a League of Nations, to be guaranteed by what now seemed a most unlikely guarantee of American power. In fear the statesmen moved and in darkness groped, not knowing that the weapons they forged in fear would wreak destruction.

The Treaty had done nothing for Russia. It had not stabilized the Far East or Middle Europe. As time would prove, it had not even solidified the Allies.[108] Reflecting upon it, Baruch could note that what repression of vengeance there had been was due to Wilson. The Treaty did not embrace all that he desired, but probably all that could have been obtained. It was, moreover, a "flexible instrument," and provision was made "whereby wrongs could be righted, wisdom and justice prevail." [109] As for Wilson, his summary was short: "If it won't work, it must be made to work." [110]

June 28 was warm and clear. The sky was bright. The trees in their marvelous young green "stood out in relief as if in color photography." Inside the Hall of Mirrors in the Palace of Versailles the shifting hundreds sat — Baruch and others eying the leaders as they came in: Wilson's smile preceding him "by about a quarter of an hour," Lloyd George expectant, Clemenceau looking dogged and tired. A weary disillusion, a feeling of anticlimax filled the air. One young Englishman wrote, "There is not a single person here among the younger people . . . who is not unhappy and disappointed in the terms."

These same young Englishmen remembered this great white hall rank with the smell of iodoform and of new rubber and leather as patched-up young Tommies were assigned new boots for their own reassignment to the slaughter mill. For Clemenceau, the Hall of

Mirrors held other memories. Images, now nearly half a century past, flickered through his mind: 1871 — and another signing, "warlike uniforms, the cries of 'Hoch!' the clicking boot heels, the cheers ... the clink of gold and steel." Now, in contrast, all he could think of was the gleam of the spectacles like crowns around the administrative heads. The crowd of hundreds was multiplied endlessly by the winking mirrors: 1871, 1919 — would this hall, these mirrors ever reflect such a scene again? A young German had the answer; he whispered, "All passes. It will seem so different in ten, in twenty years."

Clemenceau arose. The hall vibrated to his harsh cry, "*Faites entrer les Allemands.*" Now came the booted tramp, four officers — one French, one British, one Italian, and one American — and after them two Germans, "deathly pale" and staring blankly; one thin and pink of eyelids, the other with a round face like a moon. They ranged themselves before the bar. They made "cardboard bows to Clemenceau and his peers," and then "with faces like paper and jaws like iron" signed their names to "the miserable fate of their country."

But all was not yet over. One macabre touch remained. There was a stir. Clemenceau's head turned, and all others with it. There on a velvet bench between two windows Wilson and the massed hundreds saw "three ghastly masks of the hellish tragedy, with eyes unsocketed, with twisted jaws; their faces ploughed with scars — three grievously wounded men," looking unseeing on the past that had destroyed them, on the unknown future ahead.

Now the big guns crashed. Like prisoners from the dock the Germans were escorted out, and after them crowded the spectators and the Big Four. A living carpet of people awaited them. The fountains of Versailles sprayed in triumph. Clemenceau was tossed and whirled by the crowd as he passed, and pelted with flowers. Clouds raced across the sky, and after them planes, harbingers of the new age of wind and air. Now came the cheers so long withheld; later there would be the toasts and champagne. There was joy on the faces of the Americans; they had won their League and brought the New World to the Old. Yet even they felt a sense of anticlimax. They did not know that their own world would wreck their dream. But others were more aware of the future. A young Englishman made an entry in his diary that night: "To bed, sick of life." [111]

11

LOST HORIZON

MAJESTICALLY the *George Washington* moved through the summer sea. It was the Fourth of July. Peace rested on the waters; peace sounded in the voice of Woodrow Wilson as from the deck he addressed crew and passengers. This was the most glorious Fourth of July in history, for it was no longer merely an American Independence Day. Henceforth, the interests of the team "would supersede the interests of the individual." Out of this war a new freedom would come, not only to America, but "to the peoples of the world." [1] For a moment the President held them all transfixed by his vision — there was a dreamlike quality to this tranquil hour.

Yet not all was peace on the waters. Later in the day, meeting Baruch on the bridge, Wilson looked intently at him. "His eye was liquid," Baruch later recalled, "that eye that looked like flint it could flash so hard." Wilson said, "People are expecting of me what only God can perform." [2]

The future was still in doubt; yet even if much had been left undone and much had been done wrongly, the peacemakers could still look back on some solid achievement. If human nature was unaltered, new recognition was at least given to hitherto disregarded aspects of human nature. The new world, if new world there was to be, was founded upon concepts of the interdependence of men and the dignity of the individual. Even old Samuel Gompers had played his role, and it was Baruch who had warned that it would be an unfortunate circumstance if Mr. Gompers were overlooked. From Poland a friend had telephoned Baruch that the people there had great confidence in two men: President Wilson and Samuel Gompers. Baruch believed that working conditions must be improved and the rewards of the worker increased. Manual and mental work should receive a more fair recognition. Class lines should be eased.[3] This spirit was reflected in many ways in the Treaty of Versailles — notably in the recognition that "labor should not be regarded merely as an article of commerce," that child labor should be abolished, and that the eight-hour day was "the standard to be aimed at." [4]

The wonder is not that there were many mistakes in the Treaty but that there were so few. The complexities were immense. Race and language could not always determine nationality, for instance: there were Greeks who did not speak Greek, and Albanian Christians who had flooded into Greece in the wake of the Mohammedans, become Hellenized in custom and yet retained their ancient tongue. Northern Schleswig-Holstein remained Danish after years of Prussian rule. If Poland were to be allowed claims established prior to the Napoleonic wars, what of Italy and other victims of Bonaparte's conquests? [5] There were solutions, however, even for insolubles.

It was true that the great land mass and power potential of the Soviet Union had been neither stabilized nor integrated into the European scene. Cold comfort it must have been to Russia that under the Treaty of Versailles Germany accepted "definitely the abrogation of the Brest-Litovsk Treaties" and acknowledged and agreed "to respect as permanent and inalienable the independence of all the territories which were part of the former Russia on August 1, 1914," for if Germany's conquests were not recognized, neither were they returned to Russia, who was left encircled by her onetime possessions, now liberated and responsible to the Western Powers. Prisoners were coming home all over Europe, but not all the Russians were coming home. For on Wednesday, May 14, a teasing question for future years had been debated by the peacemakers — Should anti-Bolshevist Russian prisoners in Germany be returned to their country? The question was decided quickly. Very simply, the prisoners were let out and the Germans ordered to provide all needful facilities for their return to Russia, but no one was compelled to return.[6]

Although Austrians might cry that stripped of their livelihood, their raw materials, their transport, and even their watering places, they could not survive, yet boundary adjustments generally, both in terms of nationalities and of economic stabilization in the countries concerned, had been most successful. Not all could receive reparations in money or goods, but a redrawing of the boundary might provide additional taxable population and a more equitable distribution of raw materials. Rumania was doubled by her rich additions, including oil fields; Greece got fertile agricultural sections; Czechoslovakia, more than half the minerals of Austria-Hungary, coal mines, established industries, and farm areas; and Poland acquired mineral-producing sectors, the possibility of oil, and German coal fields.

Session by session, efforts had been made to eliminate the elements of disturbance, for, as the United States delegates argued, they could not go three thousand miles to report that they had settled the peace of the world if they had not truly done so.[7] They must be satisfied that the settlements were correct; they must be sure of the underlying strength of the League. Aware that the bad faith of any one country could endanger the peace of the whole, their greatest fear for the League was any appearance of impotency. No sovereignty had been surrendered; no international army formed. Would sanctions alone deter an aggressor? Wilson had heard the warning of Foch that in fifteen years France would find herself back to her frontiers of 1870; hence her insistence upon occupation of the Rhine.[8] Some semblances of a European settlement had been reached, but there were still problems. Hoover, for instance, had warned Wilson bluntly that despite the new independence of Finland, that nation was left in commercial isolation. If ever a people needed help, it was the Finns.[9] Yet great advances had been made: moral justice had been given legal sanction, and liberated peoples like the Poles and the Yugoslavs had been given national existence.

In the East were more unsettled questions. There sprawled the great land mass of China, scarcely more potent in 1919 than Russia. Yet as early as 1903 Henry Adams had written to Mrs. Elizabeth Cameron that it would be China where "the last struggle for power would come." Were Russia to organize China, so he forecast, the West could never compete, either with Asian labor or the Siberian system. "Our clumsy Western civilization" would be ended, and he set 1950 as the year when the white race would be run out.

It scarcely seemed so in 1919. China was inert. Japan, on the other hand, was aggressive, and where could her surplus energy be drained off?[10] Japan had made her own demands at the Peace Conference, including that "the Japanese nation expects from the Peace Conference the final abolition of every racial hindrance and disqualification." [11] What would recognition of this request do to the caste system of India, racial segregation in America, or the immigration policies of Australia and the rest of the Anglo-Saxon world?

In actual fact, Japan used the racial issue, which she knew was embarrassing to her allies, rather as a lever with which to bring them to her view of a much more serious question, the Shantung problem, than as a bona fide claim. In 1898, Germany had extorted from China certain railroad and commercial rights in the Shantung peninsula — a holy region to the Chinese. When Japan joined the Allies her troops, together with a few British, attacked and defeated the German Army in the peninsula. Japan then extracted from England, in a secret treaty, a promise that the German rights would be transferred to her after the war. Japan's claim was reinforced by China's "acceptance" in 1915 of the ultimatum of Japan which came to be known as the "Twenty-one Demands," by the first of which China agreed to support the transfer of the German rights to Japan. Finally, having herself declared war on Germany, China subsequently reasserted this agreement in a note of September 24, 1918. Now, at the Peace Conference, Japan demanded fulfillment of these agreements, and China claimed that the original concessions to Germany had been forcibly extorted, and that by her declaration of war against that country China had extinguished them. Consequently, claimed China, there were no "German rights" to be transferred to Japan. Both China's acceptance of the Twenty-one Demands and her later agreement with Japan were claimed to have been made only under threats of force. China claimed that Japan was simply determined to control eastern Asia through "the domination and control of the manpower of China." [12]

No issue of the entire Conference led to greater dissension among the American delegation nor to more bitter denunciation in America when the Treaty was submitted for our ratification. Wilson had been as reluctant as anyone else to concede Japan's demands, but when Italy had already withdrawn from the Conference and Japan threatened to do the same, he came to feel that to save the Treaty and the League, it was necessary to give in. So the decision was reached with few and feeble concessions on Japan's part. Wilson's capitulation was not only denounced at home as a betrayal of China, with whom the United States was traditionally friendly, but brought a wide breach within the official American delegation. It was one of the principal reasons for Wilson's demand in 1920 that Lansing resign as Secretary of State, and has been a point of bitter disagreement among Americans ever since.[13]

Baruch had questions of his own. Officially, the Economic Commission had closed its doors on June 27, one day before the signing at Versailles, but two months earlier he had concluded that the Commission's work would never be done until world trade was stabilized. In theory, this looked like an impossible task. To take only one example, Belgium had debts to the other Allies which, if left unpaid, might bog down the whole European economy. She had need of almost all the necessities of life and no credits. The United States had huge reserve supplies: underwear, khaki, hobnailed army shoes, all desperately needed overseas. How could the need and the supply meet? [14]

A typical answer was suggested by Brigadier General C. R. Krauthoff: American credits could be given Allied nations who wanted to buy surplus American supplies. A week later Baruch questioned the General on how far he felt it wise to follow this procedure. Already, the Belgians had absorbed twenty-two millions worth and wanted more.[15]

Fortunately perhaps for his peace of mind on that last serene voyage, Wilson was not tortured with visions of the future. He could measure the good and the bad of the Peace Treaty, not realizing that the abstract merits of the League of Nations were as nothing beside the question of whether Americans were ready for it. Although few shadows crossed the brightness of those sunny days, sometimes reality intruded. Baruch, like the anxious Colonel Starling, could have watched the President, haggard and pale, pacing round and round the deck, in plain sight to all stumbling each time over the same coil of rope.[16] Wilson was wrapped in his dreams, and so high were the heights he scaled that he carried even such practical men of affairs as Baruch with him.

During the trip, Wilson read to the delegation the message he was writing for Congress and asked for suggestions. Baruch said nothing. Later he met the President and Mrs. Wilson coming down the companionway, where Wilson cornered him.

"Baruch, you didn't say anything."

"I had a different idea," Baruch admitted. "In addressing Congress, you'll really have the biggest audience you've ever had. It seems you ought to explain what the League of Nations is and what it's going to do. Make the opposition attack. If you wait, you'll have to defend and then attack."

Now Wilson was silent. "I don't think he liked it," Baruch commented afterward. "He always thought that what he thought was so simple everyone could understand him. He thought they objected just to object." [17] Baruch was discovering for himself what Lansing would also belatedly observe, that for all his fine intellect Wilson's convictions were intuitive. "His judgments were always right in his own mind because he knew that they were right." [18]

Wilson had yet to find out that the issue before the country would not be the League of Nations but Woodrow Wilson. Wilson's refusal to heed the opposition had given public sympathy to the opposition, and within a few weeks' time there had been "a great reversal of sentiment." The people of America were not talking about the Peace Conference. They were worried about Prohibition and high taxes and Federal extravagance; and anyway, they felt, the next war would not come for a long time, so why worry. The press was openly warning that people were more interested in hanging the Kaiser than in the League of Nations, and that while Wilson was making the world safe for democracy, he was losing the post offices at home.[19]

As for Baruch, he was confident that the changes that had been written into the Covenant would now satisfy the fair-minded [20] and were furthermore all that could have been attempted at that time. Neither he nor Wilson seemed to understand that in general people are not fair-minded and that no changes made in the League could offset the shaky foundation upon which it had been built.

Wilson may have thought of these things, but he did not speak of them. Did not the *Literary Digest* poll show that the mass of newspaper editorial opinion favored the League? Did not the Birmingham *Age-Herald* proclaim that Wilson was strongly backed by the American people? And the *New York Times* and the Salt Lake *Deseret News?* [21]

Wilson was deaf to the dissident voices in the rear: the fierce prophecies of the Italian press, ridiculing both him and Clemenceau, warning of the resurgence of German power and the danger to France and the world when American troops were withdrawn. "Germany," bluntly stated the Italian *Epoca*, "has signed a scrap of paper." [22]

Wilson knew that Britain was for the League only if England and America clung firmly together, but of their clinging together he had no doubt.[23] The Senate? He was convinced that he could "handle" the Senate; and he was convinced of the heart of the people. The people would understand, "if certain politicians don't."

Had he forgotten that sullen White House dinner at which the Senate opposition first "bared its teeth"; the filibuster and round robin of Republican leaders, declaring that the League "in the form now proposed" was unacceptable; and the flat statement in the New York *Sun:* "Woodrow Wilson's League of Nations died in the Senate tonight"? [24] Did he remember that night in Mechanics Hall, Boston, when in spite of the faithful Tumulty's preparations, muttered boos had answered the President's denunciation of "narrow, selfish, provincial purposes . . . which have no sweep beyond the nearest horizon"? [25] America was the hope of the world; America had been founded to make men free; now America could free mankind.

A young man named Roland Hayes, who admired Wilson greatly, had slipped into Mechanics Hall that night to find out how the people really felt and why, and the animosity in those stiff rows swept the young singer like a cold blast. He could still feel the chill thirty years later. "It was very sad." [26]

Henry White had not dared tell Wilson of Lodge's "reservations," already slipped to him in a private note. Some of Lodge's suggestions made sense — with their demands that it be made "physically impossible" for Germany to break loose again in her design of world conquest, and a method as to how this could be averted: "the separation of the German Empire into component parts." [27] The people approved these suggestions, made public only when it was evident that they had failed in private. So Lodge was free — free to tell the New York *Sun* that the League was "the biggest Republican issue since the Civil War," free to be acclaimed by the French *Démocratie Nouvelle* as "the real representative of the American people." [28] Of small concern to Lodge was Wilson's fine-spun reasoning that the Senate must be spared the responsibilities of treaty-making, for if they made treaties, how then could they sit in judgment on their own creations? Senator Lodge had no desire to be spared.

As the *George Washington* docked on July 8, 1919, in tiered rows around and below the President, the homecoming soldiers were singing. New York greeted the President with destroyers, planes, dirigibles, white-haired women leaning from tenement windows crying "God bless you," cheers and surging demonstrations which brought him to his feet, hat in hand.[29] Washington greeted him with a bitter Senate, waiting expectantly for something to turn down.[30]

Bernard Baruch, meanwhile, faced problems of his own. Now that the war was won, Congress had leaped into full-scale investigations as to how it could have been won better. The Advisory Commission to the Council of National Defense was on the griddle. Republican partisans and the country were ringing with condemnation of "the secret government of the United States." As the Americus, Georgia, *Times-Recorder* noted: "The President and his administration not having been attacked for a day or two . . . Mr. Graham seized the moment." [31] The "baying pack" was off again.

Representative William J. Graham was a spellbinder from the corn country of Illinois. He was of the same ilk as Martin Dies in the nineteen-thirties; he lived to ferret, to accuse, to juggle charge and countercharge. "God save the republic" commented the Springfield *Republican.* "Is this the kind of incompetence the Republicans promised to expose?" [32]

For the Graham investigation — although its tag odds and ends dragged on for years, climaxed by the famed "Hell and Maria" boomings of Charles G. Dawes — actually boomeranged almost as soon as it began. However the headline writers had a glorious hour with their chants of " 'Secret Seven' Ruled Nation, Says Graham," and "A Super-President in Mr. Baruch." [33]

Now Graham, wittingly or unwittingly, had purposely blurred the functions of the original, almost powerless and semisecret Advisory Commission and the much advertised War Industries Board. And Baruch, with his instinct for favorable publicity, was able to make capital of this fine dividing line. If he had not exercised the power as charged, while on the Advisory Commission, he had certainly done so on the War Industries Board. So he admitted everything; and, as he said afterwards: "I won 'em all by my frankness and sincerity." [34] Smilingly he produced his records, smilingly admitted the truth of all with which they had charged him — and turned it to the Administration's benefit. As the Montgomery *Advertiser* put it, "There is no arguing with results." [35] Yes, he had wielded power, the power of the President himself, and of whatever mistakes had been made he could say: "I alone am responsible." [36]

He did say it, and the Graham Committee gasped, and latter-day commentators, taking him at his word, have written that he virtually acted as the brain of his country.[37] The original Advisory Commission perhaps reaped more than its due share of credit. The Buffalo *Express* noted that "a group of amateurs" had bungled Army supply that should have been handled by the War Department; but added that the "scattering" charges by Graham, when tallied up, only entitled the Administration to praise. "If the seven men . . . are guilty as charged," said the Buffalo *Enquirer*, "they deserve medals of honor." All the hullaballoo was "over too much foresight." Unlike Congress, the President had refused to wait until "the eleventh hour," but had carefully planned ahead for what might transpire. He had been denounced for allowing the country to remain unprepared, and now he was denounced for having prepared it. There was "no way on earth for Uncle Woodrow to please a Republican." The Republicans were not pleased, and as the Columbia, South Carolina, *Record* commented, only an investigation could give them the opportunity to claim that they might have done it all better.[38]

A Michigan newspaper wrote the epitaph of the fiasco. The whole investigation produced not "one single bit of constructive action." As for the secrecy of the American war program, should Germany have been let in on the secrets? All that Congress had uncovered were some dire reflections "upon the capacity of Congress to carry on a war." The work of the Advisory Commission had made Congress "look like the smallest potato grown." Congress was not pleased.[39]

Nor was Bernard Baruch. Despite his surface poise, years afterward he was still simmering over the kind of men who wanted to make the people believe that those who served them in the war were incompetent or dishonest, because that is how they themselves would have been, if they had had the chance.[40] The whole investigation, like so many after it, was a side show, staged to make businessmen look like profiteers. Baruch was enraged.[41]

Woodrow Wilson and his administration had won the first round. But the battle for the League of Nations still loomed ahead.

It is customary to view the great struggle over the League as a personal one between a heroic and righteous President and "a small group of willful men" who scuttled the League to gratify their spleen. Actually, the question was not so simple. Senators are not devils, although they are sometimes fools, and men of the caliber of Lodge, Hiram Johnson, Borah, Norris, La Follette, Reed, and Philander Knox are neither devils nor fools. Furthermore, the history of recent years gives validity to their belief that United States "interventionism," as opposed to "isolationism" — United States participation in a World Order — would not in itself necessarily have staved off another war.

The senators were representatives of the people, and it is by no means certain that the American people desired the burdens of responsibility. The League was viewed with the dubiousness that mankind in general entertains for anything resembling a new idea. Even sympathetic historians have conceded that there was no great demand for the League from the people.[42] Humanity, as Clemenceau might have observed, had failed again.

The League was a party fight — a Democratic Party fight, and it was largely Wilson who had made it so. With the chairman of the Senate Foreign Relations Committee, Henry Cabot Lodge, publicly committed to some kind of League, with Wilson's program in the House winning more support from Republicans than Democrats, the President had appealed for the election of a Democratic Congress. He had not made the League issue bipartisan. He had challenged the Senate and threatened it; in the Metropolitan Opera House the previous March he had shouted, "Anyone who opposes me in that I'll crush"; [43] and on May 24 he had cabled Lansing that the Senate would have to take the Treaty entire or reject it entire. But the Senate had the power. And the most powerful man in the Senate was Henry Cabot Lodge of Massachusetts.

At the time of the League struggle, Senator Lodge was sixty-nine years old. He was "Boston incarnate," a dapper figure easy to picture walking eternally up and down Beacon Street, or wittily conversing in a novel by Henry James. A small man, slenderly built, with immaculate silvered hair and beard, he focused, almost magnetized, attention. He shared, perhaps consciously, a trick of John Quincy Adams', sitting down in the Senate to listen attentively to the first florid sentences of a newcomer's maiden speech, and then rising and walking out indifferently, as if both speech and speaker were unworthy of attention. A small copy of Shakespeare was often in his pocket. "The scholar in politics," he had been termed, until Wilson's ascension; and like Wilson, he had written a number of histories and biographies, acrid, brilliant, bitter, reflecting the author as much as their subject. Watching him in action on the Senate floor, hearing his snort, seeing his sardonic grin and glittering eye, Wilson had disliked him instantly, instinctively, and probably would have done so even if Lodge had not so bitterly disapproved of Wilson.

Lodge had hated Southerners as a boy, and here we have perhaps one clue to his almost pathological hatred of the Wilson regime. Wilson was the first Southerner to be elected President since the Civil War, and his administration was rife with Southerners, many, like himself, the sons of Confederate soldiers. In fact, even the old Confederate soldiers came in his wake and Lodge saw the weathered veterans of the United Confederate Volunteers, who had fought against the flag, encamped in the national parks, picnicking around the national monuments.

Lodge had gone to Congress in 1887 at the close of the Reconstruction era, just in time to see the last of the "freemen" returning to political oblivion and their places filled once again by those "gentlemen of the South" who had plotted and made war. Three years later young Lodge had been an avid supporter of the "Force bill," the last effort of Reconstruction, calling for Federal supervision of Southern elections.[44] He was not an irreconcilable, but a Republican, and to him the party was a holy cause. The Republicans were the party of the Union, of law and order and gentlemen, and so sacred was the party to him that when his dearest friend, Theodore Roosevelt, bolted in 1912, Lodge sat the election out. The Democrats on the other hand were the party of "slavery, secession, repudiation of the public debt; fiat money; free trade; free silver; the overthrow of the courts and government ownership."[45] A statesman by inclination, Lodge had by necessity developed into a shrewd and sometimes ruthless politician, who in his own Massachusetts had welded together a constituency of Irish "more Irish than in Ireland," and of professional Yankees — British-haters who were still shooting the Redcoats off Bunker Hill. In the Senate his addresses, delivered with the unbending formality of a Spanish grandee, his learning, and powers formed a coalition of equals who penetrated his crusty exterior and loved him, of intellects who admired him, and of fawners who feared and followed him.[46]

"My first allegiance as an American," he said in 1910, "is to this great Nation."[47] Although he played from time to time with the idea of a League of Nations, he was convinced that peace could be best supported by military not moral force. In 1912, he reversed this opinion; [48] but in 1915, speaking before the students of Union College, he put himself on record as in favor of "a union of civilized nations" for the maintenance of peace and world order, but with the qualification that such a union could be maintained only "by the force which united nations are willing to put behind the peace and order of the world." [49] Speaking on the same platform with Wilson in 1916, he discussed methods that might "put force behind international peace."

In July 1919 the Senate Foreign Relations Committee went into session. For two weeks it sat behind closed doors. It was listening to the official reading of the text of the Treaty of Versailles by its chairman, Senator Lodge — that same text which had appeared unofficially in bootleg copies in the press, and which Borah had read into the *Congressional Record* the month before. [50]

Then the parade of witnesses began. Early on the roster was Bernard M. Baruch, cool and composed in the sweltering heat of the Washington summer which only heated tempers all the more.

There, ranged before him, were the "battalion of death": George Moses of New Hampshire, the Yankee newspaperman and former teacher of Greek, with the cracker-barrel wit of the country store; Pennsylvania's Philander Knox, short and rotund of body, brilliant of mind; Frank Brandegee of Connecticut and the rapier tongue sat nearby, intense, overstrung. From the West there were Hiram Johnson of California, and Albert B. Fall, the typical Western "bad man," with his handlebar mustache and soft, swirl-brimmed hat. Two strangely misassorted personalities dominated the group: shaggy-haired William E. Borah, whose piercing blue eyes burned with the light of the fanatic; and Henry Cabot Lodge, looking on with an air of bored detachment. This was the judge and the jury together, the deliberative body whose decision had been rendered even before the evidence was assembled.

When his name was called, Baruch stepped forward and faced the "bar." Although it was only 10.30 in the morning of July 31, electric fans purred overhead. Baruch was ready; he fenced; he parried; he gave nothing away, none of the doubts or dissensions of the weeks past. The Treaty was written and he was bound to it and, further-more, he was utterly convinced that the President was right and his accusers wrong. With Senators hammering questions at him, Baruch's poise remained unbroken. He would not betray weaknesses in the Treaty by showing weakness himself.

First, the Committee wanted to know America's share in the reparations payments. Baruch answered, "I think those matters would be a question for determination by the President, rather than anybody else."

Philander Knox questioned him. "The President alone, or the President in conjunction with the Congress?"

"You," answered Baruch, "would be a better judge of that."

The inquisition was continued the next day at the same hour. Patiently, Baruch explained, "No one would fix an amount against a debtor that he did not think the debtor could pay." The American delegation had fought for a fixed sum of reparations, but there was no possibility "such a short time after the sound of the cannon had died away . . . to get any adequate idea of what the bill should be . . . Germany was not in a condition to find out what she could pay . . . We soon saw it was impossible."

Why, wondered Hiram Johnson, if the United States was to receive no reparations, should it be on the Reparation Commission? "We have got a great stake in the Reparation Commission . . . even from a selfish view . . . Can you imagine the world being prosperous while one hundred thirty millions of people right in the center of the industrial population are not prosperous . . . the finances of Italy, France, and of Belgium and their industrial life depending on what they are going to receive from those people . . . It is a great big partnership . . . of vast consequence to America."

Senator Johnson leaned forward. "Is it not a fact that the whole economic section of the Treaty was drawn up by England?"

"It is not, sir, unless you call me an Englishman."

On Saturday, his wife looking on proudly and seated near her a dashing young aviator who was courting his daughter Belle, Baruch had his final say. The terms of the Treaty, he thought, were "harsh and severe, but . . . very just.[51] Chandler P. Anderson commented afterward that although obviously unfamiliar with the phases of the treaty-making in which he had played no part, Baruch made a good witness in that it was evident he was holding nothing back, and he was "very obliging and good-natured about trying to answer questions." On the reparations sections, he had little to worry about; it was generally agreed that they were in better shape than any of the others.[52]

Meanwhile, the Senate sought other witnesses. Senator Knox asked Norman Davis to recommend "a first-class expert on the League of Nations."

"I should think the President," was the surprising answer.

Knox's sneer was exceeded only by Lodge's. "We tried him once at a dinner and we did not get the information."

Key Pittman of Nevada interpolated gently that the President had said "he would be glad to give Congress any information . . . he offered to come before the Committee."

"He can come any time he wants to," snapped Senator Brandegee.

"The chairman and others" — Lodge's eyes glinted — "never saw fit to invite him," Pittman answered. In this mood and spirit, the hearings continued.[53]

The "secret agreements" and the Shantung settlement next came under fire, revealing at least that whether or not there were secret treaties there were certainly secrets kept from the United States. Once Borah observed dreamily, "I do not desire to ask anything about the Monroe Doctrine. We all understood what it was, up to six months ago."

Lansing saw his opening and took it. "I congratulate the Senator, because there seems to be a wide difference of opinion as to what it means. He may be the only man who knows." [54]

The debate continued through Monday, August 18, when it was made plain that Japan's possession of Shantung could not be broken except by a fight and that the United States would not fight. Japan could "tell the League . . . to go to the devil unless you line up certain forces to overawe her." [55]

The high spot of the hearings was the meeting of the Foreign Relations Committee at the White House on August 19. The impression given was that the Senate was on a "smelling expedition." Senator Borah arrived on foot, carrying a bound copy of the Treaty like a schoolbook under his arm. Wilson met his inquisitors with a prepared statement as to the League's goals and purposes, but Senator Lodge brushed this cursorily aside. It was on "certain points" that the Committee desired information.

Wilson gave it to them. He told them that the Monroe Doctrine was specifically recognized under Article 21. He told them that the right to withdraw from the League was "taken for granted." He told them that Article 10 was the "very backbone of the whole covenant." Finally, he suggested that the Senate submit its own interpretations as to how binding the articles were on the United States. The Senators were not mollified. Borah summed up, "The matter gets back to the point where one individual has bound Congress." [56]

Back in the committee room, the hearings continued. The Senators heard of Fiume and Trieste and Greeks that were being parceled out to Bulgaria and Italy. Traveling in their segregated trains, eating in their for-whites-only restaurants, and sleeping in their segregated hotels, they brooded over the lack of democratic institutions in India and over the Irish, jailed and shot after the uprising of 1916. Daniel O'Flaherty out of segregated Richmond, forecast that all Virginia would declare for Irish freedom. Finally, as a parting shot, fresh from Bolshevist Russia they produced a disillusioned young idealist, twenty-eight-year-old William Bullitt, whose testimony aroused international reverberations. He said that the League was "useless"; he quoted Lansing as saying it was useless. The power-politicians had sat down and rearranged the world to suit themselves. The public weal demanded defeat of the Treaty.[57] Bullitt had turned state's evidence, and the six weeks of hearings were over. Congress had found what it wanted to find. Where was the "peace without victory," the brave, new world, as promised? Congress could not "out-Wilson Wilson." [58] Borah told the Senate that Ireland was entitled to the same consideration as Poland, and that Korea and Egypt should also have been heard. Only self-determination would guarantee world peace. The Treaty of Peace betrayed self-determination and was a guarantee of war. Lodge, to cheering galleries packed with veterans from Château-Thierry, shouted, "I must think of the United States first . . . I have never loved but one flag." He could not divide his affection with the "mongrel banner invented for a League," nor to America's "everlasting meddling and muddling in every quarrel which afflicts the world." He repeated what he had said in 1912, that nothing would so guarantee world peace as a strong America, and an equally strong conviction on the part of the rest of the world that to make war on the United States "would be highly unprofitable." [59]

Wilson recognized the challenge. For him there was but one recourse left — the people, the people who had never failed him. He must tell them the truth as he saw it.

If Woodrow Wilson and Henry Cabot Lodge could be convicted of a common sin, it would be the sin of pride. Lodge could not permit the League to be Wilson's League. He would bend, he would give; but only to the point where Wilson would not give, and then he would announce in triumph that Wilson was to blame. As for Wilson, "I'll never consent to adopt any policy with which that impossible name is so prominently identified," he said.[60]

Nor could Wilson admit his mistaken judgment of people, the human failings in the dream that he had envisioned for the world. Had he done so, had he admitted, "We tried and got much, but we could not get all," he would have quieted many of his critics. This he could not do and hence his terrible vulnerability. He could not admit that his beloved League had been weakened from birth, dragged down with the weight of the Treaty. China sold out, Japan's racial claims ignored. As he had failed to embody his dream in fact, the facts came to alter themselves in his mind to fit the dream. Thus he struck out in hurt and amazement at the outcries of the disillusioned idealists, his erstwhile supporters, the liberals who saw in the League only a "hell's brew." [61]

Baruch, meanwhile, had much to do. At Eugene Meyer's, for instance, on a single evening both Admiral Cary Grayson and Senator Peter Gerry of Rhode Island came in to confer with Baruch, who was evidently "very much sought after by the Democratic officials," [62] as Chandler Anderson noted in his diary. During the same evening Baruch showed Anderson a draft of some possible revisions or interpretations to the Treaty — "not very good," Anderson thought. Baruch seemed disappointed at this judgment, but added hastily that if Anderson did not think well of it "that was enough for him." As a matter of fact, this had not been entirely Baruch's idea. Claude Swanson had come to him some days before, suggesting a kind of "trade" with Lodge.

As early as August 22, Anderson had told Lodge that Baruch had spoken to him about the possibility of arranging some compromise between the warring forces. The New Englander had flared up. It was the Republicans who had the power to make or reject such reservations as they wished, and if the Democrats did not agree, they risked having the Covenant rejected.[63]

All this was before Wilson's trip to the people. What he needed was a vacation, not a whistle-stop tour — the smoke, the heat, the crowds, the reporters. He was not well; the terrific headaches were pounding until he was almost blind with pain. But he remained determined. To Cary Grayson he said quietly that the peace of the world was at stake, and if this journey meant giving up his life, he would "gladly make the sacrifice." [64]

Baruch did not accompany him. Only in his mind's eye could he follow that gallant figure flinging words at the white-starred rows of faces below him. St. Louis and a three-minute ovation for "Wilson, the father of World Democracy." Kansas City, Des Moines, Denver, Seattle, Tacoma. Cheers and tears, parades and caravans, the streets, the windows, the rooftops blocked with people. At Oakland, California, with 12,000 gathered in the auditorium and 6000 more outside, a voice sounded: "Are we with him?" And back roared the answer: "We are." Were they? Was it the League of Nations they cheered, or the courage of the dedicated man before them? Day by day the President grew more exhausted and thinner; night after night the wheels ground and the headaches ground on, crashing louder and louder into his brain. He said, "I don't care if I die the next minute after the Treaty is ratified." [65]

He gave forty prepared speeches, beautiful speeches, beautifully wrought and phrased, and at the end of each his staff wondered how he had endured so long.

He shared his dream with the masses. He spoke of the "generous, high-minded statesmanship" of Clemenceau and Lloyd George, of the "pure light of the justice of God." He made them understand that Article 10 was not the sole item in the Treaty. But it was no use. For after him followed a tub-thumping quartet composed of one renegade Democrat, rabble-rousing Jim Reed of Missouri, and three Republicans, McCormick, Borah, and Hiram Johnson, of whom it was said "deliver us from sincere bigots." [66] From city to city they moved, drawing larger and larger crowds. Over and over they pointed out the weaknesses of the Treaty; reminded audiences that the Fourteen Points had been blunted, and that the League covenant morally compelled the United States to send American troops into European wars. Wilson had gone to Paris preaching open covenants, shouted Borah, and he had surrendered. "Who quit? Who was the quitter?" The crowd thundered back: "Wilson!" [67]

Even in his full strength, Wilson could not have coped with assaults such as this. He had none of the animal heat of an orator like

Borah, who left his Middle Western audiences shouting, hurling their hats into the air. He had not the power to dramatize his ideas in human terms — to transmute abstract concepts into human realities.[68] Nor could he realize that what mattered so much to him meant so little to other people. The people could not see any life-and-death issue in the adoption of Senator Lodge's reservations. Had America been ready for a League of Nations, Wilson might yet have won. America was not ready, and at Omaha Wilson prophesied: "I can predict with absolute certainty . . . there will be another world war if the nations of the world do not . . . prevent it." No one believed his words.[69]

Pueblo was the end. He stumbled on the single step to the platform, and Colonel Starling lifted him and stood close by. Every word was an effort for his whole body. Yet, somehow, he recharged his energies and spoke as he had never spoken before. He broke into tears — and there was not a dry eye before him. Then, like the thunder of the sea, came an ovation he was to remember the rest of his life.[70]

He moved away from the platform, his feet, once so feather-light, now as if shackled with a ball and chain.[71] He could not sleep; he was in a high fever. The pain in his head was unbearable. Yet by dawn he was dressed and shaved protesting, "No, no, no, I must keep on." [72] But the great train turned back eastward, and two days later came the cry down a White House corridor: "My God, the President is paralyzed." [73]

"The genius of a Sophocles or a Shakespeare," wrote Thomas Bailey, "never created a tragedy more poignant than that of Wilson." [74] Had he died, a martyr, that night at Pueblo, the Senate might well have been shamed into action. Instead, he lay for weeks at the point of death from a complication of ailments and an almost complete breakdown of his nervous and physical system. There were prayers in the churches, some gracious expressions in the Senate, even from Hiram Johnson. But the fight went on. *Harvey's Weekly* scoffed: "He has had his say. Now let the Senate act." [75]

He could scarcely speak. He could not sign his name. But he was master of himself always, and his first orders were that the world should not know the seriousness of his illness. So one knew and many guessed, and passers-by, gazing at the iron bars which Theodore Roosevelt had put over the lower White House windows to protect them from the children's baseballs, whispered preposterous rumors of a mad President behind those bars. The world wondered and waited.[76]

The Senate wondered, too, but it did not wait. So, on a "smelling expedition," up to the White House one day came two sheepish-faced men, Gilbert Hitchcock and Albert Fall. On the threshold of Wilson's room their feet hesitated but entered, and soon laughter broke forth from the sick chamber and echoed up and down the corridor.

"We have all been praying for you, Mr. President," Fall had ventured, washing his hands in the air like Uriah Heep, as Mrs. Wilson observed.

"Which way, Senator?" Wilson shot back.[77]

Wilson was going to get well.

During all these months of waiting and strain, Baruch had stood by. Although Josephus Daniels had noted in Paris how much the President was coming to lean on Baruch, when other associates were not helpful, Baruch was no part of the dynasty that ruled the country during Wilson's illness. His position was advisory, and he was only in the capital part of the time.[78] Perhaps it was his absence that made the President miss him. In any event, it was on his sickbed, according to Baruch, that Wilson determined to make the South Carolinian Secretary of the Treasury and formally offered him the job.* And Baruch refused. It would be a grave mistake, he pointed out, for the President to appoint a man of his wealth Secretary of the Treasury: he would be accused of personal bias.[79]

"I have no objection to wealth," Wilson said, "and I do not understand the opposition to it." But Baruch stuck to his guns; he simply felt that it would not be right.[80]

Baruch had had ample opportunity to be fore-armed. On the earlier occasion when his appointment was rumored, he was exposed to the press reports pointing out that he was earning a million dollars a year in Wall Street, and that if he advocated a tax of 60 per cent on a million-dollar income there would be those who thought it should be raised to 70 or 80 per cent or more. The New York *Sun* had commented editorially: "Bernie Baruch has a level head, a clear brain. This clear brain . . . never served him better than when he refused the distinguished honor . . . of becoming Secretary of the Treasury."

* See the subsequent chapters.

There was still a "national" prejudice against any officeholder who was a graduate of Wall Street. But this was not all that fixed Baruch in his decision.[81]

At first he had wanted the post and, despite the warnings, had planned to accept it. He had happily told his wife about it in New York, as they were getting ready to go out to dinner. She was seated before her dressing table, brushing her long black hair, and always afterward he would remember her face framed in the mirror and the fall of black hair to her waist. She turned to him, and he saw the shine of tears in her eyes. "Oh, Bernie," she said, "when are you coming home to me and the children?"

The question was answered, the decision made. Although Annie Baruch had married her husband aware of the pricks and attacks of prejudice, she had not dreamed of his going into public life, subject to the additional sneers and slurs that beset all public figures. Baruch understood. In years to come he regretted this decision. The seat in Wilson's Cabinet, the presidency of the 4-H Clubs of America, and the job of Economic Stabilizer in the Second World War were the posts that he most deeply regretted having turned down.[82]

Yet, instinct may have served him well. The Treasury? "Bernie couldn't have stood it for a week," one who was intimately associated with him in those days had asserted. By instinct Baruch knew what Dr. Alvin Johnson later pointed out: "The amount of power you have, if you take it directly, is very limited. Baruch would have been a slave in the dungeon down there." If in fact he had turned down the offer in 1918 instead of being the "general eye" of the whole war program, he would have been fettered and circumscribed, and "the notion of being tied down was repellent to him." Who today can remember the acts of McAdoo, or even of Mellon or Morgenthau? Baruch had to be free, "like an atom in space." [83]

The War Industries Board job had been what he had made it. Tradition — dating back to Hamilton's time — restricted the Treasury Department. Having tasted of the sweets of indirect power, could Baruch ever satisfy himself with limitations? Having enjoyed a signal triumph, dare he run the risk of failure? A pattern was beginning to be set in Baruch's life that was to become more and more clearly defined with the years — and would eventually greatly limit his possibilities for real public service.

Meanwhile if Baruch was not with the President, neither was

Colonel House, which was unfortunate. For in a last desperate bid
— perhaps for power, perhaps to salvage the League and the Treaty
— House, ill himself, had sent Stephen Bonsal to visit Senator Lodge.
In a remarkable interview, Lodge wrote down the minimum reservations that would be acceptable. Taking a copy of the Covenant,
Lodge wrote a few sentences. They were tremendous concessions —
reservations "decidedly milder" than those actually passed. What
became of them? No one knew. It is probable that Wilson never
saw them.[84] In his sickness a combined challenge from House and
Lodge might well have killed the President. Mrs. Wilson had to decide. She did not make his decisions for him, but she decided what
questions should be presented to him. Huge problems were piling
up: unemployment, inflation, strikes. The New Freedom was all but
at an end — and Josephus Daniels observed that Mrs. Wilson stood
between her husband and a nation "calling for his active leadership." [85] She did, for between the demands of the nation and her
husband, she chose her husband.

Wilson had once said, as for compromise, "let Lodge compromise
. . . let Lodge hold out the olive branch." [86] Now Lodge had seemingly done so — and was ignored. Colonel House later blamed
Baruch for this, claiming that Baruch prevented his having access to
the President.[87] But Baruch was no man to spurn compromise. In
fact he urged it on the President, but was convinced that the President was not open to concessions at all after his return from the tragic
tour.[88]

Yet it is possible that Wilson was not as implacable as he seemed,
for as late as October 19, Chandler Anderson wrote in his diary that
the President was "reconciled to accept reservations providing that
they were phrased so as not to amount to amendments." [89] It was a
quibble over terms, yet had the President now yielded but a fraction
of what he had surrendered at Paris, compromise might still have
been possible. He could not and would not do so. Furthermore, he
understood Lodge because he understood himself. What Lodge
wanted, he thought, was not agreement, but capitulation; and every
submission of new Lodge reservations was but an underhanded attempt "to escape any real responsibility . . . for world peace." If Wilson accepted them, he would merely be asked to accept more. Lodge
in his turn perhaps felt that he could make the concessions that he
had made, happily confident that Wilson would turn them down.[90]

The opposition was massing for action: the disillusioned idealists, the chronic dissenters, the party-line Republicans. Boldly they mapped a joint strategy — for destruction of this "unholy thing with a holy name." Porter J. McComber of North Dakota, a Republican supporter of the League with an innocence like the child who wondered where the king had left his clothes, asked how the Senate could "approve the alliance to make war to save the world and in the next breath condemn an alliance to save the world." [91] But McComber was unlettered in party warfare.

Senator Borah was the leader of the irreconcilables. No man did more to kill Wilson's dream, or the idea of American leadership in world affairs. Yet so passionate was his sincerity that even those who most bitterly opposed him did not hate him; for he himself did not hate. "I regard questions from the point of view of principle," he truthfully said. Unlike Wilson, he could separate his intellectual and emotional functions, disassociate a man from his cause. He was a far more deadly foe of the League than Lodge, for it was the League that he attacked, scarcely less than the Treaty, and he could win over even Wilson's admirers by his sincere, "very profound respect" for the President. In return, he too was granted the tribute of respect, even admiration by Wilson. He later inspired similar emotions in Baruch.[92]

Borah fought the League in terms of its own ideals and objectives. If Wilson saw the League of Nations as the only hope for the salvation of the world, Borah saw it as the destruction of the American republic. To him the whole scheme was "treacherous . . . treasonable . . . it should be buried in hell"; and when an amendment was submitted, invoking the blessing of God, Borah protested against anything that would imply such a blessing on "an infamous Covenant." He would not change his stand, he said, if Christ Himself came down and asked him to do so.[93]

Borah believed, as the founding fathers believed, that America had a divine mission to hold freedom in trust for the rest of the world. "Call us little Americans, if you will," he taunted the Senate, "but leave us the word, American." [94] He did not agree with Trotsky that the time had come "to resort to the international state." Neither did he believe that America should shirk world responsibilities; he would help his neighbor with his strength and blood, if need be — even if he did not want him for a business partner, or in a position where he may decide for me when . . . I shall act." If Wilson saw Lodge as the evil that would corrupt the Treaty, Borah saw the Treaty as the evil that would corrupt the League. He knew that Wilson had accepted the compromises of the Treaty only because the League was attached. Mr. Wilson had thought the League would humanize the Treaty. "In this, of course, I think he was greatly in error." [95]

As early as February 1919 Borah had warned that "you cannot yoke a government whose fundamental maxim is that of liberty to a government whose first law is that of force and hope to preserve the former . . . When you shall have committed this Republic to a scheme of world control, based upon . . . the combined military force of the great nations . . . you will have soon destroyed the atmosphere of freedom . . . in which alone a democracy may survive." We might become "one of the four dictators of the world, but we shall no longer be master of our own spirit." [96]

Afterward, the Senators crowded up to him, saying, "That was fine; we agree with you, but we have got to have some sort of League; everybody is for it"; and Harding, whom Borah scorned as a "moral coward," begged him to make a series of anti-League speeches in his own state of Ohio, a stand Harding personally did not dare to take. Borah was contemptuous.[97] No less than Wilson, he scorned any pandering to public opinion, although he often reflected it. "Senator Borah is not an unthinking man, but he voices the sentiments of the unthinking," the Des Moines *Register* once complained.[98]

This was true. Borah was a man of intellect, who on his rare vacations would take away with him a small bag of clothes and a big one of books. Yet, there was still the quality of drama about him that had led him at seventeen to run away from home to join a Shakespearean troupe. He was as flamboyant as his background. A frontier lawyer with a pistol on each hip, he had come to the Senate out of Boise, with its litter of law offices, saloons, and all the frontier riffraff of territorial days. Borah, although a champion of labor, had shot to fame as prosecutor of the mining chieftain "Big Bill" Haywood. A supporter of white-supremacy Senators' stand against anti-lynching legislation, he had almost singlehandedly, at risk to his own life, held back a frenzied lynching mob.[99] It was characteristic of the man and his paradoxes that he who wrecked the League was later a "prime mover" in the call for the Washington Disarmament Conference, which at worst gave men "a breathing spell of hope." [100]

Already the remote Borah had soared far beyond Idaho. He was
a kind of Senator-at-large for the United States. Baruch, who had
yet to know him, could feel his impact. Many thought him to be
a greater orator than Bryan. Writing in 1907, a *New York Times*
reporter had marveled at his "gift of speech . . . terrific, crushing . . .
tremendous . . . the highest dramatic powers." [101] The ordinary
operations of Congress ended when the words "Borah's up" were
passed through the corridors. Committee rooms emptied and the
Senate galleries were packed. This was a tribute given to no other
orator of his generation. [102]

Now all this force was turned against Wilson's dream. The Treaty
of Versailles would not mean peace, Borah told the Senate. God
was not mocked. "The Saar Basin, Upper Silesia and Danzig . . .
carry with them . . . seeds of war, the . . . weird promise of retribution." [103]

On November 19, 1919, the Senate voted on the Treaty, once with
the Lodge amendments and once without them. On the first count,
42 Democrats joined with the 13 "irreconcilables" to vote the Treaty
down. On the second, the voting Republicans were joined by seven
anti-League Democrats to defeat the Treaty on its first test. Yet
this was only the first test.

"I must get well," Wilson said, upon hearing the news. He was
getting well. He could sit up now; he could sign his name, be lifted
from his bed into a chair. But bad news still shattered him. Hence,
the anxious Grayson, Tumulty, and Mrs. Wilson still kept the day-
to-day happenings from him. There was still a chance for the Treaty
— with the Lodge reservations — but Wilson still did not see the
need for compromise. At last Baruch went to him. Could not the
President see, he argued, that without the reservations there would
be no Treaty and we would fail in our responsibility to the peace
of the world? "And Baruch, too," was the President's murmur. [104]

Then came Mrs. Wilson, with the most feminine of pleas — "for
my sake." Wilson was obdurate. "And you, too, Edith," he whispered. Suddenly he turned and pleaded with her. He had no moral
right to surrender. "Better a thousand times to go down fighting
than to dip your colors to dishonorable compromise." [105]

The Hitchcock reservations were as much as he could yield "without cutting the heart out of the Covenant." Article 10 was a sacred pledge to the dead soldiers; without Article 10 we would get nothing out of the war "but regrets for having gone in." Article 10 put the teeth into the Treaty; it could not be surrendered. Baruch, later seeing organizations without the power to implement their decisions, came to realize that Wilson was right.[106]

By January, Lodge was ready with his new set of reservations. They requested that all mandates be approved by Congress, and that the United States withdraw its sanction of the Shantung agreement. On Article 10 they proposed that the consent of Congress, rather than of the American delegates to the League, be obtained before committing United States troops to war.

It seems impossible to escape the conclusion that Lodge was playing a double game. If the League was accepted, it would be with his reservations. If it was defeated, the blame would be on Wilson. But for a moment it seemed that Wilson's strategy might work, and that if the whole Treaty was voted down, the responsibility would be placed on the Republicans. Lodge thought so, too, and wavered — when word came from the Borah camp.

A party revolt was threatening on the afternoon of January 23 as Lodge, nervous and pale, was hustled into Borah's office, where the enraged irreconcilables attacked him in language which, as he recalled afterward, no man of his years should have been forced to hear.

"Can't I discuss this matter with my friends?" he asked at last.

"No, Cabot," Borah said, "not without telling your other friends."

Lodge suggested he might resign as Majority Leader.

"No, by God, you won't have a chance," Borah retorted. "On Monday, I'll move for the election of a new leader and give the reasons." [107]

Defeat, party rupture, four years of Wilsonism, all this flashed through Lodge's mind. He bowed his head. He would stand by his commitments no less rigidly than Wilson by his. Wilson would not take a Treaty corrupted with the Lodge amendments; the irreconcilables would not take a Treaty corrupted by the League. In the end principles, no less than politics, destroyed America's role in the creation of an effective world order.

So the Treaty was voted down again and again, with the reservations and without them. Eighty per cent of the Senate was committed to a League in some form or other; in March 1919, full acceptance had been only four votes away. The slightest concessions then would have given Wilson the victory, but Wilson kept repeating that he had "no compromise or concessions . . . to make," [108] until the Hartford *Times* commented that he was himself scarcely less irreconcilable than Borah.[109]

"Infanticide," the New York *Tribune* called it, as the final vote came on March 19, 1920. For the Treaty with reservations there were 49 votes — 28 Republican and 21 Democratic; opposed there were 12 Republicans and 23 Democrats. The vote was seven short of the needed two-thirds majority of the Senators present. Lodge had "kept us out of peace," the St. Louis *Post-Dispatch* said. But Wilson did not yet surrender.

"You cannot defeat God," he said.[110]

It was with sheer incredulity that Wilson, Baruch, and the others looked on as the Congress proceeded toward a full repudiation of the Treaty of Versailles and a "declaration of peace" with Germany. A joint resolution to this effect was passed on May 15, which, Wilson declared in his veto message, placed an "ineffaceable stain upon the gallantry and honor of the United States." It sought peace without attempting to set right the infinite wrongs that Germany had committed.[111] The message took effect, and the peace resolution failed to pass over the President's veto. However, a joint resolution did get through, declaring that Congress should act as if the war was ended; and this Wilson killed with a pocket veto. Officially the war did not end until President Harding declared that it had, and requested a resolution to that effect in 1921. A few months later the Treaty of Berlin was ratified.

The epitaph of Versailles was spoken by Borah. "We do not differ as to the duty of America, we differ only as to the manner in which she shall discharge that duty." To him it seemed that the Treaty of Versailles was a "negation of moral law," based upon principles that had brought ruin to the world before and would do so again.[112]

But Wilson declined to abandon the fight. The people, he said, had yet to be heard. For this he had not long to wait.

After the Democratic convention in San Francisco, both the nominees, James M. Cox and Franklin Roosevelt, fought valiantly, warning that Wilson must not be left to die, like Moses, in sight of the Promised Land. So the "great national referendum came" and the

Democrats foundered under a wave of seven million votes — the greatest defeat ever suffered by a political party up to that time.[113] The people had spoken.

Yet the individual American delegates to the Peace Conference could look back with pride on much that they had done. Baruch, for instance, would later believe that his efforts had done much to prevent the "crippling" of Germany, and he continued to fight against the fixing of an impossible reparation. Germany should not be kept begging for freedom, he wrote in 1923.

He could take pride, too, in the fact that the "difficult clauses" under the Treaty of Versailles, on which he had worked — the tariff clauses and economic adjustments — appeared wise as time passed.[114] Yet these were empty consolations beside the bitter truth that America had forfeited her right to leadership by forfeiting responsibility. What made it more bitter was Baruch's conviction that all men at heart sought peace and adhered to the idea of a League.[115]

Why could not aggressive war be outlawed? The League was impotent without the United States. Yet even with the United States, the League rested on moral force primarily, and the world soon came to realize how flimsy a foundation that would be. Without the United States, even the semblances of moral force had vanished. The single states of Europe were defenseless, frightened, and alone; in Baruch's words, humanity was "cowering in a corner." The old game of power politics was on again, each nation for itself — France invading the Ruhr, guns bristling toward Germany. France, terrified as all were, had seen safety in a League if it could be girded up by the armed power of the United States; now she had to take care of herself. After telling us that "the frontier of freedom was in France," wrote the bitter Clemenceau, "America has forgotten it all too soon . . . The separate peace made by America, who might have been the arbiter of the peace of Europe, has thrown the old continent back into its age-long state of strife by a display of financial greed upon which the future will give its verdict." [116]

Simultaneously with the death of the dream, with the new world stillborn, the New Freedom was melting into the smoky Indian-summer air. In that tragic autumn of 1919 as Wilson lay stricken at the White House, one last effort was made to breath life into the cause to which he had dedicated himself in 1912.

The time was hardly auspicious. An "epidemic of strikes" was infecting the country, with four million workers involved — deck men, ship hands, firemen, textile workers, policemen, bakers, barbers, and steel workers. In the single week from September 11 through September 18, 151 new strikes got under way and 53 more were threatening. In United States Steel alone, 370,000 workers were involved. Their demand was for unions; their answer came from Judge Elbert H. Gary in a public statement on September 17, and in days of stubborn, reluctant testimony before a committee of Congress. No, he would not negotiate with unions, because that would close his shops to nonunion labor, and large numbers of his workmen were not members of unions and did not care to be. No, he did not favor the closed shop; he favored the open shop. Yes, if his men dared to organize, their spokesmen were subject to discharge. No, he would not answer a letter from Samuel Gompers; Gompers was not one of his employees, and he would recognize only his employees in negotiation.[117] He had some basis for his stand, for it would soon be shown that millions of nonorganized workers clung to their privileges of "choice" and of "free enterprise." One wrote: "Ninety per centum of the public is heart and soul behind that grand old man, Judge Gary." [118] A dissenting opinion was later submitted by the Interchurch Report of 1920, which denounced the "intolerable and brutal conditions under which the men are compelled to work."[119]

It was against this background that representatives of labor, management, and the general public were called to Washington for the National Industrial Conference on October 6, 1919, and charged by Wilson to produce a document of labor peace that would rank with Magna Charta, the Bill of Rights, and the Declaration of Independence.[120]

The group assembled at the Pan-American Building, amidst a shower of plans and suggestions, including some optimistic ones calculated "to eliminate all future labor troubles." [121] But the group was in no mood to be soothed by Secretary of the Interior Franklin Lane's syrupy assurances that "there can be no class in this land." Whoever was to be the next President of the United States, he would be a man "that years ago worked for wages and there can be no class where such a thing is possible." No one was convinced.

After the pronouncement by Lane and the charge by the ailing President, a fight on the rules began. Then on Thursday, Bernard

Baruch of the "public" group, of which, as he said, he had "the honor to be the chairman," arose from his chair.

Except for the merest formalities, Baruch spoke scarcely half a dozen times during the sessions. Usually he sat there half smiling and wholly unperturbed. But, involuntarily, he was a leader, this ex-Wall Streeter, this friend of John L. Lewis, whose "sympathetic attitude towards labor" was acknowledged by Gompers, this millionaire advocate of collective bargaining and the eight-hour day.

The clamor quieted. Baruch spoke, introducing a plan prepared by the Secretary of Labor, William Wilson. It was at least a collateral ancestor of the Taft-Hartley Act of thirty years later, for it called on all strikers to resume the status quo for a three-month period, after which their freely elected representatives would meet with the employers for discussion. To this California's Governor Gavin McNab appended a postscript, suggesting a Federal arbitration board to be named by the President — to consist of members of the House, the Senate, former Presidents of the United States and one woman — "for determination of all strikes between labor and capital." In the murmur of inquiry that followed submission of this plan, the majestic head of Samuel Gompers rose above the crowd, and the great labor leader laid down the dictum that neither labor nor the public could consider propositions until the employers' group had been heard.

The employers' group was heard on Friday. It submitted a statement of principles to which it would adhere, including proper working safeguards for women, equal pay for equal work, and, as for disputes, "adequate means for the discussion of questions." This was enough for capital; it was not enough for labor.

Slowly but sharply the lines began to be drawn. Debate droned on, hour by hour, and when by Tuesday it was suggested that the Conference intervene to settle the steel strike, Gavin McNab remarked acidly, "We have been here now seven days, and this is the only concrete proposition that has been submitted." Just as concrete, however, was the vote the next day on a motion of Baruch's that action be postponed until the general committee reported on collective bargaining. The public group voted yes, the employers no — feeling the strike no responsibility of the Conference — and the labor group yes. As unanimous consent was required to activate any proposition, the motion was lost. S. Pemberton Hutchinson of the employers warned sharply: "Mr. Baruch can direct all he pleases, but we cannot be forced or harried into arriving at any decision in such an important matter as collective bargaining."

Collective bargaining was the rock against which the Conference finally broke. The Associated Manufacturers and Merchants of New York demanded that the Conference "formally and officially affirm the right of every individual to work and earn a livelihood according to his individual preference, and that it is the duty of the federal government to guarantee that such right is neither abridged nor interfered with." The workers themselves seemed far less solicitous about the safeguarding of this particular "right"; but this was the credo of that "grand old man, Judge Gary." [122] How could he presume to represent the public, wondered one writer, "one of the most autocratic and undemocratic citizens of this Republic today?" [123] Nevertheless, he probably was representative of the view of much of unorganized industry. If there were numerous citizens who wrote protests to Secretary Lane, demanding justice for the organized, there were workers who sneered at special rights for the organized, terming the closed shop "an immoral, dishonest, un-American proposition," to which organized employers added a fervent "Amen." [124]

But not Samuel Gompers. Organized labor would not back down; it was fighting even for those who scorned it. Head thrown back, voice shaking, old Gompers flung down his challenge. Labor would not be confined by the dictates of Mr. Gary. Labor, no less than management, had a right to hire lawyers from the outside to represent its interests; labor could not be expected to defend itself entirely with "representatives" from its own ranks. Did not Big Steel hire legal representation to speak in its name?

Bitter recriminations followed. Over and over the employers sounded their perpetual theme — how could men from the outside know conditions in any individual company? From the side of labor, W. D. Mahon sneered, ". . . workers . . . looked to this conference to bring results." It was not enough to have "faith, hope, and Gary." Debate was even more bitter the next day as cries of "wage slavery," bribes, and aggression rent the air. J. W. O'Leary for the employers begged for a little human feeling. "You cannot secure efficient production on the basis of strained relationship."

Matthew Woll of labor repeated his group's claim to the right of legal representation as a right of democracy. Those working under industrial victimization, he charged, could not bargain; they dared not speak up themselves. Up sprang Gompers — Were not the most able men from the ranks offered bribes for their talents and their brains, salaries of $10,000 a year "to wean the loyal among the labor movement away from their fellows . . . we know our rights and are determined to assert them."

Amidst the uproar John Spargo spoke for labor, Spargo, whose back had been twisted and gnarled as he toiled in the coal mines at the age of ten; Spargo, descendant of those Dorchester laborers of 1824 who hid in the moors and fens to organize and were drawn and quartered by the British as the price for collective bargaining. His was an inheritance won by generations of suffering. The right of bargaining, he insisted, had been settled years ago; no one could take that hard-won victory away. "If you shall endanger that right, gentlemen, you may not fool yourselves into believing that this country is immune from the dangers of a wrathful and desperate proletariat."

On October 16, Baruch's "public" group offered a compromise. It was realistic in all except its comprehension of human nature, offering sops to both sides and demanding concessions in return. To the unionists the plan offered collective bargaining with representatives of their own choosing; to the employers, the open shop. With Gary conspicuously and silently absent, the public and the labor group voted yes, and, characteristically, the employers voted no. It was plain, now, if not before, that not the general public but the individual interests of capital and labor were all that counted, and that no real agreement would be possible — this despite the challenge of Dan Tobin of the Teamsters, who said it was a crime to have sat in session two weeks and to have done nothing at all.

October 21 was the eleventh day. "We hope," declared a farm organizer, J. N. Tittemore, that "we can come to some common ground . . . and have more faith in the common ordinary human being." Against the background of a resolution submitted by Thomas L. Chadbourne, calling for labor's right to collective bargaining by representatives of their own choosing, Samuel Gompers again warned the Conference that if this were voted down, untold harm would be done. No heed was paid to him.

Resolutions now came in rapid sequence. Employers' resolutions for contracts with individual workers, for shop contracts, and for another try at collective bargaining were voted down. The group was deadlocked, moving relentlessly to a standstill.

The next day Secretary Lane stood before the embattled delegates.

He had a letter in his hands, "a word of very solemn appeal." It was from President Wilson, "signed by him in his bed, lying on his back, and addressed to you." A hush fell over the hall.

Wilson's words were gentle; he offered no rebuke. But when nations were struggling to avoid war, were we "to confess that there is no method to be found for carrying on industry except in the spirit and with the very method of war?" New methods, new machinery must be found for old problems. The public expected solutions.

Gompers was the first to speak. "No man could have heard that letter read," he challenged the Conference members, "but to be moved." The delegates were moved, and under the spell of Wilson's words broke into their component parts to consider still another resolution calling for labor's right to collective bargaining by representatives of their own choice.

Eventually the exhausted policy-makers returned. One Louis Titus took the floor. "We employers have always exercised the right to be represented by representatives of our own choosing. We demand that right. Why should we not grant it to our employees?" Titus was an employer, but he spoke for the public group.

Again the vote was taken. Again the chairmen polled their groups. Again labor was voted down. Amidst the cries of bad faith, a muttering undercurrent of rumor that labor might even walk out, Gompers arose, shouting angrily of "propositions now to reinstate in the United States involuntary servitude, slavery."

The thirteenth was an unlucky day. The obituary of the National Industrial Conference was spoken by Secretary Lane. "It is impossible," he said, "for labor and capital in this conference to work together." There was no good will between men when immediate personal and selfish interests were concerned.

The virtually complete failure of the Conference has limited the space given it in history books. The most cursory glance at the records reveals that it was doomed from the start. The farmers, for example, had been classified as "employers," small comfort indeed to the landless, homeless, and voiceless "croppers," or even to the one-horse farm man, who saw no surplus cash from one year to the next. Thus, the farmer was virtually denied representation, despite warning that unless agriculture's voice was heard, no agreement between capital and labor would matter. "Don't be deluded," warned a farm spokesman, "that agriculture cannot kick." The failure to recognize the farmer's role in the national economy was ominous. Furthermore, the South had only four representatives in attendance.[125]

The Conference was further strangled by the weight of its own rules, especially by the unanimity rule. No action whatever could be taken unless all three groups agreed; and it was self-evident that there would never be agreement on measures for the general good if any group felt a threat to their own individual welfare. Wrangles over the rules laid bare animosities, speakers protesting that small craftsmen and organized labor were insufficiently represented, and from the employers' side that they were represented too much. The *New York Times* charged that organized labor had been entrenched in every group, and that Bernard Baruch "had the Public Group in his vest pocket." Public opinion might cry out against such representatives of the "general public," as John J. Raskob and John D. Rockefeller, Jr., yet these were among the men who, under Baruch's leadership, it was charged, "killed the conference" by going over to labor's side.[126]

Strange commentary indeed on a man from Wall Street. The bitterness of the attack, in fact, is the measure of how far Baruch had gone under the influence of Woodrow Wilson. He had entered by one door and come out another. He had grown. In espousing labor's side at the Conference, he had felt a new tide and had surrendered to it. He had not "gone over" to labor, but he had realized that somehow there must be a method of giving solidarity and cohesion to public opinion.

Baruch refused to concede defeat. His group lingered behind to write a report to the President. More had been accomplished, they contended, than was revealed on the surface. The Conference had at least focused the issues. It had shown the intimate relation between farming and industrial interests. One line of the report was pure Baruch: "What was not brought out clearly was that both capital and labor owe to society products at the lowest possible cost." Capital and labor had each looked to its own interest; the public group had made a sincere effort to look to the interests of the whole people.[127]

So the Conference ended, and then the fight over the League, and the New Freedom, and finally, the Wilson Era itself. In his house on S Street in Washington, Woodrow Wilson was awaiting the end. Sometimes Baruch came to see him, and it was as if a spark were

kindled between them, so that once again they were in contact with
the old hopes, the great days.

It must have been a shock to visitors as they crossed the threshold
of the cheerful south room where Wilson sat in a big chair by the
fireplace. For the room was a near duplicate of his room at the White
House: every lamp, table, pillow, and chair — even the "great Lincoln bed," topped with the American eagle — had been reproduced.
It was "the President's room" still, just as Mrs. Wilson had planned
it.[128]

There he sat, tired hands limp in his lap, the silvery-white head
drooping to one side. Only his eyes were alive, searching the visitor's
face, following his step across the floor.

"You must excuse my not rising," he would say. "I'm really quite
lame." [129] Those who knew him best, like Baruch, could notice the
changes that time and defeat were working on him. Clemenceau
came and turned away, so saddened at what he saw that he could not
keep a dinner engagement. Baruch thought of the President in Paris,
withstanding the attacks of the world's most powerful men. How
alone he was now, "yet never did his magnificent spirit waver!" He
was predicting the next world war with "absolute certainty," yet once
he admitted to Baruch: "You know, if I had not been stricken, I
would have carried through the League, but God has a mysterious
way of working. Perhaps the people of the world were not
ready . . ." [130]

No one, Baruch thought, could understand Wilson who did not
grasp the significance of his faith — in God, in people, in democracy
— which was what gave him strength to fight. He was still fighting
now. He seemed to be turning over in his mind ideas and phrases
worn thin years before; and in the evolution of new ideas every
sentence became a problem. This was painfully evident when Baruch's daughter Belle and a friend, Evangeline Johnson, called on
him, having received an appointment because of Wilson's "affection
and admiration for Mr. Baruch." Both girls were dear to Mrs. Wilson; they had worked for the League and were devoted champions of
the President. They persuaded the old warrior to make his first radio
broadcast and a last plea for the League of Nations. Laboriously he
wrote an address, "The Significance of Armistice Day," and read it,
standing, his head so full of pain that "he could scarcely see" the
typed words.[131]

He was not a lonely man. His friends came to the house as if to a shrine, Baruch, Daniels, Claude Swanson, and Carter Glass, William E. Dodd, Norman Davis, Senator Joseph Robinson, Cyrus McCormick, Frank Cobb from the New York *World*, Lord Robert Cecil, and many more.[132] As they left, particularly on Sundays or holidays, they saw the people waiting outside.

They were quiet people, "gentle and orderly." They said nothing; they asked for nothing; they were there, winter and summer. They were there in the rain and in the winter twilight: as you came down the steps you might see the dark circular patterns where someone had been kneeling in the snow. They waited by the hundreds one day, in quiet orderly groups before a theater, watching for Wilson to come out. Inside, as he moved with difficulty to his seat, the whole house rose in homage, cheering him. There were choked cheers, even sobs, as his white face flashed across a motion picture screen, and at a glimpse of his car in an Armistice Day parade up rose the cry "There's Wilson!" and an ovation such as was "given no other American."

Armistice Day was his symbol. As the young men had been sacrificed, so he, too, had been a sacrifice to his dream. But the dream lived on, and so long as he lived, wrote a wondering editor of *Collier's Magazine*, he was "The Man They Cannot Forget." He was a ghost, haunting the American soul. He was a link with greatness; he had kindled a hope in the human heart, and the hundreds who moved and waited in the Washington streets symbolized the millions who were not there, who had dreamed and awakened, who had spoken and heard only silence. They could not forget, the men and the women, and even the children. They waited "to get even the most fleeting glimpse, something that will bid them live again." [133]

His was now a voice of history. Out of a past and a nobler era he spoke to them on Armistice Day 1923. Thousands were massed before him. They were silent, but they could not hear; his voice was too weak to carry, and he leaned for support on the arm of his wife. He was broken but still undefeated. With all his old-time conviction, he denounced "sullen, selfish isolation," the "shameful fact" that we had turned our back, spurned our responsibility "in the administration of peace." "I am not one of those who have the least anxiety about the triumph of the principles for which I have stood," he said. "I have seen fools resist Providence before, and I have seen their destruction." [134]

He had had his say. On February 1, 1924, a message came: "the Chief" was steadily losing ground. The next day, past the little knots of silent people, one by one the old friends went in: Swanson, Vance McCormick, Tumulty, the tears on his ruddy cheeks. Then two men slowly climbed the steps and stood, faces averted, as an old Negro unbolted the double wooden doors. Carter Glass and Bernard Baruch had come to say farewell.[135]

Wilson knew that he was going to die. He had noticed that strange quiet in the street outside. And the people waiting. Grayson told the old Calvinist the truth and, looking at him quietly, Wilson said: "I am ready. I am a piece of broken machinery." His hand groped, touched Grayson's arm. "You've been good to me. You've done everything you could."

The doctor, choked with tears, said, "I've been with him so long. He is the gamest man I ever knew."

Grayson left the house shortly after 1 A.M. Baruch was still inside. When he came out at last, the reporters started toward him, then moved back, silent. "Baruch," one of them noted, "was grief-stricken." [136] He was also bitter. It sickened him to read what Wilson's erstwhile enemies had to say about him now — those who could have been better Christians while he was alive. Baruch saved a scrap of poetry:

> Now is his anguish over; he has won forever peace
> Great heart, great chieftain, great American
> He raised . . . a vision of the newer world to come . . .
> Beyond the shadowy border, as he passes,
> A grey light dawns and spreads, as long ago
> Above the trenches . . . The dead arise . . .
> Sharply at attention, and from afar . . . he comes
> The War President, as they presenting arms
> Salute! Now he is one with them.[137]

12

THE BARON OF HOBCAW

BERNARD BARUCH was twenty-seven years old before he first returned to Camden. Sixteen years had passed since the wheels of the Baruch buggy had creaked along the sandy ruts of Broad Street, but Camden in 1897 lay suspended between two eras. It was not yet the fashionable sporting and polo resort of a decade later, or even a stop on the highway to the Gold Coast, or the prosperous, bustling mill town of today. Dilapidation had taken over the old town.[1] Nothing had changed, Baruch mused, but the elongated bodies under the half-familiar faces and familiar names of the playmates of his youth and, walking along Broad Street, he could see the same names on the same shop windows as when he was a boy.[2] Little boys were still playing "skin the cat" on the old gymnasium pole, or shucking off shirts and pants on the run to Factory Pond. The old haunts, Hobkirk Hill, the Kennedy place, were unchanged. The old houses still stood in graying dignity under the elms. Sunning weary bones in the peace of Hampton Park slouched the same men, grayer and thinner and older now, who slid knives along chunks of weathered wood and talked of Chancellorsville and the Seven Days.

Baruch was already a hero in his home town. Although he had yet to make his first million in Wall Street, news of his early exploits had already come to the poverty-stricken little Southern hamlet. His was the American success story, the dream-come-true of every aspiring youth out of the South, who conquers the city and in triumph comes home. His own cousins in the area, Baums and Heymans and Des Portes, looked on him with special pride. His grace and good looks were freely commented upon. His bride Annie was considered "splendid" in her dignity and fine clothes, and very approachable and likable as well.[3]

It was on this visit that the seeds were sown of Baruch's later interest in the town, his chance to fulfill his mother's dream that some day he would contribute something to the people and the place from which he sprang. Nearly thirty years later he wrote that he was fond of Camden and hoped it would become a farming center rather than a resort.[4] Camden, however, went its own way. But in 1940, when the old hospital burned and there was bitterness in the words of the town's leading physician, J. W. Corbett, that the old friends of the hospital had died, that the town's two richest inhabitants were indifferent, and that people were only interested in riding and horses, the Belle Baruch Memorial Hospital arose in answer to his appeal,[5] and the donor insisted that provision must be made for all the 35,000 people of Kershaw County, Negro and white alike. Bernard Baruch had not forgotten his father's labors on behalf of the poor colored people. Nor did he forget the hospital after its completion. His generosity continued — a new X-ray machine, a larger delivery room; $33,000 here, and $61,000 there. Yet, always he insisted that all efforts must be two-way. This was his method — to help people who would help themselves. He could speak to these people in their own language.[6] His impulses were Southern, but his strict budgeting and penny-counting were Northern and confused his easygoing neighbors. High-pressure methods were not understood in Camden. "He's a great man, a brilliant man, he does a lot of good, but he's a crank," growled Dr. Corbett.[7] "He don't care how good the appeal is, he'll bring it up for next year's budget, and he won't pay a damn cent beyond that." He wanted a New York architect to design the hospital, but ran up against touchy local pride, and finally growled, "You-all go home and get your own architect." [8]

Sometimes one of the Camden neighbors would call him up when in New York, and be flattered when he recognized him, "he was such a busy fellow." Usually any plans for an interview had to be cleared through his private secretary, Miss Boyle, whose stock inquiry was: "Is it very important?"

"It's not to Mr. Baruch, but it is to me," would be the answer.

Finally, Baruch himself would take over the line.

"Shoot, shoot, shoot," would come his hasty ejaculations as a more leisurely Southern cousin proceeded to explain his current problem.[9]

Much of Baruch's generosity was unknown — his secret contributions to the support of proud old Georges Clemenceau, for instance; help for a poor woman about to be turned out of her home, an innocent man on the way to prison, a deserving youngster working his way through the University of South Carolina Law School. "He just likes to do things for people," Frances Perkins has recalled, "even if they can't help him in any way." [10] But with the power of wealth, he insisted on doing things "his" way.

His Camden neighbors insisted that he was more Southern than Northern, while his associates in the Street were equally convinced that Baruch was a New Yorker through and through.[11] Baruch himself knew that sixteen years in New York — or sixty — could not make a Yankee out of him. "South Carolina," he once said, is "flesh of my flesh and bone of my bone." [12] Yet, despite his sentimental attachment to Camden, he knew that he could never really go back home to live. He did not want to be the home-town hero, pointed out to prying eyes. Young as he was, he already craved quiet and peace and a chance to get away from it all. The South was the antidote to the fierce competitiveness of New York. Here his nerves relaxed, and it seemed as if he were a different person, as if he drew new strength from his native soil.[13]

But where would his retreat be?

His search, starting in 1897, was a long one, lasting nearly eight years. Realist that he was, he would have disclaimed sentimentality as a factor in his choice. It was a hunting ground he was looking for, he insisted — nothing more. Yet a romantic memory of his boyhood directed his feet.

He remembered a journey on an old stern-wheel steamer moving down the inland waterway. Actually, the trip had been less romantic than it seemed in memory, for a storm had hit the boat, and Bernie had "up-chucked" all the way, his nurse Minerva cowering on her knees at his side and begging the good Lord to take her to heaven! Nothing, however, could dim the glamour of his memories of Pawley's Island, near the little hamlet of Georgetown, home of his mother's relatives for over one hundred years.

At Pawley's Island Bernie had visited his great-aunt, Mrs. Deborah Sampson, whose son "Nat" was captain of the coastal vessel *Banshee*. He had swum in the warm surf, basked on the warm sands. He had wandered dreamily among the star-shaped yucca and the myrtle and the sagging "cottages" of the old rice and indigo planters, steep roofs and dormers slanting up against the wind-twisted sand dunes. Nat told such marvelous stories of the old Waccamaw country that Bernie was still thrilling to them and telling about them years after he had moved to New York.

The Waccamaw was haunted ground. Every coastal county in the South has its "River Road," and here the names of the burned and decaying plantation houses were a pageant of the Old South. Hobcaw Barony. Calais. Strawberry Hill. Friendfield. Bellefield. Marietta. Youngville. Oryzantia. Alderley. Rose Hill. Clifton. Forlorn Hope. At Clifton, Marion and his men had come up out of the swamps to be received as brothers, feted with smiles from the great ladies and with "bumpers" of amber-colored brandy; corn and sweet-scented fodder up to the eyes for their gaunt horses, and for themselves the "little rest" that they had so long deserved. Near Alderley, long ago on a June day in 1777, a strange ship had anchored in the night and visitors landed, speaking a foreign tongue; that night Lafayette first touched foot on American soil. Forty-odd years later, he would return again as a guest of the historic old Winyah Indigo Society of Georgetown. Washington himself had declared that never had he seen a place "so justly entitled to be styled a fairyland as the rice fields of the Waccamaw in the genial month of May." [14]

At Prospect Hill, President James Monroe and Secretary of War John C. Calhoun had been feted. These Waccamaw plantations had been the seats of the mighty: the Wards, the Hugers, the Alstons. Here Joseph Alston had brought his bride, the beautiful and unfortunate Theodosia Burr. But all that ancient glory was vanished now. Not a single "great house" remained; Strawberry Hill, for instance, was marked only by a row of skeleton columns and a few clay-chinked cabins dating from slavery days. A straggling bridle path through the woods marked the line of the old King's Highway, the coastal road from Wilmington to Charleston. Walking through the woods, or riding after game, you could come upon other somber reminders — an old fort in ruins, the crumbling earthworks of the men who had fought Marion, and here and there, their graves; the rusted boiler top of the Yankee ship *Harvest Moon*, and an iron cannon with the date 1864, pointing emptily toward the sky.

Gradually the houses had been burned or abandoned. At Bellefield at the turn of the century, there still loomed the skeleton of the "hanted" White Owl House, left uncompleted as the gunfire pounded down on Sumter. Nearby Rose Hill was straight in the path of the Federal gunboats, but survived for years in decay, its great ceiling stained where rare old wines had dropped from bottles shattered by Yankee soldiers marauding the attic. The dogged Colonel Mortimer Ward had held out through the bitter years in his beautiful Alderley, the carved petals and leaves of the white marble mantel as fragile as tissue paper. The house burned in the early nineteen hundreds, and then the aging colonel sold the site to Baruch.[15]

The 12,000 acres of Hobcaw Barony, comprising a number of the plantations, was one of the original baronies of South Carolina under John Locke's famous "Grand Model" for the colony, and exploration of the area by the Spaniards had begun as early as 1526. The barony was laid out by 1711 and in the division of Carolina lands among the proprietors, Hobcaw, in 1718, became the property of John, Lord Carteret, later Earl Granville.[16]

Friendfield was the heart of the barony. For over a hundred years it had been a great rice plantation, and before that had grown indigo — a "forgotten product" of a golden age. It was still a rice plantation, but its owners, Sidney and Harold Donaldson, were giving way now under the inexorable pressure of competition from Texas, Louisiana, and Asia and floods from the deforested uplands. The Northern-born Donaldsons had taken over from the impoverished Alstons after the war, and in place of the burned mansion beneath the live-oak had erected "The Old Relick," the substantial but undistinguished Victorian dwelling which after 1905 was to become Baruch's winter home.* [17] Baruch then added 5000 acres more, until his holdings comprised seven of the original ten plantations on the Waccamaw, all but Clifton, Rose Hill, and Forlorn Hope. Nearly all had been out of native hands since Reconstruction days.

Hobcaw, Baruch would always say, was the most beautiful spot in the world. It was his "Garden of Eden"; there was nothing on earth like it anywhere, he would exult then and years later. All this was his — the flaming azaleas and camellia bushes, high as trees; the white egrets and bellowing bull alligators, water lilies floating on the swamp pools and the blue-water-hyacinths, the woods blazing gold with jessamine in February and snowy with dogwood in April, the great trees bending under waterfalls of Spanish moss, and the dark

* In 1957 Baruch sold the Barony to his daughter Belle.

oceans of marshland stretching to sands of gold. For fifty years he would come there to shoot and to fish, to ride and rest and get his bearings. Here was absolute solitude, a quiet so great that you could almost hear the fall of a raindrop from a leaf. Here a man could be absolutely alone and yet could reach the cities of the world in minutes by telephone over in Georgetown.[18] In the early years before the bridge was built, the mail and telegrams were brought over twice a day by ferry. Even Georgetown itself was hidden by the luxuriant growth of swamp cypress and pine. From the front porch there was nothing to see but the slow, brown waters of the Bay, meeting place of four rivers — the Sampit, the Black, the Waccamaw, and the Santee. Along the banks stretched mile after mile of deserted rice fields, and only in recent years a lazy pillar of smoke from a Georgetown pulp-wood factory, with its accompanying smells, has risen to show the existence of any nearby human life at all.[19] Here after each success, each Wall Street triumph or political campaign, Baruch would come to rest and be restored.

It was not of romance and history, or even of peace and quiet that Baruch was thinking as he trekked the Waccamaw country back in the early years of the twentieth century. He was seeking ducks, and he found them, in untold numbers, pouring into the sun to blacken the sky. Their number was overwhelming; only those who saw could believe. No lies could equal the reality. Visitors from all over the world would agree that not in the North, South, East, or West, in Scotland, Canada, or China was there such a duck-hunter's paradise as the Waccamaw Peninsula at the end of the nineteenth century.[20]

But Baruch was no recluse. The easy, small-town life of his boyhood was his for the asking in Georgetown, six miles away. He had still his share of kin in the community: the Sampsons, Henry Clay Miller, whose great-grandmother was Baruch's grandmother, and the Kaminskis, whose grandmother was a sister of Baruch's grandmother. It was the Kaminskis, in fact, who had told him about the wonderful shooting in the area. Baruch was no outlander, although when appearing on Georgetown's Front Street, or at Ford's store, he attracted more than second glances because of his great height and wealth and reputation. Nevertheless, here he could find both escape and such easy acceptance as would never have been possible back in Camden. Here, too, were the old "Johnny Rebs," and over the whiskey, after a hunt, they would demand to know how "Bernie" had beaten out the Yankees of Wall Street.[21]

The visitors at Hobcaw, ranging through the years from Churchill of Britain to a president of the United States, could come and go without arousing undue excitement among citizens whose ancestors had played host to Washington, Lafayette, Monroe, and Cleveland. Although ships for the Indies and "the Empire" no longer moved down the Sampit, Georgetown still lingered in the afterglow of glory. The old church of Prince George, Winyah, had survived a riotous past. Erected with the proceeds of liquor taxes in 1742, once a stable for British horses in the Revolution, it still stands proudly. Also in Georgetown was one of America's most unusual clubs, the old Winyah Indigo Society. There was a Robert Mills courthouse, too, with arching twin stairways, a Masonic Temple, built in 1835, and an old slave market of ruddy brick, where overhead a great clock now marked the hours of freedom.[22] The clock was symbolic. From its romantic past Georgetown looked eagerly into a new future. The old plantations were rising from decay, new faces moved among the old-timers: Baruchs, Vanderbilts, Norrises, Huntingtons, Dr. I. E. Emerson of the Bromo-Seltzer fortune, and later, Mr. and Mrs. Henry Luce moved into the area.

River-plantation boats, fishing vessels, and sportsmen's cruisers now docked at the wharves behind the stores along Front Street. Two generations would pass before Georgetown, "a beautiful modern city" of 5000, would step forward into the new Southern industrial prosperity. But the improvements came steadily even in depression days, the white ribbons of highway, the city-owned light plant, the new Lafayette Bridge, all built under Baruch's eye, and often with his blessing.[23] Georgetown, with its power plant and its water system, was completely modern, and in its rich soil and perfect winter climate almost any crop thrived. The region was understandingly popular.[24] But much of this "prosperity" was illusory. Even Baruch, shrewd though he was in business dealings, let sentiment for his "own people" suck him into the debacle that engulfed Georgetown and the whole area. Nor was 1929 the beginning of these misadventures; in South Carolina, as throughout the farming areas, the depression had a head start of ten years.

Baruch did things for South Carolina that he would never have done for any other region. He was, for instance, a heavy stockholder

in the First Carolina Joint Stock Land Bank of Columbia, his support enabling the bank to lend $750,000 to the farmers, and bringing
his own "total help to the state" almost to the two-million mark.[25]
But not even he could stem the tide. As he wrote Alex Legge in 1925,
because of four years of bad weather and boll weevil a lot of frozen
credits in the form of real estate loans had accumulated which had
to be relieved by his personal efforts. About thirty-five banks were
involved.[26] Two years later the old Bank of Georgetown closed down.
Shaken and saddened, friends came to Baruch with the story, and of
course it was he, in company with others, nonresidents and citizens,
who opened a new bank in January 1928 with a capitalization of
$50,000. By 1932 the city of Georgetown owed Baruch some $75,000,
and the new bank closed down. Baruch's position was difficult and
delicate. He wrote Christie Benet, who then managed his South
Carolina affairs, that he did not want to be unpleasant but he would
not be made the goat.[27] He would not let other creditors have preference, nor did he favor unsound schemes involving postponement
of bond maturities. Instead, he thought there should be cuts for all
bondholders.[28]

He resisted stubbornly all suggestions that he sue the city. The
bonds, however, were only half the story. Eager as Baruch was to
get what was due him, he told Christie Benet to draw up a list of all
the depositors who had lost. He would repay them because he felt
that many had invested in the bank because of his connections with
it.

Later when he tried to help the bank, he had the unpleasant
surprise of finding that he had been classed as an owner all along, and
was facing suit for the redemption of the bank stock.

What had happened was complex. Baruch had transferred his interest in the bank to the so-called People's Investment Corporation,
ostensibly devised to interest Northerners in the possibilities of the
Georgetown area as a winter resort. This was a project congenial to
Baruch, who was spending some $25,000 a year for the study of
Carolina resources, and was also interested in the development of
hunting lands and modern dairy and truck farms. As he told his
secretary, Miss Boyle, he would have had no interest in the People's
Investment Corporation had he not believed it was in the interest of
the whole state.

He had handed over his bank stock as partial payment on a contribution of $100,000. He had no idea that as a shareholder he would thus become a partner in a kind of holding company, not only for the Bank of Georgetown, but for numerous other ailing small banks. As he said later, he could have bought up bank stock himself. Someone asked him if he tried to unload when he found out. He admitted that he certainly had.[29]

Obviously, financier Bernard M. Baruch could not plead ignorance. But a silver lining to this cloud was provided by a dear friend, James F. Byrnes, who was to become an even dearer friend as the years went by. As attorney, Byrnes's firm had helped Baruch work out income tax problems on his Georgetown loss. Later Baruch wrote to Byrnes of his appreciation for his loyal support. Everyone else had been willing to pour him down the drain.[30]

Baruch had his difficulties — at least of an extralegal nature — with his domain of Hobcaw. "Squatter sovereignty" was claimed by the Caines brothers, lank bearded men of the swamps, poachers and hunters. There were four of the "boys": Hucks and Ball, Bob and Pluty, and this universe of swamp and sky and wilderness game was theirs, they claimed. No one had dared challenge them except the Northern-owned hunt club, to which Ball and Hucks sailed up in a sloop one day, with double-barreled shotguns across their knees, swore and damned Northerners, in general and in particular. An injunction was forthwith obtained from the Federal Court, but no one dared enforce it.

But Baruch was no mere damn-Yankee member of the hunt club. He understood the Southern code. The Caines brothers had posed a challenge to his authority which no Southerner could leave unanswered and still maintain his standing among his neighbors.

He led off with strategic warfare. The legal technicalities were handled by "Captain" Jim Powell, the boss carpenter of Hobcaw, a raw-boned, blue-eyed man as tall as Baruch himself, who dared to take action against the poachers. Although bombarded with threats, Powell survived, not only alive but unwounded.

Meanwhile, Baruch proceeded to beguile the enemy. With their talents recognized when they were put on the payroll as duck guides, Bob and Pluty Caines soon decided they would rather work for Baruch than poach from him. Hucks was more stubborn. But even he succumbed when the master of Hobcaw, after watching him drop 166 ducks in succession, stepped out to congratulate him as the finest shot he had ever seen. In fact, between Baruch and Hucks Caines there sprang up a friendship founded on mutual respect and a zest for "yarning." There was no one who could imitate duck calls like Hucks, or who had so keen a knowledge of just where to place decoys.

It was Hucks's eldest son, Sawney, who had christened the so-called "President's Stand," deep in the marshes in the best duck-hunting sector of Hobcaw. The President so honored was Grover Cleveland, and Sawney, a hulking giant with a beard tumbling down his chest, had escorted the great Democrat to the "stand."

To reach it was in itself an art. Most people learned early to walk lightly and raise their feet quickly from the marsh grass, but not President Cleveland, who took his stand right there in the oozing mud. He struggled until he was breathless. Sawney was terrified. He was at home with the marsh, but not with the President of the United States. Valiantly he took a mighty "holt" on the mired, rotund form. Suddenly, sharp and empty against the horizon stood the hip boots, and up and out shot the President. Nearly waist-deep in mud, Sawney struggled back to the boat with his precious charge, where, after a good drink, Cleveland began to laugh as heartily as did Baruch when he later heard the story.

It was from the Caines boys, too, that Baruch learned some of the infinite interpretations of the term "Democrat" — Baruch shared this label but could not share Hucks Caines's fervid attachment to Cole Blease, a dark-eyed and sleek-tongued local politician and advocate for the underdog. In Caines's opinion, God's handiwork had reached its perfection in the creation of Cole Blease. Many of the South Carolina neighbors agreed.

Despite these pleasant social relations, Ball Caines remained implacable. Baruch tried to convince him that he meant business, but Ball's poaching went on undisturbed. At last Baruch had him sent to jail, and for the full nine months of his term supported the poacher's wife and children. Ball emerged still unreconciled, talking much about what he was going to do.

One day, as Baruch and Hucks Caines were coming in from rowing, Hucks suddenly spied Ball on the landing and warned Baruch. The showdown had come. Baruch told Hucks to row straight for his brother. Like pebbles skipping across the water came Ball Caines's curses. As Baruch sprang from the boat, Ball Caines raised his gun. Years afterward, Baruch could still see those double barrels — so big

they looked as though he could jump into them and not even touch
the sides. Acting almost mechanically, Baruch ran straight up to
Caines. Feet clattered along the boardwalk. There was Jim Powell
with a six-shooter. Baruch leaped forward, grabbed the barrels of
Caines's gun and pushed them up. Caines was humbled. Baruch's
poaching troubles were over. Had it been otherwise, Hobcaw might
well have become a poacher's rendezvous. Baruch knew that in the
South you were finished if you did not face down a challenge.[31]

Despite these neighborhood tensions, only once in thirty years
was the peace of Hobcaw shattered. Baruch was not there. Only at
second hand did he hear of the terrible night when a Negro sprang
from a pine thicket and dragged to the road the young neighborhood
schoolteacher, while two of Hucks Caines's little girls cowered in the
buggy, watching the struggle below.

Stiff with terror, the teacher still retained her presence of mind.
Suddenly, she called out Hucks Caines's name, and at the ruse the
Negro dived back into the woods. But within moments the news had
spread through that remote swamp country as if indeed by African
drum beat. Boats, filled with men, slid silently across the water
from Georgetown. Starlight sparkled on gun muzzles. Bloodhounds
bayed; the woods were alive with sound. From Georgetown, from
Manning, from Moncks Corner and the parishes in between,
and up "the Neck," the swamp settlers were riding, their guns
slung over their saddles. Posses were moving through the marshes,
pushing boats down the watercourses. They found the attacker, of
course, and confronted him with his victim. There was no doubt
about his identity.

At Hobcaw, the wandering posses merged. The sheriff was waiting
for them with Captain Jim Powell at his side. As the mob surged into
the yard roars sounded. A rope sprang into the light and was looped
over the branch of a tree.

Captain Powell cried out for silence and the voices died down.
Fervently he pleaded with them that to hang the man right there
near the house would disgust Mrs. Baruch and the girls with the place
thereafter. The mob muttered grimly and then Powell shouted out
a command to take the Negro.

This ruse also worked. Amidst the confusion of departure, the
fugitive was seemingly lost. A few moments later he reappeared beside the sheriff, in a boat heading for Georgetown and the county

jail. At the next session of court, he was tried for attempted rape, and hanged — legally.[32]

This was the single instance of violence in Baruch's memory. In fifty years as the "Baron of Hobcaw," he lived beside "his" Negroes, sharing their sorrows and joys in a relation little different from that of the old slavery days. Time had passed the plantation by. As Mark Sullivan noted, when sending Baruch a Christmas book, *Hunting and Fishing in Carolina*, published back in 1859, Hobcaw was something of an institution out of a storied past, a glamorous repository of the old ways of life.[33]

Here in this Carolina low-country, Baruch again heard the soft accents of his boyhood, the clipped quaint speech of the Gullah. Here, each under the shade of a live-oak tree, crouched the "dog-houses," shutters blue-painted against the spirits; and in the dawn shrilled the cries of the "drolls," the dead babies, or babies as yet unborn.[34] The Plat-eye, that fearsome spirit with one hideous eye in the middle of its forehead, still walked the fields and deserted villages of Hobcaw, or went *whish* between your legs at night. Big as an ox, or small as a cat, he haunted the woods on the night of a new moon, and in the pale light Baruch could see the Negroes clustering for protection and hear the songs with which they bolstered their courage. The brighter ones, he observed, seldom saw a "hant." But the dull ones saw plenty. Few took any chances, however, as the deserted village of Strawberry testified. Hants lingered there, and not all Baruch's new tin roofs or clapboarded cottages could bring the Negroes back again. Even as late as 1951 a young mother refused to clean and air out the Hobcaw house during Baruch's absence, saying, "Mr. Bernie, there's Plat-eye in there." [35]

In taking over Hobcaw, Baruch had assumed many of the tasks and responsibilities of his ancestors. At Hobcaw the old relation between black and white still lingered, and at church or in the fields you could hear songs that had originated right at Hobcaw, in the dim past. Each family had its cabin and garden patch. Economically, the plantation was almost a self-sufficient community as far as the Negroes were concerned. However, Hobcaw was sadly run down when Baruch took over, and "freedom" for the Negroes had long meant freedom to do nothing at all. The word that any man or woman who wanted could have work at the prevailing pay roused scant enthusiasm until the secret was out — the Negroes were to be paid for maintaining their own cabins and outbuildings. As his affection for his "people" deepened, Baruch planned a series of pensions to be paid the Negroes of the staff after his death, according to the terms of an early will. But as his own years lengthened, and the shadow of depression fell, he had a happier inspiration, and pensioners were instead given life credits at Ford's store, so long as they remained on the plantation.

Hobcaw was truly the Negroes' world. No one could be forced to leave without the master's specific orders. Even as late as the nineteen-thirties there were Negroes at Hobcaw who had scarcely ever left the plantation, some who had never even been to Georgetown, six miles away.

Nor could undesirable citizenry necessarily be evicted. Even the shrewd trader of Wall Street could be taken in by a wily old man like Morris, who explained the absence of some valued turkeys by insisting that they had drowned themselves by swallowing rain as it fell. He was forgiven, and every Christmas Morris appeared for his gift of flannel drawers,[36] whose warmth may have extended his earthly stay a little longer.

Many of the Negroes at Hobcaw had been born in slavery. Through the years, funeral procession after funeral procession moved out of the little log church, and with each, Baruch felt the snap of another link with his young manhood. By 1935 only one was left, Maum Laura, who had seemed unbelievably old when Baruch had first seen her over thirty years before. Now she lingered on, fearful that she would wake up to find herself dead. Yet she ruled her village — the shadow of the root doctor always in the background — ruled it by the weight of her age and the fear of her tongue lashings.[37]

Almost none of the Hobcaw Negroes could read or write. The plantation was out of walking distance of schools; there was no question of "equal facilities" in the form of school buses. Baruch built a little schoolhouse and hired a teacher,[38] but attendance at best was halfhearted, and only the vigilance of his daughter Belle accounted for a daily roundup of truants, including two seventeen-year-old boys whom she hauled out of a swamp by their ears. A generation later, in 1952, eighteen children were enrolled, but as many more played on in their back yards undisturbed.[39]

Yet Baruch sent some of the Hobcaw children through high school and college. He was not one to lump the Negroes collectively. If

prejudice and poverty thwarted some, so had these qualities once thwarted him. "We had all the difficulties people have," he admitted in later life. Each man had to win on his own merits. Within a few years after he bought Hobcaw, his own children would be denied admission to the school to which their mother had gone. All his life the line would be drawn. Out of his saddened wisdom, and out of half a century's residence and acquaintance with Southerners, both black and white and with all shapes and varieties of human nature, he knew that you cannot effectively legislate as to whom people will associate with. He upheld the antisegregation decision of the Supreme Court, because it was the law of the land, but he knew that law alone was not enough. The Negroes, he was sure, would in the course of time make their place in American society as other races had done. But he doubted if segregation would ever be really ended in his lifetime. Slavery, he felt, had been an evil, but no more so than the laboring of women and children in the mills of New England for fifteen hours a day at low wages. Nothing, he was convinced, had so held back the "economic emancipation of the Negro" as Reconstruction and carpetbag rule.[40]

Christmas was the gala time at Hobcaw, for black and white alike. It was celebrated in the old way, under freedom as it had been under slavery. For the Baruchs personally it was a family and a children's celebration; and whatever the great task or big deal in which he was involved, Baruch was never too busy to join his family at Hobcaw for the holiday season.

The big house usually bulged with children and young people. Christmas Eve was celebrated in the "children's playhouse," a little three-room cabin which still stands, incongruous with its tiny rooms and oversized Victorian furniture. There on Christmas Eve the lights blazed on the tree. There, too, acting as cooks and waiters, the Baruch children would serve Christmas dinner for the guests and family. Presents were given to each employee. Christmas itself was fiesta day.[41] At night, walking through the darkness, Baruch could hear the echo of thumping rafters and the "music" of clapping hands and stamping feet, and in his own barn he watched the dances which would be the rage in London or Paris, twenty-five or thirty years later. The Turkey Trot. The Charleston. The Black Bottom. There were prizes for these dancers, for the best steppers and the best-dressed steppers too.

For the Negroes, the heart of the plantation was the little white-washed church that eventually replaced the log one. The "broadaxe" preacher, who baptized and married and buried the dead, was a man of importance, second only to the root doctor. The Negroes had wanted "Mr. Bernie" to dedicate the church he had given them. Wonderingly they listened to his explanation that he could hardly dedicate a church to the Father, the Son, and the Holy Ghost, and that he would substitute a fully ordained colored preacher in his stead.

Yet there were many nights when the "Baron of Hobcaw" slipped quietly onto one of the benches, bowed his head, and reverently followed the service. In the formal sense, he was not a religious man. He adhered to no creed, but he respected all religions, and the unlettered reverence of these simple services touched his heart.

First came a field hand, leading a chant; then a second elder, kneeling and praying to the sound of stamping feet and clapping hands; prayers for crops and the stock, for fishing and shooting. Then the full tide of emotion as the cries of "Yes, Lord" and "Amen" echoed, and first one and then another began to sway up the aisles in a dance. *Clap, clap* went the hands. *Stamp, stamp,* the feet. Shadows lurched across the ceiling. The kerosene lamps shook in their brackets.[42] Again the voices lifted in prayer. Then came the preacher, the Reverend Mose Jenkins. He adjusted his gold-rimmed spectacles. He hunched over the pulpit. He picked up the mighty Bible "Miss Annie" had given him.

It came like a flood: the journey into Egypt — Pharaoh, the plagues, the flies, the locusts, the deaths of the firstborn, the pursuit. After the war there were new touches about the rifles and machine guns. Always the same old story, yet always new. To Baruch there was something very touching about this son of slaves who could tell with such drama the story of the deliverances of the Children of Israel. Years later, he could hear the echo of those feet drumming on the board floor, the clapping hands, the rise and fall of the preacher's voice, and at one o'clock in the morning the cool inrush of air and the soft voices of the congregation as they made their way home.[43]

Hobcaw was not merely a hunting preserve, nor just a winter home. Although Baruch gave up the losing battle of raising rice shortly after attempting it, the plantation was more of a farm than it had been since the end of the War Between the States. Baruch did not grow for the market, as he did not want to be in competition with his neighbors. However, he raised much of his own food, and crop experimentation was his delight, as it had been his father's. Such experiments he thought might prove of value to his state.[44]

Nevertheless, hunting was the delight of the barony. How could it have been otherwise in a paradise where the bays and rivers were alive with mullet, flounder, bluefish, and shad, where bass flicked through the waterlines of the rice fields, and tiny, sweet-fleshed oysters, crabs, pungent clams, and Carolina shrimp reveled in the marshes.[45] As for deer, Hobcaw was overrun with them. They would dart from the forest, jumping under the nose of your horse, or almost under the wheels of a car. In the early years, hunting parties used to throw a cordon around a swamp, send in drivers on horseback to herd the deer out, then pick them off as they fled past. New Year's Day always brought a big drive, with the governor and other sporting notables participating with zest. Eventually this cruel sport was ended by state law, but Baruch had ended it at Hobcaw much earlier. He did not enjoy deer hunts. But there were jacksnipe, quail, and wild turkeys, sometimes flocking across the road in such numbers that you had to stop the buggy. There were wild hogs, too, vicious animals, domesticated in ante-bellum days, and later seeking their freedom in the swamps. In the early years you could catch wildcats and otter, and Negroes told of bears and panthers in the not-too-distant past, but they had vanished into the canebrake.[46]

Although in his seventies and eighties Baruch could still bring down eight birds with seven shells, or vice versa, he never considered himself a "natural shot." [47] He was not like Hucks Caines, who used a gun as intimately as a part of his own body, nor was he a born shot like his own son. Never did he forget the day when Captain Jim Powell, cheek swollen with tobacco and right foot on the dashboard, halted the buggy and a short, fat, stubby little replica of Baruch at eight bounced gleefully to the ground, full of glee at having brought down eight ducks with the little gun which his Uncle Hartwig had given him with the admonition that it was scarcely big enough to kill bugs with.

Baruch took his son out into the marshes. There the youngster killed forty-five ducks with sixty-odd shells — good shooting at any age. It was this performance that proved the boy to be a "natural shot." [48]

In the early years duck hunting, of course, was the leading attraction at Hobcaw. Neither for Baruch nor for his guests could anything equal the delight of those morning risings at 3.30 or 4, and then the row out into the dark or the moonlight, with not a sound but the creak of the oarlocks and the *slap-slap* of water against the side of the boat. Nothing could equal this joy of health and strength, this test of skill, of drawing up the boats and putting out decoys, of a clear day and a southwest wind.

Breakfast of hot coffee and steak was waiting in a little cottage near the marshes of the President's Stand. Afterward, if it was low tide, you could walk out into the rice fields and hear the ducks there in the water, making a sound like a motorboat. They would let you come almost within fifty feet,[49] then, at a clap of your hands, they would soar up and off with a roar like musketry. Nothing was like the beauty of those ducks rising, tracing in the sky the pattern of the creeks and inlets whence they came. To the east, in the eye of the sun, you could see flock after flock breaking out of the swamps and rice fields, darkening the sky. No retriever could bring them to you — the broken clam shells cut the tender feet of the dogs. The contest was undivided, between bird and man.[50]

Hunting became Baruch's yardstick for the evaluation of character. Hunting and fishing, he believed, showed up all variety of human weaknesses, from the latent barbarian to the congenital liar who could just not resist extending the number of his killings. But this last was a weakness upon which he looked with an indulgent eye. "There's two things upon which you can never kid a man," he would drawl, "his prowess with guns or his prowess with women. Personally, I back up any and all lies that a man can tell about how good he is with the girls and guns." [51]

Snipe hunting was one of the less-publicized sports at the plantation. After seeing all the rest — the clouds of duck, the flocks of turkey, the herds of deer — the novice could see more plausibility in this mock game of going out and holding a bag in one hand, a lantern in the other, and whistling to lure the snipe, first into the light and then into the bag.

Baruch cared little for snipe hunting himself, but he was as good a sport as any of them. A snipe hunt was his test of a newcomer's fitness for entry into the "Hobcaw club." At its end, after a generous dinner, the novice would be received in full standing into the charmed circle.

One visitor was doubtful. While the bets were being laid, he tiptoed over to the hostler. Was it a good night for snipe hunting? All right, he was assured, if you liked that sort of thing. He queried Jim Powell at the buckboard and was given another encouraging, if cryptic, answer.

Hucks Caines got the bag and lantern. Bob Caines took the novice to a good stand and showed him how to wield his equipment. The others stood around, trying not to laugh. From the distance, the visitor's whistle sounded, cheerily at first, then fainter. By now, several of Baruch's companions were rolling on the ground, stuffing their fists into their mouths.

No one had to get the hunter. He came in under his own power, and at one glance at his face all stopped laughing. He began to swear. To Baruch it was all the more apparent that hunting was indeed a test of human nature, and that this particular banker had not passed the test.[52]

One rule of the plantation was never broken: no gun could be fired on Sunday. Baruch's parents had always respected their neighbor's Sabbath, and he adhered to the practice.[53]

The Hobcaw dinners, given annually by the Baron for his shooting guests, were legendary among America's business and political leaders. They inspired such tributes as that from Senator Key Pittman, whose comment was that the last Hobcaw dinner was a triumph, brilliant, delightful, and, with Baruch as toastmaster, a perfect whiz.[54] Whoever was the guest of honor — a visiting prince or Mrs. Woodrow Wilson — all were placed at perfect ease. While the "prewar stuff" lasted, good wines flowed with the conversation. Later, the understanding was that each guest would bring his own, which gave rise to heated discussions on the relative merits of Scotch, bourbon, swamp moonshine, or mountain corn between such connoisseurs as Winston Churchill and the fiery Charleston newspaper editor, William Watts Ball.[55]

Entertainment at Hobcaw was more or less of a masculine affair. Except at the holiday season, Mrs. Baruch came less frequently to the plantation in later years. Amused at a friend's refusal to accept an invitation for himself and his wife unless Mrs. Baruch wrote, Baruch explained that of course his wife would write, but that he was the one who extended the invitations because he didn't want his wife to be bothered with them.[56]

Isolated as it was, Hobcaw naturally held a greater masculine than feminine appeal. It was a man's dream hunting lodge. But all the graciousness of the South was in Baruch's gift for making his guests feel that they could give him no greater pleasure than the privilege of entertaining them. He had all that was required to play host in the old tradition. One friend expressed the opinion of many when she pointed out that as soon as you entered Baruch's house you felt that he had been born with the natural gift for hospitality. Obviously, the host enjoyed equally serious work and relaxation — a mixture that was the secret of good living as well as of being a good host. His warm human companionship gave much more than mere words of friendship could convey.[57]

To Baruch, friendship was one of the rare joys of life, and he has had a genius for making and keeping loyal friends.

Hobcaw was his headquarters. Here came his hunting "buddies," like Judge William A. Glasgow, Jr., newspapermen like Mark Sullivan, Arthur Krock, and Frank Kent, his fellow members of the Jefferson Island Club, good Democrats and good friends all: Senators Tydings, Pittman, Byrd, Byrnes, and Pat Harrison. Many of them were Southerners who could think and feel and remember as he did, and to whom politics was the very breath of life. These companions of the hunt and the fishing stream were also often the companions of his hearth and heart. Some were friends of long standing — men like Glass and McAdoo and Josephus Daniels, who by a sort of spiritual kinship came to fill the empty places left by those before them.

Of these "Hobcaw buddies," it was perhaps Senator Joseph T. Robinson of Arkansas who was dearest to Baruch. Although he was not an intellectual, Robinson's warm and courageous personality made him lovable. Furthermore, he was always the same man in the companionship of Hobcaw or in official life. He was, moreover, the most ardent hunter Baruch ever knew.

He would be out at sundown for the ducks, in the afternoon for the quail, and by evening would be sitting on a rick by the swamp watching for a turkey. Once he saw a huge gobbler rise and light on the limb of a tree. Robinson, looking at the turkey's long "whiskers" christened him Secretary Hughes. The twenty-five-pound bird was weighed in, and in view of its Republicanism was sent to President

Harding. Since no Democrats were invited to partake of the feast, Robinson swore that no Republican was again going to get such a gift from him.[58]

Another favorite hunting companion was Judge William Glasgow, who one summer accompanied Baruch to Scotland, and with whom he had a warm and bantering correspondence.[59] The company of the newspaper columnist Frank Kent always enlivened Baruch, who invited him to be his guest on the moors of Scotland in 1929, teasing his friend about his British manners.[60]

His friendships had many levels and shadings. That he enjoys the company of those "at the top" in any sphere of life has brought him companions as diverse as Francis Cardinal Spellman and Arthur Godfrey; yet he has been loyal to friends out of the past of whom the world has never heard, such as an old comrade of the mining and "bonanza" days, the union leader James Lord. There have been men he admired with whom he had little personal intimacy, such as Senator Norris and Herbert Hoover. The latter, he once said, was one of the very few who could affect his views on economic and social problems.[61]

There were political associates from whom he drifted apart under the pressure of time and onsweeping events. As Thomas L. Chadbourne once put it: they had been close friends, both tossed by the same storms, but their busy lives still found time to reach out, even for a handshake.[62] Sometimes, other factors brought about separation — as, for instance, from the Missouri senator who in 1942 wrote of his pleasure in getting a picture of Baruch and Joe Robinson.[63] Harry Truman was "most happy" to have it. Pressures of still another kind divided Baruch from the man to whom he sent a birthday cake and who, in turn, gave him valuable serum for American hospitals — Andrei A. Gromyko.[64] It was true that in more recent years individuals had to be "near the top" even to approach him. Others did not dare; even those who had known him over the years would not impose themselves upon him. But his personal feelings for those he loved never altered, and those who loved him never wavered in their turn, despite occasional temperamental differences. One of his friends said of him that he was "about the most charming man that ever walked." If he liked you, "nothing you could do could make him like you less." If he disliked you, nothing could "raise you in his estimation." [65]

Among the "Farm Bloc" Senators, with whom he was so closely associated for so long, it was only with Borah that Baruch had any real intimacy. Throughout the years others crossed and recrossed his horizon: Edwin A. Halsey, "Steve" Early, Marvin McIntire, "Pa" Watson, and Louis Howe; blunt-tongued Harold Ickes, whose early dislike of Baruch turned to genuine admiration; [66] the moody and brilliant Forrestal, Robert Patterson, and a trio of generals — John J. Pershing, George C. Marshall, and Dwight D. Eisenhower.

Of his purely political associates, probably that desperate pair, the gamecock, William G. McAdoo, and the "Happy Warrior," Alfred E. Smith, won his deepest personal affection, and it was returned in kind.

Then there were his associates in business: mentors who had helped him on the way up, like Burrill, Ryan, and Keene; that "band of brothers," the Guggenheims; the bold and fearless "Wild Westerner," George Wingfield. In a more intimate personal relation were Count René de Rougemont and Christie Benet, who knew, as few did, of Baruch's "untold amount of charity down in Georgetown county during the depression. He was the personal headquarters for keeping things going." [67] For "Dave" McGill, who looked after his hunting lodge at Kingstree, Baruch had the almost paternal affection that he invariably felt for his "protégés"; and McGill's intelligence and drive, he soon saw, made him a man worth helping. He liked the forthright brevity of McGill's annual request for a loan so that he could raise tobacco. Because he liked his neighbors, he deplored quarreling among them and did his best to patch up frayed friendships.[68]

One promising young South Carolina neighbor Baruch recommended to Eugene Grace at the Bethlehem Steel Company, where he soon did very well. "This boy is doing you credit," Grace reported. But he was five feet nine inches tall and weighed only 120 pounds. Grace suggested, ". . . if you raise any more on your duck farm . . . feed them better." [69]

A very special kind of feeling was Baruch's affection for his associates on the War Industries Board, the "team" that he had hand-picked for victory. Among them there was a strong camaraderie. All were potent, high-geared, but not necessarily the companions that he would pick to go hunting with him at Hobcaw. There were brilliant industrial specialists like Alex Legge, or J. Leonard Replogle, or

John Hancock. There was George Peek, with unmatched fighting
qualities and great idealism.[70] He felt both admiration and warm
liking for Albert C. Ritchie of Maryland, and for the emotional but
always patriotic Hugh S. Johnson.[71] During the Second World War
the brilliant Ferdinand Eberstadt became an honorary member of
this charmed circle, which included the man who could probably
claim to be Baruch's closest personal friend in this country, the loyal
Herbert Bayard Swope.

Great talker though Baruch might be, Swope could talk him down.
The whole world might defer to Baruch, but Swope would keep him
waiting in his outer office. The secret of their friendship, Swope once
said, was "the abandonment of all civility between us." The influence
of each upon the other was great. Each played the role of a kind of
jury, "from which the other seeks approval." In Swope Baruch found
more than a talented tongue and pen; he found a kind of sounding
board for his own opinions. With rare modesty, Swope had admitted
to having sometimes "a thought to help him over the marshes." [72]

Baruch and Swope met back in 1910, when Baruch was forty and
"seemed rather elderly" to the young reporter on the New York
World, who was "always ready for a fight or a frolic." There had been,
according to Swope, some "robbing" on the Exchange, and the World
was traditionally anti-Wall Street.

Swope caught sight of Baruch as he emerged from the Waldorf bar,
and caught up with him at Fifth Avenue and 34th Street.

"I'm here to ask you this question," said Swope, and asked it.
Baruch leaned his long weight against a mailbox.

"Well, you've asked it."

"And you've not answered it."

"And I'm not going to answer it," Baruch said quietly. Thus the
friendship was born.[73]

For none of his associates could Baruch ever feel quite the warmth
he had for the "graduates" of the War Industries Board, except for
those few who, like himself, served Woodrow Wilson closely —
Grayson, Glass, Daniels, McAdoo.[74] One of the great Southern newspapers, the Raleigh News and Observer, survived the depression years
because of Baruch, who assured the editor, Josephus Daniels, that his
help had been to him a great pleasure.[75]

And out of Baruch's service with Wilson came his warmest friendship of all — with Winston Churchill. Baruch was frank in telling

the great Englishman how much he meant to him.[76] In later years, during the dark struggle of atomic crisis, Churchill returned the tribute: "I value greatly your long memorable friendship. I am very thankful you have your present great responsibilities, and I sleep more soundly in my bed because I know the sentinel is awake." [77]

As we shall see, Baruch might have had intimacy with Franklin Roosevelt had it not been for Roosevelt's wary distrust of a man who in some ways was so much like himself. Occasionally, real affection broke through the tension between them. It was Roosevelt who labeled Baruch "the elder statesman," and sometimes the President would take time out for a characteristic note: "You were a dear to send me those delicious quail, which I am enjoying no end." [78] Another man in whose mind Baruch could find real comradeship was James F. Byrnes, who intellectually stood head and shoulders over many of the foremost figures of his time. With him and with Senator Harry Byrd, Baruch found a particularly stimulating companionship. He could have said of both of them what he said of Byrnes: "Isn't Jimmy Byrnes a grand person!" [79] He was at home with many South Carolinians; with the old state historian, wry, sharp-witted Alex Salley or with William Watts Ball, who in his seventies wished that he might see Georgetown once again; and Baruch's cousin, Ed Kaminski, who was "one of the last surviving South Carolina gentlemen as measured by the standards that my father taught me." [80]

He was a man of many worlds, equally at home in a ringside seat in Madison Square Garden, reading a prayer sent to him by Cardinal Spellman, or at a table in a Broadway night club. He was at home with Max Gordon — "Little Maxie," short, emphatic, pink-cheeked and blue-eyed, who could juggle compliments with Clare Boothe Luce, conjecture as to Canadian gold stocks, and comment on Bernard M. Baruch all at the same time. He and Baruch would talk in Central Park, for Gordon's tiny vault of an office contained room for only a battered desk and an equally scarred filing cabinet, a telephone directory, a calendar, the usual wallpapering of theatrical celebrities, plus his father's naturalization papers and a photograph of his dark-eyed little mother, who, upon hearing that her son had four plays on Broadway at once, only asked, "Is it honest?"

Once Gordon's theatrical fortunes faltered. He owed $300,000, was sick and "broke." Baruch offered him a loan of $50,000; Gordon declined. Impulsively, the "Old Chief" threw his arms around him and

hugged him, "You're a double mosher," * he said. Baruch did, however, insist on investing wisely what little money Gordon had left,
and the producer came back with *Over 21*, *Born Yesterday*, and *The
Solid Gold Cadillac*.[81]

Nothing in the make-up of Bernard Baruch had been more marked
than what Billy Rose has called "his utter genius for friendship." [82]
The person to whom he talks at the moment is convinced that he
means more to Baruch than anyone else. There were qualities in
him that those who knew him could find in no other man. "I cherish
your friendship as among the few things that make life any longer
tolerable," wrote Carter Glass late in his life.[83] Billy Rose told him
that he would never know what his friendship and inspiration had
meant to him.[84]

Friendship was for Baruch a reciprocal affair. To Senator Charles
Thomas, who had stood by him during the "leak" investigation in
1917, Baruch later wrote to express his gratitude for friendship in a
time of need.[85] Unknowingly he almost echoed Thomas' own words
about him, that he could never in his life have a better friend. Baruch was "distinguished in almost all respects from the common run
of men," Thomas wrote.[86]

Nothing hurt Baruch more than to be highly regarded for the sake
of his money, and he was more touched by tributes to his kindness
than by gratitude for any financial help.[87]

Baruch's correspondence is full of affection, gratitude, love. To the
old Colorado mining friend, James Lord; to Garet Garrett; [88] to
Alex Legge, to see whom in Chicago, when he was in dire grief,
Baruch made a special trip, breaking an engagement; to Harry
Hopkins, to whom he wrote hoping that his dying wife would be
spared great suffering.[89] There was a letter of comfort to a dying
White House stenographer, Marguerite Durand.[90] A depressed
Arthur Krock is encouraged to take out his frustrations on Baruch.[91]
Mark Sullivan wrote that Baruch was his "oldest anchorage," he who
had known Sullivan's wife in her beautiful prime.[92] The Negroes at
Hobcaw, Pierrepont B. Noyes, Steve Early, Robert Goelet, Gordon
Rentschler, Howard Ingels, a hundred others write of gratitude for
friendship or are sent messages of thanks or comfort.

And when, as in all deep friendships, there came moments of mis-
understanding and hurt feelings, Baruch's gift for reconciliation

* Jewish term of admiration.

equaled his friends' need for it. Herbert Bayard Swope once wrote Baruch what must be one of the most remarkable letters of the kind ever written.

> I am worried over our relations [Swope began]. I find that little wrongs . . . are of less importance than the preservation of a friendship in which affection is engaged and the qualities of respect and admiration are present.
> For fifteen years we have worked much . . . played a little; quarreled occasionally and fought frequently, but always side by side . . . For our strengths we had admiration . . . for our shortcomings we had sympathy . . .
> "Forsake not an old friend, for the new is not comparable to him" . . . Because I feel all this deeply, I am writing frankly.
> It is the only way I know.[93]

Once, imagining a coolness in his old friend Robert Bingham, Baruch wrote him such a warm letter that their relations were completely restored.[94]

He always paid a very special kind of attention to the widows of his old friends. First among these was Mrs. Woodrow Wilson, who had a claim on his affections held by no one outside his own family. To him, she was the dearest treasure of the man he had so loved and honored. To her, he was "the Baron," a friend and counselor for whom both she and Wilson had real personal affection.[95]

Easter after Easter flowers came to give her new evidence of his thought. He showered her with little gallantries, writing with an old-fashioned formality for permission to take dinner with her.[96] Because of him, she could go on living with her memories and mementos in the house on S Street, where he purchased the neighboring lot so that she might have rest and quiet. One year, with the greatest delicacy, he offered her a vacation in Saratoga, Europe, or both.[97] She wondered if he knew what it meant to her — the place that his family had given her in their hearts and home.

He kept a paternal eye on the Wilson daughters, once intervening on behalf of Margaret, who felt happier for his attention.[98]

One friendship in Baruch's life was unaltered by passing time, and no woman, with the single exception of his wife, ever exerted such influence upon him. More than a friend, more than an employee, no person outside his immediate family has had a closer association with Bernard M. Baruch than his private secretary, Miss Mary A. Boyle, who came to him as a girl in her teens and became his virtual partner in great enterprises.[99] It is possible that she was the only person since Woodrow Wilson who could influence Baruch's mind; and it is certain that there was no person to whose opinions he gave such deference.

She has deserved the tributes paid her. She has served Baruch with the same loyalty and devotion that he gave to Woodrow Wilson. She has dedicated her life to his service. She has known Baruch in his weaknesses and his strength; and yet after half a century, he was still her hero, and his portrait was in the place of honor in her home. If he was the adviser to Presidents, she was the adviser to Baruch. So close were their minds that he has trusted her implicitly to act for him. She has had custodianship of his will, his income tax dealings, his investments, his most private papers. She became fully accustomed to carrying on his affairs without detailed instructions.[100]

To his family she has given the same devotion and loyalty she gave to Baruch himself. She was his wife's confidante and dear friend, and after her death, she showed the Baruch children an affection and understanding they found nowhere else outside the family. Baruch has given her the intellectual respect he would give a man, plus the homage he would show a lovely woman. A person's sex never interfered with his judgment of the person, yet because Miss Boyle was a woman, there has been an added piquancy to their friendship. Like his children, he could always "come to Miss Boyle" with his troubles.

13

POLITICS AS USUAL

TIPPING BACK in his swivel chair, hands clasped behind his head, Bernard Baruch faced his inquisitor from the *Wall Street Journal*. "I'm tired," he said.

Baruch continued. "I see so many opportunities all around me in this wonderful country . . . to make money and they make me tired." If only he were young! [1]

Not yet fifty years old, Baruch was drained and weary from the combined impact of warmaking and peacemaking, and of a peace that was no peace. His nerves had been pounded; already the disillusion of the twenties was beginning to engulf him. A few months earlier he had been, perhaps, the second most powerful man in the nation. What would be his status now? If he had gone on making money, he once said, he could have piled it up almost endlessly.[2] But he had tired of merely making money. His great drives for money and power had been fulfilled.

By his past standards, he was not a particularly rich man, but the very idea of becoming again a Wall Street speculator was distasteful to him. As he said, he had acquired so much inside information it would have been improper for him to return actively to the market.[3] No longer was his criterion of "great minds" primarily the money they made. He was aware that many of his Wall Street cronies were "a pretty shallow set." He liked money for the power it gave, but his "extraordinary sense of reality" had left him with no vulgar illusions about what money would buy — it would not for instance, give him "a commanding place in public life." [4]

The ideal of public service still haunted him. As he said, when God and the community have been good to a man, it is only natural that he should try to pay it back.[5] He confessed to Senator Pat Harrison that the leaders did not talk to him often unless they were after money. He felt he had something more to give.[6]

You sensed his restlessness. "He is still youthful and has enormous energies and no occupation for them," almost pityingly wrote a sensitive observer.[7] Even pleasures were palling on him; he was not doing anything that he really wanted to do. He looked upon the world around him and did not find it good. Few people seemed to care what happened as long as they got "theirs." Under Wilson, America had risen to great heights. Respect for peoples, living standards, elimination of waste, had all surged forward and Baruch felt that the advance had had a spiritual source. Yet the war seemed to have drained America of idealism.[8]

Sorrow had darkened Baruch's thoughts during those years. The two greatest tragedies of his life thus far had engulfed him. In 1921 his father had died, and that same year his mother, on the fifty-fourth anniversary of their wedding day. Their union had been truly blessed. They had been honored and loved by all who had known them; they had lived to see the doctor reap the rewards of his years of struggle, and to have a President of the United States personally congratulate them on their son.[9] Now they were gone, the father whose mind and spirit Baruch had admired above those of any other man [10] and the mother whose love for a son had been merged with her pride in his career; who could write him on his forty-ninth birthday that she thanked God for him.[11]

Now this vital chain of years was broken. Grief-stricken, somehow looking strangely like Woodrow Wilson,[12] Baruch watched as four old Confederates lowered his father into the grave.[13] Never had he felt so alone. At night he lay thinking of the stamp his father had left upon his time: his battle for the pasteurization of milk for babies and for free public baths, the science of hydrotherapy, recognized by state law on April 18, 1895;[14] all the things his father had dreamed, had done, and had made better. Over and over, the words came into his head: "There is no such thing as an incurable disease, only diseases for which no cure has been found." His father was the inspiration of his desire for service.[15]

So, too, with his mother. The New York *Telegram* headline may have been sentimental, "Mrs. Isabelle Baruch Pines Away," [16] but Baruch knew the words were true. Although the doctors had diagnosed her illness as double pneumonia, in fact "heartbreak and grief over the ending of a love union that had lasted for more than fifty-three years were the cause of death." [17]

These losses seem to have aroused Baruch's own paternal instincts, making him think more as a father and less as a son. He spent hours nursing his own son through a serious bout of jaundice, and was glad just to be needed and to stand by.[18] To his daughter Belle, off for Europe, he took time to send a peremptory cablegram warning her against a certain young gentleman whom she might encounter abroad.[19] In gentler vein, he commended her to the care of his friend René de Rougemont.[20]

Travel helped to take up some of the slack of Baruch's days. His old friend, Rougemont, untangled the threads of day-to-day problems abroad, whether these involved the planning of a luncheon,[21] the selection of a Rolls or Hispano-Suiza with sufficient space for the Baruch legs, privately looking up some race horses, or giving advice as to pleasant places to visit for one who had already seen most of Europe.[22] His capacity for relaxation was limited. Dr. Alvin Johnson remembers him barking into a telephone just before leaving for a "rest" in Europe: "What's that? You say I'm holding you up. Just for that, the price has gone up two millions . . . Wireless me on the *Majestic*."

Aboard ship, Johnson heard the cry, "Radiogram for Mr. Baruch. Radiogram for Mr. Baruch." The man in New York had accepted the offer — including the extra two million dollars.[23]

It was Rougemont who arranged for Baruch's car and his French chauffeur to be at the dock waiting for one of those eighty-mile-an-hour trips to Paris. Once, Dr. Johnson has recalled, the big car went dry and coasted through the city gates to a standstill. Baruch bounced out and gave his chauffeur "hell," to which the thrifty Sartorius explained that if you took gasoline into Paris you had to pay duty on it.

Johnson, "the Professor," was with Baruch at 7 A.M. on a morning when they started for Vichy at such speed that a struck chicken leaped fifty feet in the air,[24] and he looked on through one wild evening of play when Baruch gamed with all his old-time zest, as if nothing else mattered in life.

Yet solitary trips abroad were losing some of their savor. He would get homesick for his wife and children, and once he put off a long planned trip to Scotland and a visit to Paris because of the illness of his son.[25] His interests were returning somewhat from overseas. He was looking with new eyes on a place already familiar to him — Saratoga.

Going to Saratoga was like stepping back into his boyhood. Little had changed in the old-fashioned resort since the nineties. There were still the same great trees and cool stretches of shadow, the quaint cottages embossed with gingerbread and bulging with bay windows, the smell of apple blossoms and musky boxwood. Now, however, at noon on Main Street there was a parade of farmers' Fords and sports Rolls-Royces; Saratoga was half upstate village and half county fair. You stepped backward in time behind those blazing footlights of petunias and geraniums at the foot of the slender three-story columns of the old United States Hotel, where once President Arthur had been "in residence." Here there still lingered the aura of a glamorous past, of Lillian Russell and Della Fox, of those "sporting men" who gamed at the "palace of plungers" and argued with equal avidity the points of a new trotter or of Anna Held.[26] In the twenties, as in the nineties, it was a "gaudy, riotous melange . . . abundantly and earthily American," half Continental spa and half honky-tonk, as Governor Franklin D. Roosevelt later described it.[27]

In this "paradise of gamblers," Baruch was a familiar and a conspicuous figure. As in the past, his eyes were fixed on the racing horses, the white shirts and bright breeches of the jockeys; his chair scraped forward to the cry "They're off." Baruch, however, was coming to be interested in far more than the horses. By 1927 his real wish was to see more of the mineral springs that had been the original cause of the resort's popularity.[28]

The resurrection of Saratoga Springs as a social and watering place, a substitute lure for the one hundred thousand Americans who annually went abroad for the "cure," was for Baruch a long cherished goal. It might even fulfill his father's dream of water cures, a dream to be realized, in part, a few years later at Warm Springs. He was undeterred by gibes such as that of Arthur Brisbane, that Saratoga might be healthy for gamblers and bootleggers but was less so for the fools that would patronize it.[29]

Baruch had no illusions about the Saratoga of the twenties. It was operated halfheartedly as a state park and spa, and thousands of people, in an entirely unscientific way and with no medical advice, were bathing in the waters and drinking them. The race track and gaming tables were far better organized.[30] Furthermore, by 1930, the state reported a deficit of $28,556 a year, with the water level falling.

Baruch did not believe that Saratoga Springs or any other springs were a cure-all; he was against any use of the waters except under medical supervision. Nevertheless, why could not Saratoga be fitted out like Continental resorts, the newest hotels in one sector and more modest accommodations, for those of great need and small means, in another — with mud baths and thermal stations, like those in Europe? Why should the state not have a research laboratory at Saratoga? Why should not the curative value of the waters be propagandized? The springs were radioactive, for instance, and might be of great value in the treatment of gout, arthritis, and allied diseases. Why could not the Saratoga waters be bottled and sold? If the State of New York would do its part, Baruch would do his.[31]

Yet for all his eager interest, Baruch shied off from active participation. He sincerely was sorry to decline the chairmanship of the Saratoga Springs Commission because he was not well. In fact he planned to take the cure himself.[32]

"Dear Barney," responded Governor Franklin Roosevelt, "this whole Saratoga development revolves around you." It could only be carried through by "one man in the United States . . . You must continue to be the guiding hand." [33]

Again Baruch demurred. He had already given so much of himself to diverse causes that he was exhausted. He did not want to become ill. If he were his old self, he would take on the job.[34]

Again the Governor refused to take no for an answer. A year later he was back at Baruch: "We all need you and cannot get on without you . . . I will hold it open if necessary for a hundred years until you are ready to say Yes. You are the most bashful girl I know." [35] Baruch bowed to the dictum. Under his inspiration as chairman of the Saratoga Springs Commission, new springs were unearthed, eight and a half million dollars worth of buildings erected, and the whole resort given a new lease on existence.[36] There were disappointments and drawbacks. For one thing, private funds after October 1929 dwindled away almost as fast as the resort patrons, whose "cures" could wait until the recovery of the Stock Exchange.

Yet as the nation sagged deeper into depression, the rebuilding of

Saratoga went on. A medical director was to be chosen, a $300,000 bottling works to be built, a new $75,000 bathhouse completed, and even that seemed inadequate. As a "resort of cardiacs," not for the lungs or digestive difficulties, Saratoga, if it did not become another Baden-Baden or Vichy, sustained a shot in the arm which gave it at least some semblance of health for another generation.

Baruch's own pleas of ill health, however, had been no sham. Through the twenties and thirties he was plagued by a series of minor ailments, climaxed by a serious illness and two operations. Not until his seventieth year and the coming of the Second World War did he gain the vigor of his late maturity. In bed for weeks during the spring of 1922, he wrote in discouragement that a hospital should be built for him. He still was not feeling really well a year later, and by the spring of 1924 had developed a cough which he was warned might become chronic unless he gave his voice a rest.[37] He took a cure at Vittel for his kidneys, and drank acidophilus milk, as prescribed by Admiral Cary Grayson, for his indigestion. Chronic infections, neuritis, and gout dogged him.[38] His multifold activities tired him without providing the release of dedication to a single, overwhelming cause. Usually only under crisis would he know perfect health; and being a rich man, he had, of course, time and money to tinker with his ailments. However, his gout was real, and men who had not had gout in both feet did not know what suffering was.

In the light of his subsequent vigor, it is almost amusing to read a physician's report for the year 1930, itemizing his low blood pressure, various urinary and digestive irregularities, and a heart murmur, concluding finally that Baruch's general physical condition at sixty was only adequate.[39] A London doctor prescribed a diet, recommending plenty of oranges, pineapples, raisins, onions, wheat meal and Ryvita bread, and forbidding whiskey, red wine, beef, black coffee, spinach, pears, or asparagus. (In old age, he would partake moderately of these items, except coffee, beef, and wine.)

These restrictions must have dampened Baruch's joy in the contents of his wine cellar, which was fully inventoried in 1926. There were several cases of Château Yquem, 1913; Sandeman port, amontillado sherry, ten bottles of brandy, reserve 1820; Château Lafite claret, 1891; eleven bottles of 1827 Madeira; sundry supplies of Chartreuse and kümmel; only one bottle of blackberry brandy and one of Benedictine, but nine of Cognac Bouillier and a gallon of Jamaica rum.[40]

All of which, despite his scrupulous regard for the Prohibition laws, should have made the waiting period slightly more endurable. Guests goggled at the bar in his Fifth Avenue home, complete with a brass rail and Venus perched on a shell, her charms repeated in a shining mirror. "I didn't know of this place, Mr. Baruch," stammered General Pershing. "Do you think I could get a card?" [41]

He was taking a moderate interest in New York community activities. He joined neighbors in opposition to the opening of West 52nd Street to business, but when the protest failed sold his house there and bought one on Fifth Avenue. He joined his golfing partner, Fred Edey, in helping build a new and beautiful clubhouse on Long Island. Of this, Edey wrote that the patrons fully realized that Baruch had made the club possible.[42]

Something else that exerted all its old fascination over Baruch was mining. Threaded through the list of his many securities are the romantic names — the Treadwell Gold Mining Company, the Vulcan Mining and Smelting and Refining Corporation, the Ivory Coast Group of French West Africa, in which he lost $8000, Pardners Mines — and the names of the mine shafts themselves: Pine Tree Tunnel, North-South Drift, and Hell's Hollow Dam. But of them all it was Alaska Juneau, of which its tenacious president, Fred W. Bradley, had every right to be proud, even if he did not make a cent. If he could salvage Juneau, Baruch thought, it would be one of the world's greatest mining operations.[43]

Far in the desolate North, the open-cut gold mine Alaska Juneau lay slashed against a mountainside across the Gastineau Channel. Years earlier, Bradley had brought it to Baruch's attention, and a very promising estimate of its prospects was turned in by mine engineer Dan Jackling in the spring of 1915. Financial journals had reported an issue of 400,000 shares of Alaska Juneau at $10 a share, to which was affixed the pertinent footnote: "All stock not taken by public subscription will be taken by Eugene Meyer, Jr., and Bernard M. Baruch." With this expression of confidence, the public felt secure and oversubscribed the issue five times, at which the stock rose to $15. Baruch's hopes, however, spiraled in the opposite direction. He was conscience-stricken that he had indirectly sponsored a stock flotation, for things at the mine were not well. The gold turned out to be of such low grade that it was not worth taking out of the ground unless a low-cost method of extraction could be found.

Soon the money was gone, and with it public confidence. In a single year the stock dropped to 7¾, then to 2, then to 1⅛. Bradley held on. And William H. Crocker of San Francisco, Ogden Mills, Bradley himself, and Eugene Meyer, Jr., gamely put up and saw absorbed three million more. To this seemingly ill-fated enterprise, Baruch had lent not only his name, but the most money he had ever sunk into the ground.

In his Wall Street office, Baruch pored over pictures, charts, visualized the whole backbreaking, soul-wearing scene. In 1921 the bondholders were about to foreclose, when things suddenly looked better. It was a personal triumph for Bradley.[44] Perhaps never had a single mine more challenged the ingenuity of modern man. If one difficulty was conquered, a dozen more sprang up to replace it. Then slowly Alaska Juneau began to show a profit — on eighty cents worth of gold in a ton of ore! It would have been madness to have tackled such masses of rock a decade before, without the aid of modern mining methods. Yet by 1930 all debts were paid off. In the black rock-bottom of the depression year of 1931, the first profits were made.

Less satisfactorily resolved was Baruch's attempt at a mining venture with Winston Churchill. Enchanted over the prospects in Rhodesia for development of porphyry copper, Baruch suggested a kind of British-American partnership for its development through the aid of the American Smelting and Refining Company.

Perhaps this savored too much to Churchill of America's Mexican enterprises. At any rate, he cabled back that British interests would be willing to cooperate — if the metal was to be refined in English refineries or, at least, refineries built on British soil.

To this Baruch responded with a pomp worthy of Churchill himself. Why quibble as to details? Back and forth across the Atlantic shuttled the cables — whether control by· syndicate or control by managerial voice would be preferable, and so on, but in the end no agreement was reached at all.[45] To Baruch this had been one of the last chances for adventure.

Yet mining was still as fascinating a gamble as the spin of a roulette wheel. In 1936, for instance, fabulous old Virginia City had dwindled to a ghost town of under 100 inhabitants, wild horses cropping the grass in the empty streets, lamps throwing eerie shadows over the false fronts of the empty saloons, and wind whining down the deserted mine shafts. Yet, in the Second World War with the search

on for new metals, prospectors in sweaty Stetsons and mired boots
again pounded the plank sidewalks; the saloons roared; and the sun-
scorched houses vibrated to new life. Old Goldfield, where Baruch
had journeyed in the last of his youth, was still deserted, but George
Wingfield, the buckaroo, had become Nevada's first citizen, his
Getchell Mines yielding up much gold and his fortunes spiraling
upward.[46]

Baruch's railroad ambitions, too, died hard; he was still dreaming
that one day he might own a railroad. In 1925 he abortively tried to
break into the Baltimore and Ohio, seeking something to absorb his
energies for twenty more years. He was attracted by the New York
Central, which he thought was potentially very profitable, but his
associates were afraid, and he could not go it alone.[47] Two years
later, he was wondering if the old Savannah and Atlanta, then in
the hands of a receiver, could be purchased. Could not a consolidation be arranged, linking Charlotte, Gastonia, Spartanburg and Greenwood with the Savannah and Atlanta? He wondered what would
be a reasonable price for the Norfolk and Southern, the Georgia and
Florida, and the Savannah and Atlanta.[48] But little came of all this.

To please his old colleague Daniel Willard, Baruch finally accepted
a position on the board of directors of the Baltimore and Ohio, and
thus drained off some of his surplus ambitions for railroad empire. In
Baruch, Willard found a willing ally, a "working director" who
yearned to make the railroad a valuable public utility, rather than
merely profitable.[49] In 1928 Willard urged him to use his influence
with Congress toward the passage of certain bills for the consolidation of rail lines,[50] and in 1931 Baruch used his pull to induce some
lost business to be returned. He served until 1932, when he resigned
upon his appointment to the National Transportation Committee.

Nor were his stocks and bonds entirely uninteresting to him.
Throughout his life, when at his New York office, twice or thrice or
even half a dozen times a day, a call would come from his broker.
At one time or another, he seems to have dabbled in everything from
Southern cottonseed oil to the Condé Nast publications, Hibernia
Bank stock of Birmingham, State of Idaho bonds, the Central Argen-
tine Railway Company, the City of Budapest Gold Bonds, bonds of
the Georgia and Florida railroads, of Durham and Winston-Salem,
Chelsea and Yonkers, Warner Brothers Pictures, Wesson Oil, Lea
Fabrics, Florsheim Shoes, the Royal Baking Company, the Yellow

Cab Corporation, State of Ohio bonds, McCrary stores, Bethlehem Steel, and Manhattan Railway. Unsuccessfully, he even sought an interest in the Coca-Cola Company. This might seem a grab-bag assortment to casual eyes, but not to Baruch's. He mused over his holdings (for which he had a telephone code of fruit and flowers), choosing and rejecting with the same shrewd caution which led him to scold a friend who had paid too much for a seat on the Exchange, for which Baruch had advanced the funds.[51] In reference to the oil business, he wrote a friend that he kept out of that because he never made any money in it.[52]

What else could absorb him? Well, he could muse over the lessons of modern war and of the illusory peace. In his first book, published in 1920 and entitled *The Making of the Reparation and Economic Sections of the Treaty*, he had written in an ungarnished but effective style which amazed friends who thought of him only as a practical man of affairs.[53]

Now he took up his pen again to report on the activities of the War Industries Board and the lessons that America might learn from the First World War. The book, entitled *American Industry in the War: A Report of the War Industries Board*, was issued as a government document in 1921, with an enlarged and revised edition published by Prentice-Hall in 1941.[54]

But Baruch did not continue to think of the past. The problems which arose there were carrying over into the new era. What was to become of sixty million Germans, crowded into their cramped territory, with the new mark at eighty to the dollar, children and old people enfeebled by four years of war dying day by day, universities closing, the middle class being wiped out — Baruch thought of those things and of his own kinfolk in that stricken and seething country. "Hunger is the firebrand of revolution," Senator Robert La Follette declared. Hell was "let loose in Germany." [55]

Would war come again? What of Hitler, the "strong man of Bavaria," as *Time* Magazine called him, with his proclamation of a day coming when the whole German people would be called upon "to free our country." The world laughed as "Chancellor Hitler" fired a volley of shots into a beer-hall ceiling and proclaimed himself the redeemer of Germany. But was his arrest the end? Adolf Hitler, so *Time* forecast, would still "continue to be a force to be reckoned with." [56] In Baruch's scrapbook was an account of the German "ultra-fascist movement," "der Tag," when the house would be cleaned "mercilessly of Socialists and Jews," and of the coming declaration of war on France. The Germans blamed "Barney Baruch" and other Jews for the last war. Now they wanted "to start a new war — the sooner the better." [57]

For two decades Baruch watched the rising storm signals. America must make ready its "engine of aggressive defense" for future wars. There must be a leader, "a civilian, of such repute as will secure for him the spontaneous recognition of the industry with which he is to deal," wrote Baruch, looking at the future with a clearer eye than most, and he continued: "We are of the common belief that war ought to be avoided, if possible, but that we must plan in such a way that, if war comes, we shall meet the enemy with our maximum effectiveness, with the least possible injury and violence to our people, and in a manner which shall avoid inflation and waste" in "a death grapple between peoples and economic systems." The mobilized industry of America, he thought, would be "a weapon of offense or defense far more potent than anything the world has ever seen." [58]

No Constitutional amendment would be necessary. Things could not be planned in irrevocable detail far ahead of need. Things must be kept flexible.[59] As plans were revised the leaders of industry should be informed, and as they died, substitutes found, so there would always be a nucleus of leadership ready for any emergency.[60]

Thus, in time of peace, did Baruch follow the ancient maxim to prepare for war. The nineteen-twenties were tough years for preparedness, although still in the excitement of war's aftermath, Congress did enlarge on the National Defense Act of 1916, providing for an Army Industrial College and a Planning Board to study wartime mobilization of industry. But it was only in Baruch's annual lectures at the Industrial College, and at the Army War College, that he was sure of an attentive audience.

Over and over he voiced his precepts. He argued against the draft of recalcitrant industries. For who would buy a confiscated property under the threat of reconfiscation? Where could government find the highly trained specialists to run a complex industrial organism? He favored a scheme for business to operate industries but under close government supervision.[61]

Pre-eminent in his thinking was the inflationary, backbreaking cost

of modern war in an age when war and rumors of war had become
the normal way of living. If war could not be allayed, there could
at least be an easing of the unequal burdens of conflict. No person
should be able to profit from war.

There was a relentless sequence of events on the home front during armed conflict, Baruch pointed out: first, shortages, then competitive bidding by the great agencies of government (this latter to
be offset, Baruch trusted, by a ruling that only one division of the
War Department should buy any one needed item, and all prospective purchasers should channel their requests through it).[62]

Neither then nor later had Baruch any sympathy for the all-or-
nothing school, who protested that inflation could only be controlled
by stopping the war which was its basic cause. You could halt inflation by taking the unwarranted profits out of war. Furthermore,
whenever Congress should declare either war or the existence of a
war emergency, the President should be empowered to clamp on price
controls. In peacetime shortages, the highest bidders took all. In
major modern war, this could not be permitted.

Hence, Baruch advocated price control as a device against wartime
inflation, a doctrine that would become associated with his name.
Inflation was nothing new. The Bureau of Labor Statistics could
show an almost identical pattern of rising commodity prices during
the War Between the States, for instance. So Baruch pointed out:
"The obvious norm is the whole price structure as it existed on some
antecedent date near to the declaration of war on which the normal
operation of the natural law of supply and demand can be said to
have controlled prices. That determined, we need a method of freezing the whole price structure at that level." [63]

It was as simple as that, but, in all the ensuing years and all the
labyrinth of supports, controls, credit restrictions, and "voluntary
restrictions" from Pearl Harbor to Korea, the government economists
never fully accepted it. It was easier, as Baruch cynically observed, to
let the whole price structure run riot at the pleasure of the more
vociferous pressure groups — crushing the unrepresented and un-
recognized "General Public." Yet with the money supply tripled to
pay for the war, as happened in the Second World War, prices would
have tripled, had Baruch's theory not been applied at all.

But even years later, when the blitzkrieg was under way in Europe,
and Baruch was in Washington, struggling to resurrect something
like the old War Industries Board, the New Dealers were still afraid

that government would become "a tail to the businessmen's kite." Little heed was taken of Baruch's primary concept of centralized, responsible control. In fact, at first, it was deliberately avoided.[64]

More cogently than any American of his time, perhaps, Baruch knew the rules of modern economic war. However, not until the spring of 1930, with the voice of Hitler screaming and Japan moving against China, was a joint resolution passed by Congress to consider the equalizing of burdens in case of war and to report on recommended policies; the committee was also to ascertain if a Constitutional amendment would be necessary for the commandeering of private property, and for taking the profits out of war. Hearings were held in March, with Baruch appearing on the sixth to offer his testimony to Secretary of War Patrick J. Hurley, Secretary of the Navy Charles Francis Adams, and Senators Arthur H. Vandenberg, Claude A. Swanson, and Joseph T. Robinson. Little more was heard of the idea after the hearing.

Baruch's rules were based in part on America's own mistakes in the First World War, in part on the very real successes of the German military planners. It is a comic, or perhaps an ironic, footnote to history that it was the Nazis and not the Americans who during the blitzkrieg days of the nineteen-forties were to adapt Baruch's concepts of total mobilization to their own use.

Back in 1921, thoughts of a new war were over the horizon. On Inauguration Day, the parade moved down Pennsylvania Avenue, headed by a Negro drum major, aglitter with gold and kicking his feet. In the open presidential car, the shattered figure of Woodrow Wilson shrank almost visibly from the roaring crowd, as ruddy-faced Warren G. Harding smiled and waved. It was the end of an era, the beginning of an age. "Main Street" had come to Washington. "I face the future," Wilson had quipped, "with no apprehensions other than those occasioned by Mr. Harding's literary style." [65] But Bernard Baruch, no man for mystical prognostications, had nevertheless felt a chilling qualm of apprehension upon hearing that Harding would succeed Wilson in the White House. Which was the greater tragedy, he may well have wondered, the statesman with his work over, or the politician sinking into waters beyond his depth? "I can see but one word written over his head if they make him President," Baruch had said of Harding, "and that word is Tragedy." [66]

That Baruch gave "advice" to Harding was far more myth than

fact. Baruch saw the Chief Executive without illusions. He knew that he lacked the power of decision and courage, and although a kindly man and a good companion, he lacked the qualities of a good President. Yet Baruch, like so many others, pitied him.[67]

Baruch knew Harding. All Washington knew Harding, the joiner, the Babbitt, the "best of the second-raters," the small-town newspaperman who had not wanted to be President. "I will be mighty glad if I can come back to the Senate," was his answer when the Republican boss, Boies Penrose, in the summer of 1919 asked him how he "would like to be President." [68] Yet Harding was the name Penrose muttered in a coma a year later, as the party grappled in a deadlock; and when the word came to the nominee, he begged reporters of the *New York Times*, "God help me . . . Talk to God about me every day, and ask Him to give me strength." [69]

"Harding was an honest man,"[70] is the verdict of Herbert Hoover, who brought dignity and honor to the Harding cabinet, and in a sense it is true. Hoover also knew Harding, knew of the little Green House, headquarters of the "Ohio Gang"; knew of the Justice Department, "the Department of Easy Virtue"; knew, by hearsay at least, of the White House after business hours, "the air heavy with tobacco smoke . . . every imaginable brand of whiskey . . . cards and poker chips . . . a general atmosphere of . . . feet on the desk and spittoon alongside." [71] Yet, fundamentally, Harding was an honest man, and this was the tragedy. The frankness that led him to peer over a ghostwritten speech with the guileless confession, "Well, I never saw this before . . . and I don't believe what I just read," led Penrose to issue instructions not unlike those devised for the hapless William Henry Harrison nearly a hundred years earlier — "Keep Warren at home . . . If he goes out on a tour, somebody's sure to ask him questions, and Warren's just the sort of damn fool that will try to answer them." [72]

Harding had a bad heart when he took office. However, in Herbert Hoover's opinion it was not heart failure of which the President died, but heartbreak at his betrayal by friends.[73] Colonel Starling saw Harding's face go white, his hands fall limp, as the Secret Service chief handed him the first intimations of the breaking oil scandal. Almost breathlessly, he stammered: "I am glad you brought it to me. It is something that I should know." According to Hoover, he then worried himself to death.[74]

To Baruch President Harding wrote: "Please be assured I write you just as cordially now as I was impelled to write when you remembered me as a Senator." [75] For all his weaknesses, he sought only to do good. At the time of his death, history gave him credit for his personal efforts to end the twelve-hour day in steel.[76] He had called the Washington Disarmament Conference; he had laid the "evil spirits, aroused by war," with "the healing quality of gentleness." [77] Yet he died, his "soul seared by a great disillusionment." It was his tragedy to be remembered as "the only President who neither in public nor private ever gave utterance to . . . an idea." [78] It was a time for greatness, and the greatness was not there.

Harding was the President of the twenties, of the jazz age and whoopee, of the Ziegfeld Follies, and 10,000 mourners at a gang chief's funeral, champagne cocktails at $25 apiece, of the 21 Club and William Handy and the Blues, of Harlem and Nigger Heaven, Freud and Fitzgerald, and the sign put up by the dear old lady living in a brownstone house: "This Is Not an Illicit Resort." [79] It was the time of flaming youth, and youth flamed, although Bernard Baruch must have come up with a start when the winners of the National American Dancing Contest in Madison Square Garden were not a flapper and her sheik, but his own forty-one-year-old brother and his wife, Mr. and Mrs. Sailing Baruch.[80]

Baruch himself was not too old or staid for an occasional evening of fun on the town. Flanked by such friends as little Billy Rose, he might move sometimes into that maelstrom of café society where Texas Guinan was queen and an evening for five could cost $1300, with "real roses" at $5 each and, for the lady, a $5 "baby doll." [81]

But the nineteen-twenties were far more than hip flasks and jazz babies. This was the era of the Scopes Trial and the Jovelike dome of Bryan, gleaming as if oiled under the Tennessee sun. It was Teapot Dome, which *Time* dismissed as a "public lynching" of the Republicans by the Democrats.[82] It was the court-martial of Billy Mitchell, whose "wild, nonfeasible schemes" had "betrayed the faith of the American people"; it was the tirades of Vice-President Charles G. Dawes against senatorial filibusters. It was "Uncle Joe" Cannon, retiring at eighty-six as Speaker of the House after forty-six years of service; and Borah, in his "isolated grandeur . . . politically the strongest man west of the Mississippi." [83]

Main Street America, rural America, was still the America of all the little towns huddled behind the rock-framed coves of Maine, or below the great dusty winds and empty clouds of the prairies, or around a red-clay crossroads, a sagging courthouse and a Confederate statue, young as the weary "Johnny Rebs" below were old. In all the little dusty towns life went on much as it had a generation or two before, and as it would still be going on twenty or thirty years later. The Women's Guilds met, and the Handiworkers; the missionary boxes were packed for Africa or India or the benighted children of the hills of Tennessee and Kentucky. There were the Grange and New England Town Meetings and church suppers, tables loaded with baked ham, baked beans, scalloped potatoes, baked peas, pickles and piccalilli, six kinds of cake and five kinds of pie. When the small-town public libraries opened on Saturday afternoons, the call was for Harold Bell Wright and Gene Stratton Porter. Across the country, from Maine to Indiana to Swaney's Branch, South Carolina, small boys were still growing up, learning to fish and reciting "Horatius at the Bridge" or "The Death of Benedict Arnold" at the country school declamations, scouring the town and nearby farms for loose gates, wagons, and barrels to touch off in the annual bonfire as the crackers and big guns boomed out the Glorious Fourth. Then, and thirty years later, there were still country auctions and county fairs and hose-laying contests of the volunteer fire companies. If in New York it was the hip flask and the rumble-seat convertible, in the crossroads towns all across America, boys still snuggled their girls and a jug of cider in a load of hay.[84]

Corny — sentimental — small-town stuff, jeered the sophisticates. Yet in the nineteen-twenties the farm and the small town were still the living and dying place for the great majority of Americans, and the birthplace of millions more. Basically, America was still a rural civilization with rural depths and rural narrowness, and the small-town code was the American code. If the temper of a time is measured not by the few who proclaimed it, but by the many who lived it, then the speak-easies and the country clubs of the twenties, all the whoop-de-do from New York to Paris to London, were but foam on the crest of a great wave that rose and broke, little different in essence from those that came after or before.

Mrs. Calvin Coolidge was knitting a bedspread with ten balls of yarn. And although the radio was still a jangling crackle of static, a nation peered eagerly at headlines telling that the county commissioners had ordered the snowplows to keep open the straggling dirt road between Ludlow and Plymouth, Vermont, so that a President of the United States might visit his ailing father.[85]

Not the jazz baby but Calvin Coolidge was the real symbol of the nineteen-twenties in America. For "the little fellow," as the White House Secret Service staff affectionately called him, half owl, half elf, wandering bewilderedly through the corridors in his galluses and baggy underwear,[86] was somehow the prototype of the average, middle-aged, small-town American who had come out of the nineteenth century to seek answers.

Americans liked to read of how the President entertained his breakfast visitors by "saucering his coffee" and setting it down for the cat, or how, a few days before his inauguration, he was discovered putting a black cat into a crate with a rooster, "just to see what would happen." They liked the picture of stark little Plymouth, Vermont, the five sun-bleached houses around the crossroads store where the President was born; and the picture of the President himself, sworn into office by the light of an oil lamp; Coolidge reminiscing of his mother, or lifting his eyes to the maple tree and the blue hills. "He slipped back into the life at Plymouth as easily as if he had never left there," one observer said. He never had.[87]

The people liked his peaceful platitudes no less than his homespun common sense. "It will be well," advised the man from Plymouth, "not to be too much disturbed by the thought of either isolation or entanglement . . . America," he intoned, with small comfort for the fearful, war-ridden masses of Europe, "seeks no earthly empire but the favor of Almighty God." [88]

Pronouncements such as these must have offered small comfort also to Bernard Baruch, whose sophisticated mind appreciated complexities that could not be reduced to the values of the small town. Nor was he carried away by the false materialistic prosperity that glittered around him. Yet he knew that Coolidge personally was an honest, simple man whose basic virtues had won the people. In retrospect, Baruch felt that Coolidge fitted his times.[89]

Although against the hullabaloo of the twenties the man from Plymouth stood etched with the certainty of a steel engraving, Baruch could still doubt whether such an unexceptional man, be his name Harding or Coolidge, was equipped for the White House. However, Coolidge did have a saving grace, a receptivity to advice, all

the more disarming when coupled with his frank admission that
economic and social questions were confusing to him. He and Baruch
met at a Washington luncheon during Coolidge's Vice-Presidency.
Baruch's attention was instantly drawn to the quiet man who
looked so young for his years and had a shy glint of amusement in his
eyes.

After Coolidge was sworn in as President, Baruch offered his assistance to the newcomer. From his years with Wilson, he knew
something of the strain of being President.[90] With the wry and wary
New Englander he wooed his way with ducks, and followed up a
White House dinner invitation with a gift of birds from Hobcaw.

Baruch never forgot his first actual interview. Peering down a
White House corridor, he saw Coolidge, a cigar box in his hand. A
jerk of his head indicated that Baruch was to follow him; once inside
the study, Coolidge himself knelt down and lit the fire. He held out
the box. Would Mr. Baruch have a cigar?

Conversation began. Baruch later recalled that most of the President's comments on the political situation seemed to be addressed
to the dog at his feet. But before the interview was finished, Baruch
felt the new President's warmth and sympathy.

They got down to business: "Mr. Baruch, you are a patriot?"

"Yes," Baruch answered. "I claim that I am."

The President then explained that he needed Baruch's help in the
settlement of the Italian debt question. "I need Democratic support
in the Senate. Will you help me . . . ?"

Baruch would and did. In the end, he rounded up twenty-seven
Democratic votes — at a period when Democrats were scarce enough,
even in full strength — to vote for the White House program.

It was in this period, too, during a poker game with Arthur Krock
and Herbert Bayard Swope, that a call was announced from the
White House at the precise moment when Bernard Baruch was in the
hole.

"Mr. Baruch, the President of the United States wants you on the
phone."

Baruch glanced up. Was this some joke of Krock's or Swope's to
garner their winnings? He looked down at his cards. "Tell the
President of the United States to go to hell," he allegedly said.

While Baruch was still running behind, another call was announced, this time from Secretary of the Treasury Andrew Mellon.

The message was the same. So was the answer. Not until the next day did Baruch discover that the President of the United States and the Secretary of the Treasury had indeed wanted him and that there was no joke about the calls from Washington.[91]

In January 1926, Baruch sent the White House, as requested, a memorandum pointing out that complete wartime industrial mobilization could be accomplished in four months. But he warned sharply against any sudden disarmament. Mere removal of weapons would not remove the incentive to fight. Peace could only be assured by removal of the causes of war.[92] For these observations, Coolidge offered "sincere thanks for your help," [93] and soon signed Baruch's commission as a member of the United States Commission for the two-hundreth celebration of the birthday of George Washington.

In an upper corridor of the White House one day, Coolidge cornered Baruch and offered him an important job,* but Baruch refused, saying that the President should keep it for a "worthy" Republican.

Not until six years later, with the burdens of the Presidency laid down, did real intimacy arise between Baruch and Coolidge. And then Baruch came to value him as a rare friend if not as a great President. They were serving together on the National Transportation Committee, and to his complete amazement, Coolidge authorized Baruch to use his name freely, without consulting him, in preparing findings.[94]

The Transportation group, meeting in the early thirties, achieved more publicity than solid accomplishment, although their recommendations as to the need for a sweeping consolidation of the railroads and the fierce competitiveness of trucks and buses struck straight to the heart of the railroad problem. Baruch favored no artificial respiration for railroads that should never have been built, and looked to the interests of the country as a whole, rather than to one particular branch of transportation. The natural law of change could not be denied; and the transportation question should be faced as an engineering problem. The rivers were not going to dry up, nor the highways be abandoned. He would concede that the automotive

* Baruch has forgotten just what this post was. It may possibly have involved Coolidge's plan to send him and Dwight Morrow on a mission to China, which was called off when it was decided that there was no Chinese government responsible enough to deal with.

industry should have a fair tax, and that no heavier burden should be laid on railroads. The final report, as submitted in the fall of 1932, won mixed comment, but two years later Baruch received a letter reading: "The whole railroad system of the United States has undergone a marked change for the better during the past year, largely as the result of steps taken following the report of the Committee . . . It is really remarkable how closely the recommendations of the Committee have been adopted, or are in process of being enacted into law." [95]

Alfred E. Smith was also on the Committee, and when one day he observed that the rooms in which they met were originally occupied by the American Association Against the Prohibition Amendment, Coolidge drawled that they could be disinfected. [96]

Baruch's political interests, his yen for public service, were reflected in his support of the Institute of Politics at Williams College in Massachusetts. The idea had appealed to him when broached by President Harry A. Garfield, and so, anonymously, Baruch contributed annual sums close to $25,000. In fact, the first three years' expenses of the Institute were borne by Baruch, entirely. Both the generosity and the anonymity were characteristic. [97]

Like John C. Calhoun, Baruch was convinced that politics was a science, with rules and rote like any other, and so intimately related to man's everyday living that no topic was of more importance. Therefore the work of the Institute appealed to him. Baruch further helped by suggesting old friends like Hugh Frayne and Samuel Gompers for special lectures, and even tried to get Clemenceau. He sought no tangible reward but, postponing his annual trip to Europe in the summer of 1923, was much moved as he received from the college an honorary degree of Doctor of Laws. [98] As the Great Depression closed down over the American campus, Baruch fought off his discouragement over the alumni's inability to make the Institute permanent. At least, they had blazed a trail. [99]

All these diverse activities provided no real outlet for Baruch's tumultuous energies, and the most alluring prize of all dangled always and forever beyond him. Not *every* American boy could dream of growing up to become President. A man past eighty, seated on the portico of Hobcaw Barony, looking through the white columns to the impersonal sweep of Winyah Bay beyond, Baruch once murmured wistfully, "I could have been President of the United States — if I had not been a Jew." [100]

Whether or not he was right, he thought he was. The fact is, his being a Jew may have provided a comfortably satisfying excuse for his not becoming President. It was true that he had emerged as a key man in the Wilson Era, that even former President Theodore Roosevelt hailed him as the most able man in the Administration.[101] Baruch believed also that Al Smith could have been President had he not been a Catholic. But in 1928, as in 1936, the people were not prone to shoot Santa Claus. The prosperity of the twenties was Republican prosperity; it is doubtful that any Democrat could have been elected in the wave of "normalcy." As for Baruch he had other strikes against him. "The Sidewalks of New York," for all their limitations, undeniably had more political appeal than Wall Street, and although Baruch may have emerged from the war a key man to those in the know, he was no hero to the average, hard-shooting, narrow-thinking, small-town doughboy, who cursed the "foreign" ammunition he was given to use, and looked, in vain, for American weapons that never came. Justly or unjustly, Baruch bore much of the blame for this deficiency, and was still blamed by the veterans a generation and more afterwards.

Furthermore, in these early years, Baruch lacked the platform presence of his maturity. He lacked the magnetic power which bound an audience to Eisenhower or Franklin D. Roosevelt.[102] His genius was as a man-to-man behind-the-scenes manipulator and negotiator, although this too may have been the result of a natural timidity and a disinclination to submit himself to the open blast of office. In this sense, at least, the fact of his being a Jew counted. It reinforced a natural tendency; it may, indeed, have been the primary cause of it. And the outbursts of Henry Ford during this period must have confirmed all of Baruch's worst fears.

Ford, like Baruch, personified the American dream — the man who put a continent on wheels. Ford was the prophet of the Peace Ship and the bigot of the race riots, the nonsmoking, nondrinking Henry Ford, the small-town American with a one-track mind and one idea, the man who looked for God and found Him on the assembly line.

He had looked for God and found success, and a whole continent watched him. He had the opinions of the cracker barrel and the billions of modern technocracy. Hard work, he would prate, was the key to success, and in the Ford plant men worked. Good wages were his reward for the men who put nut 14 on bolt 132, repeating, repeating, repeating, until their hands shook and their legs quivered — no time for talk, no time for laughter, three minutes for the toilet — emerging finally to doze in the streetcars on the way home, hands jerking in reflex, and brains wakening into the fear that they would "go crazy." Above the gleaming smokestacks and mountains of pig iron, a gigantic water tank shouted the name FORD across the flatness of the prairie country, "the most dramatic sight on the planet . . . the most complete ugliness in America." It was symbolic. This was the Frankenstein monster created by a rural Protestant American who dreamed of the little red schoolhouse and the Wayside Inn, never realizing that it was his own lumbering masses of metal that turned the prairie into villages and the villages into towns.[103] "War is nothing but preparedness," he declared. "No boy would ever kill a bird if he didn't first have a slingshot." [104] He wanted to "crush militarism and stop wars for all time." He had wanted the "boys" out of the "murder ditches" by the Fourth of July, and so he had sailed on his Peace Ship, this "apostle of peace," while his plants manufactured at profit weapons "for the general extermination of humanity." [105]

The tragedy of Henry Ford was indeed the tragedy of his troubled time, of the decent, rural, and small-town American who went questing after false gods. It was personified in Ford, the long, shambling figure with the angular features that reminded some of Abraham Lincoln. Where had it gone — that peaceful, idyllic nineteenth century? Why were men still troubled, with the great god Success enthroned? Ford struck out, blindly, against those who for centuries had borne the burden of the world's ills — the "chosen people."

For if Ford represented the confusions of the first quarter of the twentieth century, Baruch represented its certainties. Baruch faced the world realistically; he sought no one to blame. Instead he sought a philosophy for the new times, looking beyond individual enrichment toward the over-all improvement of all the people, in terms of the new technocracy. Mankind could never go back, and new moral values must be found to meet new challenges.

Baruch had had no quarrel with Ford. Indeed, in the summer of 1918 he had written him that he was delighted that Ford was going to run for the Senate, words he came much to regret in later years. Yet, in the spirit of that Christianity which Ford's intolerance would deny to him, his later estimate of the manufacturer was that he seemed only able to make sense in his own field.[106]

In 1920 Ford launched his Paper Pogrom, which did by words "what Nazi Germany was to do a decade later." [107] Across the masthead of his newspaper ran the banner line: "The Dearborn Independent is Henry Ford's own paper and he authorizes every statement occurring therein" — an admission little mitigated by his apologies seven years later when he was about to bring out a new car, or by his continual protests that he was only trying to tell the Jews wherein they had gone wrong, and to bring God to them.

The Jews, charged this "incredibly ignorant billionaire," were engaged in a mass conspiracy to control the country and the world. Jews were responsible for liquor, short skirts, white slavery, and the failing banks in the farm areas. Jews controlled the movie industry, sugar, cotton, the packing and shoe industries, grain, jewelry, loan companies, and the theaters, charges which many poverty-stricken Jews may only have wished were true.

Bernard Baruch was Ford's bull's-eye. Frenziedly, in his series on "The Scope of Jewish Dictatorship in the United States," he railed at Baruch's wartime control over men, munitions, and materials as power "far too great to be vested in a Jew." On November 7, 1920, he charged that Baruch had permitted his friends to profiteer; on December 11, he unveiled his "exposé" of the "Jewish Copper Kings," terming Bernard Baruch "the most powerful man in the world." Baruch during the war actually had no copper holdings at all.[108]

Banner headlines screamed Baruch's name. Baruch read the charges in his office one morning, then went home. He found his wife broken, shaken, his daughters crying. Bitterness came over him and an overpowering sense of helplessness — because of what Ford was, and what those dear to him had to endure. It was not for himself that he suffered.

Through the years he had reached a philosophy that men born into a certain set of circumstances were apt to take it for granted. As he said, "Usually, you are born into your religion. You're born into your politics . . . if you're of a minority group, you're conditioned to certain surroundings . . . There are certain protections nature provides and I've had a long life to get them." Yet, even to him, the trial had come painfully and suddenly at adolescence, before he had the "protective conditioning." [109]

Of Ford personally he would take no notice.[110] But he could not ignore the lying charge that he had profited by the sufferings of his fellow citizens and the slaughter of young men during the war. When he went to Washington in 1917 he had disposed of his interests that might have profited from the war. In the depression of 1921 he could have regained millions, but he did not care to do so. At the Paris Peace Conference all his personal expenses he had paid himself. In Paris he had used his own car; in Washington, paid his own office rent, the salary of his clerks, and the telephone bills. He could show all his private papers, account for the disposition of every penny.

But the charge had been made. Baruch might dream, but it was Henry Ford who had real hopes of becoming President of the United States — an ambition not then nearly so ridiculous as it seems in perspective. For "the people" wanted Ford, the bigots, the Klansmen, the small-town "rugged individualists," victims of the crushing forces of mass industrialism, who struck out blindly — they knew not against whom or why. And Ford's candidacy was serious enough to be taken as a threat by leaders who saw him topping popularity polls far ahead of either Harding or McAdoo. All the political crowned heads could do was to trust to the common sense of the common people, give the prophet of the Tin Lizzie enough rope with which to hang himself — which eventually he did — and let him have a fine time telling how "the Jews had started the Great War and all other wars," and "how he would run the country." [111]

The net result of the Ford campaign was to lose the Democratic Party and, incidentally, the country, the open services of Bernard Baruch, and, indirectly at least, to drive him into the backstage role he was thereafter to play. Baruch denies this. That he neither then nor later sought elective office he said, is because he never wanted anything for himself. He would not go into direct politics because he would not tell the lies the politicians have to tell. "They have to win elections," he has commented. "I won't talk politics when I know something is ethically or morally wrong. I'm for what decency demands, not for what expedience demands." He could not "play politics." He believed in the party system, but not in sacrificing his country for his party. "I could not be political in all things." [112]

Baruch may have been rationalizing here, but undoubtedly these were among the reasons he did not seek direct political office. Then, too, there was the fact that as his own particular role evolved he could and did exert a unique power. In the twenties, he did play with the idea of becoming chairman of the Democratic National Committee, but here also he was kept back by the Jewish issue as well as by his reluctance to assume political leadership.[113] The hurt had gone too deep.

In bitterness, he sympathized with a young friend rejected for a position in a bigoted small town, simply because he was a Jew.[114] He was unmoved by Mark Sullivan's protestations that the anti-Semitism was not directed against people like Baruch, that it was primarily an anti-immigration feeling, that he should be less sensitive.[115] But Baruch did not want to be the exceptional Jew among the Gentiles, to be the only Jewish member of a golf club, for instance. Hence he found small comfort in Herbert Bayard Swope's report of his unprecedented election to the Turf and Field Club.[116] Above all, he did not want anyone to hurt his family through him.[117]

It was not anti-Semitism alone but the whole temper of the time that disheartened Baruch. Of what value was able leadership if the hearts of the people were tainted? He wrote to the great Kansas editor, William Allen White, who had been fighting greed and ignorance for years whenever it made its ugly appearance. When he considered what the public was told — that statesmen were corrupt, business self-seeking, that the war was brought on by "the interests," that Catholics and Jews ran the country — Baruch had little wonder at their fanatic hatreds.[118]

As for politics — Baruch found himself continually consulted.[119] More and more people were coming to him; more and more finding out what the War Industries Board members had long since found out, that you could admire Baruch for more things than his money.[120] Annually one hundred and fifty of the nation's top business and scientific leaders, "at no small cost of time and money," gathered in New York, as Herbert Bayard Swope pointed out, "animated almost solely by a desire to pay tribute to you." [121] Baruch was the bond that held together "graduates" of the old War Industries Board. Grosvenor Clarkson, the Board historian, confessed his admiration to Baruch himself, because of "the Chief's" vitally wide range of human interests, but perhaps most of all because of the personal sacrifices he made for the war effort.[122] Herbert Bayard Swope quoted another admirer of Baruch: "I have an intense admiration for that gentleman's mentality. He does things, he doesn't talk all the time . . . he understands politics down to the ground and up to the skies, and that's the sort of man we ought to have as President of the United States." [123]

He could not be President. He could not even be chairman of the Democratic National Committee. Yet it was inevitable that he should be embroiled in politics. In spite of his clear understanding of the abuse, vilification, and misinterpretations of political life, there were some who understood what he was trying to do. One of them, Gavin McNab of California, saw in Baruch one of the few men in the East with a comprehensive view of the whole country.[124] The example and the cause of Woodrow Wilson had forever molded his thinking. With all the Southerner's zest for a lost cause, he took up the cudgels at the lowest ebb of Democratic fortunes after the debacle of 1920. The tide of party power had receded state by state, until only the "solid South" was left, and that under the leadership of old-style Southern demagogues like South Carolina's Cole Blease, who was against everything Baruch believed in.[125]

It was virtually impossible to get money, even enough to keep open the doors of the National Committee in Washington. As for "angels," the party had almost none. But Baruch insisted that he would stay on in the Democratic Party and try to make it the progressive, liberal party.[126] He would live to see the battle "won," but the winnings were not what he thought of as liberal and progressive back in the early twenties. He would live to see the party go beyond him, and the Republicans reach the goals that he had set for the Democrats more than a generation before.

Meanwhile, inside "the family," the Democratic Party itself, he indulged in strong language. There were reasons for the low state of party strength. It was no wonder that people would not give money to a party run mostly by second-raters. Unless the party organization was given a complete overhauling and new and honest men put in control, things would not improve.[127]

More than a mere desire for a house-cleaning fanned Baruch's interest in the Democratic cause. A forecast of the balloting in the Democratic convention of 1924 appeared in the *New York Times Magazine* in May. Of a total of 1098 votes, 371 were pledged to Governor Alfred E. Smith of New York and 542 to William G. McAdoo of California. In a showdown, it was forecast, many of the unpledged votes would drift to the New Yorker. McAdoo had no "reserve strength," and with the two-thirds rule, a count of 732 would be required to nominate him. Where would the additional 190 votes be found? McAdoo had few supporters in the Eastern delegations; even if nominated, it was believed he could not carry the Eastern states in the election. Four hundred delegates, enough to cost him the two-thirds majority, were openly against him. On the other hand, there was no majority for Smith. Deadlock was forecast by the political prognosticators.[128]

McAdoo was troubled by neither forecasts nor prognosticators. He charged out of the West symbolically waving a ten-gallon Stetson and two six-shooters. He seemed to some like a frontier highwayman raiding a bank.[129] The "crown prince," Wilson's "heir-apparent," the press called him — now that Wilson was not available for contradiction. And McAdoo believed it. For him, "the call" had come. No man in our history ever wanted the Presidency more than William G. McAdoo — despite his too fervent protests: "I don't care two straws about the Presidency." If he consulted his own happiness and that of his wife and children, he would not consider it for an instant. No, he insisted, he was impelled by "the same high sense of duty that makes a man volunteer to fight in the trenches for his country and to give his life, if need be." [130] No man who ever wanted the Presidency as much as McAdoo ever won it.

Almost alone among key political figures in the East, Baruch had been quietly sponsoring the McAdoo candidacy. From the first he had difficulty in holding "Mac" in check; and the candidate wrote Baruch a significant sentence in the spring of 1922, "I agree with you fully that it is better for me not to speak at this time." [131] But he saw no reason why Baruch should be sensitive about trying to capture the Democratic machine in his interest.

For a year Baruch struggled to keep the covers on his overeager candidate. He contributed thousands to the McAdoo campaign chest, but dared not give more. On May 18, 1923, Josephus Daniels wrote Baruch that when McAdoo's friends urged him to announce his candidacy he replied that "you had not thought it wise." Within a month, however, the secret was out; the impetuous Westerner could no longer be contained; and Baruch was writing Carter Glass that he favored the Californian.[132]

Baruch had no illusions as to McAdoo's capabilities. He knew his friend was no Wilson, yet he had Wilson's drive, the fanatic, god-

driven intensity of the Scotch-Irish Covenanter. To Baruch, Mc-
Adoo's fighting qualities had great appeal, as well as his efficiency and
executive ability. He would not let his party flout him as the Republicans had flouted Coolidge. He seemed to Baruch without doubt
the best man in the race.[133]

Then came the blow. Amidst the stench of Teapot Dome, the Republicans saw their chance to wreck a potential threat — and did it.
McAdoo, it was revealed, after he was no longer in an official position, had been retained as counsel by Edward L. Doheny, to whom
Secretary Fall had leased the Elk Hills oil reserves under scandalous
circumstances. The story broke in the winter of 1924 on the heels of
an impressive series of McAdoo primary victories, and in the clamor
the name of McAdoo was dragged in the oily filth. This was but a
week after Baruch had congratulated himself that amidst all the mess
of the oil scandals not a single smirch had been put upon the Wilson
Administration. Now it was hinted that McAdoo had profited hugely,
and although the charge was untrue, the damage was done. Baruch
was appalled — convinced that Doheny had involved McAdoo deliberately. The Republicans had achieved their objective, but Mc-
Adoo himself was so convinced of his integrity that Baruch reserved
judgment until he heard his side.[134]

McAdoo and Baruch met, finally, in Roper's office. There Mc-
Adoo told his story: that, after all, a lawyer was not responsible for
the morals of his clients; that nothing had happened, except that he,
as a successful lawyer, had undertaken business for a successful operator and had handled it so successfully as to receive a large fee. He
listened, unhearing, to Baruch's advice — an idea originally put forward by Arthur Krock. Baruch urged McAdoo to tell the investigating
committee of Congress that he was appearing before them to fulfill
a duty to himself, then offer to withdraw as a presidential candidate,
to fulfill his duty to the party. He should offer to go into the rear
ranks and fight for the cause. "If you do that, Mac, you'll get nominated." [135] But McAdoo paid no heed. "Damn 'em, I'm strong and
determined and if they kill me it won't be because I am spineless or
afraid of them." His determination was to hold Baruch in the fight
"and to fight forty times harder than I ever did before to down those
damned scoundrels and to . . . put back into control of the government the decent forms of morality, idealism and justice." [136]

Nevertheless, McAdoo's jig was up. Baruch's heart ached for him personally, not only for the pain the scandal had given him, but for the further price he would now have to pay.[137] Baruch decided to continue his backing of McAdoo, for he sincerely believed in his innocence and still admired his abilities. Meanwhile the candidate's optimism as to his chances was not undermined.[138]

However, nothing mattered now — not the wonderful ovations in McAdoo's native Georgia and adopted Tennessee, in Kentucky, Illinois, South Carolina, Wisconsin, Iowa, South Dakota, men cheering as he denounced the Ku Klux Klan, and in the background the white-sheeted brotherhood themselves cheering him on. According to Herbert Bayard Swope, the entire McAdoo movement in Texas had been taken over by Klan officials.[139]

If "Mac" was unavailable, who *was* available? The Democratic Party had a "cause": corruption, isolationism, high freight rates, and tariffs which had destroyed the farmer's market abroad and raised the cost of his supplies at home. But where was the candidate? There was Al Smith, of course, a meteoric figure of immigrant Irish stock, whose rise from the poverty of New York's Lower East Side had intrigued the imagination of a whole new generation of industrial-age voters. But nationally Smith was comparatively unknown. What appeal had he beyond the sidewalks of New York?

There was Franklin D. Roosevelt, an upstate Democrat and a Protestant, with the best trade name in America. Baruch had watched him from his early days as an assemblyman battling Tammany Hall: "that was the first sign we had the young man would fight." [140] As candidate for the Vice-Presidency, he had ridden out the shipwreck of James M. Cox's presidential hopes — Americans had liked his infectious grin, and all who heard him, his silvery eloquence. Here, perhaps, was the "coming man," and yet now he, who had been "one of the most graceful, vital, and handsome youths of his generation, spent hour after hour crawling over his library floor like a child," or dragging his dead weight upstairs inch by inch. Infantile paralysis had felled him. Now his mother and wife wrangled over his future while wry, gnome-like Louis McHenry Howe bustled through back corridors, arranging an appearance for Roosevelt here and a speaking engagement there, always with the stipulation that he must never be carried in the public view. But it was pretty generally agreed that Franklin D. Roosevelt's hopes, and the hopes of party leaders for him, were at an end.[141]

Not since Charleston in 1860, when the Democratic Party had sweated through sixty weary ballots and dissolved into its component parts, had there been a convention like this one in 1924. It was the North against the South, the city against the country, the East against the prairies — the low-water mark of the Democratic Party in the first half of the twentieth century, and yet its labor pains signaled the birth of a new era in party politics. However, not until more defeats would the politicos learn that the Democratic Party could not be a city party or a Southern party, but must be a coalition, united by a common desire for victory.

Madison Square Garden was a Turkish bath in that sweltering June of 1924. It seethed and steamed with heat, with sweating, close-packed bodies. It blared with the brass of bands, screeched with noise-making machines, and vibrated to music and "howlers." Baruch looked on with an interest he had not felt since 1912. On the rostrum, tall, handsome Cordell Hull of Tennessee dropped the gavel and shaped the seething pattern of delegates into order. Shortly afterward, he staggered and fell back. In the heat and noise, he had fainted.[142]

Keynote speaker Pat Harrison called the roll of Republican sins: Daugherty, Fall, the "two Secretaries of Oil." Hands, fans, handkerchiefs waved through the smoke and steam, and then the nominating speeches began. Snug in his headquarters, William G. McAdoo, confident Californian, was sure that all was "going bully." Exuberant cowboys exploded from their seats, stampeded through the aisles, as the professionals leaned back in boredom. Hull fainted again, and then again.

Delegates afterward remembered the little stir at the rear of the hall, the squeak of wheels and then the tap of crutches as Franklin Roosevelt swung himself out of his wheelchair, down the aisle, and up to the rostrum. The whole hall cheered and cheered, as all could cheer a man who was no longer a menace; all ranks closed, all bitterness was forgotten. They were not cheering for Al Smith, the "Happy Warrior," but for the man who put him in nomination — Roosevelt, with his upthrust chin and defiant grin, a warrior in battle against apparently hopeless odds. It was a "moment," one might have thought, that could never be repeated. Yet it was four years later in Houston that Roosevelt, on canes this time, again put Smith in nomination, and Will Durant wrote of him as he was then and as Baruch could have seen him in 1924 in simmering Madison Square Garden — "the finest man that has appeared at either convention . . . tall and proud even in suffering . . . pale with years of struggle against paralysis . . . nervous . . . taut . . . most obviously a gentleman and a scholar. A man softened and cleansed and illumined with pain. What in the name of Croker and Tweed is he doing here?" [143]

A lanky Oklahoman tossed a wet lock of hair from his eyes, clicked his typewriter keys, and took a breather from sentimentality. "Well," drawled Will Rogers to his newsprint, "of all bunk I ever saw collected in one building, it was in there Tuesday. It was like a menagerie at feeding time.

When Franklin Roosevelt started, he had the opportunity of a lifetime to make a name for himself comparable with the Republican end of his family. But no, he must say 'Man I am About to Name' for about 10 pages. If he had just said: 'I put in nomination Alfred Smith' . . . why the people would have classed it as a nominating speech that would have lived through the ages." [144]

The "moment" was over. The razzle-dazzle began — the band, the blare, the whoopee. For seventy-three minutes the Smith howlers sounded from floor and galleries. More names were put in nomination. West Virginia had a candidate, a Wall Street lawyer named John W. Davis. For him the weary crowd roused itself "and made a decent amount of noise for five minutes." The balloting began. Alabama, twenty-four votes for Underwood. Canal Zone, six votes for McAdoo. The clerks counted, tallied. The second roll call began. A few "favorite sons" dropped out; a few votes shifted. But Smith and McAdoo held the dead weight between them. There was no band-wagon, no "trend" either way.

On the fifth day Newton D. Baker stood before the convention. He invoked the magic name of Wilson and sparks from the old fire kindled the burnt-out delegates, and at the end of the "Little Giant's" eulogy of the League, the whole convention stood again and cheered. It was another "moment," and still another came with a statement from the platform that former Secretary Fall, Harry F. Sinclair, E. L. Doheny and his son had all been indicted. The Democrats could cheer now; if they had no candidate, they had their "cause."

Again the roll call. And again. Again. Another. And another. Thirty ballots. Forty. Forty-five. Fifty. For the last time at a Democratic convention, old William Jennings Bryan took the floor. Like a history-book figure he faced the delegates. His horseshoe mouth was twisted. As if from the past, his words echoed dimly, but his speech was "inglorious," and his old-time power was gone. The band played on, blaring and braying, as a vote changed, and as the clerk called for Alabama, the whole house joined in a roar — twenty-four votes for Underwood.

McAdoo was holding. The wise ones knew from the start that he could never win; they did not know their man. He was holding on with the same tenacious, unyielding determination by which he had won the nomination for Wilson over Champ Clark twelve years before. His "hell-bent determination" was "something near insanity or genius." Through 100 torturing ballots, he held nearly 500 delegates to a lost cause.

Again the roll call. And again. Smith was gaining, but not enough. Almost imperceptibly, John W. Davis was inching up toward third place. Men were knotted in whispering groups — there was talk of adjournment to Kansas City and of starting all over again. Now and then a loud chatter exploded. McAdoo was losing a little, one delegate here and two there. Smith "stood practically still."

The ninety-sixth ballot was called. It was the last effort of the eighth day. McAdoo's vote had dropped sharply, only 421 now. Baruch and Thomas L. Chadbourne looked at each other and shook their heads. Then they left the hall.

McAdoo was "very weary . . . very." Almost unconscious with loss of sleep, he peered groggily at them as they stood over him and read the death sentence to his hopes. He must quit, they said, for the good of the party. His head sagged. He understood. He called his floor leaders. Someone brought him a pen and paper. Then for two hours he fumbled, struggling to shape words in his mind and put them on paper. He was so tired — or was it despair? At 3 A.M. his message of surrender was read with "great emotion." A long-drawn sigh broke from the delegates, and McAdoo's vote broke with it.

On the next call, he was down to 190. Then Smith's followers began to break away. On the 103rd ballot the hall "stampeded" to John W. Davis, whom no one really wanted, and to whom no one seemed to object. The vote was tallied; he was over the top with 839. Then, while the leaders went through the formalities of nominating Charles W. Bryan for Vice-President, and Al Smith harangued them on what a good governor of New York he had been, the delegates sat in a stupor of fatigue and wished they were dead. The big fight had ended and nearly ended the Democratic Party with it.[145] Nor had any lesson been learned. Blame for the inevitable defeat would be laid on the "intellectual aristocrat," John W. Davis, who, like Cox before him, valiantly carried the flag of a lost cause. Baruch saw that once more the Democratic Party had succumbed to the splintering individualism which had so often spelled its defeat.[146]

Baruch was disgusted. Weary of lost causes, and depleted emotionally, his contribution to the cargo of John W. Davis' sinking ship was, however, $120,000, to be spent as he personally directed. This aroused a furious blast from the financial director, Jesse Jones. Had Mr. Baruch no gratitude to the party that had made him an international figure? Would Mr. Baruch, the Wall Street speculator, have any standing in the councils of the world, or influence in the affairs of the country? He should give more than any man in the United States, for the party had given him all that his millions could not buy; and, furthermore, he should pray God for the humility which makes men great.[147]

To the effrontery of this blast, Baruch responded in kind. His party relations were no matter of barter and sale. He had refused honors from the party. He had only stipulated that his money should be spent wisely. He had notified Davis that he was at his call. But he would take no further advice from Jesse Jones, and further correspondence with him would be useless.[148] Thus, angrily, Baruch dictated the first draft of his answer, but it was a letter of considered judgment that he sent in the end. As allies in a common cause, their relations were not ruptured: Jones was even a guest at a Hobcaw dinner years later. But if Baruch could forgive and forget, his antagonist did not, and his subsequent memoirs were punctuated with sly gibes at Baruch.

Baruch knew his own role to be that of the peacemaker.[149] To this end, he addressed a joint meeting of Senate and House Democratic members in the caucus room during the winter of 1926, outlining to them his plans for party unity.

But what was even more welcome to the financially and politically depleted Democratic Party of those years was the flow of Baruch's contributions to the campaign coffers and for the party deficits. These contributions were large, but the exact sums, Baruch has insisted, were no one's business but his own. With a single exception * he has never divulged the amount of money he contributed to any Senator's campaign. He bailed them out when they lost, sometimes even selected future winners, as when he, Joseph Robinson, and McAdoo thought that the chances of Alben Barkley of Kentucky looked good. He has hotly denied that he ever gave market advice to a Senator, and his "payment" for services rendered was collected in the form of a ringside seat at the Democratic convention or some great sports show. Never in his entire range of correspondence did he attempt to bring pressure to bear upon a Senator in return for contributions. It was typical of his almost paternal interest in the party that he contributed heavily to the building of the Democratic leaders' recreation center on Jefferson Island, with special quarters for the President of the United States, and of this, Senator Key Pittman wrote to Ambassador Joseph E. Davies: that Baruch had been the angel of the club as he had been of the Party. For a man who could and would give such generous help, there were, of course, receptive ears, ready for what he had to say and to appreciate the wisdom that lay behind it. Consequently his influence here came, over the years, to be even greater in the legislative than in the executive branch of the government.

But if his contributions went to the Democratic campaign chest, his admiration went to a Republican independent who alone braved the corruption of his party's machine — George Norris of Nebraska.[150]

Baruch's gift for human relations was illustrated in the years before the Convention of 1928 when he supported neither of the participants of the earlier affray, neither Smith nor McAdoo, but kept the friendship of both. He had made a new rule, never thereafter to be broken, that whatever his personal sentiments, he would back no individual candidate before the nomination. On May 27, 1927, the Brooklyn *Eagle* flaunted a headline: "Baruch Deserts Camp of McAdoo, May Aid Smith." [151] Immediately Baruch sent the clipping on to McAdoo with a spirited denial. If McAdoo were the nominee, no one would support him more enthusiastically than Baruch. But now it was more important to unite to beat the Republicans. For no man living did he have greater affection than for McAdoo — he had not "deserted" him, and he had not supported anybody.[152]

* Harry S. Truman.

Baruch knew, however, that public opinion was turning against McAdoo. And McAdoo understood Baruch's dilemma. After all, in 1924 he had had his chance. Generously the Californian wrote: "My dear fellow, any friend of mine is at liberty to support whomever he pleases." [153] McAdoo was even persuaded by Baruch's appeal that he should not allow himself to be "used" either for a third party ticket, or for a disastrous struggle of personalities within the party.[154]

Meanwhile, from the concrete and the asphalt, the slums of New York and Chicago, from the huge industrial mammoths of Flint and Pittsburgh, and the lace-curtain districts of Providence and Boston, rose the demand for Smith. It rose from the throats of millions of "new" Americans, first- and second-generation Americans, the women and men of the sweatshops and foundries, the underprivileged, the dispossessed, the migrant Negroes from the South, the second-class citizens everywhere, who found in the raucous-voiced, staunchly courageous man in the brown derby the greatest tribune of the people since Bryan. Baruch believed that the sentiment for Smith was far stronger than was generally recognized.

If Baruch retained any doubts about Smith as a sectional candidate, they were erased by his decisive victory over McAdoo in the California primary. McAdoo saw wisdom, and withdrew immediately. Baruch had deep pity for his game friend. As for Smith, Baruch observed that if he had been just a Tammany politician, he could never have done what he did in California.[155]

Old-line Democrats might write in horror of turning the party of Wilson "over to the heirs of Tweed and the saloons," but Baruch had been convinced as early as 1926 that Smith was the kind of leader that Jackson and Lincoln had been.[156] He was not afraid of Tammany Hall, Smith's religion, and his stand against prohibition.[157] His warm personal affection for Smith would not have been lessened by the Governor's appeal to the memory of the father of Baruch when he was appointing Baruch to the New York State Reorganization Commission. He felt that if Smith could be elected, it would be a tribute to our real democracy and tolerance.[158] Stories that Smith would "Tammanyize" the government were ridiculous. Even in New York state, he had snubbed the Tammany leaders.[159] He had been an able and honest governor; as a presidential candidate, he favored Federal ownership of water power, farm relief, a lowered tariff, and an amended Prohibition act; and at the pious protest against this last stand, Baruch became angry. Smith had promised to enforce the law. Had as much been done by his opponents? [160]

At first Baruch had no doubt whatever of Smith's victory. How could he fail against Hoover, the shy and self-conscious Quaker engineer with his quiet impassivity, whose name when mentioned at the Iowa State Republican Convention met with derision. Baruch had done his part to help Smith come through, pushing for the nomination of Senator "Joe" Robinson of Arkansas as his running mate, as a sop to the Southern party leadership. But it was not enough.[161]

Not until the campaign was well started did Baruch and Mrs. Franklin Roosevelt and many others begin to realize "the horror prejudice could make," [162] and the depths to which American "Christians" could sink in their persecution of a fellow Christian, all in the name of their common faith. There was really but one issue in the campaign, Baruch realized at last, and that religion.[163]

Never had such demonstrations greeted the march of a presidential candidate: Boston, with brown derbies bobbing atop a sea of white faces, old Irish women standing rapt, tears running down their weathered cheeks, little children lifted high above the crowd — and then the long lines of rails reaching into the night, the screams, the taunts, fiery crosses blazing up along the tracks, sullen, muttering crowds, whispers, rumors, threats, fears.

This was something you could not fight. You could buy space in the papers to print the truth on business conditions that Republican editors chose not to reveal. You could challenge the Republican campaign slogan of the Full Dinner Pail, unaware that your own party would be using it a generation later.[164] But you could not hold back the tides of prejudice and hatred. Courageously Baruch fought to hold the South in line, countered fear with fear and prejudice with prejudice, even raking up the ashes of Reconstruction days in his warnings to Southern leaders. He railed against the introduction of religion into politics, threatened, cajoled, but to no avail.[165] Not even the Birmingham News description of Smith as "the soundest exponent of the Jeffersonian, Jacksonian, Wilsonian program now available" made any headway, nor Franklin Roosevelt's challenge that America needed such "a leader, a pathfinder, a blazer of the trail." [166]

As early as October 4, Baruch predicted correctly to Winston Churchill that Massachusetts and Rhode Island would be the only

Northern states that Smith would carry, and that he would lose Kentucky, Oklahoma, Tennessee, North Carolina, and Florida.[167]

In spite of discouragement Baruch fought on, feeling that, successful or not, the cause was right.[168]

Baruch was a Smith adviser from the time of his nomination, suggesting a complete overhaul of the Democratic Committee, and urging that district and local leaders be given more control. On Prohibition, he pointed out that a pledge of strict enforcement of the law until it was amended would win thousands of Republican votes.

But the farm problem was his first concern. He wrote a draft of an agricultural speech for the candidate and laid down some rules of strategy. Agriculture was Smith's weak link. The spell of his voice, his genius in carrying an audience, would not be enough. He must make an agricultural speech that would be more than emotional, and it must be made from prepared copy, not the usual handful of notes on the back of an envelope. No one must mistake what he had to say. Furthermore, the nation's best-known farm leaders should be on the platform during its delivery.[169] Meanwhile, it was he who helped draft the farm plank in the 1928 platform, a contribution which George Peek forecast would later be acknowledged by history.[170]

At the White House, "Silent Cal" Coolidge shared his perception of human events and broke silence with an epitaph for the "roaring twenties." "Well," he told Colonel Starling, "they're going to elect that superman Hoover and he's going to have some trouble . . . He's going to have to spend money, but he won't spend enough. Then the Democrats will come in and they'll spend money like water. But they don't know anything about money. Then they'll want me to come back and save some money for them. But I won't do it." [171]

14

THE AGE OF THE GREAT DEPRESSION

NEITHER PERSONALLY nor theoretically did the Great Depression begin for Bernard Baruch with the crash of 1929. For him it was born in the cotton country of his boyhood; and as in his late twenties and thirties he began returning to the scenes of his youth, year by year the faces of hunger and the blight that had spread across South Carolina appeared more starkly before him. Up in Fairfield County near his Grandfather Wolfe's plantation rose the bare, red hills, more scarred and gullied even than in his boyhood. In the old sandhill country around Camden whole fields blew into dust, and the unpainted, weathered gray shacks sagged more wearily year by year. Sagging and weathered, too, were the men following the ribby mules. Little was said of the Negro, still known as the "freedman" in the South; but it was in real horror that the Greenwood, South Carolina, *Index-Journal* announced in 1922: "One hundred thousand white families in this section have an average annual income of three hundred and ten dollars ... THEY LIVE ON FARMS." [1] So driven and cowed were these tenants and "croppers," so drained of hope, that from them came not a word of protest, and for them scarcely a word of sympathy.

Nor was this the story of South Carolina alone. From the old "Cotton Kingdom" to the Panhandle moved the tenant with his span of mules and sagging wagon, perhaps fifteen dollars worth of household "furnishings," his sunbonneted wife and a houseful of knobby-kneed, towheaded children. He had no cow, no hogs, no chickens — nothing but $150, which he had borrowed at ten per cent and on which he must live, somehow, until he "made his crop." [2] "The war" had been over for half a century and more, yet its wounds still festered, and the luckless, landless poor whites, who had never plotted secession and never owned slaves, were the victims of "the old credit system," the thralldom of sharecropper to landlord, which had risen up in the war's aftermath.

The Jazz Age, the social historians called it — the Prosperity Decade. Two chickens in every pot. Two cars rolling off the assembly line for every American home. Mass production and mass plenty — this was the gospel of the nineteen-twenties — the American Way of Life. Ticker tape. Margin. Get-rich-quick. Installment plan. Easy money. But it was not "easy money" on the old cotton plantations or on the little rock-walled farms of Vermont where the President's father, John Coolidge, struggled with his maple sugar and his wood lot; or in central Massachusetts where, as late as the nineteen-fifties back-country families, oblivious both to electricity and television, lived very much as they had a hundred years before; [3] nor was there easy money on the sun-bleached farms of the dusty prairies. The economy was out of joint. Secretly, but unequivocally, in the high-water boom year of 1928 Baruch had enlightened the Democratic presidential candidate, Alfred E. Smith, about certain myths in the American way of life. The farmer, Baruch told Smith out of his firsthand observation, had no part in the American boom. In fact, it was worse than that, for he had to pay boom prices for what he bought, but he sold in a depressed market.[4] He knew what he was talking about. He had heard the despair in the cry of farm leaders excluded from the National Industrial Conference. He had been told of young South Carolinians "jumping" the debt-ridden farms and fleeing from sheriffs' warrants for new lives in South America or Australia; there was no hope for them when they were always a year behind and had to pay inflated debts with deflated dollars.[5]

Nor was the story limited to the South. From Illinois in 1925 George Peek predicted darkly: "Most people in the east, a long distance from the heart of the serious depression, are living in a Fool's Paradise, and . . . some of these days if and when the world again produces a normal crop so that agricultural prices will have a marked deflation, no power on earth will be able to withstand the wrath of the rank and file of the farmer." [6]

For Bernard Baruch, trekking southward in the spring and the fall of the year, familiarity could not dull the sharpness of experience. He could see what lay around him and understand its injustice even though he might doubt the equality of men in spite of the efforts of reformers and government to make them equal.[7] Baruch knew that he was not equal with those beasts of burden, both black and white, that sweated along the cotton rows. He knew that his superior position came not from luck alone, but from the innate superiority of the genes and chromosomes that composed him. Yet, the fact that he was a Jew could not be forgotten. In other nations and other times, men of his capacity would be crushed, denied opportunity to show their stature in the ranks of men. Not equality of men but equality of opportunity was the American ideal. Was it a fact for the Southern cotton farmer? It was not. Under the shackles of economic bondage men labored without opportunity, without hope, without chance even for escape. Baruch felt pity for them and counted himself among the "radicals" who wanted to do something for them.[8] He was a radical because of the heritage to which he was born and the memories which were his and the sights and sounds and sufferings around him. He felt himself part of the South and, loving it, was moved by its plight.[9] Sometimes he would say, "I am still unreconstructed," or tell the story of the man who said, "Baruch was first a South Carolinian, second an American, and third, a Democrat." To this he had replied that if a man was a good South Carolinian, he was good in every respect.[10]

Out of sympathy for his "own people" came action that would far transcend the limits of South Carolina. To outsiders such as Winston Churchill's confidant, Brendan Bracken, he would display not only his beautiful Hobcaw, but the great stretches of empty country around it, evoking the response: "How right you were in saying that one should not leave America without seeing something of the South . . . I shall never forget the day I spent at Hobcaw. The beauty of your ravished South is haunting." [11] Certainly, to the despair of Baruch's New York associates, who felt him completely one of themselves, the "ravished South" haunted his thinking.[12]

Baruch frankly admitted that his economic sense was pushed aside when he considered the plight of the farmer.[13] As anyone who saw them through the twenties and thirties knows, the rural slums of the deep South were as wretched as any in the world. The farmers were the depressed people of the nation, and except for teachers and nurses they were the worst-paid for what they did. "Barney Baruch," wrote a newspaper commentator, "has often expressed his desire to alleviate the desperate condition of the farmer. He has made many trips through the West and South." His observations only confirmed the bitter comment of George Peek, writing from Illinois in the fall of 1930: "There has been no rural prosperity in this section since 1920." [14]

The whole industrial boom of the nineteen-twenties Baruch sometimes saw as fictitious, for in his wiser moments he recognized the shakiness of the foundations upon which it was built — a shakiness now obvious to economists, but at that time not generally admitted. Five per cent of the nation's population during this period received a third of the national income, and the whole business structure was "exceedingly fragile," with the boasted prosperity of the times "more illusory than real," and unemployment "slowly but surely growing" through the decade.[15] This is perfectly understandable. Every business that had to do with the depressed farm economy suffered. Making up a quarter of the American population, the farmers accounted for but a tenth of industry's sales.[16]

Depressed sale of staples was at the root of the farmer's miseries; and unless a minimum price was guaranteed, Baruch forecast that they would be forced back to subsistence farming.[17] The farmer sought no special privileges, only equality. But equality was what the nation would not grant him until in the end the whole general public had to pay — and very dearly. The farmers' wrath was slow, but when aroused, terrible. The storm signals were flying in the twenties. Driving up through the Hudson River Valley, Baruch could have seen deserted farm after deserted farm whose dispirited owners had fled to the bright lights and "security" of jobs in the city. The farm population of America dropped by four million during the decade from 1920 to 1930 alone.[18] Yet agriculture was "still the nation's most important industry," for, regardless of its numerical or voting importance, it was the one industry without which the nation could not survive, in peace or in war. But by the nineteen-thirties tobacco and cotton would be selling for less than the price of the fertilizer required to grow them. Budgets, savings, hopes, plans, the long-dreamed-of education of a child, the long needed operation — all were wiped out, all at the mercy of merciless economic forces, of "free enterprise" and the law of supply and demand. Within two years' time at the First World War's end, farm incomes fell 85 per cent, and whereas six bushels of corn would buy a ton of coal in 1919, it took 60 bushels by 1921.[19]

The problem was not due entirely to the havoc of world war. It had grown with the growth of the republic, intensified under the crowding and pressures of the Industrial Age. Actually, the basic issue had changed little since the old Nullification days nearly a century before. Baruch understood, just as Calhoun had, that farmers with no bounty from the government had to sell their produce cheaply in a highly competitive market, while the high price of much which they had to buy was made possible by protective tariffs. No wonder that the farmers saw themselves as victimized for the profits of the industrial community.[20] Like an echo from Calhoun, too, sounded the bitter words of Peek, who called the agricultural South and the agricultural West natural allies "to protect agriculture against the aggressions of an industrial East," [21] and pointed out that the Civil War "was fought over five million Negroes and here we have a situation involving the property rights of nearly one third of our population." [22] The farmer had paid the costs of American industrialization.

The farmer's problems were diverse. They included mortgages and credits, which could be alternately a blessing or a curse. They included the ever-rising cost of farming itself. They included worn-out land and production on that land; the failure of world markets and the pressure of world tariffs, and most of all, the farmer's own inability to cooperate, even with others like himself; to unite either politically or economically.

The farmer's answer to all this was "parity." It was a new word in the nineteen-twenties. In laymen's terms, it meant simply a comparison between the prices at which a farmer sold his crops and the prices that he had to pay for what he bought — a gap that widened year by year. Measured against a standard of 100 in 1912, it hit a high of 118 during the First World War. It was only 81 by 1930.[23] This was the crux of the problem, the gap that had to be closed, and it was a problem that affected every man and woman in America, for the less the farmer bought, the less the industrialist could sell. With the advantage of hindsight, this truism is clear to anyone, and it was perfectly clear in 1920 to George Peek, whose farm-implement business "went broke" because of the farmers' inability to buy.

Of Peek's stubborn fifteen-year battle for the farmer, Gilbert Fite has written eloquently in his book *George Peek and the Fight for Farm Parity*. It was a fight that Peek lived to see won and which he led. He had the help of Baruch. "Baruch's work for farm relief,"

Fite has written, "is probably the least known among his many services to the nation, but actually he made one of his greatest contributions in this field, and was of inestimable help to Peek." [24] As one example, he gave $5000 to the American Council of Agriculture, and without his and Peek's contributions of this kind, it would have been impossible to have kept an organized farm lobby in Washington. [25]

Baruch now had a cause in which he could use his strength, his prestige, his money, and his energy. He could not reverse the trend of public opinion or turn back the industrial advance, but he could make his views clear and his influence felt. In so doing, he found himself in good company: with Lowden and La Follette, the elder Wallace, Norbeck, Capper, Norris, and the tempestuous Borah — the so-called "Sons of the Wild Jackass." Baruch did not care. He was not afraid of the Middle Western "radicals" — in fact he shared many of their views. [26] The onetime Wall Street speculator was to become the author in 1921 of a blueprint for farmers, written at the request of the Kansas State Board of Agriculture. In their hour of trouble the farmers were turning to him. [27]

Baruch was one with them now in this long fight that had broken into the open back in the Populist era, in the days of the Equity Society and the National Farmers' Union. Now, even the militant Non-Partisan League received his counsel, and the American Farm Bureau Federation — perhaps "the most ambitious attempt ever made to organize the farmers into a super-organization" — announced in pride, "We've retained Bernard Baruch as adviser . . . our confidence was his retainer." Incongruous though the combination of Wall Street and the "Farm Revolt" might seem, *The Outlook* recalled that on Baruch's mother's side he came of "a line of farmers," and out of his childhood memories of hungry children and "fever-stricken hovels" he realized fully the hard work farmers did against almost hopeless odds. Somehow, there must be found a way out. [28]

Beginning tentatively, cooperatives, state canneries, Chamber of Commerce campaigns stressing the iodine content of Southern-grown vegetables, all attracted Baruch's interest. Many of his efforts were only stopgap or frankly experimental, and yet were remembered with gratitude years afterwards. It was believed that had it not been for an emergency $15,000 loan from Baruch in 1922, cooperative marketing would have died in South Carolina. [29] To Governor Jonathan

M. Davis of Kansas, Baruch submitted a four-point plan, calling for
a survey of elevator and storage capacities at terminal points, for
certified inspection, grading, storage facilities, and credits to carry
over the crop when sales meant only losses.[30]

These remedies, however, were general, and Baruch knew that
something more was necessary. You must begin at the beginning,
with the land itself. Farmers on submarginal land depressed whole
areas, and perhaps the whole commodity market. Their poor output
only added to surpluses and dragged the over-all prices down. It was
almost as if a manufacturer, trying to rebuild, was confronted with
competitive plants standing idle, ready to jump into production the
moment he showed a profit. Millions of eroded acres should have
been retired.[31]

Nevertheless, the owners of this poor land had to live, and fertilizer was help, if not a cure. Cheap fertilizer and cheap electric
power were among the pipe-dream remedies of the twenties, and,
despite the cruelty with which Henry Ford had used him, Baruch
was on Ford's side in the furore over the Muscle Shoals proposal
which overshadowed the TVA controversy of a later day.

The Muscle Shoals fight took place in 1922, a little before Baruch's
wholehearted involvement in the intricacies of the farm problem.
The question was simple. Who could make cheaper power, the
United States government or Henry Ford? Which could better serve
the public, "free enterprise," or public power? And could farmers,
even for their own benefit, use the methods of collectivism?

It did not appear so. Although the Ford plan acquired such potent
support as that of the National Grange, the National Farmers' Union,
and the American Farm Bureau Federation, it was fought with vehemence by some of the more liberal farm leaders, like George Norris.
Conversely, it was attacked even more than the proposed "government ownership," by such interested groups as the National Fertilizer
Association, the American Cyanamid Company, the Alabama Power
Company, and, of course, the Chilean nitrate association. For there
was one point on which even the most diverse groups could unite —
that Henry Ford was by no means "disinterested" in any project that
bore his name.

Superficially, the possibilities appeared to be three. Should the
government take over and operate the immense but still undeveloped
nitrate plant at Muscle Shoals? Should it be operated by a combina-

tion of industries? Or by the farmers, using their own credit to build a dam for themselves, with the backing and partial control of Henry Ford and his empire? Baruch championed the third plan, although, unlike the farmers, he felt that Muscle Shoals should be developed as a war reservoir for nitrates rather than for cheap fertilizer in peacetime, which could be produced elsewhere. It is perhaps surprising that he favored Ford rather than other combinations of private industry; but it is not surprising that he felt the government proposal should only be accepted as a last resort.[32] As Gray Silver of the American Farm Bureau Federation pointed out, the government was seeking neither cheap power nor cheap fertilizer, but a return of from eight to ten million dollars a year on its investment.[33] Furthermore, the government project was to operate through the existing Alabama Power Company and distributing companies, whose profits were "enormous," but the general public was to foot the bill for the enterprise, amounting to some hundred million dollars.

The farmers, conversely, only wanted a low-priced and continuous supply of fertilizer and power at the lowest possible cost. Under the Ford plan power rates would be a fraction of those proposed by the government. Ford would assume the obligation to make the fertilizer and would be restricted to a personal profit of eight per cent. Furthermore, he would merely control, not own the company, whose direction would be under a board of nine, including seven farmers.

Henry Ford's idyllic dream of three dams along the Tennessee to serve a seventy-five-mile stretch of city, linked by power lines to the farms and the back country, looked foolish until TVA became a reality. It certainly seemed visionary to Congress, who saw nothing of Ford's much vaunted practicality in his plan. It must also have seemed visionary to Coolidge, who, however, not unaware of the vote-getting aspects of the scheme, commended it to Congress, certain that Congress would never write it into the law.[34]

There were other methods than fertilization for restoring the land. Experimental farming fascinated Baruch and had been the rule at Hobcaw for years. He wrote Governor Richard I. Manning of South Carolina about resettling people on productive land. Could not land be secretly bought, reclaimed, and manned with half a dozen families who were good truck and dairy farmers?[35] Diversification

as a remedy, of course, was nothing new and it might work for a few
families who were "set up" at others' expense, but as for the mass
of Southern farmers, how could a man buy a cow when he lacked
money to diaper his own child? How could he plant fruits and
vegetables when his landlord told him to seed the cotton in right
up to the front door? Diversification was preached — but only destitution and the boll weevil taught the lesson.[36] Meanwhile, the
farmers renewed their old demand for credits, and these were far
from an unmixed blessing. Credits were a boon here and a bane
there; they ran up a farm debt of some twelve billion dollars, which in
order to pay the farmers had to plant and plant and sell and sell.[37]
Debt meant mortgages, and 58 per cent of the farms in the country
were mortgaged; in Georgia, 90 per cent. Virtually the whole burden
of financing fell on the small-town and country banks, who were the
real owners of the crop. They had "absolute power to . . . fix the
prices of the helpless farmer, the man who while working to feed
his own family [was] also working to feed the banker's family." Furthermore, margin had to "be maintained by the borrower from day
to day as the price fell, or the crop would go at forced sale." Nor
was the banker in an enviable position, for if the crop went under,
merchants, bankers, and the whole community went under, too.
Thousands of banks failed in this way during the boom era, and the
streams of credit went dry.[38]

Small-town and rural tragedies such as these had convinced
Baruch that some extension of credits must be available to the farmer
from banks or agencies outside the section in which he lived. But
upon unrestricted credits, the goal of farmers since the era of Bryan
and free silver, Baruch bent a distrustful eye. Uncontrolled credits,
for instance, might well ruin the farmer by encouraging him to grow
at a loss,[39] whereas there was value in the Intermediate Credits Act,
supported by the American Farm Bureau Federation and other farm
organizations, which permitted a man to borrow on his crop, either
in the warehouse or in the ground, and perhaps diversify the next
year.

Superficially, overproduction, so-called, was the heart of the problem, the irony being that the more the farmer produced the less
was his purchasing power. Twice yearly across the Cotton Kingdom
the white sea rolled. In 1924 a single county in Texas produced a
seven-million-pound crop. By use of mass-scale plantings and modern

techniques, wealth was still sucked from the exhausted soil, while banks went under and the hungry sharecropper children shuffled listlessly in the dust around the community store. For those who owned the land, there was still wealth to be got from it. Despite the decline of the farm population, more and more land was stripped by the plow; with the use of new technocracy, the worker who had cultivated twenty-one acres in the eighties could take care of thirty-two now. From 1926 to 1930 farm production was one third more than in the First World War period.[40]

There seemed sometimes to be no escape from the vicious circle. The farmer could not "lay off," go on strike, or quit producing. The lower the price, the more he planted to meet his running expenses, and the more he planted, the lower the prices fell.

But Baruch had an idea. Instead of corporations to finance the growing of cotton that no one wanted to buy, why not use credits to prevent the surplus from being grown at all? Why not loan money only on condition that the grower curtail his planting by forty per cent? Then a floor should be laid, below which prices could not fall, and a ceiling above which they could not rise. Price fixing as such was not to be feared, only price fixing done in the wrong way.[41]

This idea of limiting crops was looked upon favorably by the Coolidge and Hoover Administrations, including Coolidge's Secretary of Agriculture, William Jardine, who warned however that farmers would have to be "educated" to the idea, that often it was to the individual farmer's interest to act against the group, and that you could not force restriction.[42]

But many, like George Peek, were bitterly opposed to curtailment, contending that somewhere, somehow, markets for all the goods of the earth could and should be found. This was the ideal, but how could it be achieved? As Senator Joseph T. Robinson once wrote to Baruch, "this country is bursting with production, from the factories and from the farms, from copper mines, steel mills, and what not ... Yet, there is no use for that wealth. We cannot get consumers for it. The door lies open for this consumption in the markets of the world." [43] The world has yet to solve the problem. The brain of man could invent an atomic bomb, but after the Second World War, with the people of England starving for meat and the people of Australia gorged on meat and crying out for manufactured luxury goods, the brain of man could find no way to bring these markets together.

Where Peek erred was not in his grasp of fundamentals, but in his solution. What he did not see was that although getting rid of American crops overseas might feed the hungry and provide the United States with a market, his subsequent allied proposals, amounting to a kind of farmers' tariff, walling out European surpluses from this country, would bring retaliation. Peek was a kind of economic nationalist, his primary concern being for the farmers of his own country.

Yet Baruch fell into the same trap, and less understandably, since he was convinced that foreign trade was essential to American prosperity. He felt that there could be no permanent prosperity in South Carolina with poverty in Kansas or South Dakota, no prosperity for Newark or Flint or Pittsburgh with depression in the farm regions, and that there could be no prosperity for the United States in a poverty-stricken world. To the farm leader Senator Arthur Capper, he argued vehemently that farm credits were not enough; the farmer must be free to sell his surpluses in the markets of the world. Never had there been such great demand, such great supply, or such a gulf between. What Baruch did not take into account was that America did not depend on the world for her prosperity. Never has more than five per cent of our agricultural and industrial output gone into foreign trade. American prosperity depended on markets at home.[44]

Yet the paradox is that, believing our surpluses could and should find markets overseas, Baruch, in his eagerness to help the farmer and to find an outlet for his own energies, later lent his name and prestige to a program that essentially would add a second American tariff wall to the existing one — the McNary-Haugen bills. Since under the Republican administrations of the nineteen-twenties there was no chance whatever that there would be a low tariff, other ways to raise the farmer's income would have to be found.

Industry had the benefit of organization — why did the farmers not meet it with cooperation, or, more literally, cooperatives (which Baruch supported for a time enthusiastically)? At first Baruch felt that action must be voluntary, organized by the farmers themselves. He had little sympathy with the prevalent tendency to seek help from government when men's own efforts could be effective.[45] In his original Farm Memorandum of 1922, Baruch had noted that in an age of consolidation, the farmer was still a determined individualist. He would have to organize and combine forces to create an effective marketing system.[46] From the beginning he recognized that the real purpose and strength of the cooperatives was as a means of combining bargaining power, though the farmers themselves too often regarded them as a scheme for price fixing.[47]

Baruch gave what practical help he could. He lent $35,000 to a cotton cooperative, and was much surprised when the sum was paid back.[48] He offered to put up two and a half million dollars to take care of the surplus cotton in South Carolina but, as he said, "nothing ever came of it." He was in the "buy-a-bale movement," which had the same purpose. Under his stimulus the Non-Partisan League threw its weight behind cooperative marketing and milling plans; the word went out to big business, and the squeeze went on. Southward, westward, the little streams of credit trickled and went dry. It had been highly profitable for business to sell at its own tariff-supported prices, but as farmers began organizing, efficiently or otherwise, the Sherman antitrust law was dragged out to beat them down. United States Steel could protest that it was "no combination in restraint of trade" but that cooperatives were, and cooperatives were thus subjected to intimidation. Only specific congressional action, it was found, would "permit the growers legally to co-operate," and the use of pressure-group tactics by the farm leaders only brought more howls of anguish from the big-business groups who had used those same tactics. Why, demanded that doughty champion of rugged individualism, Judge Elbert Gary, should the farmer have special privileges? Baruch's answer was curt. If the farmers were the victims of corporate organization, why should they not have the advantages of corporate organization?[49] Business did not see it this way, and, as Baruch observed, the farmer's every attempt for equality was vigorously opposed.[50]

Baruch was now no small thorn in the flesh of big business. For when the farmers' credit was shut off, he came to the rescue, even taking some semidefunct North Dakota bonds which could find no lodging elsewhere.[51] That Bernard M. Baruch who, if anyone did, knew the secrets, the methods, and the aspirations of the business world, had gone over to the enemy caused all the more anguish among the forces of corporate power.

The irony of the whole affair was that the cooperatives were taken far more seriously as a threat by business than as a program by the farmers. Even as late as 1930, only a fifth of the farmers' sales was handled by them, and the only value of a cooperative is the number of people who cooperate with it. From the first, it was evident that the Grange, the Farm Bureau, and Calvin Coolidge were far more for the movement than were the farmers. Will Rogers commented ironically: "If your stuff is not bringing as much as it costs you to raise it, why you all go in together and take it to town. Then when you sell it, you can be together to cheer each other up." [52] As Baruch himself noted, "Co-operative marketing is all right if you can get everybody to co-operate." [53]

Baruch learned his lesson when he answered an appeal from the Dakota wheat farmers, whose plight touched him,[54] urging that they cooperatively purchase an agency to which their surplus grains could be sent and held off the market for higher prices. Good as this idea was, despite the fact that it might have meant forty cents a bushel added to the price of grain, as William Allen White forecast, the plan never went through. "Rank individualist" that the farmer was, not even for his own salvation would he relinquish his inalienable right to take his chances on an individual sale. Competition against his neighbor was of more interest to him than joint warfare against abstract forces. The farmer was indeed his own worst enemy. If the Farm Bureau favored one plan, some other farm organization would jump at its throat.[55] You could often get a farmer to join an organization, but you could not keep him in it; in the year 1925 there were forty lawsuits on the breaking of cooperative agreements in one Oklahoma county alone.[56] The Burley Tobacco Growers organization was undone by the increased production of the individualists who would not join and yet took advantage of the higher prices brought about by the self-imposed restrictions of the co-op members. Furthermore, few cooperatives could get enough of a crop under their control to bring about any appreciable raising of the price.

Yet Baruch did not lose heart. What he sought and what would happen he rightly recognized as different things, and as a realist he could take men as they were and deal with them within their limitations. He pushed on doggedly, spurred by his conviction that depression in the farm belt could only mean eventual depression for the entire country.

There were other ways of uniting the farmer. There was political organization; but this, Baruch was convinced, must be within the framework of the established parties. Abortive Third Party movements provided only a highly satisfactory method of draining off zeal that might otherwise backfire into one of the major parties.[57]

A better idea would be to play the major parties off against each other — to build up farm pressure groups for whose votes the two parties would have to bid. This was an issue beyond party lines. The farmers must be welded into an aggressive fighting machine and industry must be warned that if it did not cooperate it would receive "retaliation by the agricultural representatives in the next Congress." [58] He realized that not until farmers voted for those who supported their program, regardless of party, would they be taken seriously.[59]

Ideally, as a good Democrat, Baruch would have preferred to unite the farmers in his own party. But he knew that however "natural" a working alliance of the farmers of the West, the South, and New England might be, in actuality they voted as their fathers had shot in the Civil War.[60] Pitted against all efforts on their behalf was the farmers' hidebound conservatism. The statecraft of Baruch, Peek, and the elder Wallace in helping weld together Western radicalism and Southern conservatism was a remarkable achievement. Yet they did it — and built the coalition so strong that to the embarrassment of "party-liners" it persisted for over a quarter of a century.

New figures now entered Baruch's life. Some of them, like Joseph T. Robinson, Pat Harrison, or James F. Byrnes, were to become lasting friends, united as they were to Baruch by background and political heritage. There were others whose lives were less closely entwined with his during these years — political rather than personal associates: the progressive and hard-working Gray Silver of the American Farm Bureau Federation, vigorous in his leadership toward formation of the Farm Bloc, Senator Arthur Capper of Kansas, Oscar Bradfute, and others. When the battle was over intimacy ceased, although friendship was maintained. But with William E. Borah, a kind of tenuous half-intimacy persisted for years.

Their relationship was indeed strange: Baruch, the cosmopolite and world statesman, whose ideal was Woodrow Wilson, and Borah, like Wilson an idealist and champion of lost causes yet the man who more than any other killed Wilson's dream. Under Baruch's warmth Borah's reserves melted.[61]

These two had more than a working alliance. So stirred was Baruch by the quality of the man that he even wrote a letter to a friend in Idaho asking his influence toward the re-election of Borah to the Senate, in spite of his stand on the League of Nations. Baruch considered him an honest man of courage.[62] In the end, Baruch thought better of thus advising the Republicans and did not send the letter, but he wrote a pleasant letter to Borah himself, wishing that they could more often meet and discuss matters.[63]

It was a minor tragedy that, as Borah's idealism crystallized into fanaticism and his courage into bullheaded stubbornness, this real friendship ended in bitterness. But for political purposes, at least, it had served its end. Through the twenties and even into the thirties, Borah was Baruch's link with the Western Republicans.

Baruch gave more than economic advice to the farm bloc. Because of him, candidates of both parties were found — and financed — to run against incumbents who stood against the interests of agriculture. He has given a typical example of his activity. When Senator Tom Walsh was hard pressed in Montana, Baruch promised that he would round up the farmers if Walsh would let the bill giving cooperatives exemption from the Sherman antitrust law come out of committee. Baruch then passed the word to the Farm Bureau Federation and the Non-Partisan League, and Walsh came out of Montana the victor.

Such triumphs could not go unnoticed. To O. E. Bradfute of the American Farm Bureau Federation Baruch forecast the possibility of an attack upon those who were working with them, or an attempt to wound the farmer through striking at Baruch.[64]

The attack came, for it was at this time that Henry Ford's *Dearborn Independent* gave way to the orgy of "superstition, bigotry, and hatred" in its "exposé" of "The Scope of Jewish Dictatorship in the United States," the details of which have already been described.[65] For himself, Baruch could "take it" now. He wrote a friend, with perhaps more outward than inward complacency, that the outstanding man must expect attack and jealousy. What concerned him was the cause that he served. Anti-Semitic bigotry restricted his activity in the Democratic Party. Would it also destroy his services to the farmer? His association with the farm movement, he wrote Bradfute, had given him more happiness than anything he had ever done before. However, he did not want the cause to suffer because he was identified with it, and was willing at any time that he became an embarrassment to withdraw. Fortunately, the sacrifice did not have to be made.[66]

So Baruch worked on, his inherent optimism saving him from despair at attitudes and actions that could neither be righted nor reversed. He tried "educating" the staff of the New York *Tribune* to the fact that the so-called "dirt farmer" was not ignorant, then lunched with the *New York Times* staff, too, urging round-table discussions on farm policy and the appointment of some capable farm man to the Federal Reserve Board.[67]

He had real respect for the hard-working, idealistic, but naïve Senator Arthur Capper of Kansas; but he had more than personal reasons for the large dinner party he gave the Kansan in New York in 1923. He knew that it was as necessary to allay the farm leaders' suspicions of the East as to teach Easterners that farm leaders were not horny-handed ignoramuses. The scheme worked. The New York sophisticates were enchanted with the soft-spoken, scholarly Capper. Capper, in his turn, wrote to Baruch that to meet "the big men of New York . . . in such a delightful way was a rare opportunity." [68]

In behalf of the cause, Baruch even rallied his oratorical forces and delivered an address before the Kansas Livestock Association in Wichita in January 1924, although a year earlier he had been appalled to receive a letter from the Farm Bureau requesting his inclusion in their "Speakers' Albums" for Rotary and Kiwanis Clubs. He was conscious of his amateur status.[69] Although as a national farm leader he was called to Washington to confer with other farm leaders and Secretary of Agriculture Wallace in 1922, he was aware that he had to learn by trial, error, and experiment. So too did the entire Farm Bloc, groping for the first time to unite rank individualists to find a program broad enough to include the mighty wheatgrower of the West and the applegrower on the crabbed slopes of New England; the tenant in the South, and the great truck farmers of New Jersey.

The answer seemed to be in the McNary-Haugen bills — pioneers in agricultural legislation, the ancestors, perhaps, of all the latter-day price-support experiments and the Brannan Plan, yet, compared to these, very mild pieces of legislation indeed. Four times they came before Congress, twice to be defeated there and then twice to pass, only to meet with a presidential veto. They never became law, and yet their place in history is far greater than that of many a piece of forgotten legislation moldering in dusty statute books.[70] For they were a veritable grabbag of the needs and doctrines that Baruch and the other farm leaders had been discussing over the years — they were a landmark in the history of twentieth-century agriculture.

Eventually the fight for these bills was to unite the farmers, as even the American Farm Bureau Federation had not been able to do. Their protectionist element was in keeping with the spirit of the high-tariff twenties, and the underlying concept — that agriculture, too, must have its subsidy — made them the direct ancestors of all the farm-relief measures that came afterwards.

The original McNary-Haugen bill was drawn up by two men from Baruch's old War Industries Board "team," George Peek and Hugh S. Johnson, with Baruch as "their main supporter." When the final results were laid before Baruch, he announced that he could not find a loophole in the plan.[71] Undoubtedly, as with so much of the legislation with which he has been associated, Baruch's ideas were reflected in the final results, and he was of especial value for the later versions of the bill, revised to win the support of Southern agriculturists.

What did the plan involve? First, it called for "equality for agriculture," a demand sounded by Peek and Johnson in a pamphlet written by them and circulated in 1922. Basically, it insisted on a fair relation between the prices of what the farmer sold and what he had to buy. Theoretically, it allowed a "free play in price fluctuations." Actually, it involved price fixing to the extent that it set a floor under agricultural prices. Thus it won over the supporters of various price-fixing bills then before Congress. Its goal was a no less effective system of protection for the farmer than had been enjoyed by industry for a hundred years. Now, farmers demanded that the power of government be invoked to aid them against discrimination. If bank credits could be arranged to help industry, why not to help agriculture? Finally, the proponents demanded that commodity prices bear the same relation to the general price index as they had in the ten year prewar period.

There were other features. The program would have forced farmers to cooperate in mass marketing of their products, and arranged for the government or the cooperatives to buy up crop surpluses and withhold them from the market, either to await a "short" year, or to be sold at the world price abroad. It called for the appointment by the President of a Federal Farm Board to advise the farmers on sales, marketing, and production. Finally, there was its most unique and controversial feature: the so-called Equalization Fee, devised to support the financial costs of the scheme. There was to be established a revolving fund of several hundred million dollars, raised by a tax levied upon the farmers and used to compensate the government for the cost of the price-supporting operations. In a very real sense, the farmers were to pay their own subsidy.

Was the plan economically sound? * It was damned with faint praise by some economists, who agreed that it was, at least, as sound as a protective tariff, which many agreed was unsound, anyway.[72] Some critics demurred at the added price to the consumer. It was argued that retaliatory price walls would be erected against us overseas, which may have been true; it was also argued that the plan was economically shortsighted, and that surpluses should have been prevented instead of being distributed.

It was agreed, however, that the weakest point in the plan was the fact that high prices invariably made for a larger crop, and the McNary-Haugenites never effectually answered this argument. Of course, the equalization fee was designed to take care of the difficulty with the principle of "the bigger the crop, the higher the fee." [73]

The value of the plan can be measured by the friends and the enemies that it made. The farmers believed in it; without the money for telegrams, they wrote about it in pencil to President Coolidge and to his Secretaries of Agriculture.[74] The co-ops fought it because it offered a rival program; radicals fought it because it failed to offer direct government aid. Most of all, big business fought it because it did offer government aid — because it did for the farmer something of what the tariff did for the industrialist.[75]

One other group fought stubbornly against the bills almost to the end, and in the name of principle — the low-tariff cotton farmers of the South who recognized that to sell farm produce abroad at a price below our domestic one was simply a tariff in reverse. Here

---

* Not according to Secretary of the Treasury Andrew Mellon, who condemned "the unusual spectacle of the American consuming public paying a bonus to the producers of the five major agricultural commodities." See Bibliography, Saloutos and Hicks, p. 393.

the efforts of Bernard Baruch were most effective. Continually he used his influence among Congressmen and Senators, carrying on a large correspondence with all who might lend support, and always sounding the theme of agricultural equality. An example was his attempt to allay the bitterness of Senator Robinson, who saw victory for the underprivileged men of the soil only at the cost of a principle the South held very dear. The evil of protection was to be met only by adopting the principle of protection for the farmer. For a Democratic leader, Robinson wrote Baruch bitterly, to "commit himself to the principle of the high tariff . . . permanently fixing it by causing the one class whom that system most oppresses to believe that special favors can be made general . . . is to me the acme of stupidity and hypocrisy." In long talks through long hours, Baruch struggled with this redheaded Southerner who "talked with his fists," trying to erase from his mind the prejudices of the post-Civil War years.[76] No one deplored isolation behind high tariff walls more than Baruch; but did the Democrats have the votes to beat the tariff? and, if not, what were they prepared to offer as farm relief? George Peek put the issue in a capsule: "Either the farmer is entitled to participation in the benefits of protection or others must forego the special benefits." [77] Obviously, the tariff was not to be foregone.

So, at last the farmer, united for his own protection, twice forced the McNary-Haugen bill through Congress. Not all who supported it believed in it. The comment of one congressional representative was typical: "I am for it . . . because the crowd at home are on my trail." Many voted for it under the direct "bludgeoning of one of the most skillful lobbies in Washington." [78] Many who did not in the least believe in it voted for it in the comforting knowledge that it could never become law. Coolidge would and did veto it.

Now the forces were massing for the decisive battle. Peek the Republican and Baruch the Democrat were mapping strategy to bring the question before the public — to nominate presidential candidates who would be for the McNary-Haugen bill. In the Republican camp, they set their sights on Frank Lowden — but the united support of the farmers could not withstand the tidal wave for Hoover, "one of the economic marvels of the century," as Borah termed him.[79] Hoover, like Coolidge, was irrevocably opposed to the McNary-Haugen program, but Hoover was the Republican candidate, and in an election year, in the final showdown, all good Republicans came to the aid of their party, or, as George Peek more graphically put it, were led "like sheep to the shambles on election day." [80]

As for Baruch's own party, as we have seen, they nominated the man "from the sidewalks of New York," and Baruch approved, for Al Smith was as agreeable to the general principles of McNary-Haugenism as he was ignorant of them. The farm plank in the Democratic platform was in part written by Baruch and his "team." The farm speech which was prepared for Smith was, according to General Hugh Johnson, a prophetic utterance that "called the turn on the collapse." But Smith was the victim of his own intellectual honesty. He protested, "Aw, hell, General, I don't know anything about this kind of stuff." If he used it, everyone would say he was having his speeches written for him.[81] The fact that Smith was finally forced to straddle the issue gave Republican farmers ample excuse to return to their own party, and in any case the issues of Catholicism and liquor proved of more concern than the farm problem.[82] It was a bitter disillusionment to Baruch, who felt that the farmers had come so near victory.[83]

Baruch contends that it was Borah, the "Progressive Republican," who virtually elected Hoover in one speech. Oratorically, he was still in his prime, and when he spoke, "the entire audience was likely to believe that he had just returned from a fresh conference with the gods." [84] He depicted Hoover as a kind of new "economic Moses" who would lead the farm states out of the wilderness — and into the Republican column.

The facts did not matter. Nor did the warnings in Baruch's own powerful radio address of September 28. Fifty million people were living on farms and in depressed areas; even their partial restoration to "economic equality with our industrial population would unloose such a flood of buying as would tax our capacity to supply."

"There has already been a tremendous exodus to cities," Baruch said. "Industry . . . cannot absorb this influx. It will only increase unemployment and . . . threaten a human catastrophe in the near future. Our economic system cannot stand such a violent shock. Even Mr. Hoover's proposal to spend billions in public works — evidently advanced to offset what he foresees — will not suffice." [85] So spoke Baruch a year before the crash of 1929.

A major battle had been lost but the war was not yet over. From 1928 the farmers looked ahead to the prospects for 1932. Much al-

ready had been won — more perhaps even than the fighters themselves knew. Parity had become a part of the American language,
and within a few years would be written into law. The long debate
over surpluses had paved the way for future programs of crop restrictions and controls. The farmers had been welded together as one of
the most powerful of pressure groups, which could never again be
ignored.

All this we see now. Things looked dark for the farmer in that
election year of 1928, and so sweeping was Hoover's victory that Baruch dared not even dream of the fulfillment of his dearest goals
only four years later. Instead, he came out with one of his worst
forecasts: that the farmer would always vote Republican.[86] Hoover
had lulled the fears of the West; he had even lulled Bernard Baruch.

Bernard Baruch knew "Mr. Hoover to be sound." It was thus that
he informed Bruce Barton in the blithe spring of 1929 when that
blithe exponent of businessman's Christianity interviewed the prophet
of high finance for the *American Magazine*. Baruch's words of cheerful optimism could have brought no trembling in the temple. For
Baruch voiced the phrases of the "industrial renaissance" of the
coming age of television, and the era when all mankind would have
enough to eat.

"Progress," Baruch said, "is on the march . . . the more money
people have, the more things they can buy." Was he thinking of
the farmer, of all the things that he wanted and all the money he did
not have with which to buy? Perhaps he was thinking beyond the
farmer. There was, he said, a kind of "wanting all over the world."
Then he returned to his earlier theme, that our industrial prosperity
depended on a rapidly expanding export trade. Industry, he contended, was approaching dependence on export markets; but he well
knew how the export markets were glutted.

He was concerned over the demand for tariff increases and Europe's inevitable economic retaliation. However, the war had "jarred
dead brain cells into life"; business now had "some understanding of
the laws of economics." He warned, however, that there was one foe
against which little progress had been made — panics and depressions. The average man, he said, "keeps his eyes not more than half
open . . . he who keeps his eyes open may see and be warned in time."
What did he see? "The economic condition of the world seems on
the verge of a great forward movement," he said.[87]

Did Baruch see 1929 in time? Despite the ingenious efforts of his biographer, Carter Field, to prove that he "saw the storm coming," [88] and to explain away his reasons for not issuing public warnings, it is impossible to avoid the conclusion that Baruch, too, was drugged by the lotus of the time. That most of his own assets were liquid before the Big Crash still does not disprove the conclusion. Baruch had known that a depression was coming. Bust was the inevitable sequence to boom. As early as 1924, he had predicted that the election of Coolidge would bring a period of unrestricted speculation and inflation, with lowered taxes, resulting in a stock boom and a kind of pseudo-prosperity. Earlier that same year, he had written Senator Robinson that business was sliding off, partly because new enterprises could not flourish with any hope of good profits eliminated by excess taxes.[89]

By the spring of 1927 Robinson was writing Baruch of the "tightening up" of money in his own state of Arkansas, and that business conditions were decidedly adverse. By December of that same year a Maryland landholder, ridden with debt, informed Baruch of the collapse of real estate values there. Two weeks earlier, Baruch had written Winston Churchill that conditions in this country were not as good as they were said to be in the papers. Lowered profits were showing up in business reports, and the heavy buying was really only the outcome of cheap money and a badly stretched credit base. If unemployment came into the picture, he forecast in 1927, there might even be a political reversal.[90] But the reversal did not come in time for the passage of the McNary-Haugen bill, or in time to prevent the farm collapse, which would drag all else down with it. Baruch was, admittedly, not a bit confident of the future, so long as there was no change in business. But that was in 1927.

In 1929, there were signs for those who cared to read them. And some did. Herbert Hoover, for instance, had been trying to get the stock market under control as far back as his Secretary of Commerce days. Urging a stronger Federal Reserve policy, Paul Warburg of the International Acceptance Bank warned against the orgy of "unrestrained speculation." The collapse, he said, would be complete, with a "general depression involving the entire country." Warburg knew the banks were taking in sail. This was in March of 1929, that tense month when, according to J. K. Galbraith, the real debate involved a choice between an immediate deliberate crash and a long-range inevitable one. It was a choice no one cared to make. In September, the map of the future was clearly outlined by the so-called "Sage of Wellesley," Roger Babson, who, taking the collapse of the Florida boom as warning, painted a gloomy picture of terrific unemployment and factories shut down. Unfortunately, Mr. Babson was inclined to reach his conclusions by secrets of divination known only to himself; if he was right, it was said, he was right for the wrong reasons, and the nation preferred to be wrong and respectable. What was the voice of Roger Babson beside the pronouncements of the prophets of high finance? [91]

Baruch could have issued a warning in his interview for the *American Magazine*, but he did not do so. It is true that in February he had pointed out to Swope that Coolidge and Mellon were responsible for stimulating public participation in the stock market. He was also, and rightly, concerned over lowered rates, agreed on by both the Governor of the Bank of England and the Governors of the Federal Reserve Board.[92] It is doubtful, however, that Baruch, with his own addiction to the values of the Gold Standard, saw the handiwork of his old friend Winston Churchill in this, although as Chancellor of the Exchequer in 1925, Churchill had used his influence to return England to gold, the result being a highly overvalued pound and great financial strain. In consequence, it was Britain that had had to plead for credit restrictions to be eased — and at a most fatal period.[93]

Nevertheless, the Federal Reserve Board had been helpless, largely because it wanted to be. It could, for instance, have asked Congress for power to stop trading on margin. It could have issued warnings and broken its "demoralizing silence." Herbert Bayard Swope, in correspondence with Baruch, had suggested a "tourniquet," but there was far too close a relationship between the bankers and the Reserve Board. Agreeing, Baruch did recognize the dangerous inflation already in progress and laid it squarely on the doorstep of the Federal Reserve System. The reduction of rates resulted in a complete revaluation of securities and a kind of artificial respiration for business.[94] All this he saw. Yet by 1929 his powers of prophecy did not allow him actually to predict the depression. Although he made no public warnings, such was the respect of the public for Bernard Baruch, onetime War Industries Board chief, and its increasing respect for Wall Street, that he undoubtedly would have been listened to if he had.

Baruch's contempt for the authors of economics textbooks is extreme. Had they really known the rules, he argues, they would not be writing books; they would be making money. But it is also evident that the old-fashioned rules by which Baruch accumulated his millions do not necessarily apply to the economic complexities of our time. Baruch was able to save himself and to "live like a prince" [95] through the Great Depression because he followed his old rule of getting out when he had made enough, not waiting until the market had hit the high. The truth is, he did not know when it would hit the high.

Furthermore, when the storm broke, he was too close to get perspective. Along with his more gullible associates, and even Mr. Hoover, he yielded for a time to the belief that all would pass quickly. When he found out otherwise, he secretly proposed to the most powerful Wall Street bankers that a pool be made to let the market down gradually and spare the public, but this idea was brushed aside. Was not prosperity just around the corner?

Baruch apparently thought so. Right after the crash, he wrote a friend that business would probably be bad for sixty days, or so, just long enough to assure a good investment market, and on November 15 he even cabled Churchill that the worst was over. Just in case, however, he told Joe Robinson that he thought the government should get ready a program of public works, to go into effect as soon as unemployment began to show itself.[96]

As for himself, he rode out the storm in peace, broken only by the tragedies of those around him. He had not got off wholly unscathed; he had kept some of his stocks, in which the drop had been severe, but he was still able to live in luxury, although perhaps having to curtail some of his activities.[97]

The icy wind of depression blew on high and low alike. Few could escape, and not even they could flee the misery around them. The very rich became merely rich; the rich were now only "comfortably off," and even for those, as months stretched into years, the vise of fear began to tighten as incomes grew smaller and prices fell lower — where would it all end? No one could escape the fear.

As for Baruch, he had only to look to the South — to South Carolina and home. Over the years he had lent a relative some $54,000 to sink into cotton land now worth scarcely a dollar an acre. One hundred and sixty-five banks had failed in South Carolina during the

five "prosperity years" from 1922 to 1927.[98] Up in the old Winnsboro district, Baruch's own cousins, Fay Allen and Jack Des Portes *
were struggling to hold their worn-out acres; if only "Cousin Bernard"
would help, they could escape foreclosure and sale. But Christie
Benet, even before the debacle, warned Baruch that, family feelings
aside, "If you start farming the red hills of Fairfield, you are off on a
long trip." [99] What was happening to the Des Porteses was what was
happening to the whole South. "The horrible part of the whole
situation," wrote Fay Allen Des Portes in the bitter winter of 1931,
"is these poor starving people here in our midst. The banks can't
let anyone have any money; the merchants are all broke; the farmers
can't let the poor Negroes on the farm have anything to eat. I don't
know what is going to happen. I have about four hundred Negroes
that are as absolutely dependent on me as my two little boys but I
can't help them any more and God only knows what is going to
happen to them. And what is happening to me is happening with
every other farmer and landowner in the state." [100]

What could one man do? Could one man salvage an entire state?
To his cousins Baruch wrote that he only sought to help them begin
over again.[101] Foreclosures had at last become a mere formality, and
it was virtually a gentleman's agreement now that no man would bid
in his neighbor's farm from the courthouse steps. Those eroded red
hills, scarred with tumbledown shanties, were in time to become for
the Des Porteses a highly profitable real estate development, but this
was in the future, and tragedy closed in during the fall of 1932. Fay
Allen's health broke under the strain, and he was sent to a sani-
tarium. Here, at least, Baruch could help, in one of the rare instances
that he ever exerted personal influence in patronage. The next spring
he sent a telegram to Jim Farley, saying that his cousin Fay Allen
Des Portes was coming to see him, and asking Farley to help him if
possible.[102] What happened was like the ending to a fairy tale.
For Fay Allen Des Portes, a South Carolinian with something of the
charm of his more famous kinsman, was whisked away from a dying
cotton plantation to the genial climate and cultured official society
of the Republic of Bolivia. The impression he made there as
American chargé d'affaires is revealed in a telegram to Farley from
W. B. Blaker, the general manager of an American oil company in
Bolivia. In the fall of 1935, he spoke of the great esteem and affec-

* Ulysse Ganvier Des Portes, son of Sarah Wolfe Des Portes.

tion in which Mr. Des Portes and his wife were held not only by the
American colony but by the Bolivian people. All Americans in Bolivia were thankful that those in authority had made the happy selection of Mr. Des Portes for the ministerial post.[103]

But there was no fairy-story ending for South Carolina, from which
the whites were fleeing as if before Sherman's army, and where virtually the entire Negro population was on relief. Baruch did what
he could, assuring harried and desperate Governor Ira Blackwood
that he was always ready to serve. His efforts in Georgetown alone,
where every school child in need was supplied with a winter outfit,
brought an editorial note in the Charleston *Evening Post*: "One mark
of the greatness of Bernard Baruch is that he never forgets his old
home." [104]

It was W. E. Gonzales who, as early as 1925, had suggested that
Baruch could help his native state. Baruch had tried, was still trying,
still working with the South Carolina Natural Resources Commission, striving to estimate the iron, copper, and iodine content of
locally grown food, and urging the establishment of canneries within
the state's boundaries. But these were as ripples on the flood waters.
He appeared before the legislature in the spring of 1931 with, as he
said, no magic formula, only the warning that not laws but people
alone could right circumstances; that South Carolina must pay her
just debts, and that the duty to pay lay on all, not on the few. But
privately he admitted to Gonzales that the South was in a critical
condition, and that he stood ready to do what he could.[105]

Within a few weeks, his chance came. South Carolina was about
to default on her state bonds. Would he help tide the state over?
He would do everything he could to help place the bonds.

When the bank holiday was declared, with every bank in South
Carolina closed and no certainty they would ever open again, Baruch passed the word that he would put up the capital for a new
Bank of South Carolina so that people could carry on their business.[106] The crisis passed and the need with it, but years later, W. W.
Ball, editor of the Charleston *News and Courier*, recalled that Baruch
was "thinking about South Carolina in her hour of trial." [107]

Go back. Go back in your thinking. Go back in your remembering. The pregnant woman and the pushcart with the upended bed-
spring rising above and the buckets swinging at the sides. The child

ferreting scraps from your garbage pail. See their faces — the faces
that Caldwell saw and Margaret Bourke-White photographed. Remember the lines that waited outside the banks, outside the soup
kitchens. The kids spread-eagled, hanging on to freight cars. Ella
May Wiggins lying dead on a North Carolina highway for making
ballads about the textile workers, and the twenty-six men dead at
Herrin, Illinois, for claiming the right to work.[108] Remember the
motionless, pointing fingers of the empty smokestacks in New England, and the shuffling, shuffling, shuffling sound of footsteps around
the huge bulk of the Ford plant, before the police broke through
and fired in an explosion of frenzy that somehow was never heard in
the city rooms of the newspapers.[109] Or the slow tramp, tramp,
tramp of feet, marching feet, tired feet, bare feet, broken shoes on
broken feet, children's feet, women's feet — an army marching across
Anacostia Flats and up Pennsylvania Avenue, an army encamped.
Tents and tear gas and, on a night for the first time since the burning
of Washington in 1812, flames red-painting the horizon.

Was the heart of the nation consumed in that fire? At St. Paul,
Minnesota, President Hoover pronounced a verdict. "We still have
a government in Washington," he said, "that knows how to deal
with a mob." [110]

Above it all, Baruch was burdened by the thought of his wealth.
Were he to give it all away, it would be but as a fleck of sand in a pile.
For him, as for thousands of lesser men in the Street, there were de-
pressing moments as the ticker tape reeled off in his office, but he
still had the Golden Touch, and, as if in comic irony, gold was seeping
in from Alaska Juneau, the mine abandoned by virtually all as a lost
hope nearly twenty years before.[111]

It was good to have money sometimes; good to receive a letter
like one written almost on the eve of Christmas in 1932; "Every day
in walking through the streets in the city I've thought of you. I've
met pallid faces and looked into eyes that spoke despair; and I reflected that but for the kindness of the only B. M. I would be like
them. When I could I made a vicarious sacrifice, in your name — a
hot cup of coffee, a sandwich or even a lowly doughnut . . . It
wasn't much, but who knows — it may have saved a life." Sometimes
this man would offer up, too, a silent prayer that Baruch's every hope
should be realized.[112]

All those who were solvent, in greater or lesser degree, were bearing the weight of others. When cash gave out, Baruch and the lucky ones would put up good collateral to replace the old. There was not much else they could do but wait — a whole nation was waiting — and for what? None could flee the cold fear that was clenching all. Although his health was good, Baruch was enormously depressed.[113]

How long would it last — would America last? Panic had gripped an entire people, yet with solid common sense Baruch still held on to fundamentals. People had to go through the ordinary motions of life.[114] Life would go on — life and death and birth. Men and women loved and mated and children were born. A whole generation was growing up in the Age of the Great Depression, children who knew hunger as real as the grip of their mother's hand. It would be said of them later that they knew little of love but sex, little of tenderness, loyalty, or devotion, nothing of decorum, nothing of the great power drives for prestige, for money, or for power. But they did know fear. Born to fear and bred to fear and pounded with fear, fear settled into the marrow of their bones until they became too tired and bored and pounded to fear any more. For them — the adolescents of the thirties — the screeching voice of Hitler across the air waves and the throbbing, chanting cry of "Sieg Heil! Sieg Heil! Sieg Heil!" like a pulse — Munich, Paris, and civilization dissolving into chaos — these were the realities, the high-water mark for the generation that lived with fear, the generation that was never lost because it was never found.

This was the generation of "emasculated emotions," as a perceptive woman once called it.[115] It was not disillusioned, having never known illusions. Listlessly it marched to war and fought bravely, knowing that God was on the side of the strongest artillery. Over its head would pass the Four Freedoms and the atom bomb would explode and all be anticlimax to the years and the terrors that had gone before. Man was at the mercy of the impersonal forces of Nazi or Communist terror that encased him in a uniform and sent him off to kill — for what and for whom he never knew. Individual freedom was the watchword. Freedom meant a ranchhouse in the suburbs and a pay check on Saturday; take care of yourself and let the world take care of itself. Insecurity was something you knew about; insecurity was something to fear.

Go back. Go back in your thinking. Go back in your remembering. The Hoovervilles. The Hoover wagons. The rattling, clanging bundles of junk and tin, edging along the sun-blistered scar of Highway 66 to California. The covered wagons of the thirties. The migrants. The Okies. The Crackers. The homeless, the hopeless, the dispossessed. One hundred thousand mothers and fathers and children, "washed out, pushed out, tractored out"; from Georgia and Mississippi, from Kansas and the Dakotas, from the Panhandle, from Arkansas and Oklahoma, from the seared red earth and the dried-out gray earth that blew in clouds above the dust bowls. "America was promises," [116] the poet had sung, but for these there were no promises and no hopes, and when the morning came, there was no dawn.

The year 1930, with four million men out of work, and ten million men and women and children hungry — Nineteen thirty-one, and from Arkansas, Joe Robinson was writing Baruch that nearly every bank in the state was shut down and every farmer bankrupt, "literally thousands . . . in want . . . imperative that seed, food, and feed be supplied in large quantities to those who have not yet despaired of farming." But where would help come from? This was not the story of Arkansas alone but of eleven other Southern states.[117] People who fed the poor last winter would this year have to be fed themselves, Hugh Johnson reported to Baruch.[118] Now it was 1932. Through the farming towns and areas, in the spindly children and pale, fagged-out men and women you saw the haggard evidence of the undernourishment, the look of people completely at the end of their tether. In the cities among the workmen, conditions were "deplorable"; some factories worked five shifts of their old employees, giving each a day's work, in turn.

And as if in mockery, God blessed His people with His goodness. Never had harvests been more bountiful than in that lush and sun-warmed autumn of 1931. Arkansas alone made "the best crop in its history," enough food to supply its whole needs for a year.[119] From the Atlantic to the Panhandle, the white waves of cotton rolled — and stood unpicked at five cents a pound.[120] Flies traced tracks in the dust, filming the bright new car models in the display windows, but driving out through the country, you made your way through highways crowded with resurrections from auto graveyards, and from the fields beyond rose a sickish-sweet odor of decay. Fruits and vegetables were simply rotting away in the fields; the price would not pay the cost of harvesting and transportation.[121]

Pick cherries at a cent and a half a pound! Pick pears at five dollars a ton! Red and golden carpets spread themselves beneath the fruit trees, and flies buzzed druggedly, as children dragging their way home from school paused to sag over a fence and look on with wistful, hungry eyes. In California, carloads of oranges were dumped, and like ants from an anthill came the rattling carloads of people, the children scabby with pellagra sores, and guards held them off, as men with hoses squirted kerosene on the oranges, and guards held off the men with fishing nets who had come for the potatoes dumped into the rivers. For how could you hold prices up if people were free to come and take the food away? [122]

And tractors ripped through the abandoned cottonfields and tore the abandoned old shanties off their stilts and upended them like children's playthings tossed aside. And in Florida the blue Atlantic lapped at the white shores below the white towns and the white villas and the glittering white-tile bathrooms and the rows of empty street lamps and the empty streets and the stores that had never sold merchandise and the schoolhouse that had never held children, and the lizards coiling and stretching across the empty pavements and the luxury hotels with the empty bars and the soundless game rooms, the ghost hotels with skeleton framework looming darkly against an empty horizon and chickens roosting in the upper stories.

Up and down the coast they stretched, markers of the Gold Coast and the Big Florida Boom, the boom towns, the ghost towns; and up and down the country roamed the migrants, the uprooted with their pushcarts and jalopies and jungle camps for teen-agers and never a place to call home. There was here, wrote John Steinbeck, the laureate of the thirties, "a crime that goes beyond denunciation," a sorrow beyond all weeping. Larders were bursting with plenty, and infant bellies were swollen with hunger. With every assistance, with every advantage, the world's greatest industrial machine had run down and stopped, and it seemed as if the hopes and heart of the people had stopped with it. In the eyes of the hungry there was wrath; the grapes of wrath were growing, "growing heavy for the vintage." [123]

Above the silent smokestacks and the unmoved and unmoving pinnacles of Manhattan, Bernard M. Baruch gazed from the windows of his thirty-first floor office suite on Madison Avenue and brooded in silence. To the *New York Times* interviewer-artist S. J. Woolf, who captured not only his words but the shapes and facets of his mobile features, it was as if he were thinking aloud. "In the presence of too much food, people are starving, surrounded by vacant houses they are homeless and standing before unused bales of wool and cotton they are dressed in rags."

If this was the result of "economic law," had not the time come to change economic law? The old values were gone; they had failed; somehow men must "provide against human suffering." The old values could not be restored. "We must start with new conceptions. We must forget our old ideas." [124]

"Hoover!" Hoover was the scapegoat for this human misery. In Detroit and again in St. Paul, the White House Secret Service chief, Colonel Starling, felt the "ugly mood" in the sullen, close-packed streets and saw the look on Hoover's face, stricken and bewildered, as for perhaps the first time since the Jackson era a President of the United States was openly booed, and there were cries of "Down with Hoover!" [125] The people, General Hugh Johnson informed Baruch, just blamed Hoover; they had no interest at all in fundamental causes or in the possible interrelationship of a long stricken Europe with a newly stricken America. [126]

But Hoover was not to blame. History, indeed, has come to justify Baruch's early appraisal of him as "an extraordinarily capable man," [127] and to hail the courage "with which he struggled against hopeless odds." The calamity was not of his making." [128] If responsibility is to be assigned, it must be laid primarily to the warmakers of 1914, and more immediately to the blindness of Harding and Coolidge, who permitted unbridled speculation to rampage and the creeping farm depression to blight the buying power of the nation. Other than in his lack of foresight and in his carrying on the policies — or lack of policies — of his predecessors, Herbert Hoover was no more to blame for the Great Depression than those who damned him most bitterly; and indeed, many who scoffed the loudest had hailed his philosophy and elected him in the face of Democratic warnings of disaster.

Where Hoover failed was in his inability to cope with disaster, either practically or emotionally. He was right in estimating the cause of the depression as economic, not political. But never did he see that tariff walls only walled in American goods. He spoke much of "economic law," [129] never realizing that he was a prisoner of eco-

nomic law, of the shibboleths and sacred cows of "free enterprise."
Yet in Hoover's defense it must be said that had he dared think in
terms of new concepts and a planned economy, public opinion might
well have rejected him.[130] Only the depths of suffering could reverse the thinking of an era.

Unemployment was due in large part to the failure of business, so
Hoover started the Reconstruction Finance Corporation to prime
the pump through loans to banks, insurance companies, and railroads.
Baruch was asked to head it, and, instead, suggested Jesse Jones.[131]
A plan similar to the CCC was proposed in 1932. Hoover's greatest
failure, however, was in his seeming indifference to public morale.
The man who had been "the brains of the Administration" in Harding's time, upon whom both Harding and Coolidge had leaned —
brilliant, incisive, a man of unswerving integrity — was still as shy as
if he had never left the Iowa farm from which he had sprung. He had
no small talk, no blandishments, only the strength to endure. He was
a good businessman and that was why he was a poor politician.[132]
"No President ever worked harder than Hoover, or, in his own
peculiar way, enjoyed being President more." But his "reserve and
cold manner" concealed his humanitarian heart. He could not
"break through" to the people.[133] Burdened by his own despair, he
could not lift up others. He had none of the self-confident optimism
of Al Smith or Franklin Roosevelt, who could buoy the people with
hopes and, if these failed, hand out some more. As James Cox observed to Baruch in the fall of 1932, Roosevelt might work no
miracle, but everyone thought that he would, and with the improvement in public morale business might swing up so well that it
would not matter who was President.[134]

Hoover knew despair, and despair paralyzed him.

If those four million unemployed were victims of war or pestilence,
earthquakes, or floods, cried William G. McAdoo, "their tragic condition would stir the heart." After the First World War we had appropriated millions for European relief: "Should we be less considerate of . . . our people?"[135] To Joseph T. Robinson, Baruch
wrote that he could not see why the President seemed unwilling to
distribute government-owned food to the hungry.[136] A whole year
later, the emergency having reached "the most serious proportions,"
General Johnson told Baruch that "so far as I can learn, the administration is making no preparation beyond a few futile conversations between Hoover and the Red Cross."[137] Some explanation of

Hoover's attitude is given by Colonel Starling, who wrote that the President was only seeking "the best method by which hunger and cold could be prevented." With Federal funds shrinking, he preferred a dole to a work-relief program. The dole would be more economical, for it would be sought only in cases of the greatest need and as a last resort, whereas government work would so satisfy the unemployed that they would seek no further, and the employers so that they need no longer seek to provide.[138] Hoover's logic was flawless, his comprehension of human nature somewhat less so.

In any event, he lashed out at the Democrats' insistent demand for a program of "self-liquidating public works to take care of all surplus labor at all times," [139] and at Gettysburg, in the spring of 1931, his face scarcely less marked and careworn than that of the earlier President who also had spoken there to unhearing ears nearly seventy years before, he preached his favorite doctrines of laissez faire and noninterference by the government.[140] Indignantly, Joe Robinson exploded to Baruch: "If the government is powerless in the face of immutable economic law to effect the prosperity of the nation in 1931, how could prospective administrative action two years earlier act to maintain the booming status of business?" [141] Equally logical was Baruch's observation that the traditional Republican support of the tariff, as well as the recent efforts to help the farmers, were adequate precedents for abandoning laissez faire.[142]

What could be done? Baruch had some ideas, and occasionally the President telegraphed him to come down to the White House for a day and a night to impart them.[143] As Hoover himself later said, when it was necessary to get "the Democratic point of view," he would usually consult Baruch, for whom he had real admiration and who also, he well knew, exercised great influence with the Southern senators. Furthermore, it was with a rare flight of prescience, as the Japanese charged into Manchuria two years before Hitler took over Germany, that Hoover appointed Baruch to a commission to study and prepare an American plan of mobilization. The report, when ready, was pigeonholed, and so far as is known was never consulted by President Roosevelt: "He was not interested," was Hoover's grim comment later, "in anything any of us had done." [144]

The Great Depression, however, was now the primary concern. Baruch well knew, as *Business Week* pointed out, that he was being used to head off Democratic sniping; but he did not care. He was

indifferent both to the gibe of his friends — "Don't let that man pick
your brains to get himself out of the hole he is in" — and to the fears
of party chiefs that he might betray trade secrets. Such comments
were of course embarrassing to Hoover. Once he summoned Garet
Garrett and mentioned Baruch's name. "You know what he's thinking now?"

"Why don't you ask him?" Garrett responded.

Hoover shook his head. "I can't." And Baruch, strangely enough,
understood. "I'll tell you about it," he said to Garrett, and did, knowing that the information thus imparted would find its way back to
headquarters. To Garrett privately he added, ". . . if he can use me,
I'll be his office boy." [145]

And Baruch did have some real influence during Hoover's term.
He urged the appointment of his friend Eugene Meyer to the Federal
Reserve Board, for instance; and used his persuasiveness among
Southern Democrats for the confirmation of Chief Justice Charles
Evans Hughes. But where he was of greatest value was in heading
off several somewhat hysterical measures, including a proposed peace-
time War Industries Board. [146]

He also sternly warned inflationary Democrats against the public
clamor for an issue of two billion cheap dollars to get money into
circulation. Cheap money was no answer, he pointed out to Senator
Elmer K. Thomas. Although in 1929 there were only 4.8 billions in
circulation, as against 5.6 billions in 1931, credit, not cash, was the
basis of business, and credit would be impaired by the issue of two
billion paper dollars. England, Baruch reminded Senator Thomas,
reflecting as traditional a view as any of Hoover's, maintained credit
by balancing its budget, not by going off the gold standard. Paper
money to "pay off" the soldiers' bonus would only delude them. All
who had saved would be cheated. [147]

He outlined this program of reconstruction, the so-called "Robinson Plan," in more detail to Cordell Hull. [148] First the budget must
be balanced and the dollar stabilized. Then two billion dollars in
tax-exempt bonds could be lent to the cities and states for revenue-
producing projects — such as slum clearance, or tunnels under
rivers. [149] Something would have to be offered the people to give
them hope for the coming winter; they would have to be freed from
the dread of destitution. Public works meant public buying power.

Whether Baruch was right or wrong in his recovery program depends in large part on one's political philosophy. So far as gold is concerned, his vision seems blurred, for as Franklin Roosevelt was to point out afterwards, the buying power of the world was being stymied because of purchases already made, and the cash on the barrelhead piling up uselessly in the coffers at Fort Knox. But as for the balanced budget versus deficit-spending, like isolationism and Christianity, budget-balancing was talked about but never really tried. It is true that the younger J. P. Morgan was soon to acclaim Roosevelt's move in going off the gold standard, which Baruch viewed stubbornly as a surrender of the holy-of-holies. As for deficit spending, some critics of Roosevelt have charged that his failures stemmed from the fact that he never really spent enough, and it is a fact that until the nineteen-forties and the Second World War he never ran a deficit much over four billion dollars. Two points, however, are certain: that it took war-spending to bring back prosperity, and peacetime spending afterwards soared to incredible heights.

The balanced budget, which has been defined as a matter of faith rather than of thought, was an *idée fixe* with Baruch — a policy sacred with promises and hoary with tradition which had to be abandoned under the impact of reality. For in a sense, a balanced budget put the government in a strait-jacket. To balance your budget would prevent any kind of tax relief that might allow for consumer-spending. In fact, it meant an increase in taxes. It meant reduced spending, even for relief or pump-priming needs. In the end, it might even have meant the second alternative to be posed by Franklin Roosevelt after his inauguration: the complete liquidation of our national economy and starting over from the bottom, rather than throwing in funds to stem the tide.

Baruch, however, went along with the more traditional thinkers in seeing unemployment not as a problem of the Federal government but of the states. The argument that states were so financially depleted that they could not do the job would have had small weight with one who realized that all national revenues came from the states and the people in the states. Furthermore, it could be maintained that only local groups would know who was most in need or most deserving and who could do the necessary work most economically. Yet, despite the conservatism of this plan, Hoover evinced little interest in it, and on May 27, 1932, Baruch made to Joe Robinson a bitter confession of failure.[150]

This defeat came at the end of a month of tergiversation. Since

April, Baruch had been urging the President to balance the budget by immediate reduction of a billion dollars in administrative costs, plus a sales tax — which last would certainly have been no great help toward Mr. Hoover's re-election. In any event, the President had retorted that such a reduction would leave only a half-billion for the Army and Navy at half their present strength; and would also mean the turning of the prisoners out of jail and an over-all reduction of public services. Two and a half billion dollars of the budget, Mr. Hoover explained, were for fixed contractual expenses.

Baruch, not carrying the burden of the practical details of administration, demurred. Erroneously he assumed that there were no items too permanent to be "overhauled." He pinned the President down sharply as to what expenditures were really uncontrollable. It could hardly have been pleasing to the Chief Executive to have Bernard Baruch point out that mail contracts were not budget items, or their disagreement on the amount of the uncontrollable funds, ranging from $2,285,000,000 to $1,700,000,000. Furthermore, observed Baruch, miscellaneous items alone added up to $917,000,000. It might be true, as the President claimed, that depressed business conditions made necessary a revision of the government's estimates of revenue, but it was also true that there remained nearly $800,000,000 in "miscellaneous" funds.[151]

In any event, there is no record in the Baruch Papers of any written answer to Baruch's communiqué of May 25.

So Baruch waited. A world was breaking into chaos and he could not see the future. He had advised his old friend John Golden a month after the crash of 1929 to change his General Electric stock for United States Steel, to buy Radiator and sell Radio, and to hold on to American Smelting and Refining; but in the dark uncertainties of the nineteen-thirties when besought by a friend for advice, he replied shortly that the depression would last until farmers and others who produced real wealth could operate profitably.[152]

He was waiting — a whole people was waiting, unbreathing. There was no warmth, little hope in that dire spring of 1932. Summer cooled into autumn and autumn into winter and Baruch tried to remember what it had been to see people happy. The chill, the dread, reached into the White House; despair reached out to everyone.[153] In this uncertain world, the only certain thing was that Franklin Roosevelt would be the next American President.[154]

15

ELDER STATESMAN

ONE DRAMA was in Berlin. The other was in Washington. One voice was a machine-gun staccato; the other, a trumpet of hope. Twelve years before the lightning of the first atomic blast flashed across Los Alamos, the principles of the Atomic Age were generated in two world capitals, four thousand miles apart: positivism versus negativism, creation versus destruction, two mighty forces rushing blindly and unseen toward each other. Adolf Hitler became Chancellor of the German Reich on January 30, 1933; on March 4, Franklin D. Roosevelt became President of the United States. On March 23 in Berlin, Hitler was granted dictatorial powers by the German Reichstag; almost simultaneously in Washington, Roosevelt was voted emergency powers by the American Congress. Across the world, in two great capitals, two great peoples began their battle with destiny. Across the world, the peoples were waiting.

No one who does not remember can understand the feeling in the United States on that fourth of March. It was a journey into the unknown, a shock from a giant electric battery, revitalizing the nerve cells of a nation. It meant not only a "new deal," but a "new order." It was "a call to arms . . . a crusade to restore America to its own." Sobered with the weight of history, an Associated Press correspondent wrote: "Outwardly, all the traditional pageantry of inaugurations held sway. But . . . never was there such a day, for beneath the panoply of parade ran a waiting and a wanting new to inaugurals." [1]

The voice said "My friends" and embraced a continent. The people could not see the smile. They did not hear the triumphant echo of the President's laughter. They did not know what manner of man this was behind the microphone, any more than the people of Germany knew what manner of man Hitler was — whether Savior or Man on Horseback — and they were too beaten and weary to care. The voice said, "The only thing we have to fear is fear itself," [2] and a tremor ran through the nerves. Across a continent, behind the cash registers of cheap restaurants, from the counters of grubby little stores, from open windows, in the closeness of a family circled around a radio set, the voice sounded, and a look of hope crossed the hopeless faces. Children looked on, wondering; the children would not forget that hour. Children whose older brothers and sisters huddled in hobo jungles, or marched with the Young Communists' League, children born in the shadowy aftermath of the First World War, who could remember nothing but hunger and insecurity and fear, children who would grow up and remember no other President but Roosevelt — they would remember. They would remember the look on their mother's face, and the sudden shine of tears in their father's eyes.

It did not matter what the man had said. The voice had been the voice of a friend; it was as if they could see the moving hands and nodding head and the smile, almost as if he were in the room beside them. "I felt," one girl said, "that he was thinking of me." [3] No miracles occurred; bolted factory doors did not swing open in a week's — or a month's — time. Empty stomachs remained empty. But a whole nation lived on words and hope, on action filling the vacuum of inaction, on the sheer fascination of watching the big show. What happened did not matter, so long as things continued to happen. Dynamics replaced fear. So it was in the United States. So, too, in Germany. The difference was a difference in the nature of the two people, not entirely of political systems. The "Unofficial Observer" of the New Deal, "Jay Franklin," might openly compare it to fascism, but fascism stripped of its political aggressiveness, and endeavoring to "bring under a new regime of law and administration those great areas of economic conflict" which parliamentary democracy alone had been unable to control.[4] Yet, the New Deal was an outgrowth of the American faith. In brief, its basic concept was that of governmental responsibility. It was not creation, but adaptation. Roosevelt did not invent it. He inherited it — from Wilson, who had foreseen it, from Bryan, who had called for it, and Jefferson, who had dreamed it; and perhaps even from Andrew Jackson, who had practised it one hundred years before. Jackson had seen that financial tyranny, no less than political tyranny, was the enemy of freedom. Now, unbraked, economic privilege had wrecked its own privileges, and in the midst of plenty had left millions of people hungry. Economic security was not the alternative to political freedom; it was the reverse of the coin.

The New Deal was revolution, a "bloodless economic and social revolution," based on the premise that the economic balance could no longer be maintained by the functioning of economic law alone. It was not so much change as rediscovery, a reillumination of government as a positive instrument, as well as a negative barrier, whose function was to make liberty, equality, and opportunity available to every American. This was a big job. It was conceived in big terms. But Americans, in that low-water hour of 1933, were not afraid of bigness in government, because the basis of that bigness was free men.[5]

Not since Lincoln had an American president on his inauguration inherited such a burden of disaster. Franklin D. Roosevelt knew it. He saw and thought in pictures. And there were many pictures to be etched on a man's mind back in the winter of 1932–33, whether his name was Franklin Roosevelt or Bernard Baruch, whether he traveled from Washington to Warm Springs or from New York to South Carolina. The Jersey Flats — a dun-colored plain, broken by the weird shapes of habitation, the piled wreckage of plywood and paper, rags and tin, around which human beings crouched and crawled or moved to and fro like figures out of the *Inferno*. To see that wasteland under the skyway was like lifting a lid off hell. No one who saw it could forget it. No one could look away from that stretch of sodden grass and seeping smoke, this human dumping ground of the cities' waste, from which the odors of burning trash and garbage rose fetid by day, and flames leaped and jerked by night. Above, the flashing cars roared away to their escape. From the Jersey Flats there was no escape: this was the end, the potter's field before the grave, the last stopping place of human forms that moved and spoke and bred and birthed and died, but for the most part crouched, silent, unspeaking, unmoving, waiting.

New York. Jersey City. Hoboken. Elizabeth. Newark. Trenton. Philadelphia. Baltimore. Washington. Miles and miles of reeking alleys and rotting slums, crumbling brick towers walling in the

dreams, the lives, the hopes of creatures who stared now at the peeling plaster or into the vacuum of the air shaft, or out at the flying
train or the racing cars; the child sprawled across a fire escape, the
pallid woman alone in a room, staring through a dust-grimed window.

The South — from the air a vista of flame-colored fields hemmed
in green, of brown rivers moving silkily beneath the shadow patterns
of the trees or the stiff old iron bridges where the troops of Lee might
have marched. That was from the air; from the train or the car you
saw the pictures. You saw the great steel fence around the closed
factory building and the light glinting off the three rows of barbed
wire strung around the top, a fence to bear the weight of hundreds,
maddened by want of work and want of food, who would break in
those silent buildings and wreck and crash and destroy. You saw the
shuttered windows of the Farmer's National Bank, and the farmer
stretched out across the steps, asleep, the white skin glinting through
the rents in his overalls, and the red dust falling soundlessly from his
bare toes. You saw, too, the elderly house of the elderly Confederate
relict, with the paint hanging in strips from the clapboards, curtains
drawn genteelly against the poverty within.

You saw the schoolhouse closed in the city, with dust graying
across the windows, and the children squatting silently in the sunlight at home. You saw the towheaded youngster sagging in the tire
swing, too listless to lift her bare feet from the ground. You saw the
newspaper headline of the young father who received his dismissal
notice from the college with the big half-empty classrooms, went
home, took his hunting rifle, stole to the garage, and shot himself.
You saw, mirage-like, the smokeless chimneys and the empty factory
windows, and always the men waiting, shoulders drooping and faces
lifted to watch the racing car or the flying train.

You saw the sag in the shoulders of a man in a white collar and a
threadbare business suit, waiting at the end of a bread line. No
matter how well-brushed his clothes or polished his shoes; no matter
if he had his head high, you could always tell a man on relief by the
sag of his shoulders.

Sharecroppers. The face of the woman who crawled from under
the cabin floor after a rain and said to Margaret Bourke-White:
"Sometimes I tell my husband we couldn't be worse off if we tried." [6]
Tar-paper and tin roofs. The fields of the South and the West, bone-
bare, blown dry, scarred with gullies and pock-marked with shacks on

rickety stilts, or log cabins tilted against stone chimneys, little different from the cabin where Lincoln was born, except for the tin cans of geraniums lining the walk outside. America was a free people, but freedom had limits. You had the right to speak and the right to protest, yes; but you had no right to work and no right to eat, only the right to die.

Colonel Starling, who remembered the last sad years of the Wilson regime and now again was sadly superintending the building of runways and portable ramps from wing to wing of the White House, heard the creak of the wheelchair, and then the echo of laughter in the corridors. Franklin D. Roosevelt was laughing. He laughed even as his wheelchair rolled down to the East door, and he struggled up, painfully, to walk the ninety feet to the reviewing stand.[7] "The Laughing Revolution," a historian would term his administration.[8] It was with a kind of "grim determination of joy" that Roosevelt stood up to start the administration that began in calamity and ended in war.[9] Nothing could be done, the more conventional economists said, and yet he was doing it.[10] Nothing frightened him — there was no human problem, he believed, that was beyond human solution. The country that had lost faith needed, above all, a leader with faith in himself.[11] Mrs. Roosevelt once said that no one could give her a greater sense of security than her own husband. He was the thirty-second President of the United States, and, if his mission failed, he said, he would be the last.[12]

"I stuck with him for the glorious Hundred Days," Bernard Baruch would say afterward,[13] and it is significant that his all-out dedication to the all-out New Deal only lasted that long. Not even he could withstand the excitement of that time. For it was war. Franklin Roosevelt was a war president from the moment he lifted his hand and voice in the oath of office. "From 1933 to 1945 we were always in a crisis," Frances Perkins wrote later.[14] Above all, there was action, filling a void, releasing a paralysis of fear. "We are going to make a country," the President said, "in which no one is left out." [15] He spoke words and he offered action. On March 9, the Banking Act to reopen the sound banks and to sequester gold; on the twentieth, the Economy bill, with a fifteen per cent cut of all salaries and veterans' pensions. Finally, on the last day of the month, the President signed the bill creating the Civilian Conservation Corps, which took thousands of young men off the streets and put them to constructive work out of doors. May brought the Agricultural Adjustment Act (AAA), the Federal Emergency Relief Act, and the TVA. In June came cancellation of the gold clause in Federal and private bonds, which many saw as the end of the world; the Emergency Railroad Transportation Act, the Home Owners Loan Corporation, and the National Industrial Recovery Act (NIRA), which included a $3,300,-000,000 public works program. It was a beginning.

Much ill was done, hastily done, and soon to be undone. It did not matter; we were "on our way." The erstwhile Republican Harold L. Ickes said, "A new America is developing in the womb of time." [16] Gerald Johnson wrote truthfully, "It was a moment that will not be forgotten while anyone that experienced it survives." [17]

The New Deal was the miracle of a man, a miracle of action rather than of ideas. Roosevelt succeeded in those Hundred Days where an even greater man might have failed. Hoover, with his magnificent intellect and dogged courage, had been shaken by the spectacle of the great American industrial machine shuddering to a stop.[18] But the self-confident Roosevelt only threw back his head and chortled at "Old Dr. Skinflint," while rallying a crusade of the people against "chiselers," "economic royalists," and "malefactors of great wealth." The people shrank from identifying themselves with Hoover, that saddened man, too weary even to smile, who rode at Roosevelt's side on Inauguration Day. But all were one with the laughing man on crutches, who found so many scapegoats for the evils that dogged them. It had taken the rock-bottom level of the depression to produce in the people "the state of mind that would permit the spending." [19] Hoover had been crucified, his little spending denounced by the same man who would pour out billions when the moment and the mood of the people had changed. Franklin D. Roosevelt was the man of the hour.

Bernard Baruch had known Roosevelt for a long time. Back during the First World War, Baruch had watched him, eager and energetic, chafing at the leash in Josephus Daniels' office. He could remember that white face lifted above its crippled body, before the roars and raucousness of the Democratic convention of 1924. But, most of all, he would remember him at Hyde Park.

Occasionally Baruch would make the pleasant journey up the Hudson to the sprawling old house of the Roosevelts, pleasant with the patina of age and gracious living. Even today, when Hyde Park has become a shrine, it has that crowded, untidy, lived-in look that it had when the "country squire" drew his strength from its peace, and the children and grandchildren frolicked around him.

For Baruch, there was peace, too, as he walked past the quiet of the rose garden and into the shadowy hallway, where splotched hunting prints lined the walls, and the collection of stuffed birds, shot by the young Franklin, gathered dust on the recessed bookcase to the left of the door.[20] If Baruch's appointment was strictly political, he might be ushered to a small room in the back, where the walls squeezed around a huge desk littered with knickknacks, with the big round-shouldered man smiling behind it. But in pleasant weather the visitor would be shown right down the hall through the long library and a French window, to the murmur, "The family is on the lawn."

It was like a print out of Currier and Ives, that family group: the statuesque elderly lady with her ruffled frock and curled white hair; nearby the gracious younger woman in a white dress and tennis shoes, a velvet band around her hair, brisk hands busy with the knitting in her lap. On the great lawn below romped a litter of children and dogs, and in their midst the big man who played as if he were one of them, or sat lounging in his chair, a book unopened upon his knees, eyes fixed on the children and the shining expanse of the river beyond.[21]

Roosevelt turned to greet his visitor. Baruch would have been struck, as all were, by the initial impact of that great frame above the helpless legs; [22] and then he was embraced by the smile and held in the warmth and light of it. But he was not bedazzled. He had known Roosevelt too long to have illusions about him.

To the people at large, Franklin Roosevelt could always be reduced to fairly simple fundamentals. They recognized him as the patrician that he was, yet did not question his devotion to the common man. They sensed, perhaps, that with him, as with Jefferson, his love of man had come out of his love for his own acres, that in the river and hills and great fields he had envisioned the kind of America in which all men could find their own Hyde Parks. This was a subject in which he, the country squire, and Baruch, the Carolina planter, could find kinship.

So pervading is the Roosevelt legend today that it is hard to remember a time when he was comparatively unknown. To most people it was as if he had burst upon the scene full-armed, a crusader to lead them out of the darkness. They did not remember the arrogant young assemblyman, nor Wilson's impulsive and volatile Under-Secretary of the Navy, nor the invalid he had become, battling against almost insuperable odds of weakness and pain. They knew nothing of the crucible in which he had been tempered, nor what manner of man had emerged. They never did know, really, for he was continually at cross-purposes with himself.

Baruch had realized in the spring of 1932 that what the country had to have as President was a tough man.[23] Was Roosevelt tough? No one knew. Laughter is always suspect in politics, and charm scarcely less so, and one got rather a "lightweight" impression of Roosevelt in his early years. Baruch had looked with understandable skepticism on Roosevelt's early financial misadventures, such as an experiment with mechanical salesmen, in order to release workers for "constructive labor." Nor had the trial run of the New Deal in Albany, which for all its good record of social justice had put the state some ninety million dollars in the red, overly impressed him.[24] What manner of man had Roosevelt become?

Frances Perkins has paid tribute to the "Divine Providence" that intervened to save Roosevelt from "total paralysis, despair, and death." [25] But the instruments of Providence were human. His mother, "Madam Roosevelt," as the Hyde Park natives called her, longed for her son to retire from the distasteful rowdiness of politics. But the team of Eleanor Roosevelt and Louis McHenry Howe used Roosevelt's latent ambition as a weapon and labored to free him from his mother's possessiveness. Mrs. Roosevelt has admitted that without pushing her husband might have been just "a nice young society man." [26] Alvin Johnson contends that the paralysis may even have been the making of him.[27] And Elliott Roosevelt adds that without Louis McHenry Howe his father would never have been President of the United States.[28]

Louis McHenry Howe has been called "the most singular personality in American politics." [29] Stress upon the Roosevelt-Hopkins relationship has overshadowed Howe. Hopkins long outlived his predecessor, but he was not the New Deal.[30] And it illuminates Roosevelt's peculiar needs that Howe and Hopkins were so much alike.

They were alike temperamentally and physically. Both were invalids, living on their nerves, irritable, often bedridden and wracked with pain. Each recognized greatness and himself as the instrument of greatness. They never questioned Roosevelt's ends, only his means. Neither was really "the man behind Roosevelt." But each lived at the White House.[31]

Yet of Hopkins and Howe, Howe was the wiser, according to Mrs. Franklin D. Roosevelt, who adds that he was "the biggest man from the point of view of imagination and determination" whom she had ever known.[32] Shrewd Harold Ickes called him the one individual who could or would "tell the President what the facts are, no matter how unpleasant they appear." As Mrs. Roosevelt has pointed out, confidants like Hopkins and Howe "became jealous of outside advisers such as Mr. Baruch and made it difficult for cordial relations to exist."[33] Howe was frank to grant this. "A politician," he said, "can have only one adviser."[34] Baruch was one of his real friends, but given the chance, Howe might render Baruch's influence less, that his own might be more.

For Roosevelt was Howe's work of art, his aim and purpose in life. He never wavered from his goal. Howe had looked into the face of a man and said: "I decided that the greatest adventure of which I could think was to put that man in the White House."[35] And he announced his determination, with Roosevelt on his sickbed, facing a verdict that he would never walk again. During the weeks when Roosevelt, filmed with sweat, lay struggling to move just one toe; during months when the Hudson River neighbors chattered glibly of "poor Frank" and the utter collapse of his future hopes; during years when the name of Roosevelt seemed forgotten, Howe was always there, waiting, planning, scheming, pushing Mrs. Roosevelt into organization work and speechmaking, always keeping the long-range campaign going. Letters vibrant with Roosevelt's own buoyance were dispatched across the country. Roosevelt was "on his way."

Yet had he been Louis Howe's "man," as has been charged, Roosevelt would hardly have gambled the long years of planning and preparation on the "Republican" year of 1928. Howe dared not risk '28, and his face was cast in gloom that election night when the Republican tidal wave rolled across the nation and the State of New York while Roosevelt, his mother, and Frances Perkins waited hour after hour, almost alone, while the slow trickle of votes that elected the Governor of New York spelled the defeat of Herbert Hoover four years later.[36] Roosevelt was suddenly the Democrat who could

win in a Republican year. Next, he had to choose whether he would
be his own man or Al Smith's. And he did so.

But these were preliminary skirmishes. The boldness and drive of
the primary campaign of 1932 gave some of the answers. Then, for
the first time, Baruch became sure that Roosevelt was a fighter.[37] He
felt that it took real courage for Roosevelt to come out openly before
his nomination against the premature payment of the soldiers' bonus;
and one day after the declaration of the Bank Holiday on March 5,
1933, Baruch telegraphed the Executive his congratulations on his
courage.[38] What Baruch recognized in Roosevelt was a capacity to
act, and the insight that even wrong action was better than inaction.

A crippled man leading a crippled nation — there was irony in it,
and triumph, too. As Senator Vandenberg later declared, Roosevelt
was "a gallant soul . . . a superb example of personal courage . . . in a
sodden, saddened world." [39]

He was, moreover, a politician, and he learned his politics from
Louis Howe. Howe knew every stratagem of the trade. "Shifty and
tricky himself," he encouraged the same tactics in Roosevelt; for the
outsider, it was often hard to tell where Roosevelt began and Howe
left off. Here was the origin of Roosevelt's pleasant nods of the
head, his unvaryingly cheerful "Yes, I see" and "That's very interesting" which misled so many of his visitors, and which Bernard Baruch came to understand very well.[40]

The less perceptive contended that Roosevelt did not know his
own mind. Roosevelt knew his mind perfectly, and knew when not
to express it — another trick that he had picked up from Howe. Express sympathy for all, but "promise nothing" was Howe's rule; the
law of politics was to be all things to all men.[41] So Roosevelt was the
friend of the rich, a "jolly big brother" to the crippled invalids at
Warm Springs, and a kind of father-image to the poor. His charm
was all-encompassing. The comment of a British labor leader was
typical: "I have never met a man whom I liked so much so quickly." [42]
He was diplomat and demagogue, dictator and democrat, his inborn
conservatism offset by the desire to do new and startling things; and
all this added up to "the most skillful political leader of our times."
He could get "the goods" out of both political parties. Professing to
be the champion of the Left, he saved the country for the Right. He
could make a fighting speech for the liberals and act with the utmost
conservatism. His drives and compulsions, shooting off in a dozen dif-

ferent directions at once, let him see all sides, and like and be liked "by such oddly different types of people." He had to have a new interest every day. He was at once world-weary and aglow with the zest of living, charitable and vindictive, with a bitterness that cost his country the talents of some splendid public servants.[43]

His associates Frances Perkins and Henry Morgenthau, Jr., found him perhaps the most complicated human being they had ever known; even his sympathetic biographer and friend, Robert Sherwood, admitted his inability to peer into the man's "heavily forested interior." [44] He had the breadth and vision of genius: in a sense, even his weaknesses made him great, for they led to spurts and flights of the imagination of which a more integrated man would not have dreamed. They spelled the triumph of TVA and the tragedy of Yalta. Yet these variables added up to a kind of grand simplicity which the people, at least, could understand.

Roosevelt was not like Woodrow Wilson. Wilson, for all his intellect, was essentially a simple man, in whom greatness burned direct and untrammeled. To some who had known Wilson, Roosevelt did not seem a great man at all, but "merely a great personality," a self-salesman whose primary concern was to get votes.[45] This is not necessarily a condemnation. Roosevelt well knew what Wilson never knew, that political earnings alone can buy the right to statesmanship. Whether his ultimate motivation was his power-drive or a yearning to serve mankind can never really be judged.

To Mrs. Roosevelt, learning politics as she sat knitting, watching the ebb and flow of great men passing her parlor windows, came a disturbing thought. She watched Bernard Baruch: to her, he seemed one of the wisest and most generous people she had even known.[46] Yet, as she saw him with her husband and felt the clash of those two great egos, she was struck with a realization. Both spoke of the past and of their common country as only those speak who know it, who have talked with old people who, in their turn, have talked with those who remembered many things long forgotten. Roosevelt's father, for instance, a boy of eight when Andrew Jackson left the White House; Baruch's great-grandmother, who had danced with Lafayette! Yet what Mrs. Roosevelt saw went deeper even than this. Half subconsciously, she came to realize how much her husband and Bernard Baruch were alike. They were alike in their adaptability, or "elasticity," as she called it, in their zest for living and the game of politics, their "eagerness and boldness of personality." Baruch was less exuberant, less overwhelming perhaps, yet the same basic inclinations were there. Both had the same eager extroversion, the same love of people, and both loved to be leaders. But with Roosevelt, leadership was a psychological necessity; only by domination could he free himself from overdomination. "Franklin," Mrs. Roosevelt would sometimes say, "must always have the final power." [47]

Both were given to soaring flights of the imagination. On seeing the Sahara, Roosevelt was inspired with grandiose plans to irrigate it. Baruch might muse on Africa, concluding that time could be telescoped some three centuries there by immediate installations of radio, television, and airfields, dispensing with such antiquated anachronisms as railroad and telegraph lines. Of the human factor, of the difficulty of juxtaposing modern technocracy on a primitive, barbaric people, he seemingly did not think at all.

John Hancock once compared Baruch's mind to a kind of porpoise, plunging down here and coming up there. "He's spooky about intuition," Hancock said. If he was tired he would not even look for an answer. He would sleep on it and the next morning the answer would be there. Yet he was "coldly logical," for within a day or so he could work backward through the steps that had led to the conclusion, and you could follow him through the process. This last Roosevelt could not do, and his contempt for logic was extreme. [48]

The differences between Roosevelt and Baruch grated all the more because of their likenesses. In the pre-presidential days, Roosevelt had asked Baruch for advice on economics, and had even listened. But now, almost boastfully, Roosevelt declared that he never read economics, or that he "might experiment a little with silver." [49] To Baruch this was heresy. [50]

But Baruch himself had committed the fatal heresy, not only of betting on the wrong horses in 1924 and 1928, but in 1932 of failing to bet on the right one. His role as a New Dealer was thus from the first ambiguous. If the New Dealers had doubts about him, it is perhaps because he reserved so many doubts about the foremost New Dealer. Arthur M. Schlesinger, Jr., has a story that in 1931 Baruch told the elder Morgenthau that if "Frank" were nominated, he would not give one penny to the campaign. Morgenthau protested. Had not Roosevelt been a good governor? "Yes," Baruch admitted, but he's so wishy-washy." [51]

Thus, Baruch's cardinal sin was his failure to issue a pre-convention endorsement of Roosevelt's candidacy, and this may have opened the door to those who were resolved to deny him influence. That he put party unity above the divisive battles of personalities, that he was merely following his habitual pattern, as established after 1925, of pre-convention public silence did not matter to the Roosevelt crusaders. Furthermore, as the "Unofficial Observer" put it, Baruch's propensity for being all things to all men diminished his usefulness to any one cause or one man.[52]

Baruch, of course, had his share of enemies who hastened to tell Roosevelt that he was against him.[53] He was convinced that Roosevelt believed it. Vehemently he denied the story of a secret meeting and a combine of Judge Daniel F. Cohalan, William Randolph Hearst, and himself to "stop" anybody.[54] Eventually he appealed to the candidate himself. He had always felt that their personal relations were such that they could discuss this question frankly. However, he did not pledge Roosevelt his support. He would be for the candidate whose program was best for the country.[55] Roosevelt, who appreciated this kind of hedging and knew that Baruch would never desert a ship that proved seaworthy, nevertheless shot back an "aside" about people who professed friendship to him but emitted false statements behind his back in the blissful assurance that they would never be repeated to him. As for Baruch, why did he not come up to Albany sometime this winter "to stay with us?" [56]

On March 26, 1932, Roosevelt called Baruch in for a discussion of "the situation in general and the economics of it in particular." "You have such clear thinking processes and such a fund of information," the Governor wrote, "that I should much like to get your slant." [57]

Baruch responded with canny shrewdness, advocating such general programs as slum clearance and varied public works programs. But he was far more concerned about where and how to get the money than was Franklin Roosevelt. He could agree with the Governor that the expenditures of large sums by the government would spur employment as the money sank back into industry. Two billion dollars worth of bonds he thought might be sold, or funds be lent to the cities and states. To administer such expenditures would require a courageous leader of sound judgment. And then he harped on his perpetual theme, which whether right or wrong would certainly have not been enough in itself — the necessity of a balanced budget, because otherwise, who would dare to invest in industries which needed the money? [58]

In June 1932, smiling, conciliatory, still silent, Baruch arrived at the Democratic National Convention in Chicago. Excitement sparked the air. This was the year of victory, and Room 1702 at the Congress Hotel was virtually the "anteroom to the White House." For there, hunched, gasping for breath, and weighing less than one hundred pounds, sat a figure who might have stepped out of the pages of Dickens — or of medieval folklore. Louis McHenry Howe pulled the strings. Roosevelt would win, he knew, if he could get the nomination — but how could he get the nomination?. Numerically, the cards were already stacked against him: segregated here and divided there, for Garner, for Ritchie, for Smith, and who would be the first to yield?

In Baruch's pocket lay a letter from Owen D. Young, "declining" a nomination that would never be offered him. And around Baruch surged an oddly assorted company: the flamboyant General Hugh S. Johnson; Wilson's doggedly loyal Admiral Cary Grayson and his wife; Morton Schwartz, the banker; the magazine publisher Condé Nast, and with him the beautiful blond editor of one of his magazines, *Vanity Fair*, who wore a blue polka-dot dress and typed doggedly to Baruch's dictation, with amateur slowness and two fingers. Clare Boothe Brokaw * was wide-eyed at the hurly-burly of her first political convention. Mark Sullivan, dropping in on the party, saw Baruch and Johnson pacing the floor as they argued about the national debt. He looked wonderingly at the slender girl, thinking it a pity on that warm June day that such beauty and youth should be chained to the political machine. Not in his wildest dreams would he have dared imagine that the girl in the polka-dot dress within a few years would herself be a speaker at a national convention.** [59]

Who was the Baruch party for? Who was Baruch for? No one knew, and Baruch was almost pulled to pieces by the candidates who were pursuing him. James F. Byrnes was convinced that his friend's affections were divided between Newton D. Baker and Albert Ritchie; Clare Brokaw was equally sure that he was still for Al Smith. This was true, according to Baruch himself. Secretly, he would have pre-

* Now Mrs. Henry Luce.
** A Republican convention, by the way.

ferred Smith above all other candidates, but Smith would not let anyone really work for him.[60]

There were others with claims to his support. The old war horse William McAdoo probably had first place in his affections. By virtue of ability, not "availability," Owen D. Young seemed the most qualified, and by virtue of party regularity, "Bert" Ritchie was the logical nominee.[61] This was Baruch's private opinion, and Ritchie simmered because he kept it private.[62] But why should Baruch waste his chance for future political influence by coming out for men who had scarcely more likelihood of being nominated than Will Rogers of Oklahoma? However, he had nothing to do with the nomination of Roosevelt, he frankly said later. He never moved hand or foot for him.[63]

Here, Baruch's much vaunted political sagacity seems wanting. He had not been "right" since Wilson; he had backed a loser in 1924, and again in 1928. So despite the proof in his private correspondence that he had initiated a new policy of backing no one before the nomination, it was not believed at the time, and, as we have seen, almost all of the candidates seemed to have some claim upon him, Roosevelt alone excepted. Baruch's "neutrality" was thus viewed either as outright opposition, or as an attempt to play in with whoever was nominated, and it won no favor in the Roosevelt headquarters. "For Roosevelt Before Chicago" was a phrase with pregnant meaning.

Nevertheless, Baruch was not a party to any movement to "stop Roosevelt," either at Chicago or before it. He had foreseen the New Yorker's nomination, and he was too shrewd a politician to contest the inevitable.

Even more mysterious than Baruch's pre-convention stand was his role in the convention itself. His "party" went its separate ways. Clare Brokaw was for Smith; Hugh Johnson busied himself "stopping" Roosevelt. Despite rumors of a Southern "break" to Baker, there was a missing cog in the wheel — Bernard Baruch, who certainly had no reason for preferring Baker to Roosevelt. Furthermore, South Carolina in convention had gone on record for Roosevelt the previous fall, and now at Byrnes's behest was swinging into line. Long since, Baruch had halted a half-serious move for South Carolina to give him a "favorite son" nomination. Despite the alleged "great demand," Baruch had no desire to see either himself or valuable time wasted, and, with his innate fear of the ridiculous, squelched the movement of his native state.[64]

Undercurrents were grim, however, in that depression year of 1932. Grimness even edged the gentle humor of Will Rogers. "The Republicans — " he drawled, why attack them? "They did the best they could with what they had."

Beneath the hoopla and jubilee, rumors of deals were plentiful. Without deals, there would have been no nomination of Abraham Lincoln, nor of Franklin D. Roosevelt. But Baruch was a party to none of them; peacemaking was his only concern. He did arrange a kind of nonpolitical "make up and make friends" interview between those two perpetual adversaries, Smith and McAdoo, and what was said the newspapers could only guess. Apparently an attempt was made, under cover of good drinks and good talk, to "soften" Al Smith for the inevitable, much as McAdoo himself had been softened four years before.

The moment the nomination was official, Baruch with Hugh S. Johnson at his side walked straight up to Jim Farley. "We're yours to command," he said.[65] At the Congress Hotel he offered his hand to a now mollified Howe, saying, "My President has been nominated. What can I do to help?" [66]

The next morning Jimmy Byrnes was urging Homer Cummings and Farley to make friends with Baruch, who after all was the Democrats' most important business contact.[67]

This was a party committee matter. Farley's predecessor, wealthy John J. Raskob, a forefront leader in the "Stop Roosevelt" movement, in answer to Baruch's warnings against policy statements before the nomination had retorted that he hoped this marked no attempt to dictate to the National Committee.[68] Now a new Administration was in the offing and so, quickly, the word was passed down the line to Baruch: Would he like to be party treasurer? This he politely declined; his favor did not need to be curried. He was all-out for the ticket.

Promptly his pledge was channeled on to headquarters, who were assured that Baruch would contribute as much as the party deemed wise. The assurance was hardly necessary.

For, as Frank Kent cynically observed, once the hostilities were over, Baruch stood ready, a fountain pen in one hand and a checkbook in the other. It might well have been in that depression year that Franklin D. Roosevelt could have won the Presidency had he stayed home and chatted with neighbors from the big porch at Hyde Park. But this was an uncertainty. The certainty was that the Democratic Party was no less bankrupt than the banks. The name of Baruch was of course thus doubly blessed; but from Baruch's own point of view, even more important was his opportunity for other services. For instance, the nation's second Democrat, Al Smith, had sulked sullenly ever since the convention; and it was no secret that the Tammany chieftain's ultimate capitulation to Roosevelt, the "old potato," as well as much of the flow of bright new coin through the arid party coffers was due to Bernard Baruch.[69]

In 1932, for the first time since 1916, Baruch had some opportunity to throw his weight: he was no longer regarded, as he had complained so bitterly that he was a few years previously, merely for his financial contributions.[70] The President-elect appreciated his shrewdness and gave him a chance for real influence in the campaign.

The Democratic nominee for the Presidency of the United States waved his arm. "This is the Brain Trust, Bernie, and you're the Professor Emeritus." [71]

His head just grazing the doorway of the tiny study at Hyde Park, Bernard Baruch scanned the faces before him. There was Howe, long ears dragging his collar, deep-set spaniel eyes gazing mournfully. There, too, was Professor Raymond Moley of Columbia, slant-eyes narrowed in suspicion; and his colleague, the curlyheaded and boyish Rexford G. Tugwell. Sitting in was Baruch's and Roosevelt's old friend, Judge Samuel Rosenman. This was the original "Brain Trust." Later there would be additions and substitutions. The limits of Baruch's participation were set by the President-elect in his introduction. Baruch was never to be "quite in the inner circle, not in the real Brain Trust." [72] His correspondence reveals that he saw the nominee only three times between the convention and the twentieth of December. His role had been cast: adviser to the advisers, Elder Statesman without portfolio.[73]

"The failure to use Baruch is the most glaring wastage of good brains in an Administration which prides itself on preferring intelligence to political regularity," John Franklin Carter, Jr. (Jay Franklin) commented some two years later.[74] Actually, Baruch was "used" more than this particular writer knew, although the line of demarcation between him and the "inner circle" was deep and strong. This was not entirely due to personal distrust on the part of Roosevelt, nor even of his closest advisers such as Howe, who, with Rosenman, selected the original Brain Trust. There were solid reasons why Baruch was not permitted to exercise his talents. For, to the general public, Baruch was the epitome of the damned — a New York man, a Wall Street operator.[75] Thus, he could not be elevated. Wilson had dared flout public opinion with Baruch, but not Roosevelt at the very moment when Wall Street had just been tried and found guilty of the greatest depression in history. Public opinion demanded a whipping boy, and Wall Street was it. But even if Baruch had not come out of Wall Street, his facility at money-making was suspect. Frances Perkins has recalled the jealousy and awe felt at an intellect which operated so that "coming out of a scramble where all lost, he would make money." [76] Baruch understood the situation perfectly. He was obnoxious to many around the President. Along with many others whose patriotism and ability could well have been used, Baruch's very success kept him on the fringes.[77]

Among orthodox New Dealers, those who believed (as Baruch did) that the "natural law" played a major part in economic depressions, or that Americans should be able to grow up to become millionaires, or believed in the virtues of individualism were not acceptable. In the past, candidates had usually sought advice among financiers and industrialists, but Sam Rosenman advised steering clear of them. They had seemingly failed to produce anything constructive. Why not go to the universities? And the result was the Brain Trust.

"Damned bunch of Johnny-come-latelies," Baruch would growl afterward. "I was pioneering most of the stuff they were so proud of before they ever heard of it. You'd think they invented the whole idea of better working conditions and legal assistance for the working man."

This tight-knit group of young men — what did they know of Baruch? Did they know of his support of the Adamson eight-hour day law? Did they know that it was Baruch who had put the first private money into a public housing project? Did they know of his sixteen-year battle for preparedness, or of the twelve-year fight for farm parity, written now, at last, into the Democratic platform? Did they remember the long blight years of the Democratic Party, when Bernard Baruch had helped salvage it from virtual receivership? No. They had been back in the schoolroom. They did not see in this man of conservative instincts the courage that would bring him out on a limb sometimes where even a so-called liberal did not dare to climb.

They did not know of his sense of responsibility toward the poor.[78] To them he was "the wolf of Wall Street."

Raymond Moley has admitted that at that initial meeting of Baruch and the Brain Trust, the financier was received with far more resentment than enthusiasm.[79] He was soon shunted off to prepare some "memos" of his ideas, which, Moley wrote Roosevelt on July 16, were excellent and of great value to the campaign.[80] His May 28 memorandum on agriculture was typical. Citing the South's understanding since Nullification days of the plight of the farmer in a nation whose industry was protected by high tariffs, he pointed out that this had been a basic cause of Secession.[81]

It was Moley who suggested that Baruch's reports be amplified into speeches. In his book *After Seven Years*, Moley expressed the gratitude of the Brain Trust for Baruch's subsequent "loan" of hard-hitting General Hugh S. Johnson for the speech-writing brigade, and especially for his "magnificent draft speech" blasting the economic ideas of Herbert Hoover. Speaking for the group, Moley wrote of Baruch: "We gradually came to look upon his generous intellectual contributions with admiration, respect and gratitude." [82]

A final expression of thanks came from the candidate himself. On August 30 he asked Baruch to hold himself in readiness for consultation, as one of "only a few people whose judgment I value . . . It would help me in a very practical sense if you would give me your thought on matters from time to time." Moley was to be the "clearinghouse"; any call or letter coming from him was to be interpreted as coming directly from Roosevelt.[83]

Among other suggestions made by Baruch during the campaign was the creation of a Farm Board to buy surpluses when prices fell below the world price plus the tariff. These could then be sold abroad, losses to be recouped for the government by a sales tax on the entire crop. The larger the surplus, the larger the tax, and the less the price. This, of course, was McNary-Haugenism all over again, and again Baruch suggested that a trial be made with wheat alone. The idea of crop control is also implicit in this memo, but how it was to be achieved, he did not say. Certainly no plan of destroying crops crossed his mind. He favored Roosevelt's idea of buying up marginal lands. Current farm policies, he thought, set farmer against farmer and county against county. Why not tax the processors of wheat and cotton and distribute the ensuing fund to the

farmers, proportionately to their sales? — an idea which was repeated in a famous clause of the AAA.

The campaign roared on. Baruch dictated his memos. Day by day,
week by week, studies of agriculture, of finance, of the regulation of
industry, prepared by Baruch and members of his "team" contributed
facts and ideas for Roosevelt's campaign addresses. Nor were Baruch's contributions theoretical. By following press criticism of
Roosevelt's campaign addresses, he was able to suggest rebuttals.[84]

When the votes had been counted, there was some public clamor
that Baruch should be in the Cabinet. "It's your job now," the California Republican Committeeman Mark Requa wrote. "Go to it." [85]
During the next few weeks, Baruch was "spoken of" for the Treasury,
the State Department, the ambassadorship to England, Federal Railroad Coordinator, and a dozen or so other plump "plums." Meanwhile, the silence from headquarters fairly reverberated. Baruch went
down to Warm Springs, where the nominee laughed and chatted and
sucked on his upthrust cigarette holder and dropped a hint, no more,
that the "professor emeritus" might be his choice for chairman of
the American delegation to the forthcoming London Economic Conference. Back home, Baruch conferred with Moley, also Tugwell,
and others, for study and discussion of the Conference.[86] Morgenthau had asked to see him over the weekend to discuss agriculture.

Meanwhile, rumors started as to a "break" between the adviser and
the nominee. On December 20, Baruch wrote the President-elect,
spurning any charges of disloyalty and disclaiming any desire for
office.[87]

Was Baruch bowing out in the name of party loyalty, to save the
President from embarrassment, or was he saving face by declining
an office that might never be offered him? Or was this a last-minute
attempt to force Roosevelt's hand? If so, silence still engulfed
Albany and Hyde Park. Nor can this letter be taken on its face
value alone without comparison with a note to McAdoo some six
weeks later. Not at Warm Springs, before his election, or since, had
"the Governor" consulted Baruch on a single appointment or on
any connection with his administration.

That letter brought results that Baruch did not intend. For one
thing, it brought McAdoo and a suggestion that Baruch rebuffed
promptly. "I'm going to see the President; is there anything you
want?" the Senator from California queried.

"Only to be left alone," Baruch said.

McAdoo persisted. "Mr. Hearst says he wants the President to name you Secretary of State."

Baruch countered, "I don't know those people very well and I don't think I'd fit in." In view of the later antics of the more frenzied Brain Trusters, this was a masterpiece of understatement.* [88]

His friends, generally, viewed his stand as a wise one. General Pershing wrote that Baruch would be most valuable as a private citizen.[89]

Baruch preferred power to responsibility. Roosevelt was going his own way. Sooner or later, if Baruch accepted office, a "break" would inevitably come, and any break between him and the President would wreck his power and usefulness in the Administration. Baruch knew the rules of the game, and the first of these was loyalty. He urged McAdoo to support the President's policies and, if he was dissatisfied, to take up the matter in private.[90]

Human vision could scarcely grasp the immensity of the task that lay ahead. When Woodrow Wilson had left office, the United States had won a war and worked for a peace based on the principles of malice toward none and charity for all. Now, twelve years later, Baruch foresaw the end of an era of shortsighted materialism in the capital. The Republicans had declined to do anything about either the tariff or farm prices. More machines, which meant increased production per worker, had pushed two million people out of their jobs. Meanwhile, the Hawley-Smoot Tariff had frozen the commerce of the world. Baruch believed that some of this would be righted under a Democratic regime, and he had some ideas of what must be done in the immediate emergency. Only by a balanced budget, Baruch kept repeating, and the maintenance of a sound currency, some beer taxes for an added possible $500,000 revenue, a lowered tariff and restricted production would things right themselves.[91] Roosevelt thought differently.

Between the President and Baruch, the areas of disagreement were now becoming broad. Instead of a balanced budget and a rigid gold standard, the Administration intended to apply new and frankly ex-

---

* Carter Field in his biography of Baruch says that he was offered the position of Secretary of the Treasury, but declined, mistrusting the President's monetary policies.

perimental cures to an unprecedented crisis. Baruch and the President might have the same ends, but their means were different indeed, and Roosevelt's means were a vital part of the whole New Deal program. Both, for instance, espoused "sound money," but Roosevelt had never defined sound money as necessarily based on the gold standard. Vital differences of concept thus helped eliminate Baruch from the chairmanship of the delegation to the London Economic Conference; Roosevelt could never have appointed as his personal representative a man who saw something sacred about the properties of gold. How far apart were Baruch's ideas and those of the Administration appears in a speech which he delivered at Johns Hopkins University only a few days before the inauguration. He denounced the weakness that "wants something to lean on." Banks, railroads, farmers, workers, all were turning toward Pennsylvania Avenue, all "blind to the fact that government by its very nature leans against everybody." Our sole remaining reliance was the Federal credit, and there were those who proposed to destroy it "by one universal act of repudiation." Thus spoke Baruch, out of turn, and the ensuing confusion was great.[92] He was told that he had done incalculable injury to the Democratic cause, and that thereafter he would no longer be "available" for consultation within the financial circles of the party.[93]

Since now the President did not let Baruch know what was in his mind, he was "flabbergasted" when the repudiation of the gold clause in government bonds was announced to the country. Baruch was not alone. The indignation of Senator Carter Glass can be imagined only in terms of the salty explosiveness of that picturesque character.

"Have you talked with Carter Glass?" someone asked Roosevelt immediately afterward.

"No, I haven't dared," was the President's reply.[94]

Six months later the Virginian was still smarting. "How much of your newly minted gold," he wrote Baruch, "are you going to exchange for the government's paper promises to pay, which the government has already officially repudiated?"[95]

As far as the public was concerned, Baruch followed the advice which he had given to McAdoo. The President knew that Baruch would be perfectly frank if they talked things over, but as for public announcements of disagreement with the Administration, that was not to be feared from one who thought so highly of loyalty and party unity.[96] In April 1933, Baruch told Senator Key Pittman that

there was so much of the legislation then under consideration with
which he was out of sympathy that he would rather not appear before
congressional committees,[97] and he later expressed his sympathy for
Joe Robinson, the Democratic leader of the Senate, who had to
follow the same rule of loyalty, however much it went against his
private beliefs and convictions.[98]

But the New Deal in those days was not content with silence. It
was a crusade, and crusaders want approbation, not lack of criticism.
To its adherents, there was a halo around the New Deal just like the
one that an old lady in Charlotte, North Carolina, once saw over
Roosevelt's head. Baruch, who saw no halos, was definitely "outside." Things were not helped by the press, which, ignorant of the
true state of affairs, started referring to Baruch as the "Assistant
President." In spite of their differences, Baruch still saw the President as a man of enormous courage and self-assurance who was bringing back to the country qualities that had been sadly lacking over
the past years, and he wrote the President a warm and affectionate
letter of congratulations on April 10, 1933.[99]

16

TOO LUMINOUS A MAN

DOWN TO WASHINGTON in that spring of 1933 came Bernard M. Baruch. After the March rains the grass was limpid in young green; below the Senate Office Building, dogwood creamed white in bridal finery. Even in the old tree-shadowed streets of Georgetown and the southeastern section, where white and Negro voices slow as rivers in the South flowed over wrought-iron gateways, there was a quickening of life. The proud white Capitol rose above the brick-dust slums around it, like a pond lily in a muddy pool. Even now, Washington can sometimes give the illusion of a sleepy Southern town, but in 1933 it was already the tense capital of a nation at war. Beyond the white patternings and geometric precisions of the capital was a nation of shifting uncertainties. It was spring, but ahead loomed the terrible winter of 1933–34. Ahead were the years of the dust bowl and the "Okies," human surplus out of Oklahoma and Arkansas, Georgia and eastern Texas, inching along the road — to a last frontier. Outside Washington was a nation laced with bread lines and dotted with soup kitchens, women and men whose spirit had all but broken, exhausting savings, credit, friends, and relatives — before the final indignity of requesting charity. None needed to starve, according to the relief agencies. Many chose to do so.

In March the Bonus Marchers returned to Washington, and the nation held its breath. It was a test, all knew, the return of this ragtag army to the capital that had driven them away with tear gas, herding them before the trampling horses' hoofs. What would be their greeting now, as assembling peacefully for redress of their grievances they gave democracy a second chance? What would happen now?

The answer was — nothing very much. Tents flecked the greenery like so many withered dogwood petals. Roosevelt rode by, waved his hat, and smiled. Miraculously, out of somewhere, hot coffee appeared and was served, unendingly. A car drew up and a tall woman descended, while inside "a very weary and gnomelike little gentleman" slept — Louis Howe, who had inspired Mrs. Roosevelt to visit the Bonus Marchers. As natural and as much at home as if she were welcoming friends at a Hyde Park garden party, she moved among her uninvited guests with that serenity the whole country would come to know. The men hung back at first — the horror of that earlier visit still lingered. Mrs. Roosevelt stepped into the food line, explaining that she just wanted to see how they were getting on, and the last reserves broke down. Soon she was leading them in "There's a Long, Long Trail," and as her car drove off the calls trailed after her: "Goodbye. Goodbye and good luck to you." She had offered them nothing. She had brought them nothing. But suddenly they and she and the country were one, united by their common disaster.[1]

Youth was the keynote of the early New Deal. Youth was spilling out over the placid streets of old Washington, buzzing through the somnambulance of the typical government office. As Frances Perkins has written: "For the first time in years, young people — under forty-five and even under thirty — were used in government policy-making and administration." [2] Conversation at Washington cocktail parties was the most brilliant in the country. Baruch might feel that the New Dealers sometimes lost sight of people,[3] but people were always the cornerstone of the planning. How many trees were saved by the CCC is an uncertainty, but young men were saved and salvaged for the country for which they were later to die. Nevertheless, there is truth in Frank Kent's commentary: "Confusion is the keynote of this administration — confusion and coyness. Boy Scouts in the White House . . . a government by Pink Pollyannas, first-name slingers, mothers' little helpers. What a sweet mess!" [4]

The panorama of the new was played out against a backdrop of the old. In the Senate cloakrooms Baruch could see faces out of the past, men who transcended shifts in presidential administration and had already cut their names in history. Norris. Borah. Johnson. With especially pleasurable recognition, he looked on the lanky McAdoo, Pat Harrison, Joe Robinson, and crusty, impassioned little Carter Glass, who were not only a bridge between Roosevelt and

Wilson but between the present and the past. Glass was a living link with history. A big-nosed, redheaded seven-year-old, he had stood spraddle-legged across a clay road in the spring of 1865, howling defiantly at a mounted Union officer that he would grow up to be "a Major like my father, and shoot Yankees." He could remember the Beauregard Rifles and the hoofbeats of the Second Virginia Cavalry, the Stars and Bars flying from the windows as the flag-draped coffin of Stonewall moved up the valley. He had read his Shakespeare and Plato by the light of a kerosene lamp, pledged his Lynchburg *News* "to uphold . . . the honor and welfare of the South," dipped his astringent pen in defense of Bryan in 1896 and of Wilson in 1912. He had been Wilson's friend to the end, and the love and loyalty that he had given the great Virginian he would have gladly given to Franklin Delano Roosevelt, but in the nineteen-thirties, nearing seventy, the "Father of the Federal Reserve System" had already outlived his time. The repudiation of the gold clauses, the attempted "rape" of the Supreme Court aroused his indignation. Eyes swimming with tears, he broke with Roosevelt, telling a hushed Senate Chamber: "It is painful to disagree with the occupant of the White House, whom I love and respect." He lived on into the nineteen-forties as frail as a china doll, shrunken and old; lived to see his principles "eclipsed," and to dream of a kind of heaven where he might commune with "the spirits of Patrick Henry, Clay and Calhoun . . . Cleveland and Woodrow Wilson." He was one of the last of the Jeffersonian liberals, who believed simply, without qualification, that the best government was the least government; and he instilled similar beliefs in his colleague Harry Byrd, to the discomfiture of more than one Democratic president.[5]

This pre-eminence of youth necessarily limited Baruch's impact on the early New Deal. Yet, even if they had to assert themselves by pelting reporters with snowballs, as did Carter Glass upon emerging from a White House conference, older men like Glass could not be counted out, for bills they opposed rarely came to a vote, and were voted down if they did.[6] Actually, it was this yeasty ferment of youth and age which made up the New Deal version of the Democratic Party, a hodgepodge embracing such variegated figures as Tennessee's Hull and Boston's James M. Curley, Harry Hopkins and Harry Byrd, Bernard Baruch and Huey Long. Yet, the common denominator uniting all was a belief in the underlying concept of the New Deal.

At first Baruch could not focus his thoughts and conclusions as to the philosophical essence of the New Deal. He could not sharply draw the line as to where collective responsibility might begin and individual responsibility end, but of this much he was certain: "makers and doers" could give up more than they were giving up. All the economic, political, or financial thinking that he did was based on the necessity of aiding the unemployed. He had early recognized, as Roosevelt had, that the need for action overrode all. To Winston Churchill, who had published a statement on the futility of the New Deal, Baruch explained that it was a part of the world-wide demand for a more equal distribution of the good things of life. On the wisdom with which this demand was met depended the welfare of man.[7]

"Mr. Baruch," Mrs. Roosevelt once said, "understood the New Deal." [8] He understood it — and could not wholly accept it. His was not the fanatic zeal of those young idealists, rolling up their sleeves to make America over on the pattern of their dream. Nor did he share the blind hatred of so many of his own friends, who saw the experiment solely as an instrument for diminishing the returns on their investments. He endorsed the New Deal's ends without always accepting its means, realizing the necessity for change while aware of the danger. Roosevelt's genius he saw as that of the humanitarian. "He gave the lowly a feeling of equality." [9] This was a moral value, and it was in terms of moral values that Baruch weighed and measured the New Deal. Like Roosevelt, he knew that what counted was the improvement in people's lives. Roosevelt had awakened the country's conscience.[10] Many of the New Deal social reforms might be on the road to socialism, but this could not be allowed to prevent action in the crisis.[11] It was the duty of the Federal government to deal with national economic problems. No New Dealer could have stated it more patly.[12]

Even in later years when age had tempered his liberalism and his bitterness at Mr. Truman's "Fair Deal" recolored his thought, Baruch could still support the fundamental purpose of the Roosevelt Revolution. "To lift the levels of human dignity and living is a proper function of government," he told the students at the College of the City of New York. The end of laissez faire meant a community responsibility for the individual welfare. The question was no longer Should the government take action? but How can the action of government be made just and fair? This was the moral dilemma of our time.[13]

Blind opposition by bankers and businessmen to the entire New Deal program angered Baruch, and he worked doggedly on manufacturers, seeking to make them cooperate in the solution of problems of unemployment and conditions of work. If they would do so progress would be much swifter.[14]

The New Deal, he said later, did "a wonderful lot of good." It was sometimes punitive. It was sometimes intolerant. But "something had to be done to clean things up . . . the stock exchange, the banks, the relationship between employer and employee . . ." [15]

Baruch was not deceived. The year 1929 had been the logical consequence of 1919, just as 1933 was the logical consequence of 1929. It was inevitable that the robber barons had been fought by the trust busters at the turn of the century; and inevitable, too, that the same massed corporate power was harnessed for the salvation of the free world in 1917. Bigness was inevitable. This was the lesson of the first half of the twentieth century. Not small business and small businessmen, but mass, consolidated, corporate power was the genius of America. Power could destroy and power could build; power could not be conquered, but it could be controlled. But who was to share in the profits of consolidated power? Corporate power could not be legislated out of existence, but it could die of its own internal weaknesses. Corporate power might be assembled by individuals, but it could not exist without the masses. And only big government could see and plan for all. Already Franklin Roosevelt was being damned as the executioner of finance capitalism when, in fact, he may well have been its savior.

"There is nothing wrong in the conception of the New Deal," Baruch said in retrospect. "It is simply a question of administration." [16] The men with ideas were often totally devoid of executive ability. Often, too, they were ignorant and vindictive. Even before the inauguration Baruch was disturbed by Roosevelt's fondness for the advice of intellectuals who seemed to Baruch to lack the practical experience necessary for solving the country's problems. They would go off the deep end and try to do overnight what ordinarily might take a hundred years. Louis Howe later shared Baruch's fears. "One of the mistakes we made," he conceded, "was in taking a great idea from some professor or some enthusiast and then giving him $50,000,-

ooo to carry it out. We should have taken his idea and given it to some practical fellow." [17]

Harold Ickes once defined a New Dealer as "an individual who believes and subscribes to the end that privileges, even if necessarily not equally shared, shall be within the attainment of anyone who has the ability and the character to put his hands on them." [18] Baruch agreed wholeheartedly that government should provide equal opportunity to all citizens.[19]

Baruch came to believe that instead of giving all an equal opportunity, the New Dealers often wished to make all men equal — an impossibility, the pursuit of which led to all sorts of governmental aberrations. As was natural to one who had lived under Reconstruction, he profoundly mistrusted concentrated governmental power.[20] Furthermore, he felt that as wards of the government men and women lost their self-respect no less surely than as wards of big business.

Baruch's indirect but real contribution to the New Deal was made to the NRA. There has been a fairly general opinion that he should be credited both with the organization of NRA and with the appointment of General Hugh S. Johnson as its head. This is incorrect. Baruch's assistance was never asked in the drafting of the National Industrial Recovery Act,[21] and throughout 1933 he kept a wary hands-off attitude toward the experiment. Yet the basic idea stemmed from the old War Industries Board, and into it went much of the philosophy of self-regulation by business which he had championed years before.[22] Baruch had even proposed to the Boston Chamber of Commerce in the spring of 1930 that there should be formed a "Supreme Court of Industry."

As for the appointment of Johnson, this was an entire surprise to Baruch. One evening, having heard a rumor, Baruch dropped in to call on Frances Perkins to ask, "What's this gossip I hear they're going to take Johnson?" Miss Perkins confirmed it. Baruch laughed. Suddenly, sobered, he warned, "He's been my number three man for years, but he's not a number one man." He went on to describe the General as a nervous, unstable man, frequently ill, who would vanish sometimes for days on end. "I have to keep him under control . . . Tell the President to be careful; Hugh needs a firm hand." The fact was that Baruch had "lent" Johnson to the government, at Raymond Moley's request, some time before. The General had been no early Roosevelt enthusiast, and the President was not averse to making a convert by giving him a job.

Johnson burst into action with the energy of a drill sergeant. "The air will soon be filled with dead cats," he shouted, and it soon was. He combined a sense of the divinity of his assignment with the tub-thumping of a Huey Long or a Father Coughlin. In soberer moments he could say that the NRA was "not magic . . . it is a frank dependence on the power and willingness of the American people to act together as one person in an hour of great danger." But in more elevated mood he would call NRA a "Holy Thing . . . the Greatest Social Advance Since the Days of Jesus Christ," as the headlines quoted him. Most of the time Johnson presented his organization as a crusade — the greatest show on earth — a combined "hog-calling contest and torchlight parade," sold to the country with all the gusto of Billy Sunday.[23]

Johnson lived up to his advance notices. Highstrung, baggy-eyed, his shaky nerves often soothed by the bottle, his moods were such that Miss Perkins sometimes thought the whole NRA "would blow up by internal combustion." But he was more than this. Perhaps no one else could have done what he did at that time. He could rally the people for his crusade. His years of work as an industrial researcher for Baruch had furnished him with facts and a knowledge of the key men in American industry which proved invaluable during the days of "code" making for the industries. Furthermore, he had a weird kind of executive ability — a near genius for getting other men to do the work for him. Finally, he had access to Baruch's advice at a time when the President would not use it. He also had access to Baruch's money. Johnson spent money as recklessly as he did energy. He was working for his country for thousands less than he had previously earned and getting nothing but blame.[24] Baruch supplied him with what he needed, with the definite understanding that it left Johnson a completely free man.[25]

Throughout, Baruch kept reminding Johnson of the great purpose underlying it all — capital and labor should be protected but never allowed to forget the general public. Any rise in prices could be justified only by present, not by past or theoretical, conditions.[26]

To organize monopoly for the public weal — this was the goal of the NRA, which permitted suspension of the antitrust laws, price fixing, and necessary action against all "chiselers" who failed to comply. Baruch gave some private advice, but Johnson was bitter that the country did not have the benefit of Baruch's wisdom at every turn.[27]

Johnson's vagaries, nevertheless, were soon getting out of hand. Daniel Roper brought up the matter at a Cabinet meeting, but at that time the President only replied that every Administration had to have its Peck's Bad Boy.[28] Later the President came to feel that Johnson's usefulness was at an end. Yet it took three months to carry out the execution, and a painful process it was — the President finally calling Johnson and urging him to take a slow boat to Europe. NRA was, after all, just a "detail."

Johnson understood. His humiliation was complete. Yet he could still say that he stood ready always to serve and return. Baruch was silent.

That Bernard Baruch might have "taken over" Johnson's job as head of the NRA is one of the untold stories of the New Deal. Raymond Moley gave him the invitation in a confidential plea on September 16, 1934, urging Baruch to take over for the reassurance of the businessmen and their nerves. No one else could quite do what Baruch could do.[29] Baruch was unmoved.

He admitted frankly to Senator Wagner that although he and Johnson did not always agree, the General had won his respect.[30] After Johnson's last battle was ended, and with his final days eased by the friendship of Baruch, he had sunk into the peace that eluded him in life. Baruch realized how useful his stalwart friend would have been in those perilous days just after Pearl Harbor.[31]

Two weeks to the day before Roosevelt's first inauguration, Alex Legge had urged Baruch to act as a balance wheel to the fanciful Henry Wallace. But Baruch knew Wallace well enough to realize that they could never run in double harness. Although he was not asked to provide ideas for the formation of AAA, Baruch did sit in on a conference of Wallace and the farm leaders on March 14, 1933, and a week later suggested George Peek to Wallace for AAA administrator.

Peek, who had been a hero to the farmers all through the bitter years of the fight for farm parity, was now a known Baruch man, and it was some measure of Baruch's influence that on the afternoon of April 5 Peek was called to the White House and told that the AAA job was his. He demurred. "I regard the problem as more industrial than agricultural," he told the President, "and Bernard M. Baruch is the best man in the country for the job." [32]

Roosevelt was embarrassed. He had talked with Baruch, he told Peek, and had offered him the job. Baruch had refused but had strongly recommended Peek.

That earlier session at the White House had been a stormy one. For Baruch had told the President that the projected AAA bill was not only unconstitutional, but badly written and completely unworkable.[33] Farm relief was essential, even before relief for business. But AAA could never work, and its method of crop control seemed to him completely unsound economically. Personally he could see little difference between telling a man what he could not drink or what he could not plant.[34]

With the advantage of hindsight, Baruch's doubts seem difficult to fathom. For whatever its faults of administration, the AAA avowedly was designed to do what the McNary-Haugen bills had attempted: "to give the American farmer the benefits of protection for that portion of his crop used domestically." [35] Had Baruch dared head up AAA, his might have been the great name in the farmers' fight for equality. He based his objection on AAA's unsound methods of crop control. Yet as we have seen, he had urged crop restriction upon the South in the twenties. There is, of course, a difference between restricting the unsown crop and destroying the growing one. Here, apparently, was where Baruch stickled, although he went on to say that crop control would end in the destruction of the South — the end of King Cotton — and here his foresight seems to have failed him completely. He did not see, apparently, that King Cotton had been dying ever since the Civil War. When Southern supplies were blockaded during that struggle, Egypt began growing the crop and taking over the trade. The labor of Egypt's fellahs replaced the slave labor that had been outlawed, and it was inevitable that the price of cotton would remain low thereafter, with cheap production and mass supply.

Baruch did not see that the end of King Cotton meant the South's salvation, its freedom from one-crop slavery. However, he did see that to restrict production and thus force the price up would only continue to inspire other nations to produce more cotton and to produce it more cheaply.[36] The trend continued. As United States production fell, world production soared, and the world grabbed the markets.[37] Once the New Dealers had hooted at Hoover's pleas for the farmers to let twenty per cent of their wheat lands lie fallow and to plow up every third cotton row. Now came slaughter and scarcity in the midst of starvation. Fifteen million people were without proper clothing and food, and the orders went out to destroy the surplus clothing and food. The poor were priced right out of the market. The farmers got no subsidies on their exported crops. Instead, they cashed government checks for reducing their acreage, while the market was flooded with foreign products.[38]

As for Baruch, he did see no reason why, when farm products fell below the cost of production, the government could not come in and protect them. He saw, furthermore, something that economists would be reconsidering twenty-odd years later. He saw that it was not the acreage but the output per acre that counted. Yet Baruch, who for more than a decade had built up a solid reputation as the farmer's friend, counted himself out of the great agricultural experiment of the New Deal. On farm matters he was not infallible, of course. Neither he nor Peek then seemed quite to realize the fact that high prices for the farmer were meaningless so long as industrial prices soared even higher.

Much of the farm record of the New Deal was something that even its most avowed partisans found weak. With taxpayers' funds pouring in to support the butter market, Wallace and Tugwell halted sale of the surplus to England at a world price lower than the domestic price. A projected sale of 800,000 bales of cotton to Germany was "quietly pigeonholed" in the State Department, despite the fact that from 1933 on Germany had been one of the largest purchasers of the American crop. By 1935 the gross farm income was still three billion short of the high mark of the nineteen-twenties, and Baruch's suggestion of exchanging cotton for manganese from Russia fell on deaf ears.[39]

Baruch's energies, meanwhile, were diverted into working out a kind of labor-saving plan for the President. His primary suggestion was that the emergency boards be separated from the Cabinet departments, linked only by a kind of liaison executive committee, chosen from both and keeping in touch with the President.[40] A real organization, he pointed out, meant that the top man established policy and the assistants carried it out. If they squabbled or lost public confidence they should be fired.[41] Furthermore, a sifting body to study plans and problems would keep unimportant matters from the President.

The New Deal cabinet was buckling to the problems before it. Who today can remember the personnel of President Truman's last Cabinet? But who can forget the first Cabinet of Franklin Roosevelt? Trippingly the names still fall off the tongue — the great and the nonentities — all somehow sharing in the fierce illumination of that first year. You saw them at the inevitable Washington parties, weaving your way among the new faces and the old — Swanson and Cummings and Dern; "Wee Willie" Woodin, "obviously elated about something from on high";[42] Ickes, the "Old Curmudgeon"; and Frances Perkins in her three-cornered hat. And for Baruch there were others of even more significance. Big Jim Farley, for instance, the gum-chewing, teetotaling son of a saloonkeeper from upstate New York, whose groundwork in the state broke counties untouched by the Democrats in seventy years. He had coined a phrase — "the name of Roosevelt is magic" — which turned out to be so true that the need for Farley was fading out, and he was now only hanging on by the coattails.[43] He was one of the palace guard, jealous of his position and wary of anyone who might threaten it.

Symbolic of the contrasts of the New Deal was statesmanlike Cordell Hull, as dignified and out of place on the Roosevelt band wagon, one writer quipped, as an old-fashioned upright piano. A soft-spoken man with the fierce pride of the mountain South out of which he had come, he had lived to see Wilsonian liberalism become outmoded. As one who had kept the faith during the bleak years, he was rewarded with the empty honor of being the figurehead for the State Department. Everyone knew that Roosevelt was his own Secretary of the Treasury, Navy, and State, and no one paid any more heed to Hull's rather tiresome warnings on the dangers of German aggression and Japanese imperialism than to old Swanson's perpetual pleas to build up the Navy to full strength. Roosevelt was bored with Hull, but Baruch appreciated his devotion, and so did Louis Wehle, who long remembered Hull's words that he had suffered humiliations "that no man in private life could accept and keep his self-respect." [44]

There was a kind of frontier poetry in Henry Agard Wallace, a gaunt, serious man whom you might see any morning between 7 and 8.15 walking from the Wardman Park Hotel to the Agriculture building. His arms swung loosely at his sides. His long head sagged upon his chest. About him was the look of the dreamer and the

mystic that he was — one whose interests ranged from agrarian genet-
ics to astronomy, and who, out of the country heritage of three
generations, would take time to "wonder at the workings of a God
who makes the rain to fall and the corn to grow." [45] In all the Baruch
Papers, there are no more interesting letters than those of Henry
Wallace; and it is characteristic of Baruch's perceptivity that he
made friends with Wallace, because he sensed that the Iowan was
very close to the heart of the New Deal.

More of the heart and poetry of the New Deal was to be found
in a shabby office on New York Avenue in which the very "odor of
Relief" clung to the faded walls. There, swinging in his battered
swivel chair, was a lank man in shirtsleeves, "seeming to be in a
perpetual nervous ferment," chain-smoking, gulping cup after cup of
black coffee, or jerking up to pace the floor and mutter, "I'm not
going to last six months, so I'll do as I please." Outside his office one
day another Middle Westerner paused and looked around. Ernie
Pyle saw a blind newsdealer leaning against the outside wall, and
inside, the water pipes banding the ceiling and the man in the dingy
shirt and the suit that might have come out of a hayloft, and he
wrote: "Your neck is sort of skinny like poor people's necks," which
seemed fitting, because in this office was fought "a holy war against
wants." Across the battered desk poured orders for 250,000 mattresses
for the poor, for the employment of writers to write poems and artists
to paint pictures and rabbis to compile Jewish dictionaries — five
million dollars across the desk in two hours' time.

"Hell, they've got to eat," Harry Hopkins said, and swung back to
his desk.

Hunger was his yardstick. He did not care whether a man was a
Republican or a Democrat, an alien or native-born. Down the line,
money would stick to greedy fingers, and even a pick-and-shovel job
on the WPA might have to be cleared through the local political
boss — Hopkins knew nothing of that. In fact, copies of his rulings
that a job on the WPA could not deprive you of your right to vote as
you pleased were presented by the disenfranchised poor of the South
in place of poll-tax certificates.[46]

Since the death of Louis Howe, Hopkins, the self-styled "office
boy," had not only stepped into his shoes but was coming to be recognized as the Number One man of the New Deal.[47] With brash
Hopkins carrying everything off with a gleeful kind of hell's-bells air,

the President could escape momentarily from his awful responsibilities.[48] Once Roosevelt said to Wendell Willkie that if he became
President, he would learn what a lonely job it was, and "discover the
need for somebody like Harry Hopkins who asks for nothing but to
serve you." Unofficial and omnipresent, Hopkins was a part of the
White House, whether trailing up and down in a worn-out dressing
gown, or puncturing official pomposity with a skeptical "Oh, yeah!"
— feet slung to the top of the nearest table.

The impact of Hopkins on the New Deal was very great. Roosevelt told Stalin to treat him "with the identical confidence you would
feel if you were talking directly to me," [49] and General Marshall has
written that the services Hopkins rendered will never even vaguely
be appreciated. Hopkins could focus F.D.R.'s many-sided thinking,
finding out what Roosevelt really wanted, and then getting it,
despite vacillations by the Chief Executive himself.[50] And yet
Baruch thought Hopkins a "bad influence" and, although courting
him personally, tried to thwart that influence.[51] Even Mrs. Roosevelt has conceded that there were sides of Hopkins that were "alien"
to her, and although he was what the President wanted, what he
needed was another question.[52] His very loyalty was a failing, for it
made his devotion too great for objectivity. He was a sounding board,
not an adviser; he did not originate policy. As Frances Perkins observed, "Harry felt inferior — even when he wasn't inferior, and this
held him back" from the kind of critical analysis or comment that
Howe made.[53] Yet it was he alone in the inner circle of the New
Deal whom Roosevelt had "tapped" for greatness — this man who
at the moment of his greatest triumph discovered that he had cancer
and perhaps one month to live. Ironically, this illness converted him
into the selfless individual who could perform such transcendent
services because he had no hope of personal gain.[54]

Nevertheless, Baruch has always felt that it was Hopkins who kept
him from Roosevelt's side, and this view has been supported by
Roosevelt's intimate friend Judge Samuel Rosenman, who said that
Hopkins' greatest disservice was his propensity for keeping from
Roosevelt "men who could have been of even greater service to
him than they were . . . He did not like Bernard Baruch and was
chiefly responsible for Baruch's absence from several situations where
his influence would have helped tremendously." [55] In contrast,
Robert Sherwood saw "a great personal affection" between Baruch

and "the charming scoundrel," as the Elder Statesman called Hopkins. For example, Hopkins accepted financial help from Baruch long after Roosevelt was dead. "Nobody ever told Roosevelt whom he wanted to see," Sherwood has declared. "If Mr. Baruch didn't see the President for a given length of time, I believe that the sole reason for that was the President didn't want to see him." Hopkins, aware of the final test of loyalty to F.D.R., was perfectly capable of shouldering the blame, of saying "I, and I alone, am responsible for keeping Baruch out of the White House" when such was not the case.[56]

But Hopkins was wary of Baruch. Once at the dinner table, Hopkins lashed into Baruch and was sharply reproved by Roosevelt. "Well, you attack him," Hopkins blustered.

"Harry, you ought to be the last person in the world to say anything against Bernie," the President countered. "I can criticize him, if I want to. But look at all he's done for you." [57]

Mrs. Roosevelt was probably correct in feeling that Hopkins had nothing against Baruch personally. "This man Roosevelt's a cripple and I'm going to keep people away from him," Baruch has quoted Harry Hopkins as saying.[58]

Mrs. Roosevelt has written that the people around her husband were "jealous of outside advisers such as Mr. Baruch and made it difficult for cordial relations to exist. However, my husband was inclined to be impervious to stories or rumors about anyone who he felt could be helpful, and since Mr. Baruch is one of the people who can ignore the past, he was always ready to be useful when called upon . . ." Not literally on the "inside," Baruch had made his place as one of the "devoted and loyal men" who believed in her husband and worked directly in the campaign, as Mrs. Roosevelt noted, along with Howe, Walker, Flynn, and Morgenthau, whose paramount interest was "in the work to be done." No injuries by others could make Mr. Baruch "feel hurt or slighted," and he was always ready to do anything that was asked of him. "No matter who suffers," he would say, "the President cannot be wrong." [59]

According to Mrs. Roosevelt, the personal relationship between her husband and Bernard Baruch remained unbroken during all the years of their acquaintance.[60] "The best friend my father ever had," Elliott Roosevelt once wrote of Baruch; Mrs. Roosevelt qualified it to "one of the best friends";[61] and an associate added flatly that

"Roosevelt couldn't let him be a good friend to him. Friendship has to be two-way." [62] Judge Rosenman has probably hit closest to the mark with his observation that ninety per cent of the time the two men shared "the most cordial of feelings" and ten per cent of the time Roosevelt would get irritated.[63] For Roosevelt's propensity was for talking his visitors down, and, of all men, he was least likely to relish a hair shirt. As one newspaper observed: "The President likes Baruch personally, but hates to get his ears pinned back. Baruch, suavely but firmly, pinned them back." [64]

Roosevelt enjoyed criticism no better than other egotists, and when his own mighty ego came into collision with Baruch's, the impact was terrific. Undoubtedly, too, their unconscious rivalry increased the tension between them. Roosevelt wanted to be helpful. He did not want to be told. With his almost pathological horror of domination, he did not really want an adviser; he wanted an instrument, and Baruch was too old. Past sixty, he could no longer give that blind, almost worshipful adoration which he had offered once to Woodrow Wilson. Instead, from the vantage point of his superior years, he occasionally took a Dutch-uncle approach to Roosevelt.[65]

Roosevelt demanded not only loyalty but sacrificial loyalty — the willingness to be blamed and even purged for Roosevelt's mistakes, to be dropped from sight temporarily, if a human sacrifice was demanded. To be "in" with Roosevelt, you had to be willing to be kicked out by him. Baruch, although sometimes playing the role of whipping boy, could not readily sacrifice his prestige for power. He was not constitutionally adapted to the back seat. There was indeed some truth to the charge that when he could not get Roosevelt to do what he wanted him to do he went up on Capitol Hill, where his power bloc of Southern "Old Masters," as Ickes has described them, was nothing less than formidable.[66] Furthermore, Baruch's near-guarantee of a favorable press must have been irksome to a President less blessed.[67]

"Why do they treat my boss so badly?" Hugh Johnson complained. Raymond Moley had the answer. If Baruch were invited down too often, the impression would be given that he was running everything. "Bernie," explained Moley gently, "you're just too luminous a man." [68]

Yet, Cordell Hull has pointed out that Baruch was often permitted to render services "of the most vital and lasting nature." [69]

When the New Deal "got into trouble," Robert Sherwood has said, "we would send for the Old Man." [70]

Roosevelt would growl sometimes, "Old Bernie, anything good he says he did, and anything bad is because I didn't take his advice." Irritated, he would sometimes burst out, "You're the stubbornest man I ever met." [71] And at that Baruch would just look at him and smile, and the President would smile back, because he knew that no one was more stubborn than he was. But sometimes the President could be generous, could speak words of praise that would heal over years' misunderstandings. "Bernie," he would say, "after all, I have a greater trust and confidence in you than in anyone else." And Baruch, in his turn, could assert that he had never had a quarrel that lasted with F.D.R. The President finally created a new title for him, the G.O., the "Great Oiler." [72]

The evidence of the New Dealers themselves is contradictory as to what part Bernard Baruch played. Some said that he had no influence at all; others, that his was a kind of off-and-on influence, and some that he was a constant factor throughout. "Baruch was there from the beginning," states Judge Rosenman. He was not a New Dealer, yet he was rather "consistently cordial to the New Deal." [73] He did much to prevent cabals against it and more to keep a rein upon it; he was the conservative weight, the countercheck to the left-wingers. According to Thomas Corcoran: "The New Deal was a course of constant accommodation . . . Mr. Baruch had a great deal of effect in shaping it — on the conservative side. He had a great deal to say about its underlying economic principles . . . He had a great effect in shaping its workability — when he could get a crack at it . . . When the New Deal understood what it was trying to do, Baruch was there." [74]

With one pre-eminent figure in the New Deal, Baruch's influence never weakened. No one better perceived the steadying value of Baruch's advice on the volatile Chief Executive than Mrs. Roosevelt, and none maneuvered more adroitly for the President to have the benefits of that influence.

> I hope you will see Franklin before long [ran a typical letter]. I am particularly anxious to see your plan carried out for refugees, selfishly, because I think it will help solve many of our international problems. At the same time I am

anxious to see us let business have some of the reforms which they think will solve their problems, not because I agree in toto, but because I think there is much in psychological effect.

I want to see us make a drive for some fundamental changes in attitude and that I would like to talk to you about.[75]

During Baruch's serious illness in 1939, she wrote: "I think of you often with great affection and deep gratitude for all you are and all you do for me . . . Please take care of yourself. Some of us feel you are very important to us and to many others." [76]

He, in his turn, was "always defending her." [77] He was at her side for whatever and whenever she needed him. "Mr. Baruch looks on me as a mind, not as a woman," Eleanor Roosevelt once mused with a twinkle.[78] Theirs was the working partnership of friends with great admiration and respect for each other. He saw in her a rare blending of mind and heart and promised his support to her and the President as long as he was needed.[79] To him she wrote impulsively, "You are a wonderful person . . . I count as one of my blessings your friendship . . . There are few people one trusts without reservation in life and I am deeply grateful to call you that kind of friend." [80]

When the Roosevelts came to Washington, she was already the eyes and legs of the President, and it was no surprise to Baruch when Roosevelt turned impulsively to her to find out what was going on. Within a month after the start of the New Deal, the President dispatched her on a scouting trip to the Southern Appalachians. It was the first of many such expeditions, and in those days Mrs. Roosevelt could pass virtually unnoticed, not yet having been made the victim of press attacks scarcely equaled in savagery since Rachel Jackson's time.[81] Occasionally she went alone, but more often with companions, and one of her frequent escorts was Bernard Baruch. Of those journeys, particularly into the coal-mining country near Morgantown, West Virginia, Mrs. Roosevelt has written that with only a little leadership there could easily have developed if not a people's revolution, at least a people's party.[82]

Men could prate of the "American standard of living" and the "American way." There in the Southern hills Mrs. Roosevelt and

Bernard Baruch learned the truth. This, too, was America — Logan
County, Arthurdale, Bloody Run, Scott's Run. Here were men,
family men, who subsisted on relief of one dollar a week for five
years, and children who did not know what it was to sit down at a
table and have a proper meal.

Mrs. Roosevelt saw the gleam in the eyes of the famished little
boy, frightened as the rabbit he clutched, and the scornful pity that
crossed the face of his older sister. "He thinks we are not going
to eat it, but we are."

In Logan County evicted families huddled together in waterlogged
tents. None could leave the area: all were in debt to the company
store, and in virtual debtors' prison, for their only choice was to stay
or to go to jail.

There was typhoid at "The Run," the water supply for a whole
town trickling from a single spigot. Sewage rotted in the children's
play pool — "the filth was indescribable."

They went into the cabins. One of Mrs. Roosevelt's other companions, a man high in the business world, looked into one house and
came out fast. Outside, he vomited. Fiercely he pushed into Mrs.
Roosevelt's hand some money, protesting that he would give her anything, anything she wanted, if only "she would not make him go in
again."

But after Mrs. Roosevelt's fast-moving feet, Baruch's tall figure
moved into that black and hideous world where nothing ever was or
could be clean. For him, too, these were "living conditions such as
he had never seen before." He could unfold his long length onto a
stool or the bare frame of a bed, look and stare at the family possessions: one pair of pants and a coat for a whole family; one soleless
pair of shoes, two or three cups or chipped plates, and a single pan.
He could see the look in the eyes of a hungry child gnawing a carrot;
he could see a whole family of subnormal children sleeping on a pile
of rags on the floor.[83] And he never flinched. It afterward seemed to
Mrs. Roosevelt one of the marvels of her experience of human nature
that this stately man of conservative background should have been
the one who stood by her to the end, and who could offer her $22,000
for her school the minute she needed it.[84] This was a school that she
founded at Arthurdale, near Morgantown, taking in four villages. To
her surprise, she found that Baruch sometimes visited it on his own.
"I have hoped that he got as much satisfaction as I did out of the
change in the children in six months," [85] she has written. He, too,

was inspired by the admiring affection in the eyes of those people as they looked at her.[86]

To Eleanor Roosevelt on these missions Baruch gave inspiration, money, and hardheaded advice. Most of all, he wanted to give her a chance. In the idea of the Rural Resettlement Administration — originally conceived by Louis Howe — he had no faith at all. It wouldn't work; it would never work; and yet he promised to help her with it.[87] This dream of a rural industrial community, part-time factory work supplementing subsistence farms, was Jeffersonian. It belonged to a vision from which America had turned away. It was as visionary as any scheme of the New Deal — this dream world of a simple, semi-agricultural, semi-industrial, decentralized America — and out of it came failure, and later the triumph of the TVA. Baruch issued the necessary warnings, sometimes with bitterness — as at Arthurdale, West Virginia, where, despite a model housing program and community school, the houses were priced too high.[88] There was no outlet for the produce of a factory, and the soil was exhausted.

Promises had been held out. It was cruel to put people on their feet only to strike them down again — to place them in homes with no means of staying there. Even the five-acre plots allotted were insufficient for subsistence without supplemental work in the nonexistent factory. These were tragic mistakes. At the very least, the betrayed homesteaders should be given their houses.[89]

By June of 1936 Baruch was even more certain that without factories the scheme and all the little communities would close down; yet he wrote Mrs. Roosevelt that if she decided to go on against his judgment, he would help her.[90] And he was as good as his word. Mrs. Roosevelt knew where she could write that there is "no free clinic anywhere in West Virginia." [91] She knew who it was who, as late as 1937, enlisted the aid of the Guggenheims for dental clinics for the Arthurdale children. She could write her mentor: "I think your letter to Mr. Tugwell is going to result in making the cost to homesteaders within their income." [92] And he, in his turn, could congratulate her on getting a radio contract to take care of Arthurdale, or pledge that together they would buy a pottery kiln, which might be the very thing that would salvage Arthurdale.[93]

In more somber mood, he was sometimes bitter.[94] In economic terms, the experiment had failed. Even Mrs. Roosevelt from her little stone cottage at Val Kill realized the fallacy of that idyllic dream of the little subsistence farm and the little crafts shop. As soon as their trade was learned, the young men would leave: they did not want the way of life on the land, but the way of life that money could buy. A few villages survived the early depression years, but very few outlived the entire era.

"Our partnership needs reviving; I need advice," Mrs. Roosevelt wrote Baruch at the end of 1937.[95] He gave her advice and sometimes his purse for her still struggling depression victims: the sick young expectant mother, whose son gave his quart of milk a day to her; the Massachusetts housewife, ruined by the crash of stocks, her husband broken down, two sons in college, and a surprise addition to her family. There was a job for the young husband who, losing home, car, and furnishings, could not even live with his wife and children; and there was rent money for a community center in east Harlem to keep the children off the street. Yet to Mrs. Roosevelt's plea for $800 to help send a Negro girl to college, Baruch demurred. He thought it wiser to give the sum in South Carolina, where it would be enough for four girls.[96]

When the government fell down on the first slum-clearance program in New York City, it was Baruch who found and supplied the money. Housing was a question of which he had thought for forty years; and as the energies of the New Deal burst out in a wave of slum clearance, he issued a warning against the restoration of neighborhoods in such places as New York, where opportunities for earning a living were less than in a small town, as was clear to anyone who observed the number of unemployed in the streets of New York.[97]

The wild horses were plunging and the reins were held by Roosevelt, whom somehow Baruch could view neither as dictator nor demagogue. Nor could he get too shocked at John L. Lewis,[98] whom he had known since the Versailles days in France, and who with his coal code of September 1933 had achieved what was perhaps "the greatest single victory of organized labor in fifty years." [99] Lewis behaved only as any man might behave who had been at hard labor in the mines since his thirteenth year, wrestling with mules, miners, and the self-interest of many operators. Baruch, who could remember Bryan and the Populist pleas of the nineties, could not be overdisturbed by the bank reforms, the stock market reforms, the power projects, and the breaking up of the holding companies. He could not even don mourning for Roosevelt's "betrayal" of his promises to balance the budget — a promise which he thought was impossible to fulfill without the equally impossible restoration of foreign trade.

Did people remember that Roosevelt had frankly and openly qualified his budget-balancing "promises" in his Pittsburgh speech of October 19, 1932? "Let me repeat from now to election day so that every man . . . will know what I mean: If starvation and dire need . . . make necessary the additional funds which would keep the budget out of balance I shall not besitate to . . . authorize the expenditure of that additional amount." [100] Baruch himself, before the Senate Finance Committee in February 1933, had spoken almost the same words.

Baruch was comparatively inactive during the campaign of '36. A painful siege of arthritis gave him ample excuse to withdraw, but not in a financial sense. Also he gave heart — and hope — to another invalid, Louis McHenry Howe, who, gasping for breath on his deathbed, dreamed of a "Good Neighbor League," similar to the Citizens-for-Willkie and Citizens-for-Eisenhower movements of later years. For this, Baruch gave money and support; and of his action, Mrs. Roosevelt wrote later that "it was medicine, food and drink to Louis to know that he was still in the fighting. Those of us who loved Louis will never forget your kindness to him." [101]

Through the autumn, solicitous notes poured in from Mrs. Roosevelt, Admiral Halsey, Homer Cummings, and Mrs. Calvin Coolidge, among others.[102]

While Baruch was ill, the campaign progressed to its triumphal result, the Elder Statesman being kept up to the minute by many correspondents, including the indefatigable Jimmy Byrnes, who posted him on the local situation in South Carolina. At midnight on the day after the election, with Roosevelt the victor by an unprecedented majority, Frank Kent telegraphed to Baruch, "Do you think we can get a recount if we holler fraud?" [103]

Soon thereafter a letter arrived from Mrs. Roosevelt:

> The President is tremendously heartened by the vote of confidence he received.
> The President and I are deeply grateful for your very generous and loyal support.

Franklin hopes you can come and see him before he leaves.[104]

Baruch improved only slowly, and although he received a White House invitation to dinner on the night of Inauguration Day, he dared not risk the trip down.[105] From Joe Robinson he received a vivid account of that rain-drenched January 21, when Mrs. Roosevelt sat, the black of her felt hat running in streaks down her face and her fur coat matted, as the jubilant President, "to the great pleasure of those lined up along his way," insisted on exposing himself in an open car, "waving his hat to the multitude and taking the rain like he enjoyed it. Both he and Mrs. Roosevelt were wet through and through and he seemed to think it a great performance." [106] It was an inauspicious beginning for what were for Baruch several frustrating and fruitless years.

Within a very short period, his wife and two of his closest friends — Joe Robinson and Cary Grayson had died.[107] The death of Mrs. Baruch was sudden — and a staggering blow. In the spring of 1937 she had broken her ankle, which evoked a sympathetic cable from Churchill, who had never forgotten her kindness to him at Hobcaw when he was worn-out and ill. In May, after a convalescence of eight weeks, Baruch turned down a Washington invitation when his wife announced her intention of celebrating her recovery by giving a dinner party.[108] This was a sacrifice he never regretted, for seven months later she was dead. Incidents such as these light up a relationship carefully screened from the public. Even those close to Baruch never wholly understood his wife Annie, and John Golden's memory of the laughing, vibrant girl who used to sit with the showgirls in his front office and apply for a "job" has long since receded into vanished time.[109] Her shyness and reserve made her seem "distant" even to intimates of the Baruch family, although those who know of her years of work among her charities saw her warmer and more tender side. To some it seemed that she played little part in his life, that he was one of those men whose life existed apart. That he was proud of her there was no doubt. He showered gifts upon her — a pearl necklace, bracelets of emeralds and diamonds. He took endless time and trouble to gratify her fancies, such as with a beautiful Chinese Chippendale cabinet. Her taste was exquisite. Baruch once explained to Mrs. Woodrow Wilson, who had tried to be helpful by suggesting a present for Mrs. Baruch, that although his wife did not want that particular gift, he was most grateful for Mrs. Wilson's advice.[110]

Although he took vacations alone, he preferred them with his family. He once told George Wingfield that he might accept his invitation to spend the summer on his ranch if his family could decide on their plans. Christmas was always a Baruch family festival, he once explained to Mrs. Roosevelt.[111]

The intimacies of Baruch's family life, the sentiments and letters that he and his wife exchanged are his private affair. Only now and then has he let the barriers down. A woman reporter once commented that Baruch was at his best when discussing the relationships between men and women, and gave an illustration. "I have been studying women for almost eighty years," Baruch said, "and I still don't know anything about them. My wife was the most wonderful woman in the world."

"Why?"

"She never criticized me, not one word in all the years we were married. And whenever any question arose, she always left things to me. She always said: 'You know best.'" Men strayed, he added, only when they did not get what they wanted at home.[112]

"When you've lived with one woman forty years," he once said, "and she's borne your children and shared your griefs — well, there's nothing left for any other woman either here," touching his heart, "or in here," touching his head. "Sure, there're lots of lurid stories about me and women. I haven't denied them. Why should I bother? I wouldn't have given one eyelash of hers for their whole being." [113] One friend has recalled a summer day in Europe after Mrs. Baruch's death when he came in flushed and exultant from some good shooting. He sat back and relaxed as his valet Lacey removed his boots. "I must call up Annie and tell her about this day," he said and broke off, suddenly. No one could take her place. No one did.[114]

Of the hundreds of letters of sympathy he must have received upon his wife's death, only two have survived, but they speak volumes. From Joseph P. Tumulty came realization of "all that left your life when Mrs. Baruch passed on . . . It was great to have in your life one whose passing could bring sorrow to so many." [115] And Josephus Daniels, his warm heart reaching out to his old friend in the dark hours, added that he knew "the good God who gave you such a bless-ing will give strength to you." [116]

In the abortive Court reform plan, Baruch was on the sidelines, torn by his personal opposition to the scheme and his sympathy for his old friend, Joseph T. Robinson of Arkansas, who as floor leader faced the galling task of piloting the measure through the Senate in the face of taunts that a Supreme Court seat would be his reward.[117] The heat that summer made Washington like a jungle. On July 12, Robinson, who had earlier kept Baruch informed of his preanginal twinges, wrote his friend that he felt unusually well. Two days later, as he was leaving the Capitol, "the impact of the hot, lifeless air was like a blow at his brain." [118]

The strain and abuse and personal attack had been too much. Baruch was in New York, just boarding the *Normandie* for Europe when the message came. Abruptly he canceled his sailing and chartered a plane for Washington to put himself at Mrs. Robinson's side. She told him, simply, the truth: "No one in all Joe's life was held in greater affection by him than yourself." [119]

Robinson had been far more to him than a political associate. He had been friend, companion on the hunt and at glorious feasts of quail, duck, and Carolina moonshine. Baruch could not think of Hobcaw without thinking of him. The Court fight, the excesses of the New Deal had killed him, Baruch would always believe, and his own position in the New Deal was not improved by the alleged tele-phone call to the White House, in which he warned the President to drop the fight and "not kill any more Senators." [120]

As for Roosevelt's "purge list," Baruch was appalled at an attempt by the Executive Branch of the government to usurp the prerogatives of the Legislative. So his money flowed southward, and the presi-dential temper exploded, and it was probably the combined failure of the "purge" and the Court reform plan, that led Roosevelt to burst out that he would have read old Baruch out of the Democratic Party if he had not needed his money to help re-elect Alben Bark-ley.[121]

Baruch, did not depend upon politics for the stimulation of his energies. During the mid-thirties he turned, with all his old-time zest, to his mining interests. They were like a game to him, in which he played strictly according to the rules. Here was the lure of adventure, not only of money-making, but of distant peoples and places. From British Africa came the totally unfounded report that a party of white men had been massacred on the upper Fly; one was brought back, burning with fever, and his wife collapsed, a nervous wreck, in New York.[122] At second hand, Baruch could read of the tense moments when the natives became convinced that planes overhead were monsters swooping to devour them, and of their terror at their first sight of white men. Baruch could almost see them, huddling together in their fright.

And across his desk fell pictures of the old mining country of the Far West, word pictures by his long-term partner George Wingfield, who still dreamed of adventure around the Buckhorn, or the moldering old shafts, some of them not operated since the eighteen-fifties — shafts in Virginia City, Montana, Nevada, Idaho, the blank, treeless wastes peopled only by old desert rats, blistering in the sun.[123]

As Baruch observed to Key Pittman, a gold mine rejuvenated him. Gold mines still held a thrill.[124] Baruch purchased 11,500 shares in the Graniteville Gold Mining Company at one dollar per share, which promptly dropped to nine cents, a loss which could only be written off on tax returns. Alaska Juneau, too, was still an adventure — a going enterprise which, by 1933, produced half the gold mined in Alaska and finally a full one-thirteenth of the United States supply.[125] There was still adventure in the old fields, and on September 20, 1938, Baruch telegraphed P. R. Bradley that he was eager to hear about two gold properties Alaska Juneau could buy at not less than five hundred thousand each.[126] Baruch's untapped talents, which might have brought him fame in vastly different endeavors, found outlet here. When maps were sent him, he knew what they were about and made cogent criticisms.[127]

The human elements, too, were fascinating. Corresponding with Phil Bradley, Baruch could look back philosophically now on his stormy friendship with Philip's brother, Fred, a man of vision, the driving founder of Alaska Juneau, and with all the multifacets of genius: bitter, suspicious, high-strung, and doggedly determined. A sick man, as Baruch knew, he was suspicious of the New Yorker from the start, yet had accepted Baruch's help.[128]

Getchell and Alaska Juneau were the foremost among Baruch's mining interests in the thirties. Getchell, hailed in 1938 as the "foremost Nevada Gold Mine," was the comeback venture of Baruch's old friend, George Wingfield, whose fortunes had gone down with those of his state in 1929. Early in the decade, Baruch had also taken a 35 per cent share in the Atolia Syndicate in the history-haunted old Frémont Grant in Mariposa, California, but from this he had to withdraw. Political considerations also motivated his withdrawal from the Cyprus Mines, which had made a deal with the Germans.[129]

The New Deal might not have restored prosperity, but equally it had not wrecked the rich. Baruch's income in 1934 was the highest of any year up to that time.[130] United States census figures reveal that this was no isolated phenomenon. Huey Long used the facts and figures as fuel for his fire. "The millionaire is becoming a bigger millionaire," he said. "The poor are becoming poorer and the middle class is falling into the class of the poor." [131]

What, then, troubled Baruch? He would sit sometimes on a bench in Central Park, long before the press corps sought him out there. Sullen skies lowered over him. March winds thrust themselves at him. He could not shake his feeling of depression. His mind was echoing the great phrase of Roosevelt's First Inaugural address. He knew that America had less to fear than any other country, and yet it was still fearful. And there was something to fear — Would the overpowering influence of big business be exchanged for the autocracy of big government and our people lose their self-reliance? [132]

Baruch might have been less fearful had the New Deal obtained its objectives. But the Great Depression dragged on. Roosevelt penned the words of his Second Inaugural: "I see one third of a nation ill-housed, ill-clad, ill-nourished"; a mob circled the White House, chanting, "We don't want promises; we want jobs." In one year, the national debt was up seven billion dollars, and in spite of a three-billion-dollar public works program, 440,000 more men were out of work than in 1934. The President could win elections — could he solve depressions? More and more money was being spent to fight unemployment. More and more unemployed were swamping the relief rolls. On the credit side, the New Dealers could point to shorter hours and higher wages; to the conservation both of young men and of raw materials; to increased security in job-holding, credit, bank savings, and insurance. Industrial production was up 67 per cent in four months. Despite all this, after five years of the New Deal there were still ten million people without jobs.[133]

As late as 1938, Baruch did not believe that the situation was improving. Arranging a loan here and a job there, he could see little betterment in the status of men and women over thirty-five, for whom the industrial scrap heap seemed the only answer. Occasionally he gave way to bitterness.[134]

Did the capitalistic system carry the seeds of its own restoration? Was it true, as Louis Wehle thought, that only oncoming war could save either F.D.R. or the capitalistic system?[135] In 1940 there were still 10,000,000 unemployed and Baruch thought that the fundamental problems of the country had not been faced.[136]

Without industrial recovery, Baruch knew, there would be no recovery for the country. He had outlined his ideas in a memorandum to Roosevelt in 1936. Only new industries, he argued, could solve the basic problem. But new industries were a hazard; they could not be buffeted around as the old had been. They must be allowed sufficient profits to become strong.

The new corporate taxes were sufficient in themselves to foil the creation of new experimental industries. Payroll taxes for social security would stimulate the reliance of industry on machines rather than on men, and unemployment would be increased. He told the President of these fears.[137]

The next line of assault was Harry Hopkins. To him Baruch wrote that people starting in business could have little hope of success, since profits were taxed so high.[138]

There was no response from Mr. Hopkins.

Next, Baruch took his fight to Congress. He favored the exemption of new businesses from excess-profits taxes for five years and measures to encourage liberal dividends for stockholders.[139] We had reached the point of diminishing returns, he told the Senate.[140] Would the President accept advice from a friend? Frank Kent wondered. Baruch was troubled by no such concern. He had prepared his statement with Stephen Early looking over his shoulder, and the President had, in fact, requested it a year before. He was thus neither surprised nor unduly flattered when the presidential message of April 30, 1938, followed along the lines suggested by him.[141]

He found less audience for his suggestions for tax reform. He calculated that with every billion dollars of increased business activity the government would glean 160 million in revenue. How could such activity be restored? He suggested a four-point program: the capital gains tax on securities of new enterprises to be but 12½ per cent for the first five years; the tax on reorganized railroads to be 15½ per cent for five years; on reorganized companies other than railroads, 20 per cent for five years. But it was no use. He felt worn down with exasperation.[142]

For all his frustrations, he would look back in 1940 on the real accomplishments of the New Deal which had done well in many respects though hampered by the necessity of fast action confronted, as it was, by an emergency.[143]

Frank Kent expressed the situation: "The Right Will Prevail. The trouble is, however, that it takes so long to prevail that nobody can remember what was right." [144]

17

WATCH ON THE RHINE

ONE HUNDRED THOUSAND voices sounded danger to those who had ears to hear.

The voices were in Nuremberg in 1937, a chanting chorus of hate. Tanks ground by. Planes raked the sky, their shadows racing darkly. Higher and higher rose the voices: "*Sieg Heil! Sieg Heil! Sieg Heil!*" — great waves of sound, breaking against the car that moved between the even furrows of the massed thousands; breaking against the man with the iron cross glinting on his breast, his face set in a mold, his arm outstretched unmovingly.

Years later it would be hard to remember, harder still to believe. There was a quality of nightmare about it, of the secret evil in man's heart. This was not the twentieth century. This was something hideously ancient and forgotten, something macabre like the Black Mass — choral anthems and a twisted cross, the dedication and frenzy of a pagan ceremonial. This was a challenge to the world. "I have never heard Adolf so full of hate, his audience quite so on the border of bedlam," wrote William Shirer of that day.[1]

"*Sieg Heil! Sieg Heil!*" The voices beat at your brains; they drummed in your blood; they echoed in rhythm to marching men. All over Germany there were men in uniform, men marching and singing as they marched, men marching, goose-stepping with robot-like precision, faces like death's-heads beneath the dusk of the steel helmets. The little men were shrieking, their faces distorted against monstrous backdrops of space and sound. They moved like ants down the great shaftlike corridors between the massed thousands to lay wreaths in honor of those who had fought for "our people and our star," for Germany and "a place in the sun." [2]

This was what Germany wanted, not war, not Hitler, but what war and Hitler could bring: jobs, the end of defeat, the end of repentance, a place in the sun. As for the Jews, a typical member of the Hitler Jugend insisted: "Of course, sometimes, one Jew disappears. But what is one Jew?" [3]

Said Hitler: "The Nordic race is entitled to dominate the world." The divine will called for the victory of the fittest, the extermination of an inferior race by a superior race: the Nazis were the elite of the world. The Germans had a mission to perform, and right was what Aryan men deemed right. [4]

Baruch could not visit Germany, of course. But he could see it all in his mind's eye. He could hear the thundering footsteps and the eerie shrill of the air-raid sirens. Germany was girding for war. What of England and the rest of the world?

As a rich American abroad, Baruch had done what other rich Americans had done — seen the "sights," taken the "cures," gamed with his friends at Paris or Monte Carlo, cheered on his favorites at Ascot. But even before 1937, Baruch had been looking about him with different eyes, the eyes of Winston Churchill.

Their friendship, begun in the tension of war, had deepened in peace. In the twenties, when Churchill was writing his first series of World War histories, he sent Baruch a chapter for criticism, and Baruch was much touched by the way the book spoke of him. He was Churchill's oldest American friend, and the Englishman's usual closing, "Your devoted friend," was heartfelt. [5] Even those who had known them through the years were struck by the "warm affection and respect" Churchill showed for Baruch, [6] and Churchill's friend Brendan Bracken once wrote to Baruch: "Nature made you and Winston Churchill for each other and it does you both great good to meet." [7] For Baruch, Churchill selected the one of his paintings which he considered the "very best"; and for years photographs of Churchill have occupied the places of honor in Baruch's home. For the Douglas Chandor portrait of "the old bulldog" Baruch gave over $25,000, "the highest price ever paid for a contemporary portrait in this country." [8]

Their friendship was largely carried on by transatlantic cable. Each was a full-time reception committee for the other, each striving to show off the treasures of his own "empire." Baruch would find friends for Churchill along the line of a lecture tour, to whom the visiting lion would give the honor of luncheon or dinner.[9] He might put up Churchill's entire entourage of sixteen at the Savoy-Plaza, or give advice to young Randolph.[10] To Churchill he even made his supreme offering of "tips" on the stock market, and in October 1932, remembering a significant date three years earlier, Churchill cabled: "How good your judgment was." [11]

For Baruch's summer entertainment, Churchill might plan a motor trip through "beautiful country and highly conservative constituencies." They would see the *Victory*, Nelson's flagship, and "our latest," the *Lord Nelson*. They would take in the yacht races and tour through "jolly country" to Blenheim. Baruch, who had been suffering from gout one summer and practising austerity, looked forward to relaxing his regimen and outdoing Churchill in the pleasures of the table.[12]

Perhaps their last happy year was 1930. By 1931 the Japanese hordes had darkened China; the Storm Troops had broken from the Munich beer cellar, and when the two men sat down for their old-time discussions, realities pressed darkly around them.[13] All was the same in the sun — the pastoral peace of rural England, lean, gray ships bobbing at anchor off Spithead, the smell of peat and the rising of mist on the moors, the warm shooting clothes, the thick knit stockings, the heavy, comfortable boots with nails — the peace that comes with a hot toddy at the end of a day's shooting. All was the same, yet all was changed. And England was sleeping.

Churchill knew. Like the old war horses they were, both Churchill and Baruch sensed the coming conflict. But few shared Churchill's troubled vision of a Germany far stronger than France and smoldering with dreams of a war of liberation or revenge; of a future of atomic explosions and nuclear energy, and a time when a bomb "no bigger than an orange" might blast out a township; when some robot race, bred to tend machines, might wipe out a superior people. Churchill was warning, and for seven years his warnings had gone unheeded, for after the "war to end wars" no one cared to hear what he had to say. Some few thought that Britain was "criminally foolish" not to make use of his experience and invite him to join the government. But Baruch did not share Churchill's hope for a revived League of Nations. The League, he felt, had become an instrument of selfishness which might not have happened if Americans had participated from the beginning.[14]

Both Baruch and Churchill were well aware of the propaganda

value of the Germans' clamor against the Treaty of Versailles. And both were aware of still another danger to the east of Germany. Communism and nazism were alike, and together they were making men into beasts. Baruch foresaw that they might someday become allies.[15]

Returning home in the summer of 1937, Baruch had tried to arouse public opinion. "Baruch Reports World 'A Tinder Box,'" ran a typical headline; in Europe, but one emotion — fear — predominated. "The people of Europe," he said, "have no hope any more." Five days later, he visited the President at Hyde Park. "Anything can happen," he said.[16]

On the occasion of his annual trip abroad in 1938, a New York *Post* writer reported: "Bernard Baruch is planning to sail to England with a group of colleagues who are in complete disagreement with the policies of Prime Minister Chamberlain. Their backing will be offered to Winston Churchill." [17] For seven years, Britain had been warned of her weakness, on land, on the sea, and in the air. Publicly, Baruch could say little, for he did not believe any American had the right to criticize with our own defenses as laggard as they were — but nevertheless, any appeasement by England was a threat to America. For, if Germany conquered England, she might yet accomplish her next objective, the conquest of the United States.[18]

So, when Baruch sailed, it was on a "mission." Carefully he revisited his old haunts, looking about him with new and searching eyes. "War was coming," he said afterward. "You could see it and you could feel it." France was a country stagnated and torn with the internecine wars of splinter parties and capital versus labor. Germany was arming from scratch — not for her the leftover guns and concepts of 1917. Versailles had stripped her and freed her to build the most modern army in Europe. But France slumbered under the sunlight and the poplar trees, stores and factories closed for the "weekend," from Saturday morning to Tuesday morning or noon. At Vichy, Baruch saw Pierre Laval, who said that France could put no faith in England. As for the French Army: "Put a French rifle in a Frenchman's hand and he may turn it on his officers or himself." [19]

In England, Baruch saw Lord Inscape, the Minister of Munitions, who said, "We can't depend on the French." Marquis Childs later repeated the story of Baruch's call in London on a high government

official with the blunt question: "Can the French make shells?" The
answer had been, "I'm sorry to say in that department they must rely
on us," and Baruch felt as if he "had been kicked in the stomach."
Baruch cabled to the President a warning that France and England
would not be able to fight.[20]

Germany, he reported, had long been buying nonferrous metals and
now had sufficient stocks of copper and rubber. Japan, too, was buying
copper in America.[21] In London, it was very gay, yet always you could
feel tension. England was on a spending spree. England was dancing,
dancing in the great country houses, their doors flung open now for
the last time, gardens festooned with girls who would vanish in
blitz and fire. Laughing faces, laughing up into the faces of men
soon to be shot down over Paris, over Berlin and Munich, over London itself. "You had the feeling," Senator John Kennedy remembered, "of an era ending, and everyone had a very good time at the
end." [22]

"Don't raise our boys to be cannon fodder," cried the peace
slogans. Baruch stayed on into September, when Chamberlain came
home from Munich, waving that white slip of paper with the boast,
"I bring you peace in our time." Baruch was in London that
September day when the fear-burdened crowd surged into West-
minster Abbey to kneel before the tomb of the Unknown Soldier and
the single unflickering flame, and pray for peace when there was no
peace.[23]

Sadly Baruch went to take his leave of Churchill. "War is coming
very soon," the Englishman said. "We will be in it and you will be
in it. You will be running the show over there, but I will be on the
sidelines over here." [24]

Baruch sailed and when he stepped off the gangplank in New
York, "looking like the Southern planter he is," [25] he brushed off
suggestions that he had returned at the special request of President
Roosevelt to organize American industry for war.[26] There was some
truth to this, but, as Baruch foresaw, nothing would come of it.[27] Not
until October 12 was he summoned to the White House to deliver
his "report."

Baruch could tell the President that Germany had already spent
in 1938 some 105 billion marks on arms alone. As for us — "we're so
badly off," he commented, "it's unbelievable." We must build at
least 50,000 long-range bombers. Congress must be called back, the

Military Affairs and Naval Committees informed. Here, Roosevelt interrupted him.

"The nation is not ready." [28]

Baruch knew what he meant, knew that "getting ready" was far more than an armament program. He knew what his own task must be.

Former Ambassador Joseph P. Kennedy has declared that Baruch's influence at this time has been definitely overestimated; that at a later period it was much greater. What could Baruch have told the President that Bullitt or he couldn't have told him? Kennedy has wondered. There is some truth in this. Baruch's role was entirely different from that of an ambassador. He could say what no ambassador could say and keep his job; an ambassador's confidential findings could not be used to arouse public opinion. Baruch's memos, therefore, had not been nearly so much to "inform" Franklin D. Roosevelt as to "instruct" the American people.[29]

Baruch stayed that night at the White House, but he could not sleep. The next morning, keyed to alertness, he was up early and ushered out by way of the Executive offices. There, tipped off by Steve Early, the press corps was waiting.

A tired, terribly earnest man stood before them. "I've got something I want to say to you," he began. Briefly he explained. He had been in Europe studying industrial mobilization. Thus, he said, he felt free to give his opinions. Munich was not a peace, it was a surrender. "Mr. Hitler knew that England and France were not prepared to come to grips at this time." Had they been ready to move, there would have been quite a different story.

"I hope," Baruch continued, "that we will never be in the humiliating position in which Chamberlain found himself . . . We ought to be able to defend our homes." He added, with emphasis, "I know what I am talking about. I believe America is unprepared." Why, we could not even put a first-class army in the field.

What were the remedies? He ticked them off swiftly: a two-ocean navy, ready for any emergency, for the navy was our "first line" of defensive warfare; arms and more arms; the total organization of industry for overnight conversion to a war footing.[30] Baruch made it plain that his ideas were his own, not the President's.[31] Within twenty-four hours, however, Roosevelt dispatched the second of his notes to Hitler, Baruch commenting, "The President backed me up the next day." As he pointed out afterward, he could say things the President could not say in an election year.[32]

Baruch's task was to focus public opinion. The President outlined his instructions: "You put a burr under their tail, Bernie, and if I hear 'em holler, I'll know you're doing all right." [33]

For a week or so, in those tense days, few were in closer communication with the White House than Baruch. But, slowly, the "scare" died down. For years he was to feel that he was accomplishing little. He seemed unable to convince either the Administration or the public of what seemed so clear to him. Why could they not understand what was happening across the Atlantic? It seemed that his "mission" had failed. His drive for preparedness only got support from a handful of columnists and publishers.[34]

Hugh Johnson, Frank Kent, the Hearst papers and such isolated voices as the Washington *Star*, the Portland *Herald*, the Richmond *Times-Dispatch* and the El Paso *Times* rallied to his defense, calling him "The Man of the Hour" and entirely right in his contention that American safety depended on American strength.[35] But these were drowned out by the rabid voices of Father Coughlin and the Reverend Gerald L. K. Smith. The epithets of "International Banker," "Warmonger," and "Jewish Warmonger" were hurled around Baruch's head. Wryly he could reflect that those who warned against disaster were invariably damned as the authors of the disaster. Silently he bore the slurs and insults of crackpots who signed their letters "U.S.A." or "Croix de Feu," who damned him as a "dirty Jew," or as "Public Enemy Number One."

"Who in hell ever got cash for anything that the dead Beat English ever panhandled in this country?" wrote one. "If this Country goes to war the day After the Slaughter will begin for your kind." What had Germany "done to us Americans that can induce you to talk like we all the people in U.S.A. wants to fight for England?" [36]

There was pressure from another quarter. Coming down the graceful iron stairway of his Fifth Avenue home one day, Baruch saw in the reception room a slender blond woman with the fine beauty of Dresden china. It was Clare Boothe Luce, and she faced him trembling with indignation. The Nazi purges were not a crime against the Jews alone, but against all civilization.

Baruch tried to soothe her.[37] Was not war itself a crime no less hideous than the butcheries in Germany? Yet not hatred of Germany so much as sympathy for England stirred his deepest emotions. He knew, however, that his personal feelings were not necessarily those of his country. Not until 1939 would a newspaper of the standing of the Philadelphia *Public Ledger* concede that isolationism was out of date. If England went to war, Baruch feared that they would get no help from the United States.[38]

British repudiation of her First World War debt had stiffened American public opinion against her. America would not go to war because of Austria, Czechoslovakia, or Poland. Nor would America rearm in her own defense — although had she done so, Baruch believed, she might conceivably have called a halt to German aggression. Baruch saw South America rather than Europe as the ultimate line of American defense; but South America, with its zest for dictatorship, might be won by political penetration should Hitler bring the continent to terms. How could this be averted? Baruch suggested trade. If cheap labor from Germany's conquered provinces were to flood Latin America with goods, our own standard of living might suffer.[39]

As for neutrality — "There ain't no such animal," Baruch said.[40]

For all the outcry over the so-called "Neutrality Act," Baruch was convinced that the United States did not want to be neutral; it just wanted to keep out of war. It did not want to give up its profits and its property. It did not want to surrender its rights to the freedom of the seas. It had already picked its side. It just did not want to fight. But if Americans' fears were roused sufficiently, Baruch knew, they would fight.[41]

You could not legislate sympathies. The so-called Neutrality Act forbade the sale of arms to warring countries. Yet, as Baruch pointed out, if the United States were to recognize the plain fact that undeclared war was raging between Japan and China and invoke the Act, it would be favoring Japan.

In a scholarly article in *Current History*, Baruch strove to convey some of the facts of death and life in modern war. When Napoleon had restricted the standing armies of the German states, they hit upon the idea of universal military training, a whole nation in arms — the doctrine that finally downed Napoleon at Leipzig and doomed him at Waterloo. Furthermore, gigantic fighting armies and the furiously working populations behind them consumed from three to five times as much of everything — clothing, food, and shoes — as

was used in time of peace. Hence, in a death struggle between whole
peoples, an embargo could be as deadly as armed intervention, and
the "neutral" who denied life's necessities to both sides would himself be committing an act of war. Everything was contraband now-
adays, and if we withheld raw materials from all belligerents, the
combatants might well deny us rubber, tin, nickel, and lead, were we
attacked in the Pacific. The only way to prevent war was to refuse
to finance it.[42]

What, then, was true neutrality? Baruch's idea was as realistic as
it was cynical. Why should not the United States keep its own ships
off the seas and sell goods to any country that could pay cash and take
them away? This was not only neutrality — in that it theoretically
would treat all nations alike — but it was profitable neutrality. This
was the idea called "cash and carry," which Baruch was asked to explain to the Senate Foreign Relations Committee on April 6, 1939.

He prefaced his testimony with a brief statement. "I speak not as
anti-German, anti-English, or anti-anything . . . I am not and never
have been a banker . . . I have no interests whatsoever directly or indirectly in any manufacture of munitions . . . I should be childish if
I did not know that those things are being whispered about."

The scene was a tense one. Old memories must have stirred in Baruch as he gazed at the men grouped around the horseshoe table
under the lights. There, still formidable, still potent, were the last
survivors of that famed "little group of willful men" who had read
the death sentence on Wilson's dream: Hiram Johnson, stolid and
massive, and Borah, gray and serious beyond his years. He had his
"private sources" of information from overseas; he was convinced
that another war would mean the end of our Federal system and
Constitution, and openly avowed that he would rather see the collapse of our whole economy than another war. Even the name of
Lodge was not missing. In his place sat his thirty-nine-year-old
grandson, who had vanquished Boston's flamboyant perennial, James
Michael Curley, three years before.

Baruch's friend Key Pittman of Nevada was chairman. Still the
New Yorker's gaze moved around the table. There was Barkley, his
pink face crinkled in a smile of welcome. Grinning, too, was North
Carolina's raucous-voiced America-Firster, "Our Bob" Reynolds.
Reynolds railed against Jews and "aliens" in a South where they were
scarcely more numerous than Republicans. His sheet, *The Vindicator*,

had national circulation, and he was receiving more publicity than any subsequent Senator until the advent of Joseph R. McCarthy of Wisconsin.[43]

Now Baruch spoke. "It is easier to proclaim neutrality than to maintain it." And he warned, "To embargo the sale of implements of war under conditions that now exist might be the means of cementing into power the stronger nations and reducing weaker nations to slavery." In modern war, there was no distinction between life-giving wheat and death-dealing guns.

Having finished, Baruch took off his glasses and sat down for the cross-examination. Senator Borah led off. Mr. Baruch did not contend that this cash-and-carry plan was a neutrality proposition?

"No, sir," Baruch answered promptly.

"Don't you think," the Senator continued, "when two nations are engaged in war, we ought not to sit on the side and furnish the instrumentalities?"

"Then perhaps we ought to embargo everything," Baruch snapped.

"Well, I am in favor of embargoing everything," replied the Senator. Stolidly, he forced Baruch to agree that the cash-and-carry plan would benefit Japan or any aggressor who had the sea power to carry "the stuff" away. As things now worked, Hiram Johnson added, we were the ally of Japan in the Pacific and of Great Britain in the Atlantic. Senator Lewis Schwellenbach wondered how the United States could reconcile its pledge of responsibility for the territorial integrity of China with the furnishing of scrap steel to Japan. Baruch's answer was cryptic. "Our position," he said, "is not a very pleasant one to contemplate." Nevertheless, Japan had 70 million people on islands about the size of California. "She wants to expand — she says she has to."

"We know that we are taking sides with the stronger cause," Senator Hiram Johnson boomed.

"As soon as we treat them other than alike . . . we are declaring an economic war," Baruch persisted. Maintaining the status quo was neutrality. It was not any of our affair "to stick our nose" in Europe's business; he hastened to add that he was not unaware of the moral issues, but he was also aware of America's reluctance to face these issues. Nor did he believe in talking loudly and carrying a little stick. "My desire to keep out of war overcomes my head, my heart being on the side of no war."

What Baruch wanted was all-out military production on the part
of the United States, as the surest guarantee for keeping out of war.
But the President was reluctant and Congress was reluctant, their
feeling based not on the facts but on the reluctance of the American
people. To the people, arms meant war.[44]

What may have been an outright attempt to break Baruch had
been made in June 1935, when he had been called to give an accounting of his income at the "Merchants of Death" inquiry, headed
by the rabidly isolationist Senator Gerald P. Nye of North Dakota.
Baruch and Herbert Bayard Swope had worked two whole nights in
preparation. They were comforted, however, when they recognized
Baruch's old friend Carter Glass sneering out of the corner of his
mouth at Nye and at the "dad-bum questions" of the young prose-
cuting attorney, Alger Hiss.[45]

Nothing was "uncovered." Baruch challenged the Committee to
investigate to the limit. Neither he nor any member of his family
had anything to hide. He supplied copies of the worksheets for his
income tax returns for the years 1918 and 1919, not only demon-
strating that he had not made a dollar out of the war, but also taking
the opportunity to ram down the throats of the listeners his principles on taking the profits out of war.

The next day a very angry man stormed into the committee room.
Flushed, thinning gray hair on end, James F. Byrnes stood up to voice
his indignation at the insult of an inquiry into a man of Baruch's
integrity. The Committee hushed as Byrnes told of the amount that
Baruch had paid out of his own pocket to coordinate American and
Allied industry in the First World War. Faces softened as he told
the story that had never been told before — of those office girls of the
War Industries Board stranded in Washington at the war's end, and
of who had sent them home.

"When I saw he was under criticism on money matters before this
committee," said Byrnes, "I felt it my duty to inform the committee
of these things." Nye looked shamed. He hoped that Mr. Byrnes
was not under the impression that the Committee was critical of Mr.
Baruch's wartime record. As for Baruch, he was touched beyond
measure by Byrnes's loyalty. The whole affair boomeranged completely.[46]

But, unfortunately for his activities in war mobilization, the whisper that he was "too old" seemed to have some validity. He was floored by a long-smoldering infection and underwent a serious mastoid operation in the summer of 1939, with all mail and visitors excluded. One of the first guests to be admitted was Mrs. Roosevelt, who wrote that from a purely selfish point of view she did not like her tower of strength laid low.[47] At the request of his family, young Blanche Higgins, the nurse who had seen him through the crisis, stayed on as companion and social secretary, and under her fostering care he emerged stronger and healthier than in years. But the illness had told on him; his deafness was now plainly apparent, and at seventy he looked almost as old as he did ten years later.

President Roosevelt by this time was fully aware of the necessity of arousing public opinion in support of preparedness. The wonder is that the President was able to chart any course at all. From overseas Churchill had informed him and the world that Hitler would fight, and that without rearmament Britain would lose. From the White House steps Bernard Baruch had informed him and the world that Hitler would fight and that without rearmament the United States would lose. From the Embassy in Paris, William Bullitt repeated assurances that Hitler would never fight and suggested that Poland be made the testing ground. Had this been done, Joseph Kennedy believed, Hitler would have fought Russia only and let England alone. And from London the Ambassador had already sent home advices that, if opposed, not only would Hitler fight — he would win.

At any rate, these views of his advisers help to explain the President's contradictory policies: why Baruch, for instance, had been promised the chairmanship of a revamped War Industries Board in October 1938 and then "unceremoniously scuttled" a few weeks later. Baruch himself had not helped matters by suggesting that his old War Industries Board associates be drafted to serve with him. Roosevelt countered sharply that George Peek was *persona non grata* to him and that although he liked officers and gentlemen, Hugh S. Johnson was no longer an officer and had never been a gentleman.[48]

Baruch heard no more about the plan until the summer of 1939, when Roosevelt named a War Resources Board without either consulting or appointing Baruch, and chose young Edward Stettinius as its head. Baruch's pride smarted. He was "unavailable," he concluded, because of having annoyed the Army and Navy all through

1937 and 1938 by perpetual demands that they "hurry up." But he could see that the War Resources Board was merely one of the President's trial balloons, to be punctured neatly after the 1940 election day. So Baruch let himself be "consulted" by the Board members who wanted to save themselves, and by the New Dealers who attacked the Board as Morgan-staffed and Morgan-inspired. Eliot Janeway has commented that Baruch was thus free to take credit for the Board's successes or to deny responsibility; and "if this is not power, what is?" In any case, he had salvaged himself for future influence by not being offered up as a human sacrifice.[49]

Baruch had sent his associate John Hancock to help with the paperwork, and the result, the famous, suppressed Report of the War Resources Board, was largely of Baruch's inspiration. Actually, it was a revision of the 1939 Industrial Mobilization Plan of the Army-Navy Munitions Board, which, in turn, was drawn directly from an "outline of action" prepared by Baruch for President Wilson back in 1918. The new plan, however, dealt with new contingencies — an example, the fact that modern war was no quick jump from peace to hostilities, but a slowly encroaching thing. It recognized the need for flexibility, for civilian control of wartime powers, and it vested the final authority for coordination in the President himself.[50] Above all, it declared war on special privilege. It was a good plan. It had been requested by Roosevelt, but having received it he put it aside, only to revive it piecemeal after Pearl Harbor. For it was not, at the time of its making, good politics.

Mrs. Roosevelt has noted that "Franklin frequently refrained from supporting causes in which he believed because of political realities."[51] Had he at once gone ahead with the plan as Baruch suggested, it might not only have cost Britain the belated aid we were able to give, it might also have denied us the chance to rebuild our own war machine. The cry of "warmongers" would have drowned out all else. The very men who would blame the New Deal for Pearl Harbor denied funds to fortify the islands in the Pacific. As late as 1941, the draft extension bill squeaked through the House by one vote. Poland lay stark, blackened with destruction, when a request for ten thousand new planes was dropped from the President's budget. Congress knew what was going on. But the leaders would not move ahead of their followers.

Only slowly did opinion crystallize under the hard-hitting thrusts of those who like Baruch had the facility for asking impolitic questions. He had heard of mineral deposits called monazite sands. Could it be used in making armor for airplanes? Why were draftees armed with First World War guns? Why were not the Army and Air Force motorized, as provided under the WPA? Why could not the overlapping be eliminated between the Army Industrial College and the Army War College? Could not the Army and Navy get together even to decide how much metals and raw materials they needed, and then get the necessary funds voted? Walker Stone recalled Baruch in previous years wandering in and out of committees on the Hill, "trying to get them to stockpile tin." He had been uncomfortable to have around because he would not go for the expedient thing. He had made, as Stone said, "a great effort to build up our armed forces when we were leaf-raking around here." Now, less than ever, would he submit to expediency. His efforts were useless among those who instead of stockpiling for war had determined to legislate us out of war. But he would not desist, even though he was pessimistic as to what would be accomplished.[52]

If he could not sway public opinion, he could at least continue hammering at public officials. At first, through 1938 and 1939, he urged Harry Hopkins to take the Secretaryship of War. Then as Hopkins' "touch of flu" assumed dramatic proportions, Baruch tried overtures of a different kind. On March 8, 1939, he wrote Hopkins the train schedules for Hobcaw.[53]

On cool mornings Baruch and his guest sunned themselves in long chairs, facing the massed flame of the azaleas and the dancing white petals of the dogwood. A glass screen cut off the wind from the rear. There they talked, or, rather, Baruch did. The wind seemed to grow colder, as with passionate earnestness he repeated the words and warning of Winston Churchill. War was coming. All would be in it, and it would engulf all. We were woefully unprepared. "Harry didn't much want to listen to me," Baruch said afterward, "but I kept at him." [54]

Baruch continued to go to Washington, even if, as someone now gibed, he had to sit on a park bench to be noticed. He studied the newer members of Congress: youthful, owl-eyed Rush Holt, the "little Henry Clay"; "the man Bilbo," teacher, preacher, country editor and hater; onetime county judge Harry Truman, with his feverish good-roads complex and great personal charm. How would they stand up under fire? [55] He fought with Under-Secretary of War Louis Johnson, urging him not to resign but to present the necessary facts to the President, for Secretary of War Harry Woodring was convinced there would be no war.[56]

We called the war "phony." Only the fall of France and Belgium — the tourists' playgrounds — had meaning for the United States. America at large cared little, apparently, about the men, women, and children of Poland who fled like hunted animals through roads clogged with trucks, wagons, cars, and cavalry soldiers, now racing, running, trying to hide under a searing sky in the open fields under the shadow of wings that soared and swooped, and the drilling of machine-gun fire and bombs ripping furrows or graves ahead of them.

Dust blew in clouds. It powdered the dry tongues of babies strapped to motorcycles or slung in sidecars; it stung and inflamed their eyes. Flies swarmed. There were no places to rest in the cowering little villages, no places to bathe in or prepare milk or food, except in the homes of kindly strangers who might themselves be fleeing a few hours later.

Faces were wan and worn. Eyes were dry and seemingly sightless, but no one wept. One observer recorded that their eyes would haunt her always. Poland had been a battleground for centuries, lashed and cut like wheat for the harvest, but never before like this: the bombs hurtling down on the train of women, children, and wounded soldiers lumbering out of Cracow, again and again shuddering to a stop for the bodies to be brought out, ten and twelve at a time. Refugees were fleeing across the border. They were not afraid of death, but of living under the Nazis or Russians.

And for Americans, it was a phony war.[57]

It was not phony to Baruch, who read the eyewitness accounts sent him by Mrs. Roosevelt. Within the week, Baruch was in Washington begging the President to stop the bickering in the Army and put a fighter at the head of the Navy. If he could be of permanent service, he stood ready. But he received no summons.[58]

In April 1940, General George C. Marshall invited Baruch to inspect the Army with him at Fort Benning, Georgia, and detailed special officers from the War Department as his escort. Later, Baruch and the Chief of Staff viewed the May maneuvers of an array of

160,000 aging men. Roosevelt, unconvinced by the blitzkrieg, toyed with the idea that naval and air power alone could win a war. But Marshall had recognized that the success of the Germans in Poland was due to the coordination of ground troops and supporting planes. For Marshall, quiet, enduring, patient, with his respect for facts and irritation at incompetence, Baruch had developed an admiration never shaken in the bitter years when the "good soldier" was betrayed in the name of his own patriotism. Baruch was always convinced that it was his old friend Pershing who was largely responsible for Marshall's appointment as Chief of Staff.[59]

Marshall sent to Baruch duplicates of messages he sent the President, and a plea for the Elder Statesman to use his influence with Roosevelt. Together Baruch and Marshall could agonize over the quiet comment of the German officer leaving the capital late in 1940, that his country was making far more use of the American mobilization scheme than the Americans were; or over a House Committee's elimination of $67,000,000 from the Chief of Staff's budget during the very weeks that Europe tottered and fell; and in particular over the postponement of a projected air base at Anchorage, Alaska, while the Russians were fortifying their bases at Vladivostok. But Baruch's pleas had had effect. His brief Washington visit had much to do with canceling the cuts in the Army budget which had been occasioned by the Senate's spasm of economy. He was able to write Marshall that all was set, and that if he needed anything more he had better get it while Congress was in the right mood. This in itself was no mean accomplishment for an election year.[60]

But now Americans were beginning to watch something besides their own cavalcade. Churchill cabled Roosevelt that the entire European continent would fall with "astonishing swiftness"; the great names of the First World War — Ypres and Verdun — reeled by as if in kaleidoscope; and the French Ambassador answered Roosevelt's queries with a beating of his breast. "Mr. President," he said, "France will go on and on and on." [61] Churchill cabled that France could be saved if America would come; but not 20,000 motorized American troops could have been put into the field, and their equipment was antiquated.[62] Why the delay? Baruch did not know.

Roosevelt could offer nothing but sympathy and old guns to Englishmen standing ready to fight with pitchforks. Nothing was real. Nothing endured any more but Britons alone, armed only with one thousand years of freedom, the beaches of Dunkirk, the voice of Churchill, and the promise that they would never surrender.

But conquest was possible if surrender was not, and privately Churchill had assured Roosevelt that in any case the Home Fleet would be salvaged.[63] Former Ambassador Joseph Davies, just back from the fighting fronts, wrote Baruch that he could not understand his countrymen's complacent belief that after the conquest the war would be over and life go on as before.[64]

The crisis wore hideously on Roosevelt, yet it galvanized him into action. He was already desperately tired. Before the campaign he had confessed to Daniel Tobin that he wanted to go home to Hyde Park to rest, to take care of his trees.[65] Now Lend-Lease lifted a tottering England to her feet; scientists bent to the study of the "fission of uranium." On the other hand, the Navy was still reluctant to pool information with the Army, and movie audiences hissed the valiant Wendell Willkie's appeal for more aid to Britain. Not until that "terrible May" of 1940 had the Administration begun to think in terms of the 50,000 planes that Baruch and others had recommended almost two years before, and an army of two million men. In a memo for Baruch, Sam Lubell noted that with France gone and England threatened, the stockpiling of raw materials was only slowly being planned.[66]

Roosevelt has been denounced both as an interventionist and as criminally negligent in the rearming of his country. The evidence shows that preparedness had been his goal. He had advocated universal military training as early as 1912 and a continental American defense line one thousand miles out to sea. Although he had pleased the public by promising relief from armaments, actually he had built up the peacetime army and navy to "the highest point in history," [67] and as early as 1937 had suggested a blockade of Japan, which Britain refused, and a quarantine to "strangle Japan and Germany economically." [68] It was the people who lagged behind Roosevelt. As a responsible official in a democracy as well as a master politician, he knew that he could not move too far ahead of the people and win re-election in 1940. And if he were defeated, might not the isolationists take over entirely?

As for Baruch, he held no office and could afford to preach what he saw both to officials and the public. What he saw in these days of "gathering storm" was that there was at large in the world a force of evil which must be crushed. Then, if the spirit of the crusade could be carried over to the making of peace, as it had not been in 1919, we could hope for a world in which ideals and the spiritual side of man would control. These hopes he expressed to Felix Frankfurter on the eve of Pearl Harbor in one of the most thoughtful letters he ever wrote.[69]

Back in 1940, when the people at last stirred, it looked as though it might be too late. Picking up his paper, head held closely to his radio, Baruch knew that the country was at last blazing with demands for defense and that defense goods were only "on order." So voluminous became the unsolicited advice — over a thousand letters a day and many from high sources, all pouring in upon Chief of Staff Marshall — that Baruch suggested the appointment of a special research committee of scientists to sift them.[70]

Shortly before France fell, Roosevelt had launched his second trial balloon. He had announced appointment of the National Defense Advisory Commission — spiritual child, at least, of the Advisory Commission of the First World War. Apparently not much had been learned from experience, and although good people were named — such as William Knudsen, whom Baruch had suggested, Leon Henderson, Stettinius, and Dr. Harriet Elliott, Dean of the North Carolina College for Women * — there was no chairman. Baruch's name was missing from the list.

Baruch visited the Commission almost immediately and jotted down notes on what he found. The President was backing it up, at least, and showing a surprising ability in getting executives into line. The Army and Navy were better organized than in the First World War; there was a comfortable surplus of labor; and, he noted approvingly, Stettinius was following the experience of the old War Industries Board in the attention he paid to raw materials. Donald Nelson, a big production man from Sears, Roebuck, was an unknown quantity and a known presidential favorite, but he did seem to understand priorities. The price-control picture was still vague. Baruch strongly urged that there must be a ceiling over all prices, with a committee to make necessary adjustments.[71]

He wrote to Arthur Krock that the new advisory commission had a far easier job than its predecessor. For one thing, inflation had not reached such heights, and there were clearly outlined methods of

* Now the Woman's College of the University of North Carolina.

control. They had also, if they cared to avail themselves of it, the benefit of the earlier group's experience. The fact remained that if there were only partial controls, consumers would merely seek out noncontrolled items to buy. If one price was battened down, another would rise in its place. What else could there be but inflation when there were but 75 billion dollars in consumers' goods produced to satisfy 85 billion dollars of purchasing power? [72]

Priorities and controls, however, were but segments of a coordinated war mobilization program. Furthermore, it had to be a civilian program, as was understood by Roosevelt, who named William Knudsen and Sidney Hillman co-chairmen of the Office of Production Management.[73]

Much has been written about Knudsen's limitations, but they were so interwoven with the failings of the multilettered and multiheaded agencies in which he functioned that it is impossible to determine what he might have accomplished under different circumstances. That he was a great production man there is no doubt; nor that the "production miracle" of the Second World War was in part due to his inspiration.

It was as a production man only that Baruch had recommended him. Seated at his desk on May 28, 1940, the day the British boats moved out from Dunkirk, Knudsen answered a call from the White House. He was to head production for the National Defense Advisory Commission, that seven-headed body that was taking up where Woodrow Wilson had begun. As he told it later, he had just time enough to fly to New York and tell his company. The next day he was in Washington, had talked fifteen minutes with the President, and was set to work.[74]

Theoretically, his task was to synchronize the requirements of the military machine and the capacity of the industrial machine. Knudsen understood this. As early as the previous November he had proposed the appointment of an over-all director of industrial mobilization, with all the powers and functions later performed by the War Production Board. He knew what had to be done, but he did not know how to do it, and his appointment was a cruel misuse of great talents.[75] "I don't understand all this nonsense here," he told Baruch ruefully. His character and ability were never more vividly illustrated than in his failure. As Baruch observed, he "never hollered, never complained, went right on and did his duty like the conscript he was." "I'll only work for two people," he told Baruch, "you and President Roosevelt. I won't work for anyone else." [76] Knudsen went about his job of equipping two million Americans as he might have outfitted two million Chevrolet cars. "You bring it to the shop door," he told Stettinius of the Raw Materials division, "and I'll cut it up." [77] He was a manufacturer, not an organizer. And as the waves of protest rolled in, the hapless Knudsen was eventually "promoted" to a general's desk in the Pentagon, with three stars on his shoulders. The night the news came, Knudsen crouched at the piano, humming sad tunes as he played. "He was never happy again." [78] Meanwhile, Roosevelt, who had resolved that he would never appoint a tzar or a Pooh-Bah, continued his search for one.

Baruch kept sounding his pet theme — organization — incorporating controls, production, and priorities. On the latter, he hoped the President would make no move without first consulting him. Authority to establish and administer priorities, he felt, should be located in the Office of Production Management, established in the summer of 1940, supposedly to "schedule" requirements. Price control was apparently what nobody wanted. Typical was Donald Nelson's answer when Baruch urged him to assume the authority necessary to accomplish his task — if necessary, including rationing.[79] Nelson replied that when Baruch started discussing price ceilings, he had his doubts, but later he came to the conclusion that if we had set ceilings before prices had risen it would have stemmed the tide. However, now that prices had soared so high, and some were so out of line with others, he thought "the administering of them would be exceedingly difficult." [80]

It was, of course, much too late when the OPA was born and Leon Henderson was given the job of holding the price line — after it was irrevocably broken. The public thought it wanted controls, so Leon Henderson was given the job of selling controls. If they failed, he failed with them. He was another of Roosevelt's trial balloons; he was an "expendable."

Some called him a New Dealer, this stocky, hard-driving, "swearing-mad" man, but callers could feel the atmosphere of an earlier era as he paced from chair to chair in a ramshackle office in a temporary building, snapping his suspenders against his blue shirt, or resting one foot on a seat. "I have to make nothing but adverse decisions," he would sometimes growl; or, chomping down on a cigar or a whole pack of chewing gum, "I don't expect to last . . . but I'm going to last as long as I can." This was the man who had blasted NRA and then boosted it, who had told Johnson in teamsters' language that NRA paid no attention to the consumer, and was then hired as the representative of the consumer. He had no flair for politics, and when he played them it was he who became the victim. Someone called him a Communist. "If Henderson is a Red," Baruch snapped, "then I'm a fellow-traveler." [81]

For he had been a Baruch disciple all along. Baruch had helped salvage him for future service when he stamped out of the room and out of Washington in the winter of 1941, after bellowing that $50 a thousand feet was an "outrageous" price for Southern pine — $25 would be more than enough.[82] Baruch had convinced even the wary President of Henderson's capabilities, and when he returned, it was as price stabilizer. "I think," Baruch commented, "he is the best qualified man for this job." [83] He was the "key operating man of the moment." But it was only a moment.[84]

You would see him sometimes, looking like an aggressive laundry bag and talking like a profane truck driver, slouched on a bench in Lafayette Square, his head bent toward the shrewd-eyed, elegantly dressed Baruch. "Get this straight," Baruch might be saying. "Price control by itself will not work." [85] You had to have priorities and rationing and credit controls together. Here Henderson agreed that Baruch was "absolutely right — technically." [86] They could agree, too, that consumers' rights were less important than output for war.

But Congress would not go along. The minority, as Henderson bitterly observed, could turn on an awful lot of heat. Because of the clamor of pressure groups, the anti-inflation drive failed, as Roosevelt had guessed that it would fail, and a human sacrifice had to be offered up. The experiment was obviously damned from the beginning, because the price line could only be held if the OPA had had the power to allocate supplies, and this was the job of OPM, and could only be accomplished at the expense of the civilian economy. This was not done. Hence the OPA and its hapless boss were another casualty of the war. The people's wrath against controls would be easily turned against the custodian of controls.

So the typical headline in the spring of 1941 was: "Price Control Effort Held Ineffectual," [87] and by fall the price index was up six per cent over the March figure. Yet, despite Baruch's urgings for an over-all price-control plan, the President could still tell reporters that he had never heard of the "Baruch Plan." [88]

The next day Baruch was at Hyde Park. Gangling, white-haired, taut with purpose, he looked amazingly like the driving War Industries Board chieftain of 1918.[89] Three days later, the President sent Congress a message, demanding all-out powers over wages, prices, and rents, the kind of authority that Baruch had exercised in the War Industries Board.[90]

The press generally favored the idea, but agriculture and labor promptly sent up distress signals, although in fact they stood to benefit. Another dissenting voice was that of the *New York Times*. What Baruch wanted to do was to find the basic normal price for all commodities at some given time and freeze them there, subject to individual adjustments; the *Times* felt that it was impossible for all prices to be normal.[91] And even the press corps chuckled over an unfortunate interview of November 20, in which Mr. Baruch returned to his First World War dream of standardized clothes for women. "Mr. Baruch Walks On Eggshells," laughed the Brooklyn *Eagle*; and an echo came from the Spokane *Chronicle*, "Sweet femininity cannot abide regulation. Mr. Baruch, you are out of order." [92] Five days later a House bill embodying the Baruch proposals was voted down.

Congress still operated under the happy delusion that controls might not be needed after all. Few politicians would risk their future on an unpopular measure. Quietly James F. Byrnes came to Baruch. To force the issue of all-out controls might jeopardize Selective Service, Lend-Lease, and the whole defense program. Baruch realized sadly what he later wrote in a magazine, that "without a great surge of popular and patriotic inspiration rationing could not be enforced." The people just did not want to be controlled. Baruch hated to leave such issues as these to the "panic and hate of wartime legislation." But there was no surge of "patriotic inspiration" until after Pearl Harbor, and then it was too late.[93]

Baruch had come to accept the inevitability of war. In the spring of 1941, as an uproar sounded over a White House bill to commandeer property for national defense, Baruch gave Roosevelt complete support. There was a need to "club into line a small group" that was seeking "selfish gains in selfish ways." [94]

Production would win a war, and once the United States shifted into high gear Baruch had no fear of Germany. Mechanized warfare was our dish of tea and he realized how the news that we were at last swinging into action would impress Hitler.[95]

That Baruch was the obvious man to gear and mobilize industry was not obvious to the one man who could appoint him, although it seemed so to such diverse people as the Pulitzer Prize author Marquis James, who had spent several years with Baruch working on the Elder Statesman's memoirs; New Dealer Ben Cohen and army men like General Levin Campbell, who from "the inside . . . could see the need for his talents." [96]

Garet Garrett proclaimed him "*the* great American," and Frank Kent called him the one outstanding authority on industrial mobilization in the country. That he was not now in charge made it "impossible to explain Mr. Roosevelt on reasonable lines." But Roosevelt did not care. He knew whom the press would blame if he named Baruch, and later they disagreed. There was, too, the "international banker" propaganda of those who saw the approaching war as a mere anti-Hitler plot on the part of world Jewry. Yet Baruch's ideas had support among the most rabid New Dealers as well as among defense industrialists. And many Senators shared Bennett Clark's view that unless the President could secure a man of Baruch's experience and ability, our whole defense plans might fall into disaster. The country, thought the liberal Senator Claude Pepper, regarded Baruch as "our most eminent private citizen." Even Ickes wished he could take over and clean up the Augean stables. Baruch agreed with some of these opinions.[97]

Gradually, almost imperceptibly, the pressure was wearing the President down. By 1941 Baruch was beginning to get regular hearings at the White House. He was lunching with the President every Tuesday, dropping in on Stettinius and his War Resources Board, needling the military chiefs — in general, exerting a thoroughly "wholesome influence." [98]

Already, defense costs were exceeding the outlay for the First World War. There were two armored corps now, and a munitions program was well "under way," although still far from its goal.[99] The *New York Times* ran a headline, "Aid Bill Urged In Senate Even At The Risk Of War," and Senator Warren Austin conceded, "We will fight, if necessary." [100] But there was still no coordination, no central authority. Baruch himself, when asked if there was any real obstacle to his proposed one-man setup, shot back, "That question makes me laugh." And at the startled look of response, he added: "Well, it's been storing up here for eighteen months. Go ahead and get me into trouble." [101]

His anger had indeed been storing up a long time — ever since that post-Christmas press conference of 1940, in which Roosevelt burst out that he was sick and tired of hearing about "the necessity of appointing another Barney Baruch." To Baruch this cut was cruel in view of the attacks he was undergoing for his loyal support of the President and of his policies.[102]

He grew increasingly melancholy. While the Germans adopted our plans of 1918, we had wasted months looking for a better plan. He was seething over the fact that his daughter Belle had been able to buy an airplane as late as the summer of 1940. Fighting Bob Patterson and Jim Forrestal were his two hopes.[103] Yet the hiring of good men, he instinctively felt, was offset by the retention of incompetent ones.[104]

The President agreed fully with the basic idea of centralized control — on condition, it often seemed, that he retain the control. But the time had now come when he could no longer afford to indulge personal piques.

Worn down at last, the President offered Baruch the War Production job that Donald Nelson was later to hold. Baruch refused. There were many reasons for this refusal which at first might seem the denial of all that Baruch had been working for. "Christ, I can't do this; I can't agree to take this responsibility," Garet Garrett has recalled his words; and John Hancock, who would have been his deputy, watched him go through some "soul torsions" on the question.[105] In the last analysis, the setup in no way assured Baruch that there would be an adequate delegation of power to do the job as it should be done. Such headlines as "Defense Picture Ruled By F.D.R." were true enough. In the end, Baruch decided characteristically that he could have more real influence from the outside than in the job itself as it was set up. The legendary gambler once more declined a gamble in which public prestige might be the stake. He declined the test. So his job in the autumn of 1941 was that of air-raid warden at his summer place at Port Washington, New York.[106]

At the end of August, Baruch sat on the other side of the desk in the President's oval study, still insisting that everything depended on the appointment of a dictator over defense activities. He warned that he would not let up on his efforts to influence the President to take this step until ordered to do so by the President himself.[107]

Roosevelt shoved across the desk a number of reports showing, as he said, that armament production was already twice that of the last year of the first war when Baruch had had everything in his own hands. One thousand and fifty-four military planes had been completed in a month alone, whereas in the last war a billion was spent and not a plane produced for actual combat.

As for organization and production, the President had answers for these, too. As of that day, August 28, 1941, he had created a new organization, the Supply, Priorities and Allocations Board — and what did Baruch think of that? Baruch thought very little of it.

One more pyramid on top of a column of toppling pyramids was not the Baruch way of consolidating or focusing authority. Once again, Baruch's remarks on the White House steps made headlines, and again alienated the President.

As "Pa" Watson later observed, although he for one had never doubted Baruch's sincere affection for the President, Baruch had talked too much.[108] Even by the next January, Baruch sadly told Martin J. Gillen that he had not been wise to mention Baruch's name to the President. The St. Louis *Post-Dispatch* had already written a post-mortem: "Baruch Loses Roosevelt's Ear At Weekly Luncheons. Elder Statesman In Doghouse." [109] Baruch knew that one-man control would come, but meanwhile he paid the penalty for his frankness.[110]

The annual skit for the Gridiron Dinner was canceled on the eighth of December 1941. In it Baruch was to have appeared on a park bench as "The Man Who Used to Come to Lunch."

"Sure, Mr. President [ran the lines of the skit]. Certainly, I'll run the war for you, Mr. President."

"Let's see if the luncheon flag is up at the White House. No. Not the *luncheon flag*. A hammer and sickle? No, it's just a hammer. Couldn't be John L. Lewis. Must be Martin Dies. If I hadn't called the SPAB a 'faltering step' I'd be over there, eating corn beef hash right now." He looked out toward the White House. "Everybody eats but Bernie."

Herbert Hoover slumped onto the bench. "Twenty years

ago both of us were the biggest big shots along the Potomac, but we missed one bet. We overlooked that young fellow who was assistant secretary of the Navy." [111]

Now the time for comedy was past. Baruch had for some time been well aware of the American desire, either by threat or persuasion, to sever Japan from the Axis, perhaps even to secure her participation in a war against Germany. To this end, many thought that no price would be too high: the sacrifice of China, or a play on the race issue, anything to convince the Japanese that the triumph of Nazism would mean the enslavement of all colored peoples everywhere. Loans for Japan, bribes, access to raw materials — all were considered. Roosevelt, however, knew that the sellout of China was a deal which public opinion could not tolerate.[112] What but moral leadership did the anti-Axis powers have to give the world? Morally and militarily, appeasement was no more valid in the Pacific than in the Atlantic. So the second Roosevelt spoke loudly, although waving a little stick; and it was in real alarm that E. D. Coblentz of the isolationist Hearst papers (which had, nevertheless, been drumming for armed defense since 1937) wrote Baruch early in 1941 that in view of the President's warlike "Four Freedoms" address, he feared we should soon be involved.[113]

Within a matter of months, Roosevelt had frozen all German assets in the United States. Within months, also, Admiral Halsey was promising that if he found even a Japanese sampan, he would sink it, and by November 28, orders went out to bomb all unidentified submarines around Oahu. Four days earlier, General Marshall had notified the Far Eastern command that "hostile action" was possible any moment and from any direction.[114] Baruch was among those who questioned the wisdom of aggressiveness without power to back it up — a policy that might lead to war on two fronts. Columnist George Rothwell Brown pointed out with appalling accuracy that if war came, "It is probable that occupation of the Philippines by Japan could not be prevented." [115]

Baruch himself was a virtual stranger to the making of policy during those last days when the United States drifted into war. Hence he was startled to receive a telephone call from Raymond Moley on Tuesday, December 2. The Japanese emissary, Saburo Kurusu, wanted to see Baruch on a most secret mission.

Baruch promptly put in a call to "Pa" Watson at the White House. As Baruch told it afterward, "Watson said it was O.K."

Kurusu said: "The President would like to be the broker between the Chinese and ourselves. You must get to the President right away. The war lords are ready with guns in their hands. The trigger may go off any minute. The President must go over their heads to the Emperor. It's the only chance."

Baruch stared a moment, incredulous. He warned of the ultimate consequences to Japan of a war against the United States. Slowly Kurusu nodded his head.[116]

Baruch delivered the word. It is typical of the strained relations between them that Roosevelt never even acknowledged it. Baruch waited. Two days later, he learned that the presidential message had been dispatched to the Emperor. It arrived, but too late, having been intercepted and held up long enough for the war machine to move into action.[117]

Then at two minutes past seven on the morning of December 7, 1941, Private Joseph Lockard of the Army Aircraft Warning Service on Oahu recorded that a "flight of planes," about 132 miles distant, was "coming in fast." He passed the word on, and was told to "forget it." [118]

Franklin Roosevelt heard the news, breathed a single "No," then took up the task that had been waiting for him.[119]

18

PARTNERSHIP WITH POWER

"Mrs. Roosevelt on the line, sir," said Lacey.

Baruch started. He was dressed for travel in that Christmas holiday season of 1941, his bags already stacked in the hallway. Within a few moments he would be off for Hobcaw — telegrams had long since been dispatched to various Washington dignitaries expressing his willingness to be on hand if so ordered. No call had come. Now it was from the White House. Quickly he pressed the receiver to his ear.

The summons was unofficial. "Franklin wants you to come down for the lighting of the Christmas tree," Mrs. Roosevelt said, and paused, while Baruch hesitated. Since he had "overtalked" himself late the previous summer, communication between him and the President had been rare. "I was angry at him," Baruch said afterward of that period. "I wouldn't go near Washington."

As if reading his mood, Mrs. Roosevelt broke in, "A friend of yours wants to speak to you," and a moment later the President was on the wire. The name of a third friend was mentioned.

"I'll come right away," Baruch said.[1]

So his old friend from England wanted to see him, anyway. It was a comforting thought as his train moved through the cold and tinsel of that cheerless Christmastide, shop windows piled with goods not to be seen again for five long years. Faces staring upward as the train slowed. Young soldiers straining to them their brides of a week or a day.

It is hard now to recall the electric shock which struck the American people with the announcement on December 22, 1941, that Winston Churchill was in Washington. Later arrivals of the doughty

Prime Minister were taken in course, but this first wartime visit galvanized the people as had Roosevelt's challenge to fear back in 1933. America was facing her darkest hour. Not since the burning of Washington in 1814 had an American army retreated before foreign forces. Now Wake Island had fallen; the Pacific fleet lay in ruins; MacArthur's troops were fighting a desperate rearguard action in the Philippines. Churchill put new heart into the American people; Churchill was the best Christmas present they could have had.[2] For them — for the whole Allied world — the pink-cheeked warrior in the air-raid suit had become the symbol of resistance to tyranny, he who had shaken his fists upward as Hitler's bombers blackened the sky over London, hurling the challenge, "Do your worst, we can stand it"; or, in calmer mood, laconically announcing, "The Prime Minister is getting on with the war."

"We won't crack up, sir. No, we won't crack up," he had mumbled to a *Life* correspondent a few months earlier, teeth clenched on his black cigar. He had voiced the credo of Freedom with its back to the wall, with "hardship our garment, valor our only shield." Now, America as one responded to his jovial commentary to the Congress that "if my father had been American and my mother British . . . I might have got here on my own."[3] For the moment, he was American. It was as if he were Prime Minister of the United States, too.

So "top secret" was the visit that even Mrs. Roosevelt had wondered at the President's curiosity as he scanned the dinner list.[4] Baruch had not expected to be there. He had dictated a brief courteous note to Churchill assuring him that although he would be available always, he of course understood that there might not be time for a meeting.[5] Now, in war, he was on his way to renew the friendship begun in war, and he could have thought back to those beginnings, and of the years before when he had not known Churchill, who was already a legend in England. What a life he had lived, this unconquerable warrior, writer, painter, soldier, "naval person," statesman — an Elizabethan in the tradition of Sir Francis Drake, yet a Victorian out of the era of Disraeli and Gladstone, when the sun never set on the Empire. It later seemed to Baruch that there was no more magnificent moment in Churchill's life than when he flung out his challenge to history and time — he had "not become the King's First Minister in order to preside over the liquidation of the British Empire."

For he had known the Empire at its zenith, he one of the last living men to ride with the Lancers in a full cavalry charge. Before he was twenty-six he had marched with the Spaniards in Cuba, killed his man in bloody revolver-to-spear conflict in India, been trapped by the dervishes, taken prisoner by the Boers, had escaped and regained his regiment in time for the fall of Pretoria, written six books, and wondered audibly if he would live long enough to do all the things he wanted to do. He had married, been elected to Parliament at twenty-six and warned: "Now when mighty populations are impelled on each other . . . when the resources of science and civilization sweep away everything that might mitigate their fury, European war can only end in the utter ruin of the vanquished and the exhaustion of the victors." So in 1902 did he signal the end of the Victorian Era.

He had called for a government that would "think a little more about the toilers at the bottom of a mine . . . the condition of a slum in an English city." Later came the war, the debacle of Gallipoli, eight months in the trenches and back into the Cabinet again. His ups and downs were quixotic — through years of semiretirement he was depicted as everything the conservative mind deplored. He was brilliant, he was restless, he cried "War, war" when all were longing for peace. He was a man made for his time, although few knew it; and at every mention of his name before Munich, the expostulations burst out: "Churchill? Churchill is a visionary; Churchill is a madman; we can't have Churchill." America, with the advantage of perspective, had felt "the sheer greatness of the man." [6] Just as England, in similar perspective, could look beyond the politics to the genius in Franklin Roosevelt, so did Americans assess Churchill, laboring under the most terrible burdens ever laid upon an English leader. Nearing seventy, he was again a legend. He was one with England in her "finest hour," with that "happy breed" of Drake, Nelson, Chatham, and the younger Pitt, who had stood and fought and been gloriously unafraid. Baruch had recognized his greatness long before.[7] He might differ from his old friend, but recognition of his fallibility did nothing to diminish the homage Baruch gave. Churchill, he would often say, might be mistaken but he had never made, nor would ever make, an ignoble proposal.[8] Baruch could not always speak the words that were in his mind. But he often thought of Churchill and he felt confident that the Englishman's steadfast courage and the greatness of the empire he led would win out in the end.[9] Thinking of Churchill, the lines of an old border ballad came back to him:

"I am wounded," Sir Barton cried, "but I am not slain. I'll lie me down and bleed a while and rise and fight again." [10]

It was dusk when Baruch reached Washington. He had just time to arrive at the South Grounds of the White House and to see the tree light up as the crowd stood uncertain and shifting in the bitter cold. There were carols and prayers, "but there was little joy in our hearts," Mrs. Roosevelt recalled.[11] Afterward, "tea" was served inside, only it was a more stimulating beverage. Baruch and Churchill shook hands. There was little chance for words, less for privacy between them. Harry Hopkins, Baruch noted wryly, was omnipresent.[12] Even his bedroom was strategically placed opposite Churchill's.[13] Hopkins' tense, unkempt presence had electrified the English the previous January and, having made friends then with Churchill, during the whole of this visit he monopolized the Prime Minister's attention.[14] Baruch could note, too, how far the friendship between Roosevelt and Churchill had gone on the basis of one meeting and innumerable telephone calls — much indeed as he and Churchill had found their own way to intimacy twenty-odd years before. Roosevelt had envied Baruch's friendship with Churchill. And Churchill's "real inclination," Baruch felt, was to be with him.[15] Once it had been he and Churchill who had swapped the stories and the laughter and talked out the differences between their two countries. Now Baruch was rather on the outside. Baruch could agree with Brendan Bracken's words after the Conference of the previous August: "Winston's meeting with the President has been an immense success. Winston liked him very much. Thank God the English-speaking peoples are led by these two great men." [16] As the company now started to go in to dinner and Baruch by old custom put his hand on the back of Roosevelt's chair to wheel him in, Churchill pushed forward and intervened, looking up waggishly. "He's my baby now." [17]

At table there was much to talk about. There was no time for the little things and personalities and the questions that Americans had long wanted to ask about Ambassador Winant, for instance, Kennedy's successor in besieged London — so sensitive that the time would come when he could no longer bear to live, yet whose quiet courage had won the admiration of all England; or of Auchinleck's recent brilliant successes in North Africa. Nor was there time to hear at first hand about the blitz — for recalling that sound of shrapnel beating against the slate roofs, the blasts that sucked the blackout curtains right up to the swaying ceiling, or the flights of Nazi "nuisance planes" roaring ceaselessly over the heads of a sleepless people. Churchill might speak of the "blitzed kids in London" for whose benefit Baruch had deposited thousands of pounds in the Bank of England; or of that equally welcome donation to morale, cigars for the Prime Minister and lipsticks for more general distribution.[18] Then, warmed by hospitality and refreshment, the Prime Minister's voice would boom forth more resonantly still as he talked of how the British people had held the fort and would "lick 'em now with your aid." Churchill later frankly admitted that the role he was now playing was the one he preferred to all others. Power in a crisis was a blessing, for as he said, "At the top there are great simplifications." [19]

This was a different Christmas at the White House from earlier ones. There was no time for the traditional reading of the *Christmas Carol*. Gone was the joyous stampede of Roosevelt grandchildren up and down the corridors; the children were scattered across the country saying goodbye to fathers soon to leave for overseas. Only little Diana Hopkins wandered, waiflike, up and down halls choked with brightly wrapped Christmas parcels. Like ants, figures moved in a steady line in and out of the second-floor chamber known as the Monroe Room, dominated, not by Monroe, but by the grinning portrait of Theodore Roosevelt, brought from the apartment in New York City. The President had told his wife, "You can't rent your uncle; take him." [20] Here, the British Army had made camp, with maps and office supplies, and yet, somehow, over all was still the atmosphere of Christmas, and of the dingy old house itself, with the darkness of those Southern mansions enveloped by colonnades and trees — and the warmth and friendliness of the Roosevelt clan. The walls were papered with family pictures; the scent of wax candles and evergreen permeated the air; and carefully wrapped packages for the British guests on Churchill's staff were under the tree. Familiar faces threaded their way through the "houseful" of strangers: pretty, gay Grace Tully, Steve Early, Marvin McIntyre, "Pa" Watson, whose geniality could delight even the most disappointed visitors. But that night all merrymaking ended abruptly as the men adjourned to work.

There were moments of relaxation, of course, when F.D.R. threw back his head and howled over Churchill's impromptu recitation of some of Lear's Nonsense Rhymes; [21] or there in the Oval Study, Churchill refought the Battle of Blenheim, and Roosevelt might counter with an analysis of the naval tactics of John Paul Jones — the two "former Naval persons" united now in a camaraderie that symbolized the unity of their nations. Now, like a whiplash, Hopkins' voice would cut in. His respect for immediacies and facts, at least, won Baruch's admiration. Again and again, he would return to the point under discussion, until at last Churchill turned upon him: "You are to be named 'Lord Root of the Matter.' " [22]

Baruch felt that for himself the Christmas visit was "fruitless," which was not strictly true. It was an opening wedge for re-entry to the White House. The President obviously was feeling warmer toward his old friend, and in the following February, answering a letter of Baruch's, he wrote, "You could do me no greater honor than to say such gracious things about my Mother as you express in your note, and I am deeply moved that you feel as you do." [23] Baruch had long had a genuine fondness for the stately "Madam Roosevelt," who had died the previous fall — one of "the last truly gentlewomen," he knew, seeing in her dignity and bearing, perhaps, something of the quality his own mother had had. With her, he could assume his role of country squire. One year he escorted her to a ball at the Waldorf — the grande dame in her long gown with her high-piled hair and, hovering over her, the slender man with "old-school chivalry," paying her mutually pleasing little gallantries.[24]

Had it not been for Baruch, President Roosevelt might never have paid a last visit to his mother while she could still see him and know him. By the summer of 1941, the old lady had been ill for months, but, caught in the onrush of approaching war, Roosevelt had been putting off a scheduled visit to Hyde Park. With the privilege of a family friend, Baruch urged him not to put off the visit.

"I'll do it," Roosevelt replied.[25]

A little later the younger Mrs. Roosevelt was writing Baruch: "Of course it was providential that Franklin came that weekend. He saw his mother while she could still enjoy seeing him and the end then came quickly and painlessly." [26]

In March, as war crashed down and the self-appointed purveyors of advice swarmed in upon the capital, Baruch sent Roosevelt a quotation from Livy about those who "lead armies into Macedonia; who know where the camp ought to be placed; what posts ought to be occupied by troops . . . how provisions should be conveyed . . . when it is proper to engage the enemy . . . Therefore, if anyone thought himself qualified, let him come with the Commander-in-Chief into Macedonia; if not, let him not, on land, assume the office of a pilot." [27]

"A pure gem," Roosevelt shot back. "I may use it at a press conference, but I am not sure that the press would understand." [28]

For Baruch, as for Roosevelt, for Stimson, for all who had known the nightmare of the spring of 1940, the attack on Pearl Harbor was like the bursting of a giant abscess. Everyone might still be "running around at loose ends in Washington," but at least now with the unity of a single purpose. Even the isolationists, who were moved primarily by any civilized man's hatred of war, could lend their idealism to the common cause. Republicans took their place in the councils. At the suggestion of Felix Frankfurter, Colonel Henry L. Stimson was brought out of retirement to be Secretary of War — Stimson, who had held his first Cabinet seat under William Howard Taft and had spotted the outbreak of the Second World War back in Manchuria nearly thirteen years before. With him came Colonel Frank Knox, a man who had kicked down the stairs a Ku Klux Klansman who had offered him support, and was wise enough to accommodate himself to a President with a personal interest in the Navy. "Jim" Forrestal of Dillon, Read and Company, a Dutchess County Democrat and Baruch's friend, was also one of the "inside men."

On March 8, 1942, Baruch dictated a memorandum for the President with sundry notations: he was encouraged by the President's decision to dismiss incompetents; the new ordnance requirements were all that he had advocated two years before; defense facilities in upper New York would get by but the raw material situation was bad. Donald Nelson's plan for complete industrial mobilization was important, but a small "War Cabinet" with single control was essential to any successful mobilization program.[29]

The fact that the President seemed often brusquely to disregard Baruch [30] did not deter him from sending suggestions: Admiral Land could produce ships if only he could get the plates and labor. Airplane production could be stepped up; jurisdiction was the stumbling block. The raw materials question required vigorous attention. The price-control situation was jittery. India was hoarding gold and silver, and we should make some of our reserves available to her in exchange for needed jute, manganese, and mica. Production could be increased perhaps twenty-five per cent.[31]

On March 31 he received a note from Roosevelt asking, "What do you think we should do next?" [32]

Too often in the past, a presidential summons had meant nothing but a quick lunch and a cursory "How's your wife — how's the shooting at Hobcaw?" Things were changing now.

In the spring of 1942 Baruch had noted the appointment of a new planning board. What were they going to plan? It was cold comfort that he was not responsible for the blunders that were being made. Having known as he had known, and warned as he had warned, he had an overriding sense of failure. Was it not he who had failed, who could not make the people see? And still there were the whispers and rumors: "Bernie's too old — it's not his kind of a war."

Nevertheless, down to Washington he came in the spring of 1942. He bobbed blithely like a cork on the sea of flotsam and jetsam that was the wartime capital. The WAAC's. The WAVES. The war workers — and those that worked the war. Small-town tycoons who dreamed their country needed them and who, without their dependable "Joes," were scarcely more useful than the average clerk from the Civil Service. "Dollar-a-year" men who dreamed their country needed them and that they were future Bernard Baruchs. Spenders swarming like mosquitoes and purveyors of food and drink and entertainment for the spenders. The Supper Club. The Victory Room. The friends of Russia at the Balalaika, of Free China at the Ruby Foo, of the Free French at La Salle du Bois.

Lines. Queues. "Standing in line to help the Government . . . to get something from the Government . . . to obtain food . . . to secure a place to sleep . . . to see a motion picture . . . for elbowroom on the soda-fountain bar," or at any bar, for that matter; "for sugar and gas ration cards . . . for anything, everywhere, always standing in line — and incidentally always standing up. Hurting feet. Aching feet. Aching insteps . . . Tired ankles. Queues! Queues! Queues!" [33]

Bernard Baruch, head bowed in attention, walking down a wet street with "Tommy the Cork." The bootblack who knew that the British Navy needed more pep "and a new set of Admirals"; the waiter who stopped to predict Hitler's conquest of all Europe and looked with pitying superiority on those who tried to stave off the inevitable. Tourists, besieging the State Department for visas to gape at the ruins of England. "Nothing is sacred with the great American public," complained a Washington commentator.[34] Baruch observed that you were expected to be a bit of everything in wartime Washington.[35]

If in the east section Washington still seemed a rather sleepy Southern town, westward the capital was a kind of annex to Ten Downing Street — "Like nothing so much as London or Paris in 1917." [36] Dominating the maze and the haze and the confusion was the "inherently disorderly" nature of the Administration itself, and a President who could not say no reshuffling the ranks of the New Dealers instead of dropping the inefficient,[37] declining to delegate any real power, as Joseph Pulitzer noted editorially.[38] Roosevelt was running the war as he had run the New Deal, by inspiration rather than blueprint. Yet even his critics admitted his gift for getting action from elements with no more in common than the CIO and the National Association of Manufacturers. He granted no special privilege to special-interest groups; he threw sops to all of them. This was as bad a principle as it was good politics. Amidst all the helter-skelter disorganization and disorder sat Bernard Baruch with a blue-print for mobilization under his arm, and a perpetual plea for one-man authority on his lips. In the wilting heat of the Washington summer, the Southern-born Baruch fled the dankness of hotel air-conditioning, and in the warmth of Lafayette Square stretched his long legs gratefully into the sun. A writer from The Nation said: "He has more understanding of social issues than is common in one of his class." His vanity — which the press did not question — was at least equaled by his ability.[39]

His headquarters during his Washington stays were at the Carlton Hotel. The location was good, only a two-block walk to the White House, which loomed to the south of Lafayette Square, and the dingy wedding-cake splendor of the old State, War, and Navy building. The hotel had — and still has, in spite of not being very old — an aura of past grandeur, underscored in Baruch's rooms by the faded brocade of easy chairs and chaise longue. A baby grand piano shone darkly in one corner of his rather shabby suite; in the next room a secretary scribbled away at a rickety desk.[40]

The "team" — the inevitable Hancock, Swope, and a new member, dark and incisive Ferdinand Eberstadt — were housed elsewhere. Baruch's entourage consisted of himself, the faithful Lacey, and Blanche Higgins, still in her twenties. Thin, sandy-haired, as unassuming as her own freckles, "Higgins" was overlooked by the heedless as much as she was appreciated by the discriminating. "Higgins is a great character," Anna Rosenberg later said.[41] She had stayed on after nursing Baruch through his severe illness in 1939 and now was filling the kind of role that could only have been dreamed up by a Baruch — nurse, hostess, secretary, and companion — filling them all with warmth, wit, and a very real wisdom. In his lonely rooms, with his advancing years, it was almost as if he had a young daughter by his side again. Each would give the other the greatest possible proof of affection. When her father died he told her, "I'll be a father to you," and was. He invested her money; he watched after her welfare. The more she knew him, the more she respected and loved him. "I could go to him for anything," she once said. She found him not only a "terrific personality," but "the most tolerant man in the world." [42]

She offered to stay with him through his lifetime, but he refused, leaving her free to marry a brilliant young surgeon of her choice, and himself to play godfather and grandfather to her three children. "One of the most generous things he has ever done was to insist that Higgins live her own life," Anna Rosenberg has commented.[43] But now she was his hostess at the Carlton, routing and sometimes diverting admirals, generals, Senators, Representatives, and sundry "officials" who thronged the anteroom, drinking Baruch's liquor, scattering ashes over his belongings, and variously wasting his time.

"It was gosh-awful," a friend later recalled. The apartment was like the Union Station. There were people who needed to see him and people who wanted to see him and people who just wanted to see an important man. This was "Dr. Facts," the man who had "done it" in the First World War.

He never seemed to be tired. Up, shaved, fed, ruddy-cheeked, he would see a visitor as early as 8.30 in the morning in his suite, come down to joke with the girl at the magazine counter, handle an unending stream of telephone calls, and perhaps sit up with visitors as late as midnight.[44]

On weekends he usually returned to New York, and although he had given up his own racing horses, he and Herbert Bayard Swope renewed their vigor at the track, where they could be seen peeling off bills and lustily cheering their favorites on.

It was out of this melee at the Carlton that the Park Bench Statesman legend was born. Baruch fled the crowding and the air-conditioning, the jingling of the telephones and the ruffling of papers, the endless interviews and interruptions. He fled to the park bench because there was no office space for him in Washington. Those who needed him soon knew where to find him — on bench number six, one among others, bleached by sun and eroded by rain. There in the thick Washington sunlight Baruch sat, sometimes with Leon Henderson, sloppily dressed,[45] sometimes with Donald Nelson, or the "Great Dane," William Knudsen. Baruch urged them all on, promised his support, and was willing to be told if he was too urgent. The job was all that mattered.[46]

These men of the headlines — he knew how brief was their hour, just as he well knew that Roosevelt had no intention whatever of being judged by the performance of his subordinates. He would only give power without responsibility, or responsibility without power. Roosevelt's faith was in momentum, not methods; in the masses, not the leaders, bestirring themselves into action. Eliot Janeway has said flatly that the American people are constitutionally "incapable of making history by following a blueprint and distrust men . . . who do so." [47] Yet few men short of the President himself gained a greater measure of affection and prestige through the war years than the man with the blueprint, Bernard Baruch. He did not underestimate morale. He knew that in the end the people would "sense what to do and do it." [48] Yet the question remains how much faster the people might have won the war had they combined planning with their momentum. Only history can surmise what the outcome might have been had Roosevelt been the same kind of leader on the home front as he was of the military.

It was Baruch's strength with the people that they sensed that he wanted nothing for himself. It was his weakness with Roosevelt that the President and many close to him felt that Baruch was after the big job, which was not so. Nor did he want to scuttle Roosevelt's ideas. He would merely have superimposed planning upon them.

He knew, however, that mobilization was foredoomed so long as seven men were doing one man's job. Politics was still taking precedence over preparedness; time outran decisions. We had failed to budget our resources either for ourselves or our Allies. The nation would offer money but not sacrifice; and the pinch came in "getting money turned into weapons." [49] According to one woman worker, the union slowdowns, the high wage scales, the waste of time and labor were nothing short of "criminal negligence." Some unions seemed to be more interested in fighting speed-ups than the war; munitions makers had almost to be bribed to start powder manufacture, having no desire again to be damned as warmakers. With plants by the miles and bookkeeping by the millions, there was still the lag between "on hand" and "on order." [50] Labor used for expanding plant capacity was lost to essential production; and expansion was not synonymous with output. Nor did the tax laws offer adequate protection for builders of surplus plants that would be useless in peacetime. Many war plants, Baruch knew, were overmanned 25 to 50 per cent. Yet they still paid full time for a half-day, with the surplus workers having to stand around and pretend they were busy.[51]

Even so, the railroads could not carry freight as fast as industry could produce it. Two million farm families were "frozen" on unprofitable marginal land, and consumers were buying further and further ahead as shortages loomed nearer. The sugar shortage was evident as early as the spring of 1941, when the sugar ships were dispatched to Manila for rubber. Yet there was less than a ten per cent increase in sugar production in Louisiana, because Congress and the Department of Agriculture could not agree as to the dates of the grinding season.

By the winter of 1942 the East Coast oil shortage was already desperate. The building of a pipeline between eastern Texas and New Jersey had broken down in a wrangle over authority. Shortages of steel were increasingly acute, and of tin, as well. Months earlier Baruch had urged an exchange of our surplus cotton and wheat with England for her surplus of the white metal. England had agreed, but not Washington.[52]

If Baruch's sole objective of the war years could have been summed

up, it would have been, "Get production." Such books as *They Were
Expendable*, or *They Fought with What They Had*, Walter Karig's
narrative of unpreparedness for an obviously inevitable war, were
shocking to the public, whose own self-willed blindness had caused
the situation. The Army planned; the Navy planned; the industrialists planned — and none in terms of the whole. Baruch knew that
what was needed were troubleshooters, and they would not let him
get troubleshooters for fear he would have to take over too much of
the job.[53] His own writings were "the granite structure that covered
the whole production field." [54] Central authority and over-all controls
— this was the "Baruch-Hitler system," as it was described in a news
story as early as 1941. It was Germany's "secret weapon," and we did
not have it.[55]

In September 1941 Baruch had suggested to the President that a
committee of three be named to survey the defense and production
picture, and then a single head of wartime production be named.
William O. Douglas, Wendell Willkie, and John Hancock were
selected for the survey; [56] and on a Sunday evening in January, Hancock received a call from Robert Patterson at the War Department.
"When are you coming to Washington?"

Hancock jumped the next train. He arrived just in time for his
morning appointment at 7.30. Patterson met him on the corner of
20th and F Street, holding the "bulldog edition" of the paper in
his hand. It carried the story that Donald Nelson had been chosen
head of the War Production Board, with full control over the entire
wartime productive capacity of the United States, "such as was
exercised in the First World War by Bernard Baruch . . . Baruch, a
close White House adviser, long has urged the necessity of making
such a concentration of authority."

In the cold Washington dawn, Hancock and Patterson stared at
each other. Patterson frowned. "Very funny. I guess I don't have
any more for us to talk about." [57]

The new War Production Board itself was not in any sense the
creation of Bernard Baruch, though in part it contained the idea that
he had been voicing since 1938, the discarded idea of the Baruch
Report of a year later.

As for Donald Nelson, if he had been determined upon as Roosevelt's man, the time had come to boost him. "He makes a noise like
a dividend," was Baruch's commentary to Roosevelt, after conversa-

tion with Nelson at the close of a White House dinner.[58] It seemed as though the only person surprised at Nelson's appointment was Nelson himself, who appeared quite overwhelmed when confronted with the news at the White House and with a well-prepared demonstration by his office staff afterward.

But the wily President had surrendered nothing that mattered. No battle of the Second World War was fought more furiously than the battle for controls. Baruch knew perfectly well that the new War Production Board lacked the essentials of power — the authority to fix prices and set controls. If the government created scarcities, then it must create price ceilings and priorities. If it fixed prices, it must also put a ceiling over wages. Furthermore, any working program rested on the ability of the "mobilizer" to think and act, and the ability of the President to choose men who could think and act.[59] So thought Baruch; but all this did not trouble the President, for he knew that no one would run the show but himself. He could feel safe in granting Donald Nelson power that he would never use. As Stimson noted, Roosevelt, having tinkered with boards and commissions, finally "gave real power to the wrong man." [60]

It did not seem so at first. "A Single Boss At Last," answered the headline in the Baltimore Sun, "big, decisive Donald Nelson." [61] There was indeed reason to believe in the popular picture of Nelson as a "strong man." He looked the part: this pipe-smoking, deceptively placid-appearing, small-town big-business man, avowedly from the wrong side of the tracks of Mark Twain's Hannibal, Missouri. He could pound his desk and make the inkwells jump. The firm cushioning of his six-foot frame, the eyes, "dead steady and direct," inspired confidence. He had had a lot of publicity the year before in the Saturday Evening Post as a onetime $70,000-a-year purchasing man for Sears, Roebuck, and in a similar job on the National Defense Advisory Commission had saved the taxpayers some $100,000,000. In his first ten days on the Commission he had "made things hum." He had stabilized methods of procedure; served notice on all private industry that public contracts came first; commandeered hoarded inventories, yet handed out much excess, nonstrategic material. He had moved swiftly to block plant expansion except for war purposes. Finding ten signatures on some official correspondence, he had even dared eliminate some of the sacred paperwork.[62]

The Advisory Commission had been the training school for Nelson's present post — every contract from machine guns to army socks had passed over his desk, and bills ranging from ten to seventy million dollars a day. He seemed to have the qualities Knudsen lacked: the imagination to encompass the whole picture. He saw the need for a careful coordination and spacing of defense orders. Furthermore, he thought, why should not the Army emulate Sears, Roebuck? Why should it compete with civilians and crowd the buying market for blankets in the early autumn? Sears, Roebuck would buy in the late winter and spring. To facilitate hurry-up orders he had even inventoried the milling capacity of the country, knew how many looms were idle and at what periods. Baruch evidently succumbed to the popular enchantment, and wrote David Lawrence, as late as the summer of 1942, that Donald Nelson was a much stronger man than was generally believed.[63] In fact, the highest praise for Nelson's accomplishments, both as planner and producer, has been voiced by a biographer of Baruch, Morris Rosenbloom.[64] And as we can look back on it today, the American industrial accomplishment under Nelson's leadership is impressive, even measured against the intrigues, suspicion, blindness, failures, and other derelictions of duty that infested the wartime scene.

The day of Nelson's appointment, he and Baruch lunched together, and for a time thereafter Nelson clung to the Elder Statesman with almost embarrassing ardor. He said afterward that the inspiration of Baruch was his first line of strength, that merely by hearing Baruch speak he could return home comforted, buoyed, and supported. Night after night he haunted Baruch's apartment, and hours after Baruch had sunk into bed and was asleep, he was still there, seeming to draw strength from the invisible support of the man who had "done it before." Nelson worked tremendously; no one in Washington put in longer hours.[65] And Baruch strove to help him despite official indifference to his help, despite such comments as, "We do not want to depend on old reputations. We want to make new reputations for new men." [66]

Nelson had purposely set up the War Production Board so that there were all shades of opinion in it. But was his purpose to unite those crosscurrents, or merely to placate them? There would be no time for wrangling, Nelson forecast; yet to outsiders it often seemed as if there was time for little else. Men with "new reputations to make" scorned the limitations of chart and blueprint.[67] They must be free to plan according to the need and mood of the moment. New

Dealers must improvise according to the techniques of the New Deal.

For a time, however, Donald Nelson and his men consulted Baruch freely; Baruch was welcome to sit in on War Production Board meetings at any time. He commended Nelson's plan for joint committees of industry and labor and Nelson listened attentively as the older man outlined the principles of mobilization for a world ruled by war. Military power was not industrial power, but superior utilization of its industrial power might make a weaker nation the winner. Industrial mobilization was a slower process than military mobilization; a citizen army could be trained long before industry was ready to equip and support it.

Years before, Baruch had written that the dollar must be mobilized before the man. Specifically, he urged a four-point program including a study of the ability of the national productive plant to meet war requirements, and of the potential expansion of various industries; a Raw Materials and Manufacturers' division to be made the central point of contact between the manufacturers and the government; the creation of a facilities division to plan for new industries and to expand old ones, as well as to arrange for workers' housing; and finally, a continuous study of materials, facilities, and the modernization of machinery. Always the balance of materials, plant capacity, and manpower must be kept in mind.[68]

One of Nelson's first acts in his new job was to call industrial leaders to Washington. They met in the big conference room of the War Production Board, which looked smaller than it was because it was so overcrowded with executives, businessmen, Army brass and Navy glitter, VIP's and those who thought they were. What they were waiting for, no one knew. Suddenly the room became quiet. All eyes turned toward Nelson and the white-haired figure by his side.

Baruch was introduced. He explained that Nelson had asked him to "stop by" to urge the cooperation of industry in reconversion and rearming. Production, he said, would win the war. He spoke for only seven minutes, yet at the end even the most avid opponents of the government program were sitting in attentive silence. Baruch thanked them and departed as quietly as he had come. Then, one after another, each of the assembled representatives of industrial might arose to put his company at his country's disposal.[69]

Ordinarily, Nelson's greatest concession to Baruch's wishes was to

grant the Elder Statesman his company for weekend "rests," during
which Baruch would din into his guest's ears the warning that he
must be hard-boiled. For it was no secret soon that Donald Nelson
was as "easygoing as the Mississippi, which flows past his home town."
Nelson supporters could counter with ringing defenses of his fair-
ness and "gentle Scotch strength." What could he do, they asked,
if the President insisted on going over his head? But the papers in
the Baruch correspondence bear out the criticisms of Drew Pearson.
"He is too nice," Pearson said. "He can't say no . . . he likes his
friends and can't fire them." Baruch's friend Charles Carroll added
that Nelson was not tough enough to stand up to Roosevelt, Hopkins, Hillman, and the others; or to punch the incompetents in the
nose. He would bark loudly and bite with rubber teeth.[70]

For Baruch, an "inside view" of what went on behind the portals
of the War Production Board was supplied by Charles Carroll.
Carroll, a man of idealism and driving energy, was recommended to
Nelson by Baruch. From the first he was restive that his job was not
keeping him busy, and at last took himself off Nelson's payroll. He
liked working for Nelson but had been given nothing to do that
would test his mettle, he told his mentor.[71]

Eighty-two employees of the Board, he noted, were sitting around
writing letters or otherwise wasting their time, while the men at the
front were dying for want of war materials.[72] This was the story of the
average Washington agency, becalmed, whether under Republicans or
Democrats, in peace or in war. The momentum that won the war was
supplied by the millions who cursed and snarled at the War Production Board. When the National Institute of Social Sciences
awarded a medal to Donald Nelson in recognition of the industrial
"miracle" which he had accomplished, Baruch had commented:
"The medal to be pinned upon your breast, Don, will be worn by
you, but it was won by America." [73]

Carroll railed against Sidney Hillman, Floyd V. Odlum, Maury
Maverick, and, most of all, "the Rasputin" whose boarding place was
the White House. Donald Nelson, he claimed, had failed completely to rid himself of the inefficient and undesirable deadwood
in the Board. But Carroll got small sympathy from Baruch, who, in
view of the fact that Nelson had taken him on Baruch's recommendation, regretted the younger man's role of a public critic.[74]

Baruch was, however, well aware that the errors of 1940 were the tragedies of 1942. Auto companies were still refusing to convert and still getting raw materials. Fifty-five different models of planes were on order. Steel was being siphoned off for the building of race tracks and hotels. There were surpluses of noncritical items and shortages of critical ones. The War Industries Board had had a personnel of 769; the War Production Board had some 15,000. But even had Nelson desired to cut off heads and force action, the very atmosphere of the Administration would have prevented it. He could not have put down his foot without stepping on some sacred cow. The press might declare that Nelson's powers paralleled those of Baruch in 1918. The fact was that Nelson still lacked control over prices, wages, or war contracts. He had still to share his powers and prerogatives with the War Labor Board, the Army Munitions Board, Mr. Leon Henderson of price controls, Mr. Harry Hopkins of Lend-Lease, etc., etc.[75] Conversely, it is true, however, that lacking these powers, the War Production Board, by virtue of its huge personnel if nothing else, had far more authority than the old War Industries Board of 1918. The difference was in who exercised the authority. As people in 1918 had noted, it was Baruch who made his job. And whatever the virtues and limitations of Donald Nelson, he was not another Baruch.

Baruch himself was convinced that even the semblance of centralized control, even in the hands of the wrong man, was better than no control at all. As late as July he still felt that Nelson was heading in the right direction.[76] By August, Nelson came up with an idea, at least on paper. This was the Production Requirements Plan. In effect, it permitted contractors to issue their own priorities as they took orders — and, as it unfortunately far too often worked out, to grab all items in short supply. Not even manpower went unscathed, for overzealous General Brehon Somervell, driven to distraction by Nelson's easygoing slowness, began "kidnaping" the Production chief's office staff.[77]

After a top-level meeting of the production heads in the fall, there came a reorganization and the end of Baruch's demand for one-man control, the one man who was given control having been unable to exert it. Now, authority was split six new ways. The President was still the final source of power; Byrnes was Director of Economic Stabilization; Nelson retained his title as head of WPB; Charles E. Wilson of General Electric, a first-rate man according to Stimson,[78] was put in charge of production, and Ferdinand Eberstadt, a member of the "Baruch team," in charge of priorities. As Nelson noted later: "I asked Mr. Eberstadt to come in and re-organize . . ." [79]

The inspired move in the shake-up had been the appointment of Eberstadt, a tough, hard-working man who could take a stand and adhere to it, yet with a gift for handling people. According to a re-porter for the New York *Journal-American*, who described Nelson as "a pleasant fellow, a good companion," Ferdinand Eberstadt was "one of the most capable and brightest men this writer has ever come in contact with." [80] Sympathetic to labor, he was an administrator who could master endless detail and still formulate policy.

Furthermore, Eberstadt had an idea. Nelson had muffed the problem of priorities for two years, and now Eberstadt was to solve it in a month. The Controlled Materials Plan, put into operation by Roosevelt on November 2, 1942, was the miracle of American pro-duction. It "flooded the fighting fronts with fire power." [81] It closed the gap between capacities and demand, doubled industrial output, slashed expansion, and equipped the government to operate a total war. The plan was not of Baruch's conception — it was a bigger chart for a vaster war. Yet it derived from Baruch's fundamental premise for war mobilization, that production objectives must equate with capacities.[82] This could be done, Eberstadt calculated, by con-trol of three vital metals: steel, aluminum, and copper. Control of all else would then follow. Orders for finished products were thus calculated in terms of the parts involved. Each order for 1000 tanks, for instance, spelled simultaneously an order for the necessary metal.

Eberstadt explained how it worked. On one side of the table, "you put the people who make steel, and on the other those who need it, with the government in between . . . if you let contracts for more than can be produced, then you will have tanks without tracks and guns without barrels." [83]

Upon Eberstadt now was shining some of the glory that had shone on Baruch twenty-odd years earlier. Industrially, the corner had been turned. By the end of the year, "the mobilization crisis was largely resolved"; production was three and one-half times that of the year before. Wilson, too, was doing a splendid job of breaking the bottle-necks and scheduling production. Out on the West Coast, Henry J. Kaiser, paying skilled wages to unskilled labor, or hiring skilled labor for unskilled jobs, was swinging ships on and off the assembly lines in two weeks' time, and threatening to make his own steel, if steel could not be found for them.[84] The *American Machinist* Magazine was hailing the "industry integration committees," another variant of Baruch's ideas, which brought together representatives of all manufacturers of the same product.[85] Nelson, meanwhile, had mapped his program for 1942–43. According to Rosenbloom, "The record industrial output under his leadership entitled him to recognition as one of the most important contributors to the winning of the war." [86]

There was glory enough for all. From the viewpoint of the public, the newly organized WPB was a smooth-running team. Eberstadt's brilliance, Wilson's drive and stamina were "astonishing"; and with planning came the production peaks of 1943 and 1944.[87] But what was smoldering behind the scenes could not long be concealed from public view.

The "reorganization" had scarcely been accomplished a month when Nelson suggested that Wilson schedule production operations, thus running head on against an Army ruling that only parts be scheduled, and not whole weapons. Eberstadt took the side of the Army. The fight was not yet personal, but the headlines rang with stories of the rift between the deputies. Afterward, Eberstadt said that although he read in the papers almost every day of his fights with Wilson, he had in fact never met him.[88]

Walker Stone of the Scripps-Howard chain wandered into Baruch's rooms at the Carlton. Baruch was talking to Nelson on the telephone. "You're dead wrong," Stone heard him say. "You can't dictate to the military what its requirements should be; it's your job to get out what they need." He ripped another receiver off the hook. "You're wrong," he told an anonymous Army representative. "The military does not know what industry can produce." This was Baruch in action, in his own peculiarly defined role. "Baruch was trying to prop everyone up, rather than pull the rug out," was Stone's observation; [89] and in this conscious aim he ran up against the subconscious drives of Donald Nelson.

Nelson's persecution fears had now become almost psychopathic. Baruch stared, incredulous, as Nelson announced what he was going to do, boasting that he had got three spies on his own staff now — counterirritants to the whisperers and connivers who were plotting to ruin him. Baruch begged him to desist. Professional busybodies, tossing the ball back and forth, were an inevitable part of the price of being in Washington.

But Baruch's patience was beginning to wear fine. One Sunday Nelson came to him proclaiming that Wilson could no longer remain; he was unacceptable; and only a week earlier Baruch had been urged to try to persuade Mr. Wilson to remain. Eberstadt, meanwhile, was reaching his own decision.[90]

On February 3, 1943, Eberstadt called to see Baruch and to his surprise found the older man lying stretched out on his bed. There was a listlessness about him that Eberstadt remembered with sudden recognition afterward. Eberstadt showed Baruch his proposed letter of resignation.

"Don't send it," Baruch said quickly. "There are developments you don't know about." Puzzled, Eberstadt returned to his office, then on the weekend took off for Boston. Several times he tried to call Baruch, but was unable to reach him.

In Boston on Monday, his wife opened a newspaper and read: "Eberstadt Fired." This was straight from Donald Nelson's office. What had happened during the intervening five days? He had no idea. What had happened can only be pieced together. Not Eberstadt nor Nelson nor Baruch, nor even the President, knew wholly what was going on.[91]

The previous week Baruch had dined with Nelson. "You're not doing a good job; you must make up with Mr. Eberstadt," he told him. It was a last warning. Less than twenty-four hours later, Baruch and Byrnes were at the the White House to lay before the President "substantial charges that WPB was being torn apart." They insisted that Nelson should go.[92]

Meanwhile, Stimson had joined others in the government begging the President to replace Nelson with Baruch. "No action was taken, however," Stimson wrote afterward.[93] He did not know that the authority had already been taken from Nelson. On February 5, 1943, Byrnes placed a letter in Baruch's hands:

Dear Bernie,

For a long time I have been calling upon you for assistance in questions affecting our war production. You have given unsparingly of your time and energy and your advice has been exceedingly valuable. I know that you have preferred to serve in an advisory capacity and have been disinclined to accept an appointment . . . to an administrative position. However, I deem it wise to make a change in the direction of War Production and I am coming back to the elder statesman for assistance. I want to appoint you as Chairman of the War Production Board with power to direct the activities of the organization.

The letter was inspired and composed by Byrnes, but it was signed "Franklin D. Roosevelt." [94]

This was not 1941. This time it seemed as though the President must have learned the lesson and be prepared to delegate real authority. Now we were at the very height of war, and no personal qualms should be allowed to stop a man from making his contribution. And still, tragically, Baruch hesitated. He felt his seventy-two years. He thought of the hours that he had worked during the last war, by day and by night — would he have the strength to do it again? He thought of Roosevelt. Roosevelt was not Woodrow Wilson. Would he really ever give him the powers that Wilson had given — the powers needed to do the job? If he could only think — and he was so tired; fatigue of body and brain pressed down on him. He turned to Byrnes. "I'll let you know tomorrow," he said.[95]

On the train to New York, he shifted restlessly. He could feel his heart pounding and the hot blood in his cheeks. He could not think . . . or decide. Suddenly, up came Higgins.

"Let me feel you; you're hot." Her cool hand pressed against his cheek. A moment later a thermometer popped into his mouth. The reading was over one hundred.

"But I'm not sick; I feel fine," Baruch insisted. He was still insisting as they reached the house, and he was hustled off to bed. By the time the doctor arrived, his temperature had soared to 104 degrees.

"But I can't be sick; I've got to get back to Washington; I can't let Jimmy Byrnes down," he kept insisting. By this time he was a little delirious. Eberstadt called, and leaned back puzzled when told that Baruch was unavailable. No one must know of his illness. Byrnes, the President must not know. Baruch drifted deeper into his fever.[96]

He had to get well. He had made up his mind; he knew what it was his duty to do. "Jimmy expects me down, Monday," he kept repeating. Although he could not make it on Monday, he was in the capital, weak but recovered, ten days later.

He went straight to the White House and was shown into the Oval Study. "Here I am, Mr. President, reporting for duty," he announced blithely. The President looked up, uncertainty wavering behind his smile. Baruch saw that he was holding a letter in his hand.

"Oh, Bernie — did you hear this about so-and-so?" And as he launched into a discussion of the problems of the Near East, he was relieved from his embarrassment by the announcement of a Cabinet meeting. The chairmanship of the War Production Board was never mentioned between Bernard Baruch and the White House again.[97]

Only Donald Nelson knew the end of the story. Baruch himself has always blamed Hopkins for the big switch, but in fact nobody changed the President's mind. Circumstance did that. But it was Donald Nelson who arranged the circumstances. Just who informed Nelson has never been revealed. Somehow the secret of "the letter" leaked out. Eliot Janeway believes the informer to have been Robert Nathan, intimate of both Hopkins and Nelson. In any event, Nelson was informed sometime between Saturday evening and Monday. And Nelson acted with a speed and decision that belie any theories that his mistakes on the War Production Board were due to lack of initiative.

He made a triple play. He fired Eberstadt; he confronted President Roosevelt with a *fait accompli*; he blocked Baruch; and temporarily, at least, he saved himself.[98]

Eberstadt was the victim. Eberstadt was to have been Baruch's deputy, and his dismissal made him not only politically useless but suspect to the public. Baruch would have been unable to reinstate him even had he received the chairmanship. Deprived of one of his "Big Three," it is unlikely that Baruch would have served at all. All this Roosevelt knew, and from the time he had opened his own newspaper, his hands were tied. As Janeway has written, Nelson had bluffed the President out of a commitment to the country's leading private citizen.[99]

So swift and secret had been the plays that the explosion was over before the press was aware that it had been touched off. As late as

February 18, the Washington *Times-Herald* announced that Baruch was to "come in" with complete and final power. Three days earlier, the New York *Herald Tribune* carried a story that Nelson was to lose his power, although retaining his title, and that Baruch and Byrnes were "taking over." That same day the New York *Post* reported that Baruch was "convalescing." Eberstadt was fired just as the press was discovering and enumerating his virtues. But his sin had been cardinal. *PM* on the seventeenth charged the brilliant New Yorker with urging the firing of Nelson and his replacement by either Baruch or himself.[100]

Baruch was out of the fight, but the disputes went on. Over a year passed before Donald Nelson was sent on that slow boat to China — a journey which has spelled finis for several great men. Baruch had the consolation of suggesting a draft for his letter of dismissal. He scribbled it in pencil, employing Roosevelt's own turn of phrase. Nelson was to be the President's "Personal Representative" and "Ambassador-at-Large." [101] Baruch tucked his tongue in his cheek and dispatched the script to the White House. Earlier, Drew Pearson had forecast — as had Leon Henderson before him — that Nelson was to be "banished to Siberia . . . I mean China." [102]

When the Board finally exploded in the late fall of 1944, Baruch was among those who recommended young J. A. Krug to reassemble the pieces, and, as Krug later wrote Swope, it was only with the Elder Statesman's help that he dared to tackle the job.[103]

If Baruch was out of the War Production Board, his talents had not gone unused. His job was rubber. In the summer of 1942, he received a handwritten note from the President which began with the familiar "Dear Bernie." "Because you are an 'ever present help in time of trouble' will you 'do it again'? You would be better than all the Supreme Court put together. Sam * will tell you and I'll see you later." [104]

The President had just vetoed a bill authorizing a new agency to produce rubber and alcohol for both civil and military needs. Instead, he was asking a small committee of "distinguished and disinterested citizens" to make "a quick but adequate survey" of existing rubber supplies, plus an estimate of future needs and how to fill them. Particularly, the President wanted to know how many critical

* "Sam" probably refers to Judge Rosenman.

materials might be needed to build rubber plants, and authorized the hiring of a technical staff to recommend "such action as will best produce the synthetic rubber necessary for our total war effort, including civilian use, with a minimum of interference with the production of other weapons of war." [105]

As chairman, he named Baruch. Other members were Karl Compton of the Massachusetts Institute of Technology and James Bryant Conant, President of Harvard. Baruch accepted, briefly and simply.[106]

Baruch was no novice on the subject of rubber. As we have seen, as early as 1910 he had himself been interested in the development of raw rubber in Mexico, in the Congo, in South America, and the Indies. He had made no money out of the schemes, but he and his associates had made important discoveries.[107] Rubber had again come to his attention when he was Raw Materials chairman of the Advisory Commission to the Council of National Defense, and from the early thirties on he had haunted the Senate committee rooms with the reiterated plea to stockpile it.[108]

In the late nineteen-twenties an organization known as the Intercontinental Rubber Company had caught on to the possibilities of getting raw rubber from the guayule weed of Mexico. By 1934, 60,000 acres were under cultivation in California. The venture had excited the imaginations of diverse personalities for diverse reasons — Baruch, who saw it as a crop for the restoration of marginal lands by the CCC; [109] Henry Wallace; and the Wizard of Menlo Park, Thomas Edison, who looked ahead into a future he would not live to see. As early as 1927, hard at work in his West Orange laboratory, Edison announced that he was concentrating his efforts toward wartime relief from a possible shortage of rubber.[110] As the Nazis engulfed Europe, he warned that the slow growth of guayule would make it impractical as a source of quick supply in case of need, but the government would expend no money for new plantings and a wartime reserve. Guayule alone could furnish up to 10 or 20 per cent of the total national rubber supply, and conceivably 50 per cent, but doing so, it would seriously depress the world price down.[111] It was American policy to buy rubber abroad from the French and English possessions, so as to have a market in return for our crop surpluses.[112] It was thus of more profit to the American stockholders of Intercontinental Rubber to manufacture 3 per cent of the national supply at a high price than 15 per cent at the risk of pushing prices down. So this was done despite Baruch's plea.[113]

Baruch, however, wasted no time on spilt milk. Even by June 1940 he had been busy assembling the facts on guayule. But although 500 tons a month could be obtained from Mexico, any wartime supply would have had to be planned and planted five years before. Congress spent one million dollars and two years, incidentally, to reach the conclusions which had been revealed by the War Department some six years earlier.[114]

Who was responsible? Jesse Jones was responsible — was he not head of the Reconstruction Finance Corporation and of its subsidiary, the Rubber Reserve Corporation, with power to stockpile for all crises and emergencies? Edward Stettinius was responsible — was he not the Raw Materials chairman of the President's Advisory Commission? War Production Chief Donald Nelson was responsible, because he said that he was, and by the summer of 1942 had announced that he would take full charge of the synthetic rubber program. Senator Harry S. Truman was responsible; his watchdog committee had uncovered ghastly shortages and made suggestions, some of which would later be incorporated in Baruch's report. Congress was avowedly responsible, for upon Nelson's pronouncement it moved to set up a whole independent Rubber Authority. Fuel Administrator Harold L. Ickes was responsible, because he felt that way. Seemingly, the only individual of national stature who did not feel himself responsible was Chief Justice Harlan Stone of the Supreme Court, who Ickes thought had done "a distinct disservice to his country" by refusing to make a survey.[115] The picture, stated Ickes, was "total confusion"; to Baruch it was totally appalling. Most of official Washington seemed to him to be madmen — poached eggs looking around for pieces of toast to sit on.[116]

Baruch had inventoried the stocks on hand as of the spring of 1941: the annual average consumption of crude rubber was 620,000 tons; there were on hand about 485,000 tons, with only 255,000 in the government stockpile.[117] On seeing the advance of war, Baruch had made one last attempt through Wallace, Hull, and Byrnes to barter cotton for rubber. The project had fallen through as the big men "bickered over who was to do the job." [118]

One year later Baruch was still chafing at the unwarrantable shortages and delays. Why not call together the diverse factions and require them to fight the problem out before the meeting broke up? [119] Two weeks after Pearl Harbor, Baruch wrote Milo Perkins that a commodity like rubber should have its own section in Washington, with a chairman who would receive the demands of the Army, Navy, and civilians.[120] Once again he saw that one man must head the section.[121] When Ickes, in desperation, cried out, "To whom now can the President turn?" he answered his own question: "Get Baruch." [122]

They had "called in the old man." But consent was not unanimous. The Army, for one example, unmindful of civilian demands, protested that it was not short of rubber. And then there was a big white-haired Texan named Jesse Jones.

Mr. Jones said that Baruch's criticisms were unwarranted. He said it then and he elaborated it in his memoirs later. He charged that only the meddlers sold the President on the idea of an investigation. He pointed out that a Rubber Coordinator already existed in the War Production Board. Baruch, he said, had made criticisms that were not justified, had conceded that the Reconstruction Finance Corporation's plan would produce rubber, and was "willing to give me a little dig," because the RFC was run without him. Furthermore, erroneously, Jones insisted on the success of his efforts.[123] His figures for 1940 showed 634,000 tons of rubber on hand; and by 1942 we had the greatest stockpile in the world.[124] What he did not say was that the 1940 figure was scarcely a year's domestic supply, and that the country at war was using ten times as much rubber as it had during the First World War.

Perhaps it was Jones of whom Baruch was thinking when he commented on the "tough babies" he had to deal with. At the RFC office, Jones negotiated his loans with the deliberation of a small-town banker. His happy reports to the President that "all has already been done" were indeed reassuring; but they did not make rubber.[125]

The President began to ask more questions, and was taken aback when Jones disclosed that construction of a synthetic plant with a capacity of 40,000 tons would not be completed for some eight months.

"Well, it takes a long time to build such plants, Mr. President," Jones drawled.[126]

Less complacent was Ickes, who wrote Baruch on July 29, 1942: "I have to weep on someone's shoulder and I don't know of a better one than yours." In regard to rubber, the country was in "the worst mess possible." [127]

After Pearl Harbor, Jesse Jones had bet with himself that the war would soon be over — especially in the Pacific. He had not built up the stockpile for which 100 million dollars had been earmarked; a year later, 87 millions were still unspent. Jones had made a second gamble that the price of rubber would fall — and had gone bargain-hunting in a world market where suddenly there were no bargains.[128] While he waited, "the Axis got the rubber." Before a presidential order sealed the ports, thousands more tons of the precious stuff were shipped out to Japan. Jones had "slept peacefully on the synthetic rubber program," Ickes roared; and, in point of fact, Wallace, with his dreams of guayule and fears of Standard Oil and cartels, was no less responsible. However, "as soon" — and this soon was much too late — "as Jones was given his orders, he acted on them." [129] His happy optimism had by this time infected the President; and it was not until January 14, 1942, when Ickes himself volunteered to start a synthetic rubber program, that Roosevelt took serious note of the situation. On January 27, the President told Ickes to cooperate with Nelson; on February 23, Ickes wrote Nelson hopefully, offering his services and those of his petroleum experts. Nelson did not reply. Four days later, Ickes requested the President to announce a rubber program and to call upon the public to sacrifice and conserve. The President did not respond. Then Ickes suggested to Jesse Jones the desirability of an over-all authority to handle the rubber and pe-troleum questions. But Jones had no intention of "transferring his responsibility."

And now the country had been "caught short." Jones had failed; someone had to pull the President "out from under." Who? "You are one of the wisest men that I have ever known — perhaps the wisest," Ickes told Baruch. "Here is a job worthy even of you." [130] And within a week the presidential appeal had come.

Baruch engaged in neither regrets nor recriminations. He promptly joined his colleagues, then called in his "team." In later years it distressed Baruch (who was as modest on his great achievements as he was self-assertive on his little ones), that the result of the Rubber committee's labors was known as the "Baruch Report." Conant and Compton, he thought, were the "spark plugs" who provided the technical knowledge; he just "added to the scenery." [131] This was far from true. From the first Baruch had realized the importance of the interrelationship between fuel shortages and tire usage. Sud-denly one day at his "office" in Lafayette Square, while one scientist argued molecular chain reactions, Baruch interrupted: "When you fellows get through talking Chinese, I believe we can go ahead and declare a dividend." [132]

His idea was a three-way program of gasoline rationing, tire inspection, and recapping, all tuned to a thirty-five-mile speed limit and a restriction of five tires and one car to a family. Finally, Baruch suggested the obvious: the consolidation of all government agencies dealing with rubber under a single authority.[133]

As he said afterward, he concentrated on the report to the exclusion of everything else.[134] His able young assistant, Sam Lubell, did the actual writing job, completing it in a month, and so detailed was the analysis that it would have been remarkable had it been completed in three months. All was brought to a focus, the shortage of rubber and the surplus of answers — and the total cost to Baruch, personally, was some $50,000.[135]

To the press generally, it seemed that the report would "bring a great deal of order out of the chaos"; and the New Republic called it the "first really good job done in Washington since the war began." The New York Post spoke for the nation: "This report is hard as nails . . . This is something like war talk . . . This makes much of official Washington look pretty sick." According to the Post, much of official Washington should have long since been fired.[136]

The report had its weaknesses. It presupposed the loss of Ceylon. It presumed that no rubber at all would be sold except for commercial vehicles. It failed to take into account the fact that in great open areas like Texas, trucks traveling in low gear at 35 miles an hour consumed far more gasoline than at 40 and 50 miles an hour in high gear.[137] In a postwar post-mortem, PM damned Baruch for giving insufficient consideration to the grain alcohol and synthetic rubber programs, ignoring the time lag on synthetic rubber and the fact that Baruch had long pleaded for alcohol plants.[138]

Looking back, the solution seems obvious enough. As his colleagues recognized, however, it was Baruch's name and prestige which "accomplished the desired end" of selling any kind of program to the public.[139] Dr. Baruch prescribed and the public swallowed — a dose few believed it could take.[140] What had been needed was not so much new answers as one answer, issued with a challenge to which the people could respond. They did and, publicly at least, so did the White House. An immediate presidential directive was issued to put the Baruch Plan into effect. The New York Times announced: "Full

'Gas' Rationing Dec. 1 Ordered by the President." [141] So many persons wanted to help Baruch celebrate his seventy-second birthday and a job well done that he gave the party himself, with such "New Deal Prima Donnas" as Jones and Nelson lined up along with Byrnes, Tommy Corcoran, Rosenman, Eberstadt, Swope, and Baruch's son, then a commander in the navy.[142]

On August 16, a Boston *Globe* cartoon had shown Baruch begging Roosevelt for a rubber stockpile. And the President's answer had come characteristically: "Not a word about rubber today, Bernie. That matter has been attended to." [143] Had it been? By January 30, 1943, the New York *Herald Tribune* commented, "Byrnes Grants Priority for only 43% of Baruch Plan"; and a day later the New Haven *Register* proclaimed: "More Strife Than Synthetic Rubber Produced So Far." [144]

Baruch's job was not finished when he laid his report down. "Bill" Jeffers was a vigorous and forthright man.[145] Baruch had marshaled a vigorous "public demand" for Jeffers as "Rubber Boss." Now he felt morally compelled to back him up. Conflict arose between Baruch and even old friends like Milo Perkins when Jeffers suddenly restricted the Board of Economic Welfare's remaining authority to the search for undeveloped rubber in foreign lands.[146]

Baruch stood quietly by, seeing that Jeffers was given the support due him and smoothing down the ruffled feelings of the overzealous. "You were a great source of strength to me yesterday," Perkins once wrote him.[147] The question still was not so much how to win the war as who was to win the war; and the miracle was that the war seemed to be getting won. As Baruch noted, what was to come first — planes, ships, or rubber — was still the foremost problem. It was interesting to him how tired men struggled only to find ways to divide the small existing supply rather than seeking out new sources.[148]

By September the headlines were crying: "The Big Job Is Done," and "Mr. Jeffers Did It." [149] Undeterred by boondoggling or bottlenecks, Jeffers had rammed through his synthetic rubber program, and tires were rolling off the production lines.

As for Baruch, the rubber report marked his first foray into the field of science with results that became important in the future. A warm camaraderie had grown up among the tired hatless men in shirtsleeves, representatives of science and big business, whose "office" was a bench in Lafayette Square.[150] Baruch and the scientists emerged from those hot August days with a new respect for each other, more significant, perhaps, because it went against their preconceptions. Two years later, in answer to a complimentary letter of Baruch's, Conant wrote: "I will always have the proudest and fondest memories. I think we can all congratulate ourselves on the happy way in which the rubber program has worked out. Looking back just two years ago, it seems almost too good to be true." [151]

19

WAR FROM A PARK BENCH

To THE NATION Bernard Baruch was the "Park Bench Statesman." But to official Washington during those years of the Second World War, he was "the tall old trouble shooter." There in Lafayette Square he sat, spring and autumn alike, bundled in a heavy overcoat. His bench, to which mail was duly addressed and delivered,[1] was just off dead center of the park, near the rear end of the equestrian statue of Andrew Jackson. It was four feet six inches long, just big enough to accommodate Baruch and one average-sized Cabinet officer. Hard candy sometimes rattled in his pockets, but it was for himself, not for the pigeons or squirrels.

He rarely caused a ripple in the quiet life of the park. It was as if he belonged there, along with the newspaper photographers and the loafers, the government employees on lunch hour, the lovers, the nursemaids and the children. Pigeons rooted around his high-laced shoes. Tourists sauntered by to smile and to snap pictures of Jackson, rearing ever upward on his bronze-green charger. Once Baruch dropped his gold watch and it was later returned by a child who was playing nearby, to whom he presented a war bond. After that the children played even nearer, hoping that he would drop something again.[2]

He was a part of the park, this shrewd old man whose eyes had seen the follies of two world wars, looking, according to press accounts, "like Michelangelo's Moses turned buccaneer," [3] or like an "old wind-blown eagle." [4] These expressions were typical. During the forties the public press gushed forth fountains of almost cloying hero-worship of Baruch, for which the Elder Statesman, despite his disclaimers of super powers or super prescience, cannot be held wholly irresponsible. He had too carefully cultivated his friendships with the top moguls of journalism for that. Nevertheless, there was another and more valid reason for this hero-worship of the Elder Statesman, which increased steadily toward the decade's end. Looking back over the last quarter of a century, we can see that after the national collapse of 1929, the country sought a father-image. Franklin Roosevelt filled the bill capably, but there also was Baruch, who, if a little old for the father role, was at least "the grand-daddy of them all," and the veneration in which he was held was reflected by the nickname "Old Uncle Sam," the national symbol, itself. Then, too, and always, there must be remembered what Sherwood Anderson has termed "the myth of greatness." He points out that "most modern great men are mere illusions sprung out of a national hunger for greatness." As the politicians of the industrial age have created myths about themselves, so too have the financiers, the millionaires perhaps most of all. And finally, as Anderson says, they themselves are "children enough to believe the myth" they created. And if they believe it, why should not all America? [5]

Baruch in the Second World War was without portfolio. His influence fluctuated according to the rise and fall of public opinion. It was at a low ebb, for instance, in January 1943, after he had played host at an overpublicized "Roman feast" for Harry Hopkins and his new bride.[6] Even a one-million-dollar donation to charity could not offset the effect of the three-thousand-dollar spread for Hopkins. No elected official depended on his "public" more than Bernard Baruch, as he learned when, temporarily at least, his services were virtually dispensed with, except for the Army and Navy.[7]

Officially he had no power except to advise, although this was somewhat of an oversimplification. His self-assumed job was to try to stave off what had been the bugaboo of the old War Industries Board, the excess zeal which made each department see itself as the center around which the war rotated. Each part had to be fitted into the whole. Only through proper coordination and subordination could production objectives be reached which would beat Hitler.[8]

Some smiled at Baruch. He dreamed, they thought, of the Presidency, but knew always that it was only a dream. The newspapermen knew his very human weaknesses, that he was "pleasantly aware of being handsome . . . proud of his record of public service, of his influence in Washington, of his ability to charm people, especially women." They knew his love of lunching regularly at the White House, although recognizing always that he never kowtowed to the President.[9] They knew that his bench commanded a view of the North Portico of the Executive Mansion and that sometimes a man would come out and wave. Then a limousine would move down the drive up to the curb of Lafayette Square, and the sitting eagle would be whisked away. Yet they knew that his vanity never affected his judgment, that he was a financier who had never sold his country short. They knew him as a two-fisted fighting man whose strongest drive was what he spoke of least — patriotism, in which he could be ruthless.[10]

He was impatient at any start in postwar planning now. His one aim was to see the war won fast enough to save the lives of our fighting men.[11] He would listen to the opinions of the special pleaders and advisers, and finally a solution would emerge, perhaps even in a dream, or in a burst of creative excitement.[12] His imagination was controlled by common sense. He would listen with disarming placidity to high-flown theories, only to blurt out, "Where are you going to get the money?" He sometimes exasperated with his simple, dogmatic answers to complex questions, his belaboring of the obvious. "You don't distribute wealth," he would drawl. "You distribute poverty."[13]

Yet he was praised both by the *Daily Worker* and the *New Masses*, whose spokesman saw Baruch's ideas as bearing about the only resemblance to an over-all plan in Washington;[14] and by the Illinois *State Journal*, which proclaimed him "the most useful citizen of America."[15] Few would differ from the estimate of the Chicago *Herald-American* that his "passion for winning the war takes precedence over everything else in life."[16]

The Milwaukee *Journal* pointed out: "As for Baruch, that delightful old grizzle-top could be, if he wished, the dominating figure among the advisers of the Administration, but he is as canny as he is wise. He butts in on nothing that does not figure in his own official field." Carefully and shrewdly he avoided controversy.[17] Aware that the public regarded him "as a sage," he was enjoying his reputation and safeguarding it. One writer thought that he deliberately made few public statements so that when he did have something to say it would fall with the weight of an oracle.[18] Claiming that it was better that he remain unfettered and free, he had evolved his role of the

Elder Statesman — available, yet not responsible for the mishaps that occurred.[19] He had "sitting in" privileges in all of the departments and agencies, and was in and out of most of them, except the State and Treasury Departments. At the Treasury, where New Deal monetary theories still held sway, he felt that they would resent anything he said. As to State Department policy, he felt that he did not know anything about it.[20]

"Baruch does not want his picture in the papers," wrote a reporter for *Who* Magazine. "He doesn't want his biography published. He does not care to be interviewed . . . Baruch means what he says." [21] Nor did he want to be a prime minister, an American Disraeli. "I'm not that type." He was aware that his very gift for public relations had made it difficult for Roosevelt to fit him into the role of a subordinate, that the mystery role had magnified rather than reduced his eminence. But he also had humility. "Do you think I should bother them?" he would sometimes ask John Hancock, as he mused over the failings of some war agency or war plant. "I don't want to be a busybody." [22]

"His is a one-man show," Anna Rosenberg has commented. "He doesn't let himself get drawn into others' controversies." [23] On the Washington scene, he exerted his influence indirectly, which made it hard to measure, as it would be hard to measure his place in history. For two days, he considered the job of looking after the veterans and war workers, but again, contending that he would not be up to it, he shied away from the direct responsibility and recommended William Jeffers. He felt some responsibility also for those whose names he had suggested for positions. One man, he heard, was "pretty good." "Pretty good is not good enough."

One version of the "realist at work" was given by the commentator Henry J. Taylor, in a broadcast. "He isn't just sitting on that bench, and this is what he is doing.

"He is systematically going, step by step, to the weakest section of this demoralized structure." He was sitting down with the incompetents who could not be changed. He was practical enough to know that they would not be removed "and that the really wise task is to try to make the best use of them." He was "literally and actually holding their hands these very days and telling them to buck up." [24]

In a draft for one of his reports, Baruch had pessimistically and erroneously warned that if the trend was not reversed, the country and even the armed forces would face disaster. The First World War had been a 35-billion-dollar war. In the Second World War 106 billion dollars was budgeted for 1943 alone.[25] A new generation was having to learn by trial and error the lessons which had been learned so bitterly and at so much cost twenty-five years before.

There was so little time. "Well — what is it? Shoot!" Baruch would salute the average time-waster.[26] "Throw the shoe kissers out," he would roar. "They're just a lot of yessers . . . Get some no men." [27] But these commands were carefully worded as generalities; with individuals, Baruch characteristically avoided strife. As he said, "The people who fight you today are people you may need tomorrow." [28]

"Better ask Bernie," [29] was a catchword in wartime Washington, much as it had been in Wall Street. "Salty and peppery as ever," with more fire and energy than most young men,[30] he still had that driving ticker-tape personality that had so struck David Lawrence back in 1917.[31] He was in Washington and ready to "straighten everything out on a salary of nothing a year." His hearing aid was rumored to be a recording machine,[32] and when it went out of gear at the height of the wartime shortages, Ferdinand Eberstadt promised: "We'll get you a battery, Bernie. Your hearing is essential to the war effort." [33]

Not all his work was transacted from the bench in Lafayette Square. He would sit in his suite at the hotel ringed with telephones — he could still keep eight telephones going at once. Sometimes he would put in a dozen long-distance calls to check one fact. "What are the facts?" he would snap. "What are the facts?"

"Why are people quitting your plant?" he would ask one manufacturer. "Are you getting the steel you need? Are you getting the raw materials?" To a general — "Did that shipment arrive on time?" It was not generally known that he had seventeen researchers in addition to his "staff," all on his own payroll.[34]

To guests he would talk torrentially "in a rich mixture of Broadway words and the jargon of high finance," but always sticking to the fundamentals.[35] When fatigue closed down on him, or the summer heat of Washington, which some said was second only to Singapore's,[36] he would put on his black fedora and walk down 16th Street to the park.

No "rookie" was in more rigorous training than he. He would rise early, read the news and the items on himself with care, shave with an old straight-edged razor, and then, erect in his red bathrobe and striped pajamas, have a workout with dumbbells. He was burning up energy like a youngster, and it was then that he inaugurated his custom of dining promptly at 7.30, company or no company. "They sit around drinking cocktails when I want to eat," he complained.[37] Usually now he went to bed at nine, after a cold bath to make him sleep. Because of the pressure of his self-imposed duties, during the winter of 1942–43 he spent only three weeks at his beloved Hobcaw.[38] His health was carefully guarded by young Higgins and "the faithful stage manager and major-domo, Lacey." Still he had time to help a lady in distress, prima donna Grace Moore, stranded with her company in Houston, Texas.[39] He lunched with his bearded brother, "the Ambassador," * and a party of pretty WAVES at the Mayflower.[40] He even dropped a note of appreciation to the editor of *Iron Age* for so correct and understanding an interpretation of his views, evoking, of course, in reply an editorial entitled "Nice guy, Barney Baruch." [41]

In the maze of frenzy and discouragement and politics that was wartime Washington, Baruch moved serenely. He knew perfectly well that what had to be done would not be done without effort and often would not be done at all. "This," he would say, smiling, "will be difficult."

He was said to know that he was seeking the impossible, but it became more possible because he sought it. Some thought that he didn't even expect his advice to be taken and therefore was able to go out on a limb without being sawed off. To other observers, it seemed that frustrations goaded him.[42] He had had "great successes, but greater ambitions." He had had many satisfactions yet never had been satisfied. He had had the respect and the deference of the nation, but his ideas were accepted too late, or not at all. Fortunately, he had no romantic illusions and knew that triumph was often the result of doggedly "sticking to it." [43] Expecting little, he accomplished more than he could have dreamed. "I know of no man in America who contributed more generously and effectively to the good of our country than you have," wrote Senator Harry Byrd in January 1945.[44]

In the fall of 1942, Baruch had written a memorandum on the problems of mobilization in which he optimistically claimed that with

---

* Dr. Herman Baruch (1872–1953) was named Ambassador to the Netherlands by President Roosevelt.

the War Production Board reorganized and James Byrnes at its head the problems would be solved.[45]

That was in September 1942. The reorganization had been completed, as we have seen, answering some of the old problems and creating new ones. The appointment of Byrnes indeed solved numerous difficulties, leaving the President with the wish that he were Solomon so that he could divide Jimmy Byrnes in half.[46]

The bitterness which clouded Byrnes's later years and sent him back to the governor's chair of South Carolina, from which he gazed upon a gigantic outspread Confederate flag, cannot dull the luster of his accomplishments, he who has held more state and national offices than any South Carolinian since Calhoun. As "Assistant President" during the Second World War, he was virtually the indispensable man.

Baruch, too, had been offered the job of Economic Stabilizer and had turned it down for the same reason that he had turned down the War Production job in 1941. The position did not have adequate authority. "Stabilization" was an impossible job under the circumstances.[47] The President had chortled that Bernie wanted to be both Secretary of the Treasury and Economic Stabilizer.[48] Nevertheless, he dispatched a second emissary in the person of Harry Hopkins, who repeated the offer.

Again Baruch refused. "I don't want to take anything anybody else wants," is his recollection of what he told Hopkins. Baruch well knew the venom of the pack that would be nipping at his heels if he filled a job that might lead to the Presidency. "But I've got just the man for you — Jimmy Byrnes," and at that strategic instant, as if drawn from a hat, the Associate Justice walked into the room.

Baruch turned to Hopkins. "Harry, tell him what we've been talking about." Byrnes listened with evident interest as Baruch warned him, "It may mean going back to hog and hominy."

"Well, that's where we started, wasn't it?" Byrnes is said to have replied.[49]

Byrnes's appointment was received with muted enthusiasm, born of disillusion. For all his energy and drive (it was said that he had never had time — or money — to learn to smoke), he was known primarily as a parliamentarian and a "fixer," as a "smooth" capable politician.[50] That he would become "the strong man of the Administration" was never dreamed, and it was only when the fact was self-evident that the Milwaukee *Journal* recalled that his "was probably the best mind in the Senate during his terms there." [51] The *Daily Worker* might growl that he could only compromise differences without striking out for any basic policy, but the Indiana *Teamster* spoke out boldly, declaring: "From what we know of Byrnes, he won't favor anyone and he will be fair with everyone." [52] This was true, and it spelled his political undoing.

He was a dynamo, this small, ruddy-faced, gray-haired man with the look of a troubled spaniel. When callers overstayed their welcome, he searched for cobwebs on the ceiling or doodled or rattled his papers. *Time* wrote of his job: "Only snow-haired Bernard Mannes Baruch ever had comparable responsibility.[53] However, it was not until six months later, when he surrendered the job of Economic Stabilizer for the Office of War Mobilization and a desk in the White House, that the "Assistant President" title was real at last.[54]

When it was rumored that Baruch was under consideration for this post also, his comment was, "Director Byrnes has everything it takes to do the job." [55]

In a sense, Byrnes's authority was even greater than Baruch's had been in the smaller war. It was Byrnes to whom all agencies and officials reported — the War Department, the Navy, the War Production Board, his was the power to determine all questions and conflicts, to settle disputes between even the members of the Cabinet. He, now, was the "general eye," with the task of seeing that no single job was the most important, of looking always not on the part but on the whole.

Some journalists disliked the appointment. Could Byrnes and Roosevelt change their natures? Could Byrnes, the "fixer," become hard-fisted, and could the President keep his own fingers out of every pie? As Economic Stabilizer, Byrnes had had virtually the same powers as he had now and had not seen fit to exercise them.[56] Half the answer was given by the St. Louis *Globe-Democrat*, which observed that the former Senator from South Carolina had "never fallen for nutty notions." [57]

Baruch had stepped into the headlines with the announcement that he would be the assistant to the Assistant President, serving as usual without title or pay, but in "a more formal connection with the government" than in his job on the Rubber committee. However, ac-

cording to Byrnes, the job was purely unofficial, and Baruch remarked
that his position would "be about the same as it has always been." [58]
He continued his trouble-shooting, pleased to serve under Byrnes,
with whom he did not always agree but whose sincerity and knowledge he never questioned.[59]

 . If the park bench was called Baruch's "office," [60] his real office was
at the Shoreham, where strategy was mapped in Thursday night
sessions. These included both Byrnes and his beautiful wife and the
ever-helpful "old Diesel engine," John Hancock, of whom Baruch
once said that no man in America could surpass him.[61] Hancock
later recalled that Baruch was never happier than when he, Byrnes,
and Hancock were working together on a problem.[62]

For Byrnes, the instinctive conservative, increasing intimacy with
the White House brought increasing strain. He and Baruch were
facing the struggle between their loyalty to the Democratic Party and
the New Deal and their loyalty to their own convictions. They questioned whether they could best serve their country by submission and
working from within or by outright rebellion.

One evening as they argued on a sofa, from a nearby chair Republican John Hancock smiled complacently.

"Why're you looking so happy?" Byrnes asked.

"I'm just happy I don't have to sleep tonight with the conscience of
a Democrat," Hancock said.

 : Mrs. Byrnes added, "Thank God for one honest man in this
place." [63]

Baruch's first major assignment dealt with perhaps the greatest
of all wartime questions — manpower. Men were willing to suffer
and to die, and Baruch was infuriated that our splendid youth should
be sent across the world to fight and perhaps to die, without any
knowledge of whether they were going to be backed up at home.

Manpower was the problem — not at the front alone but behind
the lines, the manpower without which the front could not fight.
Selective Service was draining skilled workers from the plants; plant
expansion was continuing while plane production fell off; and in the
end Baruch was called in to help halt the drop in the output of war
planes. In March 1943, he had sent a memorandum to the White
House that airplane production, or rather the lack of it, was disturbing, but by October he could note that production would be close
to 8200 a month, if not bungled; and Frank Kent wrote that Ba-

ruch's part in stimulating the output should make all America grateful.[64]

First, however, there had to be a smashing of the bottlenecks. Baruch knew, for instance, that there was no real manpower shortage on the East Coast, and yet a great shortage on the West Coast, and that one California plant alone was running forty Flying Fortresses a month behind because of insufficient labor.[65] No provision had been made in law to keep work and collective bargaining going at the same time; one strike on carburetors, for instance, could halt virtually all plane production.[66] He knew that farms could be a haven for some draft-dodgers, and that men in the 38 to 45 age group, now classified 4-H, could be reclassified 1A-H.[67] He had no sympathy for wartime fathers whose urges for paternity were, as often as not, stimulated by their equally strong urge for survival.[68]

He could sympathize with his friend Bradley Dewey, who wondered if there was "any hope of our teaching fellows like Stimson to stop talking about having to treat everyone alike." War itself was unreasonable, unfair.[69] Above all, there were the "peace jitters" which periodically shook up and slowed down production.

These were tough facts, requiring tough answers. Baruch hit upon a tremendous weapon of psychological warfare. Although in assembling material for his Manpower Report Baruch had the benefit of advice from his old associates John Hancock and Fred Searls, with additional aid from Colonel Fred H. Pope and William Francis Gibbs,[70] the actual report was not the product of "the team" but of Baruch, Byrnes, Hopkins, Leahy, and Judge Rosenman.

One issue nearly torpedoed the group. A strange mélange of Old Guard Republicans and out-and-out New Dealers saw the answer to the labor shortages and slowdowns as a "work or fight" law. This was an old answer to an old question that had been knocking around even back in the First World War: "Draft labor," was the cry.[71]

The plan had heavy backing from the White House, and the vote in the War Manpower Commission stood four to one in favor.* The Albany *Knickerbocker News* told the story in a headline: "Labor Draft Bill Blocked by Baruch's Lone Hold Fight." [72] Privately Baruch had argued that if there were conscription of labor, there would have to be conscription of capital and everything else; and privately the President told an aide that he had better get old Bernie into line,

---

* Presumably Byrnes, Hopkins, Leahy, and Rosenman against Baruch.

or he'd go up on the Hill and join those labor leaders and beat hell out of the bill.[73]

Baruch did. "Labor Draft Is Slavery," roared a headline in the Newark *News*, and Baruch's views were quoted at length. Not only was the projected plan unconstitutional, but it was human "slavery" to compel one citizen to work for the profits of another. A man could be punished for not working at the job he chose but could not be held to forced labor at an appointed job. Furthermore, if all industries were commandeered, where did the President propose to find the managerial experts to run them? [74]

Baruch was of course saying nothing new. He had fought the idea from the First World War on. It was significant that the Newark *News* mentioned he had never "been regarded as a radical or even as a New Dealer." It was more significant that the President called in Judge Rosenman to say that he would not insist on conscription until he had Baruch's approval, as he was set in his opposition.[75] Most significant of all was the "cautious" headline of two months later — "F.D.R. Fears Unworkable Labor Draft." [76]

Baruch had not won this victory alone. But his stubborn fight for the rights of labor had laid the groundwork for the bitter dose they were going to have to swallow. Now with the "Labor Draft" out of the way, the Commission could really get down to work. "Don't say I'm a miracle man," Baruch told reporters. "I haven't got any rabbits I can pull out of my sleeve." [77]

Baruch's working hours were limited. It was he who would provide the final touch of judgment and experience, plus the prestige given any project bearing his name. Much of the groundwork however was done by Sam Lubell, as wary as he was wise, and by John Hancock, then past sixty. Like Baruch, Hancock's talk was rapid, direct, and "man-in-the-street"; also like Baruch's, his ideas seemed obvious until you realized, with a kind of start, that no one else had hit upon them.

During working sessions Baruch would visit Hancock daily and stretch out on a sofa, Hancock in an easy chair, Lubell in the background. Then they would begin to talk, usually on an agenda prepared by Hancock, and after long preliminary discussions the right answer would begin to evolve. Lubell would occasionally contribute a phrase, or interrupt with a sharp "Wait a minute till I get that down." At the end, neither Baruch nor Hancock nor Lubell would know which words were whose, and each would give the other credit for the ideas.[78]

Hancock once noted the quotation on the wall of the Union Station: "Be noble and the nobleness that lies in other men — sleeping but never dead — will rise in majesty to meet thine own." This, he told Baruch, "is as good an expression as I have seen, with regard to your plan of dealing with industry." [79]

The plan evolved. Baruch wrote a stinging criticism of "cost-plus" contracts which the government was making, encouraging the hoarding of labor, the hoarding of material, and a general drive toward quantity rather than quality of output.[80] For the labor-draft proposal he offered an alternative based on the idea of "labor priorities" — a concept that the hair-trigger-thinking Mrs. Anna Rosenberg had worked out in Buffalo.[81] This was a "labor budget," with manpower and materials to be pooled in each community. Manufacturers would then be stringently limited in the number of men they could hire, and workers as to the jobs they could choose.[82] He urged a tightening of the draft laws all along the line, the use of part-time shifts, and the inducement of postwar jobs to be held out to workers who would stick by the assembly line now. He wanted the rehabilitation of physical defectives.[83] As for the war plants themselves, should they fail to cooperate, their contracts could be canceled. The flow of labor should be entirely regulated by the War Manpower Commission.[84]

The preliminary suggestions were worked out by the fall of 1942 and then summarized by Roosevelt. "Following the suggestion of B.M.B.'s memo, I approach manpower needs somewhat as follows": up to January 1, 1944, the armed forces were to be increased by four and a half million and the defense workers force by five and a half million. (The Commission had recommended a total army of eight million.) The President did not necessarily agree with Baruch's estimated figure of four and a half men in the rear for every fighting man at the front, but he did recognize that the estimate was in part based on the use of all factories to the limit. Two or three million more farm workers were also needed.

"I like B.M.B.'s conclusions," was the President's observation on the suggestions as to voluntary cooperation, centralized authority, improved administration, no more restrictive laws, and a work week of from 48 to 54 hours as the "most efficient," with time-and-a-half for overtime.

The President "questioned" the suggestion that there be no further enlistments.[85] Furthermore, the final report was not concluded until the spring of the next year. It was submitted as a confidential memorandum and was not made public.[86]

This aroused suspicion. "What's in That Manpower Report to the President?" demanded the Cincinnati *Times-Star* on March 30, 1943.[87] It was released, at last, in the fall of 1943 with a simultaneous announcement by Byrnes that the proposals had been put into effect. Why it had not been made public before was also revealed. Its recommendations were harsh, its language tough, as the New York *Daily News* observed, and it made Roosevelt's "all goes well talk" look silly.[88]

Such parts as had not yet been written into law were presented in Congress by Senators Arthur Vandenberg and Homer Ferguson, who got through a favorable resolution on the abolition of the cost-plus formula.[89] On September 5, Byrnes stated that he was ready to solve the West Coast labor problem, and ten days later a plan was put into effect to alleviate the labor shortage there by readjusting and moving contracts to prevent labor hoarding. All this, it was announced, was the outgrowth of the study made by Baruch and Hancock for the Office of War Mobilization.[90]

This, of course, was an exaggeration; nor was the plan perfect, by any means. Herbert Hoover, with a luncheon invitation for "My dear Bernie," took opportunity to observe that "apparently you did not get very far in consolidating the food agencies." [91] Also, Baruch still had many problems to resolve, such as to arbitrate between those who wished turbines to be assigned to Liberty ships and those who wanted them for the Navy and Maritime Commission.[92] But the results told the story.

To the military, Baruch's ideas, drive, and persistence were of great value. He was one of the special advisers to General Levin H. Campbell,[93] and he had high regard for the "free-running horse," General Brehon Somervell and his "Don't ask 'em; tell 'em." He liked the gaunt, bald, tight-lipped General Lucius Clay and, perhaps most of all, "Bob" Patterson, a fighting Irishman with his hat brim truculently upslanted, who possibly more than any other civilian was "relentless" in seeing that the soldiers came first. Baruch could agree with Patterson's dogma that in war emergencies prices could be forgotten.[94] Nevertheless, Baruch fought military encroachments on the civilian economy.

Baruch was so hard at work in Washington in the autumn of 1943

that he did not even take time to attend the reunion of the War
Industries Board in New York on Armistice Day. Fifteen or sixteen
gathered, however, and the one who was absent was foremost in their
thoughts. Howard P. Ingels wrote Baruch afterward that the gathering overflowed with love, admiration, and affection for Baruch.[95]

As we have seen, Baruch's battle for inflation controls was important to all groups — with unchecked inflation, who was to say
whether the army or civilians suffered more? Here Baruch had been
on the firing line long before Pearl Harbor. Inflation was the greatest
danger before the country, he believed, and it could still be controlled
if Washington had the courage.[96] Despite the efforts of OPA already
discussed, Washington had not the courage to hold the line — nor
had the American people. Already the country was at the mercy of
speculators, hoarders, runaway markets, and profiteers. As Baruch
said: "Piecemeal controls were a virtual invitation to inflation" to
every "pressure group, politician, lobbyist, trade association . . . The
little fellows who cannot make themselves felt will be forgotten." [97]

He had written Senator Harry Byrd in June of 1942 that faith
and hope would accomplish the task,[98] and this was a year after
the declaration of an "unlimited national emergency," and some
time before the President had issued to Congress an ultimatum demanding a price-control bill. "Either you act before October first, or
I will," [99] and on October 2, 1942, the so-called "Stabilization Act"
had become law. It had stabilized, however, very little. Mostly it
was a document for public display and the public record — a sop to
the anti-inflation pressure groups. By using fragments of Baruch's
scheme, it offered "proof" that controls did not work.

"House Bill Is Little More Than an Imposing Title and a Pious
Prayer," PM had declared.[100] A freeze on prices with no ceiling on
wages was not even a stopgap to inflation.[101] So when Mayor Fiorello
La Guardia of New York wanted raises for the firemen and police,
Baruch snapped back that next in line would be the white-collar
workers.[102] Under the existing legislation, he forecast that wage increases were inevitable. As the Farm Bloc flatly admitted: "Everybody else is doing it." [103]

Bad as the Stabilization bill was, without Baruch it could have
been worse. Chief Justice Vinson once recalled that any advocate
of any kind of control had to fight for his life in each Congress against
"crippling amendments." Here Baruch exerted all his influence and

performed a great service. But he could not withstand the tidal wave of public opinion.[104]

At its worst, the Stabilization bill was better than the congressional bill of the summer of 1942 which Baruch had been privately told to "blast out of the water," Roosevelt secretly nodding his approval as Baruch damned the measure as a "weakling" and demanded all-out controls and authority. He wrote to Mrs. Roosevelt that he did not know whether the President had seen a plan for holding the inflation in control which he had submitted.[105] He knew the ways of politics — to ask for twice as much as you hoped for and to compromise on half.

He wrote Senator Byrd in June of 1942 pointing out that it was too late to establish a ceiling over prices and wages. There were still other plans that could be adopted.[106] If his master plan was scrapped, he was ready with something else.

Price fixing, he would sometimes say, was like a four-legged chair. It would not stand on two, or even three. One leg that had been left off was the freezing of wages. Nor were there enough increased taxes to siphon off the surplus buying power. Prices had taken a four-point leap after passage of the Stabilization Act. Builders could not build houses, but landlords could chisel on rents. The GI might have his "Bill of Rights," but the $2000-house, complete with furnace and plumbing, that he could have purchased with his savings at the beginning of the war, cost $7000 or $8000 when he came home. War loans might be oversubscribed, but it was the banks which lent billions for their purchase, and all too often buyers would sell out their holdings on the eve of the next drive. What use thrift when the dollar was being devalued by the minute, and the only alternative was to bid up prices by converting savings into luxury goods?

Later, in acclaiming Vinson for his work as Economic Stabilizer, Baruch only reflected that with such a bad law the marvel was that the results were as good as they were. He stolidly continued his own pushing, urging, for instance, that the production and distribution of food be in the hands of one man who would have under him all industries and people dealing with food. He recommended that Eric Johnston be appointed to supervise civilian needs and rationing. Federal licensing of all sellers and food distributors, he thought, might break the back of the black market. Inflation was no transitory thing. Without controls, it would be an ever-growing problem. The

only improvement over the First World War was that by law both
the buyer and the seller above the fixed price could be punished.
In fact, neither usually was.

The question of demobilization when the war should be finished
was the next major problem to which Baruch turned his attention.
His report on this subject, in concept and execution, was less successful than his surveys of the past. One reason was that both officialdom
and large segments of the private citizenry had developed a full-sized
case of "peace jitters" almost before the first American army touched
foot on European soil. With objectives gained ahead of schedule,
people were slackening down just as the need rose. Cutbacks had
begun as early as 1943 and reached their height in 1944. There was
tragedy in this foresightedness, for the Hürtgen Forest, the Ardennes,
and the horrors of the Battle of the Bulge lay in the future.

As Baruch and John Hancock observed, it was even more difficult
to demobilize intelligently than to mobilize effectually. In a sharp
exchange with curious Congressmen, Baruch pointed out that he had
no advance knowledge of when the war would end, but that someone
knew.

"Who was that?" came the innocent inquiry.

Baruch answered, "God, but He won't tell me." [107]

Nevertheless, on November 7, 1943, official announcement was
made that Baruch was to handle the war-contracts revision task. This
climaxed a series of letters in which Baruch assured Byrnes that he
and Hancock were willing to assist with demobilization problems.
They were ready to begin their study but would have to be free to
select their own assistants. Mr. Byrnes could, if he wished, assign the
whole job to his own staff, employing the aid of Baruch and his men,
or give the Baruch group full responsibility to plan for the termination of contracts, the disposal of surplus property, the re-employment of war workers, the avoidance of postwar inflation; for demobilization, public works, reciprocal trade and Lend-Lease, as well
as the conservation of natural resources, the stabilization of the currency, and the national debt.

Byrnes made it clear that he wanted Baruch to do the job but
that the President had assigned the task to him. Any formal statement of policy would have to be submitted for his approval. He reassured Baruch, however, by reminding him that they always seemed

to agree on vital matters. As for Baruch's staff, there would be no restrictions except in the case of persons embarrassing to the President. Apparently this was a reference to Eberstadt, who was as conspicuous in the actual preparation of the report as he was inconspicuous in the publication of it. Eberstadt's first suggestion was that Baruch send a group to England to study its conversion and demobilization program.

Congress was being bombarded with questions. "If I am a contractor, how do I get my money to convert . . . when the government doesn't need my shells?" If you were a soldier, how did you get back your peacetime job in a plant that had not converted? How could expanded facilities be paid for? To whom should the government dispose of a surplus war plant — to the man who had expanded and been running it, or to his high-bidding competitor? If the war should end abruptly, how was payment to be made for unfinished contracts? For if the government made a guess and paid at once when the war ended, it would be defrauded; if there was too long a wait, reconversion would be stymied and the workers would be out of jobs. Unless a manufacturer knew how much he was going to get, he could not reconvert.

Byrnes knew that his job was to stop undue cutting back of production at the same time as they planned for demobilization. So long as the fighting continued, war production had first priority. Hence, he issued orders closing down the race tracks, and, with no advance knowledge of the atomic bomb, moved to redirect the whole war machine against Japan.

Men were free now to look to the future, and although in September 1943 Baruch had feared a postwar depression, by the next summer he was convinced that there would not be one. Half the world awaited rebuilding. America's productive capacity could perform yet another miracle. It would not be scrapped until peacetime industry was ready and able to provide jobs for all.

The "Baruch Report on War and Postwar Adjustment Policies" was issued on February 18, 1944. Hard on its heels came congratulatory words from James Bryant Conant on his splendid report as it appeared in the papers. Once more, the American public was in debt to Bernard Baruch.[108]

The report suggested sweeping plans for postwar demobilization, including a back-to-work program, ways and means of getting the government out of business, a tightening up of the entire war effort, a running survey of the war agencies, an extension of price control, priorities, and the requisitioning laws that were due to expire in 1944, and an extension of credit to small business and servicemen. It called for a survey of America's remaining war materials, metals, and planes. It advised that a Work Director be appointed to supervise the "human side of demobilization," and a Surplus Property Administrator who could sell much and early without disrupting trade; who would sell at the market price and apply the profits to the national debt; who would allow no sales speculation and no subjection of the interests of one part of the country to those of another, and, above all, no sales to speculators. Only the useless should be scrapped; all non-perishable items from outside the United States should be kept, in case of another war.[109]

The report further recommended the immediate drafting of a post-war tax law, so that the harassed businessman could look ahead and know what his taxes would be. It called for engineering on a backlog of public works, but no set public works program, as yet. Toward payment of our loans to our allies, Baruch suggested that we accept supplies of iron, oil, and copper, and stockpile them. He had no faith in any war to end war.

The heart of the plan was the program for contract termination, which Baruch always credited to John Hancock. If this had not been worked out, many persons would have faced 'bankruptcy.[110] Briefly, the formula called for the government to pay 100 per cent of the cost of completed items for which it had contracted and allow a maximum profit of six per cent on articles that were incomplete and two per cent on the leftover inventory. All government-owned material should be cleared out of the plants in sixty days. These sections of the plan were accepted as government policy even before the report was officially submitted.

Perhaps this action was premature. There was much muttering under the Capitol dome when details of the report appeared in the press two days before members of Congress were provided with official copies. Besides the expected outbursts by special-interest groups, Congressmen received the report with a cool hostility, which led one paper to suggest that Baruch should learn "how to merchandise himself to Congress." [111] Baruch's customary ability to deal with Congress indeed seemed to have deserted him. Even Arthur Krock deplored the report's timing, coming at a moment when the duel between the President and Congress was so intense.

Nationally, and even internationally, the plan aroused controversy. It was acclaimed as a sound approach by such "liberal" publications as the *New Republic*, the *New Masses*, and the *New Leader*, and damned by the St. Paul *Union Advocate*.[112] It was condemned by *The Nation* for the Victorianism of its "pious hopes," and by *PM* for favoring a shutdown of the war plants that Henry Wallace wanted kept open for full employment.[113] In turn, *New Masses* denounced the "certain stripe of liberal" that denounced the Report.[114] Fiscal reformers charged it with "eroding the ideal of public responsibility in the federal government"; but such papers as the New York *Journal-American*, the New York *Herald Tribune*, and the Washington *News* saw it as three-dimensional, tough-minded, and fair in its striving to protect the government, the war contractors, and the "American way." [115] To many it seemed an insurance policy against postwar dangers.

On February 22, Senator Walter George revealed plans for an Office of Demobilization, incorporating some of Baruch's ideas but permitting the President to name the men to carry them out. Yet it was three months before the congressional committee on the matter was ready even to make recommendations; and during this time the whole question had degenerated into a party fight, with Senator Taft joining the Democrats on Baruch's side. John Hancock was appropriately named chairman of the Contract Termination Board, and William Clayton was put in charge of a Surplus War Property Administration. Baruch found this legislation a formless production. He blamed himself, because he had not convinced officials of how the work should be done.

By March, the New York *Daily News* was commenting: "There are many recommendations in the Baruch-Hancock reports on manpower and reconversion which have never been implemented." Congress was thinking of a long summer recess, others said.[116] Two days later came the announcement that Congress was working on a compromise on the Baruch proposals.

Baruch had been aware from the first, of course, that he had no authority to unravel but only to recommend.[117] As John Hancock had put it, their job was only to develop policy for operating plans.[118] But time was pressing. There had been half a dozen surveys and as yet "no co-ordinated set of plans." [119] Overnight the Navy canceled an aircraft contract, and the workers were told to get out. The War Production Board was doing nothing to find out what plants were going to close.[120] A demobilization director was not to be appointed; Secretary of Labor Perkins was not interested. On June 12, Byrnes announced that the postwar adjustment unit under Baruch was to be discontinued, although Baruch was to remain as a special adviser.

A month earlier Baruch had warned Byrnes that they must hurry, both to win the war and prepare for the peace.[121] Little had happened. The Baruch-Hancock report was fading from memory. Restively, Hancock entreated Baruch to urge Congress to put through the contract termination plan as soon as possible, without change.[122] Every plan could be improved if you had time, but there was no time. Baruch went into action. On June 15 the St. Louis *Star-Times* announced that "Baruch Blasted Reconversion Lag, Got Action." [123]

Slowly Congress moved into higher gear. The contract-termination plan was passed. Nevertheless, as Baruch ruefully admitted later, this was the only part of the program that was really adopted. "Congress threw open the doors protecting the vaults of the Treasury," and it was later contended that the nation had lost billions by not following Baruch's advice.[124] But, as General Marshall wrote Baruch, little could be accomplished until after the elections.[125]

This was unhappily true. Little could be done during the summer of 1944. Yet Baruch's personal influence was perhaps at a higher point than before, despite the cartoon in the Cincinnati *Enquirer* of January 26 to the effect that Dr. Baruch did not take mental cases like the New Deal.[126]

"Baruch Finally Gets In," ran a headline in *Pic* in February. If he had got "in," which was problematical, it was because he stuck to his guns and spoke what was on his mind. The New York *Journal-American* forecast the emergence of "a new crew of conservatives," Baruch among them; [127] and from the other side, Dr. Alvin Johnson, head of New York's New School for Social Research, called him "the only man my individualistic democracy ever recognized as chief." [128] The Denver *Post* wondered, "What Do Puzzled Nations Do Who Don't Have Any Bernard Baruch?" [129]

Once again Baruch cut a conspicuous figure in Washington. His swinging stride as he sprang from his chair and restlessly paced the floor, his mobile face, one eyebrow cocked, one corner of the mouth uptilted, his vigorous gestures with his glasses or waving an Egyptian cigarette — recalled what Clemenceau had once said of him: that "you couldn't overlook his distinction in any company." [130] His brother wrote happily from the Embassy in Brazil that he was enjoying the prestige of being the brother of Bernard M. Baruch.[131]

He was relaxed, as he was apt to be when things went his way. He could take time to quip, "As long as a nation continues to make fascinating hats, it's not in danger." [132] Or he could lean back and muse on his country, "and the path that was entered upon only 150 years ago — a little more than twice my own age. How young she is . . . Soft? Who dares say that? When did we ever fail to fight?" [133] He could even pen a line to Stuart Symington on how pleasant his good manners were.[134]

A year before, he had virtually refused to discuss the oncoming peace. "As we say down South," he would drawl, "let's catch our rabbit before we stew it." [135] Now, in 1944, he wrote to Cordell Hull that he felt war production was at last on the right road.[136] This was an understatement. Nothing, perhaps, had cheered him more than a letter from Lieutenant General Jacob L. Devers from Italy in May, telling him that the American supplies were so excellent they were cheered by the troops as the rounds of ammunition went over their heads.[137]

Now his thoughts were on the coming peace.[138] He could conjecture as to what countries' manufacturing facilities should be rebuilt first — those of the countries that were the most ready, or of the countries in the greatest need.[139] A system of priorities would have to be evolved.[140] He pleaded before the New York Herald Tribune Forum that autumn for "a world unity in which all can work," echoing Henry Wallace's hope that "supplying everyone who needs it and who is willing to work, even including the Hottentots, with a quart of milk a day, might prove an economic and social advantage."

"We failed the last time because we did not enforce the peace . . . This time we must be prepared to enforce the peace with arms and men, as well as international authority." [141]

But the war was not yet over.

Byrnes was warning against the exodus of workers from the war plants.[142] Marshall was exasperated that the War Production Board, despite the opposition of Patterson and Forrestal, was advising demobilization and relaxation of controls. Production was lagging,

which hurt the Army's procurement.[143] All this was in the summer
of 1944. Baruch had foreseen these difficulties during the previous
February, warning Krug that there must be no cutbacks until the
military gave the word.[144]

He wrote Marshall that three times he had halted the country's
peace jitters.[145] Meanwhile he hammered away at his trouble-shooting. Having promised General Marshall to keep an eye on the situation of supply, in October he advised the authorities on problems
connected with shells, trucks, and tires and remained in constant
touch with Washington.[146] He was able also to iron out several rows
between such powerful figures as Jeffers, Dewey, Patterson, and
Forrestal.

And he advised the President.

It had taken a long time, and Baruch had won his way by charm
rather than force.[147] Proof that Baruch was really on the way "in"
came with an ambiguous telegram from the White House in the
summer of 1943: "Keep right at it. Some day you will grow up." [148]
It was not easy for Baruch to be a hair shirt or a messenger boy on the
sidelines. He had to fight off not only enemies but friends and well-
wishers who shrank from the spectacle of his humbling himself to
exert influence.

More was at stake than his dignity. He measured every pound of
rubber as the life of a man, and was bitter because of the cost to the
country of Sidney Hillman's repeated determination that no "Baruch
man" should have anything to do with the war program. "God only
knows what this cost us in blood, sweat and tears," he once burst
out.[149] If he could only save one life, he was going to keep trying.[150]
And he refused to engage in the quarrels that seemed to be breaking
out all around him.[151] All he wanted, he often said, was to give good
advice, and he would humble himself as much as necessary to get a
hearing from the President.[152] When the going became too rough,
he had his sanctuary. "I'm going back to the canebrake," he would
say, "and hide in the long grass." [153]

And now as the war roared to a climax, Baruch could see Franklin
D. Roosevelt in perspective — as a great humanitarian who had had
the imagination and courage to do what had to be done during the
black days of depression; the vigorous leader of a successful war; and
now the architect of the coming peace.[154] The President had both
the imagination that could conceive Lend-Lease and the shrewd
qualities of manipulation that worked it through.

Baruch was at last beginning to appreciate the genius of Franklin Roosevelt. But it had taken Roosevelt equally long to appreciate fully the talents of Baruch, or to answer the clamor of the press, dating back to 1941, that they be put to work.[155]

Perhaps it was this new closeness with the President which kept Baruch's lips relatively sealed during the campaign and the travesty of a convention that had preceded it and nominated Harry S. Truman for the Vice-Presidency. Baruch admired Truman's effective work in the Senate. In fact had it not been for Baruch, Truman might not even have been a Senator in 1944, much less a candidate for the Vice-Presidency. For Truman had not had the President's backing in his senatorial campaign in 1940. Roosevelt backed Governor Lloyd Stark. Baruch had come to the rescue and, according to his own testimony, was the largest single contributor to Truman's campaign.[156] However, Truman squeaked through by so tight a margin that his colleague Senator Bennett Champ Clark brought him to Baruch's quarters to thank him. This Truman did "most graciously, and said he would never forget it as long as he lived." According to Baruch, he had forgotten it scarcely four years later.[157]

That James F. Byrnes, by virtue of his services, knowledge, ability, and party record, was the logical man for Vice-President in 1944 seemed clear to almost everyone except the convention bosses. Afterward Baruch observed that the people did not amount to much if everything had to be "cleared by" Sidney Hillman.[158] The Negro vote and the influence of the CIO, Baruch thought, defeated Byrnes.[159] Disappointed as to the vice-presidential nomination, Baruch mailed checks to such Senators as he thought deserving of support — Murray of Montana, Maloney of Connecticut, and Johnson of Colorado, among others.[160]

His heart ached for Byrnes, whose long record of public service had been ignored, who had had the courage and perhaps the misguided judgment to warn a certain well-known White House figure, "Harry . . . keep the hell out of my business," and who had yet made compromises on behalf of the New Deal that must now rankle sorely.[161] Baruch wrote Byrnes a warm letter of encouragement and confidence that personal disappointments would not down such a fighting spirit.[162]

The campaign ground on to its end, and those who knew, including the vice-presidential candidate himself, sensed that it was Harry S. Truman running his first presidential race against Thomas E. Dewey.

Baruch had noticed nothing more than that the President was a tired, overworked man. But in fact the light was fading fast.[163] Roosevelt's brief flare-up of energy during his Teamsters Union speech quickly flickered out; the strain of the campaign told grievously on him. Marriner Eccles was appalled by his appearance in November. He was "haggard and drawn," finding obvious difficulty with his articulation. "Often . . . his mind seemed to wander off into secret recesses, as if to escape from the pounding of the words it heard." At best, he was exhausted; at worst, in "desperate physical condition." [164]

The drama was playing out. Never in American history had there been an inauguration like Franklin Roosevelt's last, which took place on the South Portico of the White House instead of at the Capitol as usual. The tension was heightened by the fears of the days preceding. Miss Perkins saw Roosevelt a few days earlier, his face gray, his clothes flapping on his gaunt frame. "You felt his enormous fatigue." He was resting his head on his hand, and brushed aside her immediate question. "Let's talk about it another day," he said. She was frightened. Yet by Inauguration Day he had braced up; he still had extraordinary recuperative powers.[165]

None but could feel the "high emotional drama" of that gray day in January, with the evergreens black against the white snow and the Washington Monument cut sharp against a dull sky. Around the White House snow lay "in a ruled line on the privet hedge" and heavy upon the magnolia leaves. It weighted the awnings and dripped wetly down the necks of Harry Hopkins and "a figure so familiar at Presidential inaugurals as to be almost a part of them — Bernard Baruch." Harry Truman leaned gaily against a pillar and quipped: "So I'm on the pay roll once more." For a moment the sun sprang out and flashed against Mrs. Roosevelt's corsage of violets.

The President's taut face relaxed. He smiled. In a familiar gesture, he threw aside his Navy cloak. Then he spoke his few words — half fireside chat, half prayer. One writer thought they should be carved around a memorial.[166]

Time was running out fast now.

As Baruch was leaving the inaugural ceremony, the President said: "Don't leave town. I want to see you." [167]

Their appointment was set for Monday morning at twelve o'clock. Stettinius was there and Hopkins. As for Roosevelt, Baruch could only think, "The poor fellow! He was so very tired." [168]

The President said, "I want you to go to see Winston. I'll have a memo for you," and surprisingly Harry Hopkins added, "The only man who can talk to him is you." [169] Perhaps Baruch then remembered his Christmas message from Churchill: "It is always a pleasure to hear from you and usually wise to follow your advice." [170]

The Allies were dividing, even before the peace on which they must unite. One issue at point was the question of our retaining our wartime air routes, as General "Hap" Arnold hoped could be done. Russia, it was known, would not agree, but a plan could be drawn up and at least submitted to Russia for her approval or disapproval.

Another critical situation was England's shortage of food, and her fears of Russia. Baruch stressed that what was done about the Russians would be the key to the peace.[171]

On Germany Baruch could speak with authority — out of his background, his experience at Versailles. From the early days he had supported the strategy of beating Germany first, primarily by air power.[172] But the evidence is abundant that he regarded Germany both as the immediate and the potential enemy. The idea of building her up as an ally seems never to have entered his head. At this period, however, even Roosevelt was convinced of the necessity of destroying Germany militarily. As Mrs. Roosevelt has written, the President was determined that Germany should never make war again and that sentimental considerations should not make this possible. Germany must be made self-sufficient, but Europe must be freed from industrial dependence upon her. Baruch personally was certain that the Germans would try again.[173] He had no sympathy for the "Be Nice to Germany Boys." [174] In fact, at one misguided moment he had even given support to the abortive Morgenthau Plan for the complete industrial dismemberment of the German nation. Now, as in the First World War, he saw opportunity to "fix" Germany and also Japan so that they could never make war again and their sweatshop competition in the labor markets could be halted. He had no omniscient vision of the United States a decade later building the erstwhile enemies into rival economies. Instead, he saw them out of the market with an ensuing new era of prosperity for the victorious United States.[175]

It was not that he desired completely to stifle German trade. But he saw it as utterly immoral to rebuild Germany and Japan and risk a third world war, all that we might find market outlets for our machine tools and scrap iron. Germany had no normal ways to which to return except the ways of war.[176] Baruch carefully studied a memorandum from Sam Lubell suggesting that five years of forced labor for the Nazi soldiers would effectively shear the German birth rate for the next world war, and arguing that German heavy industry was not essential to Europe.[177]

Baruch's sentiments at this time were little different from those that were to underlie the agreements soon to be made at Yalta. He was, however, right in his feeling that German industry soon would be built up, whether the United States government willed it or not. He knew that after the First World War the Young and Dawes plans had restored Germany industrially at the expense of the Allies, but he agreed with John Foster Dulles that now the Allies must distinguish between Germany's moral guilt and her ability to pay.[178] If reparations were demanded, Germany would have to be rebuilt — or reindustrialized.[179] If German labor were used to rebuild the war-devastated countries of Europe, it would be a menace to the free labor of those countries.[180] A few months later, the Overseas News Agency would report that, "backed by the influx of cash of American business," German heavy industry and electrical manufacturing plants were recovering at a dizzy pace and Germany was outstripping the United States in the reconversion race.[181] Less than ten years from the day when Baruch and Roosevelt discussed means of keeping Germany from ever making war again, a headline read, "German Army Will Rise from Ashes of Defeat." [182]

Baruch foresaw another development in the future. As early as September 1944 he had written "Pa" Watson that if Germany were occupied by three different governments she would be submitted to three different experiments, and the United States would be blamed. In the end, he was convinced, such occupation would only sow the seeds of controversy between the recent Allies. The partition of Germany seemed to him the logical consequence of Russia's idea of splitting the enemy state into its component parts.

Baruch's conclusions here are typical of his strengths and weaknesses. Logically, of course, he was right, and it has been part of his hold over the public that his point of view has so often typified what the shrewd, intelligent but uninformed man-in-the-street was thinking. Common sense, on the other hand, did not always make good sense where international policy was concerned. Baruch did not have the private knowledge of the State Department. He was correct in his belief that the Germans could and would play her former enemies off against each other, but he apparently did not see that the zoning formula at least kept Russia out of Western Europe.

However, Baruch did know that Germany would ultimately have to be brought into the European community, if only to be watched in the age of mass destruction. The Ruhr could not be obliterated; it was vital for European defense.[183]

Baruch had long dreamed of two great Supreme Economic Councils: one, a kind of planning board in the United States under James F. Byrnes, to sift facts and recommendations for the coming peace conference; the other, for the reconstruction and needs of Europe as a whole — foreshadowing, perhaps, the Marshall Plan. America was to be represented upon this European council, where each nation could make its demands upon Germany, and each ascertain what it was able to contribute to the total welfare. Such a program for the recovery of Europe as a whole, Baruch thought, would raise the morale of people all over the world.[184] Through lack of planning they were being unnecessarily starved, ravaged with needless hardships.

By April Roosevelt was starting to implement the American plan. In a memo written in 1945, Baruch says that he did not discuss the European plan with Churchill because he had not yet taken it up with President Roosevelt.[185] Yet, Secretary of State Stettinius, writing in 1949 his own version of the 1945 interview, recalled that he specifically requested Baruch to help persuade Winston Churchill of the need for such a council in world organization.[186]

This, then, was Baruch's mission, or the beginning of his mission. And he was earmarked for a larger role later on — to help frame the peace for the new world that was to come. Roosevelt assured him, "You're going to sit right next to Papa." [187]

It was the President who left Washington first, for Yalta. And back from Yalta came those ghastly pictures with the look on Roosevelt's face so like that of Wilson in his last years. Jonathan Daniels was given the task of sifting through the pictures, releasing only the least shocking to the public.[188]

There has been, and there will be, adequate discussion of Roosevelt's role at Yalta. Whether the United States was "sold down the river," or whether the President did what could be done face to face with a Russia already in possession of Eastern Europe and holding most of the cards, Averell Harriman has assured us that Roosevelt's eyes were opened during the Conference, and that he returned showing "a good deal of concern," "his Dutch jaw set." When Harriman urged a firmer attitude toward the Soviets, there is evidence that Roosevelt took the advice.[189]

American servicemen in England in that April of 1945 saw a very tall, very erect old man, well past the usual retirement age, who took their salutes in the uniform of a general. After him trotted a young woman, also in uniform. They were Baruch and Blanche Higgins. Civilian travel having been precluded, they had not only been supplied with the Commander-in-Chief's plane, *The Sacred Cow*, but with the army uniforms. They inspected army posts, winding up at Patton's headquarters. But mostly they were in London.

This bombed and gutted London was not the city Baruch had known before, but he did not let sentimentality deter him from his mission. Out of delicacy, perhaps, he declined the offer of Claridge's to write off his expenses. "I want my bill," he said. "I'm not a guest of the British government." If he wanted to, he mused, he could probably charge up a million dollars in expenses.[190]

Spring bloomed, hiding the rubble and the scars. Baruch set up his "office" on a bench in Hyde Park, and there talked with two GI's about their future jobs and their hopes for postwar life. Later he established himself on a park bench in the occupied sector of Germany, despite a Nazi threat to kill him. He quietly continued on the work of his "mission." Although to Winston Churchill's concern for "the poor flaxen-haired children of Germany" he replied, "Think of the children of England," [191] Baruch was not insensitive to Churchill's and Britain's very real fears. His own thinking was undergoing a sea change and he came to see that there must be an easy flow of goods, men, and money throughout Germany.[192] In the report that he was preparing, he wrote that British officials feared Russia more than anything else.[193]

Baruch knew — all knew — that the war was nearly over. In the United States, Roosevelt was leaving for Warm Springs. "The war in Europe will be over by the end of May," he told Secretary Perkins.[194] Baruch was already receiving his accolades. Typical was a letter from a member of the War Production Board saying that to many of his colleagues Baruch seemed to epitomize what a patriotic citizen could accomplish outside of the armed forces.[195] He had saved 45 million dollars for his country in the First World War. Who could measure the value of his services this time?

Baruch wrote Colonel Stimson that he knew what the War Department had done, and that he liked to feel that he had had a part in it, to which Stimson replied, conveniently, that it had been a comfort to him to have Baruch's advice and assistance.[196]

On the evening of April 12, 1945, Churchill gave London's distinguished visitor a Cabinet dinner at "The Little Club" at the Savoy. There was an atmosphere of half-stifled excitement and joy. Victory was so near now.

Late at night Churchill and his friend Brendan Bracken left a weary Baruch at Claridge's. He retired immediately, leaving orders that his bell was not to be rung.[197]

Back at 10 Downing Street, Churchill immersed himself in work. After midnight, a secretary knocked and entered, a note in his hand. "Sir," he said, "President Roosevelt died a short time ago."

For five minutes Churchill remained silent, his face that of a man lost and alone. At last he said, "Get the palace." [198]

In the sitting room of Baruch's suite the telephone bell shrilled. Sleepily, the old man roused himself, as Higgins answered.

"Mr. Bracken wants to speak to you."

Baruch took the phone. "What's the matter, Brendan?"

"Have you heard about the President?"

"No."

"He's dead."

Baruch's hand dropped. Higgins picked up the phone. A moment later Churchill's voice was sounding. "What do you think we ought to do?"

"There's nothing to do but face it," Baruch said. "We've got to go on."

Churchill then asked Baruch if he thought he should fly over to the funeral. Baruch's answer was sternly negative. "You've got to stay here and run the show. You can keep the show together."

Baruch then notified Sam Rosenman, John Hay Whitney, and Ed Flynn, all of whom were in London. Flynn, on hearing the news, had a heart attack in his hotel room. Someone called and asked if Baruch

could take Flynn, Rosenman, and Elliott Roosevelt back with him
on the presidential plane. Baruch agreed. There was a clamor outside
his door. Slowly members of the American group in London began
to sift into the room, hovering about the bed of the tall old man as
if for support. "Now, boys, it's steady in the boat," Baruch said.[199]

In Moscow, Ambassador Harriman heard the news, and his heart
sank. At 2 A.M. in Stalin's quarters in the Kremlin the lights flashed
on and blazed into the night.[200] In the United States, glasses were
set down, the night clubs darkened; a crudely lettered sign went up on
a shop window, "Closed out of memory for FDR." [201]

In a London newspaper office, a weary cartoonist penned a wreath
of victory and laid it before an empty chair.[202]

The flags were lowering across the world. *The Sacred Cow*, wing-
ing its way across the Atlantic, was a part of that journey that was
carrying Franklin Roosevelt farther than Cairo or Teheran, farther
than that funeral train moving now through a weeping country. For
Roosevelt, it was a journey into the hearts of his people, deeper perhaps than any but two or three other Presidents had penetrated
before him. Roosevelt had fallen as much a casualty of the war as
if he had fallen on the battlefield, as Wilson had fallen, and Lincoln.
Now he was entering that shrine where Americans keep the memory
of their sons, dead that they might be free.[203]

In Washington the greatest of all Roosevelt's great crowds had
gathered, 500,000 standing in silence as the black train moved out.
"Many wept. The muffled roll of black-draped drums and the slow
cadence of marching feet" were like distant thunder.[204]

At Hyde Park the few stood for the many: the tall widow in her
black veil; Elliott, the one son among the four who could be there;
James A. Farley; the President of the United States, Harry S. Truman; and a future President, Dwight D. Eisenhower. Behind Farley
was a tall, gaunt man with white hair, "who was stopped time and
again for identification before an Army officer recognized him and
took him in tow. It was Bernard M. Baruch." [205]

There was the sound of a child weeping. From the distance the
President's Scotty, Fala, howled dismally. The three volleys sounded
with finality. Franklin Roosevelt was sleeping where he had wanted
to sleep, in the rose garden below the windows of his home, beneath
the soil of his Hudson River Valley, the land of all he had loved the
most, beneath the sun and the wind and the blue sky.[206]

Afterward, back in the President's room, Baruch in the big chair and Sam Lubell at the window, Lubell said, "If all the world would carry out their feelings today, we would have peace in the world."

And Baruch answered, "We'll go on, just as we have before." [207]

A New York *Herald Tribune* reporter tapped out a single line: "The story is over." [208]

20

FROM COSMOS TO CHAOS

Harry S. Truman looked small and uncertain in that presidential chair. He sat before the desk in the oval office, his back to the sun and the iron gates where the people had massed in silence through the April night. "Here was change," [1] the greatest change, perhaps, since Lincoln had died. As he has said, the sun and the moon and the planets had fallen on him. The prison of the Presidency had closed around him. Scarcely fifteen hours before, history had broken into a gathering in Speaker Sam Rayburn's office, and Truman, dazed after his summons to the White House, had placed a call to his own apartment.

"Hey, Dad, hurry home and dress," his daughter pleaded. "You'll make us late for the party."

"Yes, Margaret, I know," he answered heavily. "Let me speak to your mother." [2]

He had been sworn in at nine minutes past seven on the evening of April 12, 1945, under the portrait of Woodrow Wilson in the Cabinet Room of the White House and before the assembled Cabinet officers, the taut and drawn Harry Hopkins, himself just out of a hospital bed, the cameras freezing all the faces into perpetuity. "Everyone was crying and carrying on. None of us," wrote John Hersey afterward, "could believe that F.D.R. was gone." [3] It was as if a light had gone out. You had the uneasy feeling of an era ended.

The morning came. The crowds had melted silently into the darkness. America stood alone now in the raw daylight, with a war to win, a peace to make, and the long days ahead of soul-searching and stocktaking. [4] Harry S. Truman was President of the United States.

It was true that he had "never wanted to be President," that he was the "happiest man in the world as Senator from Missouri." But he had taken his assignment just the same, and although shaken and awed as all were at the death of his chief, he has admitted that he knew it was coming. "After Yalta, I knew, but I was stunned just the same. I had hoped for more time, to get ready, to study up on things . . ." [5]

Here was a key to the man. No man of our time has invoked more controversy than Truman, but friend and enemy alike have agreed that he had not a lazy bone in his body, and that he used everything he had. Often the results were extraordinary. Frances Perkins has recalled that during the depression he served under her office as unemployment director of Missouri and emerged as "one of the best operators in the Labor Department and one of the most intelligent." She offered him a promotion but was not surprised to find that he had been "tapped" to run for Senator.[6] "Always, he surprised us. He was a superior Senator." His Truman Committee had saved some "fifteen billions in waste, delay and inefficiency." [7]

He was well read. As Senator he had taken night classes in law at Georgetown University and carried his books home afterward.[8] Now he was doing his homework in the White House, leaving the office at night with briefcases bulging under his arm. David Stowe, who as an administrative aide played much the same role in the Truman Administration as was later to be taken by Sherman Adams under President Eisenhower, has recalled that his capacity for learning and absorption was "tremendous." Stowe would "brief him," packing an uncanny amount into three minutes and, by test, Truman could reel it all off word for word an hour or so later.[9] When insomnia dogged him, he would read himself to sleep with the Federal budget.

He had need of all that he could learn — and what he did learn may have staggered him. Averell Harriman has a clear memory of his saying, "I'm just not up to this job." [10] No one had told him anything. He knew nothing about Yalta, and what many thought were his mistakes at Potsdam were an implementation of that earlier tragic conference. No one had told him of the premises upon which the Yalta agreements were conceived. He had only a rudimentary knowledge of the most terrible secret of all. As chairman of the Truman Committee, he had tried to investigate some of the gigantic expenditures of the scientific and warmaking branches of the government. Stimson had gone to him to say, "I can't tell you what it is, but it is the greatest project in history . . . we . . . would appreciate your not going into those plants." [11]

Now, in a room with Eisenhower, Marshall, and James F. Byrnes, he sat to weigh the question — American lives against Japanese lives, the more than one million Allied casualties which the Army estimated it would take to invade Japan, or the unknown number of dead at Hiroshima and Nagasaki. Truman faced it with the same dogged courage with which, in the battle of "Who Run" in the First World War, his Missouri cursing had driven his men back to their guns.[12] Agreement was reached by the four men present, but it was Truman who had to make the decision to drop the bomb. "The bomb was used," he said, "only to save the lives of thousands of young Americans." [13]

Bernard Baruch had been waiting to see him. Returned from his mission, he had resumed his seat on the bench in Lafayette Square, shaking his head and warming his bones under the horse-chestnut tree. To the White House aide Jonathan Daniels, he seemed a "well-advertised professional wise man who had much to give, but nothing to ask for himself." [14]

Baruch was waiting, well stocked with his own ideas for the restoration of a normal economy. He felt that money should be lent to small businesses, and that there should be a survey of the nation's resources — a matter which Mrs. Roosevelt told Mr. Truman she believed Baruch should undertake. Why, he wondered, should surplus copper, zinc, lead, and iron be sold when there would soon be a shortage in the United States? [15] Most of all, he wished that he could talk over with Eisenhower the question of the German occupation before the General went back overseas.[16]

These were some of the problems Roosevelt left behind him. The balance of power had shifted now from Hyde Park to Independence, Missouri; but Baruch could remember that Truman had written at the time of his nomination that he would be calling on him for advice as usual.[17] Later, however, Baruch doubted that anything of real value could have been done in the confusion after Roosevelt's death.

Bernard Baruch called at the White House on Tuesday, May 5, 1945. Again Edward Stettinius was there. Baruch succinctly explained that he had gone to London at the request of President Roosevelt and that Mr. Stettinius and Harry Hopkins had suggested that certain matters be taken up with Churchill. He discussed the Army Air Transport system, and his conviction that civilian lines could use the old war routes. Some program for joint operations, he felt, might be worked out with the British and perhaps with the French. But if the United States delayed, the routes would probably be divided up.[18] He had so informed General Marshall, General Arnold, and Admiral King, and, as a result of his discussions with Churchill, had offered his services in this connection to Secretary Forrestal.[19] He had discussed the British needs and fears for the future with unqualified frankness; and he believed that he had left Britain prepared to do more for herself and to ask less of us.[20]

He then handed over his report, insisting that both Truman and Stettinius read it while he was present. Once the President looked up sharply and asked how many people had seen it.

"Only you two," Baruch said.

"I don't want you to give it to anybody," the President said. He wanted to make it the basis of his policy.[21] Baruch complied, and to this day the report has never been made public. Officially this was the last heard of Baruch's "mission," although the essence of his proposals was adopted later, with no credit given to the author.

The face of the world had altered; but the only instrument of international action, the United Nations, had no knowledge of the new force that had already ended one age and inaugurated another.[22] The delegates at the San Francisco Conference shrank from any idea of enforcing peace by arms, a preliminary Senate poll having already rejected the concept of an international police force.[23] Not ideal goals but goals on which all could agree were their aim. Arthur Vandenberg, the Republican leader in the Senate, had worked through a resolution uniting his party in favor of "responsible participation by the United States in a postwar co-operative organization among sovereign nations to prevent military aggression and to attain permanent peace." [24] The "irreconcilables" had at least reconciled themselves to a new League of Nations.

Vandenberg said he was seeking the middle ground. But for a world newborn in violence there was no middle ground, no solid ground, nothing but quicksand, abysses, the horror of the unknown.

The San Francisco Conference was announced with a blare of journalistic trumpets. Although a generation of disillusionment had dimmed the idealistic fervor of 1919, there was a moving scene on the floor of the Senate as owl-eyed Vandenberg and the old-style Southerner Tom Connally, with his flowing white mane and frock coat, arose to take their leave. Tears shone in Connally's eyes. Vandenberg, also shaken with emotion, warned that they could not "chart the millenium," and begged for the Senators' prayers. Clapping, cheering men surged across the Senate Chamber to clasp the two delegates' hands. "America was going to San Francisco," Vandenberg wrote in the aftermath of that hour.[25] Yet, his optimism soon dimmed. Only one week had passed since the body of Roosevelt had been laid in the rose garden at Hyde Park. On that day Vandenberg had written: "We have . . . lost the strongest voice through which we could hope to argue Russia out of some of the mistakes it seems determined to make."[26] Even without foreknowledge of the atomic bomb, there seemed enough to darken his and Connally's thinking as their train moved westward. The President was dead. The "unseasoned" Secretary of State, Edward Stettinius, was thought to be a mere presidential messenger, without background, without experience, but with "every good intention."[27] Already, as in the First World War, the problem of a just peace for Germany was dimmed beside the problem of a *modus vivendi* with Russia. Sounding in Vandenberg's head were Franklin D. Roosevelt's last words to him: "Just between us, Arthur, I am coming to know the Russians better."[28]

Baruch was not with the delegation. Perhaps he was being kept on ice. Roosevelt, it was known, had "earmarked" him for the hypothetical peace conference of the future. Of the activities at San Francisco, he was informed only by the newspapers.

The surprise of the Conference was the underestimated "General Manager," Edward Stettinius, who, prompted by Vandenberg to "be a Secretary of State," stood up to the Russians "like a concrete column." Under his lead there was early proclaimed the new policy of "getting tough" with the Soviets, with Truman sounding the keynote.[29] In retrospect, the value of San Francisco seems to have been its revelations of the future — not of a new world order, but of the old power struggle. At San Francisco appeared the blueprint for the future Russian policy, the alternate blowing cold and blowing hot, the perpetual crises, the complete disparity between the personal characteristics of Russians like Molotov, "an earnest able man," and the aggressiveness of his public policy.[30] Twice in the first and third weeks of June, the Conference came to the brink of explosion.

"We can get along with Russia if and when we can convince Russia that we mean what we say," was Vandenberg's reflection. Yet, somberly, the Senator wondered how we could propose to entertain a "Peace Partnership" based on mutual faith with a country in which we had no faith. Everything, in the end, depended on the Soviet Union.[31]

And so, with the United Nations established, in the next month a final wartime conference was arranged in the outskirts of the ruined German capital. Eleven days after he had witnessed the signing of the Charter at San Francisco, President Truman set sail from Norfolk on the USS *Augusta*.

Could Truman win where Wilson had lost? Before Wilson had left for Paris, Frank Cobb had predicted to Baruch that his mission was already hopeless because of the compromises and promises that had been made before the Conference started. Was the Western position already at an impasse before Truman set out for Potsdam?

It had not taken a Churchill or a Baruch to see the Soviet Union with clear eyes before the war. But with Hitler's betrayal of his pact Russia necessarily became an ally of the West. It is difficult today to recapture the realities of that dawn of June 22, 1941, when German planes opened their bombardment of some "ten villages" in Russia.[32] The following day Winston Churchill expressed the inevitable in words which only he commands: "No one has been a more consistent opponent of Communism than I have for the last twenty-five years. I will unsay no word that I have spoken about it. But all this fades away before the spectacle which is now unfolding . . . We have but one aim . . . to destroy Hitler and every vestige of the Nazi regime . . . Any man or state who fights on against Nazidom will have our aid . . . The Russian danger is, therefore, our danger . . . the cause of free men and free peoples in every quarter of the globe." [33]

And as the bloody years of the Russian travail unrolled, many forgot the past, thinking only of what Baruch expressed to Roosevelt — that, after all, the Russians were killing more Germans than any other Allied power. Roosevelt might wonder what we were going to do about Russia when the fighting was over, but many succumbed to the popular delusion that we could keep Russia reasonable through a judicious use of American aid. America's first job was to win the war.[34]

The need of the present had to be weighed against the threat of the future. Men of foresight and good will differed among themselves and changed their emphasis from day to day. In 1943 Senator Vandenberg had urged that if we were to quarrel with our Allies we at least postpone it until after victory.[35] And in 1944, James Forrestal observed that if an American suggested action according to "the needs of our security he is apt to be called a god-damned fascist . . . while if Uncle Joe suggests that he needs the Baltic Provinces, half of Poland, all of Bessarabia, and access to the Mediterranean all hands agree that he is a fine, frank, candid and generally delightful fellow who is very easy to deal with because he is so explicit in what he wants." [36] When Sumner Welles had urged on Roosevelt before the invasion of Normandy, a "tougher" attitude toward Russia, the President had concurred, but Cordell Hull had "wanted to rely on the linger-and-wait policy." [37]

As the war neared its end these attitudes became even more confused and created the atmosphere in which the Yalta meeting was held and the "zones" of the Allies were established. As the triumph came still closer, the Russian attitude became ever stiffer and the doubts of the West more clearly expressed. It was in this atmosphere of fear and suspicion that the San Francisco Conference had met, and it was to dispel this black cloud that the President set sail.

Baruch mused darkly over Truman's mission. All history, he knew, told tales of such journeys in which dedicated men had set forth with a benevolent mission. Perhaps never had there been one with more possibilities than Truman's mission now.

Baruch could only give him his hopes and his prayers. He did not pretend to know the answers. He was only "a book of reference" in which you could discover what had transpired in the past. He had seen Wilson set forth and fail. He had seen Roosevelt die before the dream took life. Truman, he felt, would not fail the hopes of mankind.[38]

How much President Truman may have accomplished is still debatable, but the great hope was not fulfilled. The Russians showed no sign of change; and this, perhaps, convinced Truman at last that a strong balance of power was all that the Soviets would understand. Fear, distrust, and aggression, built up over the years, bred fear and distrust, and from them was spawned the Cold War of a divided world.

Bernard Baruch knew nothing of that July day in New Mexico when the light of a thousand suns blazed from the sands, and a wave of hot wind broke across the desert, and the earth trembled, and that first mushroom cloud "boiled up 40,000 feet into the air." He was not one of that stricken cluster of men who huddled on the desert to see the steel tower dissolve and the great crater form. He did not see that whole great stretch of sand wink and flash from the glass formed in the moment of that mighty explosion.[39]

Nor was he so fortunate as the American newspaperman William L. White, who had first heard of the "secret" in Leningrad in 1944, when his Russian guide cheerfully remarked on the similarity of Soviet atomic research to the Manhattan Project.[40] Yet, in a sense Baruch had had his own chance at a partnership with atomic power. Still in his files is a letter, dated in the nineteen-twenties, in which Charles H. MacDowell of Armour and Company describes a development in Germany even more revolutionary than the discovery of steam. It concerned the possible use of atomic energy in the manufacture of explosives and chemicals.[41] The inventor wanted backing, and MacDowell looked to Baruch, but Baruch was looking at the danger signals of 1929 and evinced no desire for participation.

There is no evidence that this memory lingered in Baruch's mind during the Second World War years, although subconsciously he may have recalled the proposal in a letter from Edward N. Hurley, written in 1929, that if the warmaking materials of the world were placed under some kind of international control, no nation would be able to sustain modern war. Or if the businessmen of the world could unite to withhold from any one nation three or four vital materials, that nation would be paralyzed and unable to make war. Here perhaps were seeds of the later Baruch Plan.[42] But his first inkling that some great project was in the wind came when Mrs. Roosevelt sent for him while the President was at Casablanca. A professor at New York University had told her that a vital secret process was being hamstrung by red tape. Was there anything Mr. Baruch could do? Then there had been the excited young man who charged in with James Bryant Conant to win Baruch's help on a similar mission. The youth said that the professors were trying to interfere with him, and that he couldn't proceed, and it took all of Baruch's and Conant's persuasiveness to calm him down.

Now Baruch was certain that some great drama was in the making, and he regarded it with respect. He could remember assigning Leland Summers to look into a possible "death ray" during the First World War. So when a builder wanted priorities and labor for a certain project in Tennessee, Baruch had asked no questions and pushed for the granting of the application.[43] Meanwhile, over at the office of the Army-Navy Munitions Board, Ferdinand Eberstadt, who was passing out priority orders, suddenly found that his chief aide, Colonel Leslie Groves, had been transferred. In due time, Groves reappeared with a general's star on his shoulders and asked for a ten-million-dollar priority.

"What's it for?" Eberstadt asked, reasonably enough.

"The Manhattan project."

"Manhattan project . . . I thought they gave up that tunnel digging." [44]

The "secret" was well guarded, at least from those on the inside. Years later when a congressional committee was investigating the qualifications of David Lilienthal to head the Atomic Energy Commission of the United States, the irascible Senator McKellar of Tennessee demanded: "Did you know that he never knew anything about atomic energy until the bomb fell on Hiroshima?"

"Neither did I," drawled Baruch. "That is just between you and me." [45]

So the bombs fell — on New Mexico, on Hiroshima, on Nagasaki — and amidst the reverberations, the formal surrender of Japan on September 1, 1945, came as an anticlimax. This was no peace, born above the rotting desolation of Nagasaki and Hiroshima.

Shortly after Hiroshima, Baruch met with President Conant and received a "briefing" on the whole atomic energy question. He was talking it over with Byrnes during the early winter of 1945–46 when the "Assistant President" put the question to him: Would he be the American representative on the United Nations Atomic Energy Commission? Instinctively, Baruch inclined to refuse.[46]

He knew the magnitude of the task. This was the climax of a series of pronouncements and edicts, beginning with President Truman's cryptic warning of the "tragic significance" of the bomb, after his return from Potsdam. Two billion dollars had been spent "on the greatest scientific gamble in history," and the United States had won.

But Pandora's box had been opened. The United States no longer faced the horizons of peace but horrors greater than the world had yet known. None who lived through it can forget the dead weight that crushed upon the people's hearts. Peace was not now just desirable; it was necessary. "It is an awful responsibility which has come to us," the President said. The bomb was "too dangerous to be loose in a lawless world." The United States and Great Britain must be trustees of this terrible force — they who had "the secret" of its production would not reveal it until means had been found to control the bomb "and redirect its force into the channels of mankind." [47]

This was the foundation of American atomic policy. That same month of August, 1945, came publication of the so-called Smyth Report. This was a description of the technical developments of the Manhattan Project, giving what its authors saw as a minimum of basic information, and what its detractors saw as a dangerous amount. The Report threw the whole question open for public debate and for action. On October 3, Mr. Truman had sounded another call, this time for the development of atomic power at home and for its control as a world weapon of war. Power to accomplish these ends, the President thought, should be given to a national Atomic Energy Commission.

No such commission yet existed officially. The nearest approach to it was a special committee named by Secretary of War Henry L. Stimson in the spring of 1945 to look into the question of the control of atomic energy. Among the members were Stimson himself, Byrnes, William Clayton, Bush, Conant, and Karl Compton, with technical assistance from a scientific panel composed of Dr. E. O. Lawrence, Dr. Arthur H. Compton, Dr. Enrico Fermi, and Dr. J. Robert Oppenheimer, then director of the laboratory at Los Alamos.

One point was clear. Discussion of the controversial aspects of atomic energy could not be delayed until the United Nations got into operation. On October 29, a Senate Committee on Atomic Energy was set up to study, investigate, and sift through the snowfall of bills on the subject. Senator Brien McMahon of Connecticut was named chairman, and a bill, originally written by him, seeking a system of domestic controls of atomic energy that would not hamstring world agreements was finally adopted in August 1946. A joint committee of Congress on the subject was also established.

Nor was this all. On November 15, 1945, Prime Ministers King of Canada and Attlee of Great Britain along with President Truman signed a joint declaration in favor of the exchange of "fundamental scientific information for peaceful ends with any nation that would fully reciprocate." To this end the heads of the three governments had called for the establishment of a United Nations Atomic Energy Commission to work out by stages the means of exchange of scientific information to assure the use of atomic energy for peace, and for safeguards to control the new discovery against use in war.[48]

The idea of "stages" in the revelation of atomic secrets was introduced as early as November by Secretary Byrnes. As no real world government would spring up overnight, some protection might be offered by having the work proceed by degrees. On December 30 in Moscow, Byrnes announced the agreement of the Soviet government to a projected United Nations Atomic Energy Commission, to be under the direction of the Security Council. This plan was forthwith endorsed by President Truman, adopted at the January meeting of the General Assembly of the United Nations in London, and clarified by a statement from Tom Connally, then chairman of the Senate Foreign Relations Committee. In performing its duties, such a commission would necessarily have to work within the framework of the United Nations. It could make recommendations, but it could not compel action from the Senate or the government of the United States.

Now the State Department took up the question. Early in January Secretary Byrnes announced plans for a thorough inquiry into the whole question, and named a special committee, composed of Dean Acheson, John J. McCloy, Vannevar Bush, James B. Conant, and General Leslie Groves to pursue the study. Meeting first on January 14, the group agreed that a report was in order, and also approved a plan to analyze and appraise all relevant facts and proposals. To draw up the report, the State Department's committee named David E. Lilienthal of TVA, Chester Barnard, Dr. J. Robert Oppenheimer, Dr. Charles Allen Thomas, and Harry A. Winne.[49] The group settled down to work. In the meantime, Baruch had entered the picture.

He knew that this was perhaps his last great call to duty, a summons that would write his name in the history of his time, yet he hesitated. Was he once more to shrink from responsibility? He asked himself over and over why he should be chosen. The more Byrnes urged him, the more difficult he thought the undertaking. For if Russia would not even allow American newspapermen behind the Iron Curtain, was it reasonable to assume that they would ever allow inspection of their atomic resources? [50]

He pondered at Hobcaw as the dilemma still pursued him. He sat on the gallery and, with his hearing aid carefully attuned, could hear the cries of the birds and the four rivers lapping the shore. His gaze lifted to the flag, waving above the pier. He could not escape the challenge of his time. There was neither peace nor rest for him in that soft air. Sometimes the shadow of Prince, his driver, or of Higgins' successor, Elizabeth Novarro, fell across his thoughts, and he slit envelopes and read the words from Byrnes or the President himself and pushed them aside. He tried to go on with his routine — walks through his private paradise, the white sand glittering around his shoes, shooting at Kingstree, struggling through the brush, on the horse and off again. Always the one question pursued him, even by night, as his tall figure trailed its shadow up and down the great upper hallway at Hobcaw.

Did they want him, or merely his name? Byrnes had spoken of the great difficulty of finding a man whom the Senate would accept. Baruch had heard that Henry Wallace wanted the position, and he shrank from the thought. This was merely a rumor, but Baruch did not know that; and again he remembered Byrnes's face as he had told him that he was the man. All he had been able to answer was that he could not help it, and then he had come South.

Why was he the man? He could look back to the generation of Lee — yet somehow he was more modern, more in tune with the time than many men of half his years. For, out of the violent heritage of the postwar South, he knew in his bones facts of life and death forever hidden to the ruling men born into the peaceful world at the century's turn. Life for him had always been a battlefield. Conflict was his natural element. Was he not in a sense even one with this young generation of the Atomic Age, whose nerves were tuned to crisis?

Of these days of "torsions" and struggle, he remembered afterward, "I was bitterly unhappy . . . my conscience smote me." At last he could stand it no longer, called for his car, and drove to Georgetown. There in the dingy sweat-smelling single telephone booth of the hotel he put in a call to Byrnes. He would come, he said.[51]

He knew that it was better to risk making mistakes than to be afraid of making decisions. He felt that he should give his last days to this gigantic and perhaps impossible task. Lots of men had wanted the job. He did not; he was seventy-five. The cause was of such importance to mankind, however, that he could not back away. He would approach the subject with an open mind and do the best he could. There need be no use of the atomic bomb in war if men would use their common sense.[52]

The press responded to his appointment with approval. The picture of the "tall old trouble shooter" assembling his colleagues and "the facts" for the "toughest job on the horizon" gave the public new hope in the midst of fear of a death force that might shatter continents. The little Macon, Georgia, *Telegraph* spoke for the nation, echoing what Winston Churchill had written to Baruch: "We will sleep more comfortably in our beds," said the *Telegraph*, "because clear-eyed Barney Baruch is on guard." [53]

Approval was not unanimous, of course. There was some question as to Baruch's age and his scientific qualifications; left-wing newspapers and organizations scored his associates as Wall Street bankers. Yet it was pretty generally believed that he would not only handle the interests of the United States ably but would be aware of his responsibility toward humanity. Furthermore, his name and person would dignify the cause he served. "No private citizen in this country enjoys the prestige both here and abroad that is Mr. Baruch's," the New York *Herald Tribune* said.[54]

Baruch inwardly felt that he needed prayers rather than congratulations. Although Senator Vandenberg had notified him that his name need not even come before a Senate committee if he would agree that no atomic disclosures would be made without proper safeguards and without the consent of Congress, Baruch asked the Foreign Relations Committee to hold up action on his name until he had looked into the question further.[55]

Baruch had good reason to weigh his decision. For, on picking up the paper on the morning of March 28, he had received a profound shock. Here was a "leaked" version of the so-called Acheson-Lilienthal Report on Atomic Energy — a working blueprint for atomic control, hailed by both the press and the State Department as the official American plan. Baruch felt that the ground had been cut out from under him. Was he to guide policy on this most terrible of all questions — or to be a mere instrument of policy already made? He wrote to President Truman to withdraw his name.

He did more. He called the White House. If this was to be the American policy, he wanted none of it. He was ready to withdraw. But he threatened further, allegedly telling the President that he would go to the people on the air. Only the combined persuasion of Mr. Truman and Secretary Byrnes retained Baruch's services.[56]

In retrospect, Baruch's fears seem exaggerated. He must have known that a State Department committee was preparing a report, but its release almost simultaneously with his own appointment did seem to reduce seriously his possible influence on the formation of policy.[57] His objections were by no means a matter of personal pride alone. The general view seemed to be that the report was "the American policy," despite its authors' assurances that they intended it "not as a final plan, but as a place to begin, a foundation on which to build." Nevertheless, a sudden reversal now on the part of the United States, Baruch felt, would arouse much suspicion as to our good intentions.[58]

The report was not the work of David Lilienthal alone. According to President Truman, it was based upon a directive written by him, and the actual authors were Dr. Charles A. Thomas, Harry A. Winne, Chester I. Barnard, and Dr. J. Robert Oppenheimer. That it provided a foundation for the later Baruch Plan is undeniable; Baruch himself subsequently congratulated Lilienthal on his work and the guidepost that it had been as he faced his own task.[59] However, he did wish that the Report could have been talked over with him before its release. His files show that letters poured in upon him urging adoption of the Report as it stood, but he generally left them unanswered.

Many of the basic formulas of the later Baruch Plan were in the Report: [60] the demand for "inspection" of atomic facilities and not just the outlawing of war or potential atom-war activities; the stipulation that any plant engaged in manufacturing of a dangerous nature must be owned and operated by an International Atomic Development Authority; the stipulation that at some point our manufacture of bombs must cease and the transfer of atomic information to the Authority proceed in stages; and, most important of all, perhaps, the recognition that there was no real military defense against the atomic bomb, and that to safeguard ourselves there must be no immediate surrender of atomic knowledge.[61]

Sitting on warm days on the gallery at Hobcaw, on cool days in the blaze of the sun, shielded by a glass screen, Baruch studied a full copy of the Report, which had at last reached him. Now and then he scrawled comments in the margins. He could agree with the authors that only international enforcement could make inspection work, but by what means? He pondered over the Report's description of the proposed International Atomic Development Authority, with power over licensing, designs, inspection, accountability, and changing needs. The Authority would be the only agency that could operate lawfully in the entire atomic field and would have ownership of all fissionable material, but Baruch wondered how an international body could own anything.

In the last analysis, the solution was not so much arms control as world government. Such leaders as Harold Stassen and Arthur Compton had already declared that the crash of the atom bomb had made world government ultimately indispensable, even if impossible in the immediate future.

Baruch noted in the Report that the authors had wondered what the Authority might do if it suspected activities in areas to which it had no right of access, and here he paused for thought. Why should there be no right of access? he wondered. There could be no Iron Curtain over atomic activity. Yet he knew that there was not much chance of Russia's agreeing to adequate inspection.[62]

The questions that he subsequently addressed to President Truman show a keen grasp of the fundamentals of the problem confronting him. Where, for example, was the Authority to derive its authority? If from the United Nations Security Council, would its acts then be subject to veto by any one of the Big Five? There must be no veto over the Authority's acts, Baruch warned the President. He had Conant's agreement on that.[63]

When the Report asserted that the United Nations Charter must include a plan to prevent seizure of atomic energy plants and other parts of the Authority's property, Baruch only wondered, What plan? With increasing respect he read the clauses declaring that the distribution of dangerous and non-dangerous plants in each country must be based on the requirements of security rather than on the country's needs; and that the first major task of the Authority must be to gain control of raw materials. America's monopoly of the bomb could not last. The whole world must have security against atomic attack. This fact was fundamental.[64]

But there was one basic difference between Baruch's ideas and the Lilienthal concept. The Lilienthal group saw the answer to the security problem as a dispersal of the Authority's manufacturing and atomic plants through the various United Nations. Protection would lie in the fact that if any one country seized the plants or the stockpiles within its borders, the other nations would have similar plants and stockpiles and thus be free for counteraction. Secret activities, which might be a continual source of fear and suspicion, would be replaced by developments known to the entire world. All secrets would be known to the International Atomic Development Authority. This was the answer of the Lilienthal group to the security question. It may have been a good answer. But it was not Baruch's answer.[65]

The Acheson-Lilienthal Report, as Baruch and Swope saw it, would have given too much away too quickly. Already there were "leaks in every direction." Nor had Truman, Attlee, and Mackenzie King been helpful when they made their great gesture about sharing atomic knowledge with the rest of the world. We should stand ready to destroy our bombs, Baruch agreed, but only as part of an entire program for atom control. Meanwhile, atomic secrets were not to be discussed during the negotiations.[66] "I am a tough baby," Baruch told the Boston *Post*, thrusting out his jaw. "I am not an Internationalist, neither am I an isolationist. But I am an American." [67] Russia was not going to get the American atomic secrets dished up on a silver platter. The bomb was a decisive weapon. We must not surrender it until all countries were prevented from doing what we would be giving up — bomb-making. He would be recreant to his trust if he decided otherwise. Even the Russian people, he felt, might someday thank him for saving them from the folly of their own reckless leaders. For might they not prefer guaranteed assurances of peace to their own ability to make war? [68]

Yet, in fact, our having the "secret" of the atomic bomb was only the matter of a head start. The basic principles traced back to the fifth century B.C. when Leucippus evolved the atomic theory. Scientists all over the world, including Russians, had made their contributions, and Baruch, no less than Senator Vandenberg, knew that any nation might pursue the secret and successfully make a bomb within the next few years, whether we liked it or not.[69] But for the moment we did have the head start, as well as the required vast resources, and a pool of skilled workmen.

Baruch was frank to admit that how much of a secret there now was no one quite knew. Soon, at the height of the negotiations, the Russians would let drop a code word, supposedly only known to those Americans who were intimately involved in atomic matters. It was characteristic of the situation that early the next year Baruch's testimony on leaks in atomic security, as presented before a "secret" session of the Senate Atomic Energy Committee, was "leaked" by publicity-hungry Senators all over the front pages.[70]

Baruch could not start with a clean slate. We could not, for example, treat all nations alike, for the fact was that England already had the necessary information. In fact Baruch and Byrnes had discussed how far this country should go in agreeing to England's establishing a bomb-making plant. No one yet knew all the secret agreements made between Churchill and Roosevelt at Quebec and Hyde Park. Yet any American policy would necessarily be built upon these agreements.[71] Britain was our "partner," without whose consent we had already agreed not to use the atom bomb.

The Acheson-Lilienthal Report had assumed the "sharing" of information from the beginning, although no one seemed to understand just how much or with whom information was to be shared. Under-Secretary of State Robert Lovett told Senators Vandenberg and Hickenlooper that there was never any intention to share knowledge on all phases of the atomic program. So it was understandable that the British were to become angry and restive as American policy alternately yielded and withdrew. As for the Russians, despite our protests of impartiality they were the angriest of all, for not only could they read American press assertions of where the real danger and the real enemy lay, but also they were naturally angry at the thought that we shared our knowledge with some allies while denying it to them.[72]

Baruch wondered at what juncture we would cease giving information to other nations.[73] He knew that scientists should enjoy free inquiry — but they must not be free to destroy life. He could share the wonder of Vandenberg as to whether the wit of man was even competent to deal with the murderous discovery.[74] He knew that as of 1946 the United States had nothing to fear, for it was still strong, but how long would this superiority last? He could have some understanding of Russia's contention that atomic controls vested in the UN would be a violation of the rights of sovereign states, but he could not feel that national sovereignty superseded the rights of men and women to live in peace. "I am at a loss to understand," he remarked, "why national sovereignty should be made such a fetish." [75]

Of one thing, however, Baruch was certain, and that was that when processed for peaceful purposes, atomic power was 75 per cent on its way to war. What could be denatured could be renatured; the same processes used to produce "peaceful" materials could also produce bombs. There must be international ownership of raw materials — on this Baruch had come to agree with the Acheson-Lilienthal Report. If all fissionable matter was internationally owned, how then could any one nation make a bomb? The hitch, of course, was the hair-line between permissible and forbidden activity. Men like Dr. Oppenheimer were "staggered" at the size of an Authority which would be necessary to make sure no fissionable material was diverted to dangerous activities. It would be easy enough to detect the fact of secret activity, but the question would be whether the activity was dangerous.[76]

As for Russia, so far as inspection went, she may well have decided that she had less to fear from atomic attack. The operation of a totalitarian state might be far more threatened by peering and prying than by the mere possibility of future war. In fact, the first report of the Atomic Energy Commission was to word the dilemma precisely: "It seems inevitable that any system of inspection adequate to insure the detection of clandestine activities will result in knowledge and inspection of activities unrelated to atomic energy." This could not be gainsaid, for all the assurances that neither any atomic Authority nor its personnel would disclose secret information gleaned during inspection.[77] The whole core of Baruch's plan would be "absolute ownership of all fissionable material everywhere by an international corporation, with full authority to tell each country how much it could make and where it could have its plants." Thus even governments which could solve the problem of how to apply atomic energy to industry would be "totally dependent upon a source of fuel which is not under their direct control, and which could conceivably be cut off upon a moment's notice." A country that refused obedience could be forcibly restrained by the Development Authority, which would not be subject to the veto and which alone could drop bombs.[78]

Within a few years, it was expected, heat, steam, all forms of energy and industrial power might evolve from atomic production. Atomic energy was the key to twentieth-century industrial advancement. The power struggle between the capitalistic and communistic nations was becoming blindingly clear. Would Russia turn over her potential industrial power to a world Authority dominated by a majority of competitive, capitalistic nations?

For Russia's atomic development might well be the fastest of all. Her atomic growth would leap forward, unhindered as it was in this country by competitive private enterprises of coal, oil, and water power. Russia might improve her standard of living while the United States lagged behind. Would Russia dare trust an International Atomic Development Authority to allow her to outstrip the very nation that had "given" her the power? She did not dare. She believed that a world Authority would forbid Russia to develop her atom-driven electric power plants, officially on the ground that they might be a war threat, actually because they might provide industrial competition to the capitalistic West. Had not the Western democracies already demonstrated that they could outvote Russia at will? "Atomic energy for peace" was far nearer than just around the corner, Baruch told Jacob Malik, and it would open up vast opportunities for Russia. He was later to tell Gromyko that America had no desire to form a bloc against Russia; if the Russian government went down, the United States would have the burden of 175 million people on its hands, to say nothing of the millions in the Balkan and Baltic countries. Yet Dr. Edward H. Condon of the Bureau of Standards said that Russia would be "stupid" to accept any plan that would empower a potentially unfriendly body to inhibit its industrial development in its own country. What of ourselves, if we had been in the minority? Would we have surrendered our potential industrial progress to a world Authority in which the Communists held control? [79]

The Soviets were suspicious. Not only the Russians charged the United States with bad faith for continuing to manufacture and stockpile bombs: this was the point of view of much of the liberal public opinion in the world. Einstein, the man who was the first scientist seen by Roosevelt in regard to the development of the atom bomb, now felt that our continuing to make the weapon was evidence of bad faith, particularly as we would only relinquish it when the world accepted our terms. Many agreed with him, as Baruch early foresaw that they would. He knew that one of the first questions the Russians would ask would be whether we were to keep on manufacturing bombs and what we would do with those already in our stockpile.[80]

The question then was Russian rights, as against world rights — and until Russia would surrender her right of veto, would the United States dare surrender the one weapon that, for a few years at least, might hold off "the next war"? It could well be that the inflexibility of Baruch's stand created an atmosphere in which the give-and-take of negotiation was impossible. "Adopt our plan," the Americans seemed to say, "or the United States will keep its bombs." To the *New Republic* this seemed a pretty barefaced horse trade.

It was not the interests of the United States alone that were being considered. Baruch was aware that for us to destroy our bombs would not only be interpreted by the Soviets as weakness on our part, but would instill terror in the small countries across the world. For them, our bomb represented the surest protection against possible Soviet attack. Russia could remobilize her armies; we could not as easily rebuild our bombs. Hence the necessity of a *fait accompli*, or presenting to the Russians in full detail the minimum that the free world was prepared to accept. It was decided as early as May 3 that the American delegation would go to the first meeting of the Atomic Energy Commission with as nearly complete a program as could be presented; not with a take-it-or-leave-it attitude, but in the conviction that the Americans had done all they could do.[81]

In other words, the United States should offer a proposal which would provide answers for any anticipated questions. Undiplomatic? Impolitic? Perhaps. The scientists might damn Baruch for being a politician, but politics was exactly what he was not playing. Agreement with the Russians might very well be reached by asking for more than would ever be conceded and then backing down in a gesture of surrender. But how would Congress react to the apparent retreat? [82] Baruch decided that we should make no proposals we were not ready to accept ourselves.[83] That was why he had been appointed, not to deal in bargain-counter politics but to rise above it.

It was natural, of course, that the security of his own country should be uppermost in Baruch's thinking. It was not Baruch but the United States Senate which laid down the dictum that no treaty or international agreement would be accepted that would commit this country to giveaways without protection. This decision was echoed by President Truman, who wrote Baruch of the absolute necessity that raw materials be controlled at the source, and that "we should not under any circumstances throw away our gun until we are sure the rest of the world won't arm against us." [84] Senator Vandenberg added that he would not care to live in a world where Russia had the bomb. And it was in the office of Secretary of the Navy James Forrestal that the decision was made that "The means to wage war must be in the hands of those who hate war," for the United States would not "tolerate" the destruction of war let loose again.[85]

Any atomic control plan rested primarily on good faith. And where was there evidence of good faith? Was mankind now to be trusted to work a miracle that had never been worked before? What if Russia agreed and the United States Congress refused to give up the veto? What if Congress agreed and a future Congress voided the agreements? Or what if Russia agreed and then changed her mind? The acts of nations, Baruch knew, were but the magnified desires of individuals. How could you abolish the innately exploitative nature of man?

Baruch understood some of the Russian fears. In fact he was convinced that fear was their primary motivation.[86] Mutual suspicion was the barrier over which two great powers were trying to build a bridge, and charges of bad faith were hurled openly by the Russians and privately by many Americans. Fear, the enemy of all peace — fear for the safety of their own people — blocked the nations' efforts to find safety for all the peoples in the world. This, then, was the dilemma, the challenge, the immensity of the task of finding answers to the unanswerable, of shaping cosmos out of chaos.[87]

Baruch called in his "team": Swope, whose gift for vibrant prose made him the natural choice for secretary and public-relations man; Ferdinand Eberstadt, quietly planning tactics and strategy; John

Hancock, with his grasp of organization; and Fred Searls, a Western pioneering type, who was one of the world's best mining engineers. This was the group who with Baruch would speak for their country in presenting the American report to the newly formed United Nations Atomic Energy Commission.

Notes by Swope show that the first conversations of the team began about April 1, 1946, with almost daily talks after that. During this early period Baruch also interviewed Admiral Nimitz and General Eisenhower, who had just been made Chief of Staff of the Army. Both men endorsed Baruch's stand that the bomb must be under the control of laymen not of the scientists, whom "the brass" feared most of all.

This was scarcely an auspicious beginning for Baruch's relations with the scientists, who quite naturally had a proprietary feeling about the bomb, no less than did the military. Baruch was caught in the squeeze, open to attack from all sides. Many of the scientists had publicly declared for the Acheson-Lilienthal Report before Baruch got into action, and their declarations continued long afterward. With each group seeking to create a favorable public opinion, only confusion resulted.

The first formal meeting of the American delegation to the United Nations Atomic Energy Commission was held April 4, 1946. It was a general-policy discussion. For four hours of that day Baruch was absent. From eleven until three he was closeted with a lean, fine-drawn, and reluctant man named J. Robert Oppenheimer.

Nothing in the record of that talk or in the letters exchanged afterward gives any inkling of the tragic difficulties Oppenheimer was later to encounter. The two men quickly reached the kind of mutual understanding that usually rose between Baruch and men who had the chance to talk with him personally.[88] Apparently Oppenheimer had no mystical illusions as to the sanctity of science, but was a hard-headed man who could appreciate Baruch's sincerity even when he disagreed with him. In any event, he pledged his assistance in every way, to which Baruch responded by telegram that he was eager for Oppenheimer's advice.[89]

But relations between Baruch and Vannevar Bush of the Carnegie Institution were strained from the start. Perhaps each distrusted the other. Bush led off in his opening words to Baruch with, "You're the worst qualified man in the country for this job."

Baruch took it with a grin. "Doc," he said, "you couldn't be righter." Then, with a strategy that left Bush nonplused, he looked at him with complete innocence and queried, "What shall I do, Doc?" Should he resign?

"Oh, hell, stay in," Bush grumbled, then added, "It would all blow up if you got out." [90] For he knew, as they all knew, that Baruch's prestige, more than that of the scientists or military, was what might put through an atomic program. Furthermore, there would have been small chance of the Senate's approving an out-and-out scientist like Bush as chairman.

On April 4, Baruch officially urged Byrnes that the special State Department Committee on Atomic Energy, headed by Dean Acheson, plus the Board of Consultants, headed by David Lilienthal, be invited to submit their ideas and advice to Baruch's group. Bush, who had personally done so much of the spadework on the bomb, answered Byrnes on the sixteenth. [91] Bush thought that it was not really necessary that Acheson's committee be reconstituted, although of course all the members would be willing to help as individuals. Baruch's group took this in the spirit in which it was meant. The scientists had no wish to be consultants to a bunch of Wall Streeters. "They felt we were defiling the plan," Eberstadt said afterward. [92] John Hancock observed of Bush: "It would surely be unfortunate if other scientists should take his view of being unwilling to co-operate." [93]

Bewildered, Baruch was enlightened by the politically knowing Jimmy Byrnes. The scientists' pride was hurt. They had expected one of their number to have Baruch's position. Bush had thought that he was in the running. So had some of the others. Baruch decided not to worry about it.

But the scientists had not deserted Baruch en masse. President Conant of Harvard, for instance, who had served with Acheson on the original State Department committee, now obtained for Baruch the services of Dr. Richard Tolman, Dean of the Graduate School of the California Institute of Technology, who became a valuable member of the organization. As originator of the theory of motion colloids, he was secure in his scientific achievements; he had been on the Manhattan Project, and Baruch felt that he had never known a wiser man. Baruch could work with him, and Tolman worked for Baruch. He labored mightily, writing scientists all over the country for help, carrying so much of the burden, in fact, that Baruch was gravely con-

cerned over his health. He was able to assemble for advisory purposes a scientific panel, including A. H. Backer, Arthur Compton,
C. A. Thomas, Harold Urey, and Oppenheimer. Harry Winne, a
vice-president of General Electric and also a member of the original
Lilienthal group, announced that he was willing to do anything. Baruch and his "team" had also the services of Major General Thomas
F. Farrell, deputy to General Groves, and his pleasant disposition, as
well as his wisdom, won the admiration of everyone.[94] On May 6,
John P. Davis of the Strategic Bombing Survey assured Baruch that
he would open that group's papers to the Commission. Belatedly, on
May 31, Lilienthal said that "Our purpose — all of us who worked on
the Report — is to try to be helpful." [95] Harold Urey, while pledging
his own services, wished that American scientists as a whole would
offer public support to the Baruch Plan.[96] This they could not do,
for they still thought Baruch's theories were more political than
scientific. As John Hancock noted, during the whole first month the
scientists talked world politics and the politicians ignored the scientific aspects of the question.[97]

The first sessions of the American delegation were held in Washington. On April 12, it was decided to set up permanent headquarters at the Empire State Building in New York, but there was
much going and coming between the two cities. John Hancock, for
instance, received a hurry-up call on April 17 to join Baruch and
Byrnes in Washington. He had just time to throw some clothes into
a suitcase and catch the 7.30 train. He met Byrnes, Baruch, and Fred
Searls at the old State, War, and Navy building the next morning.

Fundamental questions were raised. Baruch had ideas on many of
them. He had also jotted down some queries. How much could the
public understand about major weapons? Would not the broad-
casting of vital information theoretically allow a small nation to
wreck a large one? Furthermore, what was going to be the relation of
his group to a United States Atomic Energy Commission, plans for
which were already under way? Finally, and most basically, was Baruch to be a genuine policy-maker, or was he to carry out already established policies? Apparently he received satisfactory answers, for
certainly he was surprised as well as indignant when, back in New
York, Sir Alexander Cadogan, the British delegate to the United
Nations, remarked casually, "I understand that the Acheson-Lilienthal Report is to be the basis for the American proposal."

"Who told you that?" Baruch demanded.

"Acheson," came the answer.

Shortly afterwards, Baruch confronted Acheson in his office in Washington. "Is this true?"

"Yes," the Under-Secretary of State said.

"Then you'd better get another messenger boy," Baruch retorted. "Western Union don't take 'em at my age."

"What do you mean by that?"

"Exactly that."

Acheson then suggested that Baruch talk the matter over with Alger Hiss, head of the Department's section on international affairs. Baruch remembered Hiss from the Nye investigation. "I won't see him," he said.

"Well," Acheson added, "if you get out, it will raise the devil."

"That won't be a circumstance compared to what will happen when I tell the people why," Baruch said.

Baruch's next port of call was the White House. Byrnes accompanied him, and the atmosphere was strained. The President's ruddy face was rigid. There was defensiveness in his tone as he challenged Baruch, "You aren't going to run out on me, are you?"

This touched Baruch on the raw. "I'm not going to run out on the American people," he said. But he did not forget the purpose of his mission and challenged the President in his turn. "Who's going to write this report?"

"Hell, you are," Harry Truman said.

That was enough for Baruch. In later, more bitter years, he once remarked that, whatever you might say about Truman, he did "stick." [98]

Byrnes elaborated by letter on the President's position. Although the President determined policy and transmitted it through the Secretary of State to the Baruch committee, as a practical matter, the President took good advice. Despite the favorable reaction of the public, the Acheson-Lilienthal Report was definitely not to be the final official policy. Byrnes anticipated no difficulty. Baruch would advise the Secretary of State, who in turn advised the President. [99]

Thus was Baruch's responsibility made clear. His views were of great importance in the formulation of American policy on the bomb, but they would not have been so had they not won the approval of the President, and subsequently of the Congress. Furthermore,

American policy was necessarily based on agreements made months or years before, with none of which Baruch had been concerned. He had to build from the policy already laid down, but he would do so with a determination to protect American interests.[100]

The White House interview was still not the last word. The next scene was staged at Blair House. It was two o'clock on the afternoon of May 13. Dean Acheson was there. So were Bush and Conant. So were Lilienthal and his board, and Baruch and his, with the Secretary of State presiding over it all. Herbert Bayard Swope was ready with the key question. "Mr. Acheson, what *real* provision is there for inspection? What are you going to do if they *don't* behave?"

Acheson recognized with whom the question had originated. He turned to Baruch, who quietly nodded. Acheson answered, "I suggest it be left to juridical interpretation." [101] This was his answer. It was not the answer of either Bernard Baruch or President Truman.

Baruch later reflected that it was often the preference of diplomats for compromise over facing problems squarely, which led to wars.[102]

Walking one day in Rock Creek Park, Baruch saw four servicemen and startled them by coming up. "My name is Baruch," he said. "I hope you won't mind my intrusion. But seeing the four of you sitting here, looking so happy, I decided to come over and ask your advice on a lot of problems that have been bothering me."

So for a few minutes Baruch exchanged opinions with the young men who had fought for the peace he was now seeking to save. They spoke of army morale, the proposed draft of strikers, the fact that scientists, as such, were no more peacemakers than was Henry Ford. One of the boys put a question: Why couldn't we "get along with the Russians?" Baruch answered, and somehow unburdened his troubled heart. We had entered the lists with one hand tied behind us, he explained. Because of the Potsdam Conference, we were already committed to certain things. Our only ace was the bomb, and we did not want to have to use that.[103]

So the Baruch Plan began to evolve — a suggestion here, an idea there, each fitting, puzzle-like, into place: John Hancock, the plodder, breaking suddenly into quotations from Disraeli; Searls, with his Western gusto; and Swope — nothing was quiet with him around. Baruch was intrigued with the idea of international ownership of raw materials, but Hancock foresaw all manner of Russian objections to joint ownership with capitalistic nations.

Already, Hancock thought, we had oversold the idea of commercial power plants, under either national or international control. Any national authority must necessarily be under the control, although not the ownership, of an international authority, with "complete access to the resources of each nation and authority to assess them." [104]

So control rather than ownership became a part of the plan.

Of his own part, Baruch said afterward: "My associates deserve equal credit. Never were there such men as I had." Yet it was he who gave the vital spark. Ferdinand Eberstadt has recalled that individual contributions of "the team" were somehow magnified and illumined by Baruch. Furthermore, it was he who had chosen the team and coordinated its work.[105]

Much of the imaginative inspiration, however, came from Eberstadt. He and Baruch sat in the late spring sunshine one day on a bench in Lafayette Square and looked into the future. "You are on the threshold of your greatest accomplishment," Eberstadt said. "You are offering the world one of the most elevated programs ever given mankind — one which, if fo1lowed, not only can solve the atom, but the entire problem of war." [106]

The end of war — the immensity of that dream shook Baruch. This was no mere "job" he and the team were engaged on; this was a challenge to human nature itself. Few greater tasks had ever been given a man. "The last great hope," "man's last chance for survival" — words, phrases, clichés, dusty and dull, shone now with a new light. There was only one answer: international law with teeth in it, the start perhaps of an actual government of the world.

Restlessly at night, Baruch pondered. Would man ever learn? Would the horrors of Stalingrad, of Dachau, of the fall of France and the invasion of Germany — the "victory" in which all lost — would these instill terror into the human heart any more than had the siege of Londonderry, the retreat from Moscow, or the stand at Verdun? Was the bomb any more of a Damocles' sword than gunpowder had been in its day? Was the imagination of man sufficient to grasp the horror of what he had created? To win a war was impossible, but did that make war itself impossible? Some words of the chemical warfare expert General Alden H. Waitt echoed in Baruch's mind; the atom was but the beginning. Gas and biological warfare the general had talked of — and of toxic biological agents, thousands of times more effective than gas.

Baruch turned in bed, groped for a light and scratch pad and mused over the notes that he would dictate the next day. War, he knew speeded up the processes of history. If the bomb could be eliminated, why not gas, rockets, biological warfare? If you could reach an accord about one weapon of mass destruction, why not about all the others? He mused a moment over the question of controls and safeguards. Why, indeed, could you not take the final step and outlaw war itself? History was filled with man's futile efforts to end war, but that need not mean that the effort must be abandoned.

Had not General MacArthur insisted that the new Japanese Constitution outlaw war? Why then could it not be written into the Constitution of all countries that war was a crime, with the guilt resting on the individual who took part in it? This would give validity, even if after the event, to the controversial Nazi crime trials in which already the United States had committed itself to the doctrine that citizens could be held to account for the actions of their government.

Elimination of the bomb would necessarily be the first step. Next must come the end of standing armies, the visible threats of one nation against another. His imagination leaped another boundary line — the end of arms and armies would free the energies of mankind for the elimination of illness, poverty, inequity, misery. An international police force might be the safeguard that would give nations a sense of security against an aggressor. The only thing lacking was man's will to bring the dream to pass.[107]

The idea was still gripping him when he visited Byrnes on May 26 to outline his tentative plans for a report. He mentioned his dream — admitting it was only a dream so far. If his group was making any new contribution, it was simply this: whatever agreement was made had to stick. It could not be violated by anyone, and the safeguard must be swift and certain punishment. There could be no question of veto, because while you argued you could be destroyed.[108] He did not claim that elimination of the veto would assure united action against an aggressor. Nor could he guarantee that control of the atom bomb would necessarily stop its use in war.[109]

Only by the elimination of war itself could instruments of destruction be really controlled and destroyed.[110] He bent forward, eagerly. Was he to be limited merely to control of the atomic bomb or could the question include all weapons? This was his hope — the end of all instruments of destruction. How, otherwise, in this age of limitless science could man survive the horrors of all-out war? [111]

After such heights came the natural despondency of reaction. On May 29 he wrote Byrnes that he felt he himself could only undertake the presentation of the American views and begin the negotiations. He wondered if some permanent man should not be considered, for all this would take a long time. At his age he would never have undertaken it, had he not felt that whatever powers were left in him he must give. Furthermore, he wanted to remain only so long as he had the ability to meet the demands of the situation. [112]

Byrnes knew Baruch and Baruch's doubts in the face of responsibility. There is no recorded reply.

Perhaps this seeming official indifference is responsible for the depression that closed in more darkly upon Baruch in the days ahead. The newspapers still guessed that the Acheson-Lilienthal Report would provide the real basis for the American proposals. There was no public denial. Finally, on June 6, Baruch called Byrnes on the telephone. If these reports were true, why not have someone else speak, someone who could advocate the Acheson-Lilienthal program wholeheartedly? Was there to be now a reversal of position? He had waited patiently for word from Byrnes and the President. Now he could wait no more and he had lost faith that he could cooperate successfully with them. Was his report or the previous one to be the official American policy? [113]

Promptly, Byrnes invited Baruch to Washington. At 2.45 on the afternoon of June 7, Baruch went to the Secretary of State's office, a draft of the plan in his hand. It was of his own inspiration and conception, although Swope had supplied much of the phraseology, including part of the majestic beginning. [114] Baruch knew that a short address would more dramatically focus attention, but, consciously, he had sacrificed literary effects in order to leave no doubt whatever as to his meaning. "You'll spoil a beautiful speech by putting in the proposals," one adviser had told him. But he knew that if he did not put them in the Russians would say that he had hidden his hand — and he knew, also, that this was the speech of his life and perhaps never would he have such an audience again. There must be no questions unanswered, no loopholes unplugged, no opening for uncertainty or confusion. The whole plan must be there. [115]

From the State Department, Baruch and Byrnes proceeded to the

White House. There Baruch saw the President and was "astounded" at the grasp he had of the situation. He was particularly strong about the veto, Baruch recalled afterward. The President was on Baruch's side.

Of what use was a treaty, without provisions for enforcing it? Baruch demanded.

"I quite agree with you," Mr. Truman said. He added reminiscently that if Stimson had had the free world behind him when the Japanese invaded Manchuria fifteen years earlier, the Second World War might never have occurred. "What a different world it might have been," Truman said pensively.

The President then took Baruch's proposals, read them, initialed them, and approved them, paragraph by paragraph. "No man," commented Baruch in retrospect, "ever had the backing he gave me. He never wavered." [116]

Now the speech lay ready, waiting. On June 5 came a cheering message from Oppenheimer. "You must know that my thoughts and hopes are very much with you these days." [117] On the eve of delivering the speech, Baruch received a telegram from President Truman, wishing all members of the Commission godspeed and voicing his awareness of the extraordinary importance of the task before them. Nothing could concern the people of the world more. A few days later the President added, "The peace of the world and the welfare of mankind is in your hands." [118]

Perhaps no man in our history stood weighted with a feeling of more responsibility than did Baruch when, "looking like everyone's grandfather," [119] he arose on the afternoon of June 14, 1946, to present to the world his country's plea for peace.

The press corps was there; the dignitaries of the world were there, their shadowed faces brightening in the hope struck off by the words they had waited so long to hear. [120] Even Gromyko looked happy, it was noticed. For a brief moment there was faith — and hope. Momentarily it seemed as if at least the whole non-Soviet world was on the side of sanity. [121]

Light fell on the chiseled features and white head of the speaker and outlined his tall figure against the beige-draped walls of the Hunter College gymnasium. He talked simply, directly, sometimes even haltingly, and this very hesitancy underscored the seriousness of his purpose. He was aware of the weight of his mission as he spoke of "the most important subject that can engage mankind — life it-self." [122]

So he spoke, with visible pride in his role. "A revolutionary speech," said one commentator, "the first cry of a new world strug-gling to be born." [123]

"My fellow citizens of the world," he began. "We are here to make a choice between the quick and the dead.

"That is our business. Behind the black portent of the new atomic age lies a hope which, seized upon with faith, can work our salvation . . . We must elect World Peace or World Destruction.

"Science has torn from nature a secret so vast in its potentialities that our minds cower from the terror it creates." Yet terror had never halted the use of deadly weapons. Science which had given men the most terrible weapon of all offered no answer "to lift its use from death to life." The answer to the world's "longing for peace and se-curity . . . the promise of a new life, freed from the heart-stopping fears that now beset the world" could be found only in "a meeting of the minds and the hearts of our peoples. Only in the will of man-kind lies the answer."

Here, now, were assembled representatives of the peoples of the entire world. "The peoples do not belong to the governments but . . . the governments belong to the peoples . . . War is their enemy . . . Anything that happens, no matter where or how, which menaces the peace of the world . . . concerns each and all of us . . . We find ourselves here to test if man can produce through his will and faith the miracle of peace, just as he has, through science and skill, the miracle of the atom."

What, then, did the United States propose?

Swiftly he outlined the four basic points of the plan: (1) "Mana-gerial control or ownership" by a world Authority "of all atomic energy activities potentially dangerous to world security"; (2) "power to control, inspect, and license all other atomic activities"; (3) "the duty of fostering the beneficial uses of atomic energy"; and (4) "re-search and development" to make the Atomic Authority "the world's leader in the field of atomic knowledge."

"I offer this as a basis for beginning our discussion.

"But I think the peoples we serve would not believe — and with-out faith nothing counts — that a treaty merely outlawing possession or use of the atomic bomb" would be sufficient for world security.

What the peoples wanted were safeguards, "an international law with teeth in it." To this end, the United States was prepared to contribute its part.

When a proper system of controls had been set up and punishments agreed upon, the United States would propose that all manufacture of bombs be stopped, and that the Authority be left in possession of full information as to the techniques for the production of atomic energy. Penalties should be invoked for any illegal possession or use of an atomic bomb; illegal possession or separation of material for use in a bomb; seizure of any plant or property under control of the Authority; any willful interference with activities of the Authority; and creation or operation of any dangerous projects, without permission by the Authority.

"It would be a deception," Baruch continued firmly, " . . . were I not to say . . . that the matter of punishment lies at the very heart of our present security system. It . . . goes straight to the veto power . . . so far as it relates to the field of atomic energy . . . There must be no veto to protect those who violate their solemn agreements not to develop or use atomic energy for destructive purposes.

"The bomb does not wait upon debate. To delay may be to die." An illegal seizure of a plant "might permit a malevolent nation to produce a bomb in twelve months," perhaps in an even shorter time. "This shows how imperative speed is in detecting and penalizing violations . . . The solution will require apparent sacrifice in pride and in position, but better pain as the price of peace than death as the price of war."

What did he propose? The Authority should set up a complete plan for the control of all forms of atomic energy but strive to avoid the domestic concerns of the nations involved. The Authority must inventory the raw materials of the world. It must "control and operate all plants producing fissionable materials in dangerous quantities and must own and control the product of these plants." It must have "sole and exclusive right to conduct research in the field of atomic explosives," for "only by maintaining its position as the best-informed agency" could it draw the line between potentially dangerous and nondangerous activities. And a major function of the Authority should be promotion of the peaceful uses of atomic energy. All nations should be encouraged in this goal "under reasonable licensing arrangements," although Baruch warned that there was no hard and fast line between dangerous and nondangerous activities. "Constant re-examination" would be necessary.

He came now to the crux of the question — the right of entry, search, and examination. "Any plant dealing with uranium or thorium after it once reaches the potential of dangerous use" must be subject not only to inspection but to operation by the Authority. All intrinsically dangerous activities must be so operated. This would greatly reduce the problem of inspection, since any "visible operation by others than the Authority [would then] constitute an unambiguous danger signal."

"Adequate ingress and egress for all qualified representatives of the Authority must be assured . . . Important measures of inspection will be associated with the tight control of raw materials for this is a keystone of the plan." Prospecting, survey, and research in relation to raw materials would be carried on for the primary purpose of seeing that no one else was conducting "surreptitious operations . . . in the raw materials field." Members of the Authority must necessarily, therefore, be competent scientists, and be chosen on an international basis.

Control should come into effect by successive stages. As the controls were set up, the United States would yield its national knowledge of atomic matters to the Authority. All national authorities for control must be subordinate to the International Atomic Development Authority.

These were the essential part of the plan, the framework from which might arise a world Authority to control a deadly weapon of war. It was a plan worthy of a man of vision but not visionary, who dared dream but could also plan. It was a plan for a world that still had hope — a giant step for those who dared take it, but would any dare? The issue was far more one of ethics than of physics.

"Before a country is ready to relinquish any winning weapons it must have more than words to reassure it," Baruch said flatly. "It must have a guarantee of safety not only against the offenders in the atomic area but against the illegal users of other weapons — bacteriological, biological, gas — perhaps — why not? — against war itself.

"In the elimination of war lies our solution, for only then will nations cease to compete with one another in the production and use of dread 'secret' weapons . . . This devilish program takes us back not merely to the Dark Ages but from cosmos to chaos." If atomic weapons could be controlled, why not others as well? "When a man learns to say 'A' he can . . . learn the rest of the alphabet, too . . . Peace is never long preserved by weight of metal or by an armament race . . . We must embrace international co-operation or international disintegration."

"The light at the end of the tunnel is dim," Baruch concluded, "but our path seems to grow brighter as we actually begin our journey. We cannot yet light the way to the end." "The way is long and thorny but supremely worth traveling. All of us want to stand erect with our faces to the sun, instead of being forced to burrow into the earth like rats.

"The pattern of salvation must be worked out by all for all." [124]

Praise rose in a clamor. "There is not type in any newspaper office anywhere big enough to emphasize the importance of the American proposal today," ran a typical comment.[125] There was still magnificence in America. Thousands of messages poured in — from Robert Sherwood, Henry Stimson, Cardinal Spellman, and a "Bull's-eye" from James Forrestal. A joint telegram declaring that this battle cry that the bomb could not be vetoed was a powerful link to imprison both the war-lords and war itself, was signed by Justice William O. Douglas, Ely Culbertson, and John Foster Dulles.[126]

But Congress was dubious. Congress had scented softness to communism in the Acheson-Lilienthal Report, and many felt that the Baruch Plan should never have been presented at all without prior consultations with the Senate. Typical of the most reactionary opinion was that of Senator McKellar of Tennessee, who, on being informed what the plan was about, burst out, "Then I pray God that we will never have the agreement." [127] With some exaggeration the New York *Journal-American* proclaimed: "A stunned capital reacted adversely today to the proposal." Broken down, the leading senatorial opposition seemed to come from Capper of Kansas, Capehart of Indiana, and Knowland of California, who saw in the plan a peril to our national security.[128] Opposition came too from left-wingers who sought immediate and universal disarmament, with the United States at once ceasing the manufacture of atomic bombs. Some wondered if Baruch really meant what he said, if Russian agents would really someday have access to American mineral deposits. And would the

United States Senate back him if he did? [129] This was a moot question. At least thirty Senators went on record that the plan was neither tenable nor backed by public opinion.[130] But the measured verdict of Vandenberg held weight: Baruch's report was "more important to the peace of the world than anything that happen[ed] here." From the White House came the official command: "Back Baruch." [131]

The radio commentator Gabriel Heatter reported that in Russia the Baruch proposals were on the front pages, although the London *Daily Worker* gave a grim forecast of coming events by predicting that the Soviet Union would fight the proposals.[132] There were enthusiastic endorsements of the plan from *The Nation* and from the Liberal Party of New York.[133] But for Baruch, perhaps the most stirring tribute came from Winston Churchill. He had cabled for the text of the "historic" speech, read it, and then saluted his "old and honored friend . . . the leading elder statesman of America, knowing well his wisdom and value. There is no man in whose hands I would rather see these awful problems placed than Bernard Baruch's." [134]

Endorsements were beginning to come in from the scientists too: Karl Compton wrote that he was hearing "universally favorable comments." [135] For, whatever their personal scruples, the scientists knew that to control atomic energy was "scientifically feasible," and Arthur Compton went so far as to agree that until controls were developed, the United States should keep the armed authority.[136]

According to Leo Cherne of the Research Institute of America, many of the atomic scientists abroad, in France, in Holland, in England, in Belgium, were reacting with "a sense of relief and gratitude" to the briefest descriptions of the proposed program.[137] More endorsements poured in during the next few weeks — from sources as diverse as the League of Women Voters, the Church Peace Union, the faculty of Immaculate Heart College, and the American Veterans Committee; from movie producer Samuel Goldwyn, and the United Council of Church Women. By September one survey reported that 78 per cent of the American people favored the Baruch Plan.[138]

This was what counted. Those who read and those who heard felt a chill along their backs, the bringing to focus of ten thousand years of conflict. They knew that there was not much time. They knew, as Baruch said, that the choice made might be whether mankind lived or died in the next generation. It was this fact, perhaps, rather than its details that aroused enthusiasm in European centers. The plan, for all its faults, was a bold facing of the facts of life in a world of death and war, worthy of one who had sat at the feet of Woodrow Wilson. It was a sophisticated and unflinching declaration of America's coming of age. It brought the support of facts to the platitudes of San Francisco.

Officially, Soviet Russia was still silent. The "Great Debate" had yet to begin. Meanwhile, having done all that one man could do, Baruch chose to relax.

On the evening of the eighteenth, he entertained fellow members of the Atomic Energy Commission at a supper at the Stork Club. "We're going to forget the bomb and all other troubles," he said.[139] Tensions eased over clinking glasses; steaks sizzled off the grill. There was ice cream laced with brandy, and fresh strawberries, and the bursts of laughter that mark a sudden release from strain. Baruch beamed beneficently. The room echoed with vibrant talk before the group set out to watch the Conn-Louis fight at Madison Square Garden and have a final "libation" at Baruch's apartment.[140] Gromyko and Baruch posed arm in arm and smiling.* For the Elder Statesman, the first round of his battle was over. Win, lose or draw, the die was now cast — and social pleasantries did not weaken his resolve.

* The caption read: "Baruch and Gromyko in Accord on Louis." New York *Journal-American*, June 20, 1946.

21

DON'T LET THEM TAKE IT AWAY

OFFICIALLY NOW, the Baruch Plan was the American Plan. Yet, the background to the "Great Debate" which opened on June 14, 1946, at Hunter College was a confused one. America, along with the rest of the world, was groping toward peace, while Russia, it seemed, was moving toward war. The Senate was arguing for national control, and the Russians were alternately blowing cold in New York and warm at the United Nations sessions in Paris, where, to the amazement of everyone, such details as the French-Italian frontier line were cleared up in a few hours' time, with a simple "We accept" from Molotov.

"While we are in an agreeing mood, why not finish up the Dodecanese?" Byrnes had queried, weary after two weeks of futile discussion.

"Very well; we agree that the Islands shall go to Greece," answered Molotov sweetly, offering at least "temporary relief" to those who weighed the new Russian tactics in Paris against the old tactics in New York.

Andrei Gromyko was young, but his methods were as old as Russia herself.[1] The early meetings of the Atomic Energy Commission gave a preliminary measure of the Soviet spokesman and his program. The Americans realized quickly the formidable nature of their antagonist. From the first, the dark, slender Russian assumed leadership by virtue of his own capabilities no less than the power behind him. He was not affected by early attempts to rebuke him, as at the first working session on June 28 when the French representative requested French translations of what went on. Gromyko said that he had no objection.

"Nobody asked whether you had any objections," the chairman, Dr. Herbert Evatt, responded.

Once Gromyko wrangled over a name until a French delegate suggested using a number instead. On the whole, however, the Russian was helpful, even conciliatory, with a gift for facilitating routine procedure.[2] Under his lead, in early July, the Russians accepted the majority rule for decisions of the Atomic Energy Commission, waiving their previous insistence on a two-thirds vote.[3] Sometimes he directed the entire flow of the meetings, which was hardly surprising, considering his familiarity with both the procedure and personnel. For Gromyko was on virtually every committee of the Commission, including those staffed by second-string men from the other delegations. Nothing escaped him. After the delivery of the Baruch Plan, he had shrewdly cross-examined the Elder Statesman on how much solid backing the plan would get from the American Congress.[4] Apparently tireless, he was the very personification of the iron and steel of his country. Most of the time he was formal and correct, as were all the Russian delegates. Stiffly, by note, Gromyko thanked Baruch for the gift of a birthday cake, delivered during the presentation of his own atomic energy proposals — "My family and I enjoyed it very much." [5]

Yet, at other times he was thoroughly human. He could smile at Baruch's characterization of their relations: "Gromyko says No; I say No . . . and we understand each other perfectly." Nor was he without some pleasantries of his own. "I do not contemplate that we will have something to co-ordinate in the near future," he observed dryly during debate on a proposed coordination committee.

"Isn't Baruch wonderful for a man of his age?" someone once asked him.

"How about John Hancock over here?" Gromyko countered. "He signed your American Constitution and he's still going strong." [6] It was possible to view a Russian as a man, and to his colleagues, like Ferdinand Eberstadt, the Soviet representative seemed courteous, intelligent, and understanding, "defending with skill his difficult position." [7] Baruch found him an agreeable man with a closed mind.[8]

Baruch characteristically took little active part in the discussions. He remained in the background until his services were needed, seeming now more of a mediator than an advocate. Occasionally he intervened, once suggesting that one mouthpiece per country was sufficient.[9]

Early signs pointed to future agreement, on ends if not on means.

Praising the Baruch Plan as "generous and most broad-minded," Monsieur Alexandre Parodi did not think it irreconcilable with the Soviet Union's hopes for general international disarmament.[10] The Polish delegate, too, could endorse the basic ideas of both the Russians and the Americans, although warning that the most important factor was to know that atomic bombs were no longer being produced. Verbally, the Commission could agree to make recommendations as to the peaceful uses of scientific findings, on the control of atomic energy to insure its use for peace, on the elimination of atomic arms and mass destruction, and on necessary inspection or "observance," as the Russians put it, to prevent violation of those agreements. Men could agree that war was an abhorrent thing, and even Gromyko, the representative of the "atheist" power, could strike a common chord when appealing to the ancient traditions of mankind, proving that certain moral "norms" made it a crime to destroy a peaceful population in war.[11]

June 19, 1946 — when Gromyko made his counterproposals, blasting a rift between the communist and capitalist nations — was in many ways a portentous day. Reluctantly President Truman was signing a bill to stockpile critical materials. Senators Connally and Vandenberg were planning to confer with Secretary Byrnes over pending treaties at the Paris Conference. In Tokyo, the Soviet representative had charged General Douglas MacArthur's representative with trying to force his opinions on the Allied Control Commission. The Arab League was demanding a new regime in Palestine. Byrnes had proposed to unify, economically, the United States Zone in Germany with any other zone, and the United States was considering the withholding of German reparations from Russia in retaliation for her stripping of Manchurian industry. A new jacket encased an old cover in the bookstore windows: Pierrepont B. Noyes's The Pallid Giant, a 1927 novel of an atomic civilization destroyed ages past.[12] And Gromyko arose and stood before the Atomic Energy Commission.

There was very little new in what he had to say. His cleverness was apparent from the first. He was famous for his ability in dodging questions, and the loopholes in his idea stretched wide. He had no plan to prevent the use of atom bombs other than the destruction of such bombs, and, afterward, an international convention to consider the possibilities of permanent disarmament. He called for penalties for the violators of any agreements, but these were to be applied only after bombs were manufactured, or the next world war had begun. For inspection he offered no provision at all.

It was easy to say that negotiations should start on the points of agreement as to the danger of atomic energy, the elimination of atomic weapons, the punishments for makers of war. But although both plans left the door open, the differences were fundamental, striking straight to the heart of the Baruch Plan. True, these disagreements were on means rather than on ends, but only ironclad means would make the desired ends possible.

Baruch at least had been forewarned. Gromyko had shot his bolt in a talk in Baruch's rooms, the results of which the Elder Statesman had imparted to Acheson the day before Gromyko delivered his statement. He was not disturbed by Gromyko's obsessive call for the outlawing of the bomb. The bomb was not so much the point at issue as war itself. All wars were inhuman. Modern ones simply made killing easier.[13]

On the day of Gromyko's speech, an informal meeting of the French, Canadian, Australian, and American delegations was held at three in the afternoon to map plans to "cross-examine" Gromyko on his proposals. But the scheme was dropped. Instead, at a press conference afterward there emerged the rotund and reassuring figure of John Hancock. The Americans were not discouraged by the Russian proposals, he assured the press, for they saw them as "by way of argument rather than a final Soviet position."[14]

This was propaganda war with a vengeance, and it was Baruch who was planning the strategy. It was his idea to hold the press conference, and his decision that Gromyko must never be allowed to feel that there was a "gang-up" on him. Baruch pointed up this stand a few days later in a talk with the Canadian and American delegates. Every benefit of the doubt must be given the Soviet Union. Perhaps even now the various delegations did not understand each other. Baruch was convinced that news should be interpreted daily to our radio commentators, and that every day the wavering delegations should be told what the American proposals really meant.[15] If the negotiations were to fail, there must be no scrap of blame on the American side. Only if we had made every effort to reach agreement would our conscience be clear, whatever the outcome.[16]

There would be no yielding on fundamentals. The problem was

too big for horse-trading: we could not sacrifice the irreducible minimum of safety — elimination of the veto, inspection, and safeguards. These were Baruch's major contributions to the plan, and in evolving them he had relied much on his experiences at the Versailles Conference and during its aftermath. But American public opinion was by no means united in approval of his methods. Dr. Chester I. Barnard, for instance, publicly begged Baruch to drop his demand for the elimination of the veto and for "swift, sure and condign" punishment of violators of atomic agreements. "All you are doing," Barnard warned, "is creating a blind alley which will give the Russians their opportunity to dance up and down indefinitely." [17] But Harold Urey agreed with Baruch that the veto was unthinkable on atomic questions.[18] This point Baruch stressed repeatedly; he was only against the veto on this one question. Obviously, no offender should sit in judgment of his own guilt. He was not dissuaded by Gromyko's sophistry, his reiterated insistence that the veto had been established, not at the urging of the Soviet Union, but by President Roosevelt and Prime Minister Churchill, who felt that the principle of the unanimity of the great powers meant the maintenance of peace. Without the abrogation of the veto in atomic affairs, the Russians might later veto what they agreed to today. Nor had he patience with those who discounted inspection because it could not be foolproof. Should all law and order be done away with because there were murderers and thieves at large? [19] Subsequent pictures of Gromyko and Baruch would be entitled "The Inflexibles," and the Birmingham, Alabama, News later commented that despite all his fine intentions, Baruch's "touch of private petulance . . . and a tendency to regard his own point of view as the last word led him to unfortunate threats on behalf of the United States." [20]

However, a far heavier club was swinging over the negotiations than any words of Bernard Baruch's. The timing may have been deliberate. In any event, it was tragic as far as the negotiations for trust and mutual cooperation were concerned.

Not two weeks after Gromyko's speech, a bomb hurtled down upon a fleet of ships at Bikini, and "Naval power, as we have known it," was reported to have "met its end." Around the doomed ships water "writhed about like a living monster"; deadly tides swirled toward the shore; fish in the depths and helpless animals on the decks or in the cabins of the ships absorbed the dose that meant death for them. "The radioactivity — that is the thing," commented a Russian observer. At first, only ten per cent of the living creatures were dead, but in three weeks one third more, and a third of the rest dying. "One out of every two men of the original force" would have succumbed to the telltale drowsiness, the weariness, which made the lifting of an arm a superhuman effort; and then the sleep from which there was no awakening. "So loomed the world of the future — of robot planes drilling death into cities — of contaminated fields and men and women with the germs of death in them fleeing to the hills and caves to die as civilization rotted in the rear."

"The Society of Man as now constituted is through," forecast the San Francisco *Chronicle*. "Either there will be a new society built to a new blueprint or there'll be none at all." [21]

This was Bikini, where, perhaps, the United States overplayed its hand. For if this was an attempt to intimidate Russia at a strategic moment, the effort failed. It certainly was of no help to the men laboring for the success of the Baruch Plan. Baruch had known that Russia did not trust her fate in her neighbors' hands, and the demonstration at Bikini was certainly not calculated to inspire trust. Baruch therefore leaned over backward to assure the Russians that in the atomic negotiations, at least, every consideration would be given them. From the first, Eberstadt and Swope had put no trust in Russia's good faith,[22] and had endeavored to persuade John Hancock, whose belief in the ultimate goodness of man was blinding him to the threats which became daily more clear. Baruch, too, started to work on Hancock, but in the process an ironic reversal occurred. Baruch, who would begin "hard-boiled," would end up in a tolerant mood, with Hancock vehemently urging the "get-tough" policy. "Bernie threw his arms around me, his eyes dancing," as Hancock later recalled it. "Here you are," he said. "You presume to be brought up a Christian, to do unto others as you would they should do unto you. And here I was brought up under the old Hebrew Law of an eye for an eye and a tooth for a tooth, and darned if I don't believe we've changed sides." [23]

Baruch was too shrewd to look for any wholesale reversal of human nature. He was balancing, he knew, the eternal yearning of man for peace against the fears and drives that had always made peace impossible. But Russia must be wooed so long as a shadow of hope remained. This was the policy he had resolved on; and never until these final days had his colleagues been so impressed with his "knowledge and force of character." [24]

So, at a staff conference on August 1, Baruch advised that the United States draw out the Russians on their ideas as fully as possible, and avoid humiliation to them, even if it meant humiliation to ourselves. So far, things had not gone too badly.

But the iron hand was inside the velvet glove. There could be no surrender of essentials. The goal was "a unanimous report" favoring the American plan; no alternative could be considered.[25] The Americans had made the choice between a cautious step forward, promoting the Acheson-Lilienthal plan, or a bold step forward, toward the complete control of the most deadly weapon of war. It was in the tradition of Americans to reach for the ideal, as they had done at Philadelphia in 1787.[26]

At the suggestion of John Hancock, Baruch did a good deal of educational work among members of other delegations, showing up the various Soviet counterproposals.[27] On minor points, however, he was conciliatory; and John Hancock spoke for the group when he wrote that he saw no point in attacking Gromyko in public sessions, since he still hoped to win him over.[28]

There was one powerful argument that could be used, but it cut both ways. In 1928 at the meeting of the Preparatory Commission for the Geneva Disarmament Conference of 1932, the Soviet Union had demanded effective disarmament. The U.S.S.R. had called for the abolition of armed forces and the banishment of deadly weapons of war. She had furthermore proposed an international authority or commission with permanent representation from every country signing the agreement and complete access to "every facility for the full investigation of all activities of the State, of public associations, and of private persons which are connected with the application of disarmament." Here they had sought authority to transcend the League of Nations. Here was no veto; all decisions would have been made by majority vote and would have been binding on all. Here, in a sense, was the Baruch Plan, proposed in 1928 — and it was the Western powers who had turned it down.[29]

This, of course, was why it was not produced to challenge the Russians. "It would have put them on the spot . . . made them terribly defensive," Ferdinand Eberstadt thought. But the Russians could well ask, if we had refused a partnership with the Communists in 1932, how then could the Communists be expected to take us into partnership now? [30] The subject was not brought up. Hugh Gibson publicly recalled, however, that the League of Nations had considered various inspection plans and found them "impracticable and calculated to foment ill will between states" — a statement which was not helpful to the American negotiators.[31] What the Soviets now called for, a general disarmament convention, "depending for its enforcement solely upon international good faith and respect for treaties," had seemed plausible in those prewar days, but where was evidence of such trust in 1946? As Baruch later put it, the Russians could not conceive our offer to be in good faith because "They doubtless felt that if they had done it themselves, it would not have been in good faith." [32]

Meanwhile, Ferdinand Eberstadt decided to put the Russians to the test and convince the optimists of what he himself had been convinced all along. Early in August Eberstadt called on Gromyko in his rooms and was received with the courtesy always characteristic of the Russian. Eberstadt wasted no time on pleasantries, however. "If you are prepared to accept a plan, the details are not really important. If not — " Eberstadt hung on the words, "our only problem is when to quit."

Gromyko looked shrewdly at his visitor and finished the sentence. "And how," he said. It was the answer Eberstadt had expected.

He went straight to Baruch. "Boss," he said, "this thing is a short sale. I want to get out."

A look of alarm crossed Baruch's face. "We can't do that," he answered instantly. "We must go on until the people generally come to the opinion we have." The world must be shown. If we failed after holding out every possible olive branch, every possible inducement to the Soviets, the world would know who was to blame. Baruch was still willing to give them the benefit of the doubt — did the Russians really understand the plan yet? Eberstadt was certain they did, "a damn sight better than either the French or the English," he said. So, slowly, Baruch began to map his final strategy, warmly seconded by Swope. If the Soviets would not accept our proposals, then even greater safeguards should be demanded. "Appeasements lead to compromise," said Swope. It must be made clear that the United States was not backing down.

But the American delegation was still divided on the means to be taken. As late as September 10, Baruch was still countering Eberstadt, who wanted a break or showdown to come now to awaken the public to the need for preparedness. Swope chimed in, "Mr. Baruch should see the President."

Baruch was obdurate. True, we were losing ground — the Russians must be told what the situation was — but the other delegates would not go along with us if we strove to force the issue. Later even Eberstadt was to admit the wisdom of taking a course sufficiently slow to show that the blame lay on the other side — that the Soviets in insisting on the letter of the United Nations Charter were actually destroying its principles. "The great thing Bernie did," he said, "was to prevent us from being victimized." [33]

Nevertheless, Baruch had now to face the somber realization that the dream of universal peace he had cherished during the spring was indeed only a dream. Even as late as August 7 he had thought that into the Constitutions of every country might be written clauses for the outlawing of war and allowing the inspection of armed forces. But now the last hopes were fading. Eberstadt's idea that Baruch and Gromyko might go together to Moscow for a personal plea to Stalin was answered by *Pravda's* cartoon of Baruch with one hand watering bombs in a flowerpot and the other hand pulling them up. As for Stalin, Baruch felt he was as bad as Hitler.[34] By September 25, Stalin was quoted in the *New York Times* as saying that atomic bombs were not "crucial" in war, and that England and France could not make a "capitalistic encirclement" of the Soviet Union, even if they wished to do so.[35] General Groves had informed the Baruch group that the Russians would have bombs in five to seven years, regardless of what we said or of what we did or did not give away.[36]

Then came the explosion.

It came not from the Soviet Union, but from the United States, and not from an irresponsible source but from a supposedly responsible member of the President's Cabinet. What it did was wreck the American strategy of awing the Russians by a show of united public opinion. It was, in fact, one of the weirdest episodes in American public life, for, as Secretary of State Byrnes said, the President and he had spent fifteen months building a bipartisan foreign policy upon which the world could rely, and Henry Wallace destroyed it in a single day.[37]

On July 23, at the height of the atomic energy debates, Wallace had dispatched a twelve-page, single-spaced typed letter to President Truman in which he had condemned the increased Army budgets, the bomb tests in the Pacific, and what "must make it look to the rest of the world as if we were only paying lip service to peace" while arming for war. Where, he asked, was the mutual trust and good faith on which any lasting peace could be founded? As for the Baruch Plan, it only told the Russians that if "they are 'good boys,' we may eventually turn over our knowledge of atomic energy . . .'" Wallace put some leading questions: What if the Russians surrendered their uranium and we then ceased to negotiate? Who was to determine the timing of the "stages" for release of information, a point elaborated by the *Daily Worker*, which observed that Baruch's attention was so directed toward the procedure of stages that he ignored the content of the stages.[38]

Truman read Wallace's letter, and although he "could not agree with his approach . . . let him know that [he] appreciated the time he had taken to put himself on record." He then sent a copy of the letter to Byrnes.[39]

On September 12 Wallace was booked for a foreign policy speech. The President had not read it, but prior to its delivery announced to a press conference that it had his approval. He explained later in his memoirs that he should have said that he was only approving the fact that the Secretary of Commerce was going to make a speech.

Wallace spoke, blasting American foreign policy in general and our treatment of the Russians in particular. Belatedly the President disavowed his words. From capitals around the world flashed the question: Was America going to change direction? To which Truman sturdily reiterated that there would be no change. On the seventeenth, Wallace released his letter of July 23.

The next day the erring Cabinet officer was called to the White House, where he gave a preview of his coming actions by agreeing to a one-sentence joint statement of policy, issued in his name and the President's. This, he promised, was the end, but he had scarcely reached the White House steps before he spilled over some more, and then again to reporters waiting at his office.[40]

History is still too close to Henry Wallace to appraise him fairly. He has been called a traitor and a fool; also "very able, clear-thinking, high-minded, a man of patriotism and nobility." [41] His letters to Baruch are among the most interesting in the Elder Statesman's entire collection; they are also almost completely impractical. The Providence *Journal* found him irresponsible on a matter of terrible responsibility, and pointed out that he was known for disregarding facts that did not jibe with his point of view.[42] The Baltimore *Sun* commented that Mr. Wallace's addiction to "running amok in the international china shop" was only just beginning to be apparent.[43] To the press generally, the name-calling contest was primarily a clash of personalities "between an elder statesman and a dreamer of dreams, between an old and wise man and an idealist whose head is so far in the clouds his feet rarely touch the solid earth." [44] It was characteristic that much of Wallace's letter had been written before presentation of the Baruch Plan, and he had not subsequently bothered to alter it.

There was publicly as yet no recognition that the "Great Debate" was really an opening battle in the Cold War. The harm that Wallace's action wrought to Baruch's basic strategy was not understood.

Baruch understood, however. The Wallace letter appeared in the morning papers of Wednesday, September 18. By sheer coincidence, Baruch and John Hancock happened to be in Washington to make a "progress report." After a lengthy interview, they emerged from the White House looking grim. Both declined to comment to the newspapers.[45]

Back in New York the next day, Baruch called Wallace and asked him to come in. Wallace promised to call back, and here began a game of hide-and-seek which lasted some ten days. Under pressure, Wallace finally agreed to see Baruch on Sunday. Baruch then issued a short statement to the press. There was no change in United States policy.

New headlines blared on September 20. The Wallace doctrine had been disavowed, and his resignation was already in the President's hands. This was partly the result of Baruch's work — at the White House he had won a promise that Wallace would be confronted with the choice of retraction or resignation. But Baruch was not yet satisfied.[46]

Forthwith he dispatched a telegram to Wallace, reiterating his intention of seeing him on Sunday. The misstatements must be corrected, Baruch told Wallace and told the press. Late in the day, Wallace telegraphed that he could not come. Baruch telegraphed back that he must.

Wallace telephoned the next morning. He won nearly a week's grace, but agreed finally to meet with Baruch on the morning of Friday, September 27, at the Empire State Building. Baruch had already informed the President of the projected interview, and added that he was sending a memorandum to the White House to set the facts straight. Truman politely expressed his appreciation, then, according to Baruch, gave him a free hand to deal with Wallace as he saw fit.

The meeting hardly resulted in an entente cordiale. Wallace was unsmiling and defensive. "I know that what I am going to say you won't like," he began.

Baruch's entourage was angry. "No nation has a right to show the trump card during negotiations," Hancock said.

"Where was I wrong?" Wallace inquired.

"Mr. Wallace, here's what you said." Hancock read aloud some of the pertinent points.

"I have a right to write the President," Wallace insisted.

"You have no right to write these things when with five minutes on the phone with either Baruch or me you could have been set right," came the answer. Swope added, "You . . . should have checked with our group on the facts." [47]

Eberstadt had tried patiently to explain why Wallace's idea of a package deal was unworkable; in any case, he doubted that the Russians would accept it. Slowly Wallace agreed that Baruch's idea on "stages" was sound. Baruch began to explain the veto. Dictating an account of the session afterward, he recalled that Wallace finally agreed fully with this explanation.

Wallace then offered a suggestion of his own. Couldn't the Baruch group meet with him and others to work out a new plan? Quick glances were exchanged by the members of the American delegation. They knew that Wallace was seeking a compromise settlement with the Russians. All he wanted was that the United States stop making bombs, and this of course was impossible. To reverse established policy at this date was beyond consideration. Eberstadt wearily pointed out the disadvantage the United States would be under if the whole debate were started over again, and reluctantly Wallace agreed that the time was not right. But he still felt that bomb manufacture was wrong.

Baruch had reminded Wallace that he was not unique in desiring peace and that he should have his facts straight before making statements.

At last a rough draft of a statement was drawn up and tentatively agreed to by all. Wallace's representative was to work out his own comments in conjunction with Swope, and later Wallace himself was to telephone his agreement. But nothing happened. According to Baruch, Wallace reneged. According to the friends of Wallace, his "last concession" was handed to Eberstadt, who took it, read it, and then said coldly that if he were not heard from in ten minutes all was off.[48] Baruch then sent his statement to the White House with quoted comment from Wallace which made it look as if the Secretary of Commerce had backed down on much of what he said. Wallace promptly issued a counterblast, his own version. President Truman did little to help matters by snapping that this was a Baruch-Wallace fight, with the implication that he would wash his hands of it. Exasperatedly, Baruch called a press conference for the morning of October 2, 1946.

From behind his desk he faced the reporters unflinchingly. His customary benignity was absent. This was a step he regretted to take, he said. It marked the first major difference he had had with a public official. He had made all possible efforts to avoid a showdown. But Mr. Wallace had refused to correct the errors, "which were caused by the fact that he was not fully informed." He read the text of a telegram then on its way to Wallace: "Yours is a responsibility for impairing the support of the American proposals . . ."

A reporter interrupted: Had support for the American proposals been impaired by Wallace's action?

"I think his action has confused the people," Baruch answered. Wallace had made a statement, repeated it in Chicago, then had it printed "to be distributed to millions . . . We are . . . taking up delicate negotiations . . . and I can tell you this . . . it didn't do us any good." [49]

Ninety per cent of the press supported Baruch's stand. Some few felt that Wallace had performed a public service by forcing Baruch to clear up several ambiguities in his program, and claimed that Baruch could not deny that the plan rested on American control of the bomb, which we ought to scrap in the interests of good faith. Pretty generally, however, it was agreed that Wallace was "unstable." [50]

Baruch, amidst the wreckage of the "united front," had turned his attention to the possibilities of a future in which his plan had failed. On the strength of reports from Fred Searls, he warned the State and Commerce Departments and General Groves that machines to be used for atomic construction were both on order and on shipboard for the Soviet Union. Their spy system was in perfect running order.[51]

Baruch addressed the New York Herald Tribune Forum in October. The world was "making heavy weather." Fear, he told his audience, lessened with knowledge. Perhaps the dream of freedom from fear could be realized, but fear was also frequently a constructive thing. The fear of storm led us to build shelters.

He quoted Thomas Paine. "Would you rather have peace in our time and death and destruction for our children, or would you rather face the issue now?" He cited Churchill's "seven tests of freedom": free speech, free courts, freedom from violence by mobs, the right to peacefully overthrow a government, just and decent laws, freedom from search or seizure, and the dignity of the individual. "Freedom cannot die, but death comes to those who abandon it," Baruch warned. The world could no longer be partitioned, or put into separate spheres. All faced a common danger; all must "stand guard." Although all nations knew the formula, as yet none but the United States had been able to make a bomb.[52]

With the United States showing marked signs of internal dissension, the Soviets had — and took — ample opportunity to pursue a new "peace offensive" to confuse the world. Hope sputtered anew on September 26 as headlines read: "Russia Supports U.S. Atom Report."[53] Even Baruch, it was said, rejoiced in the "forward motion." Actually, the Soviets had voted only to adopt the report of the Scientific and Technological Commission, which acknowledged the principle of controls. But this was enough to catch the Americans off guard. Stalin publicly pooh-poohed the importance of the bomb as a weapon, and was publicly and speedily answered by General Eisenhower.[54] Then Vishinsky doused the new hopes, reiterating all Russia's old arguments in a new and more vituperative form. In answer Baruch said: "I do not propose to reply to the oratorical Niagara of Mr. Vishinsky . . . The world, littered with the fragments of broken promises, will not accept any plan which purports to be a control, unless it is an effective control . . . the Russians have

never advanced one single thought as to a course of action that will
free the world from the threat of atomic destruction." [55]

Two weeks later, Molotov denounced Baruch as a warmonger in a
speech that excited national indignation and shocked even Baruch
himself.[56] All pretense of amity was ended. Commenting editorially,
the Philadelphia *Bulletin* charged that the Russian leader's "dis-
tortion of the motives of Bernard M. Baruch was shameless . . .
the worst form of political mudslinging." On October 30, in the
dark paneled hall at Lake Success, Baruch spoke. "The gentleman's
slander of my personal motives is of little importance," he said,
"but it is of great importance what his country does about peace . . .
As to his attempts to insult me, that's been tried before." He paused.
"The last who did were Hitler and Mussolini." [57]

As early as October 5, Swope and Eberstadt had agreed that the
American plan must be brought to a vote in December. On October
22, Eberstadt sent a memorandum to Baruch, stating that Sir Alexander Cadogan of Great Britain thought that the vote should be
taken before Egypt, Mexico, and the Netherlands — who were temporary members of the Security Council — were retired.[58] There was
still another reason for haste. Baruch learned that Russia was going
to make counterproposals to the Security Council.[59]

On October 28, Baruch called the White House. The longer the
delay the worse for the American plan, he told the President. Should
they proceed now or stall? Now the United States had ten votes to
two, but for how long no one could tell. Three sure votes were leaving the Council. The President listened and gave the word to go
ahead. Approval also came from the Secretary of State.[60] Afterward
Baruch said that only Byrnes's and the President's support made it
possible to accomplish what they did.[61]

On November 13, ten of the twelve nations represented on the
Atomic Energy Commission voted to make a full accounting of the
Commission's progress to the Security Council by the last day in the
year. The motion was made by Baruch and supported by Great
Britain, France, China, Brazil, Canada, the Netherlands, Mexico,
Australia, and Egypt. Russia and Poland "abstained." [62]

Having won this round, Baruch talked softly. He urged that we
must be patient, because in truth the plan was not easy to understand. The feelings of other nations must be considered; time and

public opinion might soften the Soviet opposition.[63] Thus Baruch spoke publicly. Privately he expressed his mistrust of Russia's motives.[64]

The next step was to present the American plan as a resolution for a formal vote. This Baruch did at the Commission's first night meeting on December 5. A statement by Molotov on the previous day that the Soviet Union accepted the principle of no veto of "day to day operations" of the UN's control body, as well as favoring "effective inspections," led to premature optimism.[65] The San Francisco Chronicle hailed "The Dawn of a New Day." [66] A wave of optimism spread across the country at these concessions which the Christian Science Monitor called an "electrifying abandonment of the veto power." [67] Baruch was more wary. Although he announced that "apparently, it is a complete victory," he was well aware that there were hitches in the Russian concessions. Molotov had said that no nation should be allowed to interfere with measures for inspection and control "once these are adopted by the Security Council." [68] Since the veto resided in the Council, it could still be applied in establishing methods of control and inspection. Moreover, what were to be considered as "day to day operations"? Just as Russia undoubtedly hoped, the Soviet announcement increased confusion and disunity in the country. Wallace, the Political Action Committee, some of the atomic scientists, and, for very different reasons, isolationist Senators, lined up in opposition to the Baruch Plan. It was against a clouded background that Baruch presented his resolution on the evening of December 5.

The resolution incorporated the American plan as first presented to the Commission on June 14. The motion was that this should become the official recommendation of the Atomic Energy Commission of the United Nations to the Security Council. However, there was a new angle introduced by Baruch, who urged that the Report be adopted by the UN Assembly "as a recommendation to the Security Council by the end of this year." The American made an eloquent appeal for the adoption of his resolution.[69]

Again he uttered the old words, "to delay may be to die." There was an "imperative necessity" for speed. Crisis and danger might habituate us to fear so that "the keen edge of danger is blunted, and we are no longer able to see the dark chasm on the brink of which we stand." His dream was for a world where "men can walk erect again, no longer bent over by the . . . fear the atom strikes into their hearts." He listed again the conditions that alone could give the dream life: (1) an International Authority; (2) full inspection; (3) no veto on atomic energy questions. "We welcome co-operation," he said, "but we stand upon our basic principles even if we stand alone."

"The Atomic Energy Commission cannot escape its duty . . . I entreat all to join in the enterprise so that we may show speed as well as wisdom . . . The stakes are greater than ever before offered mankind . . . Peace and Security." If the atom were controlled, so eventually might all other weapons be controlled, and the world enter the first era without war. "For myself, as I look upon a long past and too short a future, I believe the finest epitaph would be: 'He helped to bring lasting peace to the world.' " [70]

It was announced that "Mr. Baruch's resolution will be considered next week." [71]

Tributes poured in upon him. Bert Andrews of the New York *Herald Tribune* said that he spoke for virtually every reporter in Washington in offering Baruch their respect, their love, and their admiration.[72] From a workman came a scribbled postal, addressed to the "Hon. Bernard Baruch, Somewhere in N.Y."

"I work at the Building Bus. And I have interviewed all kinds of workmen . . . they like Myself . . . are proud to have a Man like you in our Midst. With Common Sense. Thank God. Thanks to you. Happy New Year." [73]

More formal was the comment of Captain Alberto Alvaro of the Brazilian delegation: "Mr. Baruch . . . expostulates in generous and noble terms without which the whole reason of living would not have any meaning." [74] From Texas came assurance of people "praying for you as you worked"; and from Myrtle Beach, South Carolina, the declaration: "We, the people, thank you deeply . . ." [75]

Two days after delivery of the speech, the *New York Times* ran a headline: "Molotov Accepts Curb On All Arms." Again this grandstand play caught the West napping, confused Baruch's design, and widened the rift between the Soviets and the United States as delegates wrangled over which should be outlawed first, the atom bomb or all other weapons of destruction.[76] On December 9, Baruch wrote publicly of his surprise that the Russians had at last agreed on the right of search, if not of punishment. "We find our Russian friends apparently of one mind with America, even to the discarding of the veto." [77] Did Baruch mean what he said, or was he calling the Russians' bluff? On the seventeenth he tried to force a showdown vote on his plan in the Atomic Energy Commission. Optimistically he declared: "A new spirit has come into being. It is our privilege and duty to give flesh to that spirit . . . This is a treaty that is meant to be kept." Canada's delegate, General Kenneth P. McNaughton, remarked that "Mr. Molotov's statements give us all reason to believe that we are in agreement on the essentials, that atomic energy must be controlled." [78]

That same day, James L. Tyson of *Time* Magazine was writing Baruch: "From the way the Russians are talking . . . it looks as though you have won a great victory." [79] But now new instructions arrived from Moscow. Gromyko pleaded for more study. "Why is it so necessary to rush along and try to reach hasty decisions?" [80]

On December 20 a vote on Baruch's resolution was reached. But the issue was not yet squarely faced. By a count of ten to one, Russia and Poland again "abstaining," the Atomic Energy Commission declared that it "approves and accepts the principles" on which the American plan for world control of atomic energy "is based." Baruch's actual resolution of December 5 was to be sent to a working committee for "some changes." [81] A whole new field of debate was opened up, making it possible for Canada to come forward with her own "New Plan." An almost entire rewriting of the American proposals was forecast, as at least thirty changes were required to make the plan conform to the General Assembly Resolution of January 24, 1946, which had provided for the formation of an Atomic Energy Commission and limited its authority. A tide of protest was rising against Baruch's demand for the elimination of the veto. Even the *New York Times* argued that the veto was meaningless, that if a violation occurred, the other nations would automatically go to war in self-defense. Furthermore, the *Times* expressed the belief that Baruch was trying to go too fast and too far with his insistence that the Commission members "stand up and be counted by the end of the year." [82]

With a prospect of relaxation in the official stand, the chorus of counterattack rose louder, and American public opinion stiffened. "Don't let them take it away" was the cry of some of the press.[83] Baruch had no intention of doing so. On the twenty-eighth, speaking tensely, and in the strongest language he had yet used, he turned the isolationist hue and cry into a formidable weapon. The American people, he warned, would withdraw support from the United Nations if a criminal could escape the consequences of his acts.[84] The situation was becoming critical, for now even the British were backing down. After leading Baruch to believe they were in complete agreement with his plan, they had suddenly decided that they wanted national governments, not an international Authority, to own and run the atomic plants. Sir Hartley Shawcross of the British delegation had even suggested that the American plan be put into treaty form and then laid aside until all other weapons of destruction were "controlled" by similar plans — a surrender to the Russian tactics of slowdown and delay. It was also suggested that the Baruch Plan be split and voted upon section by section, so that there could be no doubt in anyone's mind as to what was being decided.

Sir Alexander Cadogan, who had seconded Baruch's speech and proposals, finally tossed in a bomb of his own. What had transpired in the minds and instructions of the British overnight Baruch did not know, but the meaning of their words was unmistakably clear. "His Majesty's Government has concluded," Sir Alexander said, "not to accept the Baruch Plan."

Baruch, in the tradition of several American statesmen before him, knew when to go into a rage. He went into one.[85] When the final vote of the Atomic Energy Commission was taken on December 30, Sir Alexander Cadogan was firmly on Baruch's side. Once again, Gromyko shook out the limp, frayed phrases of appeal for an international disarmament convention, pausing only when John Hancock asked just how he proposed to make such a convention effective. The question was not whether a convention would be useful, but whether it would guarantee the world that atomic energy would not be used in war.[86]

The vote was taken. The count was, as expected, ten yeas and two abstentions — Russia and Poland. No nation actually voted against the report. Despite the months of tergiversation, the *New York Times* reported that the Plan approved conformed exactly with the Baruch proposals of June 14. No one had given an inch.

He had completed the task to which he had been summoned. The Plan had been reported and was now before the Security Council. Because his work and that of his associates was finished Baruch submitted his resignation. He expressed appreciation of the "continuing aid" of all who had assisted him. He would hold himself in readiness to answer any call the President might make. Truman replied with congratulations for Baruch's skill and patience in handling negotiations, adding that he was reluctant to accept the resignation.[87]

Baruch resigned to a fanfare of headlines and controversy. James Reston of the *New York Times*, not usually a Baruch admirer, felt that the resignation would weaken the American position in the United Nations and was scarcely calculated to impress the world with America's seriousness of purpose. In Reston's opinion the Elder Statesman had been arbitrary, not about the veto "but in his tactics with commission members." [88] Ironically, to avoid this was one of the reasons why Baruch had stepped down. As he wrote to Dr. Oppenheimer, he did not want to push everybody too hard. Yet even the sympathetic *Time* Magazine, commenting on his "months of inflexible diplomacy," was critical of his tactics, especially his ultimatum to Gromyko. The insistence upon "punishment," *Time* thought, was as unrealistic as it was undiplomatic, for any nation so immoral as to invoke modern war would certainly refuse punishment, whether or not legally permitted a veto.[89]

Johannes Steel, writing in *World Affairs* saw Baruch's withdrawal as "sinister," and claimed that it made all further negotiations impossible. "It was a diabolically clever maneuver because whoever now represents the United States in the United Nations Atomic Energy Commission is under the shadow of the Baruch veto." [90] The *Christian Science Monitor* saw the "World Capitals Stunned by Baruch's Resignation," [91] and some papers now forecast a softening of Administration policy. Yet Baruch, as early as May 6, had informed Byrnes that his work would be done when the Atomic Energy Commission reported to the United Nations.

Back at his New York office, Baruch now found time to pay tribute to the loyal men who had worked with him. He wrote that each had done more than his duty and deserved the gratitude not only of his own country but of all the world. They had made Baruch's success possible.[92] Fred Searls replied that never did a group have such a good leader, a leader who had sheltered them, supported them, settled their differences — and steadied them with his wisdom and courage.[93] Tolman, thanking Baruch for a set of Thoreau, said that he knew he had served with a truly great man.[94]

Sifting through the pile of mail on his desk, Baruch could enjoy the tributes. "You and the other members did your best and you did a Damn Good Best at that," wrote a South Carolina admirer. "Please, don't retire. You're too young a man for that," came a typical appeal.[95] He had fought the good fight, but without real victory.

Now, lounging at Hobcaw with John Hancock, Baruch wrote Edwin C. Hill that after about a week's rest he had found that he was not willing to let time pass him by.[96] If another call was to come, he would be ready.

He had not lost interest in the atomic question. His Plan was the plan of his country, and the threat that he might carry the fight to the public may in itself have forestalled crippling amendments to the Plan under pressure from those who would have yielded ground.[97] Perhaps of even more weight was a grass-roots poll, showing 50 per cent of the American people for the plan, 12 per cent against it, and 38 per cent undecided.[98]

Three years later, the Baruch Plan was still very much alive, and a headline read: "Truman Asks Ban on A-War. Backs Baruch Plan at U.N. Ceremony." [99]

Shafts of sunlight were spearing through clouds that hung like lead. Speaking before a rainbow of fifty-nine flags, President Truman pledged that the United States would continue to support the Baruch Plan until a better one was evolved. It was "a good plan, and the only workable one so far advanced." He spoke with emphasis and conviction. Vishinsky, it was noted, sat staring at the sky, and at the end politely applauded.

Baruch was not on the dais. But some few of that cheering crowd of 750,000 who pelted the President with ticker tape and cries of "Hello, Harry" noticed the erect old man in the black homburg who towered head and shoulders over the other spectators at the intersection of 57th Street and Madison Avenue.

The years dropped away; the long-drawn struggle continued; again and once again, the Russians rejected the American atomic energy plan.[100] The long struggle ended in a cold war, not in peace. It revealed the old world of enemies, not a new world of friends.

22

A BOOK OF REFERENCE

THE CROWD at the East River docks that morning in January 1946 was small but expectant. They clustered about Pier 90, watching and waiting. A small boy in ear muffs was taking notes on a scratchpad. The photographers circled around, setting up their lights.

A stir rippled through the crowd. The familiar figure of Bernard Baruch, in a long black coat and brown hat, walked along the pier and stopped for a word with a customs official. At 9.15 the *Queen Elizabeth* docked. The gangway was lowered, and Baruch went aboard.

At 9.30 he reappeared, beside him a stubby figure, pink and pleased in a blue yachting coat, jaw jutting, cigar uptilted, fingers parted in the V-sign. The crowd went wild: "Do it again, Winny!" Churchill took it all with a waggish grin, "too honest to pretend he wasn't satisfied with himself." [1]

Here he was, at last, "Old Man England," John Bull himself, the indomitable figure of victory, even in the shadow of personal defeat. With Roosevelt gone, Winston Churchill was more than ever the captain, the commander-in-chief, not only of the forces of the Empire, but of the whole Allied world.

For Bernard Baruch and Winston Churchill this meeting marked the renewal of friendship. [2] During the war they had met only occasionally and under stress of critical affairs. Occasionally, also, Baruch had sent to the Prime Minister most welcome food parcels. Afterward, with Roosevelt dead and Churchill out of power, the easy transatlantic camaraderie of the old days in the twenties and thirties was resumed. Churchill might inform Baruch that he had arranged luncheons and dinners with important people, or he could ask Ba-

ruch, as he planned an American visit, to give him a large, private dinner. Although Baruch's apartment was headquarters for Churchill's
family on their visits to this country, the American never taxed
Churchill's friendship and would write him that he need never concern himself about seeing anyone who turned up with an introduction
from Baruch.[3]

Customarily, a Churchill visit involved an exchange of a multitude
of cablegrams, and the Englishman might write that he had little
time and less strength, and was hoping for a quiet visit with his faithful friend.[4] The visits, however, always turned into triumphal tours
for the man who in his seventy-fourth year painted twelve good pictures, almost finished the third volume of his history of the Second
World War, and "seemed to grow younger every day." [5] His agenda
might include calls from the Duke of Marlborough and Lord
Camrose on the day of his arrival, and in the evening a "family dinner" of fourteen. The next day he would be off for Washington and
an official cocktail party, and dinner with "Number One." * Friday,
back in New York, he would dine at the Ritz with Henry Luce and
the *Time, Life,* and *Fortune* editors; Saturday, with Governor Dewey;
Sunday would be a quiet day at home; on Monday would come a
dinner with the *New York Times* staff; on Wednesday, luncheon with
General and Mrs. Eisenhower, and so on.[6]

The climax of his 1946 visit came with a "private dinner" of three
hundred given by Baruch at Sherry's on the evening of March 18.
The guests, showing Baruch's range of friendships, included Billy
Rose and Cardinal Spellman.

Politically Churchill and Baruch did not always agree, but they
kept their personal and political relations entirely separate, and each
was careful to avoid using friendship to influence the other against
what he saw as the best course for his country.[7]

This is not to say that they did not try to persuade one another,
particularly where the interests of the world rather than of their re-
spective countries were concerned. For instance, in discussing the
recognition of Red China, Churchill wrote, "If we recognize the bear,
why should we not recognize the cub?" To which Baruch replied
that we should not recognize the bear if we had it to do today, nor
was it wise to forget that a cub in time grew up.[8]

Sometimes, if their political differences were wide, they would be

* President Truman.

silent,[9] or Churchill might cable, "You have been much in my mind lately, for I feel you are thinking about our problems." [10] Often Baruch was thinking about these problems in a way that left much to be desired from the British point of view. Scarcely was the war over before he was being flayed almost daily in the British press, and the BBC was claiming that the only voice raised against Britain's aspirations was that of Bernard Baruch.[11]

For Baruch feared that those "aspirations" were merely for American financial help, and he did not believe that Britain's problems were so simply to be solved. Their settlement was part of the problem of reweaving the whole fabric of Europe. And that fabric depended chiefly on what was done about Germany.[12]

But he had made one profound miscalculation. With their incredible fortitude and with no territory lost, Baruch erroneously thought that the people of the British Empire would emerge from the war stronger than before, especially with the elimination of Germany and Japan as economic competitors, and with the opening of their markets to the output of Great Britain. The situation was still nebulous when he had talked with Churchill at 10 Downing Street during the days of his "mission," pointing out that the American stand was that we should contribute only $1,750,000,000 as a recovery "loan." His view was little altered by a memorandum from the United Kingdom Treasury, to which he affixed pertinent comments.[13]

As early as 1943, Baruch had had a very real fear that the British would turn to the Labour Party in their first postwar election, though the Conservatives were too near the scene to see it.[14] So in a memorandum to Representative Clare Boothe Luce he had pointed out that no nationalized industry should be permitted to subsidize its exports to compete with ours.[15] Socialism meant a disastrous chain reaction. If England had only one buyer of cotton — the government — would not the American government have to become the one seller? [16] William Clayton thought not, but Baruch was not convinced.[17]

The so-called Hoover Plan of giving relief funds only to non-socialistic nations had Baruch's backing but was condemned by one Washington reporter as a method of "using American economic power as a blackjack against progressive social measures." [18] To Baruch it seemed only reasonable to withhold money from foreign powers who were seeking to nationalize their industries for competition with ours. Senator Stuart Symington has recalled the substance of a handwritten note he received from Baruch during the late nineteen-forties. It had pointed out that, having lent and given billions to nations whom we wanted as allies, we were now competitors with them in the markets of the world for materials essential for our security and theirs as well.[19]

Furthermore, Baruch thought loans to nations who had nothing to sell were cruel deceptions, because without exports they could not repay.[20] Instead of loans he favored purchases by the United States of perishable raw materials, which would stimulate production, provide backward or war-ravaged countries with both employment and dollars, and raise living standards generally.[21] Loans might stave off starvation; they would not restore employment or the productivity of a people. Britain's problem was not so much a lack of pounds as a lack of the work that would produce them. American dollars could not long hold the pound at an artificial level.[22]

Furthermore, America had paid her share of the costs of the war. We had sacrificed over 400,000 men in all the services. We had put 14 million men and women into uniform. We had gutted our natural resources. We had given 50 billion dollars in aid, most of which would never be repaid. We had given 21 billion more in gifts. Was there in all history, Baruch wondered, any finer generosity? [23]

Thus, in a memorandum on the British problem for the State Department, Baruch warned that we must control our giving lest we again be disregarded as we were after the First World War.[24] He had once outlined this principle to Jesse Jones, in regard to a projected international loan. Payments should be doled out, not handed out in a lump sum. Then, in case of a change of government, they could be stopped.[25] Finally, instead of giving millions to a socialistic British government for use in industry, why could not the money be lent directly to private British industry, and then we would get it back? This he put flatly up to Churchill; British industry would repay. To Ambassador Harriman this plan seemed impractical; and, as it had in the First World War, the question arose: Could private citizens of a foreign state undertake obligations to the American government, and would our government accept them? [26]

The Nation, horrified that Baruch advised no loans to governments nationalizing their industries, warned that this would only speed the process of nationalization.[27] Baruch thought not. Why should we fit our society to theirs when ours had twice saved the world? [28]

In point of fact, Winston Churchill, idolized in America and defeated in England, and Bernard Baruch were not nearly so far apart in their private thinking as their public views made them seem. Louis Adamic was not far wrong when he described the pair as "the chief ideologists of the counter-revolutionary international." [29] Another left-wing writer, like Adamic a genuine idealist, granted that Baruch's "reasoned support of free enterprise," coupled with his "extraordinary influence in national and international affairs commanded attention and respect." Regarding free enterprise, he had a "burning faith in its superiority over any other system. In this Americans all but unanimously agree with him. Unfortunately, several hundred million peoples in other countries have come to think otherwise." However, free enterprise and socialism had to find a *modus vivendi*, and with this, in fact, Baruch could agree. [30]

One of England's basic difficulties was that, even while the war was going on, she could not make up her mind whether she wanted a weak and defeated Germany or a strong one, rebuilt as a buffer against Russia. What Baruch did not then realize was that Britain saw more clearly in her confusions than America in her certainties. To the American public Germany was the enemy. Britain recognized that there might someday be another enemy, and in self-protection sought an Anglo-American alliance, which Baruch deprecated as a violation of the principles of the United Nations. [31]

In 1944 Baruch had been perusing again his Versailles papers, one of the most complete libraries of the kind in existence, and wrote Stettinius that he was glad the State Department was to study these documents. [32] This, as he often said, was his second time around. Would the mistakes of Versailles be repeated? We had failed before because we did not enforce the peace; would we do the same again? Or would we guarantee the political integrity of those who sincerely sought peace? This was our second chance and perhaps our last. [33]

We have seen that Baruch's attitude toward our Russian allies during the war was based on the primary necessity of beating Germany as quickly as possible. We have seen his patience and firmness during the negotiations at the United Nations. Neither of these attitudes was the result of naïveté or lack of experience with the Soviet Union.

One of the little-known chapters of Baruch's life is that of his relations with the U.S.S.R. They had begun during Lenin's life, when Lincoln Steffens once mentioned Baruch as an ideal man to help in the Russian leader's plans for industrializing his country. According to a long manuscript in the Baruch Papers, Lenin and the Commissar for Foreign Trade, Leonid Krassin, sent a message by Steffens inviting Baruch to visit the Soviet Union and map a program for the tapping of Russia's limitless natural resources and the development of her industries. Baruch's varied experience made him the ideal adviser, and as any such program would need heavy financing from foreign sources, his financial connections were not to be overlooked. Baruch was tempted, as any man would be, by this job of limitless scope. However, it was the Russian people in whom he was interested, not the dictatorship under which they were governed. Baruch made stipulations which were not found acceptable, and the matter was dropped for the time being.

Lenin died and Stalin seized his power. By 1926 the Soviet regime had received diplomatic recognition from all the great powers except the United States. Although under the New Economic Policy of Lenin there had been enormous gains in Russian production, both agricultural and industrial, there was continued unrest among the peasants, who felt no security under the new government. The violent dissension within the Communist Party which was to lead to the expulsion of Trotsky and the adoption of the first Five Year Plan, was seething below the surface. Krassin was by this time the Soviet Ambassador in Paris, and he was instructed to approach Baruch once more.

As the story has been told, the interview was arranged with the "utmost secrecy." Baruch refused to go to the Soviet Embassy, and Krassin dared not call at the Ritz. They met in a hired suite at Versailles, and there, before Baruch's wondering eyes, Krassin displayed the treasures of the Soviet Union. Here was an empire grandiose enough for Baruch's gaudiest dreams — the metals from the Urals, oil from Baku, timber and pulp from Karelia and Siberia, the great ore deposits at Krivoy, iron, coal and steel from the Donets. And from all this was to arise a heavy industry: steel plants, automobile factories, pipelines to the Black Sea, fisheries and canning plants on the Volga, canals between the Volga and the Don, rail lines, a merchant fleet, a net of modern highways, and heavy industrial development.

Krassin looked up at Baruch.

"This is our heritage . . . Mr. Baruch . . . do for us in peace what you have done for your own country in war."

There it lay at Baruch's feet, "a tender of fabulous wealth," the dream of Peter the Great. To rouse this sleeping lion, to turn the Russian economy forward a century, no price would have been too high. "We were willing to let Baruch name his own terms," Lenin had said back in 1923. "It meant a fortune to the man."

In his initial interview with Steffens, Baruch had proposed raising the necessary capital by means of concessions. Private American services would advance the money for huge industrial developments at a "certain determined profit," which would be very large for the first five years, smaller for the next, and at the end of a fifteen-year period, the investors would have their money back, plus a big return on their investment. Russian labor would be used and trained for management throughout the fifteen-year period; and at the end of the time the properties should revert to the Russian government. The plan had been turned down.

Now Baruch agreed to undertake the reorganization of the industrial structure of Russia and would devote all his time and energy to it. But he was not seeking personal gain and would pay his own expenses. He would start as if Russia were a "primitive country," as indeed in one sense she was, with her peasant millions living without gas, without heat, without lights or sanitation, in an empty countryside little changed in a thousand years. He would have to do things his own way. First things came first: food for the people, clothes for their backs, shoes for their feet, roofs over their heads. "In bold strokes" Baruch painted "the cost in blood, agony and death of any attempt to do in a few years the normal work of decades," the strain of building a heavy industry on the backs of an exhausted people. It was almost as if he foresaw the terrible winter of 1932–33, when the villages were turned into cemeteries.

He was ready to proceed to Russia, providing the government would agree in advance to an immediate agricultural and medical program, to postpone the great power enterprises, "to tackle the light industry first and abolish terror."

His conditions were laid down with a finality that closed the discussion. The sun was setting as Baruch held out his hand. Baruch had spoken for the dignity of the individual, Krassin for "mass welfare"; Baruch for the consumer-goods capitalism of peace, and Krassin for the heavy-industry capitalism of war.[34]

Baruch's faith in capitalistic methods and "know-how" made him long to put on the show before Russian eyes. If the genius of capitalism as a practical fact were to clothe, feed, and generally remake the lives of the Russian people, would they continue to dally with communism? This was why Baruch had insisted on the primary construction of a light industry. Communism, he felt, arose from poverty. End poverty and you would end communism. He had, as he always had, great respect for the character and strength of the Russian people. In 1926 no less than in 1946, he felt that the world was an economic whole, that a healthy, prosperous, competitive Russia would be a mighty force in advancing the civilization and progress of the world.

But once again Baruch's stipulations were not acceptable, and the great chance died.

In 1936, Hugh Johnson wrote an indignant denial of a story that Baruch, Bullitt, and Litvinov had together arranged for the recognition of Russia by the United States three years earlier. In the first place, wrote Johnson, Baruch had never even met Litvinov, and regarded Bullitt's enthusiasm for Russia with amused tolerance.[35]

The truth was that he favored recognition of Russia under one condition — impossible from the Soviet point of view — that there be complete freedom of travel in each country for the citizens of the other. If the Russians saw how people lived in America, they would not for long tolerate communism in their own country.[36]

His experience on the Atomic Energy Commission made Baruch increasingly doubtful of Russian motives. He wrote John Snyder in the summer of 1947 that he felt Russia would never give up any of the German territory it held, and that our future policy should be predicated upon where we would have to stand if we stood alone. We should draw a line and hold it, no matter what the cost; and once such a line were drawn, he believed the Russians would not dare step across.[37]

The immediate answer was the Marshall Plan. Two years later Baruch told Mrs. Roosevelt that the Marshall Plan was what he had advocated in the report of his "mission," which he was to have given her husband if he had lived, and which he had submitted to President Truman in 1945. He added that the reconstruction of Europe not piece by piece but as a whole was what anyone who had any knowledge of world problems would have urged.[38] The idea went along with his plan for an over-all survey of world needs and the depletion of natural resources.

This is, of course, not to be construed as crediting Baruch with the paternity of the Marshall Plan. As we know, his "Report" was shelved. The initial concept of the Plan may have been his, but the general idea occurred almost simultaneously in the minds of various important officials; a program like the Marshall Plan was the obvious solution. Baruch's ideas were more detailed and would have made the Plan more long-range: he wanted no stopgap solution of two or three years.

Yet neither Byrnes nor Truman ever spoke to Baruch about his more detailed suggestions. Finally Baruch wrote to the President in 1947, warning him that the government was not thinking far enough ahead.[39] But he refrained from sending a bitter note to Marshall which he had written, saying that he was not in sympathy with the way reconstruction in Europe had gone and that no attention had been paid to his recommendations.[40] Instead, for months before and after the actual release of the Plan in June 1947, he sat down with the General and discussed the problems at hand. The original sum projected to finance the Plan was 27 billion dollars; it was then reduced to 17 billion, and finally down to 14 billion. The actual results, Baruch thought, could have been achieved for about 40 per cent less. He tried valiantly to convince Marshall of his own view of the bargaining power of American aid. We should insist on cooperation between the European nations which we help. We could not otherwise carry the load alone.[41]

A year later, in 1948, Mrs. Roosevelt, after a global fact-finding mission, showed Baruch her report to President Truman. "If you think it is not good," she wrote, "I can always change it when I am talking to the President."

She reported that both the French and Germans were still exhausted from the war; that Britain was going to pull through because of her stubbornness and fortitude, but that England took the attitude that she made the policies and the United States accepted them. "That has got to be remedied." As for Russia — Russia was offering the gullible a brave new world and doing a better propaganda job than the United States.[42]

Baruch read this with interest, but there was nothing that he could do. His own last great hope for world peace was to be unfulfilled. Day by day, with mounting concern, he watched the breach between Russia and the United States widening.

Some way must be found. Quickening in Baruch was the lingering hope that the atomic energy plan might yet be accepted, if it were fully understood. He wanted to talk with members of the Politburo; he wanted to look over the Russian activities, perhaps again offer them help in raising their living standards. The Marshall Plan had striven to do this. It had been offered to Russia and rejected. But the Russians had sought out Bernard Baruch once before — [43] Despite the waning of diplomacy on the personal level, Baruch still felt that a shrewd trader might win.

What Baruch wanted was a "peace offensive," made by the Americans rather than the Russians, to take the initiative in the propaganda war. This he urged upon Marshall. We should make a proposal with which the Russians must either agree or split their ranks.[44]

Russia might break her long-term agreements, but she was open to immediate solutions of immediate questions. Baruch felt that Russia was right in her demands for secure boundaries, for reparations, and for a trade outlet by warm, open waters. In return, we had a right to demand the withdrawal of the Red army from Germany, the liberation of the satellites, and the disbandment of the Comintern.[45] Baruch was correct in thinking that Russia's demands were realistic and perhaps even just in terms of her own needs for security. But were they calculated to give security to an atomic world faced with the specter of Russian aggression?

The idea found initial favor not only in Washington but at the Kremlin. For Andrei Gromyko, after listening to Baruch's often repeated doubts as to whether or not the Soviet leaders really understood his plan for the control of atomic energy, invited him to Moscow to explain it to members of the Politburo.[46]

Baruch visited Washington. The necessary visas were obtained. He was already in Europe during the summer of 1948 when he fell suddenly ill. Aware of the grim lessons of sick men practising diplomacy, Baruch, wracked with arthritis, notified Gromyko that he would have to return home to recuperate before undertaking the long laborious journey.[47]

But the trip was never made. Partly this was due to the necessities of an election year. A peace mission to Moscow must be more than a campaign gesture, as Truman's abortive attempt to send Chief Justice Fred Vinson on the same mission at the very height of the electioneering proved. Such a mission would have made sense several months earlier, but with the United Nations in session could only be interpreted as bypassing that body. Baruch thought that the only proper person to go now would be either the President or the Secretary of State. Privately he continued to urge Marshall on toward a peace "settlement."

The next spring came headlines: "U.N. Agog as Baruch and Gromyko Chat." For half an hour the two had sat "buddying up publicly" in the lounge. Someone heard the word "visa." What were they talking about?

"Fishing," Baruch said with a grin.[48]

Gromyko had repeated his invitation to Baruch to go to Moscow to explain the American atomic energy proposals — dormant now, but still not superseded — and this time the invitation had been backed up by Stalin himself. Baruch was to have full access to the Politburo. He could visit any Russian embassy in any country as the guest of the Soviet Union. But Baruch did not go.[49]

In Washington the Truman Administration denied any official knowledge of a plan for Baruch ever to have gone to Russia, and also quashed hopes of an American peace offensive with an indirect presidential statement: "We have no intention of making any new approach to the Soviet Union . . . We stand by the Baruch proposals."[50]

Back in South Carolina the next winter Baruch told the local press: "Every discouragement was shown [in this country] against my going to Russia." His trip would have been useless, for it would have lacked official sanction. As Baruch said: "I was *persona non grata* at the White House then. I thought I got the hint not to go — a very broad one."[51] For Baruch's services as an adviser to President Truman had been abruptly and permanently terminated.

Ostensibly the cause of the break, as Baruch wrote to Jonathan Daniels, was the Elder Statesman's refusal to serve on the Democratic Fund-Raising Committee for the 1948 campaign.[52] Actually, the showdown had been in the making for some time and its causes were much more deep-seated. The splendid backing that the President had given to Baruch during the atomic bomb negotiations marked perhaps the last time that the two were in complete accord.

First of all, there was the question of clashing personalities. Harry Truman was a complex man, and the much talked of humility with which he undertook the burden of the Presidency was not his only characteristic. The other side of the coin was the cockiness and self-confidence which were to become more and more evident as time passed. His very real success during the first days of his Administration was scarcely calculated to diminish these traits.

As Frances Perkins has said, Truman "knew what he was about." [53] He knew it by instinct — the sure instinct of the born politician. Furthermore, he had absorbed the basic political philosophy of Franklin Roosevelt that the principal function of government was to improve the living conditions of the people, and in the uncertainties of the postwar period the Fair Deal was still the expression of the people's aspirations.[54]

The President whom Harry Truman most admired was Andrew Jackson, and as a fighter he had in him much of "Old Hickory." But he also had a real kinship with Andrew Johnson, "the Tailor from Tennessee," [55] who had proved that courage and hard hitting could make a good President of a "little man." "I wasn't going down in history like Pierce or Buchanan or Chester Arthur or Benjamin Harrison — he was one of the most mediocre presidents we ever had," Truman once roared toward the end of his term. "I wasn't going to be one of your arm-rolling, cheek-kissing mollycoddles!" [56] Truman was not going to be mediocre. He ran his office with executive efficiency. The very fact that he lacked Franklin Roosevelt's imagination was in its way a virtue. It made him easier to work for, and allowed him to make his policy, pick the man to carry it out, delegate power, and then let him alone. He was not a President harried by doubts or self-mistrust. He felt little need for an adviser, no matter how experienced.

Also, he had pride — and so did Bernard Baruch. It could have been hard for Truman to read in the newspapers that it was "about time that the President took advantage of all the splendid knowledge that Mr. Baruch possessed." [57] It was an ordeal for Truman to "be told," particularly by a man of Baruch's conscious pride and prestige. His resentment may well have been heightened by the memory of his personal obligation to the Elder Statesman. It may be true that Harry Truman would, in that senatorial campaign of 1940, have "found the money somewhere else," as has been claimed, but the fact was that it was Baruch who had furnished it, thus indirectly helping to send the Missourian back to the Senate and thence to the

White House. It is understandable that Harry Truman would chafe as he heard Baruch credited with the major successes of his Administration.

In short, Baruch was an uncomfortable person to have around, and in the first year of his Presidency, Mr. Truman had offered him the ambassadorship to London. Baruch found little appeal in the job now that Churchill was no longer in power,[58] and knowing that the President was more than apt to be his own ambassador as well as Secretary of State, he declined the appointment.[59]

Meanwhile, Truman made it clear that he neither desired nor needed the Elder Statesman, and in a sense he was right. "Baruch's hard-headed suggestions ran almost directly counter to the White House policy after the war's end," [60] and he found Truman's economic theories "revolting." Baruch adhered to the old-fashioned doctrines: he was convinced that someday there must be an end to government borrowing — you could not run up the national debt for ever.

Even before the war was over, Baruch had realized that there would be no postwar depression at least for several years, that no matter what was done or left undone, there would be full employment.[61] With workmen in their own Cadillacs, farmers in their own airplanes, hillbillies in their own shoes, and, as an ironic footnote, the "rich" in their own kitchens, there would be no return to the bleak years.[62] But Baruch saw that full employment, plus high wages, plus limited supply, spelled inflation. And when you added the need for stepped-up mobilization, caused by the Russian threat, and the ensuing gigantic government expenditures, the answers were all the more clear.

Instead of effective deflationary measures being taken, in the thirty days between June 15 and July 15, 1946, when the OPA was dying, the price index had been allowed to rise 5½ per cent through yielding to the selfishness which had replaced the sacrificial unity of a nation at war.[63]

Baruch had broken into the vicious circle of soaring prices and wages with a denunciation of the latest wage increase as "a break in the line," and was answered by the President's contradiction and a tax cut of some twenty billion dollars.[64] In 1947 Baruch called for an excess-profits tax to finance the Marshall Plan, and found that Wall Street, too, shuddered at any threat to the picnic of inflation.

A year later, at Baruch's suggestion of rolling back farm prices, the
stock market again recoiled, and the futility of such suggestions was
well expressed by a Senator: "Brilliant but impossible . . . Can you
imagine rolling back farm prices in an election year?" [65] And Senator
Blair Moody commented, "One of the most constructive analyses of
his long career appeared to get Baruch exactly nowhere." [66]

Next, the Elder Statesman butted his head against that most unyielding of walls, organized labor. Of what use were increased wages
when prices only moved higher in proportion? Baruch had asked
John L. Lewis, who dropped in at Hobcaw late in 1945.[67] Lewis
merely suggested that they talk the matter over later.[68] They did.
But labor was not interested in other "segments of the economy," not
Lewis, nor Murray, nor Baruch's old friend Jim Lord. Baruch's only
victory came when the labor committee of the National Association
of Home Builders urged adoption of a 44-hour work week, the so-
called Baruch Plan.[69] Meanwhile, steel prices were raised five dollars
a ton, and in turn the President got the steelworkers a raise in wages.[70]

Could a flood be halted? Why did not the men on fixed incomes,
the scientists and educators fight? Baruch wondered. James B. Conant answered that he doubted their effectiveness with Congress but
felt that a nonpartisan citizens' committee of business, professional,
and labor men might be of some value.[71] Nothing came of it, and
Congress merely diddled around. Every act of the Administration,
Baruch felt, had been inflationary.[72] For the first time since 1933 he
became seriously worried about the credit of the United States.[73] In
the summer of 1948 Baruch wrote to Secretary of the Treasury
Snyder that the President had made a serious mistake when he turned
down stand-by controls.[74]

As to taxes, Baruch had agreed with Senator Olin D. Johnson of
South Carolina that to avoid inflation they must not be reduced until
at least a year after the end of the war, and then in a gradual, sys-
tematic way.[75] If, however, corporation taxes were lowered, the same
should be done for personal income taxes.[76] Baruch was also interested in Senator McCarran's proposal that small businesses should
be allowed to plow back into expansion part of each year's profits,
which would be exempt from taxation.[77] But he deplored the tax bill
brought forth under Secretary Vinson reducing taxes some six billion
dollars, with corporations getting the entire advantage and private
citizens and the debt-ridden Treasury the disadvantage.[78]

So distressed was Baruch by these questions of inflation that in February 1948, when Senator Charles Tobey asked him to appear before his committee on price control and rationing, he telegraphed that the pressures of the moment made any statement by him of doubtful value. Furthermore, he had no knowledge of the Administration's program.[79]

Perhaps the people were ahead of the politicians. Upon boarding a plane from New York to Washington, Baruch heard the pilot say, "I like your plan, Mr. Baruch." He snapped back that some people would not like it. To which the pilot responded that some people had to take castor oil.[80] And a week later, as David Lilienthal parted from Baruch and got into a taxi, the driver asked if his companion was not Bernard Baruch. When Baruch spoke, many listened. He did not care "what view the politicians might take nor how reluctant the farmers might be to cut prices." All would have to take it on the chin.[81]

In another great postwar problem that led to strong feelings on all sides, Baruch was concerned directly to a certain degree, and through his colleague Ferdinand Eberstadt intimately. This was the question of the unification of the armed services — a problem both delicate and important. Eberstadt was assigned by Secretary Forrestal the task of drawing up the report on which the unification act should be based, and Baruch kept in close touch. Baruch had for some years enjoyed close personal relations with Forrestal, and had been a source of strength and stability to the highstrung younger man. Forrestal wrote in 1944, "Without your patience . . . the beating at times might have been impossible." And again, "You have this curious effect upon men: your praise makes them search their souls to see whether they can live up to it . . . I will have to work harder than ever now not to let you down." [82]

And Baruch responded that he felt like a proud father toward Forrestal.[83]

In January 1948, Baruch saw the President for the first time in a year.[84] There was still no open break, however. Baruch was still a Democrat and a loyal one, as he was to prove during that spring of 1948 when delegation after delegation secretly visited the old man and begged him to urge Truman not to run for re-election. It was not his program to which they objected; it was simply that Truman lacked political appeal. He was a "dead duck," they said, an albatross around the party's neck. Republican victory was in the air, and to win, the Democrats felt they must have a man with a magic name.

The magic name was Eisenhower, and with no knowledge that he would accept a nomination, the party powers were ready to jump on his bandwagon. Baruch faced them contemptuously — the ADA group, Claude Pepper, Dan Tobin, Leon Henderson, William Douglas, James Roosevelt. Baruch was accused of agreeing with them, for on May 3 the New York *Daily News* carried a story: "That superstatesman Bernard Baruch is said to hold the key to the door that would usher in Ike Eisenhower as a Presidential possibility." [85]

If he held the key, he did not use it. He knew the drive would fail politically, if for no better reason. It could split the party, rupture the convention, and in the end Truman would be renominated, as Hoover had been. To repudiate Truman would be to repudiate the party's record. Scornfully Baruch turned down their proposals that he try to dissuade the President from seeking a second term.

"Why foul your own nest?" he said. [86]

The astute political commentator Sam Lubell, long close to Baruch, contends that at this point Baruch, whatever their political differences, "felt nothing but personal friendship towards Mr. Truman." [87] Also, he was sorry for him. Not even Hoover at his lowest ebb had been treated by his own party with the contempt leveled at Truman — and this in the face of a record that included the atomic energy proposals, the Marshall Plan, the Truman Doctrine, the Berlin airlift, recognition of the new State of Israel, and the bold carrying on of the Cold War. Whatever his personal failings, the President had made decisions perhaps as momentous as any made by Roosevelt and had carried them out with courage and forthrightness.

Yet so savage were the attacks, "so disgraceful . . . the language and conduct of Democrats about their own Commander-in-Chief," that even many Republicans were genuinely sorry for him. Clare Boothe Luce, no political amateur herself, wondered shrewdly if in the end the attack would not boomerang and create a national wave of sympathy for the beleaguered man. [88]

The Republicans met and nominated "the next President of the United States," Thomas E. Dewey. The campaign was a formality; they were planning an inauguration. Baruch called in Sam Lubell and asked him what he thought Truman should do. Without waiting for an answer, he took out a memorandum. This was what he was going to tell him.[89]

Baruch did not tell him. Late in June he obtained an interview with the President, told him about the men who had tried to get him to urge Truman not to run, told him he would be renominated, and said that he thought the suggestions he made might improve the chances of his re-election. Truman listened intently.

First, Baruch said, Truman must not accept the nomination at the White House. "You go down to Philadelphia and accept it." There was something else he must accept — the challenge in the Republican platform. He could call the Republican bluff, divest them of their ammunition even before election day. He should call Congress into special session and dare the Republicans to make their platform promises good.

"By God, you've got something there," Harry Truman supposedly said.

He left his chair, walked restlessly up and down the room as Baruch ticked off his other proposals. He nodded when Baruch urged an anti-inflation drive. Why should young men be halted in their careers for military service and big business go on amassing profits? Baruch urged a soft-pedaling — for the moment — of Truman's drive for the Fair Employment Practices Committee. But when he suggested that a peace overture be made to Russia before October 15, the President showed little interest.

Whatever else Baruch's visit may have been, it was definitely a "gesture of political friendliness." [90] Definitely, also, Baruch was not fighting Truman's renomination. As a matter of fact, before sailing for Europe, he made a contribution of $2500 toward the expenses of the Democratic delegation from Missouri at the national convention.

Before leaving the White House Baruch was cornered by Attorney Clark Clifford, who made an appointment to see him in New York before his departure. There, together they went over President Truman's acceptance speech. Baruch then sailed. In Philadelphia, the Democrats met in "the dullest, dreariest, most dispirited gathering ever assembled . . . to pick a President." Truman's worst enemies had, at least, to admit that he had what they lacked — courage and self-confidence. Perhaps the unkindest cut of all had been the defection of James Roosevelt, to whom Truman wrote bitterly: "Here I

am, trying to carry out your father's policies. You've got no business
trying to pull the rug out from under me." [91]

Senator Alben Barkley boomed, "We are assembled here for a great
purpose," then, with an expression of pained blankness, examined
his manuscript to see what the purpose was. Yet his speech performed
a minor political miracle. It was as Southern as "hawg and hominy,"
and it brought the delegates to their feet, cheering.

The heat was excruciating. The convention hall was like a boiler
room. In an anteroom President Truman waited while the delegates
wrangled through the night. Never was an acceptance speech set to
be a greater flop than Truman's. He bounced onto the stage at last,
a smiling little man, crisp in a white linen suit, glasses shining under
the glare of the television lights.

He spoke. He was "Give-'em-Hell-Harry," a humble little man no
more. The speech was plain as a cracker barrel, the speech of back-
country Missouri, of the Elks, the Junior Order, the American Legion.
It was warm. It was demagogic. It was alive and full of fight. He
was calling Congress back into session July 26, "Turnip Day." The
Republicans had made their promises. "Let 'em make good." The
delegates roared. This was the miracle. A whole party, doomed to
defeat, was for a moment magnetized by the hope of this one man.
This was not only a fighting speech; it was a victory speech. From
the press gallery Clare Boothe Luce wrote in warning "The end of
the Philadelphia Story was not yet." [92]

In the opinion of Sam Lubell, it was the adoption of Baruch's
suggestions that gave Truman a fighting chance to win.[93] Baruch
was perfectly confident, cabling Truman from abroad that his stock
was rising. Averell Harriman, who visited him in Paris, found Baruch
the only American he saw who thought Truman had a chance to
win.[94] The betting odds were two to one against him.

Yet, shortly after Baruch's return from Europe, he came face to
face with the President at the ceremonial opening of International
Airport at Idlewild and Truman looked at him as though he had never
seen him before.[95] Then on September 17 Baruch received a letter
from Louis Johnson, asking, in the name of the President, that he
serve on the finance committee of the Democratic National Committee.[96] This request had been made in many previous campaigns,
and Baruch again gave the answer he had always given. He explained
that he never served on such committees, nor made political state-

ments. All of this was well known to the press as his established policy.[97] Upon receipt, however, of this response, Harry S. Truman sat down and wrote Baruch a letter, and mailed it.

Baruch was appalled. He hastened to Washington "in great distress," as he said afterward, not to see Truman, but to ascertain whether the whole thing had not been the mistake of some secretary. He found that it was no mistake. Truman had "written it personally and meant every word of it." [98]

Rumors of its contents began to seep into the press, but still giving Truman the benefit of the doubt, Baruch felt that he had written in anger, that the President was beset on every side, and would later either withdraw it or apologize.[99]

The break still might not have been irrevocable. Baruch declined to fight. The President was in a state of nerves and frustration; the campaign did not look very promising. He had been deserted by the bosses — the Jake Arveys, the Hagues and the Kellys; by the left-wing Wallace followers, and by the Southern States Righters. His party had been split three ways; there were four candidates for the Presidency. The Republicans, starved for victory after the famine of sixteen years, were baying at him in the most vicious chase of a generation. And now Baruch, as Truman thought, had joined the Hearsts, the McCormicks, and the Scripps-Howards. Mrs. Roosevelt sadly wrote Baruch: "I am sorry the President wrote you as he did." [100]

The press would not let up on the story. Suddenly, in late October, Westbrook Pegler hit upon what he thought would be a death blow to Truman's hopes. He published the purported details of an off-the-record conversation between Pegler and Baruch. President Truman, the Elder Statesman was quoted as saying, was "a rude, ignorant, uncouth man." [101] Frenziedly, Mrs. Roosevelt wrote Baruch, begging for a denial.[102]

Baruch was again appalled. He had not authorized anyone, least of all Pegler, to speak for him.[103] That he had said something of a derogatory nature about Truman, he did admit; and later, in bitterness, added that he could not have done better than Pegler if he had tried. Nevertheless, the exchange had taken place several months before, and Baruch was furious at its being raked up as a campaign issue. Whatever his personal views toward an occupant of the White House, he never permitted himself the luxury of getting angry in public, or of publicly condemning a President of the United States.[104]

To General Omar Bradley he wrote that he wanted no controversy, that it should be the purpose of all, as it was his, to uphold the dignity of the presidential office. He sympathized with anyone bearing the burden of the Presidency.[105] It was probably true, as the St. Louis *Star-Times* hopefully speculated, that before the blast from Pegler, the Truman-Baruch breach was not beyond repair, but now it was too late. The Washington *Times-Herald* described Baruch's words, as reported by Pegler, as "the strongest [attack] that has been directed against any occupant of the White House by any man of comparable prominence and leadership in modern times. Baruch is probably the No. 1 layman of the Jewish community in the United States." [106]

Pegler had won his objective. Truman, stung, retaliated bitterly, releasing a "garbled account" of his original letter. Mr. Truman was sorry to find that when the going was rough, there were those that would take but not give. Loyalty, for Baruch, was "a one-way street." The outburst, plus the "Truman Letter" itself, wrought "political devastation in the New York Democratic strongholds." The insult felt by the Jewish community may even have carried the state for Dewey; and the New York *Journal-American* reflected that Baruch must have been pretty sure Dewey was going to win, or he would never have risked having the White House door slammed in his face.[107]

Truman continued to brood over Baruch's forgetfulness and "ingratitude." Baruch looked back to the Roosevelt "purge" of 1940 and marveled at how much Truman had forgotten. He, Baruch, charged with influence-seeking, he who had refused even to help his cousin Gabriel Baum get a postmastership lest it restrict his freedom to criticize Administration policies.[108] He had contributed heavily to the current campaign, and what had he sought for himself? How many Democratic Senators then in Congress would not have been there had it not been for him?[109]

It was understandable now that Baruch was reported to have told a friend "what a great man Dewey was and what a fine President he would be . . . He had almost a fervor in his eye." [110] At the Lexington Avenue polling booth at 5.45 A.M. the morning of election day, Baruch was asked by a reporter what kind of election it would be.

"A good one," he answered informatively.[111]

At Republican headquarters, the "victory party" went on late into the night. Deserted, Harry Truman retired early, and awoke to find that he was to be the next President of the United States. The voters had looked at who was against him and and had decided. Ed Sullivan wrote that the people loved Truman, and they did, but there were many that he did not love. His cocky self-confidence was restored; he had done what no one thought he could do, but he had suffered "a sore humiliation that a man of pride . . . could not forget." [112]

Baruch commented: "As a life-long Democrat . . . I am most gratified, particularly since the President and both branches of Congress are of the same party." [113] Now he felt it his duty to help pay off the party deficit.[114] He had given $2500 to the House and Senate campaign fund, as well as making numerous private contributions to the campaigns of individual Senators and Representatives; [115] and Louis Johnson thanked him warmly for his part in the "grand victory." [116] Senator James Murray said flatly, "The Democratic party is indebted to you more than any other individual I know of." [117]

Harry Truman did not thank him. Four years later, when it was reported to the President in the last days of his term that Baruch had remarked "One thing you can say for that guy — he'll stick," Truman replied in bitterness, "That's more than I can say for him. I never deserted Bernard Baruch. He ran out on me when the going was tough. And I don't forget that." [118]

23

THE AGE OF CRISIS

THE MORNING the gunfire sounded in Korea, Bernard M. Baruch was up, shaved, dressed, and at the telephone by 7 A.M., two hours before his usual time. With his old friend Senator Harry Byrd and a number of acquaintances in the news services, he discussed the possibility of immediate war with Russia. He talked to Secretary of Defense Louis Johnson about the whole military picture. He put in a call to Carl Vinson regarding the possible extension of the draft.

When he emerged from his bedroom, he found the reporters waiting for him. He brushed them off peremptorily. "Got no facts yet," he said. "Can't act intelligently till the facts are in. When you got 'em, then you act. Talk afterwards."

He put in the usual working day at his office, dashed home for an hour's talk with a columnist about Korea, old-age pensions, and the armed strength and weakness of the country. He tucked the columnist alongside him in a cab and hurried to a benefit party being run by Jinx Falkenburg McCrary. Crisis, as always, had electrified him. "I feel great," he said. "Been running like a race horse since seven. I told those fellows —"

Back home, he changed to receive a dinner guest. Then he was off downtown again, and back in time to watch a baseball game between the Yankees and the Senators on television. More friends piled in. Baruch, just two months short of his eightieth birthday, was still going strong at midnight when his nurse, Elizabeth Novarro, ordered him off to bed.[1]

Throughout the day his telephone had been ringing — that day and the days afterward. But one call did not come. For the first time in thirty-five years, in a period of national emergency or disaster, no call came from the White House for Bernard Baruch.

As after the First World War, so in the four years between V-J Day and the opening of hostilities in Korea, Baruch had exerted every energy to prepare his country against the threat of armed aggression and to place it in a position that would deter any foreign power from making such a threat.

While the fighting was still going on in Europe and the Pacific, Secretary Forrestal had written to Baruch suggesting that England and the United States adopt identical machine tools. He wrote: "It seems to me that in future wars, on the assumption that we aren't going to fight the British, this might be profitable to study." [2] There is no copy of an answer to this letter in the Baruch Papers, but the idea obviously remained in Baruch's mind, since he brought it up two years later. Forrestal answered that Baruch's "prodding" contrasted sharply with the general lack of interest.[3]

"Hemispheric solidarity," with the United States arming its southern neighbors, seemed to Baruch a possibility late in 1945, but there were objections from the Administration.[4] His ideas for a united Europe were at least forerunners of the Atlantic Pact. Writing to Mrs. Roosevelt in 1948 Baruch wondered why the nations of Europe did not unite into the legendary unbreakable bundle of sticks. Otherwise, each might be broken one at a time.[5] And to a similar proposal to General Marshall, the military leader replied that he only wished he had thought of that himself; Baruch said the General planted more ideas than he knew.[6] A year later Baruch could write with pride that the idea of an Atlantic Pact had never even been mentioned until he had suggested it to the Vandenberg Committee.[7] This may have been true, although certainly the basic idea of an Atlantic community of nations was not his alone. Nevertheless, he had been called to the White House and spent ninety minutes outlining the plan to President Truman.[8] To Vandenberg, Baruch wrote that if an Atlantic alliance went through, the Senator would have done more for peace than any other man.[9]

Baruch realized, as did so many others, that it was on ourselves and our own preparedness that we must in the last analysis depend. Stand-by plans for industrial mobilization, the stockpiling of essential raw materials, the dispersal of manufacturing plants, universal military training, and the development of the hydrogen bomb — these were the elements of national security as he saw it, and he pursued them with determination.

Above all there must be legislation, planning, and organization to prepare the country's industry for immediate conversion to a war footing in the event of an emergency. Because this had not been done in the past, according to Senator Harry Byrd, "millions of lives were lost and billions of dollars spent." [10] Now it must be accomplished while we had the sole control of atomic weapons. Were men too blind to see this? Baruch responded with anger to General Omar Bradley's suggestion that the Munitions Board and the National Security Resources Board might "lead us to the point you had in mind." To wait upon the boards and upon the usual leisurely congressional operations, he thought, would be suicidal, especially as they in turn were waiting for the President, who kept insisting that we were setting up a peaceful, not a wartime establishment, and who was waiting himself for public opinion.[11]

In perhaps his last official request of the Elder Statesman, President Truman had asked that he aid in establishing a program for general mobilization, but the proposal was in such general terms that Baruch replied with equally general discussion.[12] After the break between the President and Baruch, a running fight got under way as to whether or not the Elder Statesman's staff had prepared a mobilization plan and submitted it for White House approval. Baruch said that it had, and that failure to act upon it had been a "needless invitation to disaster." [13] Truman said that it had not, and the battle raged publicly, since the principals were not speaking privately. Truman declared that Baruch was "pretty badly informed." Baruch snapped back that he only hoped the President was better informed on other matters than on this.[14]

Sailing for Europe on June 30, 1949, Baruch decided that he had had his say. "The weather is hot," he snapped. "Mr. Truman has enough trouble without me bothering him." [15] Pressed further, he added, "I never discuss what a President tells me or what I tell a President." [16] But he took to the ship-to-shore telephone from the Queen Elizabeth to suggest that President Truman examine the White House files. A plan by Arthur M. Hill and Ferdinand Eberstadt had been submitted in May or June of the previous year. Hill declined comment. Baruch insisted, "The record will justify what I said."

It did. The subsequent publication of the Forrestal Diaries showed that both Truman and Baruch were right. A plan had been submitted; Baruch had considered it a mobilization plan, and the President had not.[17] In any event, the President had the last word in rejecting Baruch's "Push-Button Defense Idea." [18] The White House thought this was not the appropriate time to put stand-by controls on the books. More effective legislation could be obtained under the stress of imminent war.

In London Baruch placed a wreath on the statue of Franklin D. Roosevelt in Grosvenor Square. "In this unsettled world," he said, "individuals without definite responsibilities . . . should not be talking . . . Their chatter might disturb men with delicate tasks on their hands." [19] Thus, outwardly he held his peace, but he wrote Louis Johnson, the new Secretary of Defense, that although he understood why the official could take no position, in view of the President's feelings, while the necessary legislation was being placed on the books the nation could be destroyed. This responsibility Baruch refused to have on his conscience.[20]

He still had friends in high places. He wrote to Stuart Symington, then chairman of the National Security Resources Board, that he now had some hopes for real action. Was anything going to be done? Or were we going to study ourselves into defeat? [21]

He would not cease his drum-beating as long as the country was in danger. At a seminar at Columbia University, in May 1950, he repeated his plea for a stand-by plan of mobilization, with General Eisenhower concurring.[22] On May 28 he sounded a call for stand-by powers to draft industry.[23] Korea was only days away, but Congress again fiddled around. Mobilization plans were an old story to the Congress. In 1949 the draft of a bill had been worked out, but even Baruch had thought it invoked too much power, and it was voted down. Late in 1949 another had been prepared which, from Baruch's point of view, merely wrote "creeping" mobilization into law. Baruch responded to Louis Johnson, who had sought advice, that the bill had no provision for a universal military training law, for a work-or-fight clause, for price control, for elimination of profiteering, or for rationing of scarce essentials. In fact the whole scheme seemed like nothing so much as "a water barrel with only one side to it." [24]

Nor had he any more luck with his pleas for a raw materials stockpile, of which the New York *World-Telegram* stated in 1949, "Baruch Stockpile Plan Would Have Armed Us." [25] There was no stockpile, nor were we armed. He urged the plan again in 1950, just before the outbreak in Korea, and still nothing was done.

Of course, the major reliance of the country was on our head start in nuclear weapons, and what we vainly thought of as the secret of their manufacture. When in August 1949 the President reported that the Russians had exploded an atomic bomb, much of the myth of American invulnerability was exploded with it. On the following January 17, Baruch announced his conviction that the United States should proceed with the manufacture of a "super bomb" of a thousand times the power of the type used during the war.[26] This was two weeks before Mr. Truman gave the directive to the Atomic Energy Commission to "continue its work on all forms of atomic weapons, including the so-called hydrogen or super-bomb." Baruch was pleased by the President's "wise" handling of the question.[27] But even more than ever now, Baruch realized that saving the world from atomic holocaust depended on strong international control of the new weapons.

That the Korean War, when it came, was the outgrowth of American policy in the Far East can never be proved or disproved, but that it came as a completely unexpected blow to the American people is certain. Furthermore, we were in a state of almost utter unpreparedness for the conflict. Months before, Baruch had warned that our policies seemed to ignore the possibility of war — particularly in the Far East.[28]

Once the war came, President Truman moved with a swiftness and decision worthy of the man who had given the word for Hiroshima, for the development of the hydrogen bomb, for the Truman Doctrine, and for the Berlin airlift. His courage never shrank from responsibility, and he never faltered during the terrible months of alternating defeat, victory, and again defeat which unfolded in Korea.

Harry S. Truman — "the people gone to Washington" — faced this new trial from behind his White House desk, at once neat and disorderly, cluttered with eight timepieces, three ship's clocks, a piece of wood from the old White House, blackened with the flames from the burning of Washington, a miniature picture of Andrew Jackson, the "three wise monkeys," the framed headline from the Chicago Tribune, "Dewey Defeats Truman," all items in neatly spaced rows. To the right was a portrait of Franklin Roosevelt in his sea cape; behind, the framed photographs of Mrs. Truman and their daughter. Thus was he fortified in his prison cell, yet he sat decisively in that chair where he had at first looked uncertain and small. Stubbornness, courage, forthrightness — these were in the stance of his stocky body, in the strongly marked ruddy face, the sudden flash of his eyes. He had proved that he could do the job. Two years earlier, Forrestal had written: "We are very fortunate in having Mr. Truman . . . a conserver of the things we want to keep." Baruch conceded that he had the courage, if he only had the facts.[29]

John Hersey has recorded a vivid memory of a day when the President received a "terrible message from General MacArthur"; after holding in and planning for hours, his emotions were revealed only by flushed cheeks and tight lips. In a calm voice of "absolute personal courage" he said: "This is the worst situation we have had. We'll just have to meet it as we've met all the rest." [30]

The ill winds from Korea at least brought with them another chance for an all-out mobilization and anti-inflation program. They also brought Bernard Baruch back to Washington, if not to the White House. Into the Senate caucus room he strode, dapper in a white linen suit, his son, Commander Baruch of the Naval Reserve, at his side. That same month, President Truman had sent to Congress a cautious program for partial controls, partial mobilization. Baruch thought it did not go far enough.[31]

He strode up and down before the committee table, leaning forward to catch the Senators' questions, waving his hearing aid in front of him. "I don't want to duck anything," he said.[32] He glowered over his spectacles. "Our highest military authorities have stated, unequivocally, that from now through 1954 will be the period of maximum peril for this nation." The situation, he thought, was "sufficiently grave to warrant an over-all ceiling across the entire economy . . . prices . . . wages . . . rents, fees, and so on." As prices rose, the value of every dollar shrank. And prices were now zooming.

How soon should such a plan go into effect? the Senators asked him.

"Right now. Toot suite. Today . . ." While we were stocking our homes with refrigerators and television sets, the Soviets were stocking tanks and radar.[33]

Fervently he pleaded that the costs of war should be met by new taxes. How high should taxes go? Baruch raised his hand. "Higher than a cat's back," he drawled, as Senator Paul H. Douglas of Illinois chortled with delight.

Senator Capehart wondered if Congress should tear up the President's bill and write it over. Baruch thought not. "Don't tear it up. Just add to it those sections we've been talking about," he said.

But he had no patience with those who opposed the immediate imposition of all-out controls. Guns or butter was our choice. "It seems like my hearing aid is out of order and I'm hearing things I heard before," he said.

Was he going to see President Truman? "No," snorted Baruch, and stalked out of the caucus room. Equally dramatic was the way he had changed the political atmosphere in a few hours' time. The House Banking Committee went into session again with a hastily drawn-up "Baruch amendment," and this failed to come out of the committee room by a single vote, ten to nine. But all was not lost. The political lions and lambs began lying down together, such diverse elements as Senators Bricker, Sparkman of Alabama, and Wayne Morse of Oregon lining up in favor of the plan, to say nothing of Lister Hill of Alabama and Hubert Humphrey of Minnesota. The *New York Times,* declaring that Baruch was the "economic conscience" of the nation, wrote editorially that if one could judge "by the events of the last three weeks in Washington, Mr. Baruch has never been a more vital force in American affairs than he is at this very moment." [34] He had come down on what was thought to be a hopeless errand and had "electrified Congress with the voltage of an idea." [35]

The President spurned Baruch's proposals, telling a press conference that such drastic steps were not necessary. Yet many of Truman's own advisers — among them Averell Harriman and Dean Acheson — had already urged much more rigid controls.[36] Nor did Baruch himself give up. By July a new "built-by-Baruch plan" came to the Senate, calling for a rollback of prices to their highest level in the month preceding the invasion of Korea and for stand-by wage and rationing controls.

The White House still stood firm. But within three days Senate leaders saw this as a workable compromise on the whole issue.[37] Baruch, according to one columnist, had "darn near worked a miracle," [38] and the final bill, as passed, embodied the substance of his plan.

Yet, although Congress gave him power to invoke a general price ceiling, if necessary, the President found it wise to await the outcome of the November elections. Meanwhile the power rusted on the shelf; pensions and savings shrank smaller and smaller, and prices soared. Writing to Senator Byrd on September 3, Baruch noted that since the attack in Korea, lead had gone from 10 to 15 cents a pound, zinc from 10 to 17, copper from 18½ to 24½; and that in addition the government had competed in its purchases against the "scare buying" of the general public. Senator Byrd added that of the 53 billion dollars spent between July 1, 1946, and 1949, only 20 per cent had gone for new weapons of war, and only 600 million for tanks and guns. The question in Washington was whether this continuing price spiral could be curbed without the all-out wage and price controls advocated by Baruch.[39]

Baruch did not think so. "Soothing syrup" would not cure "the body politic," he told an audience at the Mayo Clinic on October 19. We knew the remedy but dared not use the knife. "Inflation must be halted" if our American way of life was to be preserved. Prices were still rising. Only now did the Mobilization Director, Stuart Symington, urge that even indirect controls be given a try. Slowly, almost imperceptibly, the price scale began to level off. Two years later, in retrospect, Mr. Truman listed as one of the three outstanding accomplishments of his Presidency the fact that the price index had leveled off and held — a few months after Korea.[40] But this did not mollify Baruch, who always contended that twenty billion dollars had gone down the rathole of inflation after the Korean War began, and all unnecessarily. He did not blame the CIO for striking for higher wages; the strike could have been averted had the Administration used the powers granted it.

Nor was the piecemeal program of "creeping mobilization" conducive to overawing the Soviets, now, two years after the start of the war in Korea, when we were already in danger of losing our superiority in the air. The inflation could have been prevented. The segments of the economy could have been held in balance and the armed forces have been supplied with what they needed, with the minimum amount of dislocation to the civilians. The so-called mobilizers had chosen the path of expediency rather than principle. To save freedom, it was sometimes necessary temporarily to give up some elements of freedom.[41]

Baruch's blasts were too frequent — and too well timed — for any real reconciliation to occur between him and the President, despite the hopes of those close to both men. So far as Truman was concerned, Baruch had lost his post as adviser to Presidents. Baruch was forced to appeal to public opinion.

He refused, however, to worry much about the feud. "I don't bear any animosity toward Truman," he said in the winter of 1950. "Why should I when I know that he's wrong and I'm right?" [42]

Where he felt the President deserved credit he gave it to him, publicly and privately. Truman had been "unlucky" in having the worst job thrust upon him perhaps any President had ever had. He had been crippled by his "Missouri gang" scarcely less than Harding by his "Ohio gang." [43] Baruch had genuine admiration for Truman's plan to stimulate production and living standards around the world, and he recognized that in the last analysis a victory for the President was a victory for the United States.[44]

Truman, good hater though he was, strove to make up. After Baruch had called the hard-pressed General Marshall our greatest global strategist, the President sat down and wrote him a gracious note. A few days later, the two met unexpectedly at Marshall's Virginia place. Baruch was visiting there; the President had dropped in. The meeting was brief but cordial. According to the St. Louis *Post-Dispatch*, Truman could not have been "more charming or agreeable." Mrs. Roosevelt, long a would-be mediator, confided to the public she hoped now that "both gentlemen will forget their differences" and that the President could thus derive "some benefit from the Elder Statesman's advice." She was sure of Baruch, "since in every crisis his great desire is to serve his country." [45] In August, back from twenty-two days abroad, Baruch told reporters that his current relations with Truman were "quite good." In any case, there was never a breach between him and the office of the Presidency. "I certainly don't want to quarrel with a man who has the responsibilities Mr. Truman has." And he added, "He's seeking peace in the tradition of Woodrow Wilson and Franklin D. Roosevelt and we should support him wherever we can." [46] Thus, he again assumed his role of courtier.

Actually, Baruch's reputation for wisdom and disinterested patriotism had so grown over the years, that his influence depended but little on presidential approval. Even after the break with Truman he was making arrangements for consultations with Stuart Symington, Secretary of the Air Force, Louis Johnson, Secretary of Defense, Lewis

Strauss of the Atomic Energy Commission, and David Lilienthal, among many others in high office. General Omar Bradley, Wayne Morse, Secretary Snyder, all wrote Baruch of their dependence on him for advice and counsel.[47]

And on the bench in Lafayette Square, he still sat dispensing nuggets of wisdom in the sunlight. "Now, in the afternoon of my life, I reaffirm my faith in this country of ours — this infinitely potent, this quick-rewarding, this slow-to-anger, bold, independent, just and loving mother of us all . . . We oppose slavery, whether imposed by the state or the individual." [48]

Although at the last there was no real reconciliation, even before the "pleasant chat" at General Marshall's, at the suggestion of Anna Rosenberg and Marshall, President Truman offered Baruch a place on the Universal Military Training Commission. Again the Elder Statesman, now approaching eighty-one, pleaded his age and declined. In later years, when asked if he would go to Washington if called by Truman, he replied as he always would have replied, "Of course. You don't turn down a call from the President." [49]

He knew well enough however, that no call would come. He could be content — with an expression of faith from Mrs. Roosevelt, who in a handwritten note said, "You have done all you could for your country. God bless you, dear, kind friend." [50]

24

SOUTH CAROLINA WAS HOME

THE NEGROES at Hobcaw tell the story. "One day in de spring dey was lots of excitement around Hobcaw. Everybody roun' de place dey was busy a-buildin' and a-buildin'. Dey go build a railing on de pier out by de President's Stand. And dey go build little runways all over de place, and we think Mr. Bernie goin' to have some old lady come visit him. Yeah. And den one day in come de sogers from Fort Jackson. And den in come de Marines from Parris Island. And den in comes de Secret Service men with this Filipino valet. And he say, 'De President of de United States, he comin' here.' And we say, 'Oh, yeah!' But it's true." [1]

So in after years the Negroes of Hobcaw recalled that April of 1944 when the exhausted President, Franklin D. Roosevelt, came to Hobcaw to gather strength for his last toiling year. He came in secrecy; it was days before his presence was known; and the families at Hobcaw were held almost as prisoners to keep the secret. No one was permitted to leave the plantation. Children could not even visit from the Georgetown high school. Baruch's chauffeur, Prince, a young Second World War veteran, has recalled that one day a week a single member of the community was allowed to go into Georgetown to buy groceries, but even he was not permitted to speak except on business, and a Secret Service man shadowed him every step of the way. There are ten thousand people in the Georgetown area, but they, too, played their parts. At first, so many planes hovered over the town, with boats racing up and down the rivers, that rumors grew that a German submarine was hiding nearby. But when the special Pullman lay at rest on a siding, and jeeps raced up and down the country roads, and Marines stood guard at Baruch's gate, and searchlights picked out commuting homecomers to Pawley's Island, the big secret was a secret no more, although the conspiracy of silence was still maintained.

The President had days of sun-warmed peace and exercise, breakfasts of fragrant coffee and hot breads, fresh-caught fish and fruits, hours of peace, without the intrusions of newspapers or telephones, and long leisurely evenings of talk with his host. He cast for bass in the ponds, snagged eels from the pier, went crabbing in the Black and Waccamaw Rivers. At night, driving through the great corridors of trees, he might see the deer, blinded by the headlights, motionless, against the mossy trunks. He had left Washington tired, he who "couldn't bear to be tired," as Frances Perkins has observed. At Hobcaw he slept twelve hours a night, sopped up sun and strength in his shirtsleeves, and slowly "some of the tired lines smoothed from his face." Although he did not gain strength as quickly as had been hoped, he returned with a new vigor, and those close to him have agreed that without this interlude he might never have survived the rigors of his last year. Mrs. Roosevelt commented afterward that "Hobcaw was just the right place for Franklin who loved the country and the life there. I have always been grateful to Mr. Baruch for providing him with this holiday." [2]

In later years Baruch delighted in showing visitors "the President's room," a downstairs chamber overlooking the slope of the lawn to the bay and a sun-blistered little pier where a pole stood on which the President could have seen the American flag rising with the rising sun. The room in Roosevelt's time was decorated in tones of muted red and yellow, with a mahogany bed and over the mantel an etching of Harvard beating Oxford in a boat race of 1876.

For Baruch, this presidential visit marked a crowning achievement. For his years of service he had asked nothing but recognition; that of all the places the President might have chosen for rest Hobcaw had been his preference, touched his host deeply. Although perhaps it was too late for intimacy between him and the President, Baruch's serene wisdom heartened Roosevelt, and a degree of mutual understanding and appreciation was reached that had never been attained before. Mrs. Roosevelt bustled in briefly during the visit, attracting as much interest from the Negroes as did her husband. She left, satisfied that her long hoped-for wish that Mr. Baruch would find "Franklin" in a cooperative frame of mind had been accomplished.

Roosevelt was beginning to see Baruch as Herbert Hoover has described him — "one of the great characters of our time, a beneficent influence at all times and all places." [3] The substance of Baruch's and Roosevelt's talks at Hobcaw has never been revealed by Baruch. Undoubtedly plans were discussed for the peace that lay ahead.

The Hobcaw house of 1944 was not the "Old Relick" of earlier years. On December 29, 1929 — a disastrous year for any financier — fire swept the old house, amid ragged cries and thundering feet and sudden panicky terror. Although all were saved, family and servants, but little else remained. In the later inventory, it appeared that only two articles of furniture, the sideboard and a victrola, were salvaged. Like his mother sixty-five years earlier, Baruch, sick at heart, watched the "Old Relick," his home for twenty-five years, dissolve in fire.[4]

Would he build again? Sometimes he doubted it. His children had grown up and were leading their own lives, and a new house would be strange to them. Yet two days earlier he had written Charles Michelson that the new house would contain the old memories.[5]

The "Old Relick" had been a link between the past and the present, and its destruction was a symbol, perhaps, that the past was gone. Young Bernard was married and launched on his own way; it was comforting during this sad holiday to receive from Key Pittman praise of the young man's rare abilities and good sense [6] and a forecast that "in him you will have a worthy successor." Renée, once her father's constant companion [7] and hostess at Hobcaw, was in love with Robert Samstag, a young Princeton graduate and Wall Street broker, whom she later married. Belle loved Hobcaw, and of all Baruch's children, it was she who most shared his tastes. A vigorous woman, now over thirty, Belle was setting up her own establishment at the adjoining plantation of Bellefield, which her father had put in her name. Here she entertained her own friends as well as her father's guests, including President Roosevelt, cooking for them and waiting upon them as she had done in her childhood. Senator Joseph Robinson once commented that "Miss Belle" was simply wonderful because she always said and did the things which made her guests "comfortable and happy without seeming to make an effort," and never bored them with excessive attention.[8]

Although a new Hobcaw could not be the same, there was something in it that could never change. There were still the same sights and smells and sounds, still the live-oak and the cypress and the lean silhouette of the Carolina pine, the fans of the yucca and the swords of the palmetto. Still the great azalea hedges, towering up fifteen feet and flowered with pink stars flecked with gold; still the same crunch under your feet of last year's dried and yellow magnolia leaves. The sanded walks were still swept into their old patterns; sunlight glanced fiercely off the drive made of crushed white tabby shells. Up from the riverbank still rose the smell of honeysuckle mingled with the earthy pungency of box hedges. There was still the same play of light and shadow inking the pines and painting the maples in bright green and cutting the old rice marshes into bars of green and gold. Wild turkeys crossed the sand roads, pink-flushed in the sunset; deer moved shadowlike through the forest. There were still the old rice fields blazing gold against a horizon of blue, and the half-drained wraiths of the canals wavering in the tidewater as it flowed down to the sea. Not a sound broke that stillness save the water lapping milkily at the pier.

The long, slow work of rebuilding began. There were architects, builders, and all the inevitable irritations with architects and builders. Baruch's original idea was for a Spanish villa, in keeping with the early history of the peninsula, but it was decided that it did not fit into the traditions of the "New South." [9] So the Hobcaw house was planned, a spacious but simply designed dwelling, with iron grillwork in the rear and six plain white columns upholding the portico on the front. As the house rose, square and stoutly built of brick with white trim, Baruch's spirits rose with it. Mrs. Baruch wanted a double floor in the attic so that people walking overhead would not be heard, and Baruch selected a corner suite for her on the second floor. Together they agreed on the organdy curtains for the bedroom and the glazed chintz slipcovers. Below the windows the lawn sloped gradually to the bay, and through the fine lace of the hanging moss Annie Baruch could watch the haze on the horizon, shadowing into purple and then into jade.

Years later, nearly twenty years after she was dead, the little suite remained as she had left it. Standing in a window, looking down on the river silvered with sunset, Baruch could almost feel her there beside him and understand, perhaps, what the Negroes meant about spirits lingering in the house. Nothing had changed in her little study with its quaintly patterned pink and white wallpaper, the pink sofa

or the pink chaise longue piled high with pillows. In the adjoining
bedroom there was still the little maple four-poster and the bottles on
the dressing table. The flowered chintz of the easy chair had faded
comfortably over the years. No one could really ever occupy these
rooms again, as no one could occupy Mrs. Baruch's place in her husband's heart.

With the new house completed, Baruch succumbed for a time to
reaction. Scattered references to the possibility of selling Hobcaw
appear in his correspondence from 1932 to 1935.[10] But he was no
man to indulge feelings of gloom very long. The tie between him
and Hobcaw was too strong to be broken. Once again, the dinners
were served, with such guests as Arthur Krock, H. G. Wells, Ogden
Mills, and Irving Berlin. It was the old Baruch who wrote to Byrnes
that he had a big house and a night watchman who could help his
guests to bed in case of need. His cellar was as good as ever and
branch water never was lacking.[11] Once, while "in residence," he
received an offer of a quarter of a million dollars if he would merely
survey a certain industry and suggest remedies for its problems. He
refused. But that night after dinner, he became fascinated with the
idea of what might have happened if he had taken on the job. He was
deep in his plans when a woman guest dozed off peacefully, lulled by
a big fire and a big day. Baruch growled, "I'm going to bed, Novarro.
This is the first time anybody ever went to sleep in the middle of a
quarter million bucks' worth of free advice." [12]

Although years earlier he had written that he did not intend to
interfere in "local South Carolina politics," it was natural that Southern politics in general, and South Carolina problems in particular,
were in his mind. Foreseeing that the AAA would cripple cotton
farming he once wrote bitterly that he could scarcely contain himself
when he thought of the plight of the South.

In these same terms, he faced the critical Negro question, with a
clear recognition of how much the North would demand and how
far the South was prepared to go. None, for instance, deplored the
horrors of lynching more than he, or was more convinced that the
South would have to revise its laws in the light of modern times.
This was the price, he believed, that would have to be paid for states'
rights. Southern problems must be solved by Southerners in a Southern way before outsiders took over, as they had once taken over the
problem of slavery.[13] The misrepresentation, bigotry, and prejudice

that had brought a revival of the Ku Klux Klan also lay heavily on his heart.[14] In the spring of 1937 he and Senator Robinson had talked long and earnestly on the race question, Baruch expressing his hope for a ringing declaration of the whole South against the lynching horror. Although this was not to be realized, he became one of a group of distinguished South Carolinians who agreed to see to it that lynchers were punished.[15] Baruch was to put up much of the money to guarantee enough law-enforcement officers for this purpose. Meanwhile, he was convinced that the Negro, like other minority peoples before him, would come into a pride of race and heritage and awareness of the great history of his people in Africa. Yet he was aware that you could not hasten progress, and himself ran into difficulties when he attempted to give some of his land near Georgetown for a Negro playground.[16]

The South had to handle its own problems, including the questions of labor and farm tenantry. It reads almost quaintly today that Baruch thought that the Southern states should agree on a maximum forty-hour week and a minimum wage of eleven dollars.[17] But that was in the depression-ridden thirties, and a revolutionary idea for its time.

He believed in states' rights, but not as a substitute for the human rights that every person in the state was entitled to. Poor laboring conditions in the South inevitably dragged down the standard in other sections of the country. Farm tenants must be given the opportunities due human beings, and this must be done by the states, or else the Federal government would undoubtedly step in.[18]

These were some of the problems to which Baruch applied himself, sitting in the sun in the garden at Hobcaw, or later at "Little Hobcaw," his "long thoughts" reaching far into the past of the South which he loved, and far into its future. Admittedly, he was first concerned with his own immediate low-country region. About the problems of the Piedmont area he knew little.[19] Years earlier he had foreseen the industrial renaissance of his native state: South Carolina had the water and the climate; the North would realize this, if the State itself did not do so first. If he could not wholly agree with one enthusiast that the discovery of iodine in South Carolina was comparable to the oil strikes in Oklahoma, he could, at least, telegraph $13,000 for additional research on the matter [20] and try to get the Continental Can Company to start a factory in the locality.

Finally, the governor named him chairman of the Advisory Council of the South Carolina Natural Resources Commission, which studied the iodine and mineral content of the state's fruit, vegetables, and milk, also the value of the iron in South Carolina oysters in the treatment of anemia.[21]

Although Baruch felt that his own Georgetown had little to offer in a war program, South Carolina's war-born industrial prosperity eventually flowed into Georgetown and engulfed even Hobcaw itself. In the end, more and more of Baruch's thinking and planning was done up at Little Hobcaw in Kingstree, not under the long portico at Hobcaw. The new future for South Carolina in a very real sense ended the old past at Hobcaw. Guests who came there in the late forties and early fifties were aware that they were seeing something they were "not likely to see again in this land." You knew, somehow, that you were lingering in an afterglow. The "great days of the hunt" had vanished long before, with the deerhounds and foxhounds and beagles, the English shotguns, the stable of stamping horses.[22]

One of the last great dinner parties at Hobcaw was treasured in the memory of a young Charleston woman, Beatrice Ravenel, who was there with her uncle, Baruch's old friend the Charleston editor, William Watts Ball. Long afterwards she recalled the tall, stately old man coming out into the drive to greet them and open the door of their car.

The party left their wraps in "the President's room," and after a glass of sherry were seated at three dinner tables. First there were oysters from the Hobcaw waters, then partridge and duck which had been shot on the place, baked ham, fruit cake, and "excellent white wine." Attention alternated between the smiling old man with the white hair and the dark-eyed dark-haired Ball, fiery and intense at seventy-three.[23] Coffee was served in the long drawing room overlooking the Waccamaw, with its massive fireplaces at either end. Afterward, the company was free to roam about the house, admiring the big gracious rooms, the sporting prints, the trophies, the portrait in the dining room of Belle on her horse Souriant.

The Korean War finished what the First World War had begun. Over in Georgetown were mills, television sets, and high schools. Like a bubble, the old patriarchal society that had flowered and grown on the plantation for over two hundred years burst. First the young people went, one by one, then whole families. And looking on was the patriarch, who had struggled with the new age of atomic power and still reigned as master amidst the vestiges of the past. He delivered his ultimatum. "You can do so, if you want to," he told those who wished to move away, "but you can't come back." [24]

In a sense it was the end of Hobcaw, and everything happened within two years time. There were no more bounties of a full month's wages at Christmas time, no more bridal outfits, no more $450-checks for funerals. Baruch had felt it his "duty and obligation" to see that the Negroes were properly paid; he had even invented work for them to do. He had hired a schoolteacher for them, and if any were likely students he had sent them through college. Their security had been complete. Now they had "gone off and become modernized." By 1953 the new clapboards and the new tin roofs on the old cabins glared blankly into the sun. The church stood empty. The schoolhouse was silent. "It's a good thing for me," Baruch said. "Now, I've nothing to do." But there was bitterness in his words. The hurricane of 1954 completed the ruin, laying waste miles of park-like woods and fields, crashing down pines and oaks that had stood through the centuries. The golden age of Hobcaw Barony was over, and, although opened occasionally during the winter, it would never be the same again, never again a Negro drawling, "Mr. Bernie, we must have a kind of slow hurry." [25]

But Baruch was unchanged. At eighty-three he made a rightabout-face in his life with all the resilience of a man fifty years younger. He could still enjoy life to the full, still come in from an afternoon of fishing with his daughter, hair tousled and cheeks flushed, looking like that happy young man who had shot 228 ducks on a single day some forty years before.

His life at Hobcaw was over officially early in 1957, when he made formal transfer and sale of the property to his daughter Belle. But, actually, he had made the change-over from a plantation sportsman to a gentleman-farmer several years before, and supervised his crops of cotton, corn, and tobacco with no less zest than he had put into the duck hunts of the past. Duck-hunting was, in fact, still possible, but he had marked it off his list since the imposition of the game laws. It was no fun to get up at 4 A.M. to shoot four birds!

Little Hobcaw now became his base of operations. This 1000-acre farm was the outgrowth of the hunting lodge at Kingstree in some of the best quail country left in the United States. At Big Hobcaw the thickets and foliage were too dense for quail. So for nearly half a century Baruch and his friends had been coming forty-five miles up-country to the wide stretches around Kingstree, lunching in the open at Cooper's store, then mounting horses for the ride through the long, lean second-growth pine, its blue-and-violet-tinted trunks hemmed in by glittering roads of white sand.

Kingstree itself, a straggling community of some 3700, bounded by the clear waters of the Black River on one side and by the Atlantic Coastline Railroad on the other, was, far more than Georgetown, a typical low-country town. It has the wide side-streets, shadowed by trees, a few fine old ante-bellum houses, a courthouse designed by Robert Mills, and in the Square, the inevitable "Johnny Reb" leaning on his rifle. It is a trading center for cotton and tobacco whose streets on Saturdays are jammed with Negroes.

Here Baruch took less interest in community activities than he had in Georgetown. But he became a familiar sight in the village, nevertheless, his white hair shining under the red hunting cap, his tall figure looming up suddenly in front of the little hotel, where he repaired into the single dark booth to place his telephone calls to New York, London, or Capitol Hill.

Actually, Little Hobcaw was the home of his nurse, Elizabeth Novarro. It was she who planned the farm, laid out pecan trees, and tended the infinite varieties of rare camellia bushes. Baruch had built the brick dwelling for her, and it differed only in size from the typical suburban residences that dotted the South in the nineteen-forties and nineteen-fifties. Soon this house, like the larger one, bore Baruch's unmistakable stamp. A painting of Mecca by his friend Sir Winston, signed "W.S.C.," its pinks and blues conveying both the great heat and the long shadows of that sacred place, hung over the pine mantelpiece. The sofas and easy chairs were rich emerald green, and the inevitable sporting prints adorned the walls. The place had a more lived-in look than Baruch's more formal abodes: copies of the five newspapers that he read daily — the *Christian Science Monitor*, the *New York Times*, the New York *Journal-American*, the *Daily Mirror*, and the Charleston *News and Courier* — littered the chairs. The little sunroom was his real habitat, with its big fireplace bordered with blue tiles, the comfortable wicker furniture, and the little mounted statuette of Baruch himself, gun uplifted, pursuing the flying ducks.

Here, as at Hobcaw, sport was always in his mind. "I think I would have died," he once said, "if it hadn't been for quail." Nothing had changed — not the cries of the bluejays or the robins, or the tingling autumn air, like the first bite out of a cold, crisp fall apple; nor the smell of woodsmoke, nor the woods in their flaming reds and browns and gold, nor the gentle gray of the plowed fields, nor the golden waves of the broom sedge and the dark-massed pines against a hard blue sky; not the "houn' dawgs," eager and perky in the ears, proudly capering; nor the rise and fall of the Negro voices, nor the sturdy old horse he rode, its back broad as a divan. Nothing had changed, not even the mules in the fields, arrested in motion as the dogs pointed and the shots rang out and up came the whir of the covey. Baruch, of course, could not hear them, but his shooting average remained incredible over the years. In 1954, for instance, he dropped 15 birds with 13 shots. "Some shoot with both eyes open," he once observed, "and some with one," and he was afraid that "most beginners shoot with both eyes closed." One memorable exception was Clare Boothe Luce, who brought down two on her first attempt, and then four. Baruch was flabbergasted. But she could never do it again.[26]

Riding through the woods, Baruch could savor the companionship of old friends, like big ruddy-faced Dave McGill, who has said of him, "He's a very easy man to hunt with," [27] or it might be his driver, Ely Wilson, at his side. And in the spring of 1953, Baruch marveled at the "beginner's luck" of Senator Robert Taft, who brought down four birds the first day and four the second.

Back home, there was the bourbon waiting to hit you "on the first belt," and the warmth and crackle of the fire, toward which Baruch would lean eagerly. Despite his splendid health, he was always cold in later years and demanded a fire even on hot days. Then he would sink back into an easy chair and sip and pontificate as the rubber boots were removed and the shadows and tall tales lengthened, and Baruch and his guests leaned back to await the dinner hour, "all full of lies and triumph." [28] Sleep would come, long and deep, and then in the morning the drowsy sunlit hours on the porch facing the lake, browsing through the papers and the mail, pausing to give advice or a loan to his Negro neighbor Tom Cooper, or just letting go and stretching out his nerves in the Southern sun.

Sport, whether he was spectator or participant, was still a consuming passion of Baruch's at eighty and beyond. After his serious operation in 1939, he had planned to recuperate by spending the month of August with a pack train in the High Sierras, and was only dissuaded by his doctors, who warned him that his eardrum would burst if he went higher than 1500 feet. As croupier of a five-cents-a-spin roulette game, he could be as tense as at a no-limit crap game, playing with the same zest with which he had raked in millions on Wall Street. "You can't stop people from gambling," he would drawl. He admitted that he trembled every time the Red Sox hitter Ted Williams stepped to the plate. "He's so destructive." [29]

His horses for hunting birds were usually old plugs, but he got a vicarious enjoyment by feasting his eyes on his daughter's fine stallions. Really to revel in the joys of horseflesh, Baruch went yearly for at least a few weeks to his old haunt, Saratoga.

Baruch knew horses, and although he had sold the greater part of his own stable at the end of the First World War, his attention was aroused in the late twenties by a "fast, rugged, game" Irish-bred stallion named Happy Argo. Happy Argo himself could not win races, for his wind was broken. But in 1931 Baruch gave him to Mrs. Cary Grayson in Virginia for service as a "free stallion," and yearly some of his fast, strong progeny appeared on the track. Looking on, you would see Baruch, making "sentimental wagers." He would rather see a Happy Argo colt win than watch Seabiscuit or Man o' War.

He was always happy at Saratoga. When he passed through the white gate of the stable yard he left the twentieth century far behind. It was like a circus day out of his childhood. You could see the red buckets swinging beside each door of the stable and hear the nervous stamps echoing from within, and watch the black stable boys with their wide white grins, tumbling out of shanties built long before the Civil War. Then came the grooms in bright sweaters, leading out the stiff-legged thoroughbreds, their forelegs bound in white bandages.[30] And there, a part of the scene, would be Baruch, seated easily under a tree, long legs stretched out, eyes lifting now and again from his Racing Form. He was a part of that shifting, sweating, swearing crowd of spectators at the rail and at breakfast afterward at the Jockey Club, with coffee strong and heady as the talk, interrupted occasionally by Baruch seeking another serving of flapjacks.

Once at Belmont, Baruch lost $2000 in hundred-dollar bills. A track employee found it and received a $500-reward. "In all my years of race-going, I've never had so much kick out of anything," Baruch commented. "It proves that everyone at the race track is honest" — at least, he added, it was better to think this than to imagine everyone as dishonest.[31] In any event, he was happy even with "incongruous companions" at the track, shrewd and shifty racing owners and plungers. Baruch was always catholic in his choice of companions.[32]

From some friends Baruch became separated over the years, primarily because of the difficulties of age and distance. "Don't you ever need me to argue with any more?" Garet Garrett once wrote him.[33] And although he saw little of him in later years, Baruch took the time and trouble to write a cheering note to Senator William E. Borah when he had been operated on at Johns Hopkins, evoking from the usually restrained Westerner a warm "I cannot express to you the feeling of appreciation I experienced." [34]

Jimmy Byrnes, one of the last of the old original crowd of Southern Democrats who were his friends, was always especially dear to him; as were the "team" of John Hancock, Ferdinand Eberstadt, and Herbert Bayard Swope, who was perhaps the closest of all.

Swope had retired in 1929 from the New York World, after making the paper almost synonymous with his name. As Baruch wrote Ralph Pulitzer, Swope had put the paper first in his life — he had never seen greater devotion.[35] He had a mind filled with irrelevant facts, from the specifications of an old-type cannon to the Japanese definition of an elder statesman as one whose responsibility was to keep the Emperor from making a mistake.[36] For thirty years Swope had been close to Baruch and to history. He had been a leader in the fight to expose the Teapot Dome scandal, and had labored for months in Texas to break the back of the Ku Klux Klan. Now he had time, if not to relax, at least to enjoy his big pillared house on Long Island, where millionaires, sportsmen, and show people mingled in a heady mixture.

One man, then very young, took Baruch on in a crap game and had the luck of the beginner, for at the end Baruch owed him $77. Later the older man offered to drive his lucky opponent back to town and "bawled him out" the whole way. It was just a case of incredible luck, Baruch insisted. "Given another half hour, I'd have had you in my debt hundreds of dollars. You're too insecure to gamble that way." The young man, lanky, horse-faced Robert E. Sherwood, was so impressed that he never touched dice again.[37]

In town you would see Baruch sometimes in the smoky, untidy

clubhouse of The Lambs, that fabulous establishment off Times
Square, and sometimes at the old German restaurant, Lüchow's,
where one day in 1951 the American Society of Composers, Authors,
and Publishers feted John Golden on his seventy-seventh birthday.
The atmosphere was like that of a German liner in the early nineteen-
hundreds. Golden, vigorous and vital, with the carriage of a young
man, threw back his black hair and sang "Poor Butterfly." Baruch,
wearing his eighty-two years with grace, was charming the still
beautiful old lady at his side. She was Mrs. Charles Dana Gibson,
one of the famous Langhorne sisters of Virginia, and for her Baruch
inscribed a few lines of poetry when he escorted her later to the
"Gibson Girl Ball." [38]

The theater still drew him, although as his hearing failed his
"first nights" became less frequent. In his eighty-sixth year he would
be donning a dinner jacket to quip with Bob Hope at a televised
banquet of the Friars Club. In earlier years he had been a familiar
figure at the Colony, the Stork Club, and 21. Now he preferred quiet
dinners at the Waldorf with a group of friends, or at Dinty Moore's
before the theater.

At his Fifth Avenue apartment Baruch entertained at quiet, conservative dinners with old friends, "no brawls, no body punches," as
Billy Rose wonderingly observed. As host, he knew how to put a newcomer at ease and would always see and hear the guest who needed to
be drawn into the conversation. He had a small boy's enthusiasm for
the latest fad or trick food, and upon hearing Mrs. George Marshall
explain how carrot juice had improved her eyesight, he immediately
called for a drink of the beverage. He quaffed lustily and, beaming
down on the assembled guests, announced, "I see better already." [39]

In recent years, Baruch has often had his meals served on a card
table in front of the television set, but on state occasions guests were
shown into the beautiful dining room, with its Chippendale sideboard, the Chinese silver wall-hangings and exquisite china. Here
there were always attractive women, good talk, and good food and
wine. There was never any pomposity. Once when Baruch was the
guest of honor at a large dinner, the company was quieted to hear
words of weighty wisdom from the great man. As a leading question
he was asked, "Now, Bernie, what do you think is the most important
topic in contemporary life?"

Baruch grinned. "Why," he observed, "I guess it's the same as it
always was, how to make a living."

Or again, when asked what he considered a rich man, Baruch replied, "I'm glad you asked me that. I'll tell you what I consider a rich man — any man who spends a little less than he makes." [40] The atmosphere was so easy around him that once when he was entertaining a little refugee boy, the child sat down, saw the peas, put one on his knife, and flipped it at his dignified host. [41]

Yet there were moments when he could not resist impressing or even bedazzling a guest, once welcoming a young country visitor, complete in all the splendor of full dress, with cuff links of emeralds encircled by diamonds.

Nothing annoyed Baruch more than to be used as bait to lure others to a party. One evening he dined with a person in New York who had told him that his good friend Fleur Cowles was to be among the guests. In the drawing room, Mrs. Cowles and Baruch compared notes; Mrs. Cowles had accepted the invitation because Mr. Baruch was to be in the company. They stuck it out during dinner, but as soon as coffee had been served Baruch arose and announced, "Fleur is going to take me home." In the elevator Mrs. Cowles teased Baruch about getting old, to which he replied, "I want to go to the Stork Club." They did — and remained three hours. [42]

Throughout life Baruch has been a man with a strong need for feminine companionship. There have, of course, been innumerable rumors about his affection for various ladies. Whatever truth there may be in them, diverse women have certainly responded to the diverse facets of his nature. One may speak of his "sweet, old-world quality"; [43] another, an English lady, found that "you think he is going to kiss you, but he doesn't." [44] His sense of chivalry is as much a part of him as his hearing aid. When a man in Central Park said of a passing woman, "Isn't she gorgeous? Ever see such complexion, figure?" Baruch silenced him with: "A beautiful woman only asks for attention, not appraisal." [45]

At times he seemed to treat women as though they were delightful little creatures whose chief function was to make life more pleasant for men. Again he could say: "A woman can do almost anything a man can do. Sometimes they do things better." Many of his women friends would agree that he had the consummate gift of making them feel like women and yet of appreciating their minds too.

Of all the intelligent men and lovely women friends Baruch has had in his later years, the friendship of few has meant more to him than that of Clare Boothe Luce. And in few of his friends has he had greater faith. It was Baruch who encouraged her to send her first play to Max Gordon, and although it was rejected there was no doubt about *The Women*, which arrived a few weeks later. When after her daughter's tragic death Mrs. Luce became a Roman Catholic, she received the sympathetic understanding from her old friend which many others did not give her. Baruch certainly agreed with the tribute of Brendan Bracken, which he passed on to Mrs. Luce: "Clare is one of the few who add zest to the drab lives which we are forced to live in the twentieth century." [46]

And there was young Blanche Higgins Van Ess, his former nurse, over whom he watched as though she were one of his own children after she was married and had a brood of her own. When Hobcaw was open, he would sometimes invite Mrs. Van Ess to pay him a visit with her children, encourage her to sleep late, the children playing around and climbing over him as if he were a mountain. He would watch them paternally, sometimes anxiously. "Don't you think you ought to take her coat off?" he might ask. On appropriate occasions he sent the children handwritten notes of rare charm that would be treasured in later years. Mrs. Van Ess once said of Baruch: "Once he's a friend of yours, you can do anything. And he never says anything unkind. Maybe to your face but never behind your back." [47]

Another one of his "children" was the effervescent Fleur Cowles. In every crisis of her life he would give her advice, then thank her for seeking his help. Once, near Christmas, she was startled to hear his voice on the telephone late at night. He had not been well but had sent Miss Novarro out for a change and was alone. Would she come over? Mrs. Cowles slipped on a coat and went at once. The butler showed her into Baruch's room, where the old man was lying on his bed stretched out, his eyes closed. He opened his eyes and took her hand. He began to talk, and he talked for hours. He talked of Hoover and why he liked him. He spoke of Truman and why he did not like him, and on across the whole range and roster of his life. He had received letters and cables and telegrams from all parts of the earth this Christmas season, yet had sought out this one warm personal friend.[48]

That same year a quaint friendship sprang up between him and seventeen-year-old Virginia Leigh, who lived in the same apartment house and became much attached to the courtly gentleman who would arrive at her door carrying a twenty-five-cent bag of cherries with the greetings, "Virginia, my spies told me you were at home."

She felt the nostalgia of his memories as he would murmur that her grandmother had been a beautiful woman. "You know, you look a lot like your grandmother." But he would brush aside her political curiosities: "My dear, this hearing aid of mine is out of order. Did I ever tell you about the time I went to the races with your grandmother?"

The mystery of the hearing aid was soon revealed to Virginia; it was Baruch's insurance against boredom. If he was interested, he tuned you in. If bored, he nodded pleasantly and faded you out. To Virginia he confessed that New York contained at least one well-known bore whom he had not tuned in for ten years! [49]

There were admirers who would write that if he ever needed them, they would take the first plane to reach his side.[50]

There was Roosevelt's devoted secretary, "Missy" LeHand, whose last years were made comfortable by Baruch. There were affectionate epistles from his old friend Hedda Hopper.[51]

At the Colony Club he had once refused the plea of a woman selling bonds. Later he wrote that she looked so sad he was sending her a check for $10,000, even if it meant he had to give up smoking for a week.[52]

Always like a shadow, like a counterpart, was the one of whom he had said back in 1903, "I'll give her a chance." That had been the beginning, and he could say fifty years later that he would "trust her with everything in the world" he held dear. That was Mary Allen Boyle, whose position in his life has been unique, and of whom he has admitted, "She's the only one on earth who can get me to change my mind." [53]

One other bright feminine light of his later years deserves mention. Asked whom she would invite if she had a choice of six for dinner, Jinx Falkenburg McCrary once named Mr. and Mrs. Eisenhower, Mrs. Roosevelt, Bernard Baruch, Mary Martin, and Miss Martin's husband, Richard Halliday. One night in 1951, Jinx and her husband, Tex, spoke of a projected trip to Paris. Instantly Baruch said that he was going over in July. Would they like to come with him and be his guests and meet General Eisenhower? Before they could gasp their acceptance, Baruch said, "Now, we must watch Arthur Godfrey's Talent Scouts," and had the television set turned on. Five minutes after the show, the redheaded entertainer himself walked into the room.

Tex and Jinx left with a "Goodbye, we'll see you in Paris!" Godfrey pricked up his ears. The upshot was that he took a week off from his television show and flew over, too, where Baruch and his party met him at the airport in Paris.

They had dinner at Maxim's, then Baruch had a superb time showing them Paris before he retired, leaving the "young people" to go out on the town. The next day, as planned, the quartet sat in SHAPE with General of the Army Dwight D. Eisenhower. As Jinx later recalled, Mr. Baruch led the conversation, Tex asked the questions, Godfrey listened, and she looked on, enraptured by the magnetic General.[54] Afterward, Godfrey flew home to report to his audiences. Unless the nation supported mobilization, controls, everything the General needed, "by golly, we'll lose the war here before we even fire a shot." The public responded enthusiastically, but the first wave of unfavorable publicity soon broke. Baruch came in for his share of the criticism. The junket was described as ridiculous. Baruch had had his pick of brains. Why had he taken Godfrey to sit in at the conference?[55] The fact is that from his first meeting with the television star Baruch had been astounded at the depth of his thoughts and the breadth of his questions, and Godfrey had admired Baruch's dignity and wisdom and had fired queries at him on economics and military affairs and politics in the broadest sense.[56] The Elder Statesman was struck by the quality of his mind. But it was his influence that really counted. Baruch did not have an air and television audience of some eighty million people. Eisenhower himself had told Godfrey, "Arthur, you've got to go back and be a Billy Sunday." He had done it, and it had taken courage. Baruch had warned, "They won't fight fair." No one would answer his arguments; they would just say that he did not know what he was talking about.[57]

His New York apartment was a reflection of Baruch's formalities — which had nothing to do with pomposity. Visitors would be shown into a stately hall and then into one of the two long drawing rooms. They were comfortably furnished but with something of that bare, ordered look that comes in a big house with too many servants with too little to do. Yet the rooms still bore the imprint of Baruch's personality. Not, perhaps, in the rarely opened sets of books, or the mantel décor of green porcelain peacocks and stallions facing each other resolutely on either side of a tiny Buddha; or in the rather feminine flowered chintz that covered the sofa and easy chairs; but in little things — the lacquered cigarette box by the telephone and the scribbled writing pad, the round ashtray from the Stork Club, a current book that he was dipping into, or a tin of his favorite butter drops. His tastes were found too in the bronze of the "Discus Thrower," reflected in a carved mirror, the two rows of sporting prints hanging over a corner sofa, the massive television set, the cut gladioli and zinnias, and the rows of photographs on the tables — his wife, young and lovely, his son and daughters, and all who had been close to him through the years: Cardinal Spellman in his scarlet robes; Churchill glowering from the top of the television set; Clare Boothe Luce, Woodrow Wilson, Anna Rosenberg, Byrnes, Marshall, Franklin Roosevelt, Mrs. Woodrow Wilson, and many more, to say nothing of the youthful Baruch himself, stripped to the waist in boxing pose.

If in a mellow mood, Baruch might show a guest around the apartment, into the formal drawing room, dominated by the Chandor portrait of Churchill. Baruch would pause. "Doesn't he look like a bulldog?" His gaze would then sweep the room, resting on the lovely things his wife had collected, the Chippendale desk, for instance, with its delicate lacework in wood. "The most valuable and beautiful piece in the house," he would say, "is in here — the most famous table in the world. It belonged to Lord Chesterfield, but I'm not sure which it is, that one, or the other." He would smile deprecatingly. "I don't know anything about it, really; my wife bought it. I'd say, 'Buy what you like,' and she'd buy. 'You'd better give me a limit,' she'd say, 'or I'll never stop.'" [58]

Baruch's headquarters were down the hall. Here was his small study with his desk and a comfortable sofa and walls lined with political cartoons covering fifty years. Guests also became familiar with the little Empire reception room with delicate furniture and a portrait of Baruch in his middle years, sitting in front of the White House. Next was a guest room, with a landscape signed "Winston Churchill" over the bed. The whole effect was of luxury and good taste.

He was "at home" with his surroundings, whether in South Carolina or New York — that city, which, in spite of its cosmopolitanism was absolutely American from the highest building to the deepest subway.[59] "I guess I am a typical New Yorker," he once said, "because I was not born here and am the son of Jewish immigrants."

Always he has been concerned about his city — the smog, for example, and the sewerage system. He gave funds for the purchase of a little park near one of the early Baruch Baths, $85,000 in land and cash for a new park on the East Side,[60] and funds for a clubhouse for chess players in Central Park. He also gave the money for the first public housing project in New York, including the Simon Baruch Homes settlement, south of Houston Street on the Lower East Side, although he has always felt that private enterprise could supply adequate housing for the poor if money were not devaluated by inflation.

As a voting resident of New York, Baruch has taken a moderate interest in the civic enterprises of the city. He was, for instance, at the age of eighty sworn in as an Honorary Commissioner of Borough Works. This ceremony was conducted at his Central Park bench by the Borough President, Robert Wagner, and was followed by animal crackers all around for the children playing in the park, among them a handsome little boy, born with only one arm, who has become a favorite companion of the Park Bench Statesman.[61]

When in the city, Baruch's interests radiated from his big thirty-first floor office in the Fuller Building, carpeted, tiled, luxuriously furnished in mahogany and fitted out with a complete kitchen for the benefit of the staff. This office is presided over by Miss Boyle, and the staff includes a stenographer, a filing clerk, a bookkeeper, a switchboard operator, and, in recent years, a research assistant. Behind the front rail a desk is always kept for Sam Lubell, who still drops in occasionally to give an "assist" on an especially important address or paper.

Baruch's long office at the rear embraces the city in its view — river to shining river, with the spire-like towers between. From his great desk he can look at the oil paintings of the "Old Relick" and the "President's Stand" on the walls, or the bookcases of achievement, the filed volumes of the papers of the War Industries Board, the Versailles Peace Conference, or the National Industrial Conference.

This is the setting where Baruch still pored over the ticker tape and received three or four telephone calls a day from his brokers. He would always make money, although in 1953 he said publicly that he had so little left people would be surprised. Years earlier, General Johnson revealed that Baruch, "the most faithful, kindly, and considerate man" he had ever known, had given so much away that he was no longer one of the world's richest men. "I've known Bernie to give a million dollars to the Red Cross without making it public," Herbert Hoover once said.[62]

This was an example of hundreds of instances of similar generosity. Baruch has always been proud of not being a "sucker." He would not be taken advantage of where he knew the circumstances, and he made it a point to know the circumstances. He always preferred to match a man's efforts rather than to make effort unnecessary. He carefully chose the recipients of his generosity.

His gifts varied from $1000 toward the purchase of the Lee Mansion in Virginia to contributions in the hundreds of thousands for army relief and to alleviate the sufferings of the war victims in Europe. To religious charitable appeals Baruch responded generously — no less so for the Little Sisters of the Poor than to the United Jewish Appeal, which received a donation of $50,000 in 1939. Once the Saturday Evening Post offered him $3500 for an article and was appalled to have Baruch discover that Calvin Coolidge had been paid $5000 for a similar contribution. Baruch sent back his check and held out for the same amount. Receiving it, satisfied, he returned it to the editors and told them to give it to their own charity.[63]

Generally speaking, Baruch's charities could be divided into three major classifications — personal, educational, and medical. He aided deserving old friends, one of whom felt as if he had "a bank in heaven," and another recalled that from the time of Jeremiah the name of Baruch had been blessed.[64]

Of the sufferings of his "own people," the poor of the South, he was always keenly aware. He responded to the plea of a village called Universe, on the Big Sandy Creek in Alabama, where, since the last white resident had left a year before, there were no schools at all. There was no road in or out of Universe. The farm land was the poorest in the state. The county farm agent only laughed at the eroded hills. No doctor could come. There was taxation without representation, for the landowners paid taxes but their color denied them a vote. Their appeal reached Mrs. Roosevelt and through her, Baruch. With his aid there rose a school, a cooperative, a dairy, and a new look came on men's faces as they assumed responsibility, which they never had the opportunity to do before.[65]

Sometimes he was sentimental as to where and how his money was to be dispersed. Here again, no one could force his hand. He wanted his money to go in the main where it could do great good, such as to the giant research centers like the Massachusetts Institute of Technology, or to small places where the majority of American youth studied and which no one ever seemed to remember. A college president in South Carolina, J. Rion McKissick, wrote that Baruch's donation of $10,000 was the second largest individual donation given the college in 138 years.[66]

Typical of these projects was an Annie Griffen Baruch Memorial Scholarship Fund, the income to be used for talented students in eleven South Carolina colleges, state and denominational, without regard to color or creed. Later came special gifts of a swimming pool for the state university; $5500 for the Charleston Orphanage, and a dome for the Shriner Hospital in Greenville; $8000 more for Erskine College, an additional $500 for St. Angela, and for the University of South Carolina Medical School which his father had attended. Donations totaling some $187,500 went to Clemson College, to which in earlier years he had given $25,000 for their poultry department and $10,000 for work at Sand Hills. He gave depression aid to hard-pressed little Oglethorpe University in Georgia, taking up their $400,000 bonds at the height of the depression and literally saving the life of the institution.[67]

Proceeds from the surplus timber on his Southern properties were always reserved for the South Carolina colleges, and once he wrote David McGill that if oil were ever struck on his land, the money must go to the colleges in South Carolina.[68]

In the nineteen-forties he set about the fulfillment of his life's dream. Perhaps it had all begun back in the early days in Camden when his father, the "wisest man he had ever known," had spoken the words that remained always thereafter in his mind: "There are no incurable diseases, only diseases for which no cure has been found." Perhaps it was because he still felt a faint regret that the phrenologist of his childhood had not encouraged him to become a doctor; because he envied those men who could know for themselves what it meant to snatch a man back from sickness or from death.

Perhaps it had begun in 1929 when, along with Walter Gifford, Philip G. Gossler, Darwin P. Kingsley, Morgan J. O'Brien, and Henry S. Pritchett, he had penned an "epoch-making report" on the relation of the city and Columbia University, which Dr. Nicholas Murray Butler hailed as a "literally stupendous service." He had reviewed the resources, the problems, the future needs of the university and its history since 1754, when it had been Kings College. The university and the city had grown together and must continue to do so. Columbia needed 2½ million additional dollars annually for teachers' salaries. It needed a 10-million-dollar building program, and 50 million in endowments.[69]

Baruch was the type of man, wrote a representative of the American Medical Association, who could make dreams come true — both a doer and a dreamer. A dream was coming true. Of it Nicholas Murray Butler wrote him confidentially on Christmas Eve, 1942: "I have no words to express my admiration for the magnificent benefaction which you have just made. This will do more than anything else that has been done to help not only scores but hundreds, perhaps thousands of those who are suffering from the war." [70]

For more than a year the news was not made public. Then in the spring of 1944 the details were released. Baruch had made an outright grant of $1,100,000 to Columbia and other universities for research in physical therapy. To this end, a "Baruch Committee" had been set up and, furthermore, his will had been worded so that almost all that he had at death would go toward the development of various schools of physical therapy. This was partially for work with the handicapped, not for buildings but for the training of doctors, for studies on the cure of polio and cancer and epilepsy and hypertension and for abnormal mental states.[71]

Three major centers were established immediately, including one at the Medical College of Virginia (similar to the one at Columbia) which was, of course, a memorial to Dr. Simon Baruch. Forty-eight fellowships were arranged to instruct doctors in the techniques of treatment through heat, through cold, through light, through massage, by water. Baruch, of course, kept an interested eye on all the institutions to which he had made grants, but he followed a different line of thinking here from his guiding rule in politics. Too many wealthy men, he thought, made the mistake of trying to direct personally how their money was to be spent. He would keep hands off. The project was, however, very close to his heart, and he did not want to wait for his own death for it to reach fulfillment.

In 1948 he wrote Karl Compton that he was trying, almost alone, to establish the best rehabilitation center in the world. He could no longer give time or money to any other project, for he wanted to see this realized in his lifetime.[72] He did see it completed. He gave an additional $450,000 toward the New York University Bellevue Medical Center for an Institution of Rehabilitation and Physical Medicine, agreeing to provide the additional funds necessary for the erection of the building.[73] When the cornerstone for the modern little clinic was laid in May 1950, Baruch was there, bringing with him the portrait of his father that had hung in the place of honor in his home for half a century. The Confederate surgeon, said Baruch, "was the one who made it possible." [74]

He gave of his interest and his time as well as his money. On his birthday he brought his cake down to the Center — a huge cake in yellow and white, "four tiers high, topped by a basket of frosted flowers." The circle of candles was no brighter than his face. It was the strangest birthday party he had had. The guests were a group of paraplegics and spastics, arthritics, paralytics, the lame and the halt, little children who would never walk, and old people felled by strokes. "Mr. Baruch," one said, "I want to show you what I can do." "It's hard to find words to describe a man like that," Dr. Donald Covalt of the Center said of Baruch afterward. "He has one of the warmest hearts of any man I've ever known." [75]

For Covalt, Baruch, and the director, Dr. Howard Rush, the goal had been the same: to establish the "most complete and modern rehabilitation center in the world." The same work was actually being done at Bellevue on a larger scale than at this little clinic with its eighty-four beds, but Baruch had said, "Howard, this is what I want." Bellevue was open only to the citizens of New York; "I want a center that will take care of people all over the world." [76]

His medical interests were diverse. His address before the New York Medical Society in the autumn of 1947 was hailed as a beautiful job of research, an eloquent fifteen-point program toward the goal of good health and medical care for all, delivered, as the New York *Post* said, "with the vigor of the young man he is." [77] In retrospect it seems remarkable because of a proposal, then advanced, that was later taken up almost *in toto* by the Eisenhower Administration. It was the suggestion of a new Cabinet post for health, education, and social welfare. Also, he called for a moderate version of socialized medicine in the form of compulsory health insurance, to provide for the great mass of people who were not able to take care of themselves or were not covered by voluntary health plans. "I do not fear government taking its legitimate part in medicine any more than I fear it in education or housing," Baruch said.[78]

Specific aspects of medicine interested him. At the end of the war he had written General Bradley that he had spent a great deal of time on the question of veterans and offered his services and those of his staff to the government.[79] Shortly afterward he submitted a full-scale veterans' program dealing primarily with health and employment. He had the concept of the future Veterans Service Act, stipulating that in each community there should be a veterans' center where the ex-servicemen could go, "in dignity, not charity," to learn what rights were due them. Re-employment, job training, loans were all included in Baruch's recommendations. But he stressed primarily the creation of a new medical service and a long-range psychiatric and rehabilitation program, not only for mental and emotional cripples but for paraplegics and all the victims of war's disasters.[80] Later, he was able to take an active interest in the JOB (Just One Break) program, which dealt with the fitting of all handicapped persons into jobs where they could be most useful.[81] He was also much interested in the health and problems of the old.

To Baruch health was a "great adventure," and his own vibrant constitution led him to say, "To me, old age is always fifteen years older than I am." After seventy, he seemed to draw on an extra vital force. His walk was a fluid stride. One friend, Robert Ruark, wrote flippantly: "If there was ever a fair bet to live forever, Bernard M. Baruch is that bet." He had the gift of being able to drop off at odd moments, stoking his energy with cat naps. His restless brain was still interested in everything. He wrote a lot and read a lot and pondered a lot and still could get as angry as an Irish revolutionist. He could tire a young man with his tremendous mental vitality.[82] His eye was still sharp, his reflexes a marvel.

But he was puzzled by what made some men young when they were old and others age long before their time. To Baruch there seemed "vast human waste material" in the numbers of aging individuals, "full of fears, hopes, despairs."

He wanted the answers. He subsidized publication of a book, *Gerontology*, a scientific study of the aging process, written in layman's language. And he spoke out against private pension plans because they encouraged early retirement and discouraged the hiring of older workers.

The New York *Herald Tribune* asked him to list the most important events of the twentieth century. He ticked them off: the First World War and the lessons not learned; the preventable Second World War; the New Freedom; atomic energy; the rise of totalitarianism; the advances in physical science and education without the discipline to use them. But the most important, he said, was the twenty added years of life for man.[83]

What could he do with his own prolonged life? He still "liked to make the area of contact with all phases of life as large as possible." He could look to the sky and the flash of metal wings, where the great engines droned that he could no longer hear. He had done his part to make America air-minded. After thirty years' support of air power, he had been awarded his own wings at the age of seventy-eight. They were presented him at an air show in Madison Square Garden, with Tex McCrary offering congratulations — that same Tex whose effort to get America air-minded Baruch had commended to Charles E. Wilson in the winter of 1944.[84]

He could think of his few personal regrets, such as having refused the office of Secretary of the Treasury under Wilson. His mind could reach back over the years as half-forgotten incidents came back into focus, as he browsed through Mark Sullivan's *Our Times*. Or he could discover sudden illuminations from a past behind his own, musing over *Little Dorrit* with its wonderful passage on the office of circumlocution. He could think of the memoirs he had planned to write. During the nineteen-thirties he had gone so far as to enlist the aid of Marquis James, but after a few years the project bogged down. In truth there was so much in the present that he had little time to deal with the past.

His tendency was always to look beyond himself. Only occasionally did he indulge in rambling reminiscences of past years, as he did in an unrehearsed give-and-take session before the undergraduates at Brown University, and then he looked at the past only in terms of the young people's future.

Money-making was a specialty, he told them. You could not make money "and do something else. None of the great artists, none of the great painters, none of the great political figures have ever been money-makers, but you have to make up your mind what you want to do. If you want to make money you've got to study the things which go into money-making . . . And after you get the money, you had better be careful that the government doesn't destroy its purchasing value because you won't have very much left." [85]

He still looked to the horizons of his country, to the good earth from which all wealth came. It was fitting irony, perhaps, that the man who had reaped the treasures of the earth in his youth should now think of cultivation and future harvests, and urge Congress to institute a twenty-billion-dollar survey of our natural resources. He who had twice helped mobilize his country for war knew that time and riches were running out, that in the future we would fight as other nations fought, as a "have-not" country. He read with interest such books as *Our Plundered Planet* and *Road for Survival*, and, in answer to an appeal from William Vogt, wrote a foreword to the latter book so that it might get a hearing among people who could do something about the gigantic conservation problem. "Mankind," Baruch wrote, "must reach a sound, healthy relationship with [its] total environment, not only if it is to survive, but if it is to raise its standard of living." Later that year of 1948 he addressed the New York Herald Tribune Forum on the same general subject.[86]

Several noble sentences stand out: the struggle was "largely one of man against himself, between the instincts that make wreckers and those that make creators. As old as the Biblical conflict between the forces of light and darkness, this struggle is also as new as atomic energy." Atomic energy could answer the conservationists' dream, for where coal and oil burned away in giving heat, fissionable material reproduced itself. The day would come when men could farm the sea, manufacture food by mixing sunlight and sea water. The sea might even be distilled for irrigation. True, men were still shrinking the earth's resources faster than science was expanding them. Men, living in fear of another war, lacked trust in their capacity for self-government. Their faith had to be reborn if the land was to be saved. "We dare not face the future with complacency, but need not face it with despair." [87]

His own state of South Carolina had turned Baruch's interest toward conservation. When he was a boy the land in the South was often cleared by fire. Through his young manhood the bitter harvest had been reaped: of raw-bone clay and rivers red with silt, the naked roots of trees, from which the last clinging lumps of topsoil had blown away, the denuded hills, the scarred and empty fields. He had seen death and then, like spring, the wonder of rebirth. Through modern methods of conservation, fostered by the New Deal, Baruch had seen South Carolina bloom again, and nothing could have stirred him more.

"You are my people," he told the members of the South Carolina legislature upon the unveiling of his portrait there in the old shell-scarred State House, beside all the great men of South Carolina's past, the Rutledges and the Pinckneys, Calhoun and Hampton, Ben Tillman, and James F. Byrnes.[88] Byrnes had joked about the two hanging together although they were hung separately.* [89] At the moment when his older daughter pulled the cord unveiling the portrait and Baruch saw himself surrounded by Lee and Wilson and Jackson, he was so stirred that for a moment he could not speak.[90]

On another April day two years later, the Camden *Chronicle* had a banner headline: "Camden's Most Illustrious Son Comes Home." [91]

There his old neighbors, visitors, and dignitaries from across the state had gathered to do him honor. His children and "kin" were at his side. But it was another Camden to which he came home in memory: the old schoolroom with the bundle of switches in the corner; Factory Pond, the Race, the freshets; the uptown boys and the downtown boys; the hickory nuts in the fall; the hunting dogs racing across the fallen leaves; and Minerva, who still was alive, still able to stumble across the stand at Hampton Park and clasp in her arms the "little toad" who had kept her "on the jump" so many years before.[92]

And then there were the ones that could not be there. As Baruch said: "The thoughts of my parents were ever in this state. If they could look down and see the welcome being attached to one of their sons, I know their cup of happiness would be complete." [93]

It was April in South Carolina, like the Aprils of seventy years before, with dogwood, white floating in the green, and the scarlet blaze of azaleas, the sunlight warm on your back, and all the sights and sounds and smells of seventy years before — and he the center of it all. He was so touched by the spontaneous warmth of this celebration that he was overcome by the excitement and when he went back to New York had to remain in bed several days.[94]

It was as a South Carolinian, too, that Baruch in 1951 addressed perhaps the only men in the world who could still call him "son" —

---

* The portrait of Byrnes was hung in the Senate Chamber, Baruch's in the House.

three of the twelve surviving men who had fought under Stonewall and Lee, met together at the last encampment of the United Confederate Veterans. "What should America be afraid of now?" he asked the tired old men nodding in the convention hall.[95] And as a South Carolinian he attended the inauguration of James F. Byrnes as Governor of his native state, under the shining green leaves of the magnolias and the palmettos. This was his state, South Carolina, with the best all-around climate and the greatest agricultural possibilities in the world. No pastures were greener. South Carolina was home.[96]

25

MR. BARUCH

ON THE TWENTY-SIXTH of May, 1947, *Time* Magazine observed that Bernard Baruch had gone a whole week without getting an award.[1] However, things picked up the next day when "America's number one citizen"[2] appeared before the Fraternal League of the Jewish Educational Committee to receive their citation for brotherhood. In the days and weeks following he garnered the Boy Scouts' Silver Buffalo for "distinguished service to boyhood," the Cardozo Memorial Award from the legal fraternity, Tau Epsilon Rho; an honorary doctorate of laws from Rutgers; he was cited as the world's foremost humanitarian by the Jewish War Veterans, and a bust of him was unveiled at the Army War College. All this was just a sampling. In a year's time he had received the plaque of the New York Kiwanis Club as the city's "outstanding citizen of the year," the Freedom House Award, the American Hebrew Medal, and had shared with Trygve Lie the first annual award of the Good Neighbor Foundation. He had been the guest speaker at the centennial celebration of the alumni of the College of the City of New York and at the thirty-seventh anniversary of the Boy Scouts of America. He had been presented the ten-millionth ball of American-made rubber, and the award of the Metropolitan Temple Brotherhoods for his services to humanity. When the presentations slacked off a bit, the press stepped into the breach and told the story of the green china cat that Baruch's mother had presented to him for luck some forty-five years before. "It worked," was the journalistic comment. This had apparently been true, although his doubting father had whispered in his ear, "Don't put your faith in it."[3]

The era of Baruch hero-worship was at its peak. What started as a trickle had become a flood. Baruch had written to General Levin Campbell in the spring of 1946 that he had come through the war without getting any important recognition.* This was when he was unexpectedly awarded the Medal of Merit. But now he was heavy both with age and honors — this "grand old man" who, as Henry Luce described him, walked "unterrified through the foam of human illusions." [4] Since the First World War, when the image of the Wall Street man began to fade from the public mind, Baruch's press had been good and, more recently, better and better. He was in his seventy-seventh year when one man wrote to him that he would be the only logical Democratic candidate for the Presidency in 1948 if he were twenty years younger.[5] That same year a friend wrote from California that everywhere sounded the same refrain: "If we only had Bernard Baruch as President of the United States, the most intelligent man in the whole country." [6] Even Walter Lippmann, a newspaperman with whom Baruch has never been close, succumbed to the tide of adulation, with the declaration that perhaps there has been no man in our history held in such esteem.[7]

Having repeatedly refused the responsibilities of important public office, he had cultivated the friendship of the newspapermen, fully aware that, as Anna Rosenberg has said, "you can be wise, but if you only talk to yourself, it's no good." [8] His resource was influence on public opinion, and he knew how to get it. He endeared himself to the newspapermen, Walker Stone has declared, because he never lied to them and never talked down to them, and never used them for trial balloons.[9] Therefore, they had been only too glad to aid in building up the image. One correspondent wondered if Baruch really realized how Main Street and the little hamlets felt about him. *He* knew, because he had tested the sentiment.[10] At a liquor store in Dover, New Hampshire, in Broken Bow, in a courthouse square down South, or at a crosswalk in New York City, the name of Baruch was greeted with recognition. "A call from Baruch," said one enthusiast, "is like a summons from the White House." [11] There was a constant demand for more concrete information about him. The press supplied a series of short biographical sketches, and there was a brilliant three-issue "Profile" by John Hersey in *The New Yorker*.[12]

---

* Although in 1944, after a poll of the leaders of church and industry, he was given the *Churchman* award for his "vision and greatness of heart." *The Churchman*, May 8, 1949.

By 1952 he was listed in the New York *Herald Tribune* as one of the 100 most important people in the world.[13] Everything was "news" about him, even his hot-weather drink of tea, vinegar, and cloves.[14] He delighted in being photographed holding a child up to a drinking fountain in the park. He got a healthy and sometimes naïve enjoyment out of the results of his fame, such as his ability to stop the traffic while the lights changed at 57th Street. From the taxi at the head of the left-hand column came the cry: "Go on, boss, I'll hold 'em." "I'll hold 'em, too," came an answer from the other side. When he was sixty-seven, his bout at fisticuffs with a recalcitrant taxi driver became legend. He was by now a favorite with the taxi drivers, whose acknowledged favorites are few. Sometimes they would slow down before a building on the corner of East 66th Street. "You know, Bernard Baruch lives in that building. A great fellow." [15]

One night diminutive Billy Rose was ignored by the major-domo of a night club as he requested a table for "a very tall man." But when the "tall man" arrived, there was pandemonium as the waiters tumbled over themselves in their haste to escort Bernard Baruch to a table.[16]

The prestige of being named Bernard Baruch was less pleasing to a retired German cavalry veteran living quietly on West 92nd Street. He could endure the five or six telephone calls a day for his famous namesake which his wife referred to the Madison Avenue office. He evolved a pat answer for the perpetual and insistent inquiry, "But you *are* Bernard Baruch, aren't you?" At first he opened the sundry mail, most of which stated that Mrs. So-and-so had money to invest and would Mr. Baruch advise her what to do? At last he automatically forwarded, unopened, all mail bearing an unfamiliar postmark. But he could never quite get used to a sudden telephone call from Dwight D. Eisenhower, or an abrupt "This is Henry Kaiser, listen, Bernie," or to receiving fifty dollars worth of flowers at New Year's time from Cardinal Spellman, or that night in 1944 when the telephone rang and the impersonal operator in Washington said quietly, "The President wants to speak to you." [17]

The popularity of Bernard Baruch was dramatically shown one spring day in 1953 when he attended a matinee of the Danny Kaye show at the Palace Theater in New York. Midway in the midst of slapstick, muggery, all-American folksiness, and the poignant child-like quality of Kaye's humor, the blond-haired comedian came down to the footlights. He swung his legs over the orchestra pit, smoking and chatting companionably as the lights went up. Then he stood and raised a hand for silence. "Ladies and gentlemen," he shouted, "we have in our midst one of the great Americans of all time, an elder statesman, whose name will go ringing down the corridors of history. I give you Mr. Bernard M. Baruch."

As Baruch stood up, the crowd went wild. There was an avalanche of sound. The shouting, the cheering, the clapping, the stamping went on and on, until in sheer weariness Baruch resumed his seat, but there was no slackening of sound. The uproar continued, and Baruch stood up again — for a second bow. The demonstration lasted nearly ten minutes. It was a spontaneous outpouring of the people's affection.[18]

Oddly enough, the admiration which Baruch has aroused in the American people has not always been shared by a vocal minority of the Jewish population. To the masses of those of his inherited faith, he has been as much or more of a hero than to the rest of Americans, but to four groups he has seemed far less. The strictly orthodox have found that he was not religious enough, according to their definition; the political liberals have found him too conservative; and the Zionists have often become bitter at his failure publicly to support their programs. Intellectuals too have felt that Baruch has neglected the great scholarly aspects of the Jewish heritage. But, the truth is that in his own mind Baruch is not primarily a Jew but an American. "Why should any man kick," he asked in 1951, "who can do what I have done? Here's this wonderful country, and look what it's done for me!" [19] We have already seen Baruch's generosity to many Jewish causes, but that generosity was not limited to appeals from any one creed or race. A story is told of a conversation between Baruch and a certain rabbi who sharply demanded, "Aren't you ever going to do anything for your people?"

"You're damned right, I am," Baruch replied. "I'm going to do everything I can for my people. They're the American people." [20]

Although he was quick and violent in his reaction to whatever seemed to suggest that he or any other Jew was to be judged on a different basis from other Americans, by the same token he insisted that all were Americans first and should act as such. When the bigots of the Ku Klux Klan burned their fiery cross near Hobcaw one late summer night in 1951, Baruch slept for months with a loaded gun at hand. Yet he scorned to be sorry for himself, or to grant his fellow Jews the privilege of being sorry for themselves.

For the victims of Hitler's bestiality, Baruch naturally felt the compassion of any decent person, and when he came to know of Dachau and Buchenwald, he for a time sympathized with Morgenthau's plan to reduce Germany to the simplest agricultural society. Never, he thought, should the Germans be allowed to get into the society of decent people again.[21] Yet on soberer thought, he was wise enough to know that there was no way to punish the German people for their crime. The evil was in men's hearts and would break out another time unless it were made impossible. The only answer was to take care that the crime could not occur again.

As for the refugees, Jewish and others, who were wandering over the face of Europe seeking to escape the madness of the times, Baruch had a plan. He dreamed of a "United States of Africa," on land voluntarily relinquished by the colonial powers, where all the homeless and the victimized could find asylum and start a new nation, founded neither on race nor religion. Baruch approached President Roosevelt. Although there would be no racial or religious bias in the new state, the population originally would be largely Jewish, and Baruch proposed that all Americans of Jewish antecedents be called upon to contribute one tenth of their wealth. He himself would contribute five million dollars, and guaranteed to get a million from each of the Guggenheims. The President listened and several weeks later wrote Baruch, "The big thing we talked about is by no means dead. It will revive if Hitler and Mussolini do not slam the door in our faces." But this was 1939, and the door was very soon slammed.[22]

Israel, Baruch always felt, was only a halfway solution. He realized what the Arabs would feel, after their long tenure of the land, and he also knew the Jewish attitude toward the Arabs. Furthermore, he objected violently to founding a state upon a religion, and if the Zionists denied that this was their intent, then Baruch doubted the very existence of such a thing as Jewish nationality. If Israel was not being set up on a basis of either religion or nationality, then what was to be its basis? No one quite seemed to know. One thing that Baruch knew was that a war between the new Israel and the millions of the Moslem world would benefit no one.

So far as his religious convictions went, Baruch held them to be entirely his own affair. Although he was not a great synagogue attendant, he has nevertheless been an enrolled member of the West End Synagogue all his life, and he became hot with fury over a charge that he did not keep the Holy Days. He has probably been one of those people who speaks little of what means most.

A multifaceted man, Bernard Baruch has never been adequately summed up. He once came near the truth himself, when he said, "I am a man of legend — a man of many faces." [23] It is significant that a famous portrait painter once gave up in exasperation, deciding that he could never get that complex face onto canvas. One who was close to Baruch over many years has said that he could never make a statement about him without wanting to qualify it. "You could live beside him for years and never predict him." He was great and he was small. He could be closefisted and perhaps the most generous man alive. He could find pleasure in Winston Churchill and in Billy Rose. He was naïve and sophisticated, vain on little things, and humble on great ones. He was ruthless and he was tender — and greater than the sum of his parts. [24]

As one friend, Mrs. Christie Benet, has pointed out, his facets were as diverse as those of a diamond, but his essential motivation was simple. All in him was centered about his country — that country of which he said: "Let us cherish our own, hug it to our bosom and defend it every moment of every day of every month in every year." [25]

Yet it was not alone his patriotism, or his many-faceted mind, or his services to his country which made up his claim to greatness. It was, possibly, the quality of maturity which he had achieved over the years — the growth from one who takes to one who gives. He had achieved a security that enabled him to pick brains where he found them, and to disregard conventional appraisals of people and values.

And his personal traits, as much as his larger qualities, endeared him to the variety of people who were his delight and his power. It was only his closest friends who had come to know the glints of humor that lightened the somewhat austere and elegant figure of the statesman.

But the last chapter has not yet been written, and it is not yet time for a final summing-up of Bernard Baruch. Powerful and close associations were kept green even in his later years, and political days were not yet ended. There were still those controversial American visits of England's Elder Statesman, and in them Baruch played his old role of friend and guide.

There was the great convocation at the Boston Garden in the raw New England spring of 1949, in the great barnlike room, with its wooden chairs and the red-painted pipes along the wall. Churchill had indulged in some "obvious posing," had stepped down to the front of the platform, peering impishly forward, before giving a V-sign. He had snatched off his glasses, ignored his script, still the showman, still the master of "the art of timing" — and still a symbol of Britain's lonely fight, and of the "darkling hour" in which the world groped. He spoke at last with his old majesty, out of the "depths of his twentieth century disillusion." Again he sounded the challenge to his time. "Let us then move forward together in discharge of our mission and our duty, fearing God and nothing else." [26] As Baruch foresaw, within eighteen months he was again Prime Minister. He was like Niagara Falls in one of his favorite stories, with which he had delighted newspapermen during his American visit in 1944. Had the Falls changed much, a young reporter wanted to know, since Churchill had last seen them in 1900? The Englishman gazed at the cataract, then said thoughtfully: "The principle seems the same. The water still keeps falling over." [27]

Baruch was asked to play a major role at the exercises at the Massachusetts Institute of Technology that day. President Karl Compton had telegraphed, asking him to fill in for President Truman, who had canceled his scheduled address on short notice. Baruch was urged to speak "on some aspect of our hopes, opportunity, responsibility for the future. Your stature and wisdom would save the situation." [28]

But tactfully, Baruch stepped into the background, choosing merely to introduce his old friend. Of this ceremony, an eyewitness wrote: "I think the most interesting thing at the convocation was to see the greatest living American totally subordinate himself in the public eye to the greatest living Englishman. I think it was quite wonderful." [29]

In their private interviews, however, back in Baruch's New York apartment, where Churchill dined at ease in his siren suit, Baruch had no hesitation in speaking to his old friend firmly. He picked up where he had left off earlier conversations with Churchill during his postwar visits to Britain. "If you do your part," he told the great Englishman, "we'll do more." England must hold up her end in the world-wide recovery program. He agreed with Mrs. Roosevelt that British influence had made us do certain things, particularly on the Palestine question, which lacked a long-range view.[30]

But also he was laying the groundwork for the new Administration, soon to take over, and for the man who he well knew would be the next President of the United States, and whose policies would be the same, whatever his political party.[31]

Strategically, Baruch played his part in this turn of events. "Baruch says: 'Don't Draft Eisenhower,'" read a New York *World-Telegram and Sun* headline on August 2, 1951.[32] Another headline had a different tone: "General Eisenhower's Job Won't Bar Him From '52 Race, Truman Thinks." Baruch had pointed out that careless talk of the Presidency did a "great disservice" to the man whose present task was probably "the most important assignment an individual has held in our lifetime." Never had he seen a man so "thoroughly imbued with the idea of preserving the peace of the world." But he had warned Eisenhower personally to go slow, since the mess in Washington was so great.[33]

President Truman, on the other hand, saw nothing in the General's overseas post to interfere with the possibilities in 1952 if Eisenhower happened to be "in that frame of mind." General Eisenhower was doing "a magnificent job," would continue to do it so long as duty called him, and would always put his country first.

It was abundantly clear that if Eisenhower filled his immediate assignment well, and only if he filled it well, he would be a logical candidate. "Washington is a place where results only are applauded," wrote Doris Fleeson.[34]

Jay Franklin saw through the palaver immediately. "Shrewd Bernard Baruch has put over a fast one on Mr. Truman," he wrote. For it was no secret in Washington that if Baruch said it was a fine day, Truman would reply that it was raining cats and dogs. Baruch now seemed to squelch the Eisenhower presidential boom. So Truman snapped back that everything was ready for Eisenhower to run for the White House the next year.[35] One newspaper even commented that it looked as though "the Baruch interview had needled Mr. Truman into launching an Eisenhower candidacy . . . General Eisenhower, at the moment, is clearly the strongest of the Republican possibilities . . ."[36]

Baruch had long known and esteemed Eisenhower, who had been

one of the bright young officers at the Army War College, where Baruch had so often lectured. Long before Baruch had heard of him, Eisenhower had avowedly been one of those who had enjoyed "sitting at his feet and listening to his words." But Baruch was not long unaware of the potential of this young officer, who as early as 1922 saw with Baruch the inevitability of another world war, and who shared his faculty for belaboring the obvious.[37] Baruch admittedly had so great a fondness and admiration for Eisenhower that he even felt it might influence his judgment. You could see, he felt, why his soldiers were so fond of him.[38] As for Eisenhower, he told Herbert Bayard Swope in 1946 that he was deeply conscious of his personal debt to Baruch. America needed more men like him.[39]

A remarkable file in the Baruch Papers contains a series of letters signed "Ike." Many of them are handwritten to his counselor and friend. Their humility is incredible, from a man who had already reached such stature, both as myth and hero, the man whose forceful leadership, General Marshall had written Baruch, should have much credit for the winning of the war.[40]

The war was scarcely won before Eisenhower wrote Baruch of his doubts about filling Marshall's place as Chief of Staff, saying that the momentous issues of peace were staggering to contemplate. He felt deeply the need of advice from men like Baruch, who faced the problems of the present day with the wisdom of the past. He would be grateful for any suggestions that Baruch might offer him.[41] He agreed with Marshall that universal military training was the keystone to our national security, and that we must plan before our forces were trimmed by public apathy. Baruch's private telephone number, he thought, would be of value to him.[42]

Baruch was present in the pouring rain when Eisenhower was sworn in as president of Columbia University. The downpour was so intense that Eisenhower decided to shorten his prepared speech and urge the spectators to take cover. But suddenly the sun shouldered its way through the clouds. Eisenhower read a paragraph, then halted informally, muttering something about "those darned glasses." Finally he spoke the words that raised the hopes of liberals among the President-makers across the country. "The facts of communism shall be taught here . . . its ideological development, its political methods, its economic effects, its probable course in the future . . . Conceal something from a boy or girl and he'll grow curious about it." [43]

As time went on, Eisenhower continued to write to Baruch. What he was concerned with primarily was the question of the ever-growing paternalism in Washington. Why could not a committee of the best minds be set up to study where the line could be drawn between individual and governmental responsibility? [44]

Time passed. Eisenhower had gone back to Europe as Supreme Commander at SHAPE and returned to the United States amid rumors that he would accept the nomination of either or both parties. All campaigns seem regrettable and low in retrospect, but the campaign of 1952 reached considerable depths, considering the caliber of the two candidates.

Officially, Baruch kept out of the fracas. According to Mrs. Luce, he gave the same advice to Stevenson that he gave to Eisenhower. On his return from Europe on August 4, he had said flatly that he could not back either candidate until he saw which had the greater wisdom and the fortitude to oppose inflation.[45] "Efforts to smoke him out" during an interview in California were futile. Baruch donned a white sombrero, slumped down on a bench under a giant redwood tree, and snapped to the circle of reporters, "I'm not elderly and I don't know what Presidents you think I've advised."

As for the presidential race, he would not come out for either candidate before the election. He never had. If he had wanted to endorse General Eisenhower, he would have done so outright. He understood the English language.[46]

Had he changed his mind about President Truman since he was last quoted? Baruch played with his hearing aid. "This thing goes out at the damnedest times," he said. He relaxed, stretched his legs out into the warm California sunshine. "What wonderful dreams a man could dream here," he reflected.[47]

Back home, Baruch touched off a flurry of newspaper headlines and speculation by playing host to Adlai Stevenson at a breakfast conference at his apartment. Stevenson arrived without a police escort. Tongues were set wagging, probably the more since neither participant had anything public to say. It was concluded by the New York *Journal-American* that by visiting an avowed enemy of President Truman, Stevenson had at least demonstrated that he intended to run his own campaign.[48]

The next day Baruch lunched on a card table facing his television set and watched closely the appearance of Governor Stevenson before the convention of the American Federation of Labor. He made no comment afterward, but took a collection of letters from both Stevenson and Eisenhower and studied them carefully. Eisenhower's, he concluded, were the more thoughtful and penetrating. The telephone jingled; Baruch pressed the receiver to his ear. "Why, yes. Yes, General. Come right up." A few moments later the shrill of police sirens cut the air. Walking to the window, Baruch observed a few pedestrians on the sidewalk across the street, feet dragging, their heads turned almost backward.

The elevator zipped up. "Ike" bounced out, ruddy, vibrant with energy, in fighting fettle for the campaign about to begin. His bright smile flashed across his face. For thirty-five minutes he and Baruch were closeted, ranging over the whole field of foreign policy, Korea, inflation. The *New York Times* telephoned: Would Mr. Baruch pose for a picture with General Eisenhower? "Certainly not. He didn't pose with Mr. Stevenson," Miss Novarro snapped, and clicked down the telephone. As Eisenhower was waved out, she told Baruch, "The *New York Times* wanted you to pose for a picture . . . but I told them that you wouldn't."

"Pose with General Eisenhower! Why, of course, I'll pose with General Eisenhower. Let me at him," and Baruch dived toward the elevator.

"Here, you can't go like that." In an instant, Miss Novarro had stripped him of his summer-weight cord coat and thrown a formal black one over his shoulders. He leaped into the elevator. Baruch hurriedly told the doorman to have the General wait. "I'm going to have my picture taken with you. I'd be so proud of that." [49]

To the reporters Eisenhower said only that he had paid a call on an old and dear friend. And would Mr. Baruch vote for the General? Baruch grinned all over his face. "When you see me look at him, you can tell I don't hate him," he said. He threw his hands into the air and retreated inside, muttering, "The people don't have to be told how to vote. If they haven't seen enough and had enough." [50]

The cat was out of the bag. That grin of Baruch's was splashed across the country, and was less wide the next morning when, lounging comfortably in his siren suit, he was roused by a long-distance telephone call from Anna Rosenberg, once a fervent Eisenhower supporter. Baruch fought off the attack valiantly. "I couldn't help it, Anna," he said. "They insisted I pose with General Eisenhower." Why hadn't he posed with Mr. Stevenson?

"No one asked me," he said.[51]

Quiet settled down again over Baruch's headquarters until he was roused by a bitter charge of President Truman's that Ike was willing to accept "Nazi-like and anti-Semitic practices in the McCarran Act." The statement was carefully worded and could have applied to anyone who had voted for or supported the McCarran Act. But the implication, especially in view of Eisenhower's German ancestry, was plain. Baruch was furious. Eisenhower was having a rough time. He still did not know how to return the brickbats.

Now Baruch moved into action. Eisenhower headquarters made public a letter that he had written the candidate six weeks before. It was effusive and it had been unsolicited, a spontaneous, handwritten missive, reading in part: "Since I have known you as a major, I have grown to respect and admire your character, ability, gentleness but firmness and above all, the high purposes that have motivated you. Your abhorrence of cant, hypocrisy, and intolerance in all fields of human relations" had added affection to Baruch's respect and admiration. He signed it, "Affectionately, Bernie." [52]

Eisenhower responded in a speech on October 20: "They have charged me only lately, when they overstepped themselves, with being anti-Semitic and anti-Catholic. Ladies and gentlemen, I leave the answers to those two to my good friends, Cardinal Spellman, Rabbi Silver and Bernard Baruch." [53]

On November 4, 1952, twenty minutes before the opening time, Bernard Baruch was waiting at the Lexington Avenue polling booth. Once in, he emerged hastily. "The damned thing won't work. You can't pull the lever." To the reporters he admitted, "I did vote for the General . . . They wouldn't let me vote more than once." [54] He had cast the third Republican ballot of his life, the two others having been for Theodore Roosevelt and Thomas E. Dewey.

He issued an official congratulation to James F. Byrnes who had almost carried his state for Eisenhower. Meanwhile, as the votes were tallied, one of the first telephone calls the President-elect made that election night was to Baruch, thanking him "for his all-important support." [55]

Baruch already had his role blocked out in the Eisenhower Administration. According to Alvin Johnson, what he wanted was to bring the American and British administrations close to each other, with himself as "the liaison officer between Eisenhower and Churchill." [56]

In one important instance he got his wish during the historic meeting of the two men early in January, 1953, which the President-elect had suggested be held at Baruch's New York apartment. There were good reasons for this. Churchill was again Prime Minister of Britain; he wanted to talk to Eisenhower; time was pressing; and so it was arranged that they talk informally. A "social call" on Bernard Baruch enabled the Prime Minister to make a "private visit" in this country. Had the visit been "public" his calendar would have been clogged with needless appointments with officials of the outgoing Truman Administration in Washington, and he might never have had a chance for lengthy conversations with Eisenhower at all.

Although it was the first time Eisenhower and Churchill had met since the General had given up his Atlantic Pact command, they were old friends. Baruch well knew of the mutual affectionate regard between them.[57]

To the press Baruch's part in the conference seemed remarkable, in view of the fact that he was then eighty-two, "a life-long Democrat and not very rich any more." [58] Although no information was released as to the topics discussed, the three men posed for the photographers characteristically, Eisenhower bent forward, intent, Baruch with his hearing aid, and Churchill with his cigar. How much actual part Baruch played in the discussions, however, is not known. If he gave advice, there is no evidence that it was followed.

Despite his personal friendship with the new President, Baruch was to play no great role in the Eisenhower Administration as a "presidential adviser." For one thing, he was getting very old. All who have known Baruch have appreciated his shrewdness, the disinterested quality of his thinking, and, most of all, his fervent desire to serve. Under Eisenhower, as under the Presidents of the past, the door to the White House was open; the President was receptive to any advice that he might care to impart, but he was not sought out. Occasionally there would still come a letter on the familiar White House paper, suggesting that "Bernie" stop by, on his way to or from Little Hobcaw, but the relation was essentially personal.

Before the Eisenhower Administration took over, however, the cheap jerry-built raw-wood stands for the inauguration were springing up like weeds along Pennsylvania Avenue. Washington, in the closing days of the Fair Deal, looked like a lumber yard.

Bernard Baruch, or any tourist visiting the capital in that hazy December of 1952, could feel the sleepy, unbuttoned, tensions-all-ended air. Everyone had time, even the President, although his mouth still tightened at mention of the name of Eisenhower. At the White House, tall, white-haired Bill Simmons, the chief usher, typed doggedly. But the President could find time to reminisce with callers in his office, to talk of Jackson and Johnson and the "Federals" in Missouri, of Quantrill's Raiders, of the old days, of the New Deal and the passing days of the Fair Deal, and the great names of those days — Wallace and Hull and Roosevelt.

Some things were unchanged: the white rise of the Capitol dome, the dignitaries eating at the Carlton; in Lafayette Square the pigeons still pecked at the dried bread crumbs, although the bench where Bernard Baruch once sat looked scarred and bleached by sun and rain. Time was in suspension, ticked off only by the unresting clocks. Appointments, even at the Pentagon, could be made almost at the lifting of a telephone receiver, or you could wander in and out of the swinging latticed doors of the executive offices in the old State, War, and Navy building, tiered like a wedding cake under its mansard roof.

Easily available in his high-vaulted office was lanky David Stowe, a sharp-eyed man, physically relaxed, with that same air of geniality and hardness that Truman had. In offices like his had lived and breathed the New Deal and then the Fair Deal. There had been a lot of history since this Renaissance "palace" towered skyward in the eighteen-seventies. Lots of files had been filled and emptied, and they were being emptied now. No, nothing was being burned, as the newspapers said. Everything was being returned. The business of government now was receipting; every item sent out had to be re-ceipted for.

Stowe could smile now. He could lean back in his chair. The old era was ending, all that had begun with such hope and youth and resilience twenty years before. It was ending where it had begun, in old Washington, the White House, the old State Building, the Treasury, the Civil Service building — not differing so much from the new modern Washington, except that in the new buildings there was no more gold work or frescoing, no more Grecian columns between the office doors, no old mahogany or iron stairways spiraling upward, no more high-vaulted ceilings where the Washington heat could rise and cling before the days of air-conditioning, no more swinging doors.

Harry Truman was leaving, and a wave of sentiment was breaking across the country toward the little man. "America Wishes You Well," wrote columnist H. I. Phillips. "The folks" loved "a spunky guy." He was more like "the average American than any president in years." He was "a plain, everyday homespun type to be encountered at the Kiwanis Club luncheon and the Elks' clambake." Fate had thrown him into the ring with the atom bomb, the Cold War, the threat of world destruction, and he had faced them all with unyielding courage. The pompous had thrown up their hands in horror at his letters and verbal outbursts, then sneaked around the corner to whisper: "That Truman's a corker. He sure does sling it out with the best of them."

"Relax, Harry," wrote Phillips. "Sit around in your socks and undershirt, write all the letters you feel like, look up at that picture of your mother and tell her you tried to 'plow a straight furrow' and do your best as you saw it. You can say that again and again." [59] Out of office, on a subsequent trip to New York, Truman was mobbed by crowds shouting "Hiya, Harry," taxi drivers muttering their thrill over carrying "a President of the United States," turning right on "No Turn" signs, the police only smiling and waving them on. New York was his. Somehow, the people were his and he was the people. "I'm as puffed as a pizened pup," he said. "I thought I was a has-been. Guess I'm a still-is."

The years of bitterness and passion and partisan hatreds were melting away, and the vision only of the spunky little man remained. Phillips predicted that "a hundred years from now you may shape up as a guy whose batting average was extra good." Stowe had no doubt of it. To him, Truman was great even beside the greatness of his predecessor. "He's a terrific character." And had he been running, he might even have beaten Eisenhower, Stowe thought. But he knew it was all over the night in New York that he began talking to the taxi drivers. "I talked to three in one night, just to see, you know. And they all said: 'If the little fellow was running, I'd vote for him, but I guess I'll vote for Ike.'" For the record, Stowe added that Truman never said, as was reported, "I am running this campaign." He had heard Truman talking. He had warned, "There's a man with a mike." When the playback was heard, it sounded: "I am . . . running this campaign." The word "not" had been deleted.

Stowe relapsed into bitterness. "The people don't always know what's good for them," he said.[60] So too said Frances Perkins, one of the few last original New Dealers left in Washington. The years had rested lightly upon her. She looked almost unchanged from those first pictures of the first woman Cabinet officer of twenty years before. The trim tricorne hat still rode the waves of lustrous hair, only faintly powdered with gray. Her trim figure was rigid and unbowed. So, too, were her convictions. She would talk steadily, erect at her desk, her hands playing with a letter opener. She was still the New Dealer. She appreciated the goals of President Truman no less than his accomplishments; he had seen what she had seen, and Roosevelt and Al Smith before him, that the purpose of government was to help those who could not help themselves.[61]

No longer a New Dealer, perhaps, but a founder of the New Deal was the short, bustling figure over in the classic Greek temple opposite the Capitol. Mr. Justice Frankfurter left court sessions with a rush and a supercharged intensity that belied his seventy-two years. He was dignified without being pompous, alert, eager. His office was lined with bookshelves, crowded with tumbled and well-read piles of books; a new biography of Sidney Hillman was on his desk. His eyes were bright; beneath the gray-white hair his skin was sallow but unlined, drawn tight over the bones of his face. He talked of age and youth. He had seen men of twenty or twenty-one as fit to sit on the bench as he was; and men like Baruch, he thought, were listened to for their past rather than their present views and contributions.[62]

But horse-faced, tobacco-chewing Chief Justice Vinson, with the baggy clothes and the bags under his eyes, thought differently. To him Baruch was a sage, a seer. And Vinson, too, was a wise man, big and sad and shrewd. He had been in Washington a long time. He also had been a part of the New Deal, but was not really a New Dealer at all.[63]

Only at the Pentagon Building now was the stream of activity flowing on — the currents of peace or war flowing on irresistibly, admirals and generals pouring out of Anna Rosenberg's office, with here and there a young sergeant happily "at war" at a Pentagon desk.

You had to wait for Anna Rosenberg. In the office of the Under-Secretary of Defense there was no relaxing. War went on and the

imminence of war, even at the end of the Fair Deal. She looked
her age. Her dark, waving short hair was shining with gray. She
was haggard under her make-up. But you felt her quality of compassion, that rare combination of intellectual sharpness and emotional
warmth. Photographs of those of whom she was fond were framed on
the walls, Truman in the outer office, Marshall and Baruch within.

Unlike the more cynical Frances Perkins, she did not say that "the
people have been fooled." But she would not stay on with Eisenhower, although she had been one of his original supporters. She
spoke of him with pity, perhaps because she knew what he would
have to suffer, what Marshall had already suffered, what any military
man has to endure who has civilian responsibilities to bear.[64]

And the Senate went on, changing and unchanging as the Presidents changed. There were still the walls papered with pictures of
Lincoln in the office of Senator "Wild Bill" Langer, and pictures and
busts and statuettes of Lincoln in the office of bespectacled, pudgy
Homer Capehart. Senator Paul Douglas also had Lincoln on the
wall, but Madison and Jackson too, among others. There were no
pictures of statesmen on the walls of Senator Joseph McCarthy's
office. It was the floors that were piled knee-deep there with reports
of the McCarthy "hearings."

Senator Byrd's outer office displayed pictures and maps of Virginia. The inner office displayed the Senator himself, back to the
window, framed by three walls of cartoons of Harry Byrd. He sat
before an untidy desk on which he could instantly find what he
sought, surrounded by a white-capped sea of paper-strewn carpet.
Guarded and yet genial, relaxed and drawling, the curly-haired Byrd
had been there a long time and would be there longer. He had no
ambitions nor any illusions that he could ever be President. His
shrewd gray eyes saw everything in terms of the South and Virginia.
He was content with the power he exercised in his state and in the
Congress, and wise enough to know that he would get no more.
With Baruch he had long consulted; he still continued to do so.

It was quiet in the Senate Office Building, quiet except for the
office of Senator Taft, soon to be Majority Leader, soon to guide an
untried President. Taft, who had gallantly seen the fall of his life-
long hopes, his dream of the office for which he had virtually been
born and trained and nurtured; Taft, "Mr. Republican," waiting now
only to serve and to die. His country came first, symbolized by that

quiet, starkly bare office of his, with only the American flag stretched
out across the wall. Someone later complimented him on the smooth
flow of White House–congressional relations. And he looked up and
smiled with that boyishness and tilt of the head characteristic of him
and said, "But the credit for that should go to the President. He
believes in team play." [65] Taft had been there a long time; he would
not be there much longer.

There were new faces and new personalities, like bushy-haired
young John Kennedy, scion of the Boston Irish as his predecessor
had been the scion of the Boston Brahmins. Theirs had been a battle
dating back over a generation, when Lodge's grandfather, "the old
Senator," had defeated Kennedy's grandfather, "Honey Fitz" Fitz-
gerald, then mayor of Boston. Both were out of Boston, out of
Harvard, both barely out of their twenties upon their election to the
Senate, both had the same distinctive grace. Kennedy was the complete antithesis of Senator McCarthy: his utterances were scholarly,
statesmanlike, without a trace of demagoguery, although his power-
drives were no less consuming. Like many a young Washington
officeholder before him and since, he would drive his little sun-faded
blue car past the White House and dream what it might be like "to
go there." His office had six work-strewn desks, scattered copies of
the Boston *Post*, no sofas, only straight-backed chairs. His inner office
was decked with well-filled bookcases and framed letters from Daniel
Webster and Andrew Jackson. He crackled with nervous energy.

Another vibrant personality on the Washington scene was hard-
bitten Stuart Symington. Behind his very neat desk, Symington
dominated his inner office. A strikingly handsome man, he exuded
strength and ambition, smiling winningly beneath the blue eyes, the
black brows, the thick gray hair. He walked with military erectness.
Forthright, dogged, somehow militaristic, it is not surprising that
he was a favorite of Baruch's, one of Baruch's "boys."

This, then, was Washington between the eras, before the changing
of the guard, before the prayer for "the power to discern clearly . . .
for all the people, regardless of station, race or calling" that Eisenhower delivered on his inaugural day. The guard changed. Then
you saw the sights and scenes of Republican Washington — the Republicans ravenous after twenty years' famine, the women of the
party waiting two hours in a stifling White House corridor, passing
in looping lines through the East Room and finally to Mrs. Eisen-

hower, looking young and radiant and happy and really shaking your hand.

So did Republican Washington begin the New Era. So ended the New Deal. And as before, always part of the Washington scene was Bernard Baruch, the man who still repeated his old warnings, no matter how often they had been heard — and discarded — before.

He spoke again and again, warning that all would become "ashes in our mouths" if defense efforts were not intensified, that while budgets were being cut and the calculated risk was being taken, the Communists in Berlin were throwing up street blockades and the truce negotiators at Panmunjom were threatening to renew the fighting.

Some were tiring of his Cassandra-like prophecies. "Baruch's gone one-track, obsessed with controls," was David Stowe's comment.[66] Baruch cared little. Baruch's position squared entirely with what he had said all along. The fact that he and President Eisenhower did not agree on the question of controls did not halt his plea.

So he came down to Washington in the spring of 1953 to plead once again for stand-by mobilization and stand-by controls, because "the surest deterrent against another war would be to so narrow the gap in our mobilization that no enemy could delude himself into thinking he could overwhelm us with a surprise blitz attack." The next war, he thought, would explode in a "big smash" if stand-by powers were not on the books. He repeated his old warning: "To wait is to die." The issue was unchanged; to face it might mean the only chance of peace.

This appearance of Baruch's was put on television and millions across the country watched the Elder Statesman, his long head leaning on his hand. He sat at a small table with his briefcase and a microphone at his side. Sam Lubell was beside him, lips outthrust, stoic-faced.

Senator Homer Capehart, the Indiana Republican, said gently: "You've had great experience in life . . . Now tell us how we can convince the American people."

Baruch: "Senator, the American people understand this better than you think."

Capehart: "Well, I wonder. I've been accused of being un-American, a Communist, everything, for being for controls."

Baruch's eyes narrowed. "We all get accused of things. This really is a very simple thing. We know what ought to be done. We go all around it."

"Should we presume that the Russians have an atom bomb?"

"It is well to presume that they do have."

The men in the background looked at Baruch with reverence, some few with skepticism. Over and over again, the Senators rehashed the same old questions, and Baruch shot in the answers and the warnings, quickly, gruffly. There was no choice between strengthened defenses and a balanced budget. "We can afford to do exactly what Russia makes us afford. You'll have nothing left if the Russians get this country."

Vehemently, he gestured with one hand. The Administration had not had the courage to use even the controls that had been voted, he charged. He thrust his face forward, his head hunched between his great shoulders. "If you put a ceiling on everything, everything will be easier. War is not a game of mumblety-peg . . . You're never going to have people satisfied."

One Senator wondered why Congress could not just impose an over-all freeze if war came.

"Would you vote for that?" Baruch promptly demanded.

The Senator hedged. It would be uncomfortable to have the threat of controls hanging over us all the time.

Baruch's voice saddened. "It will always hang over our heads so long as the threat of war hangs over our heads." You could never get perfection.[67]

And what of President Dwight D. Eisenhower, sitting now at that desk in the Oval Study where Truman had sat, that desk, bare now of all but a blotter and a pen, a single clock, and the appointment calendar for the day, a desk stripped for action with military efficiency? Responsibility was carving new lines in his face. His was now the responsibility.

He had heard Baruch's theories before. Together they had studied the lessons of inflation in two world wars and the disaster that had ensued, as the economy had raced on, headlong. Together they had resolved that this must not happen again. The President knew the sincerity of Baruch's fight for the white-collar man, the farmer, the laborer, for all who were the victims of inflation, and without whose economic health the nation could not be healthy.

He knew Baruch's plan for a program of stand-by controls — and as President of Columbia had endorsed it. As President of the United States he had not moved to put it into effect. Why? He knew that it was right — theoretically. But as President of the United States he had to face the responsibility for making it work and he knew what the results would be.

As President, Mr. Eisenhower could see what the general public could not see — and what the Presidents before him had seen — the gulf between the excellence of Baruch's theories and the difficulty of putting them into legislation. The Elder Statesman's concepts were those of a man who did not have to face ultimate responsibilities. Not since the War Industries Board days had Baruch had to take the responsibility for putting his theories into effect, except over short periods of time. The very astuteness that had won him millions in Wall Street had held him back from the ultimate tests that might have immortalized his name.

The trouble with his stand-by mobilization plan, from a practical, operating point of view was that it would set up a system of controls which would go into effect immediately upon the outbreak of war. In this troubled time, how could you tell when there was going to be a war? Could our bold but fragile economy function with the sword of Damocles hanging over its head? Baruch had simply failed to take into account what might happen in peacetime, with an economy operating under the continuous threat of controls in a world where almost every day saw a new threat of war.

So now, moving farther and farther away from active participation in public affairs, Baruch had time to focus his philosophy of life. He voiced it frequently these days, in a series of public addresses, blunt, peppery, full-flavored. "People don't like to hear unpleasant facts," he once snorted. "They like to hear Pollyanna talk. People hate the truth when it works a hardship on them. A lot of people think I'm an unpleasant person because I tell them unpleasant truths." [68]

Young people enjoyed talking to him. He spoke their language. He was never happier or in better form than when matching wits in an unrehearsed question-and-answer session at Brown University, perhaps, or at The Citadel. Often he would give out such gruff and common-sense advice as he imparted to Gretta Palmer in a *Ladies' Home Journal* interview called "If I Were 21."

If he were, he said, he would get a job, any job. "If it wasn't just the job I'd hoped for, I wouldn't worry too much about that." Making a success of the job at hand, however uncongenial, was the first step toward obtaining the job you really wanted. "Help, hustle, and carry the briefcase for the boss," he suggested.[69] "Do little jobs and don't worry if they are beneath you." He did not apparently share the sentiments of George Bernard Shaw, who defined the secret of success as "to offend the greatest number of people." [70]

He qualified his homilies with off-the-record asides: "I'm not trying to reform the world, for I can't even reform myself." There was a kind of Benjamin Franklin quality to his platitudes. "Be quick to praise," he advised young people at a youth forum. "Keep yourself tidy . . . Interest yourself in politics. If you're governed badly, it will usually be your fault.

"Be polite. If you are, others will be polite.

"Be helpful, that is the first definition of success.

"Don't pity yourself." [71]

He spelled out more specific advice to a student in a press interview. "Avoid taking easy courses, for that makes slovenly thinking and action in after life . . . Do a thing because it gives you joy in the doing and not for thanks." There was "a kind of bitter-sweetness" in the knowledge that you had fought the battle well, even though you lost.[72]

In his eighty-fourth year Baruch began a new career. He became a special lecturer in economics at his old alma mater, the College of the City of New York, meeting classes in the new Bernard M. Baruch School of Business and Public Administration which stands on the site of the old college he attended nearly seventy years before.

In his three major lectures he gave the distillation of nearly eighty-five years of life and thought. Much of what he said was not new. Often he repeated observations that he had made in earlier speeches. But in talks such as these were crystallized what at City College Baruch called "A Philosophy for Our Time."

The three lectures give a general view of his philosophy, although in other talks at other colleges he developed specific points more fully. It is characteristic that the majority of his public addresses have been before educational institutions and have dealt more or less with education. Virtually all the great issues in which he has been interested over the years have been basically questions of education, which he has come to feel is the key to the whole American system. Systems of government have sprung up elsewhere, resting not upon man's strength but his weakness, on his unwillingness to correct conditions by correcting himself. Totalitarianism was the proof of man's incompetence and weakness. Was this to be the fate of the United States? Could education halt this tide?

The old simple faith in the certainty of progress was gone. In these dark years of the twentieth century man smelled the stench of the gas chambers; he saw the rebirth of human slavery; and with miracles performed almost daily in the laboratories, man fumbled like a child in his attempts to govern himself. The only freedom man could really ever have was freedom to discipline himself. This was what the free world was fighting for — to maintain the right to self-discipline instead of having the disciplines of slavery and tyranny thrust upon it by a conquering enemy. It was not enough to believe in self-government. You had to make it work.

Education could provide the answer.

Men must make self-government work, first, by thinking their problems through, and, second, by disciplining themselves to whatever duties might be necessary. No form of government in itself could save man. Our freedom as individuals would depend upon how much responsibility we would assume ourselves. "To paraphrase Thomas Jefferson, that government is best which governs least because its people discipline themselves."

Education, Baruch said, was basically united to democracy. Without it, democracy was meaningless. Yet "book learning" alone was not enough. The men who wrote the Constitution had been well versed in the classics, but they had also learned "to blend living experience with moral values." Their minds drew a clear distinction between good and evil, between principle and expediency. Most important of all, they knew how to think.

Today, thinking had become a neglected art.

This, Baruch thought, was where the institutions of learning had fallen down. This cut to the core of the controversy over subversive influences in the schools. "There would be no problem in teaching our students about communism, about Buddhism, or about any other subject, if the students had learned how to think, how to organize . . . how not to fall victim to labels . . ." The Soviet system, for instance, was no outgrowth of the liberal tradition. It was a reversion to those same dark ages against which liberalism had revolted.

The dogma of the divine right of kings had been overthrown, but the Soviets had revived an even older dogma, that the people were not to be trusted to guide their own affairs.[73] The Communists knew the power of discipline, but they could not deviate from the line. Our task was to teach young men and women not what to think, but how to think. As for communism in the United States, it was not a political philosophy, it was a criminal conspiracy.

Utterances such as this brought outcries from the left wing, who conveniently forgot that it had been Baruch who had paid for the passage home of men in the Abraham Lincoln Brigade, after they had fought against Franco in the Spanish Civil War. This action has laid Baruch open to attack from the right, but his comments were typical: "I probably wouldn't agree with a single political opinion they have, but any American who's willing to fight for his own beliefs in democracy is good enough for my money." [74]

Neither the liberals nor the conservatives could pin a label on him, he contended. "If you tie me up to a particular thing, you just circumscribe me," he once said. His own political philosophy was simple. He would, he said, rise and fall on what he could call individualism. Industrial capitalism, free enterprise, and democracy were synonymous.

What was the dominant yearning of our time? Baruch tried to put it into words during the first of his three lectures at City College. It was May; the windows were open. Warm air ruffled the thick white hair of the man on the speaker's platform. He spoke forcibly and at length. His words were no less stirring than his delivery. This was the dominant yearning of our time: to be freed from fear of war, of brainwashings, of dictatorship, and, perhaps most of all, of those "cyclic spasms which have characterized man's history up to now." Not for him, the old "do-nothing" philosophy. Man did not have to lie down humbly and submit to flood, famine, fire, or the effects of his own stupidities. Savages might crouch in terror before lightning; we had made electricity our servant. The very germs that once threatened to wipe out the human race had become the antibiotics that destroyed germs.

This was the challenge of our time, progress without relapse, freedom from the age-old cycle of breakdown and build-up. For the philosophers there was the comforting fact that over the centuries these chills and fevers, these tremendous upheavals which sometimes meant the destruction of entire civilizations, had averaged out into a general improvement of man's stature, though this was, of course, small comfort to the poor mortals who had been the victims of the advance. Yet mankind could avoid "both dumb submission and blind revolt." Man did not have to submit mutely to the laws of supply and demand. Baruch was for free enterprise — but with traffic lights. Valiant efforts could be made to control the workings of natural laws. The valleys of economic depression could be filled and the peaks of speculative inflation leveled.

Natural laws could be adapted, as well, to the most fearsome problem of the modern world, atomic energy. To demonstrate the basic principle of atomic energy, Baruch held out his arm. From the shoulder down to the wrist, the production of fissionable material was the same, regardless of its ultimate use. Yet, with a twist of the wrist, a would-be aggressor could turn "peaceful" fissionable material into a means of international blackmail and destruction. There could be no insurance against destruction without controls; controls, not agreements, were what mattered. He had striven for a complete system of controls, for, as he said, "if we can control one weapon, we can control them all." President Eisenhower's proposal for an international atomic pool was but a single step. It could not itself solve the basic problem. We dared not accept less than an effective over-all plan.

In his second lecture Baruch strove to find the clues to "the natural laws that govern human affairs." The law of supply and demand, he still thought, was "the most basic of all human laws." But it was only a part of the whole economic picture. "Nothing," Baruch said, "may I repeat, nothing has cost this country and the rest of the world more, except the losses and maimings of war itself, than the failure to grasp the enormous difference in the workings of supply and demand under conditions of war and conditions of peace."

Ever since 1914 we had either been going into a war or coming out of one. "Yet through this period most economic thinking assumed we were dealing with peacetime problems." But there were two major differences between the economic systems of peace and war, particularly in regard to the functioning of the law of supply and demand. In war, the supply had to be increased and demand restricted. This was the lesson of the First World War. Instead of applying it in the Second World War, all the old errors were repeated "until we finally ended up where we should have begun." Only a general price ceiling over the entire economy at the outset of a conflict could keep the economy in hand. Failure to impose this ceiling had increased the cost to the taxpayers of the Second World War by some 200 billion dollars. It posed the ultimate threat of a new depression, for no inflationary cycle could be continued indefinitely.

In fact, with our complex peacetime society Baruch felt that a floor had to be kept under the economy, but there should be a downward adjustment of the sky-high ceilings of war. He favored insurance against poor crop years, but wartime incentives to production could not be continued. As for the "surpluses," they were genuine wealth, which man in his ignorance had not yet learned to use.

One of the most significant changes of modern times, he felt, was the extent to which the old philosophy of "leave things alone" had been replaced by government intervention. It was no longer even a debatable question whether it was the government's duty to prevent another depression. "That was yesterday's battle. *Laissez faire* is dead. Today virtually every phase of society is subject to some government control. The issue is whether such control can be made just and fair."

Yet no problem, Baruch warned, was solved merely by having the government take care of it. Government was not a substitute for the people, but the instrument by which they acted. If individuals failed to discharge their personal duties, then government could become a deadly instrument. In the end, a free government rested upon free citizens who acted and thought in terms of freedom.[75]

Thus spoke Baruch in the twilight of his life. How he delivered his message was scarcely of less interest to listeners than what he had to say. His delivery was casual, unstudied, and highly informal; there was a complete lack of conscious elocution or of oratorical embroidery. His platform voice was baritone, rather heavy, sometimes a little harsh, and very vigorous. To his listeners, his vitality seemed incredible: the octogenarian seemed to have the secret of perpetual youth.

"If I had to sum up the career of Bernard Baruch in one sentence," one of his oldest and closest friends once said, "I would term it frustration." [76] No one would deny this with more vehemence than Baruch himself. He is not an introspective man. He would think it unmanly to probe his own subconscious motivations, just as he has shied off violently from those who have attempted to search his deeply forested interior. At the age of eighty-five Baruch could say of himself,

"Always the thought of tomorrow has buoyed me up. I have looked to the future all my life. I still do." He added, "I've had a happy life, wonderful parents, a wonderful wife, wonderful children and wonderful friends — and an occasional chance to serve my country. What more could any man ask?" [77]

Is it not ironic to see frustration or even tragedy in the life of the American success story incarnate? Thousands of young men have come out of the South, dreamed of conquering the city, and have failed, but Baruch succeeded and became the personification of their dream. He was the direct antithesis of that other South Carolinian who fought the battle of a Lost Cause and lived to see its defeat. Modern, materialistic, industrial America could well consider Calhoun a defeated man, but how could it so consider Baruch?

But let us go back to the young man whose ideal was J. P. Morgan, and who when snubbed by the Titan of the banking world became the sporting "Wolf of Wall Street." Let us remember the young millionaire who found something lacking in the satisfactions of wealth and, having sought an outlet for his talents, became the disciple of Woodrow Wilson, dedicating himself to public service. Yet today it is how Baruch made his millions which is of overweening concern to a money-minded people grappling for millions of their own. And in public service, what has Baruch sought? Has it not been the concrete achievements of "Dr. Facts?" Yet as we have seen, he declined to strive for the War Industries Board post even though it was obvious that the job was made for him. He refused the position of Secretary of the Treasury and regretted it the rest of his life. He would not become chairman of the Democratic National Committee when his party sorely needed his abilities to rebuild it. He has never submitted himself to the test of an election for public office, though he has lived through times when his services in such a position would have meant much to the country which he has so loved. He has been ready, often, to serve when a job has carried sufficient authority and prestige to allow him to succeed. It has not been a conviction of inadequacy that has held Baruch back from the assumption of responsibility, but an unwillingness to risk the rebuff of an unfavorable public opinion should he fail. Although his convictions have often been ahead of popular trends, they have never been too far ahead; and as has been said, flexibility has been one of Bernard Baruch's most useful secrets of survival. Some critics have seen the result as a series of platitudes which win a following just because they express the reactions of the average man. Such views as that the budget should be balanced in the depression, that there is a sacredness in the financial properties of gold, and that self-reliance is the key to success have seemed to more sophisticated economists and political thinkers old-fashioned or even absurd.

Has Baruch subconsciously, though sincerely, voiced his nostrums from an uncanny sense of how far the public would follow him? He has advised the men on the firing line wisely and well, but his has not been the responsibility for carrying out the advice. The times when he has been of most conspicuous service — in the War Industries Board, the Rubber committee, the Atomic Energy Commission — have been when he overcame his fear and put himself to the public test.

Here, then, is the tragedy. Baruch, unwilling to face defeat — Baruch, who has always had to win — has taken refuge behind his legend. Neither by accident nor against his will has Bernard Baruch become the greatest living American legend — perhaps the greatest in all our history who has not held a major political office.

How can his reluctance to take the risks of the political cockpit be explained? Perhaps it is the result of those cruel slights and attacks which have hurt not only him but his family — the attacks of racial bitterness and prejudice. But beyond this there was something more. Having at least cooperated in creating Baruch the Myth, Baruch the man has become its victim. Behind the myth, Baruch has felt such a necessity for operating as fully as possible that he has put himself often in the position of lavishing his advice on at least partially reluctant officials. To be always known as the Adviser of Presidents involves the necessity of advising Presidents who may be no idolaters of Baruch. That much of the advice has been good, coming from a luminous intellect, makes it the more tragic that it has not always been welcome to those who were bearing the brunt of public office with all its exposure to denunciation and attack. The infantryman in the trenches looks with a sour eye on even the wisest orders from a secure headquarters well behind the lines.

One may well summarize Baruch as a man whose influence was great, but how much greater he would have been, how much more glorious his success had he dared to risk failure.

APPENDIX

President Wilson's Letter Appointing Mr. Baruch
Chairman of the War Industries Board

The White House
Washington, March 4, 1918

My Dear Mr. Baruch:

I am writing to ask if you will not accept appointment as Chairman of the War Industries Board, and I am going to take the liberty at the same time of outlining the functions, the constitution and action of the Board as I think they should now be established.

The functions of the Board should be:

(1) The creation of new facilities and the disclosing, if necessary, the opening up of new or additional sources of supply;

(2) The conversion of existing facilities, where necessary, to new uses;

(3) The studious conservation of resources and facilities by scientific, commercial, and industrial economies;

(4) Advice to the several purchasing agencies of the Government with regard to the prices to be paid;

(5) The determination, wherever necessary, of priorities of production and of delivery and of the proportions of any given article to be made immediately accessible to the several purchasing agencies when the supply of that article is insufficient, either temporarily or permanently;

(6) The making of purchases for the Allies.

The Board should be constituted as at present and should retain, so far as necessary and so far as consistent with the character and purposes of the reorganization, its present advisory agencies; but the ultimate decision of all questions, except the determination of prices, should rest always with the Chairman, the other members acting in a cooperative and advisory capacity. The further organization of advice I will indicate below.

In the determination of priorities of production, when it is not possible to have the full supply of any article that is needed produced at once, the Chairman should be assisted, and, so far as practicable, guided, by the present priorities organization or its equivalent.

697

In the determination of priorities of delivery, when they must be determined, he should be assisted, when necessary, in addition to the present advisory priorities organization, by the advice and cooperation of a committee constituted for the purpose and consisting of official representatives of the Food Administration, the Fuel Administration, the Railway Administration, the Shipping Board, and the War Trade Board, in order that, when a priority of delivery has been determined, there may be common, consistent, and concerted action to carry it into effect.

In the determination of prices the Chairman should be governed by the advice of a committee consisting, besides himself, of the members of the Board immediately charged with the study of raw materials and of manufactured products, of the labor member of the board, of the Chairman of the Federal Trade Commission, the Chairman of the Tariff Commission, and the Fuel Administrator.

The Chairman should be constantly and systematically informed of all contracts, purchases, and deliveries, in order that he may have always before him a schematized analysis of the progress of business in the several supply divisions of the Government in all departments.

The duties of the Chairman are:

(1) To act for the joint and several benefit of all the supply departments of the Government.

(2) To let alone what is being successfully done and interfere as little as possible with the present normal processes of purchase and delivery in the several departments.

(3) To guide and assist wherever the need for guidance or assistance may be revealed; for example, in the allocation of contracts, in obtaining access to materials in any way pre-empted, or in the disclosure of sources of supply.

(4) To determine what is to be done when there is any competitive or other conflict of interest between departments in the matter of supplies; for example, when there is not a sufficient immediate supply for all and there must be a decision as to priority of need or delivery, or when there is competition for the same source of manufacture or supply, or when contracts have not been placed in such a way as to get advantage of the full productive capacity of the country.

(5) To see that contracts and deliveries are followed up where such assistance as is indicated under (3) and (4) above has proved to be necessary.

(6) To anticipate the prospective needs of the several supply departments of the Government and their feasible adjustment to the industry of the country as far in advance as possible, in order that as definite an outlook and opportunity for planning as possible may be afforded the business men of the country.

In brief, he should act as the general eye of all supply departments in the field of industry.

Cordially and sincerely yours,

WOODROW WILSON

Mr. Bernard M. Baruch,
    Washington, D.C.

BIBLIOGRAPHY

BOOKS USED during the preparation of this study are listed below. The greatest part of the research was done in the private and public papers of Mr. Bernard M. Baruch at his New York office in the Fuller Building, 597 Madison Avenue. These included an unfinished manuscript memoir covering his early life to the First World War period. Mr. Baruch did not begin saving his papers until he entered public life during the First World War.

Various other manuscript collections were consulted in the preparation of this book, including letters and papers in the possession of Mr. and Mrs. Ulysse Ganvier Des Portes of Winnsboro, S.C., and of the late Marion Heyman of Camden, S.C. Manuscript collections used included the Barnett A. Elzas Papers at The New-York [State] Historical Society; the Diary of Vance McCormick, the Diary of Chandler P. Anderson, the Confidential Diary of Robert Lansing, the Tasker H. Bliss Papers, and the Woodrow Wilson and Ray Stannard Baker Papers, all in the Manuscript Division of the Library of Congress. The papers of Colonel Edward M. House at Yale University and of Franklin D. Roosevelt at Hyde Park were consulted. Assistance also came from the American Jewish Archives.

Adam, Pearl H., *Paris Sees It Through* (London and New York, 1919).

Adams, Henry, *The Education of Henry Adams* (Boston and New York, 1930). Riverside Lib. Ed.

Adams, Samuel Hopkins, *Incredible Era* (Boston, 1939).

Agar, Herbert, *The Price of Union* (Boston, 1950).

Allen, Frederick L., *The Great Pierpont Morgan* (New York, 1949).

—— *Only Yesterday* (New York, 1931).

Bailey, Thomas A., *Woodrow Wilson and the Great Betrayal* (New York, 1945).

—— *Woodrow Wilson and the Lost Peace* (New York, 1944).

Baker, Ray Stannard, *What Wilson Did at Paris* (Garden City, N.Y., 1919).

—— *Woodrow Wilson: Life and Letters* (New York, 1927–39). 8 vols.

Ball, William Watts, *The State That Forgot* (Indianapolis, 1932).

Barrett, Richmond, *Good Old Summer Days* (New York and London, 1941).

Barron, Clarence, *More They Told Barron*, Arthur Pound and Samuel Taylor Moore, eds. and arrangers (New York and London, 1931).

—— *They Told Barron*, Arthur Pound and Samuel Taylor Moore, eds. and arrangers (New York, 1923).

Baruch, Bernard M., *American Industry in the War* (New York, 1941).

———— The Making of the Reparation and Economic Sections of the Treaty (New York and London, 1920).

Beard, Charles A. and Mary R., A Basic History of the United States (New York, 1944).

Binkler, W. E., American Political Parties (New York, 1943).

Birdsall, Paul, Versailles Twenty Years After (New York, 1941).

Blum, John M., Joe Tumulty and the Wilson Era (Boston, 1951).

Bolick, Julian, Waccamaw Plantations (Clinton, S.C., 1946).

Bolles, Blair, How to Get Rich in Washington (New York, 1952).

Bonsal, Stephen, Unfinished Business (New York, 1944).

Borah, William E., American Problems (New York, 1924).

Bowers, Claude G., The Tragic Era (New York, 1940). Blue Ribbon Ed.

Burnett, Philip M., Reparation at the Paris Peace Conference (New York, 1940). 2 vols.

Byrnes, James F., Speaking Frankly (New York, 1947).

Caldwell, Erskine, and Bourke-White, Margaret, You Have Seen Their Faces (New York, 1932).

Canby, Henry S., Age of Confidence (New York, 1934).

Cash, E. B. C., The Cash-Shannon Duel (Boykin, S.C., 1930).

Chesnut, Mary Boykin, A Diary from Dixie, Ben Ames Williams, ed. (Boston, 1949).

Churchill, Winston S., Amid These Storms (New York, 1932).

———— The Grand Alliance, Vol. III of The Second World War (Boston, 1950).

———— Their Finest Hour, Vol. II of The Second World War (Boston 1949).

———— The Unknown War (New York, 1931).

———— The War Speeches of the Rt Hon Winston S. Churchill, Charles Eade, comp. (Boston, 1953). 3 vols.

———— The World Crisis (New York, 1931). 1 vol. ed.

Clarkson, Grosvenor B., Industrial America in the World War: The Strategy Behind the Line, 1917–1918 (Boston and New York, 1923).

Clay, Cassius M., The Mainstay of American Individualism (New York, 1934).

Clemenceau, Georges, The Grandeur and Misery of Victory (Boston and New York, 1930).

Coffin, Robert P. Tristram, Primer for Americans (New York, 1949).

Coffin, Tristram, Your Washington, Gordon Carroll, ed. (New York, 1954).

Coit, Margaret L., John C. Calhoun: American Portrait (Boston, 1950).

Coker, Elizabeth Boatwright, Daughter of Strangers (New York, 1951).

Colby, Arundel, The Gary I Knew (Boston, 1928).

Coulter, E. Merton, The South During Reconstruction (Baton Rouge, 1947).

Cowles, Virginia, Winston Churchill (New York, 1953).

Daniels, Jonathan, The End of Innocence (New York, 1954).

———— Frontier on the Potomac (New York, 1946).

———— The Man from Independence (New York, 1950).

Daniels, Josephus, The Wilson Era: Years of Peace, 1910–1917 (Chapel Hill, N.C., 1944).

———— The Wilson Era: Years of War and After, 1917–1923 (Chapel Hill, N.C., 1946).

Diamond, William, The Economic Thought of Woodrow Wilson (Baltimore, 1943).

Early, Eleanor, New York Holiday New York, 1950).

Eccles, Marriner, Beckoning Frontiers (New York, 1951).

Eisenhower, Dwight D., Crusade in Europe (Garden City, N.Y., 1948).

Elliott, Margaret A., My Aunt Louisa

and *Woodrow Wilson* (Chapel Hill, N.C., 1944).

Elzas, Barnett A., comp., *Jewish Marriage Notices from the Newspaper Press of Charleston, S.C., 1775–1906* (New York, 1917).

Falkenburg, Jinx, *Jinx* (New York, 1951).

Farley, James A., *The Jim Farley Story* (New York, 1948).

Field, Carter, *Bernard Baruch: Park Bench Statesman* (New York and London, 1944).

Fite, Gilbert, *George Peek and the Fight for Farm Parity* (Norman, Okla., 1954).

Fleming, Walter F., *Documentary History of Reconstruction* (Cleveland, 1906).

Flynn, John, *Country Squire in the White House* (New York, 1940).

——— *Men of Wealth* (New York, 1941).

Ford, Worthington Chauncey, ed., *Letters of Henry Adams* (Boston and New York, 1930–38). 2 vols.

Forrestal, James B., *The Forrestal Diaries*, Walter Millis, ed. (New York, 1951).

Galbraith, John K., *The Great Crash* (Boston, 1955).

Garraty, John A., *Henry Cabot Lodge* (New York, 1953).

Garrett, Garet, *The Driver* (New York, 1922).

Gee, Wilson, *The Place of Agriculture in American Life* (New York, 1930).

Gilbert, Clinton, *Mirrors of Washington* (New York, 1921).

Glass, Carter, *An Adventure in Constructive Finance* (New York, 1927).

——— *The Facts About the Fiscal Policy of Our Government* (Washington, 1933).

Goldman, Eric, *Rendezvous with Destiny* (New York, 1952).

Gossler, Philip G., *Columbia University in the City of New York, 1754–1929* (New York, 1930).

Gould, John, *And One To Grow On* (New York, 1949).

Grew, Joseph C., *Turbulent Era* (Boston, 1952). 2 vols.

Grund, Francis, *Aristocracy in America* (London, 1839). 2 vols. in 1.

Gunther, John, *Inside U. S. A.* (New York, 1947).

——— *Roosevelt in Retrospect* (New York, 1950).

Hadley, Hamilton, *The United States: Guardian of Atomic Weapons* (New York, 1946).

Hemingway, Ernest, *Men at War* (New York, 1952). Avon. ed.

Hennig, Helen, *Great South Carolinians* (Chapel Hill, N.C., 1940–49). 2 vols.

Hitler, Adolf, *Mein Kampf* (New York, 1939).

Holbrook, Stewart, *Lost Men of American History* (New York, 1946).

Hollis, Christopher, *The American Heresy* (New York, 1930).

Hoover, Irwin Hood, *Forty-two Years in the White House* (Boston and New York, 1934).

Hopper, Hedda, *From Under My Hat* (New York, 1952).

Hull, Cordell, *The Memoirs of Cordell Hull* (New York, 1948). 2 vols.

Ickes, Harold L., *The First Thousand Days, 1933–1936*, Vol. I of *The Secret Diary of Harold L. Ickes* (New York, 1953).

——— *The Inside Struggle, 1936–1939*, Vol. II of *The Secret Diary* (New York, 1953).

——— *The Lowering Clouds, 1939–1941*, Vol. III of *The Secret Diary* (New York, 1954).

Janeway, Eliot, *The Struggle for Survival* (New Haven, 1951).

Johnson, Claudius, *Borah of Idaho* (New York, 1936).

Johnson, Gerald W., *Incredible Tale* (New York, 1950).

Johnson, Hugh S., *The Blue Eagle*

from *Egg to Earth* (Garden City, N.Y., 1935).

Johnson, Walter, *William Allen White's America* (New York, 1947).

Jones, Jesse, *Fifty Billion Dollars* (New York, 1951).

Kennedy, John F., *Why England Slept* (New York, 1940).

Kessler, Harry C. U., *Germany and Europe* (New Haven, 1924).

Keynes, John M., *The Economic Consequences of the Peace* (New York, 1920).

———*A Revision of the Treaty* (New York, 1922).

King, Edward, *The Great South* (New York, 1875).

Kirkland, Thomas J., and Kennedy, Robert M., *Historic Camden* (Columbia, S.C., 1905–26). 2 vols.

Korovine, Eugene A., *The U.S.S.R. and Disarmament*, in *International Conciliation* No. 292 (Worcester, Mass., and New York, 1933). Carnegie Endowment for International Peace pamphlet.

Lansing, Robert, *The Peace Negotiations* (Boston, 1921).

Lawrence, David, *Woodrow Wilson* (New York, 1924).

Lawrence, William, *Henry Cabot Lodge* (Boston, 1925).

Leonard, Jonathan, *The Tragedy of Henry Ford* (New York and London, 1932).

Levin, Nathaniel, *Year Book of the Charleston Congregation of Beth Elohim* (Charleston, S.C., 1883).

Lochner, Louis, *America's Don Quixote* (London, 1924).

Lodge, Henry Cabot, *The Senate and the League of Nations* (New York, 1925).

Longworth, Alice Roosevelt, *Crowded Hours* (New York, 1933).

McAdoo, William G., *Crowded Years* (Boston and New York, 1931).

McCann, Kevin, *Man from Abilene* (Garden City, N.Y., 1952).

Martin, Franklin, *Digest of the Proceedings of the Council of National Defense During the World War* (Washington, 1934).

Moley, Raymond, *After Seven Years* (New York, 1939).

Morris, Lloyd, *Incredible New York* (New York, 1950).

Muzzey, David, *A History of Our Country* (Boston, 1937).

Myers, Gustavus, *History of the Great American Fortunes* (Chicago, 1908–10). 2 vols.

Nelson, Donald, *Arsenal of Democracy* (New York, 1946).

Nevins, Allan, and Commager, Henry S., *America: The Story of a Free People* (Boston, 1942).

———*Pocket History of the United States* (New York, Pocket Books, Inc.).

New-York Historical Society Collections for 1885, *The Burghers of New Amsterdam and the Freemen of New York*.

Nichols, Thomas L., *Forty Years of American Life* (London, 1864). 2 vols.

Nicolson, Harold, *Peacemaking, 1919* (New York, 1931).

Noyes, Pierrepont B., *While Europe Waits for Peace* (New York, 1921).

Obear, Theus, *Through the Years in Old Winnsboro* (Columbia, S.C., 1940).

Perkins, Frances, *The Roosevelt I Knew* (New York, 1946).

Pike, James, *The Prostrate State* (New York, 1874).

Pool, David De Sola, *Portraits Etched in Stone* (New York, 1951).

Reznikoff, Charles, and Engelman, Uriah Z., *The Jews of Charleston* (Philadelphia, 1950).

Richards, William C., *The Last Billionaire* (New York, 1948).

Robinson, Donald, *The 100 Most Important People* (New York, 1952).

Roosevelt, Eleanor, *This I Remember* (New York, 1949).

Roosevelt, Elliott, *As He Saw It* (New York, 1946).

Roosevelt, Theodore, *Autobiography* (New York, 1913).

Rosenbloom, Morris, *Peace Through Strength* (New York, 1953).

Rosenman, Samuel, *Working with Roosevelt* (New York, 1952).

Saloutos, Theodore, and Hicks, John D., *Agricultural Discontent in the Middle West* (Madison, Wis., 1951).

Schlesinger, Arthur M., Jr., *The Crisis of the Old Order*, Vol. I of *The Age of Roosevelt* (Boston, 1957).

Schriftgiesser, Karl, *The Gentleman from Massachusetts* (Boston, 1944).

Seager, Henry R., and Gulick, Charles A., Jr., *Trust and Corporation Problems* (New York and London, 1929).

Seymour, Charles, *Woodrow Wilson and the World War* (New Haven, 1921).

———, ed., *The Intimate Papers of Colonel House* (Boston and New York, 1926–28). 2 vols.

Simkins, Francis, *Pitchfork Ben Tillman* (Baton Rouge, 1944).

Sherwood, Robert, *Roosevelt and Hopkins* (New York, 1948).

Smith, Alfred E., *Up to Now* (New York, 1930).

Smith, Henry A. M., *The Baronies of South Carolina* (Charleston, S.C., 1931).

Smith, Lillian, *Killers of the Dream* (New York, 1949).

Smith, Rixey, and Beasley, Norman, *Carter Glass* (New York, 1939).

Smyth, Henry De Wolf, *Atomic Energy for Military Purposes* (Princeton, 1945).

Stanwood, Edward, *A History of the Presidency* (Boston and New York, 1928). Rev. ed. 2 vols.

Starling, Edmund W., and Sugrue, Thomas, *Starling of the White House*

(New York, 1946).

Steffens, Lincoln, *Autobiography* (New York and London, 1931). 2 vols.

Steinbeck, John, *The Grapes of Wrath* (New York, 1934).

Stettinius, Edward, *Roosevelt and the Russians* (New York, 1949).

Stiles, Lela, *The Man Behind Roosevelt* (New York, 1954).

Stimson, Henry L., and Bundy, McGeorge, *On Active Service in Peace and War* (New York, 1948).

Thomas, Henry, and Thomas, Dana Lee, *50 Great Americans* (New York, 1950).

Tocqueville, Alexis de, *Democracy in America* (New York, 1904). 2 vols.

Trollope, Frances, *Domestic Manners of the Americans* (New York, 1832).

Truman, Harry S, *Year of Decisions* (Garden City, N.Y., 1955).

——— *Years of Trial and Hope* (Garden City, N.Y., 1956).

Unofficial Observer [John Franklin Carter], *The New Dealers* (New York, 1934).

U. S. Dept. of State, *The International Control of Atomic Energy: Growth of a Policy* (Washington, 1946).

——— *A Report on International Control of Atomic Energy, Prepared for the Secretary of State's Committee on Atomic Energy by a Board of Consultants* (Washington, 1946).

U. S. Steel Corporation, *United States Steel Corporation: T.N.E.C. Papers* (New York, 1940). 3 vols.

Vandenburg, Arthur H., Jr., ed., *The Private Papers of Senator Vandenberg* (Boston, 1952).

Vernadoky, George, *A History of Russia* (New Haven, 1954). 4th ed.

War Industries Board, Bernard M. Baruch, Chairman, *An Outline of the Board's Origins, Functions, and Organization* (Washington, 1918). Pamphlet.

Wecter, Dixon, *The Age of the Great Depression* (New York, 1948).

Wehle, Louis, *Lost Threads of American History* (New York, 1954).

White, William Allen, *Masks in a Pageant* (New York, 1928).

———— *A Puritan in Babylon* (New York, 1938).

———— *Woodrow Wilson* (Boston and New York, 1924).

White, William L., *Bernard Baruch: Portrait of a Citizen* (New York, 1950).

Wilson, Edith Bolling, *My Memoir* (New York, 1939).

Woodward, C. Vann, *Reunion and Reaction* (Boston, 1951).

WPA, Federal Writers' Project, *South Carolina: A Guide to the Palmetto State* (New York, 1941).

INDEX

theater, 54–55, 76, 105–6; first jobs, 62–63, 67–68; and gambling, 66–67; interest in mining, 68–69, 345, 458–60; begins Wall Street career, 69–74; courtship and marriage, 74–75, 77–78; first seat on Exchange, 75, 76; first Wall Street coup, 78–79; tobacco negotiations for T. F. Ryan, 81–83; second seat on Exchange, 83; on Wall Street, 84–85, 88, 91–92, 93–101, 113–14; rules of success, 95–96; trip to Mexico, 120–21; friendship with Wilson, 136–37, 145–46; political contributions, 144, 372, 427–28, 543, 625, 629; conceives idea of War Industries Board, 147; appointed to Council of National Defense, 148; in War Industries Board, 165–220; personal finances during war, 179; philanthropies, 197, 314–15, 358, 381, 452–54, 494, 658–62; social life, 197–98; sends WIB girls home, 215–16; appointed to Peace Conference, 224; offered Treasury post, 228–29, 229n., 295; aid to South Carolina, 319–21, 381–82, 399–401, 644–46, 665–67; on segregation, 326; friends, 331–38; parents' death, 340–41; periods of ill health, 344, 474; interest in railroads, 347; securities holdings, 347–48; books by, 348; belief in policy of preparedness, 349–51; and Democratic party, 364, 371–72; ideas on agriculture, 375, 378–89, 430–31, 443–44; on balanced budget, 410; break with Roosevelt, 431–34, 448–50; death of wife, 456–57; urges preparedness and mobilization, 468–73, 477–82, 486; testimony before Senate Foreign Relations Committee, 471; offered WPB job, 486; advises F.D.R., 496–97, 542–43; asked to head WPB, 511–12; work on Rubber Committee, 513–20; urges inflation controls, 534–36; works for demobilization, 536–41; work on Atomic Energy Commission, 560–87, 588–607; relations with U.S.S.R., 613–17; and break with Truman, 619–21, 623–25, 626–28, 632; love of sport, 649–50;

women friends, 653–55; New York apartment, 656–57; interest in medicine, 660–63; voting record, 679; viewed by Jewish people, 671; City College lectures, 691–93

Baruch, Bernard M., Jr., 180, 258, 341, 635, 642

Baruch, Dr. Simon, 3, 4, 6–7, 11–12, 23–24, 25, 26, 31, 52–53, 111–12, 199

Baruch, Hartwig, 22, 29, 41, 75, 76

Baruch, Herman, 526n.

Baruch, Renée, 104, 180, 258, 642

Baruch, Sailing, 43, 353

Baruch Plan on atomic energy, 575–87; debate on, 558–608

Baruch Report on rubber, 517–18

"Baruch Report on War and Postwar Adjustment Policies," 537–38

Baum, Gabriel, 628

Baum, Herman, 4–5

Baum, Mannes, 4–5

Baum, Marcus, 12

Bedford, Alfred C., 212

Beneš, Edouard, 235

Benet, Christie, 198, 320, 333, 400; Mrs., 673

Berlin, Irving, 644

Bikini, 592–93

Bilbo, Theodore G., 476

Bingham, Robert, 337

Black, John, 104

Blake, Katherine Devereux, 38–39

Blaker, W. B., 400

Blease, Cole, 322, 364

Bliss, Gen. Tasker H., 146, 249

Bonus Marchers, 435–36

Bonsal, Stephen, 297

Borah, William E., 192, 288, 290, 291, 293, 298, 299–300, 302, 333, 353, 389–90, 394, 395, 471, 472, 651

Bourke-White, Margaret, 402, 415

Boyle, Mary Allen, 258, 338, 655, 658

Bracey, Creola, 7, 23

Bracken, Brendan, 378, 464, 493, 549, 654

Bradfute, Oscar, 389, 390

Bradley, Fred W., 345, 346, 459

Bradley, Gen. Omar, 628, 632, 639, 663

Bradley, P. R., 459

INDEX